2009
AQA
Biology AS
Student Workbook

AQA *Biology AS* 2009

Student Workbook

First edition 2008

ISBN 978-1-877462-18-4

Copyright © **2008** Richard Allan
Published by **BIOZONE** International Ltd

Printed by REPLIKA PRESS PVT LTD using paper
produced from renewable and waste materials

About the Writing Team

Tracey Greenwood joined the staff of Biozone at the beginning of 1993. She has a Ph.D in biology, specialising in lake ecology, and taught undergraduate and graduate biology at the University of Waikato for four years.

Lissa Bainbridge-Smith worked in industry in a research and development capacity for eight years before joining Biozone as an author in 2007. Lissa has an M.Sc from Waikato University.

Richard Allan has had 11 years experience teaching senior biology at Hillcrest High School in Hamilton, New Zealand. He attained a Masters degree in biology at Waikato University, New Zealand.

Purchases of this workbook may be made direct from the publisher:

www.biozone.co.uk

UNITED KINGDOM:

BIOZONE Learning Media (UK) Ltd.
P.O. Box 23698, Edinburgh EH5 2WX, **Scotland**
Telephone: (131) 557 5060
FAX: (131) 557 5030
E-mail: sales@biozone.co.uk

AUSTRALIA:

BIOZONE Learning Media Australia
P.O. Box 7523, GCMC 4217 QLD, **Australia**
Telephone: +61 (7) 5575 4615
FAX: +61 (7) 5572 0161
E-mail: info@biozone.com.au

NEW ZEALAND:

BIOZONE International Ltd.
P.O. Box 13-034, Hamilton 3251, **New Zealand**
Telephone: +64 (7) 856 8104
FAX: +64 (7) 856 9243
E-mail: sales@biozone.co.nz

Preface to the 2009 Edition

This is the first year Biozone has offered a workbook specifically designed to meet the needs of students enrolled in the AQA biology course. The specific nature of this workbook allows both students and educators to locate material rapidly and easily. The chapters are organised into blocks of related information aligned to the AQA units. The introduction to each chapter provides learning objectives for divisions within each unit, and clearly directs students to the required activities. Tabs identifying "**Related activities**" and "**Web links**" will help students to locate related material within the workbook and indicates web links and activities (including animations) that will enhance their understanding of the topic. See page 8 to find out more about these. Supplementary material and extension activities are available with a limited photocopy licence on Biozone's **Teacher Resource CD-ROM**. A guide to using the Teacher Resource CD-ROM to best effect has been included in the introductory section of the workbook and can be used in conjunction with the course guide. The TRC also contains glossary lists and crosswords to test vocabulary in a student friendly manner. This workbook will be regularly updated to keep abreast of new developments in biology and to reflect changes to the AQA biology course. Biozone continues to be committed to providing up-to-date, relevant, interesting, and accurate information.

A Note to the Teacher

This workbook has been produced as a student-centred resource, and benefits students by facilitating independent learning and critical thinking. Biozone's workbooks motivate and challenge a wide range of students by providing a highly visual format, a clear map through the course, and a synopsis of supplementary resources. In modern biology, a single textbook may no longer provide all the information a student needs to grasp a topic. This workbook is a generic resource and **not a textbook**, and we make a point of referencing texts from other publishers. Above all, we are committed to continually revising and improving this resource **every year**. The price remains below £11 for students, as a reflection of our commitment to providing high-quality, cost effective resources for biology. Please **do not photocopy** from this workbook. We cannot afford to supply single copies to schools and still provide annual updates as we intend. If you think it is worth using, then we recommend that the students themselves own this resource and keep it for their own use. A free model answer book is supplied with your **first order** of 5 or more workbooks.

How Teachers May Use This Workbook

This workbook may be used in the classroom to guide students through each topic. Some activities may be used to introduce topics while others may be used to consolidate and test concepts already covered by other means. The workbook may be used as the primary tool in teaching some topics, but it should not be at the expense of good, 'hands-on' biology. Students may attempt the activities on their own or in groups. The latter provides opportunities for healthy discussion and peer-to-peer learning. Many of the activities may be set as homework exercises. Each page is perforated, allowing for easy removal of pages to be submitted for marking. This has been facilitated this year by the back-to-back format of two page activities. Teachers may prescribe the activities to be attempted by the students (using the check boxes next to the objectives for each topic), or they may allow students a degree of freedom with respect to the activities they attempt. The objectives for each topic will allow students to keep up to date even if they miss lessons and teachers who are away from class may set work easily in their absence. I thank you for your support.

Richard Allan

Acknowledgements

We would like to thank those who have contributed towards this edition:
• Sue Fitzgerald, Mary McDougall, and Gwen Gilbert for efficient handling of the office • Will Robinson and Bardoe Besselaar for their artistic contributions to this edition • Corel Corporation, for use of their eps clipart of plants and animals from the Corel MEGAGALLERY collection • TechPool Studios, for their clipart collection of human anatomy: Copyright ©1994, TechPool Studios Corp. USA (some of these images were modified by Richard Allan and Tracey Greenwood) • Totem Graphics, for their clipart collection of plants and animals • 3D models created using Poser IV, Curious Labs and Bryce.

Photo Credits

Royalty free images, purchased by Biozone International Ltd, are used throughout this workbook and have been obtained from the following sources: Corel Corporation from various titles in their Professional Photos CD-ROM collection; IMSI (International Microcomputer Software Inc.) images from IMSI's MasterClips® and MasterPhotosTM Collection, 1895 Francisco Blvd. East, San Rafael, CA 94901-5506, USA; ©1996 Digital Stock, Medicine and Health Care collection; ©Hemera Technologies Inc, 1997-2001; © 2005 JupiterImages Corporation www.clipart.com; ©Click Art, ©T/Maker Company; ©1994., ©Digital Vision; Gazelle Technologies Inc.; PhotoDisc®, Inc. USA, www.photodisc.com.

The writing team would like to thank the following individuals and institutions who kindly provided photographs: • Alan Sheldon, Sheldon's Nature Photography, Wisconsin for the photo of the lizard without its tail • Adam Luckenbach and the North Carolina State University for use of the poster image on sex determination in flounder • Clinical Cases for the photo of the lung affected by asbestosis • Dan Butler for his photograph of a wounded finger • Dept. of Natural Resources, Illinois for the image of the Illinois prairie chicken • Ed Uthman for the photo of the atherosclerotic plaque in the carotid artery • PASCO for their images of probeware • PEIR digital library for the use of the photo of an unobstructed coronary artery • Stephen Moore for his photos of freshwater insects • University of Florida for the image of the strawberry runners • Ute Frevert for the photo of the malaria sporozoite • Dr Roger Wagner, Dept of Biological Sciences, University of Delaware, for the LS of a capillary • www.coastalplanning.net for the image of a marine quadrat

Photos kindly provided by individuals or corporations have been identified by way of coded credits as follows:

BF: Brian Finerran (Uni. of Canterbury), **BH**: Brendan Hicks (Uni. of Waikato), **BOB**: Barry O'Brien (Uni. of Waikato), **CDC**: Centers for Disease Control and Prevention, Atlanta, USA, **EII**: Education Interactive Imaging, **EW**: Environment Waikato, **FRI**: Forest Research Institute, **GW**: Graham Walker, **JDG**: John Green (Uni. of Waikato), **RA**: Richard Allan, **RCN**: Ralph Cocklin, **TG**: Tracey Greenwood, **USDA**: United States Department of Agriculture, **VM**: Villa Maria Wines, **WBS**: Warwick Silvester (Uni. of Waikato), **WMU**: Waikato Microscope Unit.

Special thanks to all the partners of the Biozone team for their support.

Cover Photographs

Main photograph: The western lowland gorilla (*Gorilla gorilla gorilla*) is a subspecies of the western gorilla (*Gorilla gorilla*). It is the most widespread and common of all the gorillas, and is found in several African countries. All gorilla species are critically endangered. Human poachers, leopards, and death from the Ebola virus are the main threats to the survival of the western lowland gorilla.
PHOTO: Auke Holwerda, from iStock Photos www.istockphoto.com

Background photograph: Autumn leaves, Image ©2005 JupiterImages Corporation www.clipart.com

Contents

Note to the Teacher iii
Acknowledgments & Photo Credits iv
How To Use This Workbook 1
Activity Pages 2
Explanation of Terms 3
Resources Information 4
Textbook Reference Grid 7
Using the Internet 8
Using the Teacher Resource CD-ROM 10
AQA AS and A2 Biology Course Guide 11

Skills in Biology

Objectives and Resources 12
Terms and Notation 14
Hypotheses and Predictions 15
Planning an Investigation 17
Experimental Method 19
Recording Results 21
Variables and Data 22
Transforming Raw Data 23
Data Presentation 25
Drawing Bar Graphs 26
Drawing Histograms 27
Drawing Pie Graphs 28
Drawing Kite Graphs 29
Drawing Line Graphs 30
Interpreting Line and Scatter Graphs 33
Drawing Scatter Plots 34
Taking the Next Step 35
Descriptive Statistics 37
Interpreting Sample Variability 39
Biological Drawings 41
The Structure of a Report 43
Writing the Methods 44
Writing Your Results 45
Writing Your Discussion 46
Citing and Listing References 47
Report Checklist 49

Unit 1: Biology and Disease

Concept Map for Unit 1 50
The Causes of Disease 51

Macromolecules & Human Digestion

Objectives and Resources 53
Biochemical Tests 54
Carbohydrates 55
Amino Acids 57
Proteins 59
Enzymes 61
Enzyme Reaction Rates 63
Enzyme Cofactors and Inhibitors 64
The Human Digestive Tract 65

Stomach and Small Intestine 67
The Large Intestine 69
Absorption and Transport 70
The Control of Digestion 71

Cell Structure and Function

Objectives and Resources 72
Animal Cells 73
Eukaryotic Cell Diversity 75
Cell Sizes 76
Cell Structure and Organelles 77
Prokaryotic Cells 79
Optical Microscopes 81
Electron Microscopes 83
Cell Fractionation 85
Identifying Cell Structures 86
Identifying Electron Micrographs 87

Processes Across Exchange Surfaces

Objectives and Resources 89
Cell Processes 90
Lipids 91
The Structure of Membranes 93
The Role of Membranes in Cells 95
Active and Passive Transport 97
Diffusion 98
Osmosis and Water Potential 99
Ion Pumps 101
Exocytosis and Endocytosis 102
Cholera 103

Gas Exchange at the Lungs

Objectives and Resources 104
Introduction to Gas Exchange 105
Breathing in Humans 106
The Human Respiratory System 107
Measuring Lung Function 109
Gas Transport in Humans 111
Respiratory Diseases 113
Diseases Caused by Smoking 115
Tuberculosis 117

The Human Heart

Objectives and Resources 118
The Human Heart 119
Control of Heart Activity 121
The Cardiac Cycle 123
Review of the Human Heart 124
Exercise and Blood Flow 125
Cardiovascular Disease 127
The Health Benefits of Exercise 129

Activity is marked: • to be done   ✓ when completed

CONTENTS (continued)

Immunology

Objectives and Resources 131
- Targets for Defence 133
- Blood Group Antigens 134
- Blood 135
- The Body's Defences 137
- Blood Clotting and Defence 139
- The Action of Phagocytes 140
- Inflammation 141
- Fever 142
- The Immune System 143
- Antibodies 145
- Antigenic Variability in Pathogens 147
- Acquired Immunity 148
- Vaccination 149
- Types of Vaccine 151
- Monoclonal Antibodies 153
- Disease and Public Health 155

Unit 2:
The Variety of Living Organisms

Concept Map for Unit 2 157
- Variation 158

The Role of DNA

Objectives and Resources 160
- The Genome 161
- Prokaryotic Chromosomes 162
- Eukaryote Chromosome Structure 163
- Nucleic Acids 165
- Creating a DNA Molecule 167
- DNA Molecules 171
- The Genetic Code 172
- The Simplest Case: Genes to Proteins 173
- Meiosis 174
- Crossing Over 176
- Crossing Over Problems 177

Variety and Complexity

Objectives and Resources 178
- Genetic Diversity 179
- The Founder Effect 180
- Population Bottlenecks 181
- Genetic Drift 182
- Selective Breeding in Crop Plants 183
- Selective Breeding in Animals 185

Biochemical & Cellular Diversity

Objectives and Resources 187
- Chloroplasts and Cell Walls 188
- Haemoglobins 189
- DNA Replication 191
- Mitosis and the Cell Cycle 193

- The Cell Cycle and Cancer 195
- Differentiation of Human Cells 196
- Human Cell Specialisation 197
- Plant Cell Specialisation 198
- Root Cell Development 199
- Levels of Organisation 200
- Animal Tissues 201
- Plant Tissues 202

Adaptation and Specialisation

Objectives and Resources 203
- Transport and Exchange Systems 204
- Surface Area and Volume 205
- Gas Exchange in Animals 207
- Gas Exchange in Insects 209
- Gas Exchange in Freshwater 210
- Gas Exchange in Fish 211
- Stomata and Gas Exchange 213
- Adaptations of Xerophytes 215
- Mammalian Transport 217
- Arteries 218
- Capillaries and Tissue Fluid 219
- Veins 221
- Root Structure 222
- Transpiration 223
- Uptake in the Root 225

Classification and Evidence
of Phylogeny

Objectives and Resources 226
- The New Tree of Life 227
- The Species Concept 228
- Behaviour and Species Recognition 229
- DNA and Taxonomy 230
- Classification System 231
- DNA Hybridisation 233
- Immunological Studies 234
- Protein Comparisons 235

Evolution and Biodiversity

Objectives and Resources 236
- Antibiotics 237
- Evolution of Drug Resistance 238
- The Basis of Resistance 239
- Global Biodiversity 240
- Britain's Biodiversity 241
- Loss of Biodiversity 243
- Tropical Deforestation 244
- Agriculture and Diversity 245
- Measuring Diversity 247

INDEX 249

Activity is marked: ⬝ to be done ✓ when completed

How to Use this Workbook

This workbook is designed as a resource that will make the study of biology more enjoyable. It is suitable for students in their AS year of AQA biology. The course guide on page 11 (or on the Teacher Resource CD-ROM) indicates where in the workbook the material required by your course is covered. This workbook will reinforce and extend the ideas developed by your teacher. It is **not a textbook**; its aim is to complement the texts written for your course. It provides the following resources for each topic:

Guidance Provided for Each Topic

Learning objectives:

These provide a map of the topic content. Completing the relevant learning objectives will help you to satisfy the knowledge requirements of your course. Your teacher may add to or omit points from this list.

Topic outcomes:

This panel provides a summary of the content of the AQA Unit to which this topic applies. See page 11 for a synopsis of the content requirements for your course.

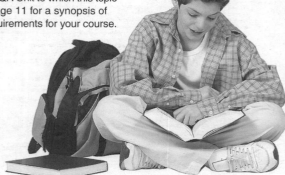

Key words:

Key words are displayed in **bold** type in the learning objectives and should be used to create a glossary as you study each topic. From your own reading and your teacher's descriptions, write your own definition for each word. Use only the terms relevant to the learning objectives assigned by your teacher. Free glossary worksheets are also available from our web site.

Use the check boxes to mark objectives to be completed.
Use a **dot** to be done (•).
Use a **tick** when completed (✓).

Comprehensive textbooks

The **Textbook Reference Grid** on page 7 lists the major comprehensive textbooks available for your course (these are texts providing coverage of the majority of course topics). The grid provides the pages or chapters from each text relevant to each topic in the workbook.

Supplementary texts:

References to supplementary texts, which have only a restricted topic coverage, are provided as appropriate in each topic.

Supplementary resources from Biozone

Supporting Presentation MEDIA are noted where appropriate. Other resources relevant to topics in the workbook are provided on the **Teacher Resource CD-ROM** (purchased separately). See page 10 for details.

Periodical articles:

Ideal for those seeking more depth on a specific topic. Articles are sorted according to their suitability for student or teacher reference. Visit your school, public, or university library for these articles.

Internet addresses:

Access our database of links to more than **800** web sites (updated regularly) relevant to topics covered in the manual. Go to Biozone's own web site: **www.biozone.co.uk** and link directly to listed sites using the *BioLinks* button.

Activity Pages

The activities and exercises make up most of the content of this book. They are designed to reinforce the concepts you have learned about in the topic. Your teacher may use the activity pages to introduce a topic for the first time, or you may use them to revise ideas already covered. They are excellent for use in the classroom, and as homework exercises and revision. In some cases, the activities should not be attempted until you have carried out the necessary background reading from your textbook. Your teacher should have a model answers book with the answers to each activity. This workbook includes a small amount of material that could be regarded as extension. Although you may choose not to complete these activities, our workbooks still represent exceptional value.

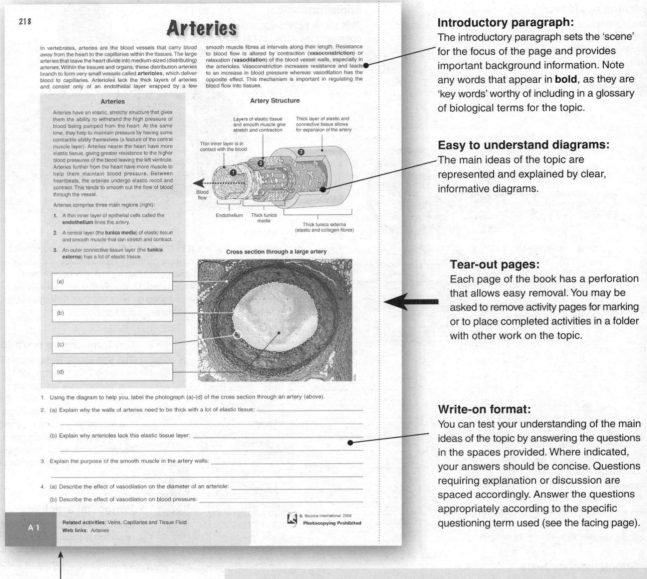

Introductory paragraph:
The introductory paragraph sets the 'scene' for the focus of the page and provides important background information. Note any words that appear in **bold**, as they are 'key words' worthy of including in a glossary of biological terms for the topic.

Easy to understand diagrams:
The main ideas of the topic are represented and explained by clear, informative diagrams.

Tear-out pages:
Each page of the book has a perforation that allows easy removal. You may be asked to remove activity pages for marking or to place completed activities in a folder with other work on the topic.

Write-on format:
You can test your understanding of the main ideas of the topic by answering the questions in the spaces provided. Where indicated, your answers should be concise. Questions requiring explanation or discussion are spaced accordingly. Answer the questions appropriately according to the specific questioning term used (see the facing page).

Activity code and links:
Activity codes (explained right) help to identify the type of activities and the skills they require. Most activities require knowledge recall as well as the application of knowledge to explain observations or predict outcomes.

Use the **'Related activities'** indicated to visit pages that may help you with understanding the material or answering the questions.

Web links indicate additional material of assistance or interest (either web pages or pdf activities). You can access these from:
www.biozone.co.uk/weblink/AQA-AS-2184.html

Activity Level
1 = Generally a simpler activity with mostly "describe" questions
2 = More challenging material (including "explain" questions)
3 = Challenging content or questions (more "discuss" questions)

(b) Describe the effect of vasodilation on blood pressure:

| A 1 | Related activities: Veins, Capillaries and Tissue Fluid |
| | Web links: Arteries |

Type of Activity
D = Includes some data handling and/or interpretation
P = includes a paper practical
R = May require research outside the page
A = Includes application of knowledge to solve a problem
E = Extension material

Explanation of Terms

Questions come in a variety of forms. Whether you are studying for an exam or writing an essay, it is important to understand exactly what the question is asking. A question has two parts to it: one part of the question will provide you with information, the second part of the question will provide you with instructions as to how to answer the question. Following these instructions is most important. Often students in examinations know the material but fail to follow instructions and do not answer the question appropriately. Examiners often use certain key words to introduce questions. Look out for them and be clear as to what they mean. Below is a description of terms commonly used when asking questions in biology.

Commonly used Terms in Biology

The following terms are frequently used when asking questions in examinations and assessments. Students should have a clear understanding of each of the following terms and use this understanding to answer questions appropriately.

Account for: Provide a satisfactory explanation or reason for an observation.

Analyse: Interpret data to reach stated conclusions.

Annotate: Add **brief** notes to a diagram, drawing or graph.

Apply: Use an idea, equation, principle, theory, or law in a new situation.

Appreciate: To understand the meaning or relevance of a particular situation.

Calculate: Find an answer using mathematical methods. Show the working unless instructed not to.

Compare: Give an account of similarities and differences between two or more items, referring to both (or all) of them throughout. Comparisons can be given using a table. Comparisons generally ask for similarities more than differences (see contrast).

Construct: Represent or develop in graphical form.

Contrast: Show differences. Set in opposition.

Deduce: Reach a conclusion from information given.

Define: Give the precise meaning of a word or phrase as concisely as possible.

Derive: Manipulate a mathematical equation to give a new equation or result.

Describe: Give a detailed account, including all the relevant information.

Design: Produce a plan, object, simulation or model.

Determine: Find the only possible answer.

Discuss: Give an account including, where possible, a range of arguments, assessments of the relative importance of various factors, or comparison of alternative hypotheses.

Distinguish: Give the difference(s) between two or more different items.

Draw: Represent by means of pencil lines. Add labels unless told not to do so.

Estimate: Find an approximate value for an unknown quantity, based on the information provided and application of scientific knowledge.

Evaluate: Assess the implications and limitations.

Explain: Give a clear account including causes, reasons, or mechanisms.

Identify: Find an answer from a number of possibilities.

Illustrate: Give concrete examples. Explain clearly by using comparisons or examples.

Interpret: Comment upon, give examples, describe relationships. Describe, then evaluate.

List: Give a sequence of names or other brief answers with no elaboration. Each one should be clearly distinguishable from the others.

Measure: Find a value for a quantity.

Outline: Give a brief account or summary. Include essential information only.

Predict: Give an expected result.

Solve: Obtain an answer using algebraic and/or numerical methods.

State: Give a specific name, value, or other answer. No supporting argument or calculation is necessary.

Suggest: Propose a hypothesis or other possible explanation.

Summarise: Give a brief, condensed account. Include conclusions and avoid unnecessary details.

In Conclusion

Students should familiarise themselves with this list of terms and, where necessary throughout the course, they should refer back to them when answering questions. The list of terms mentioned above is not exhaustive and students should compare this list with past examination papers / essays etc. and add any new terms (and their meaning) to the list above. The aim is to become familiar with interpreting the question and answering it appropriately.

Resources Information

Your set textbook should always be a starting point for information. There are also many other resources available, including scientific journals, magazine and newspaper articles, supplementary texts covering restricted topic areas, dictionaries, computer software and videos, and the internet.

A synopsis of currently available resources is provided below. Access to the publishers of these resources can be made directly from Biozone's web site through our resources hub: **www.biozone.co.uk/resource-hub.html**, or by typing in the relevant addresses provided below. Most titles are also available through amazon.co.uk. Please note that our listing any product in this workbook does not, in any way, denote Biozone's endorsement of that product.

Comprehensive Biology Texts Referenced

Appropriate texts for this course are referenced in this workbook. Page or chapter references for each text are provided in the text reference grid on page 7. These will enable you to identify the relevant reading as you progress through the activities in this workbook. For further details of text content, or to make purchases, link to the relevant publisher via Biozone's resources hub or by typing: **www.biozone.co.uk > Resources > Textbooks > UK**

AQA Specific

Hirst, K., and M. Bailey, 2008
Collins AS Biology for AQA
Publisher: HarperCollins Publishers Ltd.
Pages: approx. 256
ISBN: 978-0007268214
Comments: *Fully revised edition to support the 2008 AQA biology course. Real world contexts and summaries aid student learning. A companion web site is available.*

Potter, S. 2008
AQA AS Biology
Publisher: Philip Allan Publisher
Pages: approx. 269
ISBN: 978-1844892174
Comments: *Written to meet the new 2008 AQA specification. Material is presented with a how science works theme and colour illustrations. Student knowledge is tested with questions throughout. A teacher's answer guide is available.*

Toole, G., and S. Toole, 2008
AQA Biology AS Level: Student's book
Publisher: Nelson Thornes LTD.
Pages: approx. 246
ISBN: 978-0748782758
Comments: *Designed to meet the new 2008 AQA specification, this text uses learning objectives, examiners tips and summary questions to aid student learning. Diagrams and photos are used to help explain difficult concepts.*

Indge, B, M. Rowland, and M. Baker, 2000
AQA Biology Specification A: A New Introduction to Biology (AS)
Publisher: Hodder & Stoughton
Pages: 240
ISBN: 0-340-78167-X
Comments: *Written specifically for the AQA biology specification A. AS content is covered in full, with assignments for each area to build skills and knowledge.*

Exam Board Independent

Boyle, M., D, Boyle and K. Senior, 2008
Collins Advanced Science: Biology, 3 ed.
Publisher: HarperCollins Publishers Ltd.
Pages: approx. 624
ISBN: 978-0007267453
Comments: *Revised edition. Includes how science works features, stretch and challenge boxes, and putting science into context.*

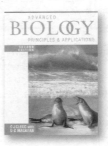

Clegg, C.J. and D.G. MacKean, 2000
Advanced Biology: Principles and Applications 2 ed.
Publisher: John Murray
Pages: 712
ISBN: 0-7195-7670-9
Comments: *Student study guide also available. A general text with specific references for use by biology students of the AS and A2 curricula in the UK.*

Kent, N. A. 2000
Advanced Biology
Publisher: Oxford University Press
Pages: 624
ISBN: 0-19-914195-9
Comments: *Each book comes with a free CD-ROM to help with specification planning. Book is formatted as a series of two page concept spreads.*

Williams, G., 2000
Advanced Biology for You
Publisher: NelsonThornes
Pages: 464
ISBN: 0-7487-5298-6
Comments: *Covers the content for AS-level specifications and the core content of most A2 specifications.*

Supplementary Texts

For further details of text content, or to make purchases, link to the relevant publisher via Biozone's resources hub or by typing: www.biozone.co.uk > resources > supplementary

Barnard, C., F. Gilbert, F., and P. McGregor, 2007
Asking Questions in Biology: Key Skills for Practical Assessments & Project Work, 256 pp.
Publisher: Benjamin Cummings
ISBN: 978-0132224352
Comments: *Covers many aspects of design, analysis and presentation of practical work.*

Cadogan, A. and Ingram, M., 2002
Maths for Advanced Biology
Publisher: NelsonThornes
ISBN: 0-7487-6506-9
Comments: *Covers the maths requirements of AS/A2 biology. Includes worked examples.*

Freeland, P., 1999
Hodder Advanced Science: Microbes, Medicine, and Commerce, 160 pp.
Publisher: Hodder and Stoughton
ISBN: 0-340-73103-6
Comments: *Combines biotechnology, pathology, microbiology, and immunity in a thorough text.*

Fullick, A., 1998
Human Health and Disease, 162 pp.
Publisher: Heinemann Educational Publishers
ISBN: 0435570919
Comments: *An excellent supplement for courses with modules in human health and disease. Includes infectious and non-infectious disease.*

Indge, B., 2003
Data and Data Handling for AS and A Level Biology, 128 pp.
Publisher: Hodder Arnold H&S
ISBN: 1340856475
Comments: *Examples and practice exercises to improve skills in data interpretation and analysis.*

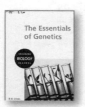

Jones, N., A. Karp, & G. Giddings, 2001.
Essentials of Genetics, 224 pp.
Publisher: John Murray
ISBN: 0-7195-8611-9
One of several titles in the Advanced Biology Reader series providing comprehensive coverage of genetics and evolution (including cell division, molecular genetics, and genetic engineering).

Jones, A., R. Reed, and J. Weyers, 4th ed. 2007
Practical Skills in Biology, approx. 300 pp.
Publisher: Pearson
ISBN: 978-0-131775-09-3
Comments: *Provides information on all aspects of experimental and field design, implementation, and data analysis. Contact www.amazon.co.uk*

Morgan, S., 2002
Advanced Level Practical Work for Biology, 128 pp.
Publisher: Hodder and Stoughton
ISBN: 0-340-84712-3
Comments: *Caters for the investigative requirements of A level studies: experimental planning, techniques, observation and measurement, and interpretation and analysis.*

Cambridge Advanced Sciences (Cambridge UP)
Modular-style texts covering material for the A2 options for OCR, but suitable as student extension for core topics in other courses.

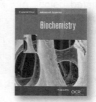

Harwood, R. 2002.
Biochemistry, 96 pp.
ISBN: 0521797519
Methodical coverage of the structure and role of the main groups of biological molecules. Questions and exercises are provided and each chapter includes an introduction and summary.

Jones, M. and G. Jones, 2002.
Mammalian Physiology and Behaviour, 104 pp.
ISBN: 0521797497
Covers mammalian nutrition, the structure and function of the liver, support and locomotion, the nervous system, and senses and behaviour. Each chapter includes an introduction and summary.

Nelson Advanced Sciences (NelsonThornes)
Modular-style texts covering material for the A2 specifications for Edexcel, but are suitable as teacher reference and student extension reading for core topics in other AS/A2 biology courses.

Adds, J., E. Larkcom & R. Miller, 2004.
Exchange and Transport, Energy and Ecosystems, revised edition 240 pp.
ISBN: 0-7487-7487-4
Includes exchange processes (gas exchanges, digestion, absorption), transport systems, adaptation, sexual reproduction, energy and the environment, and human impact. Practical activities are included in several of the chapters.

Adds, J., E. Larkcom & R. Miller, 2003.
Molecules and Cells, revised edition 112 pp.
ISBN: 0-7487-7484-X
Includes coverage of the basic types of biological molecules, with extra detail on the structure and function of nucleic acids and enzymes, cellular organisation, and cell division. Practical activities are provided for most chapters.

Illustrated Advanced Biology (John Murray Publishers)
Modular-style supplements for AS and A2 level biology courses.

Clegg, C.J., 1999.
Genetics and Evolution, 96 pp.
ISBN: 0-7195-7552-4
Concise but thorough coverage of molecular genetics, genetic engineering, inheritance, and evolution. An historical perspective is included by way of introduction, and a glossary and a list of abbreviations used are included.

Clegg, C.J., 1998.
Mammals: Structure & Function, 96 pp.
ISBN: 0-7195-7551-6
An excellent, clearly written supplementary text covering most aspects of basic mammalian anatomy and physiology. Note: This text is now out of print from the publishers, but many schools will still have copies in their collections and it is still available from amazon: www.amazon.co.uk

Clegg, C.J., 2003
Green Plants: The Inside Story, approx. 96 pp.
ISBN: 0-7195-7553-2
The emphasis in this text is on flowering plants. Topics include leaf, stem, and root structure in relation to function, reproduction, economic botany, sensitivity and adaptation.

6

Biology Dictionaries

Access to a good biology dictionary is valuable when dealing with biological terms. Some selected titles are listed below. All are available from www.amazon.co.uk. For further details, link to the relevant publisher via Biozone's resources hub or by typing: **www.biozone.co.uk > resources > dictionaries**

Clamp, A.
AS/A-Level Biology. Essential Word Dictionary, 2000, 161 pp. Philip Allan Updates.
ISBN: 0-86003-372-4.
Carefully selected essential words for AS and A2. Concise definitions are supported by further explanation and illustrations where required.

Collin, P.H.
A Dictionary of Ecology and Environment 5 ed., 2001, 560 pp. Peter Collin Publishers Ltd
ISBN: 0747572011
A revised edition, with over 9000 definitions from all areas of ecology and environmental science, including climate and energy conservation.

Hale, W.G. **Collins: Dictionary of Biology** 4 ed., 2005, 528 pp. Collins.
ISBN: 0-00-720734-4.
Updated to take in the latest developments in biology and now internet-linked. This dictionary is specifically designed for advanced school students, and undergraduates in the life sciences.

Henderson, I.F, W.D. Henderson, and E. Lawrence.
Henderson's Dictionary of Biological Terms, 1999, 736 pp. Prentice Hall.
ISBN: 0582414989
This edition has been updated, rewritten for clarity, and reorganised for ease of use. An essential reference and the dictionary of choice for many.

King, R.C. & W.D. Stansfield **A Dictionary of Genetics**, 6 ed., 2002, 544 pp. Oxford Uni. Press.
ISBN: 0-19-514325-6
A dictionary specifically addressing the needs of students and teachers for an up to date reference source for genetics and related fields. More than 7000 definitions and 395 illustrations.

McGraw-Hill (ed). **McGraw-Hill Dictionary of Bioscience**, 2 ed., 2002, 662 pp. McGraw-Hill.
ISBN: 0-07-141043-0
22 000 entries encompassing more than 20 areas of the life sciences. It includes synonyms, acronyms, abbreviations, and pronunciations for all terms. Accessible, yet comprehensive.

Thain, M. **Penguin Dictionary of Biology**, 2004, 750 pp. Penguin.
ISBN: 0-14-101396-6
Concise reference with definitions to more than 6000 terms. It covers fundamental concepts, core vocabulary, and new advances in the subject.

Rudin, N.
Dictionary of Modern Biology (1997), 504 pp. Barron's Educational Series Inc
ISBN: 0812095162.
More than 6000 terms in biosciences defined for college level students. Includes extensive cross referencing and several useful appendices.

Periodicals, Magazines and Journals

Articles in *Biological Sciences Review (Biol. Sci. Rev.)*, *New Scientist*, and *Scientific American* can be of great value in providing current information on specific topics. Periodicals may be accessed in your school, local, public, and university libraries. Listed below are the periodicals referenced in this workbook. For general enquiries and further details regarding subscriptions, link to the relevant publisher via Biozone's resources hub or by typing: **www.biozone.co.uk > resources > journals**

Biological Sciences Review: *An informative and very readable quarterly publication for teachers and students of biology.* Enquiries: Philip Allan Publishers, Market Place, Deddington, Oxfordshire OX 15 OSE.
Tel: 01869 338652
Fax: 01869 338803
E-mail: sales@philipallan.co.uk
or subscribe from their web site.

New Scientist: *Widely available weekly magazine. Provides summaries of research in articles ranging from news releases to 3-5 page features on recent research.*
Subscription enquiries:
Reed Business Information Ltd
151 Wardour St. London WIV 4BN
Tel: (UK and intl):+44 (0) 1444 475636
E-mail: ns.subs@qss-uk.com
or subscribe from their web site.

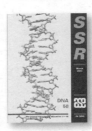
Scientific American: *A monthly magazine containing mostly specialist feature articles. Articles range in level of reading difficulty and assumed knowledge.*
Subscription enquiries:
415 Madison Ave. New York. NY10017-1111
Tel: (outside North America): 515-247-7631
or subscribe from their web site.

School Science Review: *A quarterly journal published by the ASE for science teachers in 11-19 education. SSR includes articles, reviews, and news on current research and curriculum development. Free to Ordinary Members of the ASE or available on subscription.* Subscription enquiries:
Tel: 01707 28300
Email: info@ase.org.uk *or visit their web site.*

Biologist: *Published five times a year, this journal from the IOB includes articles relevant to teachers of biology in the UK. Articles referenced in the workbook can be identified by title and volume number. The IOB also publish the Journal of Biological Education, which provides articles and reviews relevant to those in the teaching profession. Archived articles from both journals are available online at no cost to IOB members and subscribers. Visit their web site for more information.*

Textbook Reference Grid

Guide to use:
Page numbers or chapters in the grid refer to the material in each text that is relevant to the stated topic in the workbook.

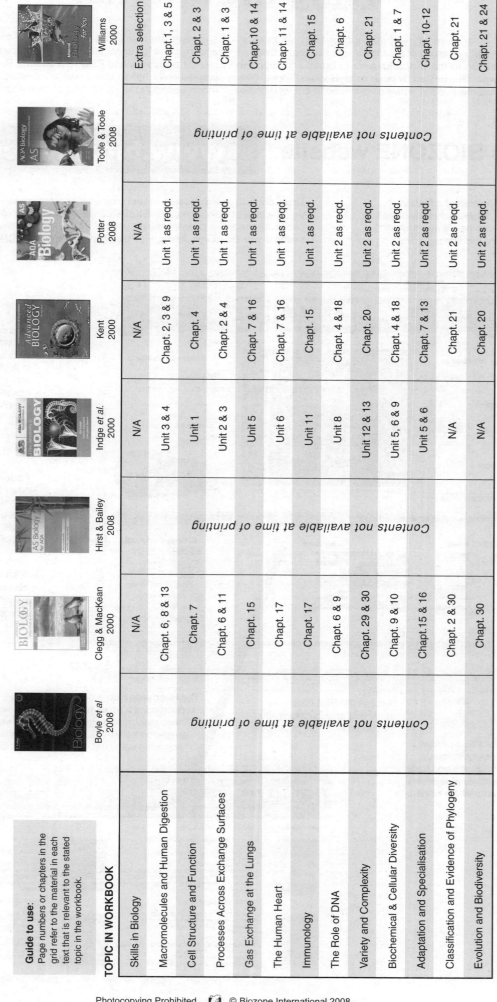

TOPIC IN WORKBOOK	Boyle et al 2008	Clegg & MacKean 2000	Hirst & Bailey 2008	Indge et al. 2000	Kent 2000	Potter 2008	Toole & Toole 2008	Williams 2000
Skills in Biology	Contents not available at time of printing	N/A	Contents not available at time of printing	N/A	N/A	N/A	Contents not available at time of printing	Extra selection
Macromolecules and Human Digestion		Chapt. 6, 8 & 13		Unit 3 & 4	Chapt. 2, 3 & 9	Unit 1 as reqd.		Chapt.1, 3 & 5
Cell Structure and Function		Chapt. 7		Unit 1	Chapt. 4	Unit 1 as reqd.		Chapt. 2 & 3
Processes Across Exchange Surfaces		Chapt. 6 & 11		Unit 2 & 3	Chapt. 2 & 4	Unit 1 as reqd.		Chapt. 1 & 3
Gas Exchange at the Lungs		Chapt. 15		Unit 5	Chapt. 7 & 16	Unit 1 as reqd.		Chapt.10 & 14
The Human Heart		Chapt. 17		Unit 6	Chapt. 7 & 16	Unit 1 as reqd.		Chapt. 11 & 14
Immunology		Chapt. 17		Unit 11	Chapt. 15	Unit 1 as reqd.		Chapt. 15
The Role of DNA		Chapt. 6 & 9		Unit 8	Chapt. 4 & 18	Unit 2 as reqd.		Chapt. 6
Variety and Complexity		Chapt. 29 & 30		Unit 12 & 13	Chapt. 20	Unit 2 as reqd.		Chapt. 21
Biochemical & Cellular Diversity		Chapt. 9 & 10		Unit 5, 6 & 9	Chapt. 4 & 18	Unit 2 as reqd.		Chapt. 1 & 7
Adaptation and Specialisation		Chapt.15 & 16		Unit 5 & 6	Chapt. 7 & 13	Unit 2 as reqd.		Chapt. 10-12
Classification and Evidence of Phylogeny		Chapt. 2 & 30		N/A	Chapt. 21	Unit 2 as reqd.		Chapt. 21
Evolution and Biodiversity		Chapt. 30		N/A	Chapt. 20	Unit 2 as reqd.		Chapt. 21 & 24

Using the Internet

The internet is a powerful resource for locating information. There are several key areas of Biozone's web site that may be of interest to you. Go to the **BioLinks** area to browse through the hundreds of web sites hosted by other organisations. These sites provide a supplement to the activities provided in our workbooks and have been selected on the basis of their accurate, current, and relevant content. We have also provided links to biology-related **podcasts** and **RSS newsfeeds**. These provide regularly updated information about new discoveries in biology; perfect for those wanting to keep abreast of changes in this dynamic field.

The BIOZONE website: www.biozone.co.uk

The current internet address (URL) for the web site is displayed here. You can type a new address directly into this space.

Use Google to search for web sites of interest. The more precise your search words are, the better the list of results. EXAMPLE: If you type in "biotechnology", your search will return an overwhelmingly large number of sites, many of which will not be useful to you. Be more specific, e.g. "biotechnology medicine DNA uses".

Find out about our superb **Presentation Media**. These slide shows are designed to provide in-depth, highly accessible illustrative material and notes on specific areas of biology.

Podcasts: Access the latest news as audio files (mp3) that may be downloaded to your ipod (mp3 player) or played directly off your computer.

RSS Newsfeeds: See breaking news and major new discoveries in biology directly from our web site.

Access the **BioLinks** database of web sites related to each major area of biology.

The **Resource Hub** provides links to the supporting resources referenced in the workbook. These resources include comprehensive and supplementary texts, biology dictionaries, computer software, videos, and science supplies.

News: Find out about product announcements, shipping dates, and workshops and trade displays by Biozone at teachers' conferences around the world.

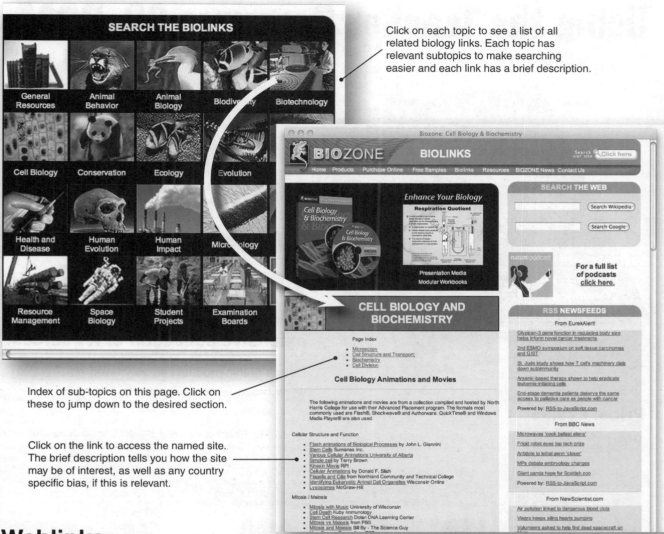

Click on each topic to see a list of all related biology links. Each topic has relevant subtopics to make searching easier and each link has a brief description.

Index of sub-topics on this page. Click on these to jump down to the desired section.

Click on the link to access the named site. The brief description tells you how the site may be of interest, as well as any country specific bias, if this is relevant.

Weblinks:

Go to: **www.biozone.co.uk/weblink/AQA-AS-2184.html**

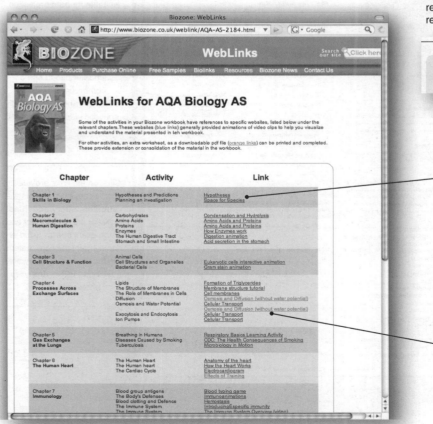

Throughout this workbook, some pages make reference to additional or alternative activities, as well as web sites that have particular relevance to the activity. See example of page reference below:

Related activities: Plant Cells, Animal Cells
Web links: Eukaryotic Cells Interactive Animation
RA 2

Web Link: provides a link to an **external web site** with supporting information for the activity

Web Link: provides a link to a downloadable **Acrobat (PDF) file** which may provide an additional activity or a different activity with an alternative set of features.

Using the Teacher Resource CD-ROM

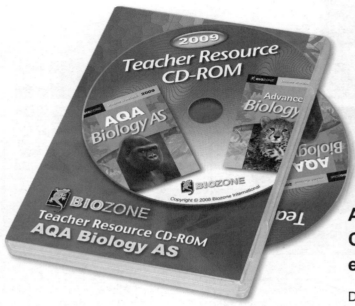

Price: £29.95

Supporting resources for this workbook

Acrobat PDF files supplied on CD-ROM provide hyperlinks to an extensive collection of resources.

Details of this product can be viewed at:
www.biozone.co.uk/Products_UK.html

NOTE: Photocopy licence EXPIRES on **30 June 2009**

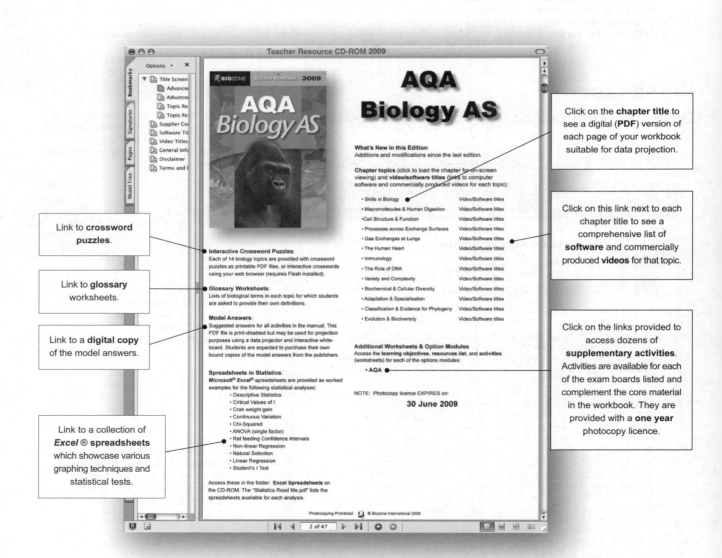

Link to **crossword puzzles**.

Link to **glossary** worksheets.

Link to a **digital copy** of the model answers.

Link to a collection of *Excel* ® **spreadsheets** which showcase various graphing techniques and statistical tests.

Click on the **chapter title** to see a digital (**PDF**) version of each page of your workbook suitable for data projection.

Click on this link next to each chapter title to see a comprehensive list of **software** and commercially produced **videos** for that topic.

Click on the links provided to access dozens of **supplementary activities**. Activities are available for each of the exam boards listed and complement the core material in the workbook. They are provided with a **one year** photocopy licence.

Candidates taking the new AQA AS biology course (to be first taught in 2008) must complete all of Units 1-3. Until the new A2 course is available for teaching (2009), the old A2 specifications apply.

AS Module | Topics in AQA-AS workbook

Unit 1: Biology and Disease

1.1	Pathogens, diseases caused by pathogens, lifestyle factors and disease.	The Causes of Disease
1.2	The human digestive system, carbohydrate and protein digestion, condensation and hydrolysis reactions, enzymes and enzyme activity, biochemical food tests.	Macromolecules & Human Digestion
1.3	Prokaryote and eukaryote cell structure, organelles, microscopy, cell fractionation. Plasma membranes, membrane transport. Cholera and membrane permeability, oral rehydration solutions.	Cell Structure & Function Processes across Exchange Surfaces
1.4	Structure and function of the human respiratory system, gas exchange surfaces, lung disease (TB, smoking related disease).	Gas Exchange at the Lung
1.5	Structure and function of the human heart, cardiac cycle and control, coronary heart disease and risk factors. Blood vessels	The Human Heart Adaptation & Specialisation
1.6	Immune response, phagocytosis, antigens and antibodies, humoral and cellular responses, antigenic variability, vaccines, monoclonal antibodies	Immunology

Unit 2: The Variety of Living Organisms

2.1	Species variation, causes of variation. Distribution, mean and standard deviation.	Variation Skills in Biology
2.2	Structure and function of DNA, genes the genetic code, amino acid coding, eukaryotic and prokaryotic chromosomes, meiosis.	The Role of DNA
2.3	Genetic diversity, selective breeding, the founder effect, genetic bottlenecks.	Variety & Complexity
2.4	Biochemical diversity, haemoglobin structure and function, oxygen dissociation curves, effects of carbon dioxide. Plant cell structure and organelles. Carbohydrate structure and function.	Biochemical & Cellular Diversity Macromolecules & Human Digestion
2.5	DNA replication, mitosis and the cell cycle, cancer and the cell cycle.	Biochemical & Cellular Diversity
2.6	Cellular specialisation and organisation, plant and animal tissues, cell differentiation.	Biochemical & Cellular Diversity
2.7	Exchange surfaces, SA:V ratio, animal and plant gas exchange systems, xerophytes. Mammalian circulatory system, structure and function of blood vessels, lymphatic system and tissue fluid. Plant transport system, structure and function of dicot roots, transpiration, translocation.	Adaptation & Specialisation
2.8	Classification, principles of taxonomy.	Classification & Evidence of Phylogeny
2.9	Genetic evidence for classification, DNA hybridisation, immumological evidence, protein comparisons, courtship behaviour.	Classification & Evidence of Phylogeny
2.10	Antibiotic resistance, evolution in bacteria, gene transmission.	Evolution & Biodiversity
2.11	Biodiversity, measuring biodiversity, effects of deforestation and agriculture on diversity.	Evolution & Biodiversity

Unit 3: Investigative and Practical Skills in AS Biology

3.1 - 3.4	Assessment of planning and implementation of practical work, collection and presentation of raw data, data analysis and evaluation, ability to select and retrieve information and communication skills.	Skills in Biology

A2 Module (Spec A) | Topics in A2 workbook (unless indicated)

Module 5: Inheritance, Evolution and Ecosystems

14.1 14.2	Meiosis and causes of variation. Mendelian inheritance, use of chi-squared. Polygeny.	Sources of Variation Inheritance
14.3 14.4	Hardy-Weinberg principle. Allele frequencies and selection. Speciation. Species concept and the five kingdom classification.	Population Genetics and Speciation Biodiversity and Classification
14.5	Ecosystem numbers and distribution. Diversity indices. Succession.	Populations and Interactions Practical Ecology
14.6, 14.8	Biochemistry of photosynthesis. Respiration, respiratory quotient, ATP.	Cellular Metabolism
14.7, 14.9	Ecological pyramids. Energy transfer between trophic levels. C and N cycles.	Energy Flow and Nutrient Cycles
14.10	Deforestation and forest conservation.	Populations and Interactions

Module 6: Physiology and the Environment Biology only

15.1	Dicotyledon water uptake and transport. Potometers, Xeromorphic adaptations.	● TRC: Physiology & the Environment
15.2 15.3	Homeostasis, blood glucose control, thermoregulation. Liver and kidney function.	Homeostasis
15.4- 15.7	Gas exchange, digestion and absorption, metamorphosis and insect nutrition.	● TRC: Physiology & the Environment
15.8- 15.10	Nervous systems, receptors and stimuli, behaviour (reflexes, ANS, taxes, kineses).	Responses & Coordination

Modules 8a/9a: Written synoptic papers
Modules 8b/9b: Centre assessed coursework

Practical and investigative work.	Skills in Biology

A2 Module (Spec B)

Module 4: Energy, Control, and Continuity

13.1- 13.3	The role of ATP and the biochemistry of photosynthesis and respiration.	Cellular Metabolism
13.4- 13.7	Sensory reception, reflexes, hormones, homeostasis and nervous systems.	Homeostasis Responses & Coordination
13.8	Structure and function of skeletal muscle.	Muscles & Movement
13.9- 13.10	Meiosis and fertilisation, inheritance, sex determination, variation.	Sources of Variation Inheritance
13.11	Natural selection and speciation.	Population Genetics and Speciation
13.12	Taxonomy and the five kingdom classification.	Principles of Classification

Module 5a: Environment

14.1 14.2	Energy transfer and trophic levels. Carbon and nitrogen cycles.	● TRC: Energy Flow and Nutrient cycles
14.3	Biological and physical sampling methods.	Practical Ecology
14.4	Populations and ecological succession.	Populations & Interactions
14.5	Human environmental impact: hedgerows, monocultures, pesticides, pollution.	Populations & Interactions ● TRC: Human Impact

Module 5b: Coursework

Candidates will be assessed on planning, implementing, analysis, evaluation, and synthesis of principles and concepts.	AS: Skills in Biology A2: Practical Ecology

Option Modules

Module 6: Applied Ecology	● TRC: Option Module 6
Module 7: Microbes and Disease	● TRC: Option Module 7
Module 6: Behaviour and Populations	● TRC: Option Module 8

Skills in Biology

Learning Objectives

□ 1. Compile your own glossary from the **KEY WORDS** displayed in **bold type** in the learning objectives below.

Investigating Biological Problems *(pages 14-22)*

□ 2. Demonstrate an understanding of the meaning of the following terms: **compare**, **contrast**, **define**, **describe**, **discuss**, **explain** (or account for), **evaluate**, **identify**, **illustrate**, **list**, **outline**, **state**, **suggest**, **summarise**. A correct understanding of these terms will enable you to answer questions appropriately *(see page 3 for help)*.

□ 3. Explain what is meant by the **scientific method**. Understand its importance to science and the acquisition of new scientific knowledge. Explain the purpose of each of the common features of all science:
   • *Observing and measuring.*
   • *Hypothesising and predicting.*
   • *Designing and planning investigations.*
   • *Recording and interpreting data.*
   • *Drawing conclusions and communicating findings.*

□ 4. Recall the role of **observation** as a prelude to forming a **hypothesis**. In your practical work, you will make observations, and use these to formulate a hypothesis, from which you can generate testable predictions. In Units 1 and 2, you will use your skills in planning and implementing an investigation in an experiment in which the effect of manipulating one variable on another is investigated.

□ 5. Define and explain the purpose of each of the following variables in a controlled experiment:
   • **Independent variable** (manipulated variable)
   • **Dependent variable** (response variable)
   • **Controlled variables** (to control nuisance factors)

□ 6. Describe an appropriate method of systematically varying the independent variable. Determine the **control** for your investigation, explaining how it acts as a reference against which the responses to treatments can be reliably interpreted. Explain how you will ensure controlled variables are kept constant. Identify any **assumptions** made in the investigation.

□ 7. For your own investigation distinguish clearly between:
   • A **data value** for a particular **variable**, e.g. height.
   • The individual sampling unit, e.g. a test-tube with an enzyme at a particular pH.
   • The sample size, e.g. the number of test-tubes in each treatment.

□ 8. Determine the amount of data that you need to collect in order to reasonably test your hypothesis. For your investigations based in the laboratory, determine the **sample size** (e.g. the number of samples within each treatment) and the number of **treatments** (the range of the independent variable).

□ 9. Determine the type of data that you will collect (e.g. counts, measurements) and how you will collect it. Have a clear idea about how you are going to analyse your data before you start and appreciate why this is important. Understand why it is desirable to collect **quantitative** rather than **qualitative** data.

□ 10. Identify different methods for systematically recording data: tables, spreadsheets, and software linked to **dataloggers**. Decide on the method by which you will **systematically record** the data as they are collected.

□ 11. Identify **sources of error** in your experimental design and explain how you will minimise these.

□ 12. Recognise that all biological investigations should be carried out with appropriate regard for safety and the well-being of living organisms and their environment.

Collecting Data *(pages 21-22, 41-42)*

□ 13. Collect and record data systematically according to your plan (#10). Critically evaluate the **accuracy** of your methods for data collection, any **measurement errors**, and the repeatability (**precision**) of any measurements.

□ 14. Make good **biological drawings** as a way of recording information where appropriate to your investigation.

□ 15. Demonstrate an ability to use **SI units** and an appropriate number of **significant figures**. Understand the relationship between the appropriate number of significant figures and the accuracy of a measurement.

Transforming Raw Data *(pages 23-24)*

□ 16. Understand the difference between **raw data** and **transformed data**. Explain why data are often transformed before analysis or graphical presentation. Evaluate the need for transformation with respect to the data you collect.

□ 17. Describe the effect of transformation on data of different types. Demonstrate an ability to carry out a variety of common data transformations: totals, percentages, rates, reciprocals, relative values, and logs. Understand when each of these data transformations would be appropriate.

□ 18. If necessary, modify a table used for data collection to a formal table that can be included in the report. Include space in the table for transformed data.

Drawing Graphs *(pages 25-34)*

□ 19. Describe the benefits of graphing data and explain why data are often presented in a graph rather than in a table. Recognise the **x axis** and **y axis** of graphs and identify which variable (dependent or independent) is plotted on each.

□ 20. Demonstrate an ability to present data appropriately using different types of graphs. Note that the graphical presentation that is appropriate will depend largely on the type of data involved. Review the guidelines for the presentation of data in the following formats:

- ☐ **Bar and column graphs**
- ☐ **Histograms**
- ☐ **Pie graphs**
- ☐ **Kite graphs**
- ☐ **Line graphs**
- ☐ **Scatter diagrams**

☐ 21. Demonstrate an ability plot scatter diagrams and use these to identify **correlation**.

☐ 22. Explain what is meant by a **line of best fit** and when it is appropriate to use it. Draw lines of best fit to graphs with plotted points. Use error bars to place your line or try a computer generated fit.

Data Analysis *(pages 35-40)*

☐ 23. Distinguish between a **statistic** and a **parameter**. Demonstrate an understanding of the calculation and use of the following **descriptive statistics**:

  (a) Sample **mean** and **standard deviation**. Identify when the use of these statistics is appropriate.

  (b) **Median** and **mode** (calculated from your own, or second hand, data). Explain what each statistic summarises and when its use is appropriate.

☐ 24. Discuss the use of **standard deviation** as a measure of dispersion around the mean, related to the true population parameter (the population mean).

☐ 25. Identify trends and relationships in your data for later discussion, including any **positive** or **negative** **correlations** between variables.

☐ 26. Evaluate unexpected or conflicting results and any outlying data points (on line graphs and scatter plots), and be prepared to discuss these in your write-up. Include reference to the limitations of your apparatus and techniques, the effects of these limitations, and how they could feasibly be minimised.

Writing a Report *(pages 43-49)*

☐ 27. Write up your report. Give it a concise, descriptive title, and organise it into the following sections:

  ☐ **Introduction**: Explain the aim, outline your hypothesis, and summarise the current state of the knowledge in the topic area.

  ☐ **Materials and methods**: Describe how you carried out your investigation in a way that allows the method to be reproduced by others.

  ☐ **Results**: Use text, graphs, and tables to describe your results, but exclude any discussion of them at this stage.

  ☐ **Discussion**: Discuss your findings fully, including any unexpected results, and with reference to the work of others.

  ☐ **Conclusion**: Summarise your findings with respect to your original hypothesis. Explain the importance of drawing conclusions only about the variable that you planned to investigate (even if this means that your hypothesis is not accepted).

  ☐ **Bibliography**: List all sources of information, including personal communications.

Skills in Biology

See the 'Textbook Reference Grid' on page 7 for textbook page references relating to material in this topic.

Supplementary Texts

See pages 5-6 for additional details of these texts:

■ Barnard, C., *et al.*, 2007. **Asking Questions in Biology**, 3 edn (Prentice Hall).

■ Cadogan, A. and Ingram, M., 2002. **Maths for Advanced Biology** (NelsonThornes).

■ Indge, B., 2003. **Data and Data Handling for AS and A Level Biology** (Hodder Arnold H&S).

■ Jones, A., *et al.*, 2007. **Practical Skills in Biology** (Pearson).

■ Morgan, S., 2002. **Advanced Level Practical Work for Biology** (Hodder and Stoughton).

See page 6 for details of publishers of periodicals:

STUDENT'S REFERENCE

■ **Drawing Graphs** Biol. Sci. Rev., 19(3) Feb. 2007, pp. 10-13. *A guide to creating graphs. The use of different graphs for different tasks is explained and there are a number of pertinent examples described to illustrate points.*

Working spreadsheets support this topic:

Teacher Resource CD-ROM
- **Statistics spreadsheets**

■ **AS: A Word at the Start?** Biol. Sci. Rev., 13(1) Sept. 2000, pp. 6-8. *A useful summary of the importance of understanding the facts, reading carefully, and accurately communicating your knowledge when answering examination questions.*

■ **Size Does Matter** Biol. Sci. Rev., 17 (3) February 2005, pp. 10-13. *Measuring the size of organisms and calculating magnification and scale.*

■ **Percentages** Biol. Sci. Rev., 17(2) Nov. 2004, pp. 28-29. *The calculation of percentage and the appropriate uses of this important transformation.*

■ **The Variability of Samples** Biol. Sci. Rev., 13(4) March 2001, pp. 34-35. *The variability of sample data and the use of sample statistics as estimators for population parameters.*

■ **Experiments** Biol. Sci. Rev., 14(3) February 2002, pp. 11-13. *The basics of experimental design and execution: determining variables, measuring them, and establishing a control.*

■ **Descriptive Statistics** Biol. Sci. Rev., 13 (5) May 2001, pp. 36-37. *A synopsis of descriptive statistics. The appropriate use of standard error and standard deviation is discussed.*

■ **Dealing with Data** Biol. Sci. Rev., 12 (4) March 2000, pp. 6-8. *A short account of the best ways in which to deal with the interpretation of graphically presented data in examinations.*

■ **Describing the Normal Distribution** Biol. Sci. Rev., 13(2) Nov. 2000, pp. 40-41. *The normal distribution, with an introduction to data spread, mean, median, variance, and standard deviation.*

■ **Statistical Modelling** New Scientist, 17 Sept. 1994 (Inside Science). *Useful presentation of data; distributions, normal curves, and histograms.*

■ **The Truth is Out There** New Scientist, 26 Feb. 2000 (Inside Science). *The philosophy of scientific method explained clearly and with examples.*

■ **Statistical Sampling** New Scientist, 10 June 1995 (Inside Science). *Hypotheses, sampling methodology, significance, & central limit theorem.*

■ **Estimating the Mean and Standard Deviation** Biol. Sci. Rev., 13(3) January 2001, pp. 40-41. *Simple statistical analysis. Includes formulae for calculating sample mean and standard deviation.*

■ **Correlation** Biol. Sci. Rev., 14(3) February 2002, pp. 38-41. *An examination of the relationship between variables. An excellent synopsis.*

■ **Ecological Projects** Biol. Sci. Rev., 8(5) May 1996, pp. 24-26. *Planning and carrying out a field-based project (includes analysis and reporting).*

■ **Fieldwork - Sampling Animals** Biol. Sci. Rev., 10(4) March 1998, pp. 23-25. *The appropriate methodology for collecting animals in the field.*

■ **Fieldwork Sampling - Plants** Biol. Sci. Rev., 10(5) May 1998, pp. 6-8. *Methods for sampling plant communities (transects and quadrats).*

TEACHER'S REFERENCE

■ **Biology Statistics made Simple using Excel** SSR 83(303), Dec. 2001, pp. 29-34. *An instructional account on the use of spreadsheets for statistics in A level science (excellent).*

See pages 8-9 for details of how to access **Bio Links** from our web site: **www.biozone.co.uk**. From Bio Links, access sites under the topics:

STUDENT PROJECTS > **General**: • AP Biology training • Biology in motion • Potato cores in salt solution • Mr Knight's AP lab activities • StudyZones.com > **Skills in Biology**: • A level biology essays • Scientific investigation • Study skills - biology • The scientific method • Tree lupins • What is plagiarism • Woodlice online > **Statistics**: • Statistics glossary • Chi-square lesson • What is a P value? ... *and others*

Terms and Notation

The definitions for some commonly encountered terms related to making biological investigations are provided below. Use these as you would use a biology dictionary when planning your investigation and writing up your report. It is important to be consistent with the use of terms i.e. use the same term for the same procedure or unit throughout your study. Be sure, when using a term with a specific statistical meaning, such as sample, that you are using the term correctly.

General Terms

Data: Facts collected for analysis.

Qualitative: Not quantitative. Described in words or terms rather than by numbers. Includes subjective descriptions in terms of variables such as colour or shape.

Quantitative: Able to be expressed in numbers. Numerical values derived from counts or measurements.

The Design of Investigations

Hypothesis: A tentative explanation of an observation, capable of being tested by experimentation. Hypotheses are written as clear statements, not as questions.

Control treatment (control): A standard (reference) treatment that helps to ensure that responses to other treatments can be reliably interpreted. There may be more than one control in an investigation.

Dependent variable: A variable whose values are determined by another variable (the independent variable). In practice, the dependent variable is the variable representing the biological response.

Independent variable: A variable whose values are set, or systematically altered, by the investigator.

Controlled variables: Variables that may take on different values in different situations, but are controlled (fixed) as part of the design of the investigation.

Experiment: A contrived situation designed to test (one or more) hypotheses and their predictions. It is good practice to use sample sizes that are as large as possible for experiments.

Investigation: A very broad term applied to scientific studies; investigations may be controlled experiments or field based studies involving population sampling.

Parameter: A numerical value that describes a characteristic of a population (e.g. the mean height of all 17 year-old males).

Prediction: The prediction of the response (Y) variable on the basis of changes in the independent (X) variable.

Random sample: A method of choosing a sample from a population that avoids any subjective element. It is the equivalent to drawing numbers out of a hat, but using random number tables. For field based studies involving quadrats or transects, random numbers can be used to determine the positioning of the sampling unit.

Repeat / Trial: The entire investigation is carried out again at a different time. This ensures that the results are reproducible. Note that repeats or trials are not **replicates** in the true sense unless they are run at the same time.

Replicate: A duplication of the entire experimental design run at the same time.

Sample: A sub-set of a whole used to estimate the values that might have been obtained if every individual or response was measured. A sample is made up of **sampling units**, In lab based investigations, the sampling unit might be a test-tube, while in field based studies, the sampling unit might be an individual organism or a quadrat.

Sample size (*n*): The number of samples taken. In a field study, a typical sample size may involve 20-50 individuals or 20 quadrats. In a lab based investigation, a typical sample size may be two to three sampling units, e.g. two test-tubes held at 10°C.

Sampling unit: Sampling units make up the sample size. Examples of sampling units in different investigations are an individual organism, a test tube undergoing a particular treatment, an area (e.g. quadrat size), or a volume. The size of the sampling unit is an important consideration in studies where the area or volume of a habitat is being sampled.

Statistic: An estimate of a parameter obtained from a sample (e.g. the mean height of all 17 year-old males in your class). A precise (reliable) statistic will be close to the value of the parameter being estimated.

Treatments: Well defined conditions applied to the sample units. The response of sample units to a treatment is intended to shed light on the hypothesis under investigation. What is often of most interest is the comparison of the responses to different treatments.

Variable: A factor in an experiment that is subject to change. Variables may be controlled (fixed), manipulated (systematically altered), or represent a biological response.

Precision and Significance

Accuracy: The correctness of the measurement (the closeness of the measured value to the true value). Accuracy is often a function of the calibration of the instrument used for measuring.

Measurement errors: When measuring or setting the value of a variable, there may be some difference between your answer and the 'right' answer. These errors are often as a result of poor technique or poorly set up equipment.

Objective measurement: Measurement not significantly involving subjective (or personal) judgment. If a second person repeats the measurement they should get the same answer.

Precision (of a measurement): The repeatability of the measurement. As there is usually no reason to suspect that a piece of equipment is giving inaccurate measures, making precise measurements is usually the most important consideration. You can assess or quantify the precision of any measurement system by taking repeated measurements from individual samples.

Precision (of a statistic): How close the statistic is to the value of the parameter being estimated. Also called **reliability**.

The Expression of Units

The value of a variable must be written with its units where possible. Common ways of recording measurements in biology are: volume in litres, mass in grams, length in metres, time in seconds. The following example shows different ways to express the same term. Note that ml and cm^3 are equivalent.

Oxygen consumption (millilitres per gram per hour)

Oxygen consumption ($mlg^{-1}h^{-1}$) or ($mLg^{-1}h^{-1}$)

Oxygen consumption (ml/g/h) or (mL/g/h)

Oxygen consumption/$cm^3g^{-1}h^{-1}$

Statistical significance: An assigned value that is used to establish the probability that an observed trend or difference represents a true difference that is not due to chance alone. If a level of significance is less than the chosen value (usually 1-10%), the difference is regarded as statistically significant. Remember that in rigorous science, it is the hypothesis of no difference or no effect (the null hypothesis, H_0) that is tested. The alternative hypothesis (your tentative explanation for an observation) can only be accepted through statistical rejection of H_0.

Validity: Whether or not you are truly measuring the right thing.

Hypotheses and Predictions

Scientific knowledge grows through a process called the **scientific method**. This process involves observation and measurement, hypothesising and predicting, and planning and executing investigations designed to test formulated **hypotheses**. A scientific hypothesis is a tentative explanation for an observation, which is capable of being tested by experimentation. Hypotheses lead to **predictions** about the system involved and they are accepted or rejected on the basis of findings arising from the investigation. Rejection of the hypothesis may lead to new, alternative explanations (hypotheses) for the observations. Acceptance of the hypothesis as a valid explanation is not necessarily permanent: explanations may be rejected at a later date in light of new findings. This process eventually leads to new knowledge (theory, laws, or models).

Making Observations

These may involve the observation of certain behaviours in wild populations, physiological measurements made during previous experiments, or 'accidental' results obtained when seeking answers to completely unrelated questions.

Asking Questions

The observations lead to the formation of questions about the system being studied.

Forming a Hypothesis

Features of a sound hypothesis:

- It is based on observations and prior knowledge of the system.
- It offers an explanation for an observation.
- It refers to only one independent variable.
- It is written as a definite statement and not as a question.
- It is testable by experimentation.
- It leads to predictions about the system.

Generating a Null Hypothesis

A hypothesis based on observations is used to generate the **null hypothesis (H$_0$)**; the hypothesis of no difference or no effect. Hypotheses are expressed in the null form for the purposes of statistical testing. H$_0$ may be rejected in favour of accepting the alternative hypothesis, H$_A$.

Accept or reject the hypothesis

Testing predictions may lead to new observations

Testing the Predictions

The predictions are tested out in the practical part of an investigation.

Designing an Investigation

Investigations are planned so that the predictions about the system made in the hypothesis can be tested. Investigations may be laboratory or field based.

Making Predictions

Based on a hypothesis, **predictions** (expected, repeatable outcomes) can be generated about the behaviour of the system. Predictions may be made on any aspect of the material of interest, e.g. how different variables (factors) relate to each other.

Related activities: Experimental Method
Web links: Hypotheses

A 2

Useful Types of Hypotheses

A hypothesis offers a tentative explanation to questions generated by observations. Some examples are described below. Hypotheses are often constructed in a form that allows them to be tested statistically. For every hypothesis, there is a corresponding **null hypothesis**; a hypothesis against the prediction. Predictions are tested with laboratory and field experiments and carefully focused observations. For a hypothesis to be accepted it should be possible for anyone to test the predictions with the same methods and get a similar result each time.

Hypothesis involving manipulation
Used when the effect of manipulating a variable on a biological entity is being investigated. **Example**: The composition of applied fertiliser influences the rate of growth of plant A.

Hypothesis of choice
Used when species preference, e.g. for a particular habitat type or microclimate, is being investigated. **Example**: Woodpeckers (species A) show a preference for tree type when nesting.

Hypothesis involving observation
Used when organisms are being studied in their natural environment and conditions cannot be changed. **Example**: Fern abundance is influenced by the degree to which the canopy is established.

1. Generate a prediction for the hypothesis: *"Moisture level of the microhabitat influences woodlouse distribution"*:

   _____

2. During the course of any investigation, new information may arise as a result of observations unrelated to the original hypothesis. This can lead to the generation of further hypotheses about the system. For each of the incidental observations described below, formulate a prediction, and an outline of an investigation to test it. *The observation described in each case was not related to the hypothesis the experiment was designed to test:*

   (a) **Bacterial cultures**

   Prediction: _____

   _____

   Outline of the investigation: _____

   _____

   _____

   _____

   _____

   _____

Bacterial Cultures

Observation: During an experiment on bacterial growth, the girls noticed that the cultures grew at different rates when the dishes were left overnight in different parts of the laboratory.

   (b) **Plant cloning**

   Prediction: _____

   _____

   _____

   Outline of the investigation: _____

   _____

   _____

   _____

   _____

   _____

Plant Cloning

Observation: During an experiment on plant cloning, a scientist noticed that the root length of plant clones varied depending on the concentration of a hormone added to the agar.

Planning an Investigation

Investigations involve written stages (planning and reporting), at the start and end. The middle stage is the practical work when the data are collected. Practical work may be laboratory or field based. Typical lab based studies involve investigating how a biological response is affected by manipulating a particular **variable**, e.g. temperature. Field work often involves investigating features of a population or community. These may be interrelationships, such as competition, or patterns, such as zonation. Where quantitative information must be gathered from the population or community, particular techniques (such as quadrat sampling) and protocols (e.g. random placement of sampling units) apply. These aspects of practical work are covered in *Advanced Biology A2*. Investigations in the field are usually more complex than those in the laboratory because natural systems have many more variables that cannot easily be controlled or accounted for.

Planning

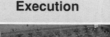

- Formulate your hypothesis from an observation.
- Use a checklist (see the next activity) or a template (above) to construct a plan.

Execution

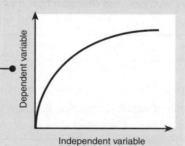

- Spend time (as appropriate to your study) collecting the data.
- Record the data in a systematic format (e.g. a table or spreadsheet).

Analysis and Reporting

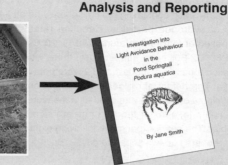

Investigation into Light Avoidance Behaviour in the Pond Springtail *Podura aquatica*

By Jane Smith

- Analyse the data using graphs, tables, or statistics to look for trends or patterns.
- Write up your report including all the necessary sections.

Identifying Variables

A variable is any characteristic or property able to take any one of a range of values. Investigations often look at the effect of changing one variable on another. It is important to identify all variables in an investigation: independent, dependent, and controlled, although there may be nuisance factors of which you are unaware. In all fair tests, only one variable is changed by the investigator.

Dependent variable
- Measured during the investigation.
- Recorded on the y axis of the graph.

Controlled variables
- Factors that are kept the same or controlled.
- List these in the method, as appropriate to your own investigation.

Independent variable
- Set by the person carrying out the investigation.
- Recorded on the x axis of the graph.

Assumptions

In any experimental work, you will make certain assumptions about the biological system you are working with.

Assumptions are features of the system (and your experiment) that you assume to be true but do not (or cannot) test.

Examples of Investigations

Aim		Variables	
Investigate the effect of varying ...	on the following ...	Independent variable	Dependent variable
Temperature	Leaf width	Temperature	Leaf width
Light intensity	Activity of woodlice	Light intensity	Woodlice activity
Soil pH	Plant height at age 6 months	pH	Plant height

Related activities: Variables and Data, Experimental Method
Web links: Space for Species

A 2

In order to write a sound method for your investigation, you need to determine how the independent, dependent, and controlled variables will be set and measured (or monitored). A good understanding of your methodology is crucial to a successful investigation. You need to be clear about how much data, and what type of data, you will collect. You should also have a good idea about how you will analyse the data. Use the example below to practise your skills in identifying this type of information.

Case Study: Catalase Activity

Catalase is an enzyme that converts hydrogen peroxide (H_2O_2) to oxygen and water. An experiment investigated the effect of temperature on the rate of the catalase reaction. Small (10 cm^3) test tubes were used for the reactions, each containing 0.5 cm^3 of enzyme and 4 cm^3 of hydrogen peroxide. Reaction rates were assessed at four temperatures (10°C, 20°C, 30°C, and 60°C). For each temperature, there were two reaction tubes (e.g. tubes 1 and 2 were both kept at 10°C). The height of oxygen bubbles present after one minute of reaction was used as a measure of the reaction rate; a faster reaction rate produced more bubbles. The entire experiment, involving eight tubes, was repeated on two separate days.

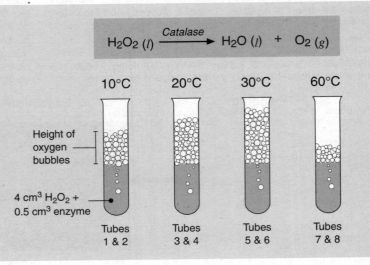

1. Write a suitable aim for this experiment: _____

_____

2. Write a suitable hypothesis for this experiment: _____

_____

3. (a) Identify the **independent variable**: _____

   (b) State the range of values for the independent variable: _____

   (c) Name the unit for the independent variable: _____

   (d) List the equipment needed to set the independent variable, and describe how it was used: _____

   _____

4. (a) Identify the **dependent variable**: _____

   (b) Name the unit for the dependent variable: _____

   (c) List the equipment needed to measure the dependent variable, and describe how it was used: _____

   _____

5. (a) Each temperature represents a treatment/sample/trial (circle one):

   (b) State the number of tubes at each temperature: _____

   (c) State the sample size for each treatment: _____

   (d) State how many times the whole investigation was repeated: _____

6. Explain why it would have been desirable to have included an extra tube containing no enzyme: _____

   _____

7. Identify three variables that might have been controlled in this experiment, and how they could have been monitored:

   (a) _____

   (b) _____

   (c) _____

8. Explain why controlled variables should be monitored carefully: _____

_____

Experimental Method

An aim, hypothesis, and method for an experiment are described below. Explanations of the types of variables for which data are collected, and methods of recording these, are provided in the next two activities. The method described below includes numbered steps and incorporates other features identified in the previous activity. The method can be thought of as a 'statement of intent' for the practical work, and it may need slight changes during execution. The investigation described below was based on the observation that plant species 'A' was found growing in soil with a low pH (pH 4-5). The investigators wondered whether plant species 'A' was adapted to grow more vigorously under acid conditions than under alkaline or neutral conditions.

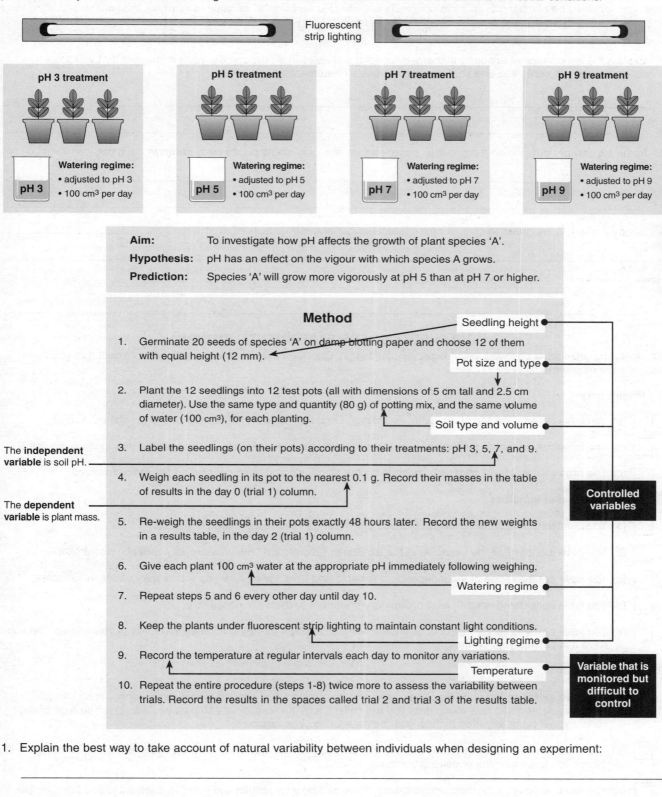

Aim: To investigate how pH affects the growth of plant species 'A'.

Hypothesis: pH has an effect on the vigour with which species A grows.

Prediction: Species 'A' will grow more vigorously at pH 5 than at pH 7 or higher.

Method

Seedling height

1. Germinate 20 seeds of species 'A' on damp blotting paper and choose 12 of them with equal height (12 mm).

Pot size and type

2. Plant the 12 seedlings into 12 test pots (all with dimensions of 5 cm tall and 2.5 cm diameter). Use the same type and quantity (80 g) of potting mix, and the same volume of water (100 cm^3), for each planting.

Soil type and volume

3. Label the seedlings (on their pots) according to their treatments: pH 3, 5, 7, and 9.

The **independent variable** is soil pH.

4. Weigh each seedling in its pot to the nearest 0.1 g. Record their masses in the table of results in the day 0 (trial 1) column.

The **dependent variable** is plant mass.

5. Re-weigh the seedlings in their pots exactly 48 hours later. Record the new weights in a results table, in the day 2 (trial 1) column.

6. Give each plant 100 cm^3 water at the appropriate pH immediately following weighing.

Watering regime

7. Repeat steps 5 and 6 every other day until day 10.

8. Keep the plants under fluorescent strip lighting to maintain constant light conditions.

Lighting regime

9. Record the temperature at regular intervals each day to monitor any variations.

Temperature

10. Repeat the entire procedure (steps 1-8) twice more to assess the variability between trials. Record the results in the spaces called trial 2 and trial 3 of the results table.

Controlled variables

Variable that is monitored but difficult to control

1. Explain the best way to take account of natural variability between individuals when designing an experiment:

_____

_____

_____

_____

Replication in experiments

Replication refers to the number of times you repeat your entire experimental design (including controls). True replication is not the same as increasing the sample size (n) although it is often used to mean the same thing. Replication accounts for any unusual and unforseen effects that may be operating in your set-up (e.g. field trials of plant varieties where soil type is variable). Replication is necessary when you expect that the response of treatments will vary because of factors outside your control. It is a feature of higher level experimental designs, and complex statistics are needed to separate differences between replicate treatments. For simple experiments, it is usually more valuable to increase the sample size than to worry about replicates.

2. Explain the importance of ensuring that any influencing variables in an experiment (except the one that you are manipulating) are controlled and kept constant across all treatments:

_____

_____

3. In the experiment outlined on the previous page, explain why only single plants were grown in each pot:

_____

_____

4. Suggest why it is important to consider the physical layout of treatments in an experiment: _____

_____

_____

_____

YOUR CHECKLIST FOR EXPERIMENTAL DESIGN

The following provides a checklist for an experimental design. Check off the points when you are confident that you have satisfied the requirements in each case:

1. **Preliminary:**

☐ (a) You have determined the aim of your investigation and formulated a hypothesis based on observation(s).

☐ (b) The hypothesis (and its predictions) are testable using the resources you have available (the study is feasible).

☐ (c) The organism you have chosen is suitable for the study and you have considered the ethics involved.

2. **Assumptions and variables:**

☐ (a) You are aware of any assumptions that you are making in your experiment.

☐ (b) You have identified all the variables in the experiment (controlled, independent, dependent, uncontrollable).

☐ (c) You have set the range of the independent variable and established how you will fix the controlled variables.

☐ (d) You have considered what (if any) preliminary treatment or trials are necessary.

☐ (e) You have considered the layout of your treatments to account for any unforseen variability in your set-up and you have established your control(s).

3. **Data collection:**

☐ (a) You have identified the units for all variables and determined how you will measure or monitor each variable. You have determined how much data you will collect, e.g. the number of samples you will take. The type of data collected will be determined by how you are measuring your variables.

☐ (b) You have considered how you will analyse the data you collect and made sure that your experimental design allows you to answer the questions you have asked.

☐ (c) You have designed a method for systematically recording your results and had this checked with a teacher. The format of your results table or spreadsheet accommodates all your raw results, any transformations you intend to make, and all trials and treatments.

☐ (d) You have recorded data from any preliminary trials and any necessary changes to your methodology.

Recording Results

Designing a table to record your results is part of planning your investigation. Once you have collected all your data, you will need to analyse and present it. To do this, it may be necessary to transform your data first, by calculating a mean or a rate. An example of a table for recording results is presented below. This example relates to the investigation described in the previous activity, but it represents a relatively standardised layout. The labels on the columns and rows are chosen to represent the design features of the investigation. The first column contains the entire range chosen for the independent variable. There are spaces for multiple sampling units, repeats (trials), and averages. A version of this table should be presented in your final report.

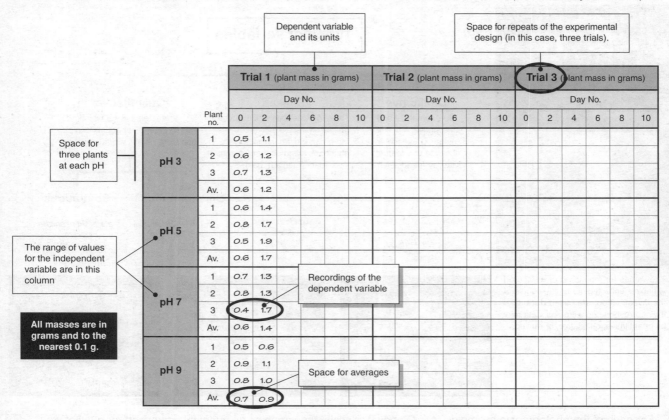

Dependent variable and its units

Space for repeats of the experimental design (in this case, three trials).

Space for three plants at each pH

The range of values for the independent variable are in this column

All masses are in grams and to the nearest 0.1 g.

Recordings of the dependent variable

Space for averages

	Plant no.	Trial 1 (plant mass in grams)						Trial 2 (plant mass in grams)						Trial 3 (plant mass in grams)					
		Day No.						Day No.						Day No.					
		0	2	4	6	8	10	0	2	4	6	8	10	0	2	4	6	8	10
pH 3	1	0.5	1.1																
	2	0.6	1.2																
	3	0.7	1.3																
	Av.	0.6	1.2																
pH 5	1	0.6	1.4																
	2	0.8	1.7																
	3	0.5	1.9																
	Av.	0.6	1.7																
pH 7	1	0.7	1.3																
	2	0.8	1.3																
	3	0.4	1.7																
	Av.	0.6	1.4																
pH 9	1	0.5	0.6																
	2	0.9	1.1																
	3	0.8	1.0																
	Av.	0.7	0.9																

Skills in Biology

1. In the space (below) design a table to collect data from the case study below. Include space for individual results and averages from the three set ups (use the table above as a guide).

Case Study
Carbon dioxide levels in a respiration chamber

A datalogger was used to monitor the concentrations of carbon dioxide (CO_2) in respiration chambers containing five green leaves from one plant species. The entire study was performed in conditions of full light (quantified) and involved three identical set-ups. The CO_2 concentrations were measured every minute, over a period of ten minutes, using a CO_2 sensor. A mean CO_2 concentration (for the three set-ups) was calculated. The study was carried out two more times, two days apart.

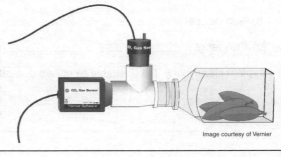

Image courtesy of Vernier

2. Next, the effect of various light intensities (low light, half-light, and full light) on CO_2 concentration was investigated. Describe how the results table for this investigation would differ from the one you have drawn above (for full light only):

_____

_____

Variables and Data

When planning any kind of biological investigation, it is important to consider the type of data that will be collected. It is best, whenever possible, to collect quantitative or numerical data, as these data lend themselves well to analysis and statistical testing. Recording data in a systematic way as you collect it, e.g. using a table or spreadsheet, is important, especially if data manipulation and transformation are required. It is also useful to calculate summary, descriptive statistics (e.g. mean, median) as you proceed. These will help you to recognise important trends and features in your data as they become apparent.

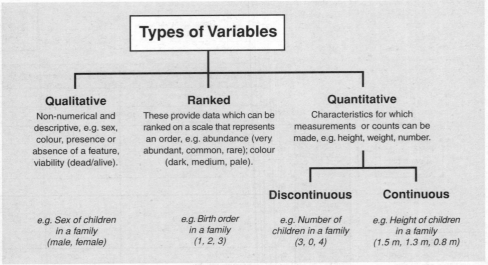

Types of Variables

Qualitative

Non-numerical and descriptive, e.g. sex, colour, presence or absence of a feature, viability (dead/alive).

Ranked

These provide data which can be ranked on a scale that represents an order, e.g. abundance (very abundant, common, rare); colour (dark, medium, pale).

Quantitative

Characteristics for which measurements or counts can be made, e.g. height, weight, number.

Discontinuous

Continuous

e.g. Sex of children in a family (male, female)

e.g. Birth order in a family (1, 2, 3)

e.g. Number of children in a family (3, 0, 4)

e.g. Height of children in a family (1.5 m, 1.3 m, 0.8 m)

The values for monitored or measured variables, collected during the course of the investigation, are called **data**. Like their corresponding variables, data may be quantitative, qualitative, or ranked.

A: Leaf shape

B: Number per litter

C: Fish length

1. For each of the photographic examples (A – C above), classify the variables as quantitative, ranked, or qualitative:

   (a) Leaf shape: _____

   (b) Number per litter: _____

   (c) Fish length: _____

2. Explain clearly why it is desirable to collect quantitative data where possible in biological studies: _____
   _____
   _____
   _____
   _____

3. Suggest how you might measure the colour of light (red, blue, green) quantitatively: _____
   _____

4. (a) Give an example of data that could not be collected in a quantitative manner, explaining your answer:
   _____
   _____

   (b) Sometimes, ranked data are given numerical values, e.g. rare = 1, occasional = 2, frequent = 3, common = 4, abundant = 5. Suggest why these data are sometimes called **semi-quantitative**:
   _____
   _____

Related activities: Descriptive Statistics

Transforming Raw Data

Data often have to be transformed as a first step in the initial analysis of results. Transforming data can make them more useful by helping to highlight trends and making important features more obvious. Data transformations may be quite simple (e.g. percentages, totals, and rates) or they may be more complex transformations used before statistical procedures (e.g. log transformations). Some of the simple transformations are outlined below.

Transformation	Rationale for transformation
Frequency table	A tally chart of the number of times a value occurs in a data set. It is a useful first step in data analysis as a neatly constructed tally chart can double as a simple histogram.
Total	The sum of all data values for a variable. Useful as an initial stage in data handling, especially in comparing replicates. Used in making other data transformations.
Percentages	Provide a clear expression of what proportion of data fall into any particular category. This relationship may not be obvious from the raw data values.
Rates	Expressed as a measure per unit time. Rates show how a variable changes over a standard time period (e.g. one second, one minute or one hour). Rates allow meaningful comparison of data that may have been recorded over different time periods.
Reciprocals	Reciprocals of time (1/data value) can provide a crude measure of rate in situations where the variable measured is the total time taken to complete a task, e.g. time taken for a colour change to occur in an enzyme reaction.
Relative values	These involve expression of data values relative to a standard value e.g. number of road deaths per 1000 cars or calorie consumption per gram of body weight. They allow data from different sample sizes or different organisms to be meaningfully compared. Sometimes they are expressed as a percentage (e.g. 35%) or as a proportion (e.g. 0.35).

Skills in Biology

1. (a) Explain what it means to **transform data**: _____

   _____

   (b) Briefly explain the general purpose of transforming data: _____

   _____

   _____

2. For each of the following examples, state a suitable transformation, together with a reason for your choice:

   (a) Determining relative abundance from counts of four plant species in two different habitat areas:

   Suitable transformation: _____

   Reason: _____

   (b) Making a meaningful comparison between animals of different size in the volume of oxygen each consumed:

   Suitable transformation: _____

   Reason: _____

   (c) Making a meaningful comparison of the time taken for chemical precipitation to occur in a flask at different pH values:

   Suitable transformation: _____

   Reason: _____

   (d) Determining the effect of temperature on the production of carbon dioxide by respiring seeds:

   Suitable transformation: _____

   Reason: _____

3. Complete the transformations for each of the tables on the right. The first value is provided in each case.

(a) TABLE: *Incidence of cyanogenic clover in different areas*

Working: 124 ÷ 159 = 0.78 = 78%

This is the number of cyanogenic clover out of the total.

Incidence of cyanogenic clover in different areas

Clover plant type	Frost free area		Frost prone area		Totals
	Number	%	Number	%	
Cyanogenic	124	78	26		
Acyanogenic	35		115		
Total	159				

(b) TABLE: *Plant transpiration loss using a bubble potometer*

Working: (9.0 – 8.0) ÷ 5 min = 0.2

This is the distance the bubble moved over the first 5 minutes. Note that there is no data entry possible for the first reading (0 min) because no difference can be calculated.

Plant transpiration loss using a bubble potometer

Time /min	Pipette arm reading /cm^3	Plant water loss /$cm^3\ min^{-1}$
0	9.0	–
5	8.0	0.2
10	7.2	
15	6.2	
20	4.9	

(c) TABLE: *Photosynthetic rate at different light intensities*

Working: 1 ÷ 15 = 0.067

This is time taken for the leaf to float. A reciprocal gives a per minute rate (the variable measured is the time taken for an event to occur).

NOTE: In this experiment, the flotation time is used as a crude measure of photosynthetic rate. As oxygen bubbles are produced as a product of photosynthesis, they stick to the leaf disc and increase its buoyancy. The faster the rate, the sooner they come to the surface. The rates of photosynthesis should be measured over similar time intervals, so the rate is transformed to a 'per minute' basis (the reciprocal of time).

Photosynthetic rate at different light intensities

Light intensity /%	Average time for leaf disc to float / min	Reciprocal of time / min^{-1}
100	15	0.067
50	25	
25	50	
11	93	
6	187	

(d) TABLE: *Frequency of size classes in a sample of eels*

Working: (7 ÷ 270) x 100 = 2.6 %

This is the number of individuals out of the total that appear in the size class 0-50 mm. The relative frequency is rounded to one decimal place.

Frequency of size classes in a sample of eels

Size class /mm	Frequency	Relative frequency/ %
0-50	7	2.6
50-99	23	
100-149	59	
150-199	98	
200-249	50	
250-299	30	
300-349	3	
Total	270	

Data Presentation

Data can be presented in a number of ways. **Tables** provide an accurate record of numerical values and allow you to organise your data in a way that helps to identify trends and facilitate analysis. **Graphs** provide a visual representation of trends in the data that may not be evident from a table. It is useful to plot your data as soon as possible, even during your experiment, as this will help you to evaluate your results as you proceed and make adjustments as necessary (e.g. to the sampling interval). The choice between graphing or tabulation in the final report depends on the type and complexity of the data and the information that you are wanting to convey. Usually, both are appropriate. Some of the basic rules for constructing tables and graphs are outlined below. Note that values for standard deviation and 95% confidence intervals are provided in these examples. Calculating these will help you to understand your data better and critically evaluate your results. Always allow enough space for a graph, e.g. one third to one half of an A4 page. The examples in this workbook are usually reduced for reasons of space.

Presenting Data in Tables

Tables should have an accurate, descriptive title. Number tables consecutively through the report.

Independent variable in left column.

Control values (if present) should be placed at the beginning of the table.

Each row should show a different experimental treatment, organism, sampling site etc.

Table 1: Length and growth of the third internode of bean plants receiving three different hormone treatments (data are given ± standard deviation).

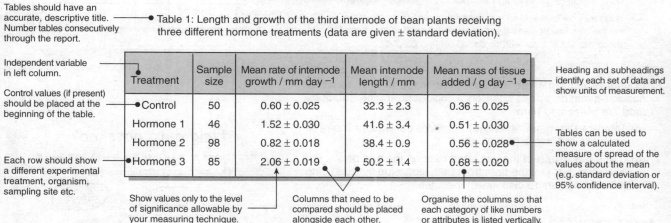

Treatment	Sample size	Mean rate of internode growth / mm day^{-1}	Mean internode length / mm	Mean mass of tissue added / g day^{-1}
Control	50	0.60 ± 0.025	32.3 ± 2.3	0.36 ± 0.025
Hormone 1	46	1.52 ± 0.030	41.6 ± 3.4	0.51 ± 0.030
Hormone 2	98	0.82 ± 0.018	38.4 ± 0.9	0.56 ± 0.028
Hormone 3	85	2.06 ± 0.019	50.2 ± 1.4	0.68 ± 0.020

Heading and subheadings identify each set of data and show units of measurement.

Tables can be used to show a calculated measure of spread of the values about the mean (e.g. standard deviation or 95% confidence interval).

Show values only to the level of significance allowable by your measuring technique.

Columns that need to be compared should be placed alongside each other.

Organise the columns so that each category of like numbers or attributes is listed vertically.

Presenting Data in Graph Format

Plot points accurately. Different responses can be distinguished using different symbols, lines or bar colours.

Label both axes (provide SI units of measurement if necessary).

Place the dependent variable, e.g. biological response, on the vertical (y) axis (if you are drawing a scatter graph it does not matter).

A break in an axis allows economical use of space if there are no data in the "broken" area. A floating axis (where zero points do not meet) allows data points to be plotted away from the vertical axis.

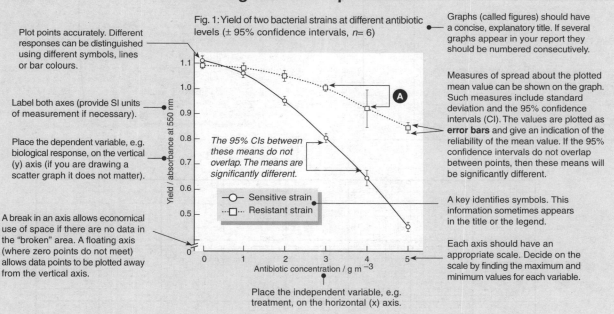

Fig. 1: Yield of two bacterial strains at different antibiotic levels (± 95% confidence intervals, $n = 6$)

The 95% CIs between these means do not overlap. The means are significantly different.

Key:
—○— Sensitive strain
···□··· Resistant strain

Yield / absorbance at 550 nm

Antibiotic concentration / g m^{-3}

Graphs (called figures) should have a concise, explanatory title. If several graphs appear in your report they should be numbered consecutively.

Measures of spread about the plotted mean value can be shown on the graph. Such measures include standard deviation and the 95% confidence intervals (CI). The values are plotted as **error bars** and give an indication of the reliability of the mean value. If the 95% confidence intervals do not overlap between points, then these means will be significantly different.

A key identifies symbols. This information sometimes appears in the title or the legend.

Each axis should have an appropriate scale. Decide on the scale by finding the maximum and minimum values for each variable.

Place the independent variable, e.g. treatment, on the horizontal (x) axis.

1. What can you conclude about the difference (labelled **A**) between the two means plotted above? Explain your answer:

_____

2. Discuss the reasons for including both graphs and tables in a final report: _____

_____

_____

_____

Drawing Bar Graphs

Guidelines for Bar Graphs

Bar graphs are appropriate for data that are non-numerical and **discrete** for at least one variable, i.e. they are grouped into separate categories. There are no dependent or independent variables. Important features of this type of graph include:

- Data are collected for discontinuous, non-numerical categories (e.g. place, colour, and species), so the bars do not touch.

- Data values may be entered on or above the bars if you wish.

- Multiple sets of data can be displayed side by side for direct comparison (e.g. males and females in the same age group).

- Axes may be reversed so that the categories are on the x axis, i.e. the bars can be vertical or horizontal. When they are vertical, these graphs are sometimes called column graphs.

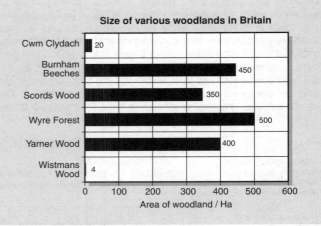

Size of various woodlands in Britain

1. Counts of eight mollusc species were made from a series of quadrat samples at two sites on a rocky shore. The summary data are presented here.

   (a) Tabulate the mean (**average**) numbers per square metre at each site in Table 1 (below left).

   (b) Plot a **bar graph** of the tabulated data on the grid below. For each species, plot the data from both sites side by side using different colours to distinguish the sites.

Average abundance of 8 mollusc species from two sites along a rocky shore.

Species	Average/ no m^{-2}	
	Site 1	Site 2

Field data notebook

Total counts at site 1 (11 quadrats) and site 2 (10 quadrats). Quadrats 1 sq m.

Species	Site 1		Site 2	
	No m^{-2}		No m^{-2}	
	Total	Mean	Total	Mean
Ornate limpet	232	21	299	30
Radiate limpet	68	6	344	34
Limpet sp. A	420	38	0	0
Cats-eye	68	6	16	2
Top shell	16	2	43	4
Limpet sp. B	628	57	389	39
Limpet sp. C	0	0	22	2
Chiton	12	1	30	3

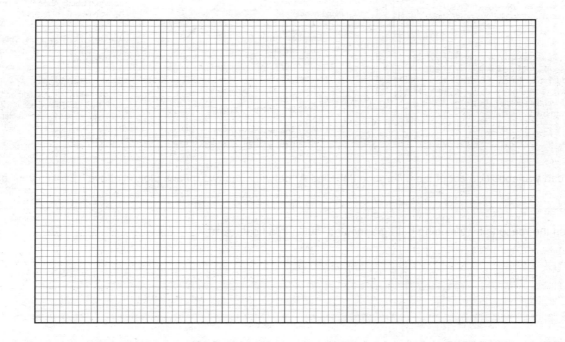

Related activities: Transforming Raw Data

Drawing Histograms

Guidelines for Histograms

Histograms are plots of **continuous** data and are often used to represent frequency distributions, where the y-axis shows the number of times a particular measurement or value was obtained. For this reason, they are often called frequency histograms. Important features of this type of graph include:

- The data are numerical and continuous (e.g. height or weight), so the bars touch.

- The x-axis usually records the class interval. The y-axis usually records the number of individuals in each class interval (frequency).

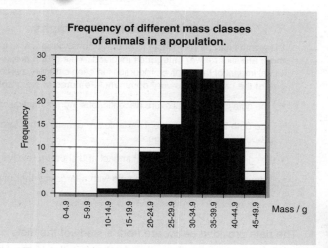

Frequency of different mass classes of animals in a population.

Skills in Biology

1. The weight data provided below were recorded from 95 individuals (male and female), older than 17 years.

   (a) Create a tally chart (frequency table) in the frame provided, organising the weight data into a form suitable for plotting. An example of the tally for the weight grouping 55-59.9 kg has been completed for you as an example. Note that the raw data values, once they are recorded as counts on the tally chart, are crossed off the data set in the notebook. It is important to do this in order to prevent data entry errors.

   (b) Plot a **frequency histogram** of the tallied data on the grid provided below.

Weight /kg	Tally	Total
45-49.9		
50-54.9		
55-59.9	LHT //	7
60-64.9		
65-69.9		
70-74.9		
75-79.9		
80-84.9		
85-89.9		
90-94.9		
95-99.9		
100-104.9		
105-109.9		

Lab notebook

Weight (in kg) of 95 individuals

63.4	81.2	65
56.5	83.3	75.6
84	95	76.8
81.5	105.5	67.8
73.4	82	68.3
56	73.5	63.5
60.4	75.2	58
83.5	63	58.5
82	70.4	50
61	82.2	92
55.2	87.8	91.5
48	86.5	88.3
53.5	85.5	81
63.8	87	72
69	98	66.5
82.8	71	61.5
68.5	76	66
67.2	72.5	65.5
82.5	61	67.4
83	60.5	73
78.4	67	67
76.5	86	71
83.4	85	70.5
77.5	93.5	65.5
77	62	68
87	62.5	90
89	63	83.5
93.4	60	73
83	71.5	66
80	73.8	57.5
76	77.5	76
56	74	

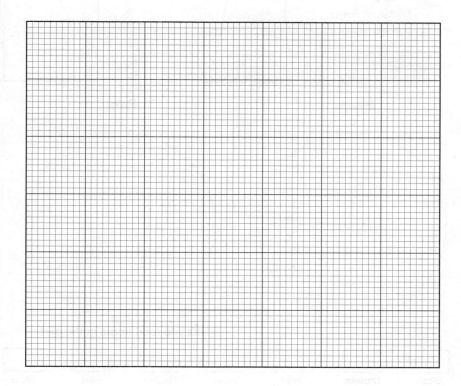

Related activities: Transforming Raw Data

DA 2

Drawing Pie Graphs

Guidelines for Pie Graphs

Pie graphs can be used instead of bar graphs, generally in cases where there are six or fewer categories involved. A pie graph provides strong visual impact of the relative proportions in each category, particularly where one of the categories is very dominant. Features of pie graphs include:

- The data for one variable are discontinuous (non-numerical or categories).

- The data for the dependent variable are usually in the form of counts, proportions, or percentages.

- Pie graphs are good for visual impact and showing relative proportions.

- They are not suitable for data sets with a large number of categories.

Average residential water use

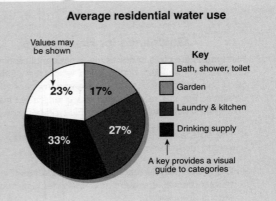

Values may be shown → 23% 17% 27% 33%

Key
- Bath, shower, toilet
- Garden
- Laundry & kitchen
- Drinking supply

A key provides a visual guide to categories

1. The data provided below are from a study of the diets of three vertebrates.

(a) Tabulate the data from the notebook in the frame provided. Calculate the angle for each percentage, given that each percentage point is equal to 3.6° (the first example is provided: 23.6 x 3.6 = 85).

(b) Plot a pie graph for each animal in the circles provided. The circles have been marked at 5° intervals to enable you to do this exercise without a protractor. For the purposes of this exercise, begin your pie graphs at the 0° (= 360°) mark and work in a clockwise direction from the largest to the smallest percentage. Use one key for all three pie graphs.

Field data notebook

% of different food items in the diet

Food item	Stoats	Rats	Cats
Birds	23.6	1.4	6.9
Crickets	15.3	23.6	0
Other insects (not crickets)	15.3	20.8	1.9
Voles	9.2	0	19.4
Rabbits	8.3	0	18.1
Rats	6.1	0	43.1
Mice	13.9	0	10.6
Fruits and seeds	0	40.3	0
Green leaves	0	13.9	0
Unidentified	8.3	0	0

Percentage occurrence of different foods in the diet of stoats, rats, and cats. Graph angle representing the % is shown to assist plotting.

Food item in diet	Stoats		Rats		Cats	
	% in diet	Angle / °	% in diet	Angle / °	% in diet	Angle / °
Birds	23.6	85				

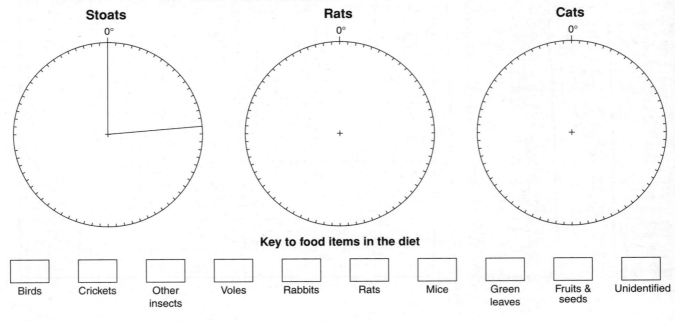

Stoats 0°

Rats 0°

Cats 0°

Key to food items in the diet

| Birds | Crickets | Other insects | Voles | Rabbits | Rats | Mice | Green leaves | Fruits & seeds | Unidentified |

DA 2 **Related activities**: Transforming Raw Data

Drawing Kite Graphs

Guidelines for Kite Graphs

Kite graphs are ideal for representing distributional data, e.g. abundance along an environmental gradient. They are elongated figures drawn along a baseline. Important features of kite graphs include:

- Each kite represents changes in species abundance across a landscape. The abundance can be calculated from the kite width.

- They often involve plots for more than one species; this makes them good for highlighting probable differences in habitat preferences between species.

- A thin line on a kite graph represents species absence.

- The axes can be reversed depending on preference.

- Kite graphs may also be used to show changes in distribution with time, for example, with daily or seasonal cycles of movement.

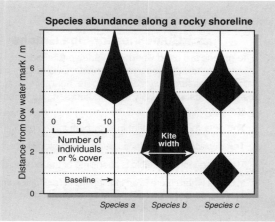

Species abundance along a rocky shoreline

1. The following data were collected from three streams of different lengths and flow rates. Invertebrates were collected at 0.5 km intervals from the headwaters (0 km) to the stream mouth. Their wet weight was measured and recorded (per m^2).

   (a) Tabulate the data below for plotting.

   (b) Plot a **kite graph** of the data from all three streams on the grid provided below. Do not forget to include a scale so that the weight at each point on the kite can be calculated.

Wet mass of invertebrates along three different streams

Distance from mouth/ km	Wet weight/ g m^{-2}		
	Stream A	Stream B	Stream C

Field data notebook

Mass per m^2 of invertebrates from 3 streams.

Stream A: Slow flowing

Km from mouth	g m^{-2}
5.0	0.3
4.5	2.5
4.0	0.2
3.5	0.7
3.0	0.1
2.5	0.6
2.0	0.3
1.5	0.3
1.0	0.4
0.5	0.5
0	0.4

Stream B: Fast, steep

Km from mouth	g m^{-2}
2.5	0.3
2.0	0.4
1.5	0.5
1.0	0.1
0.5	0.6
0	0.4

Stream C: Steep torrent

Km from mouth	g m^{-2}
1.5	0.2
1.0	0
0.5	0.5
0	0

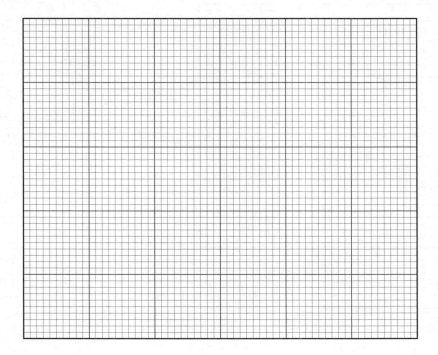

Related activities: Transforming Raw Data

DA 2

Skills in Biology

Drawing Line Graphs

Guidelines for Line Graphs

Line graphs are used when one variable (the independent variable) affects another, the dependent variable. Line graphs can be drawn without a measure of spread (top figure, right) or with some calculated measure of data variability (bottom figure, right). Important features of line graphs include:

- The data must be continuous for both variables.

- The dependent variable is usually the biological response.

- The independent variable is often time or the experimental treatment.

- In cases where there is an implied trend (e.g. one variable increases with the other), a line of best fit is usually plotted through the data points to show the relationship.

- If fluctuations in the data are likely to be important (e.g. with climate and other environmental data) the data points are usually connected directly (point to point).

- Line graphs may be drawn with measure of error. The data are presented as points (the calculated means), with bars above and below, indicating a measure of variability or spread in the data (e.g. standard error, standard deviation, or 95% confidence intervals).

- Where no error value has been calculated, the scatter can be shown by plotting the individual data points vertically above and below the mean. By convention, bars are not used to indicate the range of raw values in a data set.

Metabolic rate of a rat at different temperatures

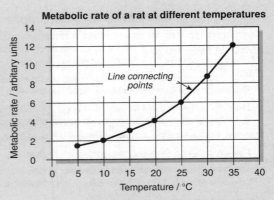

Growth rate in peas at different temperatures

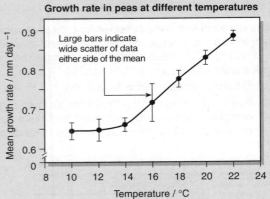

1. The results (shown right) were collected in a study investigating the effect of temperature on the activity of an enzyme.

   (a) Using the results provided in the table (right), plot a line graph on the grid below:

   (b) Estimate the rate of reaction at 15°C: _____

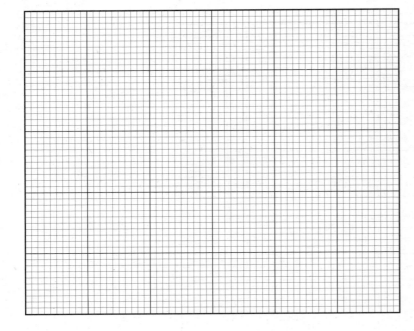

Lab Notebook

An enzyme's activity at different temperatures

Temperature /°C	Rate of reaction /mg of product formed per minute
10	1.0
20	2.1
30	3.2
35	3.7
40	4.1
45	3.7
50	2.7
60	0

DA 2

Related activities: Transforming Raw Data, The Reliability of the Mean, Interpreting Line and Scatter Graphs

Plotting Multiple Data Sets

A single figure can be used to show two or more data sets, i.e. more than one curve can be plotted per set of axes. This type of presentation is useful when you want to visually compare the trends for two or more treatments, or the response of one species against the response of another. Important points regarding this format are:

- If the two data sets use the same measurement units and a similar range of values for the independent variable, one scale on the y axis is used.

- If the two data sets use different units and/or have a very different range of values for the independent variable, two scales for the y axis are used (see example provided). The scales can be adjusted if necessary to avoid overlapping plots

- The two curves must be distinguished with a key.

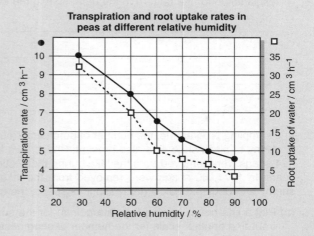

Transpiration and root uptake rates in peas at different relative humidity

2. A census of a deer population on an island indicated a population of 2000 animals in 1960. In 1961, ten wolves (natural predators of deer) were brought to the island in an attempt to control deer numbers. Over the next nine years, the numbers of deer and wolves were monitored. The results of these population surveys are presented in the table, right.

Plot a line graph (joining the data points) for the tabulated results. Use one scale (on the left) for numbers of deer and another scale (on the right) for the number of wolves. Use different symbols or colours to distinguish the lines and include a key.

Field data notebook
Results of a population survey on an island

Time /yr	Wolf numbers	Deer numbers
1961	10	2000
1962	12	2300
1963	16	2500
1964	22	2360
1965	28	2244
1966	24	2094
1967	21	1968
1968	18	1916
1969	19	1952

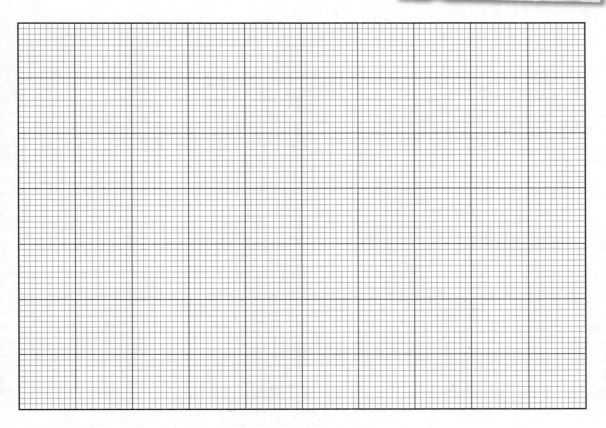

(b) Study the line graph that you plotted for the wolf and deer census on the previous page. Provide a plausible explanation for the pattern in the data, stating the evidence available to support your reasoning:

_____

_____

_____

_____

3. In a sampling programme, the number of perch and trout in a hydro-electric reservoir were monitored over a period of time. A colony of black shag was also present. Shags take large numbers of perch and (to a lesser extent) trout. In 1960-61, 424 shags were removed from the lake during the nesting season and nest counts were made every spring in subsequent years. In 1971, 60 shags were removed from the lake, and all existing nests dismantled. The results of the population survey are tabulated below (for reasons of space, the entire table format has been repeated to the right for 1970-1978).

(a) Plot a line graph (joining the data points) for the survey results. Use one scale (on the left) for numbers of perch and trout and another scale for the number of shag nests. Use different symbols to distinguish the lines and include a key.

(b) Use a vertical arrow to indicate the point at which shags and their nests were removed.

Results of population survey at reservoir

Time/ year	Fish number (average per haul)		Shag nest numbers	Time/ year continued	Fish number (average per haul)		Shag nest numbers
	Trout	Perch			Trout	Perch	
1960	–	–	16	1970	1.5	6	35
1961	–	–	4	1971	0.5	0.7	42
1962	1.5	11	5	1972	1	0.8	0
1963	0.8	9	10	1973	0.2	4	0
1964	0	5	22	1974	0.5	6.5	0
1965	1	1	25	1975	0.6	7.6	2
1966	1	2.9	35	1976	1	1.2	10
1967	2	5	40	1977	1.2	1.5	32
1968	1.5	4.6	26	1978	0.7	2	28
1969	1.5	6	32				

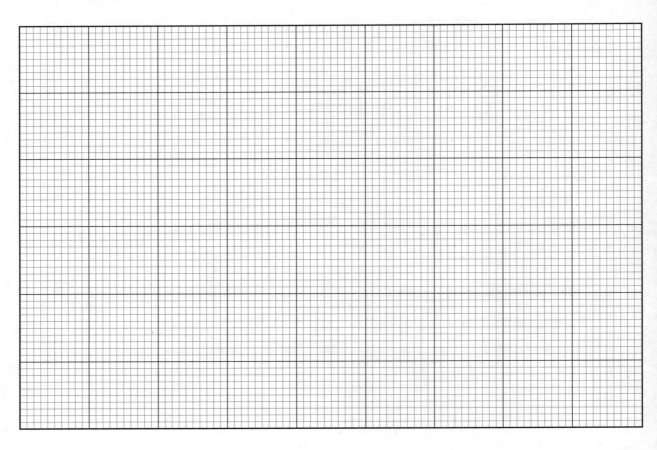

Interpreting Line & Scatter Graphs

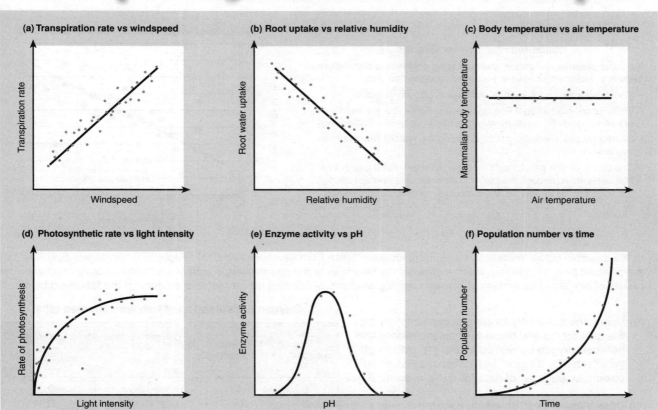

(a) Transpiration rate vs windspeed

Transpiration rate vs *Windspeed*

(b) Root uptake vs relative humidity

Root water uptake vs *Relative humidity*

(c) Body temperature vs air temperature

Mammalian body temperature vs *Air temperature*

(d) Photosynthetic rate vs light intensity

Rate of photosynthesis vs *Light intensity*

(e) Enzyme activity vs pH

Enzyme activity vs *pH*

(f) Population number vs time

Population number vs *Time*

1. For each of the graphs (b-f) above, give a description of the slope and an interpretation of how one variable changes with respect to the other. For the purposes of your description, call the independent variable (horizontal or x-axis) in each example "variable X" and the dependent variable (vertical or y-axis) "variable Y". Be aware that the existence of a relationship between two variables does not necessarily mean that the relationship is causative (although it may be).

(a) Slope: _Positive linear relationship, with constantly rising slope_

   Interpretation: _Variable Y (transpiration) increases regularly with increase in variable X (windspeed)_

(b) Slope: _____

   Interpretation: _____

(c) Slope: _____

   Interpretation: _____

(d) Slope: _____

   Interpretation: _____

(e) Slope: _____

   Interpretation: _____

(f) Slope: _____

   Interpretation: _____

2. Study the line graph that you plotted for the wolf and deer census on the previous page. Provide a plausible explanation for the pattern in the data, stating the evidence available to support your reasoning:

_____

_____

_____

_____

Related activities: Drawing Line Graphs

RDA 2

Drawing Scatter Plots

Guidelines for Scatter Graphs

A scatter graph is a common way to display continuous data where there is a relationship between two interdependent variables.

- The data for this graph must be continuous for both variables.
- There is no independent (manipulated) variable, but the variables are often correlated, i.e. they vary together in some predictable way.
- Scatter graphs are useful for determining the relationship between two variables.
- The points on the graph need not be connected, but a line of best fit is often drawn through the points to show the relationship between the variables (this may be drawn be eye or computer generated).

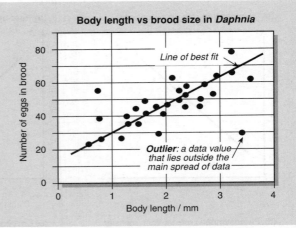

Body length vs brood size in *Daphnia*

1. In the example below, metabolic measurements were taken from seven Antarctic fish *Pagothenia borchgrevinski*. The fish are affected by a gill disease, which increases the thickness of the gas exchange surfaces and affects oxygen uptake. The results of oxygen consumption of fish with varying amounts of affected gill (at rest and swimming) are tabulated below.

(a) Using **one** scale only for oxygen consumption, plot the data on the grid below to show the relationship between oxygen consumption and the amount of gill affected by disease. Use different symbols or colours for each set of data (at rest and swimming).

(b) Draw a line of best fit through each set of points.

2. Describe the relationship between the amount of gill affected and oxygen consumption in the fish:

(a) For the **at rest** data set:

_____

_____

_____

_____

_____

_____

_____

(b) For the **swimming** data set:

_____

_____

_____

_____

_____

_____

_____

Oxygen consumption of fish with affected gills

Fish number	Percentage of gill affected	Oxygen consumption/ $cm^3 \, g^{-1} \, h^{-1}$	
		At rest	Swimming
1	0	0.05	0.29
2	95	0.04	0.11
3	60	0.04	0.14
4	30	0.05	0.22
5	90	0.05	0.08
6	65	0.04	0.18
7	45	0.04	0.20

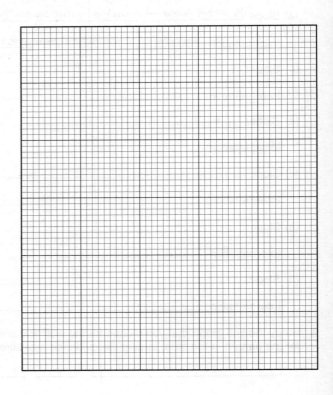

3. Describe how the gill disease affects oxygen uptake in resting fish: _____

_____

© Biozone International 2008

Related activities: Interpreting Line and Scatter Graphs

Taking the Next Step

By this stage, you will have completed many of the early stages of your investigation. Now is a good time to review what you have done and reflect on the biological significance of what you are investigating. Review the first page of this flow chart in light of your findings so far. You are now ready to begin a more in-depth analysis of your results. Never under-estimate the value of plotting your data, even at a very early stage. This will help you decide on the best type of data analysis (see the next page).

Photos courtesy of Pasco

Observation

Something ...

- Changes or affects something else.

- Is more abundant, etc. along a transect, at one site, temperature, concentration, etc. than others.

- Is bigger, taller, or grows more quickly.

Pilot study

Lets you check ...

- Equipment, sampling sites, sampling interval.

- How long it takes to collect data.

- Problems with identification or other unforeseen issues.

Research

To find out ...

- Basic biology and properties.

- What other biotic or abiotic factors may have an effect.

- Its place within the broader biological context.

Analysis

Are you looking for a ...

- **Difference**.

- **Trend** or relationship.

- **Goodness of fit** (to a theoretical outcome).

GO TO NEXT PAGE

Be prepared to revise your study design in the light of the results from your pilot study

Variables

Next you need to ...

- Identify the key variables likely to cause the effect.

- Identify variables to be controlled in order to give the best chance of showing the effect that you want to study.

Hypothesis

Must be ...

- Testable

- Able to generate predictions

so that in the end you can say whether your data supports or allows you to reject your hypothesis.

Related activities: Descriptive Statistics, Interpreting Sample Variability

36

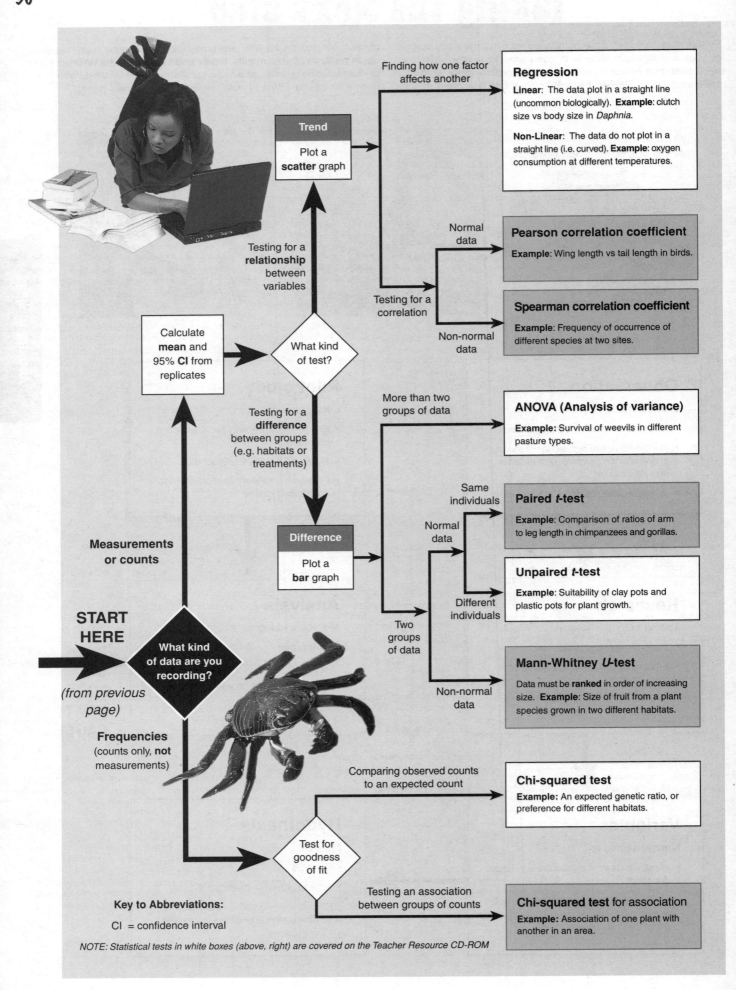

Finding how one factor
affects another

Regression

Linear: The data plot in a straight line (uncommon biologically). **Example:** clutch size vs body size in *Daphnia*.

Non-Linear: The data do not plot in a straight line (i.e. curved). **Example:** oxygen consumption at different temperatures.

Trend

Plot a **scatter** graph

Testing for a **relationship** between variables

Normal data

Pearson correlation coefficient

Example: Wing length vs tail length in birds.

Testing for a correlation

Non-normal data

Spearman correlation coefficient

Example: Frequency of occurrence of different species at two sites.

Calculate **mean** and 95% **CI** from replicates

What kind of test?

Testing for a **difference** between groups (e.g. habitats or treatments)

More than two groups of data

ANOVA (Analysis of variance)

Example: Survival of weevils in different pasture types.

Difference

Plot a **bar** graph

Same individuals

Paired *t*-test

Example: Comparison of ratios of arm to leg length in chimpanzees and gorillas.

Normal data

Different individuals

Unpaired *t*-test

Example: Suitability of clay pots and plastic pots for plant growth.

Two groups of data

Measurements or counts

START HERE

(from previous page)

What kind of data are you recording?

Non-normal data

Mann-Whitney *U*-test

Data must be **ranked** in order of increasing size. **Example:** Size of fruit from a plant species grown in two different habitats.

Frequencies (counts only, **not** measurements)

Comparing observed counts to an expected count

Chi-squared test

Example: An expected genetic ratio, or preference for different habitats.

Test for goodness of fit

Key to Abbreviations:

CI = confidence interval

Testing an association between groups of counts

Chi-squared test for association

Example: Association of one plant with another in an area.

NOTE: Statistical tests in white boxes (above, right) are covered on the Teacher Resource CD-ROM

Descriptive Statistics

For most investigations, measures of the biological response are made from more than one sampling unit. The sample size (the number of sampling units) will vary depending on the resources available. In lab based investigations, the sample size may be as small as two or three (e.g. two test-tubes in each treatment). In field studies, each individual may be a sampling unit, and the sample size can be very large (e.g. 100 individuals). It is useful to summarise the data collected using **descriptive statistics**.

Descriptive statistics, such as mean, median, and mode, can help to highlight trends or patterns in the data. Each of these statistics is appropriate to certain types of data or distributions, e.g. a mean is not appropriate for data with a skewed distribution (see below). Frequency graphs are useful for indicating the distribution of data. Standard deviation and standard error are statistics used to quantify the amount of spread in the data and evaluate the reliability of estimates of the true (population) mean.

Variation in Data

Whether they are obtained from observation or experiments, most biological data show variability. In a set of data values, it is useful to know the value about which most of the data are grouped; the centre value. This value can be the mean, median, or mode depending on the type of variable involved (see schematic below). The main purpose of these statistics is to summarise important trends in your data and to provide the basis for statistical analyses.

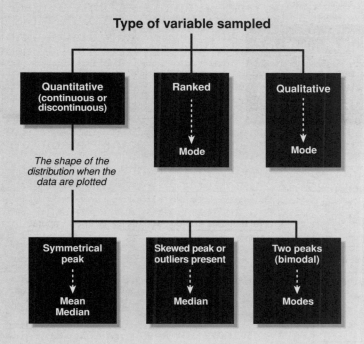

Variability in continuous data is often displayed as a **frequency distribution**. A frequency plot will indicate whether the data have a normal distribution (A), with a symmetrical spread of data about the mean, or whether the distribution is skewed (B), or bimodal (C). The shape of the distribution will determine which statistic (mean, median, or mode) best describes the central tendency of the sample data.

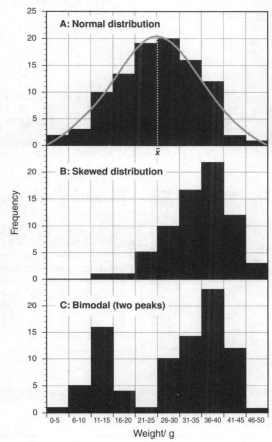

Statistic	Definition and use	Method of calculation
Mean	• The average of all data entries. • Measure of central tendency for normally distributed data.	• Add up all the data entries. • Divide by the total number of data entries.
Median	• The middle value when data entries are placed in rank order. • A good measure of central tendency for skewed distributions.	• Arrange the data in increasing rank order. • Identify the middle value. • For an even number of entries, find the mid point of the two middle values.
Mode	• The most common data value. • Suitable for bimodal distributions and qualitative data.	• Identify the category with the highest number of data entries using a tally chart or a bar graph.
Range	• The difference between the smallest and largest data values. • Provides a crude indication of data spread.	• Identify the smallest and largest values and find the difference between them.

When NOT to calculate a mean:

In certain situations, calculation of a simple arithmetic mean is inappropriate.

Remember:

• *DO NOT* calculate a mean from values that are already means (averages) themselves.

• *DO NOT* calculate a mean of ratios (e.g. percentages) for several groups of different sizes; go back to the raw values and recalculate.

• *DO NOT* calculate a mean when the measurement scale is not linear, e.g. pH units are not measured on a linear scale.

Related activities: Interpreting Sample Variability

DA 2

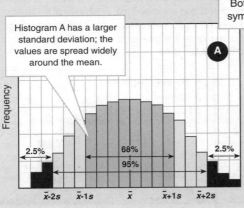

Normal distribution

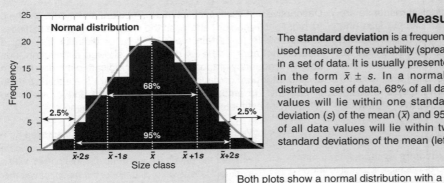

Measuring Spread

The **standard deviation** is a frequently used measure of the variability (spread) in a set of data. It is usually presented in the form $\bar{x} \pm s$. In a normally distributed set of data, 68% of all data values will lie within one standard deviation (s) of the mean ($\bar{x}$) and 95% of all data values will lie within two standard deviations of the mean (left).

Two different sets of data can have the same mean and range, yet the distribution of data within the range can be quite different. In both the data sets pictured in the histograms below, 68% of the values lie within the range $\bar{x} \pm 1s$ and 95% of the values lie within $\bar{x} \pm 2s$. However, in B, the data values are more tightly clustered around the mean.

Both plots show a normal distribution with a symmetrical spread of values about the mean.

Histogram A has a larger standard deviation; the values are spread widely around the mean.

Histogram B has a smaller standard deviation; the values are clustered more tightly around the mean.

A

B

Calculating s

Standard deviation is easily calculated using a spreadsheet.

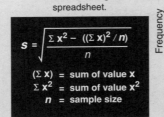

$$s = \sqrt{\frac{\Sigma\, x^2 - ((\Sigma\, x)^2 / n)}{n}}$$

$(\Sigma\, x)$ = sum of value x
$\Sigma\, x^2$ = sum of value x^2
n = sample size

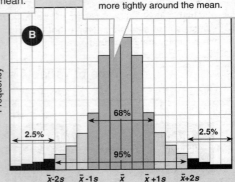

Fern spores

Case Study: Fern Reproduction

Raw data (below) and descriptive statistics (right) from a survey of the number of spores found on the fronds of a fern plant.

Raw data: Number of spores per frond

64	60	64	62	68	66	63
69	70	63	70	70	63	62
71	69	59	70	66	61	70
67	64	63	64			

$$\frac{\text{Total of data entries}}{\text{Number of entries}} = \frac{1641}{25} = 66 \text{ spores}$$

Mean

Number of spores per frond (in rank order)	
59	66
60	66
61	67
62	68
62	69
63	69
63	70
63	70
63	70
64	70
64	70
64	71
64	

Median

Mode

Spores per frond	Tally	Total
59	✔	1
60	✔	1
61	✔	1
62	✔✔	2
63	✔✔✔✔	4
64	✔✔✔✔	4
65		0
66	✔✔	2
67	✔	1
68	✔	1
69	✔✔	2
70	✔✔✔✔✔	5
71	✔	1

1. Give a reason for the difference between the mean, median, and mode for the fern spore data:

_____

_____

_____

_____

2. Calculate the mean, median, and mode for the data on beetle masses below. Draw up a tally chart and show all calculations:

Beetle masses / g		
2.2	2.1	2.6
2.5	2.4	2.8
2.5	2.7	2.5
2.6	2.6	2.5
2.2	2.8	2.4

Interpreting Sample Variability

Measures of central tendency, such as mean, attempt to identify the most representative value in a set of data, but the description of a data set also requires that we know something about how far the data values are spread around that central measure. As we have seen in the previous activity, the **standard deviation** (s) gives a simple measure of the spread or **dispersion** in data. The **variance** (s^2) is also a measure of dispersion, but the standard deviation is usually preferred because it is expressed in the original units. Two data sets could have exactly the same

mean values, but very different values of dispersion. If we were simply to use the central tendency to compare these data sets, the results would (incorrectly) suggest that they were alike. The assumptions we make about a population will be affected by what the sample data tell us. This is why it is important that sample data are unbiased (e.g. collected by **random sampling**) and that the sample set is as large as practicable. This exercise will help to illustrate how our assumptions about a population are influenced by the information provided by the sample data.

Complete sample set
n = 689 (random)

Length in mm	Freq
25	1
26	0
27	0
28	0
29	0
30	0
31	0
32	2
33	3
34	3
35	4
36	5
37	10
38	23
39	22
40	33
41	39
42	41
43	41
44	36
45	49
46	32
47	14
48	32
49	27
50	25
51	24
52	17
53	18
54	27
55	21
56	20
57	11
58	18
59	16
60	22
61	13
62	8
63	10
64	5
65	7
66	2
67	3
68	3
69	1
70	0
71	1

Random Sampling, Sample Size, and Dispersion in Data

Sample size and sampling bias can both affect the information we obtain when we sample a population. In this exercise you will calculate some descriptive statistics for some sample data.

The complete set of sample data we are working with comprises 689 length measurements of year zero (young of the year) perch (column left). Basic descriptive statstics for the data have bee calculated for you below and the frequency histogram has also been plotted.

Look at this data set and then complete the exercise to calculate the same statistics from each of two smaller data sets (tabulated right) drawn from the same population. This excercise shows how random sampling, large sample size, and sampling bias affect our statistical assessment of variation in a population.

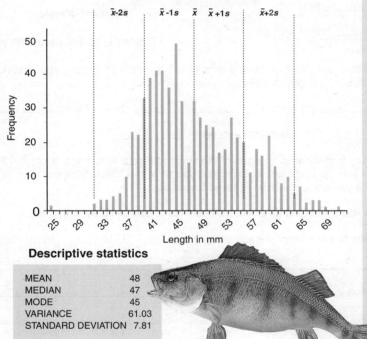

Length of year zero perch

$\bar{x}-2s$ $\bar{x}-1s$ $\bar{x}$ $\bar{x}+1s$ $\bar{x}+2s$

(Frequency vs Length in mm)

Descriptive statistics

MEAN	48
MEDIAN	47
MODE	45
VARIANCE	61.03
STANDARD DEVIATION	7.81

Small sample set
n = 30 (random)

Length in mm	Freq
25	1
26	0
27	0
28	0
29	0
30	0
31	0
32	0
33	0
34	0
35	2
36	0
37	0
38	3
39	2
40	1
41	3
42	0
43	0
44	0
45	0
46	1
47	0
48	2
49	0
50	0
51	1
52	3
53	0
54	0
55	0
56	0
57	1
58	0
59	3
60	2
61	2
62	0
63	0
64	0
65	0
66	0
67	2
68	1
	30

Small sample set
n = 50 (bias)

Length in mm	Freq
46	1
47	0
48	0
49	1
50	0
51	0
52	1
53	1
54	1
55	1
56	0
57	2
58	2
59	4
60	1
61	0
62	8
63	10
64	13
65	2
66	0
67	2
	50

The person gathering this set of data was biased towards selecting larger fish because the mesh size on the net was too large to retain small fish

This population was sampled randomly to obtain this data set

This column records the number of fish of each size

Number of fish in the sample

1. For the complete data set (*n* = 689) calculate the percentage of data falling within:

   (a) ± one standard deviation of the mean: _____

   (b) ± two standard deviations of the mean: _____

   (c) Explain what this information tells you about the distribution of year zero perch from this site: _____

   _____

2. Give another reason why you might reach the same conclusion about the distribution: _____

   _____

Related activities: Descriptive Statistics, Taking the Next Step

DA 3

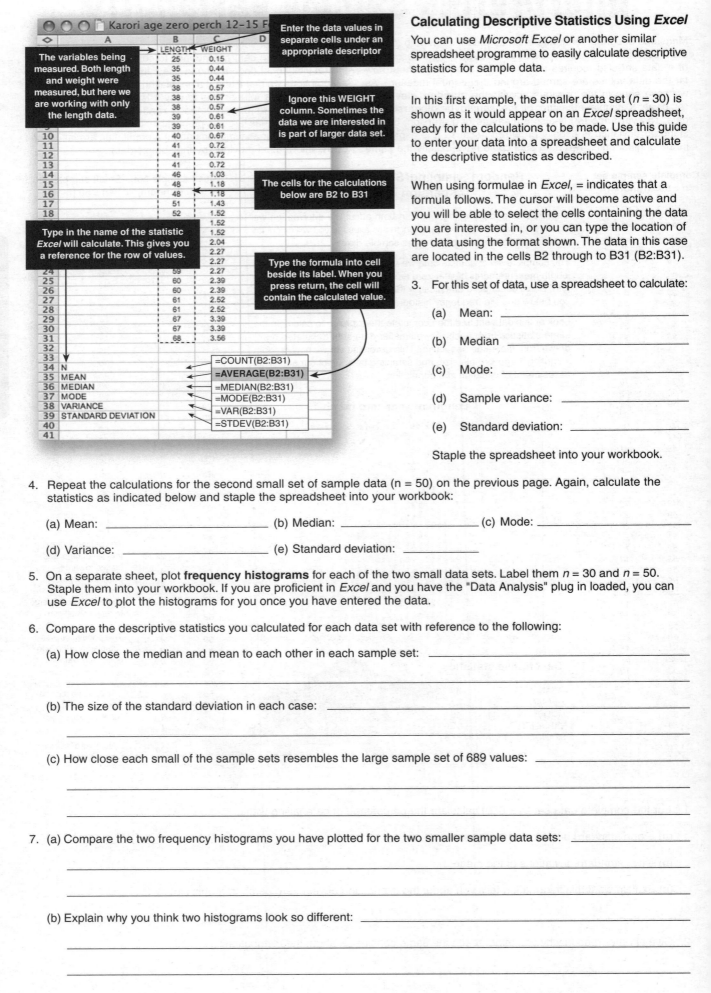

Karori age zero perch 12-15 F

	A	B	C	D
		LENGTH	WEIGHT	
		25	0.15	
		35	0.44	
		35	0.44	
		38	0.57	
		38	0.57	
		38	0.57	
		39	0.61	
		39	0.61	
10		40	0.67	
11		41	0.72	
12		41	0.72	
13		41	0.72	
14		46	1.03	
15		48	1.18	
16		48	1.18	
17		51	1.43	
18		52	1.52	
			1.52	
			1.52	
			2.04	
			2.27	
			2.27	
24		59	2.27	
25		60	2.39	
26		60	2.39	
27		61	2.52	
28		61	2.52	
29		67	3.39	
30		67	3.39	
31		68	3.56	
32				
33			=COUNT(B2:B31)	
34	N		=AVERAGE(B2:B31)	
35	MEAN			
36	MEDIAN		=MEDIAN(B2:B31)	
37	MODE		=MODE(B2:B31)	
38	VARIANCE		=VAR(B2:B31)	
39	STANDARD DEVIATION		=STDEV(B2:B31)	
40				
41				

The variables being measured. Both length and weight were measured, but here we are working with only the length data.

Enter the data values in separate cells under an appropriate descriptor

Ignore this WEIGHT column. Sometimes the data we are interested in is part of larger data set.

The cells for the calculations below are B2 to B31

Type in the name of the statistic Excel will calculate. This gives you a reference for the row of values.

Type the formula into cell beside its label. When you press return, the cell will contain the calculated value.

Calculating Descriptive Statistics Using *Excel*

You can use *Microsoft Excel* or another similar spreadsheet programme to easily calculate descriptive statistics for sample data.

In this first example, the smaller data set ($n = 30$) is shown as it would appear on an *Excel* spreadsheet, ready for the calculations to be made. Use this guide to enter your data into a spreadsheet and calculate the descriptive statistics as described.

When using formulae in *Excel*, = indicates that a formula follows. The cursor will become active and you will be able to select the cells containing the data you are interested in, or you can type the location of the data using the format shown. The data in this case are located in the cells B2 through to B31 (B2:B31).

3. For this set of data, use a spreadsheet to calculate:

    (a) Mean: _____

    (b) Median _____

    (c) Mode: _____

    (d) Sample variance: _____

    (e) Standard deviation: _____

Staple the spreadsheet into your workbook.

4. Repeat the calculations for the second small set of sample data (n = 50) on the previous page. Again, calculate the statistics as indicated below and staple the spreadsheet into your workbook:

    (a) Mean: _____ (b) Median: _____ (c) Mode: _____

    (d) Variance: _____ (e) Standard deviation: _____

5. On a separate sheet, plot **frequency histograms** for each of the two small data sets. Label them *n* = 30 and *n* = 50. Staple them into your workbook. If you are proficient in *Excel* and you have the "Data Analysis" plug in loaded, you can use *Excel* to plot the histograms for you once you have entered the data.

6. Compare the descriptive statistics you calculated for each data set with reference to the following:

    (a) How close the median and mean to each other in each sample set: _____

    _____

    (b) The size of the standard deviation in each case: _____

    _____

    (c) How close each small of the sample sets resembles the large sample set of 689 values: _____

    _____

    _____

7. (a) Compare the two frequency histograms you have plotted for the two smaller sample data sets: _____

    _____

    _____

    (b) Explain why you think two histograms look so different: _____

    _____

    _____

Biological Drawings

Microscopes are a powerful tool for examining cells and cell structures. In order to make a permanent record of what is seen when examining a specimen, it is useful to make a drawing. It is important to draw **what is actually seen**. This will depend on the **resolution** of the microscope being used. Resolution refers to the ability of a microscope to separate small objects that are very close together. Making drawings from mounted specimens is a skill. Drawing forces you to observe closely and accurately. While photographs are limited to representing appearance at a single moment in time, drawings can be composites of the observer's cumulative experience, with many different specimens of the same material. The total picture of an object thus represented can often communicate information much more effectively than a photograph. Your attention to the outline of suggestions below will help you to make more effective drawings. If you are careful to follow the suggestions at the beginning, the techniques will soon become habitual.

1. **Drawing materials**: All drawings should be done with a clear pencil line on good quality paper. A sharp HB pencil is recommended. A soft rubber of good quality is essential. Diagrams in ballpoint or fountain pen are unacceptable because they cannot be corrected.

2. **Positioning**: Centre your diagram on the page. Do not draw it in a corner. This will leave plenty of room for the addition of labels once the diagram is completed.

3. **Size**: A drawing should be large enough to easily represent all the details you see without crowding. Rarely, if ever, are drawings too large, but they are often too small. Show only as much as is necessary for an understanding of the structure; a small section shown in detail will often suffice. It is time consuming and unnecessary, for example, to reproduce accurately the entire contents of a microscope field.

4. **Accuracy**: Your drawing should be a complete, accurate representation of the material you have observed, and should communicate your understanding of the material to anyone who looks at it. Avoid making "idealised" drawings; your drawing should be a picture of what you actually see, not what you imagine should be there. Proportions should be accurate. If necessary, measure the lengths of various

parts with a ruler. If viewing through a microscope, estimate them as a proportion of the field of view, then translate these proportions onto the page. When drawing shapes that indicate an outline, make sure the line is complete. Where two ends of a line do not meet (as in drawing a cell outline) then this would indicate that the structure has a hole in it.

5. **Technique**: Use only simple, narrow lines. Represent depth by stippling (dots close together). Indicate depth only when it is essential to your drawing (usually it is not). Do not use shading. Look at the specimen while you are drawing it.

6. **Labels**: Leave a good margin for labels. All parts of your diagram must be labelled accurately. Labelling lines should be drawn with a ruler and should not cross. Where possible, keep label lines vertical or horizontal. Label the drawing with:
   • A title, which should identify the material (organism, tissues or cells).
   • Magnification under which it was observed, or a scale to indicate the size of the object.
   • Names of structures.
   • In living materials, any movements you have seen.

Remember that drawings are intended as records for you, and as a means of encouraging close observation; artistic ability is not necessary. Before you turn in a drawing, ask yourself if you know what every line represents. If you do not, look more closely at the material. ***Take into account the rules for biological drawings and draw what you see, not what you think you see!***

Examples of acceptable biological drawings: The diagrams below show two examples of biological drawings that are acceptable. The example on the left is of a whole organism and its size is indicated by a scale. The example on the right is of plant tissue: a group of cells that are essentially identical in the structure. It is not necessary to show many cells even though your view through the microscope may show them. As few as 2-4 will suffice to show their structure and how they are arranged. Scale is indicated by stating how many times larger it has been drawn. Do not confuse this with what magnification it was viewed at under the microscope. The abbreviation **T.S.** indicates that the specimen was a *cross* or *transverse section*.

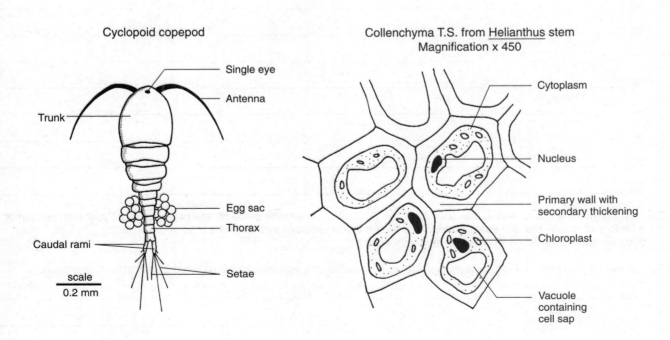

Cyclopoid copepod

Collenchyma T.S. from Helianthus stem
Magnification x 450

Related activities: Optical Microscopes

A 2

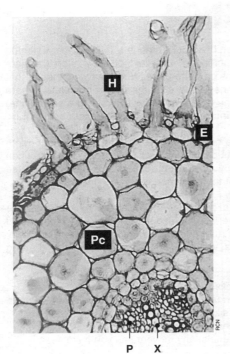

P   X

Specimen used for drawing

The photograph above is a light microscope view of a stained transverse section (cross section) of a root from a *Ranunculus* (buttercup) plant. It shows the arrangement of the different tissues in the root. The vascular bundle is at the centre of the root, with the larger, central xylem vessels (**X**) and smaller phloem vessels (**P**) grouped around them. The root hair cells (**H**) are arranged on the external surface and form part of the epidermal layer (**E**). Parenchyma cells (**Pc**) make up the bulk of the root's mass. The distance from point **X** to point **E** on the photograph (above) is about 0.15 mm (150 µm).

An Unacceptable Biological Drawing

The diagram below is an example of how *not* to produce a biological drawing; it is based on the photograph to the left. There are many aspects of the drawing that are unacceptable. The exercise below asks you to identify the errors in this student's attempt.

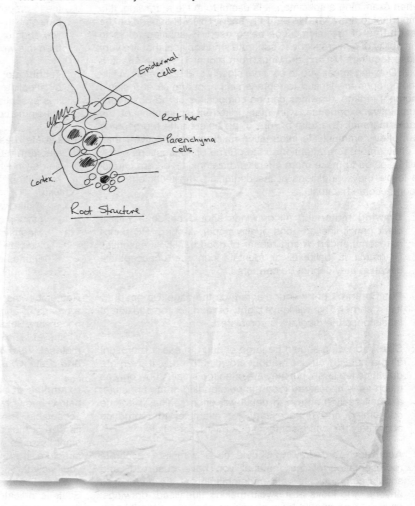

1. Identify and describe eight unacceptable features of the student's biological diagram above:

(a) _____

(b) _____

(c) _____

(d) _____

(e) _____

(f) _____

(g) _____

(h) _____

2. In the remaining space next to the 'poor example' (above) or on a blank piece of refill paper, attempt your own version of a biological drawing for the same material, based on the photograph above. Make a point of correcting all of the errors that you have identified in the sample student's attempt.

3. Explain why accurate biological drawings are more valuable to a scientific investigation than an 'artistic' approach:

_____

_____

_____

The Structure of a Report

Once you have collected and analysed your data, you can write your report. You may wish to present your findings as a written report, a poster presentation, or an oral presentation. The structure of a scientific report is described below using a poster presentation (which is necessarily very concise) as an example. When writing your report, it is useful to write the methods or the results first, followed by the discussion and conclusion. Although you should do some reading in preparation, the introduction should be one of the last sections that you write. Writing the other sections first gives you a better understanding of your investigation within the context of other work in the same area.

To view this and other examples of posters, see the excellent NC State University web site listed below

1. Title (and author)
Provides a clear and concise description of the project.

2. Introduction
Includes the aim, hypothesis, and background to the study

3. Materials and Methods
A description of the materials and procedures used.

4. Results
An account of results including tables and graphs. This section should not discuss the result, just present them.

5. Discussion
An discussion of the findings in light of the biological concepts involved. It should include comments on any limitations of the study.

6. Conclusion
A clear statement of whether tor not the findings support the hypothesis. In abbreviated poster presentations, these sections may be combined.

7. References & acknowledgements
An organised list of all sources of information. Entries should be consistent within your report. Your teacher will advise you as to the preferred format.

Flounder Exhibit Temperature-Dependent Sex Determination

J. Adam Luckenbach*, John Godwin and Russell Borski
Department of Zoology, Box 7617, North Carolina State University, Raleigh, NC 27695

Introduction

Southern flounder (*Paralichthys lethostigma*) support valuable fisheries and show great promise for aquaculture. Female flounder are known to grow faster and reach larger adult Therefore, information on sex dete might increase the ratio of female important for aquaculture.

Objective

This study was conducted to determine whether southern flounder exhibit temperature-dependent sex determination (TSD), and if growth is affected by rearing temperature.

Methods

- Southern flounder broodstock were strip spawned to collect eggs and sperm for *in vitro* fertilization.
- Hatched larvae were weaned from a natural diet (rotifers/*Artemia*) to high protein pelleted feed and fed until satiation at least twice daily.
- Upon reaching a mean total length of 40 mm, the juvenile flounder were stocked at equal densities into one of three temperatures 18, 23, or 28°C for 245 days.
- Gonads were preserved and later sectioned at 2-6 microns.
- Sex-distinguishing markers were used to distinguish males (spermatogenesis) from females (oogenesis).

Histological Analysis

Male Differentiation   Female Differen

Temperature Affects Sex Determination

Growth Does Not Differ by Sex

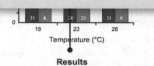

Temperature (°C)

Results

- Sex was discernible in most fish greater than 120 mm long.
- High (28°C) temperature produced 4% females.
- Low (18°C) temperature produced 22% females.
- Mid-range (23°C) temperature produced 44% females.
- Fish raised at high or low temperatures showed reduced growth compared to those at the mid-range temperature.
- Up to 245 days, no differences in growth existed between sexes.

Conclusions

- These findings indicate that sex determination in southern flounder is temperature-sensitive and temperature has a profound effect on growth.
- A mid-range rearing temperature (23°C) appears to maximize the number of females and promote better growth in young southern flounder.
- Although adult females are known to grow larger than males, no difference in growth between sexes occurred in age-0 (< 1 year) southern flounder.

Acknowledgements

The authors acknowledge the Salstonstall-Kennedy Program of the National Marine Fisheries Service and the University of North Carolina Sea Grant College Program for funding this research. Special thanks to Lea Ware and Beth Shimps for help with the work.

Skills in Biology

---

1. Explain the purpose of each of the following sections of a report. The first has one been completed for you:

(a) Introduction: *Provides the reader with the background to the topic and the rationale for the study*

(b) Methods: _____

_____

(c) Results: _____

_____

(d) Discussion: _____

_____

(e) References and acknowledgements: _____

_____

2. Posters are a highly visual method of presenting the findings of a study. Describe the positive features of this format:

_____

_____

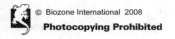

© Biozone International 2008
Photocopying Prohibited

Related activities: Hypotheses and Predictions, Report Checklist
Web links: NC State University: Creating Effective Poster Presentations

RA 2

Writing the Methods

The materials and methods section of your report should be brief but informative. All essential details should be included but those not necessary for the repetition of the study should be omitted. The following diagram illustrates some of the important details that should be included in a methods section. Obviously, a complete list of all possible equipment and procedures is not possible because each experiment or study is different. However, the sort of information that is required for both lab and field based studies is provided.

Field Studies	Laboratory Based Studies

Study site & organisms
- Site location and features
- Why that site was chosen
- Species involved

Specialised equipment
- pH and oxygen meters
- Thermometers
- Nets and traps

Data collection
- Number and timing of observations/collections
- Time of day or year
- Sample sizes and size of the sampling unit
- Methods of preservation
- Temperature at time of sampling
- Weather conditions on the day(s) of sampling
- Methods of measurement/sampling
- Methods of recording

Data collection
- Pre-treatment of material before experiments
- Details of treatments and controls
- Duration and timing of experimental observations
- Temperature
- Sample sizes and details of replication
- Methods of measurement or sampling
- Methods of recording

Experimental organisms
- Species or strain
- Age and sex
- Number of individuals used

Specialised equipment
- pH meters
- Water baths & incubators
- Spectrophotometers
- Centrifuges
- Aquaria & choice chambers
- Microscopes and videos

Special preparations
- Techniques for the preparation of material (staining, grinding)
- Indicators, salt solutions, buffers, special dilutions

General guidelines for writing a methods section

- Choose a suitable level of detail. *Too little detail and the study could not be repeated. Too much detail obscures important features.*
- Do NOT include the details of standard procedures (e.g. how to use a balance) or standard equipment (e.g. beakers and flasks).
- Include details of any statistical analyses and data transformations.

- Outline the reasons why procedures were done in a certain way or in a certain order, if this is not self-evident.
- If your methodology involves complicated preparations (e.g. culture media) then it is acceptable to refer just to the original information source (e.g. lab manual) or include the information as an appendix.

1. The following text is part of the methods section from a report. Using the information above and on the checklist on page 63, describe eight errors (there are ten) in the methods. The errors are concerned with a lack of explanation or detail that would be necessary to repeat the experiment (they are not typographical, nor are they associated with the use of the active voice, which is now considered preferable to the passive):

"We collected the worms for this study from a pond outside the school. We carried out the experiment at room temperature on April 16, 1997. First we added full strength seawater to each of three 200 cm³ glass jars; these were the controls. We filled another three jars with diluted seawater. We blotted the worms dry and weighed them to the nearest 0.1 g, then we added one worm to each jar. We reweighed the worms (after blotting) at various intervals over the next two hours."

(a) _____

(b) _____

(c) _____

(d) _____

(e) _____

(f) _____

(g) _____

(h) _____

Writing Your Results

The results section is arguably the most important part of any research report; it is the place where you can bring together and present your findings. When properly constructed, this section will present your results clearly and in a way that shows you have organised your data and carefully considered the appropriate analysis. A portion of the results section from a scientific paper on the habitat preference of New Zealand black mudfish is presented below (Hicks, B. and Barrier, R. (1996), NZJMFR. 30, 135-151). It highlights some important features of the results section and shows you how you can present information concisely, even if your results are relatively lengthy. Use it as a guide for content when you write up this section.

Results

A total of 222 black mudfish were caught in the 400 traps set be... Mean total length (TL) was 67 mm (range 26-139 mm, $n = 214$)... had black mudfish. Mudfish... ...nly amo... independence, $P < 0.001$... ...at 8 out... at 20 out of 30 wetland sit... ...ed at only... none of the 6 lake margin or 4 pond, dam, and lagoon sites. Categorical variables that distinguished ...rate disturbance scale rating; presence of emergent ...sed or peat bog substrate types; absence of fish ...orphus cotidianus) and inanga (*Galaxias maculatus*)...

Keep your statement of important findings brief.

Graphs (figures) illustrate trends in the data. Be sure to choose the correct type of graph and allocate enough space to it in the report.

Label figures and tables clearly and in sequence so that they can be referred to easily in the text.

Scientific names are included if they are known.

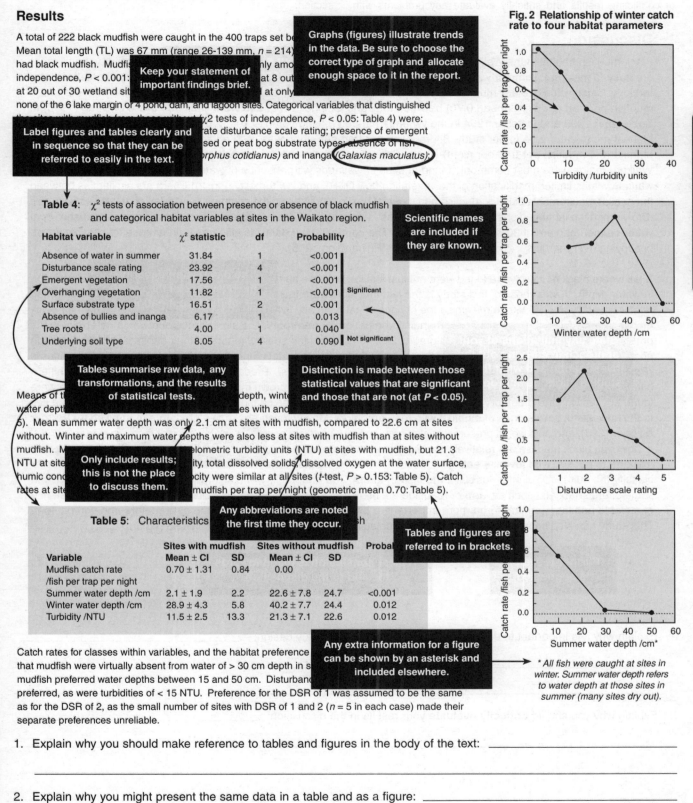

Fig. 2 Relationship of winter catch rate to four habitat parameters

Table 4: χ^2 tests of association between presence or absence of black mudfish and categorical habitat variables at sites in the Waikato region.

Habitat variable	χ^2 statistic	df	Probability	
Absence of water in summer	31.84	1	<0.001	
Disturbance scale rating	23.92	4	<0.001	
Emergent vegetation	17.56	1	<0.001	
Overhanging vegetation	11.82	1	<0.001	Significant
Surface substrate type	16.51	2	<0.001	
Absence of bullies and inanga	6.17	1	0.013	
Tree roots	4.00	1	0.040	
Underlying soil type	8.05	4	0.090	Not significant

Tables summarise raw data, any transformations, and the results of statistical tests.

Distinction is made between those statistical values that are significant and those that are not (at $P < 0.05$).

Means of th... ...depth, winte... water depth... ...es with and... ...5). Mean summer water depth was only 2.1 cm at sites with mudfish, compared to 22.6 cm at sites without. Winter and maximum water depths were also less at sites with mudfish than at sites without mudfish. M... ...elometric turbidity units (NTU) at sites with mudfish, but 21.3 NTU at site... ...ity, total dissolved solids, dissolved oxygen at the water surface, humic conc... ...ocity were similar at all sites (*t*-test, $P > 0.153$: Table 5). Catch rates at site... ...mudfish per trap per night (geometric mean 0.70: Table 5).

Only include results; this is not the place to discuss them.

Any abbreviations are noted the first time they occur.

Tables and figures are referred to in brackets.

Table 5: Characteristics... ...sh

Variable	Sites with mudfish Mean ± CI	SD	Sites without mudfish Mean ± CI	SD	Probal...
Mudfish catch rate /fish per trap per night	0.70 ± 1.31	0.84	0.00		
Summer water depth /cm	2.1 ± 1.9	2.2	22.6 ± 7.8	24.7	<0.001
Winter water depth /cm	28.9 ± 4.3	5.8	40.2 ± 7.7	24.4	0.012
Turbidity /NTU	11.5 ± 2.5	13.3	21.3 ± 7.1	22.6	0.012

Catch rates for classes within variables, and the habitat preference... ...that mudfish were virtually absent from water of > 30 cm depth in s... mudfish preferred water depths between 15 and 50 cm. Disturbanc... preferred, as were turbidities of < 15 NTU. Preference for the DSR of 1 was assumed to be the same as for the DSR of 2, as the small number of sites with DSR of 1 and 2 ($n = 5$ in each case) made their separate preferences unreliable.

Any extra information for a figure can be shown by an asterisk and included elsewhere.

* All fish were caught at sites in winter. Summer water depth refers to water depth at those sites in summer (many sites dry out).

Skills in Biology

1. Explain why you should make reference to tables and figures in the body of the text: _____

_____

2. Explain why you might present the same data in a table and as a figure: _____

_____

_____

Related activities: The Structure of a Report, Report Checklist

A 3

Writing Your Discussion

In the discussion section of your report, you must interpret your results in the context of the specific questions you set out to answer in the investigation. You should also place your findings in the context of any broader relevant issues. If your results coincide exactly with what you expected, then your discussion will be relatively brief. However, be prepared to discuss any unexpected or conflicting results and critically evaluate any problems with your study design. The Discussion section may (and should) refer to the findings in the Results section, but it is not the place to introduce new results. Try to work towards a point in your discussion where the reader is lead naturally to the conclusion. The conclusion may be presented within the discussion or it may be included separately after the discussion as a separate section.

Discussion:

Black mudfish habitat in the Waikato region can be ad[...]ses by four variables that are easy to measure: summer water depth, winter wa[...]cated by vegetation), and turbidity. Catch rates of black mudfish can be extreme[...]es ranged from 0.2 to 8.4 mudfish per trap per night (mean 0.70) between May and October 1992, and were similar to those of Dean (1995) in September 1993 and October 1994 in the Whangamarino Wetland complex (0.0-2.0 mudfish per trap per night). The highest mean catch rate in our study, 8.4 mudfish per trap per night, was at Site 24 (Table 1, Figure 1). The second highest (6.4 mudfish per trap per night) was at Site 32, in a drain about 4 km east of Hamilton. Black mudfish in the Waikato region were most commonly found at sites in wetlands with absence of water in summer, moderate depth of water in winter, limited modification of the vegetation (low DSR), and low turbidity (Fig. 2). There are similarities between the habitat requirements of black mudfish and those of brown mudfish and the common river galaxias *(Galaxias vulgaris)*. Brown mudfish inhabited shallow water, sometimes at the edges of deeper water bodies, but were usually absent from water deeper than about 30-50 cm (Eldon 1978). The common river galaxias also has a preference for shallow water, occupying river margins < 20 cm deep (Jowett and Richardson 1995).

Sites where black mudfish were found were not just shallow or dry in sum[...]al variation in water depth. A weakness of this study is the fact that sites were trap[...]ere spread relatively widely at each site to maximise the chance of catching any fish[...]nt for black mudfish in the form of emergent or overhanging vegetation, or tree roots. The significance of cover in determining the pres[...]s predictable, considering the shallow nature of their habitats. Mudfish, though noc[...] require cover during the to protect them from avian predators, such as bitterns *(Bo[...]*fishers *(Halcyon sancta vagans)*. Predation of black mudfish by a swamp bittern has [...]1). Cover is also important for brown mudfish (Eldon 1978). Black mudfish were found at sites with the predatory mosquitofish and juvenile eels, and the seasonal drying of their habitats may be a key to the successful coexistence of mudfish with their predators. Mosquitofish are known predators of mudfish fry (Barrier & Hicks 1994), and eels would presumably also prey on black mudfish, as t[...]h (Eldon 1979b). If, however, black mudfish are relatively uncompetitive and vulnerable to pr[...]s as to how they manage to coexist with juvenile eels and mosquitofish. The habitat varia[...] can be used to classify the suitability of sites for black mudfish in future. The adaptability of black mudfish allows them to survive in some altered habitats, such as farm or roadside drains. From this study, we can conclude that the continued existence of suitable habitats appears to be more important to black mudfish than the presence of predators and competitors. This study has also improved methods of identifying suitable mudfish habitats in the Waikato region.

Support your statements with reference to Tables and Figures from the Results section.

The discussion describes the relevance of the results of the investigation.

State any limitations of your approach in carrying out the investigation and what further studies might be appropriate.

Reference is made to the work of others.

Further research is suggested

A clear conclusion is made towards the end of the discussion.

1. Explain why it is important to discuss any weaknesses in your study design: _____

_____

_____

2. Explain why you should **critically evaluate** your results in the discussion: _____

_____

_____

_____

3. Describe the purpose of the conclusion: _____

_____

Related activities: The Structure of a Report, Report Checklist

Citing and Listing References

Proper referencing of sources of information is an important aspect of report writing. It shows that you have explored the topic and recognise and respect the work of others. There are two aspects to consider: **citing sources** within the text (making reference to other work to support a statement or compare results) and **compiling a reference list** at the end of the report. A **bibliography** lists all sources of information, but these may not necessarily appear as citations in the report. In contrast, a reference list should contain only those texts cited in the report.

Citations in the main body of the report should include only the authors' surnames, publication date, and page numbers (or internet site), and the citation should be relevant to the statement it claims to support. Accepted methods for referencing vary, but your reference list should provide all the information necessary to locate the source material, it should be consistently presented, and it should contain only the references that you have yourself read (not those cited by others). A suggested format is described below.

Preparing a Reference List

When teachers ask students to write in "APA style", they are referring to the editorial style established by the **American Psychological Association** (APA). These guidelines for citing **electronic (online) resources** differ only slightly from the **print sources**.

For the Internet

Where you use information from the internet, you must provide the following:
- The website address (URL), the person or organisation who is in charge of the web site and the date you accessed the web page.

This is written in the form: URL (person or organisation's name, day, month, and year retrieved)
   This goes together as follows:
      http://www.scientificamerican.com (Scientific American, 17.12.03)

For Periodicals (or Journals)

This is written in the form: author(s), date of publication, article title, periodical title, and publication information.
Example: Author's family name, A. A. (author's initials only), Author, B. B., & Author, C. C. (xxxx = year of publication in brackets). Title of article. Title of Periodical, volume number, page numbers (Note, only use "pp." before the page numbers in newspapers and magazines).
   This goes together as follows:
      Bamshad M. J., & Olson S. E. (2003). Does Race Exist? Scientific American, 289(6), 50-57.

For Online Periodicals based on a Print Source

At present, the majority of periodicals retrieved from online publications are exact duplicates of those in their print versions and although they are unlikely to have additional analyses and data attached to them, this is likely to change in the future.

- If the article that is to be referenced has been viewed only in electronic form and not in print form, then you must add in brackets, "Electronic version", after the title.
   This goes together as follows:
      Bamshad M. J., & Olson S. E. (2003). Does Race Exist? (Electronic version). Scientific American, 289(6), 50-57.
- If you have reason to believe the article has changed in its electronic form, then you will need to add the date you retrieved the document and the URL.
   This goes together as follows:
      Bamshad M. J., & Olson S. E. (2003). Does Race Exist? (Electronic version). Scientific American, 289(6), 50-57. Retrieved December 17, 2003, from http://www.scientificamerican.com

For Books

This is written in the form: author(s), date of publication, title, and publication information.
Example: Author, A. A., Author, B. B., & Author, C. C. (xxxx). Title (any additional information to enable identification is given in brackets). City of publication: publishers name.
   This goes together as follows:
      Martin, R.A. (2004). Missing Links Evolutionary Concepts & Transitions Through Time. Sudbury, MA: Jones and Bartlett

For Citation in the Text of References

This is written in the form: authors' surname(s), date of publication, page number(s) (abbreviated p.), chapter (abbreviated chap.), figure, table, equation, or internet site, in brackets at the appropriate point in text.
   This goes together as follows:
      (Bamshad & Olson, 2003, p. 51) or (Bamshad & Olson, 2003, http://www.scientificamerican.com)

This can also be done in the form of footnotes. This involves the use of a superscripted number in the text next to your quoted material and the relevant information listed at the bottom of the page.
   This goes together as follows:
      .... Bamshad & Olson reported that ....[1]

---
[1] Bamshad & Olson, 2003, p. 51

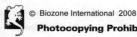
Related activities: The Structure of a Report, Report Checklist

A 3

48

Example of a Reference List

Lab notes can be listed according to title if the author is unknown.
→ Advanced biology laboratory manual (2000). Cell membranes. pp 16-18. Sunhigh College.

References are listed alphabetically according to the author's surname.

Cooper, G.M. (1997). *The cell: A molecular approach* (2nd ed.). Washington D.C.: ASM Press

| Book title in italics (or underlined) | | Place of publication: Publisher |

Davis, P. (1996) Cellular factories. *New Scientist* 2057: Inside science supplement.

| Publication date | Journal title in italics | A supplement may not need page references |

If a single author appears more than once, then list the publications from oldest to most recent.

Indge, B. (2001). Diarrhoea, digestion and dehydration. *Biological Sciences Review*, 14(1), 7-9.

Indge, B. (2002). Experiments. *Biological Sciences Review*, 14(3), 11-13.

| Article title follows date |

Kingsland, J. (2000). Border control. *New Scientist* 2247: Inside science supplement.

Spell out only the last name of authors. Use initials for first and middle names.

Laver, H. (1995). Osmosis and water retention in plants. *Biological Sciences Review* 7(3), 14-18.

| Volume (Issue number), Pages |

Steward, M. (1996). Water channels in the cell membrane. *Biological Sciences Review*, 9(2), 18-22.

Internet sites change often so the date accessed is included. The person or organisation in charge of the site is also included.
→ http://www.cbc.umn.edu/~mwd/cell_intro.html (Dalton, M. "Introduction to cell biology" 12.02.03)

---

1. Distinguish between a **reference list** and a **bibliography**: _____

   _____

   _____

2. Explain why internet articles based on a print source are likely to have additional analyses and data attached in the future, and why this point should be noted in a reference list:

   _____

   _____

3. Following are the details of references and source material used by a student in preparing a report on enzymes and their uses in biotechnology. He provided his reference list in prose. From it, compile a correctly formatted reference list:

   Pages 18-23 in the sixth edition of the textbook "Biology" by Neil Campbell. Published by Benjamin/Cummings in California (2002). New Scientist article by Peter Moore called "Fuelled for life" (January 1996, volume 2012, supplement). "Food biotechnology" published in the journal Biological Sciences Review, page 25, volume 8 (number 3) 1996, by Liam and Katherine O'Hare. An article called "Living factories" by Philip Ball in New Scientist, volume 2015 1996, pages 28-31. Pages 75-85 in the book "The cell: a molecular approach" by Geoffrey Cooper, published in 1997 by ASM Press, Washington D.C. An article called "Development of a procedure for purification of a recombinant therapeutic protein" in the journal "Australasian Biotechnology", by I Roberts and S. Taylor, pages 93-99 in volume 6, number 2, 1996.

   REFERENCE LIST

   _____

   _____

   _____

   _____

   _____

   _____

   _____

Report Checklist

A report of your findings at the completion of your investigation may take one of the following forms: a written document, seminar, poster, web page, or multimedia presentation. The following checklist identifies points to consider when writing each section of your report. Review the list before you write your report and then, on satisfactory completion of each section of your write-up, use the check boxes to tick off the points:

Title:

☐ (a) Gives a clear indication of what the study is about.

☐ (b) Includes the species name and a common name of all organisms used.

Introduction:

☐ (a) Includes a clear aim.

☐ (b) Includes a well written hypothesis.

☐ (c) Includes a synopsis of the current state of knowledge about the topic.

Materials and methods:

☐ (a) Written clearly. Numbered points are appropriate at this level.

☐ (b) Describes the final methods that were used.

☐ (c) Includes details of the how data for the dependent variable were collected.

☐ (d) Includes details of how all other variables were manipulated, controlled, measured, or monitored.

☐ (e) If appropriate, it includes an explanatory diagram of the design of the experimental set-up.

☐ (f) Written in the past tense, and in the active voice (We investigated …) rather than the passive voice (An investigation was done …).

Results:

☐ (a) Includes the raw data (e.g. in a table).

☐ (b) Where necessary, the raw data have been averaged or transformed.

☐ (c) Includes graphs (where appropriate).

☐ (d) Each figure (table, graph, drawing, or photo) has a title and is numbered in a way that makes it possible to refer to it in the text (Fig. 1 etc.).

☐ (e) Written in the past tense and, where appropriate, in the active voice.

Discussion:

☐ (a) Includes an analysis of the data in which the findings, including trends and patterns, are discussed in relation to the biological concepts involved.

☐ (b) Includes an evaluation of sources of error, assumptions, and possible improvements to design.

Conclusion:

☐ (a) Written as a clear statement, which relates directly to the hypothesis.

Bibliography or References:

☐ (a) Lists all sources of information and assistance.

☐ (b) Does not include references that were not used.

© Biozone International 2008

Related activities: The Structure of a Report, Writing the Methods, Writing Your Results and Discussion, Citing and Listing References

Skills in Biology

A 3

50

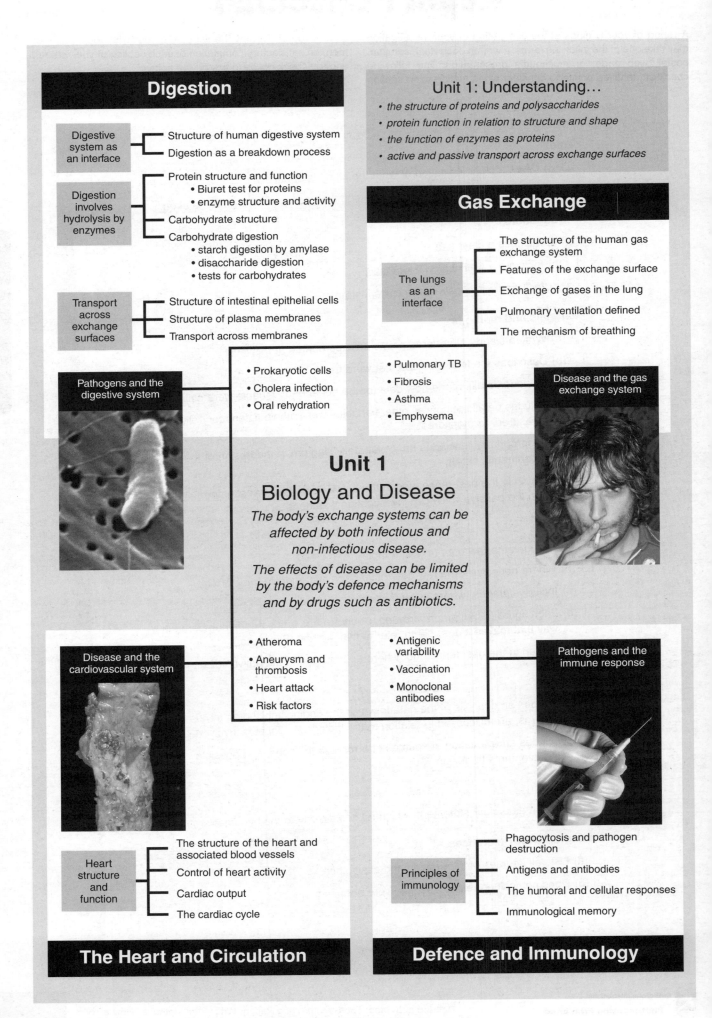

Digestion

Digestive system as an interface
- Structure of human digestive system
- Digestion as a breakdown process

Digestion involves hydrolysis by enzymes
- Protein structure and function
  - Biuret test for proteins
  - enzyme structure and activity
- Carbohydrate structure
- Carbohydrate digestion
  - starch digestion by amylase
  - disaccharide digestion
  - tests for carbohydrates

Transport across exchange surfaces
- Structure of intestinal epithelial cells
- Structure of plasma membranes
- Transport across membranes

Pathogens and the digestive system
- Prokaryotic cells
- Cholera infection
- Oral rehydration

Unit 1: Understanding…
- *the structure of proteins and polysaccharides*
- *protein function in relation to structure and shape*
- *the function of enzymes as proteins*
- *active and passive transport across exchange surfaces*

Gas Exchange

The lungs as an interface
- The structure of the human gas exchange system
- Features of the exchange surface
- Exchange of gases in the lung
- Pulmonary ventilation defined
- The mechanism of breathing

- Pulmonary TB
- Fibrosis
- Asthma
- Emphysema

Disease and the gas exchange system

Unit 1
Biology and Disease

The body's exchange systems can be affected by both infectious and non-infectious disease.

The effects of disease can be limited by the body's defence mechanisms and by drugs such as antibiotics.

Disease and the cardiovascular system
- Atheroma
- Aneurysm and thrombosis
- Heart attack
- Risk factors

- Antigenic variability
- Vaccination
- Monoclonal antibodies

Pathogens and the immune response

Heart structure and function
- The structure of the heart and associated blood vessels
- Control of heart activity
- Cardiac output
- The cardiac cycle

Principles of immunology
- Phagocytosis and pathogen destruction
- Antigens and antibodies
- The humoral and cellular responses
- Immunological memory

The Heart and Circulation

Defence and Immunology

The Causes of Disease

Disease is more difficult to define than **health**, which is described as a state of physical and mental well-being. A disease is usually associated with particular **symptoms** that help to define and diagnose it. The term **disease** is used to describe a condition in which part or all of an organism's normal physiological function is upset. All diseases, with the exception of some mental diseases, can be classified as **physical diseases** (i.e. diseases that cause permanent or temporary damage to the body). Physical diseases can be subdivided into two major groups: **infectious**

diseases caused by an infectious agent (**pathogen**) and **non-infectious diseases** (or disorders). Non-infectious diseases are often not clearly the result of any single factor, although they are often categorised into subgroups according to their principal cause (below). However, many diseases fall into more than one category, e.g. Alzheimer's disease and some cancers. Diseases can affect any of the body systems. Some of those affecting the body's exchange systems are identified below. You will examine these in more detail in this unit.

Some Diseases of Exchange Systems

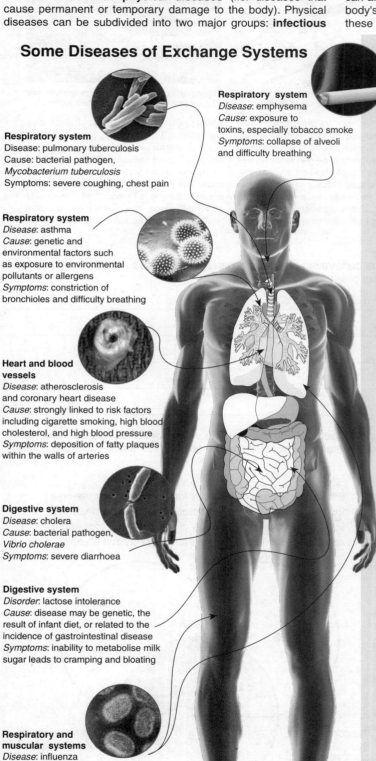

Respiratory system
Disease: pulmonary tuberculosis
Cause: bacterial pathogen, *Mycobacterium tuberculosis*
Symptoms: severe coughing, chest pain

Respiratory system
Disease: asthma
Cause: genetic and environmental factors such as exposure to environmental pollutants or allergens
Symptoms: constriction of bronchioles and difficulty breathing

Heart and blood vessels
Disease: atherosclerosis and coronary heart disease
Cause: strongly linked to risk factors including cigarette smoking, high blood cholesterol, and high blood pressure
Symptoms: deposition of fatty plaques within the walls of arteries

Digestive system
Disease: cholera
Cause: bacterial pathogen, *Vibrio cholerae*
Symptoms: severe diarrhoea

Digestive system
Disorder: lactose intolerance
Cause: disease may be genetic, the result of infant diet, or related to the incidence of gastrointestinal disease
Symptoms: inability to metabolise milk sugar leads to cramping and bloating

Respiratory and muscular systems
Disease: influenza
Cause: viral pathogen *Influenzavirus*
Symptoms: chills, fever, aches, weakness, and respiratory difficulties

Respiratory system
Disease: emphysema
Cause: exposure to toxins, especially tobacco smoke
Symptoms: collapse of alveoli and difficulty breathing

Non-Infectious Disease

Inherited Diseases
Diseases caused by genetic malfunctions. The onset of genetic diseases can be delayed, becoming apparent later in life. Examples include Down syndrome (right), cystic fibrosis, multiple sclerosis, Alzheimer's, and Huntington's disease.

Nutritional Diseases
Nutritional diseases are caused by an inadequate or unbalanced diet, or by over eating. Examples include rickets, scurvy, marasmus, kwashiorkor, and obesity (left).

Mental Disorders
Diiseases affecting a person's thoughts, memory, emotions, and behaviour. Many have an strong genetic component. Examples include biopolar disorder and depression (right).

Social Diseases
Social diseases are caused or influenced by living conditions and personal behaviour. They may or may not involve an infectious agent. Examples include sexually transmitted infections and lung cancer due to smoking.

Degenerative Diseases
Degenerative diseases are wholly or partly the result of the ageing process, and the slowing of cell renewal and repair rates. Examples include osteoarthritis, Alzheimer's disease, and many cancers.

Unit 1: Biology & Disease

Related activities: Cholera, Tuberculosis, Diseases Caused by Smoking, Cardiovascular Disease

RA 2

Types of Pathogens

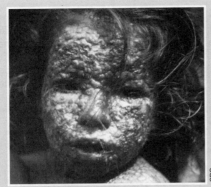

Photo: Bangladeshi girl with smallpox (1973). Smallpox was eradicated from the country in 1977.

Bacillus anthracis bacterium causes anthrax. The anthrax bacillum can form long-lived spores.

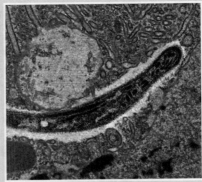

Malaria sporozoite moving through gut epithelia. The parasite is carried by a mosquio vector.

Viral pathogens: Viruses are responsible for many everyday diseases (e.g. the common cold), as well as more dangerous diseases, such as Ebola, and some diseases that have since been eradicated as a result of vaccination programmes (e.g. the *Variola* virus, which causes smallpox, above). Viruses are obligate intracellular parasites and need living host cells in order to multiply.

Bacteria: All bacteria are prokaryotes, and are categorised according to the properties of their cell walls and features such as cell shape and arrangement, oxygen requirement, and motility. Many bacteria are useful, but the relatively few species that are pathogenic are responsible for enormous social and economic cost. This is especially so since the rise in incidence of antibiotic resistance.

Eukaryotic pathogens: Eukaryotic pathogens (fungi, algae, protozoa, and parasitic worms) include those responsible for malaria and schistosomiasis. Many are highly specialised parasites with a number of hosts. The malaria parasite for example has a mosquito and a human host. Like many other pathogens, this parasite has become resistant to the drugs used to treat it.

1. "Disease can result from pathogenic microorganisms penetrating any of an organism's interfaces with the environment". Discuss this statement with reference to specific examples:

An organisms interfaces might be the the Bangladeshi girls living host cells which the micro-organism has peletrated (which has also affected her external environment the skin.

2. Non-infectious diseases are rarely attributable to a single factor. Using the example of cardiovascular disease and with reference to the data provided below, explain the role of multiple risk factors in the occurrence of non-infectious disease:

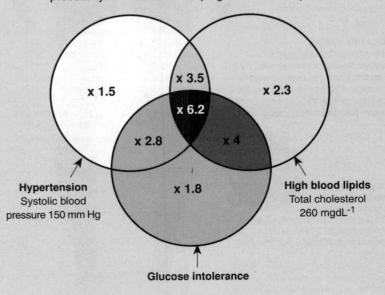

Effects of multiple risk factors for cardiovascular disease for a 40-year-old male nonsmoker. Risk is given relative to a similar patient with none of these risk factors and a probability of 1.5% of developing CVD within 8 years.

x 1.5

x 3.5

x 2.3

x 6.2

x 2.8

x 4

x 1.8

Hypertension Systolic blood pressure 150 mm Hg

High blood lipids Total cholesterol 260 mgdL⁻¹

Glucose intolerance

Macromolecules & Human Digestion

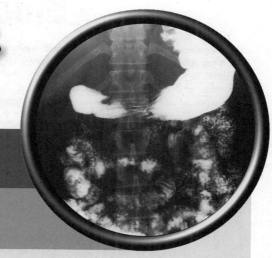

Unit 1: Biology and Disease
1.2 The digestive system

Structure of the human digestive system, macromolecules and their digestion, enzymes.

Learning Objectives

☐ 1. Compile your own glossary from the **KEY WORDS** displayed in **bold type** in the learning objectives below.

The Digestive System *(page 65-71)*

☐ 2. Identify the purpose of digestion and explain that digestion involves enzymic **hydrolysis** of larger molecules for **absorption** and **assimilation**.

☐ 3. Describe the gross structure of the human digestive system, including reference to the oesophagus, stomach, small intestine, large intestine, and rectum, and the function of these. Describe the role of the salivary glands and the pancreas in digestion.

Amino Acids and Proteins *(page 54, 57-64, 68)*

☐ 4. Describe the general structure and formula of an **amino acid**. Explain the basis for the different properties of amino acids. Recognise amino acids as the building blocks of functional proteins.

☐ 5. Describe how amino acids are joined in **condensation reactions** to form **dipeptides** and **polypeptides**. Describe the **peptide bonds** that result. Describe how polypeptides are broken down by **hydrolysis**.

☐ 6. Describe the use of the **biuret test** for proteins.

☐ 7. Describe the various functions of proteins in living organisms. Describe the relationship between the **primary**, **secondary**, **tertiary**, and **quaternary** structure of a protein and its biological function. Explain how **denaturation** destroys the activity of proteins.

☐ 8. Describe the general role of **enzymes** in digestion. Explain how enzymes work as catalysts to bring about reactions in cells. Include reference to the **active site**,

enzyme-substrate complex, enzyme-product complex, and lowering of **activation energy**.

☐ 9. Contrast the **induced fit** and the **lock and key** models of enzyme function, clearly explaining how they differ.

☐ 10. Describe the dependence of enzyme function on tertiary structure. Describe and explain the effect of the following factors on enzyme activity: temperature, pH, substrate concentration, enzyme concentration, and competitive and non-competitive inhibitors.

Carbohydrates *(page 54, 55-56, 68)*

☐ 11. Describe the basic structure of **carbohydrates** and their roles in biological systems.

☐ 12. Describe the molecular structure of a **monosaccharide** (e.g. α glucose). Give examples of monosaccharides and their roles. Describe structural isomers of glucose and their biological significance.

☐ 13. Describe how **disaccharides** are formed by **condensation** reactions and broken apart by **hydrolysis**. Identify the bond formed and broken in each case. Identify disaccharides and their functions, identifying the monosaccharides involved in each case.

☐ 14. Describe the use of the **Benedict's test** for distinguishing **reducing** and **non-reducing sugars**.

☐ 15. Describe how **polysaccharides** are formed. Compare and contrast the structure of starch, cellulose and/or glycogen, and relate their structure to their function in biological systems.

☐ 16. With reference to digestion describe the role of salivary and pancreatic amylases and maltase in the digestion of starch, and the activity of sucrase and lactase.

☐ 17. Describe the use of the I_2/KI test for starch.

Textbooks

See the 'Textbook Reference Grid' on page 7 for textbook page references relating to material in this topic.

Supplementary Texts

See pages 5-6 for additional details of these texts:

■ Adds, J. *et al.*, 2003. **Molecules and Cells** (NelsonThornes), chapters 1 and 3.

■ Clegg, C.J., 1998. **Mammals: Structure and Function** (John Murray), pp. 12-23.

■ Harwood, R. 2002. **Biochemistry** (Cambridge), chapters 2-4.

Presentation MEDIA
to support this topic:
CELL BIO & BIOCHEM:
• Molecules of Life

Periodicals

See page 6 for details of publishers of periodicals:

STUDENT'S REFERENCE

■ **Glucose & Glucose-Containing Carbohydrates** Biol. Sci. Rev., 19(1) Sept. 2006, pp. 12-15. *The structure of glucose and its polymers.*

■ **Designer Starches** Biol. Sci. Rev., 19(3) Feb. 2007, pp. 18-20. *The composition of starch, and an excellent account of its properties and functions.*

■ **Enzymes** Biol. Sci. Rev., 15(1) Sept. 2002, pp. 2-5. *Enzymes as catalysts: how they work, models of enzyme function, and cofactors and inhibitors.*

■ **Enzymes: Fast and Flexible** Biol. Sci. Rev., 19(1) Sept. 2006, pp. 2-5. *The structure of enzymes and how they work so efficiently.*

■ **Lactose Intolerance** Biol. Sci. Rev., 17(3), Feb. 2005, pp. 28-31. *The nature of lactose intolerance. This disorder is a physiological response following a genetically programmed loss of lactase.*

■ **The Pancreas and Pancreatitis** Biol. Sci. Rev., 13(5) May 2001, pp. 2-6. *The structure and role of the pancreas, including a description of secretion from the acinar cells.*

Internet

See pages 8-9 for details of how to access **Bio Links** from our web site: **www.biozone.co.uk**. From Bio Links, access sites under the topics:

CELL BIOLOGY AND BIOCHEMISTRY:
> **Biochemistry and Metabolic Pathways:**
• Enzymes • Energy and enzymes • Energy, enzymes and catalysis problem set • Reactions and enzymes • The Biology project: Biochemistry

ANIMAL BIOLOGY: > **Nutrition:** • Human anatomy online - Digestive system • Large intestine: Introduction and index • The pancreas • Your digestive system and how it works

Biochemical Tests

Biochemical tests are used to detect the presence of nutrients such as lipids, proteins, and carbohydrates (sugar and starch) in various foods. These simple tests are useful for detecting nutrients when large quantities are present. A more accurate technique by which to separate a mixture of compounds involves chromatography. Chromatography is used when only a small sample is available or when you wish to distinguish between nutrients. Simple biochemical food tests will show whether sugar is present, whereas chromatography will distinguish between the different types of sugars (e.g. fructose or glucose).

Paper Chromatography

Set Up and Procedure

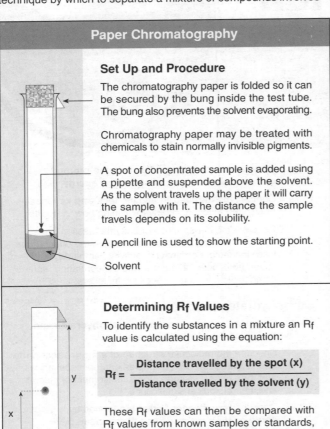

The chromatography paper is folded so it can be secured by the bung inside the test tube. The bung also prevents the solvent evaporating.

Chromatography paper may be treated with chemicals to stain normally invisible pigments.

A spot of concentrated sample is added using a pipette and suspended above the solvent. As the solvent travels up the paper it will carry the sample with it. The distance the sample travels depends on its solubility.

A pencil line is used to show the starting point.

Solvent

Determining Rf Values

To identify the substances in a mixture an R_f value is calculated using the equation:

$$R_f = \frac{\text{Distance travelled by the spot (x)}}{\text{Distance travelled by the solvent (y)}}$$

These R_f values can then be compared with R_f values from known samples or standards, for example: Glycine's R_f value = 0.50

Alanine's R_f value = 0.70

Arginine's R_f value= 0.72

Leucine's R_f value = 0.91

Simple Food Tests

Proteins: The Biuret Test

Reagent:	Biuret solution.
Procedure:	A sample is added to biuret solution and gently heated.
Positive result:	Solution turns from blue to lilac.

Starch: The Iodine Test

Reagent:	Iodine.
Procedure:	Iodine solution is added to the sample.
Positive result:	Blue-black staining occurs.

Lipids: The Emulsion Test

Reagent:	Ethanol.
Procedure:	The sample is shaken with ethanol. After settling, the liquid portion is distilled and mixed with water.
Positive result:	The solution turns into a cloudy-white emulsion of suspended lipid molecules.

Sugars: The Benedict's Test

Reagent:	Benedict's solution.
Procedure:	*Non reducing sugars*: The sample is boiled with dilute hydrochloric acid, then cooled and neutralised. A test for reducing sugars is then performed.
	Reducing sugar: Benedict's solution is added, and the sample is placed in a water bath.
Positive result:	Solution turns from blue to orange.

1. Calculate the R_f value for the example given above (show your working): _____

_____

2. Explain why the R_f value of a substance is always less than 1: _____

_____

3. Discuss when it is appropriate to use chromatography instead of a simple food test: _____

_____

_____

4. Predict what would happen if a sample was immersed in the chromatography solvent, instead of suspended above it:

_____

_____

5. With reference to their R_f values, rank the four amino acids (listed above) in terms of their solubility: _____

_____

6. Outline why lipids must be mixed in ethanol before they will form an emulsion in water: _____

_____

Related activities: Proteins, Carbohydrates, Lipids

Carbohydrates

Carbohydrates are a family of organic molecules made up of carbon, hydrogen, and oxygen atoms with the general formula $(CH_2O)_x$. The most common arrangements found in sugars are hexose (6 sided) or pentose (5 sided) rings. Simple sugars, or monosaccharides, may join together to form compound sugars (disaccharides and polysaccharides), releasing water in the process (**condensation**). Compound sugars can be broken down into their constituent monosaccharides by the opposite reaction (**hydrolysis**). Sugars play a central role in cells, providing energy and, in some cells, contributing to support. They are the major component of most plants (60-90% of the dry weight) and are used by humans as a cheap food source, and a source of fuel, housing, and clothing. In all carbohydrates, the structure is closely related to their functional properties (below).

Monosaccharides

Monosaccharides are used as a primary energy source for fuelling cell metabolism. They are **single-sugar** molecules and include glucose (grape sugar and blood sugar) and fructose (honey and fruit juices). The commonly occurring monosaccharides contain between three and seven carbon atoms in their carbon chains and, of these, the 6C hexose sugars occur most frequently. All monosaccharides are classified as **reducing** sugars (i.e. they can participate in reduction reactions).

Single sugars (monosaccharides)

Triose

e.g. glyceraldehyde

Pentose

e.g. ribose, deoxyribose

Hexose

e.g. glucose, fructose, galactose

Disaccharides

Disaccharides are **double-sugar** molecules and are used as energy sources and as building blocks for larger molecules. The type of disaccharide formed depends on the monomers involved and whether they are in their α- or β- form. Only a few disaccharides (e.g. lactose) are classified as reducing sugars.

Sucrose = α-glucose + β-fructose (simple sugar found in plant sap)
Maltose = α-glucose + α-glucose (a product of starch hydrolysis)
Lactose = β-glucose + β-galactose (milk sugar)
Cellobiose = β-glucose + β-glucose (from cellulose hydrolysis)

Double sugars (disaccharides)

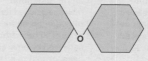

Examples
sucrose,
lactose,
maltose,
cellobiose

Polysaccharides

Cellulose

Cellulose is a structural material in plants and is made up of unbranched chains of β-**glucose** molecules held together by **1, 4 glycosidic links**. As many as 10 000 glucose molecules may be linked together to form a straight chain. Parallel chains become cross-linked with hydrogen bonds and form bundles of 60-70 molecules called microfibrils. Cellulose microfibrils are very strong and are a major component of the structural components of plants, such as the cell wall.

Starch

Starch is a polymer of glucose, made up of long chains of α-**glucose** molecules linked together. It contains a mixture of 25-30% **amylose** (unbranched chains linked by α-1, 4 glycosidic bonds) and 70-75% **amylopectin** (branched chains with α-1, 6 glycosidic bonds every 24-30 glucose units).

Starch is an energy storage molecule in plants and is found concentrated in insoluble **starch granules** within plant cells. Foods rich in starch are a good source of energy for many animals and a staple in most human societies. The starch can be easily hydrolysed by amylases (in saliva and pancreatic secretions) to soluble sugars when required. Maltose is the disaccharide product of starch digestion. Maltose is broken down to its constituent monosaccharides by the enzyme maltase (steps 1-3, right), which is secreted by the surface cells of the intestinal villi.

Glycogen

Glycogen, like starch, is a branched polysaccharide. It is chemically similar to amylopectin, being composed of α-**glucose** molecules, but there are more α-1,6 glycosidic links mixed with α-1,4 links. This makes it more highly branched and water-soluble than starch. Glycogen is a storage compound in animal tissues and is found mainly in **liver** and **muscle** cells (seen as dark areas in the photo, right). It is readily hydrolysed by enzymes (including amylases) to form glucose.

Cellulose in plant cell wall

Starch granules

Starch granules in a plant cell

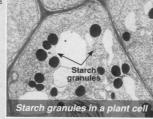

Maltose is a product of starch hydrolysis found in germinating grains

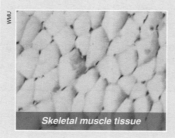

Skeletal muscle tissue

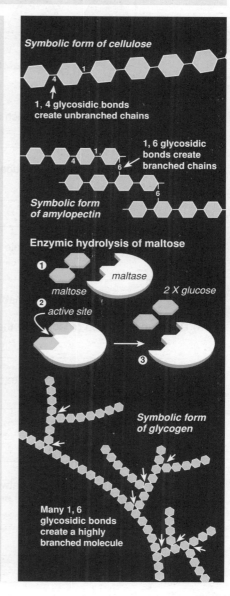

Symbolic form of cellulose

1, 4 glycosidic bonds create unbranched chains

1, 6 glycosidic bonds create branched chains

Symbolic form of amylopectin

Enzymic hydrolysis of maltose

maltase

maltose

2 X glucose

active site

Symbolic form of glycogen

Many 1, 6 glycosidic bonds create a highly branched molecule

Macromolecules & Human Digestion

Related activities: Biochemical Tests
Web links: Condensation and Hydrolysis, Lactose Intolerance

A 2

Isomerism

Compounds with the same chemical formula (same types and numbers of atoms) may differ in the arrangement of their atoms. Such variations in the arrangement of atoms in molecules are called **isomers**. In **structural isomers** (such as fructose and glucose, and the α and β glucose, right), the atoms are linked in different sequences. **Optical isomers** are identical in every way but are mirror images of each other.

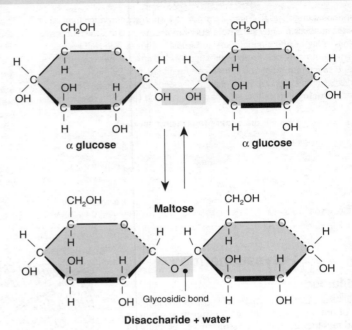

α **glucose**   β **glucose**

Condensation and Hydrolysis Reactions

Monosaccharides can combine to form compound sugars in what is called a **condensation** reaction. Compound sugars can be broken down by **hydrolysis** to simple monosaccharides.

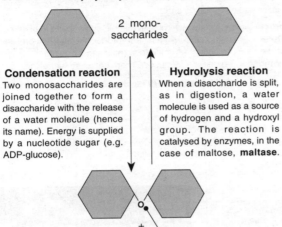

2 mono-saccharides

Condensation reaction
Two monosaccharides are joined together to form a disaccharide with the release of a water molecule (hence its name). Energy is supplied by a nucleotide sugar (e.g. ADP-glucose).

Hydrolysis reaction
When a disaccharide is split, as in digestion, a water molecule is used as a source of hydrogen and a hydroxyl group. The reaction is catalysed by enzymes, in the case of maltose, **maltase**.

Glycosidic bond
+ H_2O

Disaccharide + water

α glucose   α glucose

Maltose

Glycosidic bond

Disaccharide + water

1. Explain why polysaccharides are such a good source of energy: _____

_____

2. (a) Explain briefly how compound sugars are formed and broken down: _____

_____

_____

(b) Using an example, explain the role of enzymes in the hydrolysis of disaccharides: _____

_____

3. Lactose intolerance describes the inability to metabolise **lactose** because lactase is absent or its availability is lowered.

(a) Describe the action of lactase in the gut: _____

_____

(b) Explain why the lack of lactase leads to the symptoms associated with lactose intolerance (bloating and flatulence):

_____

_____

_____

4. Discuss the structural differences between the polysaccharides starch and glycogen, explaining how the differences in structure contribute to the functional properties of the molecule:

_____

_____

_____

Amino Acids

Amino acids are the basic units from which proteins are made. Plants can manufacture all the amino acids they require from simpler molecules, but animals must obtain a certain number of ready-made amino acids (called **essential amino acids**) from their diet. The distinction between essential and non-essential amino acids is somewhat unclear though, as some amino acids can be produced from others and some are interconvertible by the urea cycle. Amino acids can combine to form peptide chains in a **condensation reaction**. The reverse reaction, the hydrolysis of peptide chains, releases free water and single amino acids.

Structure of Amino Acids

There are over 150 amino acids found in cells, but only 20 occur commonly in proteins. The remaining, non-protein amino acids have specialised roles as intermediates in metabolic reactions, or as neurotransmitters and hormones. All amino acids have a common structure (see right). The only difference between the different types lies with the 'R' group in the general formula. This group is variable, which means that it is different in each kind of amino acid.

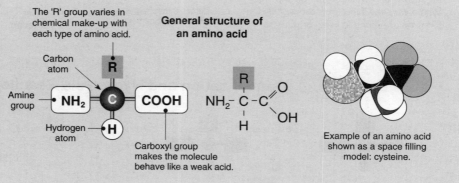

The 'R' group varies in chemical make-up with each type of amino acid.

General structure of an amino acid

Carbon atom

Amine group

Hydrogen atom

Carboxyl group makes the molecule behave like a weak acid.

Example of an amino acid shown as a space filling model: cysteine.

Properties of Amino Acids

Three examples of amino acids with different chemical properties are shown right, with their specific 'R' groups outlined. The 'R' groups can have quite diverse chemical properties.

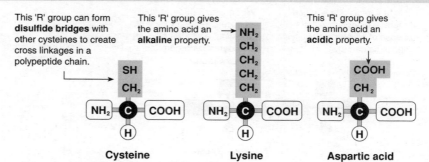

This 'R' group can form **disulfide bridges** with other cysteines to create cross linkages in a polypeptide chain.

This 'R' group gives the amino acid an **alkaline** property.

This 'R' group gives the amino acid an **acidic** property.

Cysteine   **Lysine**   **Aspartic acid**

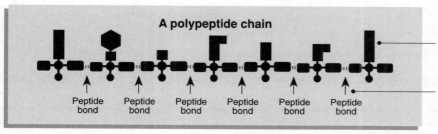

A polypeptide chain

Peptide bond   Peptide bond   Peptide bond   Peptide bond   Peptide bond   Peptide bond

The order of amino acids in a protein is directed by the order of nucleotides in DNA and mRNA.

Peptide bonds link amino acids together in long polymers called polypeptide chains. These may form part or all of a protein.

The amino acids are linked together by peptide bonds to form long chains of up to several hundred amino acids (called polypeptide chains). These chains may be functional units (complete by themselves) or they may need to be joined to other polypeptide chains before they can carry out their function. In humans, not all amino acids can be manufactured by our body: ten must be taken in with our diet (eight in adults). These are the 'essential amino acids'. They are indicated by the symbol ◆ on the right. Those indicated with as asterisk are also required by infants.

Amino acids occurring in proteins

Alanine	Glycine	Proline
Arginine *	Histidine *	Serine
Asparagine	Isoleucine ◆	Threonine ◆
Aspartic acid	Leucine ◆	Tryptophan ◆
Cysteine	Lysine ◆	Tyrosine
Glutamine	Methionine ◆	Valine ◆
Glutamic acid	Phenylalanine ◆	

1. Describe the biological function of amino acids: _____

_____

_____

_____

2. Describe what makes each of the 20 amino acids found in proteins unique: _____

_____

_____

_____

Macromolecules & Human Digestion

Related activities: Proteins
Web links: Amino Acids and Proteins

A 2

Optical Isomers of Amino Acids

All amino acids, apart from the simplest one (glycine) show optical isomerism. The two forms that these optical isomers can take relate to the arrangement of the four bonding sites on the carbon atom. This can result in two different arrangements as shown on the diagrams on the right. With a very few minor exceptions, only the **L-forms** are found in living organisms.

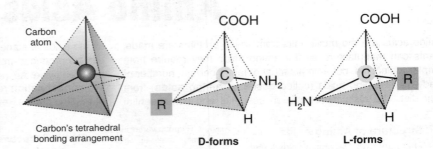

Carbon atom

Carbon's tetrahedral bonding arrangement

D-forms

L-forms

Condensation and Hydrolysis Reactions

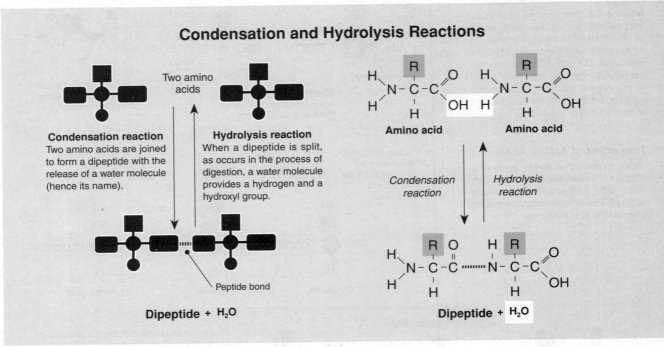

Condensation reaction
Two amino acids are joined to form a dipeptide with the release of a water molecule (hence its name).

Hydrolysis reaction
When a dipeptide is split, as occurs in the process of digestion, a water molecule provides a hydrogen and a hydroxyl group.

Peptide bond

Dipeptide + H₂O

Amino acid

Amino acid

Condensation reaction

Hydrolysis reaction

Dipeptide + H₂O

3. Describe the process that determines the sequence in which amino acids are linked together to form polypeptide chains:

_____

_____

4. Explain what is meant by **essential amino acids**: _____

_____

_____

5. Describe briefly the process of the **condensation** reaction for amino acids: _____

_____

_____

_____

_____

6. Describe briefly the process of the **hydrolysis** reaction for amino acids: _____

_____

_____

_____

_____

7. Name the optical isomeric form that occurs in nearly all amino acids in living things: _____

Proteins

The precise folding up of a protein into its **tertiary structure** creates a three dimensional arrangement of the active 'R' groups. The way each 'R' group faces with respect to the others gives the protein its unique chemical properties. If a protein loses this precise structure (denaturation), it is usually unable to carry out its biological function. Proteins are often classified on the basis of structure (globular vs fibrous). Some of the properties used for the basis of structural classification are outlined over the page.

Primary Structure - 1° (amino acid sequence)
Strings of hundreds of amino acids link together with peptide bonds to form molecules called polypeptide chains. There are 20 different kinds of amino acids that can be linked together in a vast number of different combinations. This sequence is called the **primary structure**. It is the arrangement of attraction and repulsion points in the amino acid chain that determines the higher levels of organisation in the protein and its biological function.

Secondary Structure - 2° (α-helix or β pleated sheet)
Polypeptides become folded in various ways, referred to as the secondary (2°) structure. The most common types of 2° structures are a coiled α-**helix** and a β-**pleated sheet**. Secondary structures are maintained with hydrogen bonds between neighbouring CO and NH groups. H-bonds, although individually weak, provide considerable strength when there are a large number of them. The example, right, shows the two main types of secondary structure. In both, the **'R' side groups** (not shown) project out from the structure. Most globular proteins contain regions of α-helices together with β-sheets. Keratin (a fibrous protein) is composed almost entirely of α-helices. Fibroin (silk protein), is another fibrous protein, almost entirely in β-sheet form.

Tertiary Structure - 3° (folding)
Every protein has a precise structure formed by the folding of the secondary structure into a complex shape called the **tertiary structure**. The protein folds up because various points on the secondary structure are attracted to one another. The strongest links are caused by bonding between neighbouring **cysteine** amino acids which form disulfide bridges. Other interactions that are involved in folding include weak ionic and hydrogen bonds as well as hydrophobic interactions.

Quaternary Structure - 4°
Some proteins (such as enzymes) are complete and functional with a tertiary structure only. However, many complex proteins exist as aggregations of polypeptide chains. The arrangement of the polypeptide chains into a functional protein is termed the **quaternary structure**. The example (right) shows a molecule of haemoglobin, a globular protein composed of 4 polypeptide sub-units joined together; two identical **beta chains** and two identical **alpha chains**. Each has a haem (iron containing) group at the centre of the chain, which binds oxygen. Proteins containing non-protein material are **conjugated proteins**. The non-protein part is the **prosthetic group**.

Denaturation of Proteins
Denaturation refers to the loss of the three-dimensional structure (and usually also the biological function) of a protein. Denaturation is often, although not always, permanent. It results from an alteration of the bonds that maintain the secondary and tertiary structure of the protein, even though the sequence of amino acids remains unchanged. Agents that cause denaturation are:
- **Strong acids and alkalis**: Disrupt ionic bonds and result in coagulation of the protein. Long exposure also breaks down the primary structure of the protein.
- **Heavy metals**: May disrupt ionic bonds, form strong bonds with the carboxyl groups of the R groups, and reduce protein charge. The general effect is to cause the precipitation of the protein.
- **Heat and radiation** (e.g. UV): Cause disruption of the bonds in the protein through increased energy provided to the atoms.
- **Detergents and solvents**: Form bonds with the non-polar groups in the protein, thereby disrupting hydrogen bonding.

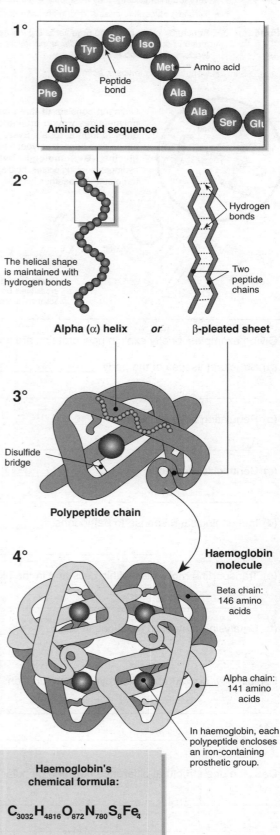

Haemoglobin's chemical formula:

$C_{3032}H_{4816}O_{872}N_{780}S_8Fe_4$

Macromolecules & Human Digestion

Related activities: Biochemical Tests, Amino Acids, Enzymes
Web links: Amino Acids and Proteins

RA 2

Structural Classification of Proteins

Fibrous Proteins

Properties
- Water insoluble
- Very tough physically; may be supple or stretchy
- Parallel polypeptide chains in long fibres or sheets

Function
- Structural role in cells and organisms e.g. collagen found in connective tissue, cartilage, bones, tendons, and blood vessel walls.
- Contractile e.g. myosin, actin

Globular Proteins

Properties
- Easily water soluble
- Tertiary structure critical to function
- Polypeptide chains folded into a spherical shape

Function
- Catalytic e.g. enzymes
- Regulatory e.g. hormones (insulin)
- Transport e.g. haemoglobin
- Protective e.g. antibodies

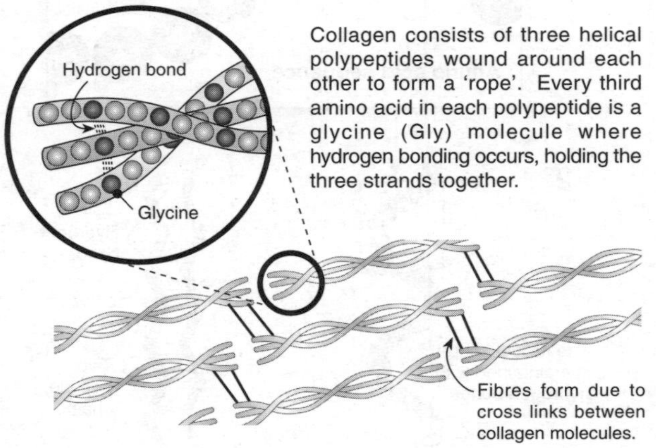

Collagen consists of three helical polypeptides wound around each other to form a 'rope'. Every third amino acid in each polypeptide is a glycine (Gly) molecule where hydrogen bonding occurs, holding the three strands together.

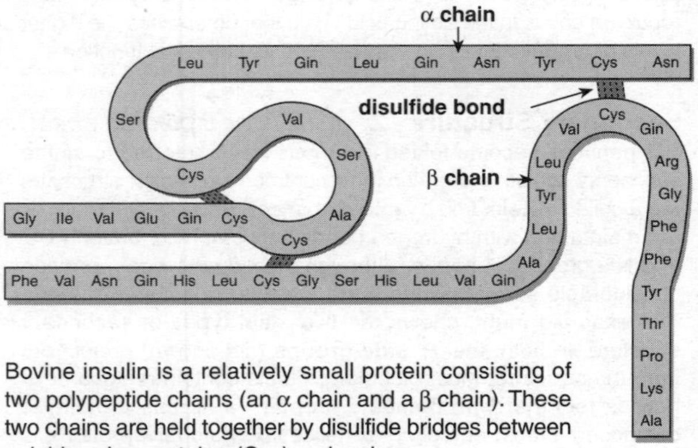

Fibres form due to cross links between collagen molecules.

Bovine insulin is a relatively small protein consisting of two polypeptide chains (an α chain and a β chain). These two chains are held together by disulfide bridges between neighbouring cysteine (Cys) molecules.

1. Giving examples, briefly explain how proteins are involved in the following functional roles:

   (a) Structural tissues of the body: _Joined together by fibrous proteins._

   (b) Regulating body processes: _Regulate the hormone (insulin) levels by Globular proteins_

   (c) Contractile elements: _Collogen. connect tendons to muscles together by fibrous proteins._

   (d) Immunological response to pathogens: _____

   (e) Transporting molecules within cells and in the bloodstream: _____

   (f) Catalysing metabolic reactions in cells: _Enzymes which are proteins speed up reactions._

2. Explain how denaturation destroys protein function: _The enzyme loses it shape and the active site altered, Substrates can no longer bind to the enzyme._

3. Describe one structural difference between globular and fibrous proteins: _Fibrous protein consists of long fibres/sheet of polypeptide chains and globular proteins are folded into a spherical shape._

4. Determine the total number of amino acids in the α and β chains of the insulin molecule illustrated above:

   (a) α chain: _21_   (b) β chain: _29_

Enzymes

Most enzymes are proteins. They are capable of catalysing (speeding up) biochemical reactions and are therefore called biological **catalysts**. Enzymes act on one or more compounds (called the **substrate**). They may break a single substrate molecule down into simpler substances, or join two or more substrate molecules chemically together. The enzyme itself is unchanged in the reaction; its presence merely allows the reaction to take place more rapidly. When the substrate attains the required **activation energy** to enable it to change into the product, there is a 50% chance that it will proceed forward to form the product, otherwise it reverts back to a stable form of the reactant again. The part of the enzyme's surface into which the substrate is bound and undergoes reaction is known as the **active site**. This is made of different parts of polypeptide chain folded in a specific shape so they are closer together. For some enzymes, the complexity of the binding sites can be very precise, allowing only a single kind of substrate to bind to it. Some other enzymes have lower **specificity** and will accept a wide range of substrates of the same general type (e.g. lipases break up any fatty acid chain length of lipid). This is because the enzyme is specific for the type of chemical bond involved and not an exact substrate.

Enzyme Structure

The model on the right is of an enzyme called *Ribonuclease S*, that breaks up RNA molecules. It is a typical enzyme, being a globular protein and composed of up to several hundred atoms. The darkly shaded areas are called **active sites** and make up the **cleft**; the region into which the substrate molecule(s) are drawn. The correct positioning of these sites is critical for the catalytic reaction to occur. The substrate (RNA in this case) is drawn into the cleft by the active sites. By doing so, it puts the substrate molecule under stress, causing the reaction to proceed more readily.

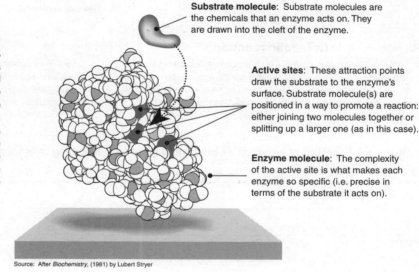

Substrate molecule: Substrate molecules are the chemicals that an enzyme acts on. They are drawn into the cleft of the enzyme.

Active sites: These attraction points draw the substrate to the enzyme's surface. Substrate molecule(s) are positioned in a way to promote a reaction: either joining two molecules together or splitting up a larger one (as in this case).

Enzyme molecule: The complexity of the active site is what makes each enzyme so specific (i.e. precise in terms of the substrate it acts on).

Source: After *Biochemistry*, (1981) by Lubert Stryer

How Enzymes Work

The **lock and key** model proposed earlier this century suggested that the substrate was simply drawn into a closely matching cleft on the enzyme molecule. More recent studies have revealed that the process more likely involves an **induced fit** (see diagram on the right), where the enzyme or the reactants change their shape slightly. The reactants become bound to enzymes by weak chemical bonds. This binding can weaken bonds within the reactants themselves, allowing the reaction to proceed more readily.

The presence of an enzyme simply makes it easier for a reaction to take place. All **catalysts** speed up reactions by influencing the stability of bonds in the reactants. They may also provide an alternative reaction pathway, thus lowering the activation energy needed for a reaction to take place (see the graph below).

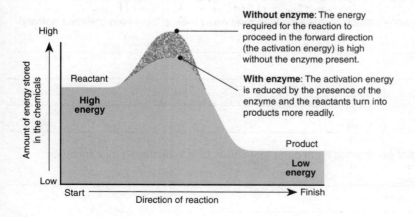

Without enzyme: The energy required for the reaction to proceed in the forward direction (the activation energy) is high without the enzyme present.

With enzyme: The activation energy is reduced by the presence of the enzyme and the reactants turn into products more readily.

Induced Fit Model

An enzyme fits to its substrate somewhat like a lock and key. The shape of the enzyme changes when the substrate fits into the cleft (called the **induced fit**):

1 Two substrate molecules are drawn into the cleft of the enzyme.

2 The enzyme changes shape, forcing the substrate molecules to combine.

3 The resulting end product is released by the enzyme which returns to its normal shape, ready to receive more.

Macromolecules & Human Digestion

Related activities: Enzyme Reaction Rates
Web links: How Enzymes Work

RA 2

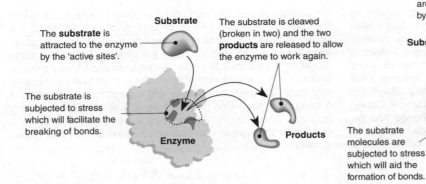

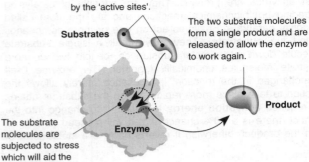

Catabolic reactions

Some enzymes can cause a single substrate molecule to be drawn into the active site. Chemical bonds are broken, causing the substrate molecule to break apart to become two separate molecules. **Examples**: *digestion, cellular respiration*.

Anabolic reactions

Some enzymes can cause two substrate molecules to be drawn into the active site. Chemical bonds are formed, causing the two substrate molecules to form bonds and become a single molecule. **Examples**: *protein synthesis, photosynthesis*.

1. Give a brief account of enzymes as **biological catalysts**, including reference to the role of the **active site**:

Enzymes are called biological catalyst because they speed up reaches. they break or join substrates together, the enzyme itself is unchanged. The part of the enzyme surface in which the chemical reaction takes place in is called the active site.

2. Distinguish between **catabolism** and **anabolism**, giving an example of each and identifying each reaction as **endergonic** or **exergonic**:

Catabolism → endergonic (cellular respiration occurs inside cells)
Anabolism → exergonic (photosynthesis, food giving out energy)

3. Outline the key features of the '**lock and key**' model of enzyme action: Enzyme, substrate, active site, products.

4. Outline the '**induced fit**' model of enzyme action, explaining how it differs from the lock and key model:

Induce fit is when the shape of the reactonts change, it differs from the lock and key model because the combine substrate is flexible and is able to mould itself orand the active site rather than closely match into it.

5. Identify two factors that could cause enzyme denaturation, explaining how they exert their effects (see the next activity):

(a) If temperature is higher than 40° Enzyme denature rapidly.

(b) Extreme acidic causes that bond, to break, therefore loses its shape.

6. Explain what might happen to the functioning of an enzyme if the gene that codes for it was altered by a mutation:

It is not going to carry out it's specific purpose

Enzyme Reaction Rates

Enzymes are sensitive molecules. They often have a narrow range of conditions under which they operate properly. For most of the enzymes associated with plant and animal metabolism, there is little activity at low temperatures. As the temperature increases, so too does the enzyme activity, until the point is reached where the temperature is high enough to damage the enzyme's structure. At this point, the enzyme ceases to function; a phenomenon called enzyme or protein **denaturation**.

Extremes in acidity (pH) can also cause the protein structure of enzymes to denature. Poisons often work by denaturing enzymes or occupying the enzyme's active site so that it does not function. In some cases, enzymes will not function without cofactors, such as vitamins or trace elements. In the four graphs below, the rate of reaction or degree of enzyme activity is plotted against each of four factors that affect enzyme performance. Answer the questions relating to each graph:

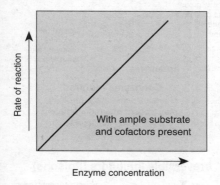

With ample substrate and cofactors present

Rate of reaction

Enzyme concentration

1. **Enzyme concentration**
   (a) Describe the change in the rate of reaction when the enzyme concentration is increased (assuming there is plenty of the substrate present):

   As the enzyme concentration is increased so does the rate of reaction

   (b) Suggest how a cell may vary the amount of enzyme present in a cell:

   _____

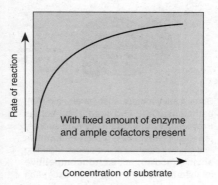

With fixed amount of enzyme and ample cofactors present

Rate of reaction

Concentration of substrate

2. **Substrate concentration**
   (a) Describe the change in the rate of reaction when the substrate concentration is **increased** (assuming a fixed amount of enzyme and ample cofactors):

   The rate of reaction increase with increased substrate concentration but it stops when it reaches maximum level even though substrate being added

   (b) Explain why the rate changes the way it does: _____

   _____

   _____

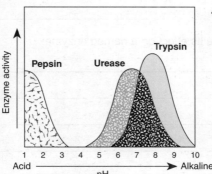

Enzyme activity

Optimum temperature for enzyme

Too cold for the enzyme to operate

Rapid denaturation at high temperature

0   10   20   30   40   50

Temperature / °C

3. **Temperature**
   Higher temperatures speed up all reactions, but few enzymes can tolerate temperatures higher than 50–60°C. The rate at which enzymes are **denatured** (change their shape and become inactive) increases with higher temperatures.

   (a) Describe what is meant by an optimum temperature for enzyme activity:

   Specific temperature in which after that temperature the enzyme denature, stops working.

   (b) Explain why most enzymes perform poorly at low temperatures:

   It too cold for the enzyme to function properly.

Enzyme activity

Trypsin

Pepsin   **Urease**

1   2   3   4   5   6   7   8   9   10

Acid ———————— Alkaline

pH

4. **pH (acidity/alkalinity)**
   Like all proteins, enzymes are **denatured** by extremes of **pH** (very acid or alkaline). Within these extremes, most enzymes are still influenced by pH. Each enzyme has a preferred pH range for optimum activity.

   (a) State the optimum pH for each of the enzymes:

   Pepsin: _1_   Trypsin: _8_   Urease: _65_

   (b) Pepsin acts on proteins in the stomach. Explain how its optimum pH is suited to its working environment:

   Pepsin is very acidic. The stomach condition too is very acidic so it works perfectly.

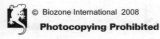

Macromolecules & Human Digestion

Related activities: Enzymes, Enzyme Cofactors and Inhibitors

RDA 2

Enzyme Cofactors and Inhibitors

Enzyme activity is often influenced by the presence of other chemicals. Some of these may enhance an enzyme's activity. Called **cofactors**, they are a nonprotein component of an enzyme and may be organic molecules (**coenzymes**) or inorganic ions (e.g. Ca^{2+}, Zn^{2+}). Enzymes may also be deactivated, temporarily or permanently, by chemicals called enzyme **inhibitors**.

Types of Enzyme

Nearly all enzymes are made of protein, although RNA has been demonstrated to have enzymatic properties. Some enzymes consist of just protein, while others require the addition of extra components to complete their catalytic properties. These may be permanently attached parts called **prosthetic groups**, or temporarily attached pieces (**coenzymes**) that detach after a reaction, and may participate with another enzyme in other reactions.

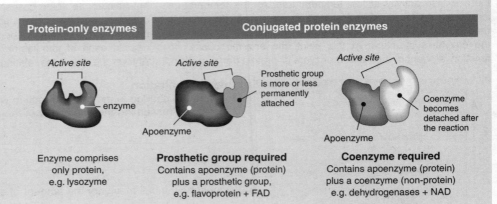

Protein-only enzymes

Enzyme comprises only protein, e.g. lysozyme

Conjugated protein enzymes

Prosthetic group required
Contains apoenzyme (protein) plus a prosthetic group, e.g. flavoprotein + FAD

Coenzyme required
Contains apoenzyme (protein) plus a coenzyme (non-protein) e.g. dehydrogenases + NAD

Reversible Enzyme Inhibitors

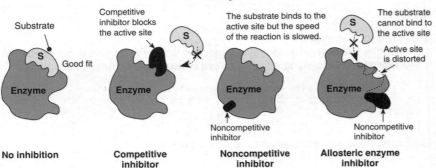

No inhibition   Competitive inhibitor   Noncompetitive inhibitor   Allosteric enzyme inhibitor

Enzyme inhibitors may be reversible or irreversible. **Reversible inhibitors** are used to control enzyme activity. There is often an interaction between the substrate or end product and the enzymes controlling the reaction. Buildup of the end product or a lack of substrate may deactivate the enzyme. This deactivation may take the form of **competitive** (competes for the active site) or **noncompetitive** inhibition. While noncompetitive inhibitors have the effect of slowing down the rate of reaction, **allosteric inhibitors** block the active site altogether and prevent its functioning.

Irreversible Inhibitors (Poisons)

Some heavy metals, such as arsenic (As), cadmium (Cd), and lead (Pb) act as **irreversible inhibitors**. They bind strongly to the sulfhydryl (-SH) groups of a protein and destroy catalytic activity. Most, including arsenic (above), act as **noncompetitive** inhibitors. Mercury (Hg) is an exception because it is a competitive inhibitor, binding to the sulfhydryl group in the active site of the papain enzyme. Heavy metals are retained in the body and lost slowly.

1. Describe the general role of **cofactors** in enzyme activity: _____

   _____

2. (a) List four **heavy metals** that are toxic to humans: _____

   (b) Explain in general terms why these heavy metals are toxic to life: _____

   _____

3. There are many enzyme inhibitors that are not heavy metals (e.g. those found in some pesticides).

   (a) Name a **common poison** that is an enzyme inhibitor, but not a heavy metal: _____

   (b) Try to find out how this poison interferes with enzyme function. Briefly describe its effect on a named enzyme:

   _____

   _____

4. Distinguish between **competitive** and **noncompetitive** inhibition: _____

   _____

5. Explain how **allosteric inhibitors** differ from other noncompetitive inhibitors: _____

   _____

Related activities: Enzymes, Enzyme Reaction Rates

The Human Digestive Tract

It is estimated that an adult consumes about 20 000 kg of food between the ages of 18 and 38 years; about a metric tonne a year. Although babies grow rapidly from birth, growth is not the most significant reason for our ongoing eating. Our bodies require a constant source of energy for the vast number of biochemical reactions that constitute **metabolism**. Food provides the source of this energy. Tube-like digestive tracts (guts) run through the body from the mouth to the anus. The digestive tract prepares the food we eat for use by the body's cells through five basic activities: eating (ingestion), movement (of food through the gut), digestion (physical and chemical breakdown), absorption, and elimination. However the different specialisations that occur in each region will depend both on the diet and the method of ingestion (prechewed, liquid, unchewed).

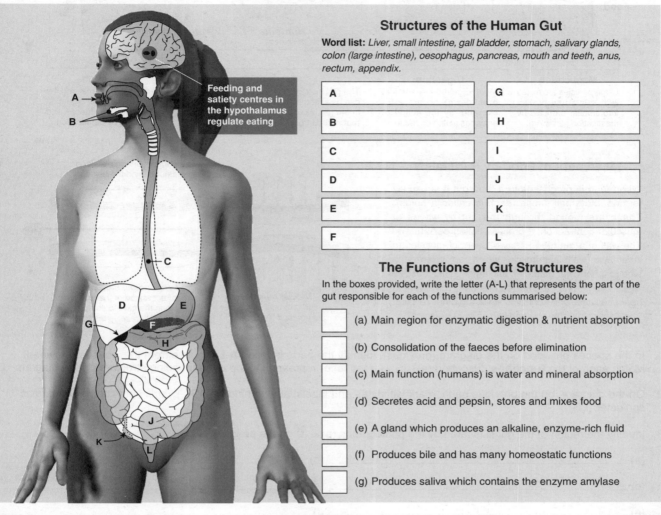

Feeding and satiety centres in the hypothalamus regulate eating

Structures of the Human Gut

Word list: *Liver, small intestine, gall bladder, stomach, salivary glands, colon (large intestine), oesophagus, pancreas, mouth and teeth, anus, rectum, appendix.*

A		G	
B		H	
C		I	
D		J	
E		K	
F		L	

The Functions of Gut Structures

In the boxes provided, write the letter (A-L) that represents the part of the gut responsible for each of the functions summarised below:

- [ ] (a) Main region for enzymatic digestion & nutrient absorption
- [ ] (b) Consolidation of the faeces before elimination
- [ ] (c) Main function (humans) is water and mineral absorption
- [ ] (d) Secretes acid and pepsin, stores and mixes food
- [ ] (e) A gland which produces an alkaline, enzyme-rich fluid
- [ ] (f) Produces bile and has many homeostatic functions
- [ ] (g) Produces saliva which contains the enzyme amylase

Macromolecules & Human Digestion

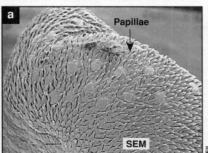

Papillae

SEM

SEM

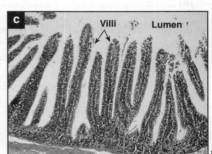

Villi   Lumen

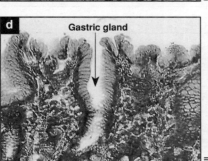

Gastric gland

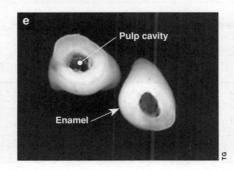

Pulp cavity

Enamel

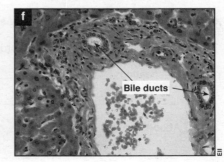

Bile ducts

Related activities: Stomach and Small Intestine, The Large Intestine, Absorption and Transport   **Web links**: Digestion Animation

RA 2

Digestive Processes in a Simple Tube Gut

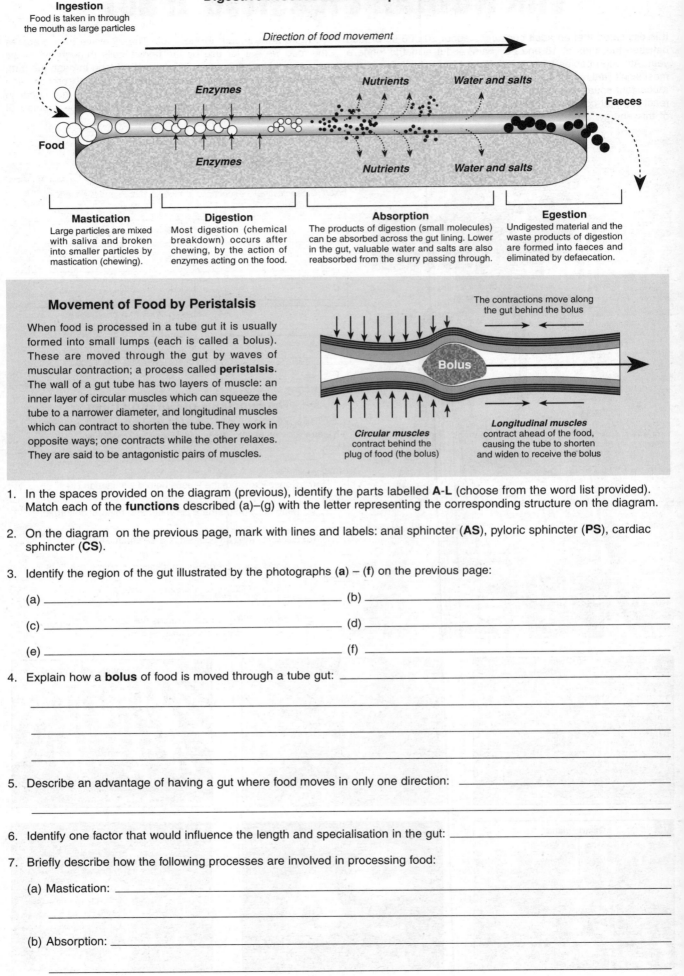

Ingestion
Food is taken in through the mouth as large particles

Direction of food movement

Enzymes

Nutrients

Water and salts

Faeces

Food

Enzymes

Nutrients

Water and salts

Mastication
Large particles are mixed with saliva and broken into smaller particles by mastication (chewing).

Digestion
Most digestion (chemical breakdown) occurs after chewing, by the action of enzymes acting on the food.

Absorption
The products of digestion (small molecules) can be absorbed across the gut lining. Lower in the gut, valuable water and salts are also reabsorbed from the slurry passing through.

Egestion
Undigested material and the waste products of digestion are formed into faeces and eliminated by defaecation.

Movement of Food by Peristalsis

When food is processed in a tube gut it is usually formed into small lumps (each is called a bolus). These are moved through the gut by waves of muscular contraction; a process called **peristalsis**. The wall of a gut tube has two layers of muscle: an inner layer of circular muscles which can squeeze the tube to a narrower diameter, and longitudinal muscles which can contract to shorten the tube. They work in opposite ways; one contracts while the other relaxes. They are said to be antagonistic pairs of muscles.

The contractions move along the gut behind the bolus

Bolus

Circular muscles
contract behind the plug of food (the bolus)

Longitudinal muscles
contract ahead of the food, causing the tube to shorten and widen to receive the bolus

1. In the spaces provided on the diagram (previous), identify the parts labelled **A-L** (choose from the word list provided). Match each of the **functions** described (a)–(g) with the letter representing the corresponding structure on the diagram.

2. On the diagram on the previous page, mark with lines and labels: anal sphincter (**AS**), pyloric sphincter (**PS**), cardiac sphincter (**CS**).

3. Identify the region of the gut illustrated by the photographs (**a**) – (**f**) on the previous page:

   (a) _____   (b) _____

   (c) _____   (d) _____

   (e) _____   (f) _____

4. Explain how a **bolus** of food is moved through a tube gut: _____

   _____

   _____

   _____

5. Describe an advantage of having a gut where food moves in only one direction: _____

   _____

6. Identify one factor that would influence the length and specialisation in the gut: _____

7. Briefly describe how the following processes are involved in processing food:

   (a) Mastication: _____

   _____

   (b) Absorption: _____

   _____

Stomach and Small Intestine

Digestion in the gut depends on both the physical movement of the food and its enzymatic breakdown into constituent components. Most digestion occurs in the stomach and small intestine. The digestive enzymes involved may be bound to the surfaces of the intestinal epithelial cells or occur as components of the secretions of digestive glands (e.g. pancreas). The structure and functions of the stomach and small intestines, and their enzymic secretions are shown on this and the next page.

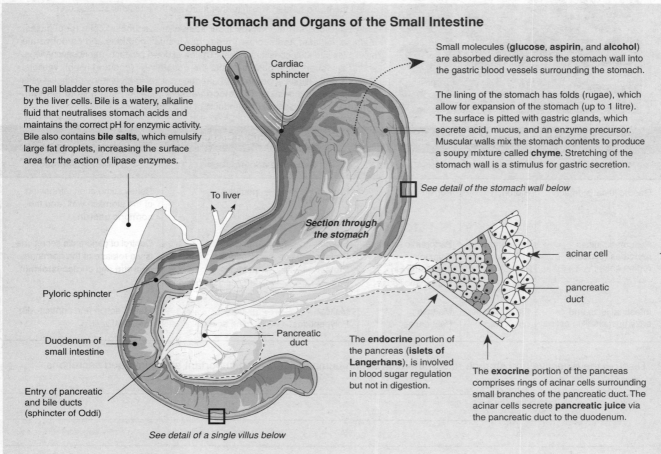

The Stomach and Organs of the Small Intestine

Oesophagus

Cardiac sphincter

The gall bladder stores the **bile** produced by the liver cells. Bile is a watery, alkaline fluid that neutralises stomach acids and maintains the correct pH for enzymic activity. Bile also contains **bile salts**, which emulsify large fat droplets, increasing the surface area for the action of lipase enzymes.

Small molecules (**glucose, aspirin,** and **alcohol**) are absorbed directly across the stomach wall into the gastric blood vessels surrounding the stomach.

The lining of the stomach has folds (rugae), which allow for expansion of the stomach (up to 1 litre). The surface is pitted with gastric glands, which secrete acid, mucus, and an enzyme precursor. Muscular walls mix the stomach contents to produce a soupy mixture called **chyme**. Stretching of the stomach wall is a stimulus for gastric secretion.

To liver

See detail of the stomach wall below

Section through the stomach

acinar cell

pancreatic duct

Pyloric sphincter

Duodenum of small intestine

Pancreatic duct

The **endocrine** portion of the pancreas (**islets of Langerhans**), is involved in blood sugar regulation but not in digestion.

Entry of pancreatic and bile ducts (sphincter of Oddi)

The **exocrine** portion of the pancreas comprises rings of acinar cells surrounding small branches of the pancreatic duct. The acinar cells secrete **pancreatic juice** via the pancreatic duct to the duodenum.

See detail of a single villus below

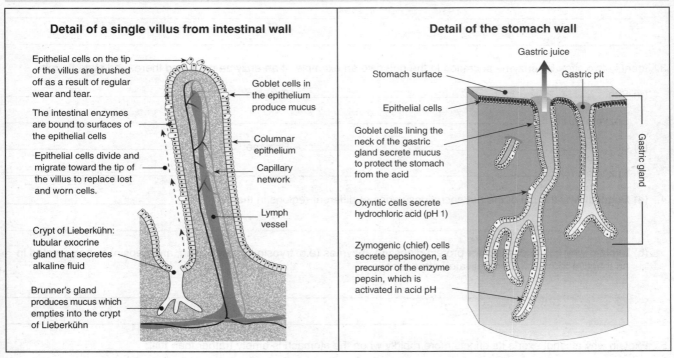

Detail of a single villus from intestinal wall

Epithelial cells on the tip of the villus are brushed off as a result of regular wear and tear.

The intestinal enzymes are bound to surfaces of the epithelial cells

Epithelial cells divide and migrate toward the tip of the villus to replace lost and worn cells.

Crypt of Lieberkühn: tubular exocrine gland that secretes alkaline fluid

Brunner's gland produces mucus which empties into the crypt of Lieberkühn

Goblet cells in the epithelium produce mucus

Columnar epithelium

Capillary network

Lymph vessel

Detail of the stomach wall

Gastric juice

Stomach surface

Gastric pit

Epithelial cells

Goblet cells lining the neck of the gastric gland secrete mucus to protect the stomach from the acid

Oxyntic cells secrete hydrochloric acid (pH 1)

Zymogenic (chief) cells secrete pepsinogen, a precursor of the enzyme pepsin, which is activated in acid pH

Gastric gland

Macromolecules & Human Digestion

1. Describe the two important roles of gut movements: _____

_____

_____

Related activities: The Human Digestive Tract, Absorption and Transport
Web links: Acid Secretion in the Stomach

A 2

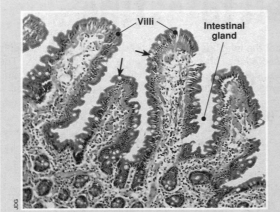

Villi Intestinal gland

Intestinal villi and microvilli

The photograph (left) shows a section through the ileum with the **intestinal villi** and **intestinal glands** (crypts of Lieberkühn) indicated. The intestinal glands secrete mucus and alkaline fluid. **Epithelial cells** lining the surface of the villi are regularly worn off and replaced by new cells migrating from the base of the intestinal glands. Each epithelial cell has many **microvilli** (microscopic projections called the brush border) which further increase the intestinal surface area.

Enzymes bound to the microvilli surfaces of the epithelial cells (peptidases, maltase, lactase, and sucrase) break down small peptides and carbohydrate molecules into their constituent parts. The breakdown products (monosaccharides, amino acids) are then absorbed into the underlying blood and lymph vessels. **Mucous cells** (white spots arrowed) produce mucus to protect the epithelial cells from enzymatic digestion. The **blood vessels** transport nutrients to the liver. **Lymph vessels** transport the products of fat digestion.

Enzyme secretions of the gut and their role in digestion

Secretion and source	Site of action	Active enzyme	Substrate and products	Control of secretion
Gastric juice: stomach	Stomach	Pepsin	Protein ⟶ peptides	Reflex stimulation, stretching of the stomach wall, and the hormone **gastrin**.
Pancreatic juice: pancreas (exocrine region only)	Duodenum	Pancreatic amylase Trypsin Chymotrypsin Pancreatic lipase	Starch ⟶ maltose Protein ⟶ peptides Protein ⟶ peptides Fats ⟶ fatty acids + glycerol	Control of pancreatic secretions is via release of the hormones **secretin** and **cholecystokinin**.
Intestinal juice and enzymes: small intestine	Small intestine	Maltase Peptidases	Maltose ⟶ glucose Polypeptides ⟶ amino acids	Reflex action and contact with intestinal wall.

2. Discuss the digestive and storage role of the stomach in humans, identifying important structures and secretions:

_____

_____

_____

_____

_____

3. Identify two sites for enzyme secretion in the gut, give an example of an enzyme produced there, and state its role:

(a) Site: _____ Enzyme: _____

Enzyme's role: _____

(b) Site: _____ Enzyme: _____

Enzyme's role: _____

4. (a) Suggest why the pH of the gut secretions varies at different regions in the gut: _____

_____

(b) Explain why it is necessary for protein-digesting enzymes (e.g. trypsin, chymotrypsin, and pepsin) to be secreted in an inactive form and then activated after release:

_____

_____

5. Explain why alcohol exerts its effects more rapidly when the stomach is empty (rather than full): _____

_____

6. Explain the role of sphincter muscles in the digestive tract: _____

_____

The Large Intestine

After most of the nutrients have been absorbed in the small intestine, the remaining fluid contents pass into the large intestine (appendix, caecum, and colon). The fluid comprises undigested or undigestible food, bacteria, dead cells sloughed off from the gut wall, mucus, bile, ions, and a large amount of water. In humans and other omnivores, the large intestine is concerned mainly with the reabsorption of water and electrolytes. Infection or disease can cause an increase in gut movements, resulting in insufficient reabsorption of water and diarrhoea. Sluggish gut movements cause the reabsorption of too much water and the faeces become hard and difficult to pass, a condition known as constipation. The semi-solid waste material (faeces) passes from the **colon** to the rectum, where it is stored and consolidated before being expelled (egested). Egestion of faeces is controlled by the activity of two sphincters in the **anus**, one being under involuntary reflex control.

Structure of the Large Intestine

A single crypt from the intestinal wall

The lining of the large intestine consists of a simple columnar epithelium. The epithelium is not folded into villi, but instead contains tubular glands called crypts, containing numerous goblet cells. The goblet cells produce mucus, which lubricates the colon wall and aids formation of the faeces.

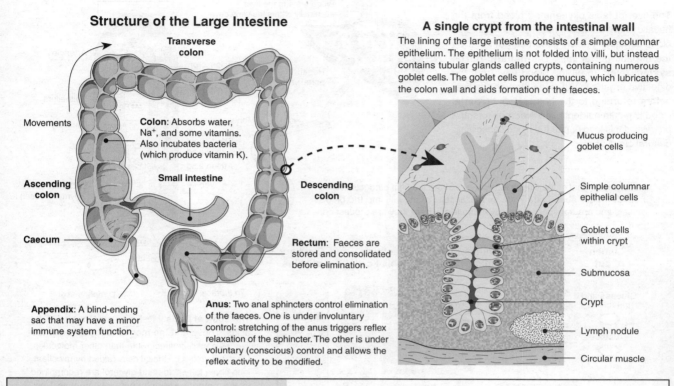

Transverse colon

Movements

Colon: Absorbs water, Na⁺, and some vitamins. Also incubates bacteria (which produce vitamin K).

Small intestine

Ascending colon

Descending colon

Caecum

Rectum: Faeces are stored and consolidated before elimination.

Appendix: A blind-ending sac that may have a minor immune system function.

Anus: Two anal sphincters control elimination of the faeces. One is under involuntary control: stretching of the anus triggers reflex relaxation of the sphincter. The other is under voluntary (conscious) control and allows the reflex activity to be modified.

Mucus producing goblet cells

Simple columnar epithelial cells

Goblet cells within crypt

Submucosa

Crypt

Lymph nodule

Circular muscle

Macromolecules & Human Digestion

Appendicitis

Obstruction of the appendix by faecal matter or some other cause can lead to an inflammation called *appendicitis*. Appendicitis usually develops rapidly with little warning over a period of 6-12 hours. The usual symptom is abdominal pain, accompanied by nausea, vomiting and a slight fever. When severe, it can be life threatening. Acute appendicitis is treated by surgical removal of the appendix (**appendectomy**). The entire procedure usually takes about one hour and is performed in one of two ways: through what is called an open operation or through the laparoscopic technique.

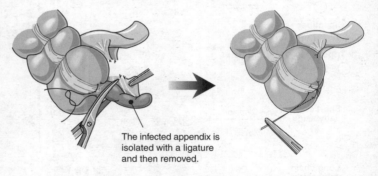

The infected appendix is isolated with a ligature and then removed.

1. Outline the main function of the large intestine: _____

2. Suggest why the lining of the large intestine consists of crypts as opposed to villi like projections: _____

_____

3. The photograph below shows a cross section through the colon wall. Label the features indicated:

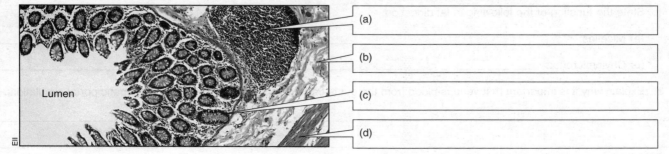

Lumen

(a)

(b)

(c)

(d)

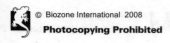

Related activities: Absorption and Transport

RA 2

Absorption and Transport

All the chemical and physical processes of digestion from the mouth to the small intestine are aimed at the breakdown of food molecules into forms that can pass through intestinal lining into the underlying blood and lymph vessels. These breakdown products include monosaccharides, amino acids, fatty acids, glycerol, and glycerides. Passage of these molecules from the gut into the blood or lymph is called **absorption**. After absorption, nutrients are transported directly or indirectly to the liver for storage or processing. Some of the features of nutrient absorption and transport are shown below. For simplicity, all nutrients are shown in the lumen of the intestine, even though some nutrients are digested on the epithelial cell surfaces.

The Hepatic Portal System

The liver obtains oxygenated blood from the hepatic artery, but it also receives deoxygenated blood containing newly absorbed nutrients via the hepatic portal vein. The **hepatic portal system** refers to all the blood flow from the digestive organs that passes through the liver before returning to the heart. Hepatic portal blood is rich in nutrients: the liver monitors and processes this load before the blood passes into general circulation.

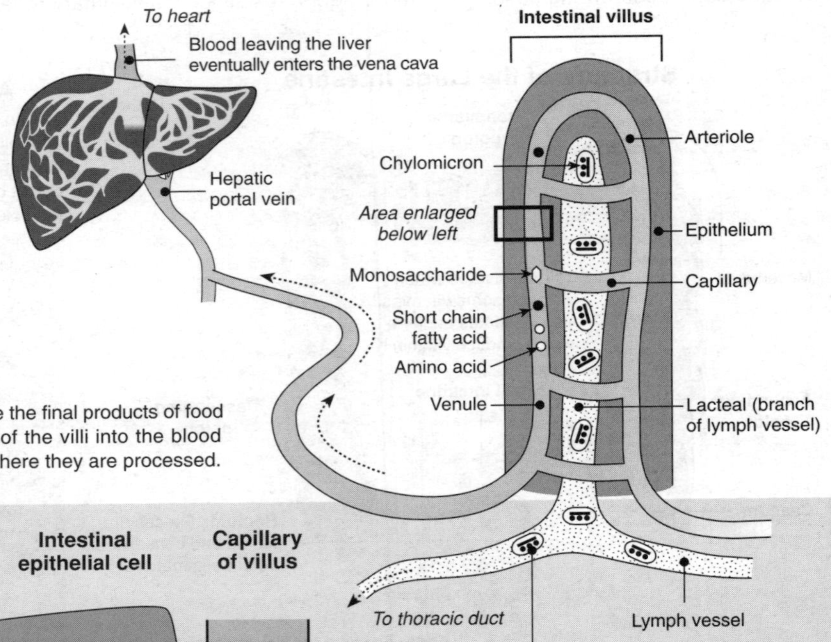

Absorption: Most of the simple molecules that are the final products of food breakdown are absorbed by the epithelial cells of the villi into the blood vessels and are transported directly to the liver where they are processed.

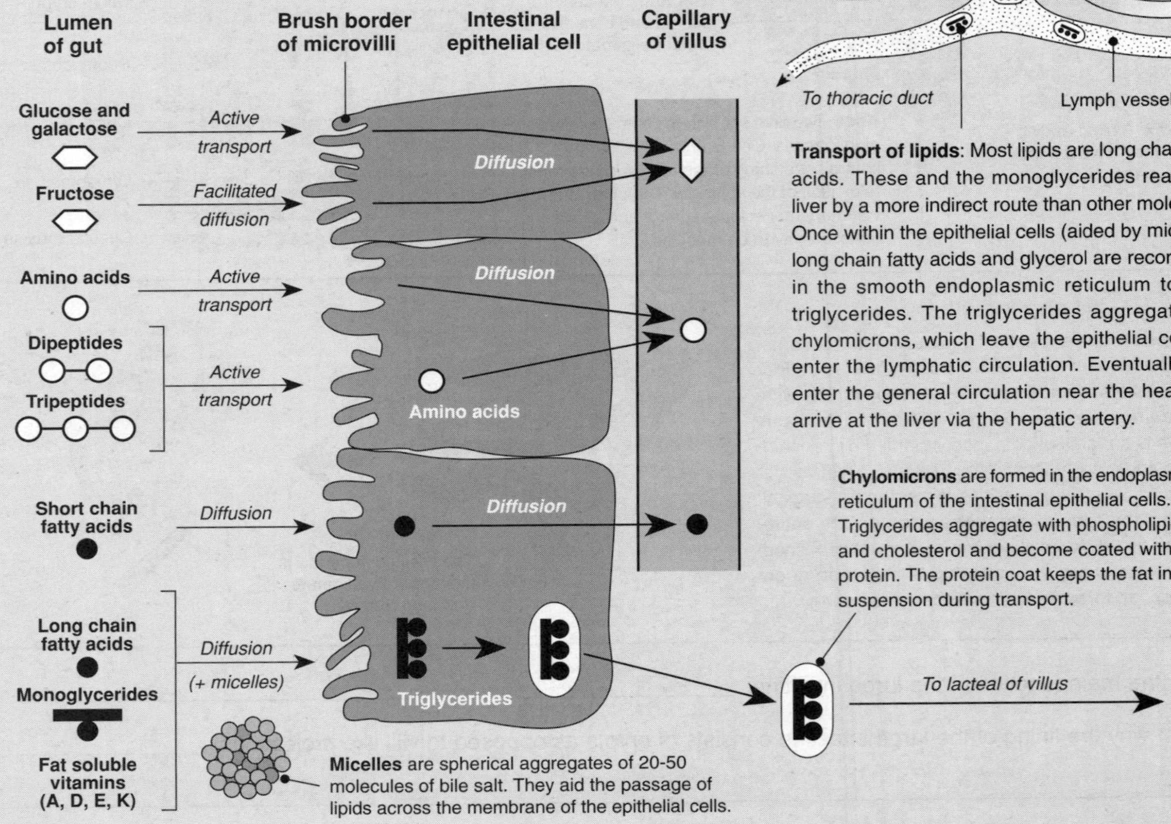

To heart
Blood leaving the liver eventually enters the vena cava
Hepatic portal vein

Intestinal villus
Chylomicron
Area enlarged below left
Monosaccharide
Short chain fatty acid
Amino acid
Venule
Arteriole
Epithelium
Capillary
Lacteal (branch of lymph vessel)
To thoracic duct
Lymph vessel

Lumen of gut	Brush border of microvilli	Intestinal epithelial cell	Capillary of villus

Glucose and galactose — *Active transport* — Diffusion
Fructose — *Facilitated diffusion*
Amino acids — *Active transport* — Diffusion
Dipeptides / Tripeptides — *Active transport*
Amino acids
Short chain fatty acids — *Diffusion* — Diffusion
Long chain fatty acids / Monoglycerides — *Diffusion (+ micelles)*
Triglycerides
Fat soluble vitamins (A, D, E, K)
To lacteal of villus

Micelles are spherical aggregates of 20-50 molecules of bile salt. They aid the passage of lipids across the membrane of the epithelial cells.

Transport of lipids: Most lipids are long chain fatty acids. These and the monoglycerides reach the liver by a more indirect route than other molecules. Once within the epithelial cells (aided by micelles), long chain fatty acids and glycerol are recombined in the smooth endoplasmic reticulum to form triglycerides. The triglycerides aggregate into chylomicrons, which leave the epithelial cell and enter the lymphatic circulation. Eventually they enter the general circulation near the heart and arrive at the liver via the hepatic artery.

Chylomicrons are formed in the endoplasmic reticulum of the intestinal epithelial cells. Triglycerides aggregate with phospholipids and cholesterol and become coated with protein. The protein coat keeps the fat in suspension during transport.

1. State the function of the following in fat digestion:

   (a) Micelles: _____

   (b) Chylomicrons: _____

2. Explain why it is important that venous blood from the gut is transported first to the liver via the hepatic portal circulation:

   _____

   _____

A 2   **Related activities**: Stomach and Small Intestine, The Large Intestine

The Control of Digestion

The majority of digestive juices are secreted only when there is food in the gut and both nervous and hormonal mechanisms are involved in coordinating and regulating this activity appropriately. The digestive system is innervated by branches of the **autonomic nervous system** (sympathetic and parasympathetic stimulation).

Hormonal regulation is achieved through the activity of several hormones: **gastrin**, **secretin**, and **cholecystokinin** (formerly called **pancreozymin**). These are released into the bloodstream in response to nervous or chemical stimuli and influence the activity of gut and associated organs.

Hormonal and Nervous Control of Digestion

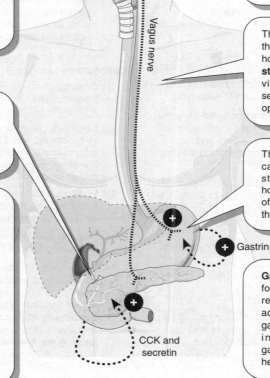

Salivation is entirely under nervous control. Some saliva is secreted continuously in response to **parasympathetic stimulation** via the vagus nerve. The presence of food in the mouth stimulates the salivary glands (and stomach) to increase their secretions. This response operates through a simple cranial reflex via the vagus nerve. The smell, sight, and thought of food also stimulates salivary (and gastric) secretion. These stimuli involve higher brain activity and learning (a conditioned reflex).

The feeding centre of the brain

The **feeding centre** in the hypothalamus is constantly active. It monitors metabolites in the blood and stimulates hunger when these metabolites reach low levels. After a meal, a neighbouring region of the hypothalamus, **the satiety centre**, suppresses the activity of the feeding centre for a period of time. Impulses from these two centres travel via the vagus nerve to stimulate the secretion of particular digestive hormones.

The secretions and muscular activity of the gut are regulated by both nervous and hormonal mechanisms. **Parasympathetic stimulation** of the stomach and pancreas via the **vagus nerve** increases their secretion. Sympathetic stimulation has the opposite effect.

The entry of food into the small intestine, especially fat and gastric acid, stimulates the cells of the intestinal mucosa to secrete the hormones **cholecystokinin** (CCK) and **secretin**.

The presence of food in the stomach causes it to stretch. This mechanical stimulus results in secretion of the hormone **gastrin** from cells in the mucosa of the stomach. This activity is mediated through a simple **reflex**.

Cholecystokinin circulates in the blood and stimulates the pancreas to increase its secretion of enzyme-rich fluid. CCK also stimulates the release of bile into the intestine from the gall bladder.
Secretin stimulates the pancreas to increase its secretion of alkaline fluid. This fluid neutralises the acid entering the intestine. Secretin also stimulates the production of bile from the liver cells.
Both secretin and CCK stimulate the secretion of intestinal juice but inhibit gastric secretion and general motility of the gastrointestinal tract.

Gastrin is secreted in response to eating food (particularly protein). Gastrin is released into the bloodstream where it acts back on the stomach to increase gastric secretion and motility. Gastrin also increases the motility of the gastrointestinal tract in general, and this helps to propel food through the gut.

Vagus nerve

Gastrin

CCK and secretin

Macromolecules & Human Digestion

1. Describe the role of each of the following stimuli in the control of digestion, identifying both the response and its effect:

(a) Presence of food in the mouth: _____

_____

(b) Presence of fat and acid in the small intestine: _____

_____

(c) Stretching of the stomach by the presence of food: _____

_____

2. Outline the role of the vagus nerve in regulating digestive activity: _____

_____

Cell Structure and Function

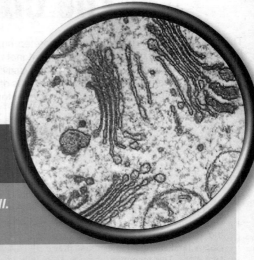

Unit 1: Biology and Disease

1.3   Cells and microscopy

Cell structure as typified by an intestinal epithelial cell.
Prokaryotic cells. Cell fractionation. Microscopy.

Learning Objectives

☐ 1. Compile your own glossary from the **KEY WORDS** displayed in **bold type** in the learning objectives below.

Features of Cells *(pages 73-80, 86-88)*

☐ 2. Recognise the contribution of microscopy to our present knowledge of cell structure. Recognise the **cell** as the basic unit of living things.

☐ 3. Use different units of measurement (mm, μm, nm) to express cell sizes and to describe a range of cell sizes.

☐ 4. Contrast the generalised structure of **prokaryote** and **eukaryote** cells and provide examples of each type.

☐ 5. Describe the structure of a **bacterial cell**, including the **bacterial cell wall** and the structures associated with it (**flagella**, **pili**), the **bacterial chromosome** and **plasmids**, and the plasma membrane. Identify which of these are unique to prokaryotes.

☐ 6. Identify the appearance, ultrastructure, and function of each of the following cellular structures or organelles in an **intestinal epithelial cell**:
   • **nucleus, nucleolus**
   • **mitochondria**
   • rough/smooth **endoplasmic reticulum, ribosomes**,
   • **plasma membrane**
   • **Golgi apparatus**
   • **lysosomes**
   • **microvilli**

☐ 7. Identify which of the cellular structures in #6 would be discernable under light microscopy, and which would require electron microscope to be distinguished.

☐ 8. Describe the role of **cell fractionation** in separating cellular components. Explain how it is achieved through homogenisation of a sample followed by **ultracentrifugation**. Explain the role of speed of centrifugation in separating the cellular fractions.

☐ 9. Use your knowledge of the cell features described in #6 to describe features and explain adaptations of a variety of eukaryotic cells. You could include specialised animal cells, fungal cells, protoctists, and plant cells.

Microscopy *(pages 81-88)*

☐ 10. Describe the basic structure of **optical** and **electron microscopes**. With respect to these, explain and distinguish between **magnification** and **resolution**.

☐ 11. Distinguish between TEM (**transmission electron microscopy**) and SEM (**scanning electron microscopy**). Recognise EM as an important tool in investigating cell structure and function, and discuss the limitations of each microscopy method.

☐ 12. Distinguish between **compound** and **stereo light microscopes**. Identify the situations in which these different microscopes would be used.

☐ 13. Interpret drawings and photographs of cell features as seen using light and electron microscopy.

☐ 14. Demonstrate an ability to correctly use a light microscope to locate material and focus images. Identify the steps required for preparing a **temporary mount** for viewing with a compound light microscope. Explain why **stains** are useful in the preparation of specimens. If required, use simple **staining techniques** to show specific features of cells.

■ **Lysosomes and their Versatile and Potentially Fatal Membranes** Biol. Sci. Rev., 17(3) Feb. 2005, pp. 14-16. *The critical importance of the lysosome membrane.*

■ **The Beat Goes On: Cilia and Flagella** Biol. Sci. Rev., 18(4) April 2006, pp. 2-6. *The structure and function of cilia and flagella.*

 See the 'Textbook Reference Grid' on page 7 for textbook page references relating to material in this topic.

Supplementary Texts

See pages 5-6 for additional details of these texts:

■ Adds, J., *et al.*, 2003. **Molecules and Cells**, (NelsonThornes), chpt. 4.

■ Adds, J., *et al.*, 1999. **Tools, Techniques and Assessment in Biology**, (NelsonThornes), pp. 13-26.

 Presentation MEDIA to support this topic: **CELL BIO & BIOCHEM** Cell Structure

See page 6 for details of publishers of periodicals:

STUDENT'S REFERENCE

■ **Transmission Electron Microscopy** Biol. Sci. Rev., 13(2) Nov. 2000, pp. 32-35. *The techniques and applications of TEM. Includes a diagram comparing features of TEM and light microscopy.*

■ **Light Microscopy** Biol. Sci. Rev., 13(1) Sept. 2000, pp. 36-38. *An excellent account of the basis and various techniques of light microscopy.*

■ **Scanning Electron Microscopy** Biol. Sci. Rev., 20(1) Sept. 2004, pp. 38-41. *An excellent account of the techniques and applications of SEM. Includes details of specimen preparation and recent advancements in the technology.*

■ **Lysosomes: The Cell's Recycling Centres** Biol. Sci. Rev., 17(2) Nov. 2004, pp. 21-23. *The nature and role of lysosomes: small membrane-bound organelles found in all eukaryotic cells.*

See pages 8-9 for details of how to access **Bio Links** from our web site: **www.biozone.co.uk**. From Bio Links, access sites under the topics:

CELL BIOLOGY AND BIOCHEMISTRY: • Cell and molecular biology online • Cell structure and function web links > **Microscopy:** • A guide to microscopy and microanalysis • Biological applications of electron and light microscopy • Microscopy UK • Scanning Electron Microscope ... *and others* > **Cell Structure and Transport:** • Animal cells • CELLS alive! • Cell breakage and fractionation • Nanoworld ... *and others*

Animal Cells

Animal cells, unlike plant cells, do not have a regular shape. In fact, some animal cells (such as phagocytes) are able to alter their shape for various purposes (e.g. engulfment of foreign material). The diagram below illustrates the basic ultrastructure of an **intestinal epithelial cell**. It contains organelles common to most relatively unspecialised animal cells. The intestine is lined with these columnar epithelial cells. They are taller than they are wide, with the nucleus close to the base and hairlike projections (**microvilli**) on their free surface. Microvilli increase the surface area of the cell, greatly increasing the capacity for absorption.

Structures and Organelles in an Intestinal Epithelial Cell

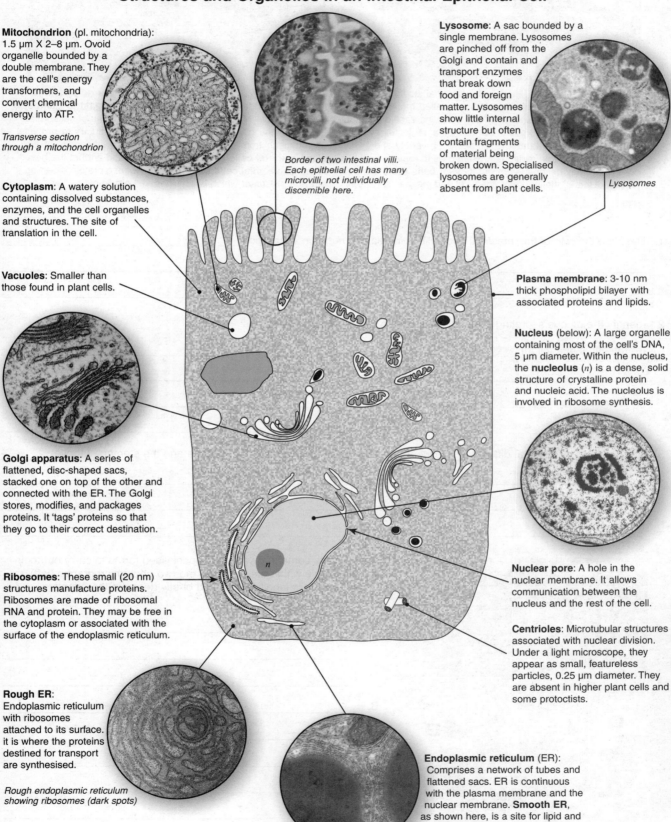

Mitochondrion (pl. mitochondria): 1.5 μm X 2–8 μm. Ovoid organelle bounded by a double membrane. They are the cell's energy transformers, and convert chemical energy into ATP.

Transverse section through a mitochondrion

Cytoplasm: A watery solution containing dissolved substances, enzymes, and the cell organelles and structures. The site of translation in the cell.

Vacuoles: Smaller than those found in plant cells.

Golgi apparatus: A series of flattened, disc-shaped sacs, stacked one on top of the other and connected with the ER. The Golgi stores, modifies, and packages proteins. It 'tags' proteins so that they go to their correct destination.

Ribosomes: These small (20 nm) structures manufacture proteins. Ribosomes are made of ribosomal RNA and protein. They may be free in the cytoplasm or associated with the surface of the endoplasmic reticulum.

Rough ER: Endoplasmic reticulum with ribosomes attached to its surface. it is where the proteins destined for transport are synthesised.

Rough endoplasmic reticulum showing ribosomes (dark spots)

Border of two intestinal villi. Each epithelial cell has many microvilli, not individually discernible here.

Lysosome: A sac bounded by a single membrane. Lysosomes are pinched off from the Golgi and contain and transport enzymes that break down food and foreign matter. Lysosomes show little internal structure but often contain fragments of material being broken down. Specialised lysosomes are generally absent from plant cells.

Lysosomes

Plasma membrane: 3-10 nm thick phospholipid bilayer with associated proteins and lipids.

Nucleus (below): A large organelle containing most of the cell's DNA, 5 μm diameter. Within the nucleus, the **nucleolus** (*n*) is a dense, solid structure of crystalline protein and nucleic acid. The nucleolus is involved in ribosome synthesis.

Nuclear pore: A hole in the nuclear membrane. It allows communication between the nucleus and the rest of the cell.

Centrioles: Microtubular structures associated with nuclear division. Under a light microscope, they appear as small, featureless particles, 0.25 μm diameter. They are absent in higher plant cells and some protoctists.

Endoplasmic reticulum (ER): Comprises a network of tubes and flattened sacs. ER is continuous with the plasma membrane and the nuclear membrane. **Smooth ER**, as shown here, is a site for lipid and carbohydrate metabolism, including hormone synthesis.

Cell Structure & Function

Related activities: Cell Structures and Organelles, Human Cell Specialisation, Stomach and Small Intestine **Web links**: Review of Eukaryotic Cells

RA 2

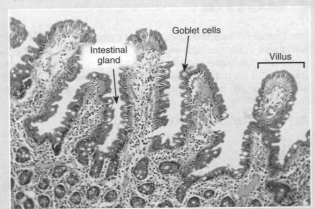

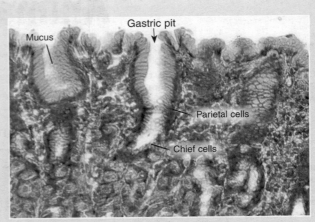

The small intestine is lined with intestinal epithelium. Each epithelial cell has finger like protrusions called **microvilli** which extend into the intestinal lumen. They act to increase the surface area for nutrient absorption. Between the projecting villi are crypts or **intestinal glands**, which secrete a variety of digestive enzymes and contain multipotent stem cells to replace epithelial cells when they become worn out. **Goblet cells** secrete mucus to protect the epithelium from chemical and mechanical stress.

The stomach wall contains numerous deep **gastric pits**, which increase its surface area. The pits open into **gastric glands**, secretory units which are lined with various types of cells. Near the top of the gland, **mucous cells** secrete mucus to protect the stomach from the acidic gastric juices. In the neck of the gland, **parietal cells** secrete hydrochloric acid and, at the base of the gland, **chief cells** secrete pepsinogen, a protein-digesting enzyme precursor which is activated in the acid pH.

1. Describe the role of the intestinal microvilli in increasing nutrition absorption: _____

_____

_____

2. Identify the mucus secreting cells and their role in the following tissue types:

(a) Intestinal epithelium: _____

_____

(b) Stomach: _____

_____

3. Discuss the fundamental differences between the histological structure of the intestine and the stomach (above):

_____

_____

_____

Neurones (nerve cells) in the spinal cord

White blood cells and red blood cells (blood smear)

4. Animal cells come in a variety of specialised forms to carry out their particular role within the body. On the two photomicrographs (left), identify the cells labelled A-C, and briefly describe the adaptive features of each:

A: _____

_____

_____

_____

B: _____

_____

_____

_____

C: _____

_____

Eukaryotic Cell Diversity

Animals, plants, fungi, and protoctistans are all **eukaryotes**; organisms whose cells are organised into complex structures and their genetic material is located within a membrane-bound nucleus.   The cells of multicellular eukaryotes show enormous variety in both their external and internal features as a result of undifferentiated cells specialising to perform specific functions. However, certain features will distinguish cells of different types. In the following exercise, identify which of the cell types belongs to each of the four eukaryotic kingdoms and describe the major distinguishing characteristics of their cells.

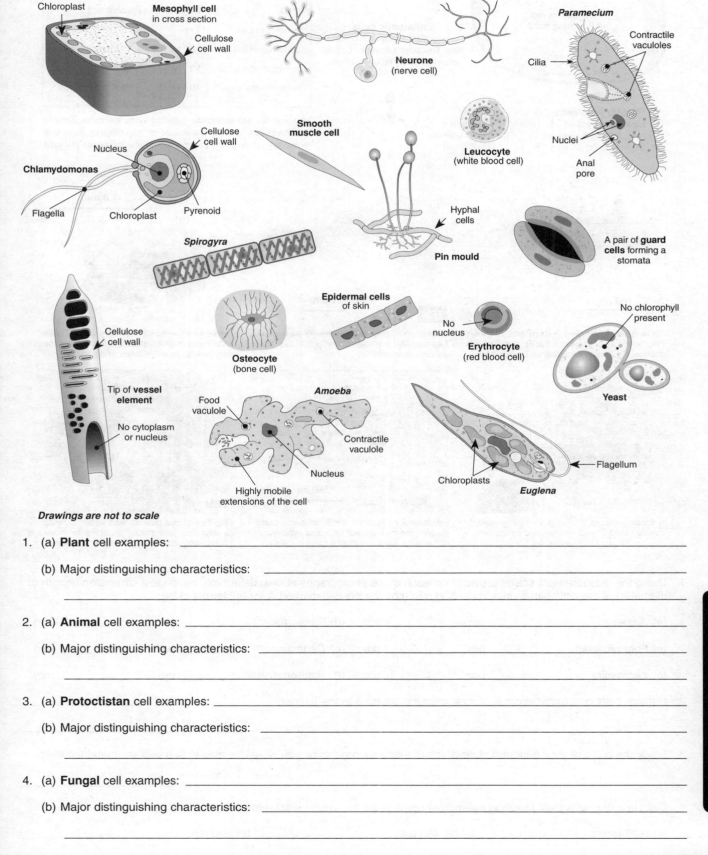

Drawings are not to scale

1. (a) **Plant** cell examples: _____

  (b) Major distinguishing characteristics: _____

  _____

2. (a) **Animal** cell examples: _____

  (b) Major distinguishing characteristics: _____

  _____

3. (a) **Protoctistan** cell examples: _____

  (b) Major distinguishing characteristics: _____

  _____

4. (a) **Fungal** cell examples: _____

  (b) Major distinguishing characteristics: _____

  _____

Cell Structure & Function

Related activities: Plant Cells, Animal Cells

RA 1

Cell Sizes

Cells are extremely small and can only be seen properly when viewed through the magnifying lenses of a microscope. The diagrams below show a variety of cell types, together with a virus and a microscopic animal for comparison. For each of these images, note the scale and relate this to the type of microscopy used (light microscopy, TEM, or SEM).

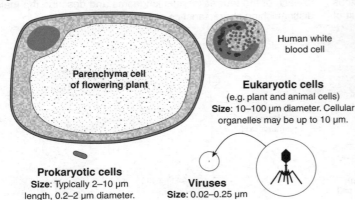

Parenchyma cell of flowering plant

Human white blood cell

Eukaryotic cells
(e.g. plant and animal cells)
Size: 10–100 μm diameter. Cellular organelles may be up to 10 μm.

Prokaryotic cells
Size: Typically 2–10 μm length, 0.2–2 μm diameter. Upper limit, 30 μm long.

Viruses
Size: 0.02–0.25 μm (20–250 nm)

Units of length (International System)

Unit	Metres	Equivalent
1 metre (m)	1 m	= 1000 millimetres
1 millimetre (mm)	10^{-3} m	= 1000 micrometres
1 micrometre (μm)	10^{-6} m	= 1000 nanometres
1 nanometre (nm)	10^{-9} m	= 1000 picometres

Micrometres are sometime referred to as **microns**. Smaller structures are usually measured in nanometres (nm) e.g. molecules (1 nm) and plasma membrane thickness (10 nm).

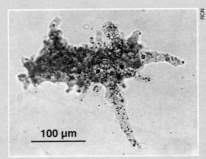

100 μm

An **Amoeba** showing extensions of the cytoplasm called pseudopodia. This protoctist changes its shape, exploring its environment.

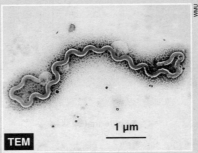

1 μm

TEM

A long thin cell of the spirochete bacterium **Leptospira pomona**, which causes the disease leptospirosis.

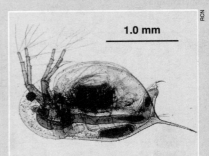

1.0 mm

Daphnia showing its internal organs. These freshwater microcrustaceans are part of the zooplankton found in lakes and ponds.

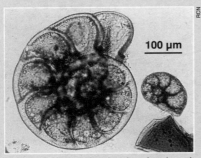

100 μm

A **foraminiferan** showing its chambered, calcified shell. These single-celled protozoans are marine planktonic amoebae.

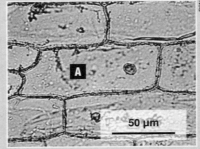

A

50 μm

Epidermal cells (skin) from an onion bulb showing the nucleus, cell walls and cytoplasm. Organelles are not visible at this resolution.

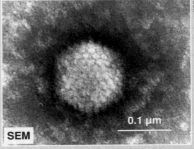

0.1 μm

SEM

Papillomavirus (human wart virus) showing its polyhedral protein coat (20 triangular faces, 12 corners) made of ball-shaped structures.

1. Using the measurement scales provided on each of the photographs above, determine the longest dimension (length or diameter) of the cell/animal/virus in μm and mm (choose the cell marked **A** for epidermal cells):

   (a) *Amoeba*: _____ μm _____ mm   (d) Epidermis: _____ μm _____ mm

   (b) Foraminiferan: _____ μm _____ mm   (e) *Daphnia*: _____ μm _____ mm

   (c) *Leptospira*: _____ μm _____ mm   (f) *Papillomavirus*: _____ μm _____ mm

2. List these six organisms in order of size, from the smallest to the largest: _____

   _____

3. Study the scale of your ruler and state which of these six organisms you would be able to see with your unaided eye:

   _____

4. Calculate the equivalent length in millimetres (mm) of the following measurements:

   (a) 0.25 μm: _____   (b) 450 μm: _____   (c) 200 nm: _____

Cell Structures and Organelles

The table below provides a format to summarise information about structures and organelles of typical eukaryotic cells. Complete the table using the list provided and by referring to a textbook and to other pages in this topic. Fill in the final three columns by writing either 'YES' or 'NO'. The first cell component has been completed for you as a guide and the log scale of

measurements (top of next page) illustrates the relative sizes of some cellular structures.

List of structures and organelles: nucleus, mitochondrion, centrioles, lysosome and food vacuoles (given), ribosome, endoplasmic reticulum, Golgi apparatus, plasma membrane (given), cell cytoskeleton, flagella or cilia (given).

Cell Component	Details	Present in Plant cells	Present in Animal cells	Visible under light microscope
(a) 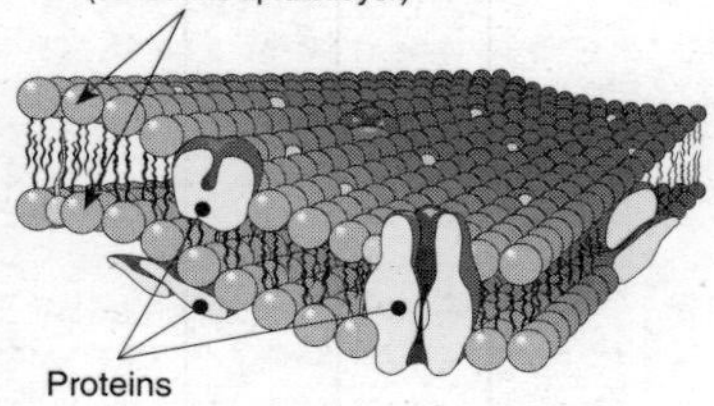 Double layer of phospholipids (called the lipid bilayer) / Proteins	Name: Plasma (cell surface) membrane Location: Surrounding the cell Function: Gives the cell shape and protection. It also regulates the movement of substances into and out of the cell.	YES	YES	YES (but not at the level of detail shown in the diagram)
(b) 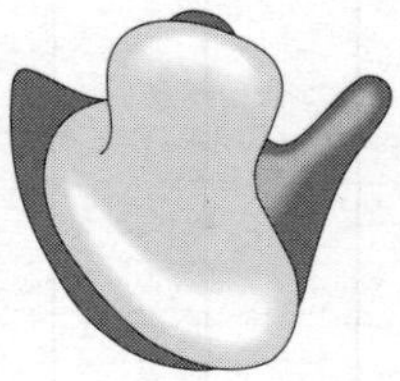	Name: Location: Function:			
(c) 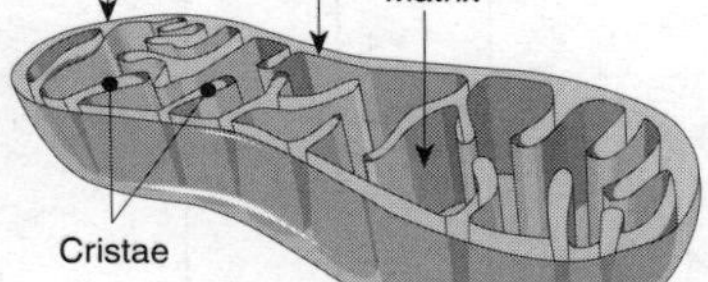 Outer membrane / Inner membrane / Matrix / Cristae	Name: Location: Function:			
(d) 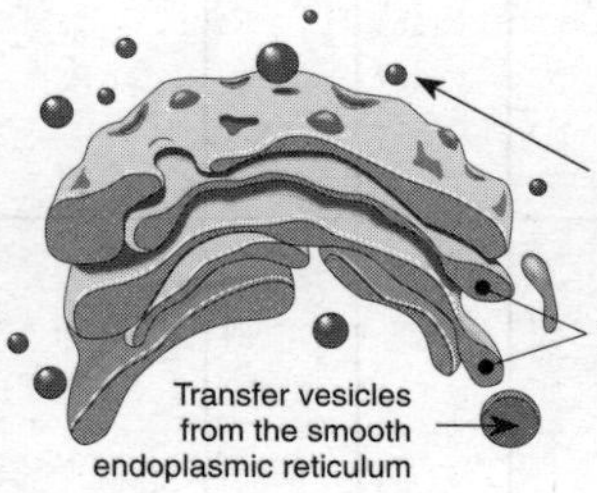 Secretory vesicles budding off / Cisternae / Transfer vesicles from the smooth endoplasmic reticulum	Name: Location: Function:			
(e) 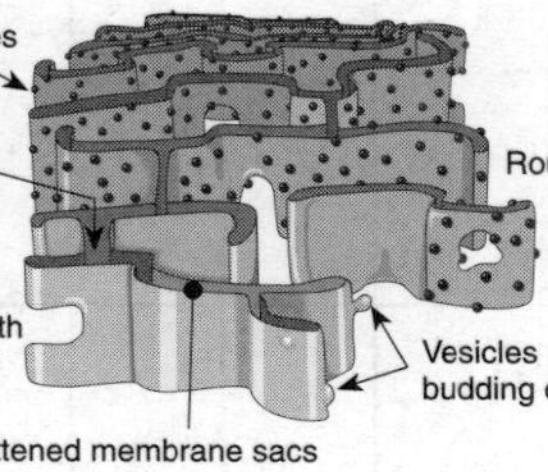 Ribosomes / Transport pathway / Rough / Smooth / Vesicles budding off / Flattened membrane sacs	Name: Location: Function:			
(f) 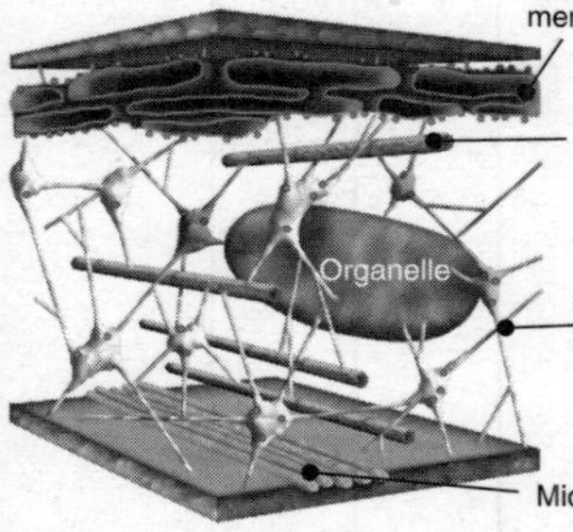 Plasma membrane / Microtubule / Organelle / Intermediate filament / Microfilament	Name: Location: Function:			

Cell Structure & Function

Related Activities: Plant Cells, Animal Cells, Types of Eukaryotic Cells
Web links: Eukaryotic Cells Interactive Animation

RA 2

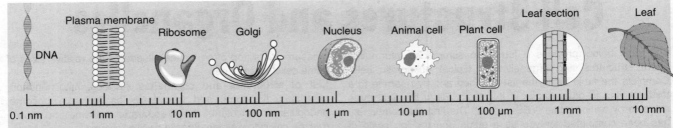

DNA | Plasma membrane | Ribosome | Golgi | Nucleus | Animal cell | Plant cell | Leaf section | Leaf

0.1 nm   1 nm   10 nm   100 nm   1 μm   10 μm   100 μm   1 mm   10 mm

Cell Component	Details	Present in		Visible under light microscope
		Plant cells	Animal cells	

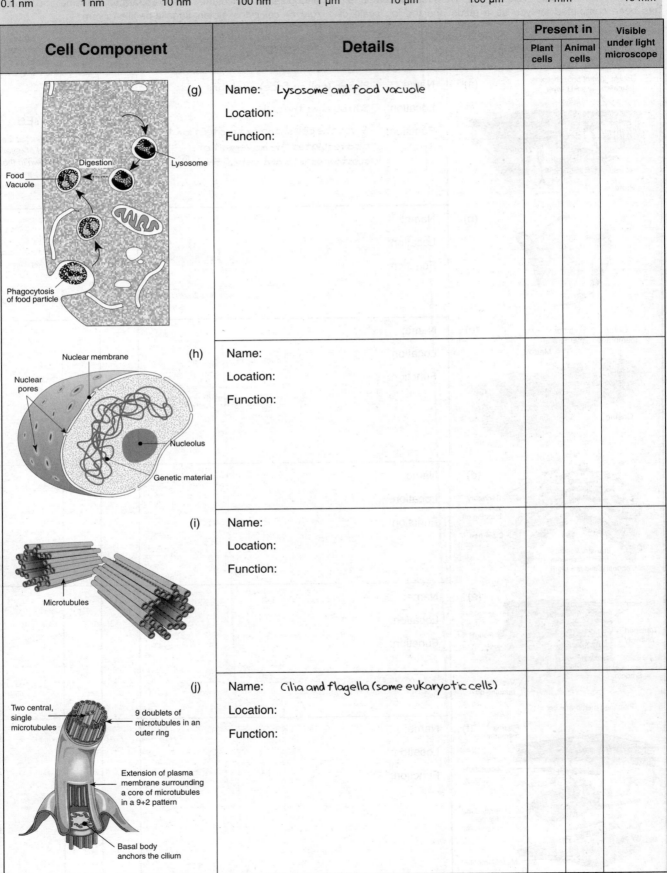

(g)

Name: Lysosome and food vacuole

Location:

Function:

Diagram labels: Digestion, Lysosome, Food Vacuole, Phagocytosis of food particle

(h)

Name:

Location:

Function:

Diagram labels: Nuclear membrane, Nuclear pores, Nucleolus, Genetic material

(i)

Name:

Location:

Function:

Diagram label: Microtubules

(j)

Name: Cilia and flagella (some eukaryotic cells)

Location:

Function:

Diagram labels: Two central, single microtubules; 9 doublets of microtubules in an outer ring; Extension of plasma membrane surrounding a core of microtubules in a 9+2 pattern; Basal body anchors the cilium

Prokaryotic Cells

Bacterial (prokaryotic) cells are much smaller and simpler than the cells of eukaryotes. They lack many eukaryotic features (e.g. a distinct nucleus and membrane-bound cellular organelles). The bacterial cell wall is an important feature. It is a complex, multi-layered structure and often has a role in virulence. These pages illustrate some features of bacterial structure and diversity.

Structure of a Generalised Bacterial Cell

Plasmids: Small, circular DNA molecules (accessory chromosomes) which can reproduce independently of the main chromosome. They can move between cells, and even between species, by **conjugation**. This property accounts for the transmission of antibiotic resistance between bacteria. Plasmids are also used as vectors in recombinant DNA technology.

Single, circular main chromosome: Makes them haploid for most genes. It is possible for some genes to be found on both the plasmid and chromosome and there may be several copies of a gene on a group of plasmids.

The cell lacks a nuclear membrane, so there is no distinct nucleus and the chromosome is in direct contact with the cytoplasm. It is possible for free ribosomes to attach to mRNA while the mRNA is still in the process of being transcribed from the DNA.

Fimbriae: Hairlike structures that are shorter, straighter, and thinner than flagella. They are used for attachment, not movement. Pili are similar to fimbriae, but are longer and less numerous. They are involved in bacterial conjugation (below) and as phage receptors (opposite).

Cell surface membrane: Similar in composition to eukaryotic membranes, although less rigid.

1 μm

Cytoplasm

Glycocalyx. A viscous, gelatinous layer outside the cell wall. It is composed of polysaccharide and/or polypeptide. If it is firmly attached to the wall, it is called a **capsule**. If loosely attached, it is called a **slime layer**. Capsules may contribute to virulence in pathogenic species, e.g. by protecting the bacteria from the host's immune attack. In some species, the glycocalyx allows attachment to substrates.

Cell wall. A complex, semi-rigid structure that gives the cell shape, prevents rupture, and serves as an anchorage point for flagella. The cell wall is composed of a macromolecule called **peptidoglycan**; repeating disaccharides attached by polypeptides to form a lattice. The wall also contains varying amounts of lipopolysaccharides and lipoproteins. The amount of peptidoglycan present in the wall forms the basis of the diagnostic **gram stain**. In many species, the cell wall contributes to their virulence (disease-causing ability).

Flagellum (pl. flagella). Some bacteria have long, filamentous appendages, called flagella, that are used for locomotion. There may be a single polar flagellum (monotrichous), one or more flagella at each end of the cell, or the flagella may be distributed over the entire cell (peritrichous).

Bacterial cell shapes

Most bacterial cells range between 0.20-2.0μm in diameter and 2-10μm length. Although they are a very diverse group, much of this diversity is in their metabolism. In terms of gross morphology, there are only a few basic shapes found (illustrated below). The way in which members of each group aggregate after division is often characteristic and is helpful in identifying certain species.

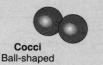

Bacilli
Rod-shaped

Bacilli: Rod-shaped bacteria that divide only across their short axis. Most occur as single rods, although pairs and chains are also found. The term bacillus can refer (as here) to shape. It may also denote a genus.

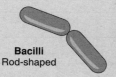

Cocci
Ball-shaped

Cocci: usually round, but sometimes oval or elongated. When they divide, the cells stay attached to each other and remain in aggregates e.g. pairs (diplococci) or clusters (staphylococci), that are usually a feature of the genus.

Spirilla
Spiral-shaped

Spirilla and vibrio: Bacteria with one or more twists. Spirilla bacteria have a helical (corkscrew) shape which may be rigid or flexible (as in spirochetes). Bacteria that look like curved rods (comma shaped) are called vibrios.

Bacterial conjugation

The two bacteria below are involved in conjugation: a one-way exchange of genetic information from a donor cell to a recipient cell. The plasmid, which must be of the 'conjugative' type, passes through a tube called a **sex pilus** to the other cell. Which is donor and which is recipient appears to be genetically determined. Conjugation should not be confused with sexual reproduction, as it does not involve the fusion of gametes or formation of a zygote.

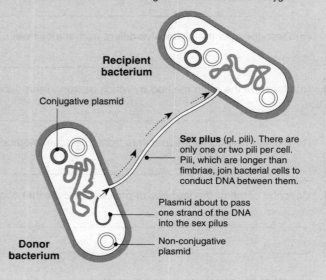

Recipient bacterium

Conjugative plasmid

Sex pilus (pl. pili). There are only one or two pili per cell. Pili, which are longer than fimbriae, join bacterial cells to conduct DNA between them.

Plasmid about to pass one strand of the DNA into the sex pilus

Non-conjugative plasmid

Donor bacterium

Cell Structure & Function

Related activities: Cholera, Tuberculosis, The Prokaryotic Chromosome
Web links: Gram Stain Animation, Structure and Function of Bacterial Cells

RA 2

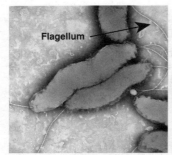

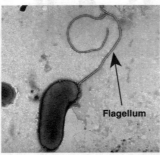

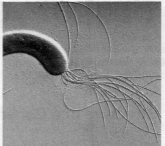

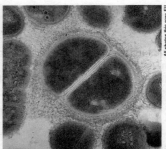

Campylobacter jejuni, a spiral bacterium responsible for foodborne intestinal disease. Note the single flagellum at each end (amphitrichous arrangement).

Helicobacter pylori, a comma-shaped vibrio bacterium that causes stomach ulcers in humans. This bacterium moves by means of multiple polar flagella.

A species of *Spirillum*, a spiral shaped bacterium with a tuft of polar flagella. Most of the species in this genus are harmless aquatic organisms.

Bacteria usually divide by binary fission. During this process, DNA is copied and the cell splits into two cells, as in these gram positive cocci.

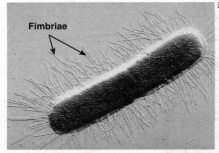

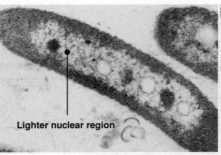

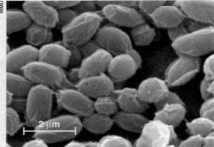

Escherichia coli, a common gut bacterium with **peritrichous** (around the entire cell) **fimbriae**. *E. coli* is a gram negative rod; it does not take up the gram stain but can be counter stained with safranin.

TEM showing *Enterobacter* bacteria, which belong to the family of gut bacteria commonly known as enterics. They are widely distributed in water, sewage, and soil. The family includes motile and non-motile species.

SEM of endospores of ***Bacillus anthracis*** bacteria, which cause the disease anthrax. These heat-resistant spores remain viable for many years and enable the bacteria to survive in a dormant state.

1. Describe three features distinguishing prokaryotic cells from eukaryotic cells:

   (a) _____

   (b) _____

   (c) _____

2. (a) Describe the function of flagella in bacteria: _____

   _____

   (b) Explain how fimbriae differ structurally and functionally from flagella: _____

   _____

   _____

3. (a) Describe the location and general composition of the bacterial cell wall: _____

   _____

   _____

   (b) Describe how the glycocalyx differs from the cell wall: _____

   _____

4. (a) Describe the main method by which bacteria reproduce: _____

   _____

   (b) Explain how conjugation differs from this usual method: _____

   _____

5. Describe some of the features of prokaryotic cells that contribute to their ability to cause disease:

   _____

   _____

   _____

Optical Microscopes

The light microscope is one of the most important instruments used in biology practicals, and its correct use is a basic and essential skill of biology. High power light microscopes use a combination of lenses to magnify objects up to several hundred times. They are called **compound microscopes** because there are two or more separate lenses involved. A typical compound light microscope (bright field) is shown below (top photograph). The specimens viewed with these microscopes must be thin and mostly transparent. Light is focused up through the condenser and specimen; if the specimen is thick or opaque,

little or no detail will be visible. The microscope below has two eyepieces (**binocular**), although monocular microscopes, with a mirror rather than an internal light source, may still be encountered. Dissecting microscopes (lower photograph) are a type of binocular microscope used for observations at low total magnification (x4 to x50), where a large working distance between objective lenses and stage is required. A dissecting microscope has two separate lens systems, one for each eye. Such microscopes produce a 3-D view of the specimen and are sometimes called stereo microscopes for this reason.

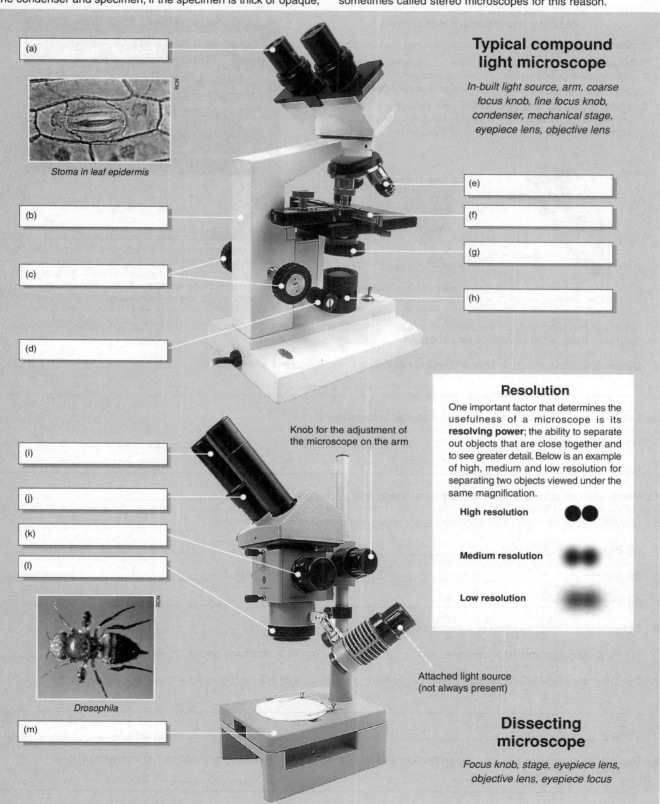

(a)

Stoma in leaf epidermis

(b)

(c)

(d)

Typical compound light microscope

In-built light source, arm, coarse focus knob, fine focus knob, condenser, mechanical stage, eyepiece lens, objective lens

(e)

(f)

(g)

(h)

Resolution

One important factor that determines the usefulness of a microscope is its **resolving power**; the ability to separate out objects that are close together and to see greater detail. Below is an example of high, medium and low resolution for separating two objects viewed under the same magnification.

High resolution

Medium resolution

Low resolution

(i)

(j)

(k)

(l)

Knob for the adjustment of the microscope on the arm

Attached light source (not always present)

Drosophila

(m)

Dissecting microscope

Focus knob, stage, eyepiece lens, objective lens, eyepiece focus

Cell Structure & Function

Related Activities: Plant Cells, Animal Cells, Types of Eukaryotic Cells

RDA 2

Pollen grains

Phase contrast illumination increases contrast of transparent specimens by producing interference effects.

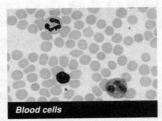

Blood cells

Leishman's stain is used to show red blood cells as red/pink, while staining the nucleus of white blood cells blue.

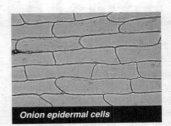

Onion epidermal cells

Standard **bright field** lighting shows cells with little detail; only cell walls, with the cell nuclei barely visible.

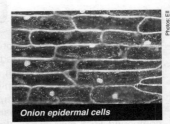

Onion epidermal cells

Dark field illumination is excellent for viewing near transparent specimens. The nucleus of each cell is visible.

Photos: Ell

Making a temporary wet mount

1. **Sectioning**: Very thin sections of fresh material are cut with a razorblade.

2. **Mounting**: The thin section(s) are placed in the centre of a clean glass microscope slide and covered with a drop of mounting liquid (e.g. water, glycerol or stain). A coverslip is placed on top to exclude air (below).

3. **Staining**: Dyes can be applied to stain some structures and leave others unaffected. The stains used in dyeing living tissues are called **vital stains** and they can be applied before or after the specimen is mounted.

Commonly used temporary stains

Stain	Final colour	Used for
Iodine solution	blue-black	Starch
Aniline sulfate	yellow	Lignin
Schultz's solution	blue	Starch
	blue or violet	Cellulose
	yellow	Protein, cutin, lignin, suberin
Methylene blue	blue	Nuclei

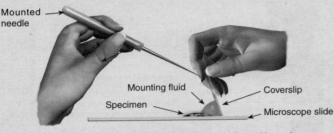

Mounted needle

Mounting fluid

Specimen

Coverslip

Microscope slide

A mounted needle is used to support the coverslip and lower it gently over the specimen. This avoids including air in the mount.

Irrigation   Specimen   Coverslip   Filter paper

If a specimen is already mounted, a drop of stain can be placed at one end of the coverslip and drawn through using filter paper (above). Water can be drawn through in the same way to remove excess stain.

1. Label the two diagrams on the previous page, the compound light microscope (a) to (h) and the dissecting microscope (i) to (m), using words from the lists supplied.

2. Describe a situation where phase contrast microscopy would improve image quality: _____

_____

3. List two structures that could be seen with light microscopy in:

(a) A plant cell: _____

(b) An animal cell: _____

4. Name one cell structure that cannot be seen with light microscopy: _____

5. Identify a stain that would be appropriate for improving definition of the following:

(a) Blood cells: _____   (d) Lignin: _____

(b) Starch: _____   (e) Nuclei and DNA: _____

(c) Protein: _____   (f) Cellulose: _____

6. Determine the magnification of a microscope using:

(a) 15 X eyepiece and 40 X objective lens: _____   (b) 10 X eyepiece and 60 X objective lens: _____

7. Describe the main difference between a bright field, compound light microscope and a dissecting microscope:

_____

_____

8. Explain the difference between magnification and resolution (resolving power) with respect to microscope use:

_____

_____

Electron Microscopes

Electron microscopes (EMs) use a beam of electrons, instead of light, to produce an image. The higher resolution of EMs is due to the shorter wavelengths of electrons. There are two basic types of electron microscope: **scanning electron microscopes**

(SEMs) and **transmission electron microscopes** (TEMs). In SEMs, the electrons are bounced off the surface of an object to produce detailed images of the external appearance. TEMs produce very clear images of specially prepared thin sections.

Transmission Electron Microscope (TEM)

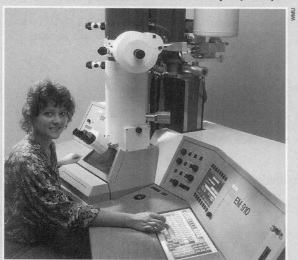

The transmission electron microscope is used to view extremely thin sections of material. Electrons pass through the specimen and are scattered. Magnetic lenses focus the image onto a fluorescent screen or photographic plate. The sections are so thin that they have to be prepared with a special machine, called an **ultramicrotome**, that can cut wafers to just 30 thousandths of a millimetre thick. It can magnify several hundred thousand times.

TEM diagram labels: Electron gun, Electron beam, Electromagnetic condenser lens, Specimen, Electromagnetic objective lens, Vacuum pump, Electromagnetic projector lens, Eyepiece, Fluorescent screen or photographic plate. **TEM**

Scanning Electron Microscope (SEM)

The scanning electron microscope scans a sample with a beam of primary electrons that knock electrons from its surface. These secondary electrons are picked up by a collector, amplified, and transmitted onto a viewing screen or photographic plate, producing a superb 3-D image. A microscope of this power can easily obtain clear pictures of organisms as small as bacteria and viruses. The image produced is of the outside surface only.

SEM diagram labels: Electron gun, Primary electron beam, Electromagnetic lenses, Vacuum pump, **SEM**, Electron collector, Amplifier, Viewing screen, Specimen, Secondary electrons.

TEM photo showing the Golgi (**G**) and a mitochondrion (**M**).

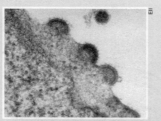

Three HIV viruses budding out of a human lymphocyte (TEM).

SEM photo of stoma and epidermal cells on the upper surface of a leaf.

Image of hair louse clinging to two hairs on a Hooker's sealion (SEM).

Cell Structure & Function

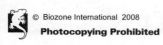
Related activities: Optical Microscopes, Interpreting Electron Micrographs

RA 2

	Light Microscope	Transmission Electron Microscope (TEM)	Scanning Electron Microscope (SEM)
Radiation source:	light	electrons	electrons
Wavelength:	400-700 nm	0.005 nm	0.005 nm
Lenses:	glass	electromagnetic	electromagnetic
Specimen:	living or non-living supported on glass slide	non-living supported on a small copper grid in a vacuum	non-living supported on a metal disc in a vacuum
Maximum resolution:	200 nm	1 nm	10 nm
Maximum magnification:	1500 x	250 000 x	100 000 x
Stains:	coloured dyes	impregnated with heavy metals	coated with carbon or gold
Type of image:	coloured	monochrome (black & white)	monochrome (black & white)

1. Explain why electron microscopes are able to resolve much greater detail than a light microscope:

   _____

   _____

   _____

2. Describe two typical applications for each of the following types of microscope:

   (a) Transmission electron microscope (TEM): _____

   _____

   (b) Scanning electron microscope (SEM): _____

   _____

   (c) Bright field, compound light microscope (thin section): _____

   _____

   (d) Dissecting microscope: _____

   _____

3. Identify which type of electron microscope (SEM or TEM) or optical microscope (bright field, compound light microscope or dissecting microscope) was used to produce each of the images in the photos below (A-H):

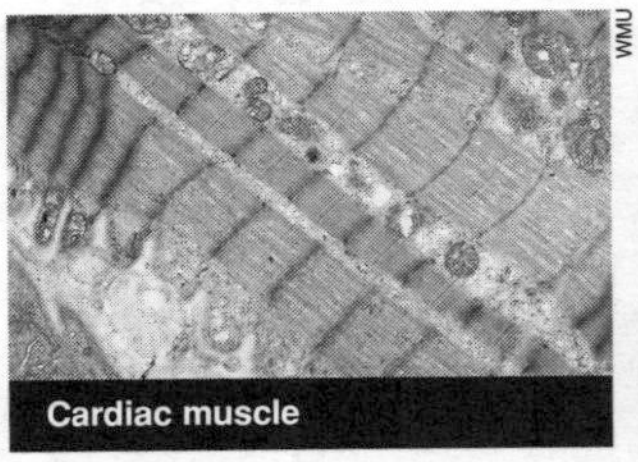

Cardiac muscle

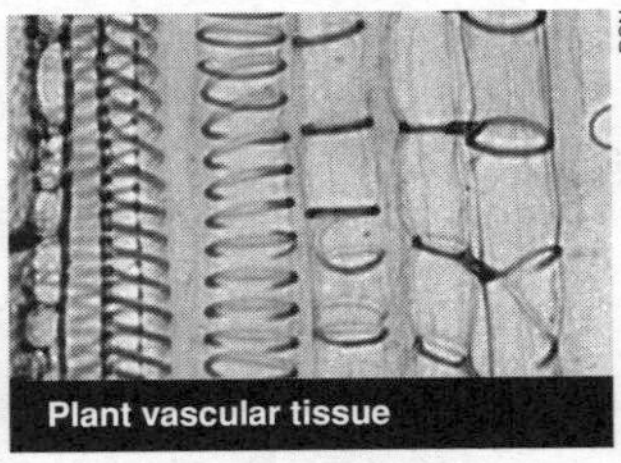

Plant vascular tissue

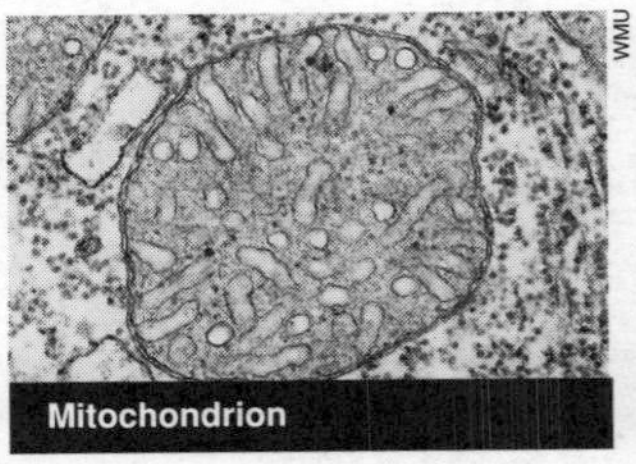

Mitochondrion

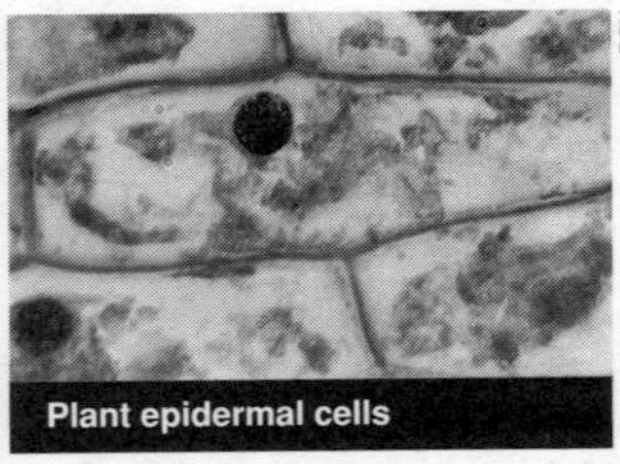

Plant epidermal cells

A _____   B _____   C _____   D _____

Head louse

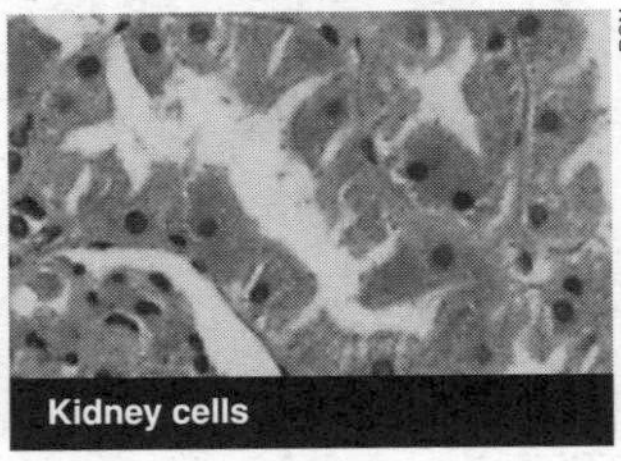

Kidney cells

Alderfly larva

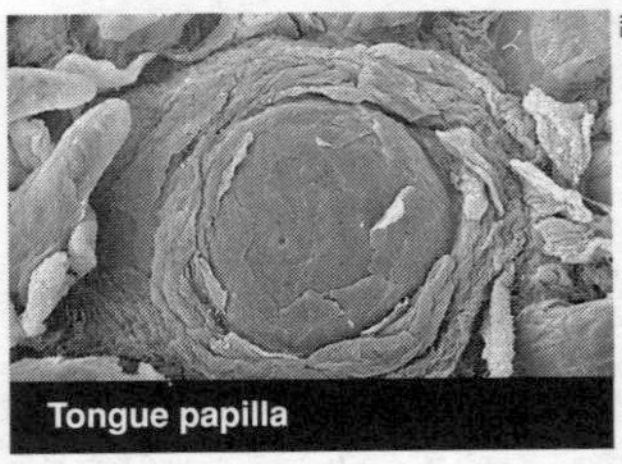

Tongue papilla

E _____   F _____   G _____   H _____

Cell Fractionation

Cell fractionation (also called differential centrifugation) is a technique used to extract organelles from cells so that they can be studied. The aim is to extract undamaged intact organelles. Samples must be kept very cool so that metabolism is slowed and self digestion of the organelles is prevented. The samples must also be kept in a buffered, isotonic solution so that the organelles do not change volume and the enzymes are not denatured by changes in pH.

Cell Fractionation

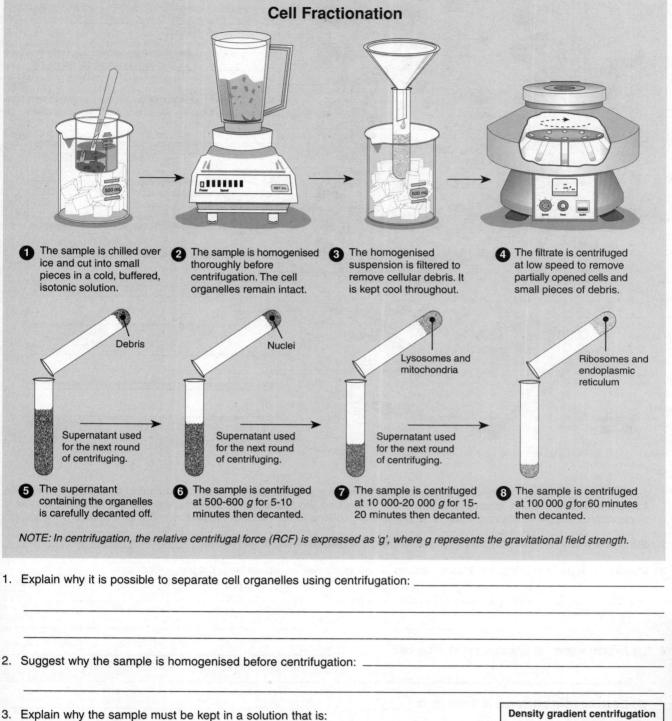

1. The sample is chilled over ice and cut into small pieces in a cold, buffered, isotonic solution.

2. The sample is homogenised thoroughly before centrifugation. The cell organelles remain intact.

3. The homogenised suspension is filtered to remove cellular debris. It is kept cool throughout.

4. The filtrate is centrifuged at low speed to remove partially opened cells and small pieces of debris.

Debris

Nuclei

Lysosomes and mitochondria

Ribosomes and endoplasmic reticulum

Supernatant used for the next round of centrifuging.

Supernatant used for the next round of centrifuging.

Supernatant used for the next round of centrifuging.

5. The supernatant containing the organelles is carefully decanted off.

6. The sample is centrifuged at 500-600 *g* for 5-10 minutes then decanted.

7. The sample is centrifuged at 10 000-20 000 *g* for 15-20 minutes then decanted.

8. The sample is centrifuged at 100 000 *g* for 60 minutes then decanted.

NOTE: In centrifugation, the relative centrifugal force (RCF) is expressed as 'g', where g represents the gravitational field strength.

1. Explain why it is possible to separate cell organelles using centrifugation: _____

_____

_____

2. Suggest why the sample is homogenised before centrifugation: _____

_____

3. Explain why the sample must be kept in a solution that is:

(a) Isotonic: _____

(b) Cool: _____

(c) Buffered: _____

4. **Density gradient centrifugation** is another method of cell fractionation. Sucrose is added to the sample, which is then centrifuged at high speed. The organelles will form layers according to their specific densities. Using the information above, label the centrifuge tube on the right with the organelles you would find in each layer.

Density gradient centrifugation

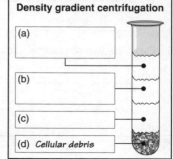

(a)

(b)

(c)

(d) *Cellular debris*

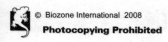

Related activities: Cell Structures and Organelles, Enzyme Reaction Rates

Cell Structure & Function

A 1

Identifying Cell Structures

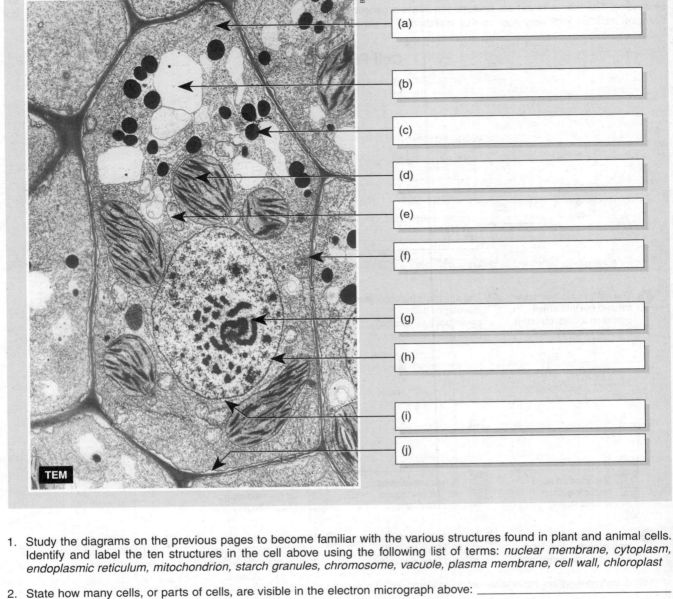

(a)

(b)

(c)

(d)

(e)

(f)

(g)

(h)

(i)

(j)

1. Study the diagrams on the previous pages to become familiar with the various structures found in plant and animal cells. Identify and label the ten structures in the cell above using the following list of terms: *nuclear membrane, cytoplasm, endoplasmic reticulum, mitochondrion, starch granules, chromosome, vacuole, plasma membrane, cell wall, chloroplast*

2. State how many cells, or parts of cells, are visible in the electron micrograph above: _____

3. Identify the **type** of cell illustrated above (bacterial cell, plant cell, or animal cell). Explain your answer:

_____

_____

4. (a) Explain where cytoplasm is found in the cell: _____

_____

(b) Describe what cytoplasm is made up of: _____

_____

5. Describe two structures, pictured in the cell above, that are associated with storage:

(a) _____

_____

(b) _____

_____

Related activities: Prokaryotic Cells, Chloroplasts and Cell Walls, Animal Cells

Interpreting Electron Micrographs

The photographs below were taken using a transmission electron microscope (TEM). They show some of the cell organelles in great detail. Remember that these photos are showing only **parts of cells, not whole cells.** Some of the photographs show more than one type of organelle. The questions refer to the main organelle in the centre of the photo.

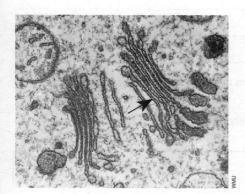

1. (a) Name this organelle (arrowed): _____

   (b) State which kind of cell(s) this organelle would be found in:

   _____

   (c) Describe the function of this organelle: _____

   _____

   _____

   (d) Label two structures that can be seen inside this organelle.

2. (a) Name this organelle (arrowed): _____

   (b) State which kind of cell(s) this organelle would be found in:

   _____

   (c) Describe the function of this organelle: _____

   _____

   _____

   _____

   _____

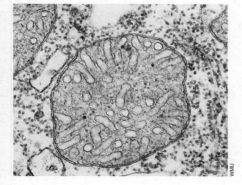

3. (a) Name the large, circular organelle: _____

   (b) State which kind of cell(s) this organelle would be found in:

   _____

   (c) Describe the function of this organelle: _____

   _____

   _____

   (d) Label two regions that can be seen inside this organelle.

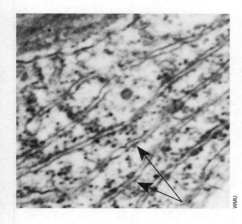

4. (a) Name and label the ribbon-like organelle in this photograph (arrowed):

   _____

   (b) State which kind of cell(s) this organelle is found in:

   _____

   (c) Describe the function of these organelles: _____

   _____

   _____

   (d) Name the dark 'blobs' attached to the organelle you have labelled:

   _____

Related activities: Electron Microscopes, Animal Cells, Cell Structures and Organelles, Chloroplasts and Cell Walls

RA 2

Cell Structure & Function

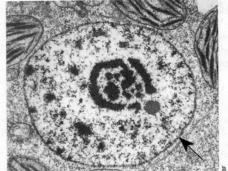

5. (a) Name this large circular structure (arrowed): _____

   (b) State which kind of cell(s) this structure would be found in:

   _____

   (c) Describe the function of this structure: _____

   _____

   _____

   (d) Label three features relating to this structure in the photograph.

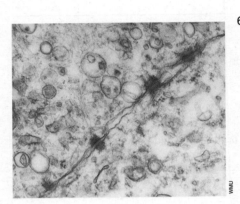

6. The four dark structures shown in this photograph are called **desmosomes**. They cause the plasma membranes of neighbouring cells to stick together. Without desmosomes, animal cells would not combine together to form tissues.

   (a) Describe the functions of the plasma membrane:

   _____

   _____

   _____

   (b) Label the plasma membrane and the four desmosomes in the photograph.

7. In the space below, draw a simple, labelled diagram of a **generalised cell** to show the **relative size** and **location** of these six structures and organelles (simple outlines of the organelles will do):

Processes Across Exchange Surfaces

Unit 1: Biology and Disease

1.3 Transport across exchange surfaces

Lipids, cellular membranes, passive and active transport processes, cholera (effect on transport)

Learning Objectives

☐ 1. Compile your own glossary from the **KEY WORDS** displayed in **bold type** in the learning objectives below.

Lipids and Cellular Membranes *(pages 90-96)*

☐ 2. Describe the properties of lipids. Describe the diversity and functional roles of lipids in biological systems.

☐ 3. Describe the **emulsion test** for lipids. Explain the basis of the test and its result.

☐ 4. Describe the structure of **triglycerides** (triacyl-glycerols). Classify triglycerides as **fats** or **oils** and explain how they are made by **condensation** reactions between glycerol and three fatty acids, with formation of **ester bonds**. Distinguish between **saturated** and **unsaturated fatty acids** and relate differences to the properties of the fat or oil that results.

☐ 5. Describe the structure of a **phospholipid** and explain how it differs from a triglyceride. Explain the importance of phospholipid structure to membranes.

☐ 6. Describe the **fluid-mosaic model** of membrane structure and use it to explain the properties of plasma membranes. Include reference to the **lipid bilayer**, membrane permeability, and the roles of **phospholipids** and **proteins** in membrane structure.

☐ 7. Describe the functions of membranes in cells, including their role in regulating the transport of materials.

Cellular Transport *(pages 97-102)*

☐ 8. Summarise the types of movements that occur across membranes. Outline the role of proteins in membranes as receptors and carriers in membrane transport.

☐ 9. Describe **diffusion, facilitated diffusion,** and **osmosis,** identifying them as **passive transport** processes. Identify the types of substances moving in each case, and the role of membrane proteins and the **concentration gradient** in net movement.

☐ 10. Identify factors determining the rate of diffusion. Explain how **Fick's law** provides a framework for determining maximum diffusion rates across cell surfaces.

☐ 11. Explain what is meant by **water potential** (ψ) and define its components. Explain the significance of water potential to the net movement of water in cells.

☐ 12. Distinguish between passive and **active transport** mechanisms. Understand the principles involved in active transport, explaining the role of carrier proteins and transfer of energy in transporting substances against a concentration gradient. Describe examples of active transport mechanisms, including **ion-exchange pumps** and forms of **cytosis**.

☐ 13. Describe the transport mechanisms involved in the absorption of the products of carbohydrate digestion. Include reference to diffusion, active transport, and **co-transport** involving sodium ions.

Infection and Cellular Transport *(page 103)*

☐ 14. Recognise that **pathogens** can affect the normal permeability of plasma membranes and contribute to imbalances in ion and water transport. Describe the **cholera bacterium** with reference to the structure of **prokaryotic cells**. Explain the symptoms of cholera in terms of water and electrolyte transport.

☐ 15. Describe the use of oral rehydration solutions in the treatment of diarrhoeal diseases such as cholera.

 **Textbooks**

 **Periodicals**

 **Internet**

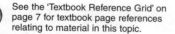

See the 'Textbook Reference Grid' on page 7 for textbook page references relating to material in this topic.

Supplementary Texts
See pages 5-6 for additional details of these texts:

■ Adds, J., *et al.*, 2003. **Molecules and Cells**, (NelsonThornes), chpt. 4 as reqd.

■ Harwood, R., 2002. **Biochemistry**, (Cambridge University Press), chpt. 5.

Presentation MEDIA
to support this topic:
CELL BIO & BIOCHEM
Cell Membranes

See page 6 for details of publishers of periodicals:

STUDENT'S REFERENCE

■ **Cellular Factories** New Scientist, 23 Nov. 1996 (Inside Science). *An overview of cellular processes and the role of organelles in plant and animal cells.*

■ **Getting in and Out** Biol. Sci. Rev., 20(3), Feb. 2008, pp. 14-16. *An excellent account of diffusion: common misunderstandings and some adaptations.*

■ **Water Channels in the Cell Membrane** Biol. Sci. Rev., 9(2) November 1996, pp. 18-22. *The role of proteins in membrane transport, including the mechanisms involved in physiological processes.*

■ **Water, Water, Everywhere...** Biol. Sci. Rev., 7(5) May 1995, pp. 6-9. *The transport of water in plants (turgor, bulk flow and water potential).*

See pages 8-9 for details of how to access **Bio Links** from our web site: **www.biozone.co.uk**. From Bio Links, access sites under the topics:

GENERAL BIOLOGY ONLINE RESOURCES
• Biology I interactive animations • Instructional multimedia, University of Alberta • HowStuffWorks • Biointeractive ... *and others* > **Online Textbooks and Lecture Notes**: • S-Cool! A level biology revision guide Learn.co.uk ... *and others* > **Glossaries**: • Cellular biology: Glossary of terms • Kimball's biology glossary ... *and others*

CELL BIOLOGY AND BIOCHEMISTRY: • Cell and molecular biology online > **Cell Structure and Transport**: • Aquaporins • CELLS alive! • The virtual cell • Transport in and out of cells

Cell Processes

All of the organelles and other structures in the cell have functions. The cell can be compared to a factory with an assembly line. Organelles in the cell provide the equivalent of the power supply, assembly line, packaging department, repair and maintenance, transport system, and the control centre. The sum total of all the processes occurring in a cell is known as **metabolism**. Some of these processes store energy in molecules (anabolism) while others release that stored energy (catabolism). Below is a summary of the major processes that take place in a cell.

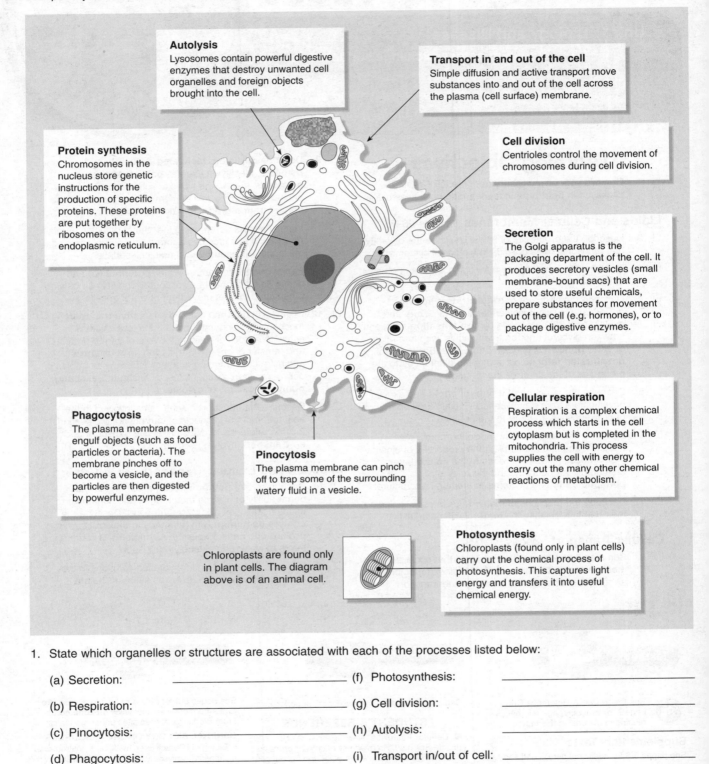

Autolysis
Lysosomes contain powerful digestive enzymes that destroy unwanted cell organelles and foreign objects brought into the cell.

Transport in and out of the cell
Simple diffusion and active transport move substances into and out of the cell across the plasma (cell surface) membrane.

Protein synthesis
Chromosomes in the nucleus store genetic instructions for the production of specific proteins. These proteins are put together by ribosomes on the endoplasmic reticulum.

Cell division
Centrioles control the movement of chromosomes during cell division.

Secretion
The Golgi apparatus is the packaging department of the cell. It produces secretory vesicles (small membrane-bound sacs) that are used to store useful chemicals, prepare substances for movement out of the cell (e.g. hormones), or to package digestive enzymes.

Phagocytosis
The plasma membrane can engulf objects (such as food particles or bacteria). The membrane pinches off to become a vesicle, and the particles are then digested by powerful enzymes.

Pinocytosis
The plasma membrane can pinch off to trap some of the surrounding watery fluid in a vesicle.

Cellular respiration
Respiration is a complex chemical process which starts in the cell cytoplasm but is completed in the mitochondria. This process supplies the cell with energy to carry out the many other chemical reactions of metabolism.

Chloroplasts are found only in plant cells. The diagram above is of an animal cell.

Photosynthesis
Chloroplasts (found only in plant cells) carry out the chemical process of photosynthesis. This captures light energy and transfers it into useful chemical energy.

1. State which organelles or structures are associated with each of the processes listed below:

   (a) Secretion: _____

   (b) Respiration: _____

   (c) Pinocytosis: _____

   (d) Phagocytosis: _____

   (e) Protein synthesis: _____

   (f) Photosynthesis: _____

   (g) Cell division: _____

   (h) Autolysis: _____

   (i) Transport in/out of cell: _____

2. Explain what is meant by **metabolism** and describe an example of a metabolic process: _____

   _____

   _____

© Biozone International 2008

Related activities: Cell Structures and Organelles, Active and Passive Transport, The Role of Membranes in Cells

Lipids

Lipids are a group of organic compounds with an oily, greasy, or waxy consistency. They are relatively insoluble in water and tend to be water-repelling (e.g. cuticle on leaf surfaces). Lipids are important biological fuels, some are hormones, and some serve as structural components in plasma membranes. Proteins and carbohydrates may be converted into fats by enzymes and stored within cells of adipose tissue. During times of plenty, this store is increased, to be used during times of food shortage.

Neutral Fats and Oils

The most abundant lipids in living things are **neutral fats**. They make up the fats and oils found in plants and animals. Fats are an economical way to store fuel reserves, since they yield more than twice as much energy as the same quantity of carbohydrate. Neutral fats are composed of a glycerol molecule attached to one (monoglyceride), two (diglyceride) or three (triglyceride) fatty acids. The fatty acid chains may be saturated or unsaturated (see below). **Waxes** are similar in structure to fats and oils, but they are formed with a complex alcohol instead of glycerol.

Triglyceride: an example of a neutral fat

Condensation

Triglycerides form when glycerol bonds with three fatty acids. Glycerol is an alcohol containing three carbons. Each of these carbons is bonded to a hydroxyl (-OH) group.

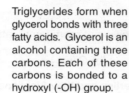

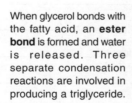

Glycerol   Fatty acids

When glycerol bonds with the fatty acid, an **ester bond** is formed and water is released. Three separate condensation reactions are involved in producing a triglyceride.

Triglyceride   Water

Saturated and Unsaturated Fatty Acids

Fatty acids are a major component of neutral fats and phospholipids. About 30 different kinds are found in animal lipids. **Saturated fatty acids** contain the maximum number of hydrogen atoms. **Unsaturated fatty acids** contain some carbon atoms that are double-bonded with each other and are not fully saturated with hydrogens. Lipids containing a high proportion of saturated fatty acids tend to be solids at room temperature (e.g. butter). Lipids with a high proportion of unsaturated fatty acids are oils and tend to be liquid at room temperature. This is because the unsaturation causes kinks in the straight chains so that the fatty acids do not pack closely together. Regardless of their degree of saturation, fatty acids yield a large amount of energy when oxidised.

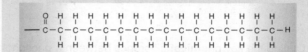

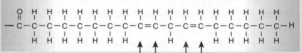

Formula (above) and molecular model (below) for **palmitic acid** (a saturated fatty acid)

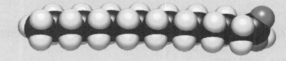

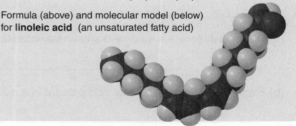

Formula (above) and molecular model (below) for **linoleic acid** (an unsaturated fatty acid)

Phospholipids

Phospholipids are the main component of cellular membranes. They consist of a glycerol attached to two fatty acid chains and a phosphate (PO_4^{3-}) group. The phosphate end of the molecule is attracted to water (it is hydrophilic) while the fatty acid end is repelled (hydrophobic). The hydrophobic ends turn inwards in the membrane to form a **phospholipid bilayer**.

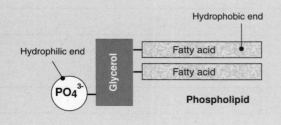

Steroids

Although steroids are classified as lipids, their structure is quite different from that of other lipids. Steroids have a basic structure of three rings made of 6 carbon atoms each and a fourth ring containing 5 carbon atoms. Examples of steroids include the male and female sex hormones (testosterone and oestrogen), and the hormones cortisol and aldosterone. Cholesterol, while not a steroid itself, is a sterol lipid and is a precursor to several steroid hormones.

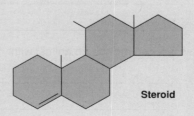

Steroid

Related activities: The Structure of Membranes, Biochemical Tests
Web links: Formation of Triglycerides

92

Important Biological Functions of Lipids

Lipids are concentrated sources of energy and provide fuel for aerobic respiration.

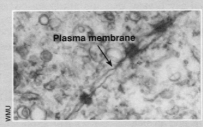
Phospholipids form the structural framework of cellular membranes.

Waxes and oils secreted on to surfaces provide waterproofing in plants and animals.

Fat absorbs shocks. Organs that are prone to bumps and shocks (e.g. kidneys) are cushioned with a relatively thick layer of fat.

Lipids are a source of metabolic water. During respiration, stored lipids are metabolised for energy, producing water and carbon dioxide.

Stored lipids provide insulation. Increased body fat reduces the amount of heat lost to the environment (e.g. in winter or in water).

1. Outline the key **chemical** difference between a phospholipid and a triglyceride: _____
_____
_____

2. Name the type of fatty acids found in lipids that form the following at room temperature:

   (a) Solid fats: _____ (b) Oils: _____

3. Relate the structure of phospholipids to their chemical properties and their functional role in cellular membranes:
_____
_____

4. (a) Distinguish between saturated and unsaturated fatty acids: _____
_____

   (b) Explain how the type of fatty acid present in a neutral fat or phospholipid is related to that molecule's properties:
_____
_____

   (c) Suggest how the cell membrane structure of an Arctic fish might differ from that of tropical fish species:
_____
_____

5. Identify two examples of steroids. For each example, describe its physiological function:

   (a) _____

   (b) _____

6. Explain how fats can provide an animal with:

   (a) Energy: _____

   (b) Water: _____

   (c) Insulation: _____

The Structure of Membranes

All cells have a plasma membrane that forms the outer limit of the cell. Bacteria, fungi, and plant cells have a cell wall outside this, but it is quite distinct and outside the cell. Membranes are also found inside eukaryotic cells as part of membranous **organelles**. Present day knowledge of membrane structure has been built up as a result of many observations and experiments. The original model of membrane structure, proposed by Davson and Danielli, was the unit membrane; a lipid bilayer coated with protein. This model was later modified after the discovery that the protein molecules were embedded within the bilayer rather than coating the outside. The now-accepted model of membrane structure is the **fluid-mosaic model** described below.

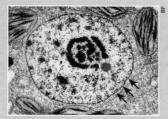
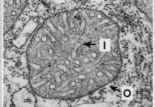
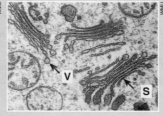
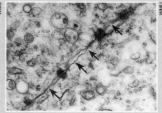

The **nuclear membrane** that surrounds the nucleus helps to control the passage of genetic information to the cytoplasm. It may also serve to protect the DNA.

Mitochondria have an outer membrane (**O**) which controls the entry and exit of materials involved in aerobic respiration. Inner membranes (**I**) provide attachment sites for enzyme activity.

The **Golgi apparatus** comprises stacks of membrane-bound sacs (**S**). It is involved in packaging materials for transport or export from the cell as secretory vesicles (**V**).

The cell is surrounded by a **plasma membrane** which controls the movement of most substances into and out of the cell. This photo shows two neighbouring cells (arrows).

The Fluid Mosaic Model

The currently accepted model for the structure of membranes is called the **fluid mosaic model**. In this model there is a double layer of lipids (fats) which are arranged with their 'tails' facing inwards. The double layer of lipids is thought to be quite fluid, with proteins 'floating' in this layer. The mobile proteins are thought to have a number of functions, including a role in active transport.

Glycoproteins (proteins with attached carbohydrate chains) play an important role in cellular recognition and the immune response, and act as receptors for hormones and neurotransmitters. Together with glycolipids, they stabilise membrane structure.

Some proteins completely penetrate the lipid layer. These proteins may control the entry and removal of specific molecules from the cell.

Generalised animal cell

Glycolipids, like glycoproteins, act as surface receptors and stabilise the membrane.

Double layer of phospholipids (the lipid bilayer).

Cholesterol disturbs the close packing of the phospholipids. It helps to regulate membrane fluidity and is important for membrane stability.

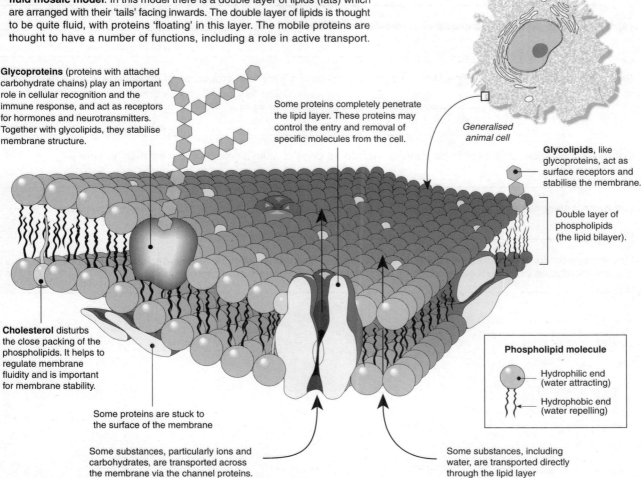

Phospholipid molecule

Hydrophilic end (water attracting)

Hydrophobic end (water repelling)

Some proteins are stuck to the surface of the membrane

Some substances, particularly ions and carbohydrates, are transported across the membrane via the channel proteins.

Some substances, including water, are transported directly through the lipid layer

1. (a) Describe the modern fluid mosaic model of membrane structure: _____

_____
_____
_____

Related activities: Cell Structures and Organelles, The Role of Membranes in Cells **Web links**: Membrane Structure Tutorial

RA 2

(b) Explain how the fluid mosaic model accounts for the observed properties of cellular membranes:

_____

_____

_____

_____

_____

_____

_____

2. Discuss the various functional roles of membranes in cells: _____

_____

_____

_____

_____

3. (a) Name a cellular organelle that possesses a membrane: _____

(b) Describe the membrane's purpose in this organelle: _____

_____

4. (a) Describe the purpose of cholesterol in plasma membranes: _____

_____

(b) Suggest why marine organisms living in polar regions have a very high proportion of cholesterol in their membranes:

_____

_____

5. List three substances that need to be transported **into** all kinds of animal cells, in order for them to survive:

(a) _____ (b) _____ (c) _____

6. List two substances that need to be transported **out** of all kinds of animal cells, in order for them to survive:

(a) _____ (b) _____

7. Use the symbol for a phospholipid molecule (below) to draw a **simple labelled diagram** to show the structure of a plasma membrane (include features such as lipid bilayer and various kinds of proteins):

Symbol for phospholipid

The Role of Membranes in Cells

Many of the important structures and organelles in cells are composed of, or are enclosed by, membranes. These include: the endoplasmic reticulum, mitochondria, nucleus, Golgi apparatus, chloroplasts, lysosomes, vesicles and the plasma membrane itself. All membranes within eukaryotic cells share the same basic structure as the plasma membrane that encloses the entire cell.

They perform a number of critical functions in the cell: serving to compartmentalise regions of different function within the cell, controlling the entry and exit of substances, and fulfilling a role in recognition and communication between cells. Some of these roles are described below. The role of membranes in the production of macromolecules (e.g. proteins) is shown on the next page:

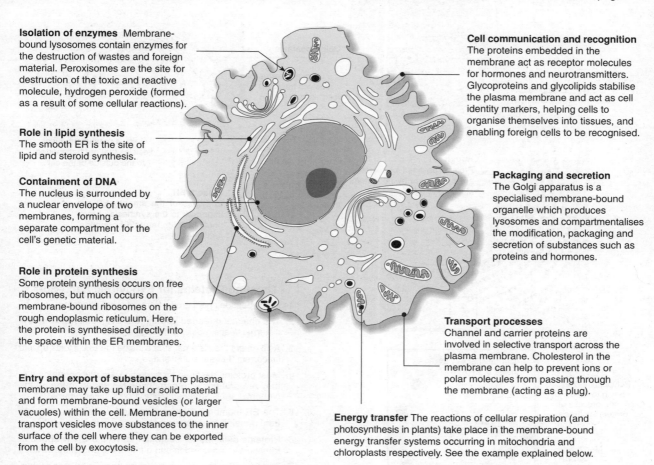

Isolation of enzymes Membrane-bound lysosomes contain enzymes for the destruction of wastes and foreign material. Peroxisomes are the site for destruction of the toxic and reactive molecule, hydrogen peroxide (formed as a result of some cellular reactions).

Role in lipid synthesis
The smooth ER is the site of lipid and steroid synthesis.

Containment of DNA
The nucleus is surrounded by a nuclear envelope of two membranes, forming a separate compartment for the cell's genetic material.

Role in protein synthesis
Some protein synthesis occurs on free ribosomes, but much occurs on membrane-bound ribosomes on the rough endoplasmic reticulum. Here, the protein is synthesised directly into the space within the ER membranes.

Entry and export of substances The plasma membrane may take up fluid or solid material and form membrane-bound vesicles (or larger vacuoles) within the cell. Membrane-bound transport vesicles move substances to the inner surface of the cell where they can be exported from the cell by exocytosis.

Cell communication and recognition
The proteins embedded in the membrane act as receptor molecules for hormones and neurotransmitters. Glycoproteins and glycolipids stabilise the plasma membrane and act as cell identity markers, helping cells to organise themselves into tissues, and enabling foreign cells to be recognised.

Packaging and secretion
The Golgi apparatus is a specialised membrane-bound organelle which produces lysosomes and compartmentalises the modification, packaging and secretion of substances such as proteins and hormones.

Transport processes
Channel and carrier proteins are involved in selective transport across the plasma membrane. Cholesterol in the membrane can help to prevent ions or polar molecules from passing through the membrane (acting as a plug).

Energy transfer The reactions of cellular respiration (and photosynthesis in plants) take place in the membrane-bound energy transfer systems occurring in mitochondria and chloroplasts respectively. See the example explained below.

Compartmentation within Membranes

Membranes play an important role in separating regions within the cell (and within organelles) where particular reactions occur. Specific enzymes are therefore often located in particular organelles. The reaction rate is controlled by controlling the rate at which substrates enter the organelle and therefore the availability of the raw materials required for the reactions.

Example (right): *The enzymes involved in cellular respiration are arranged in different parts of the mitochondria. Reactions are localised and separated by membrane systems.*

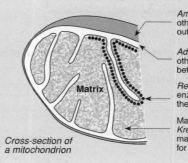

Cross-section of a mitochondrion

Amine oxidases and other enzymes on the outer membrane surface

Adenylate kinase and other *phosphorylases* between the membranes

Respiratory assembly enzymes embedded in the membrane (ATPase)

Many soluble enzymes of the Krebs cycle floating in the matrix, as well as enzymes for fatty acid degradation.

Matrix

1. Explain the crucial role of membrane systems and organelles in the following:

(a) Providing compartments within the cell: _____

_____

_____

(b) Increasing the total membrane surface area within the cell: _____

_____

_____

_____

Related activities: Cell Structures and Organelles, Active and Passive Transport   **Web links**: Cell Membranes

A 1

Cells produce a range of **macromolecules**; organic polymers made up of repeating units of smaller molecules. The synthesis, packaging and movement of these molecules inside the cell involves a number of membrane bound organelles, as indicated below. These organelles provide compartments where the enzyme systems involved can be isolated.

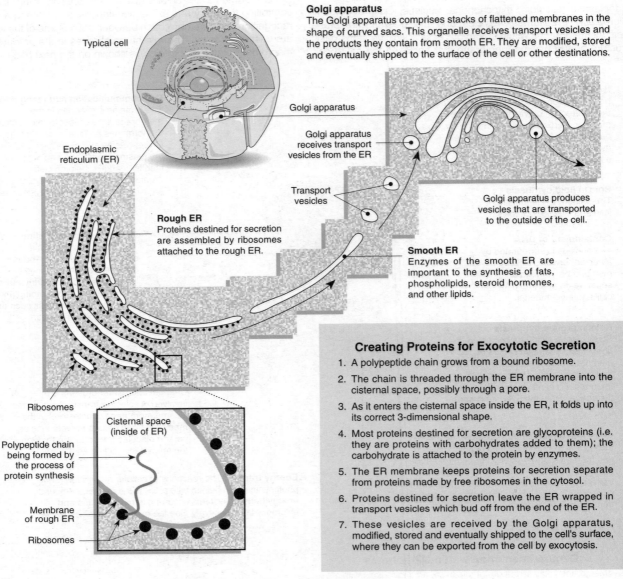

Typical cell

Endoplasmic reticulum (ER)

Golgi apparatus
The Golgi apparatus comprises stacks of flattened membranes in the shape of curved sacs. This organelle receives transport vesicles and the products they contain from smooth ER. They are modified, stored and eventually shipped to the surface of the cell or other destinations.

Golgi apparatus

Golgi apparatus receives transport vesicles from the ER

Transport vesicles

Golgi apparatus produces vesicles that are transported to the outside of the cell.

Rough ER
Proteins destined for secretion are assembled by ribosomes attached to the rough ER.

Smooth ER
Enzymes of the smooth ER are important to the synthesis of fats, phospholipids, steroid hormones, and other lipids.

Ribosomes

Cisternal space (inside of ER)

Polypeptide chain being formed by the process of protein synthesis

Membrane of rough ER

Ribosomes

Creating Proteins for Exocytotic Secretion

1. A polypeptide chain grows from a bound ribosome.

2. The chain is threaded through the ER membrane into the cisternal space, possibly through a pore.

3. As it enters the cisternal space inside the ER, it folds up into its correct 3-dimensional shape.

4. Most proteins destined for secretion are glycoproteins (i.e. they are proteins with carbohydrates added to them); the carbohydrate is attached to the protein by enzymes.

5. The ER membrane keeps proteins for secretion separate from proteins made by free ribosomes in the cytosol.

6. Proteins destined for secretion leave the ER wrapped in transport vesicles which bud off from the end of the ER.

7. These vesicles are received by the Golgi apparatus, modified, stored and eventually shipped to the cell's surface, where they can be exported from the cell by exocytosis.

2. Explain the importance of the following components of plasma membranes:

   (a) Glycoproteins and glycolipids: _____

   _____

   (b) Channel proteins and carrier proteins: _____

   _____

3. Explain how cholesterol can play a role in membrane transport: _____

   _____

4. Non-polar (lipid-soluble) molecules diffuse more rapidly through membranes than polar (lipid-insoluble) molecules:

   (a) Explain the reason for this: _____

   _____

   (b) Discuss the implications of this to the transport of substances into the cell through the plasma membrane:

   _____

   _____

Active and Passive Transport

Cells have a need to move materials both into and out of the cell. Raw materials and other molecules necessary for metabolism must be accumulated from outside the cell. Some of these substances are scarce outside of the cell and some effort is required to accumulate them. Waste products and molecules for use in other parts of the body must be 'exported' out of the cell.

Some materials (e.g. gases and water) move into and out of the cell by **passive transport** processes, without the expenditure of energy on the part of the cell. Other molecules (e.g. sucrose) are moved into and out of the cell using **active transport**. Active transport processes involve the expenditure of energy in the form of ATP, and therefore use oxygen.

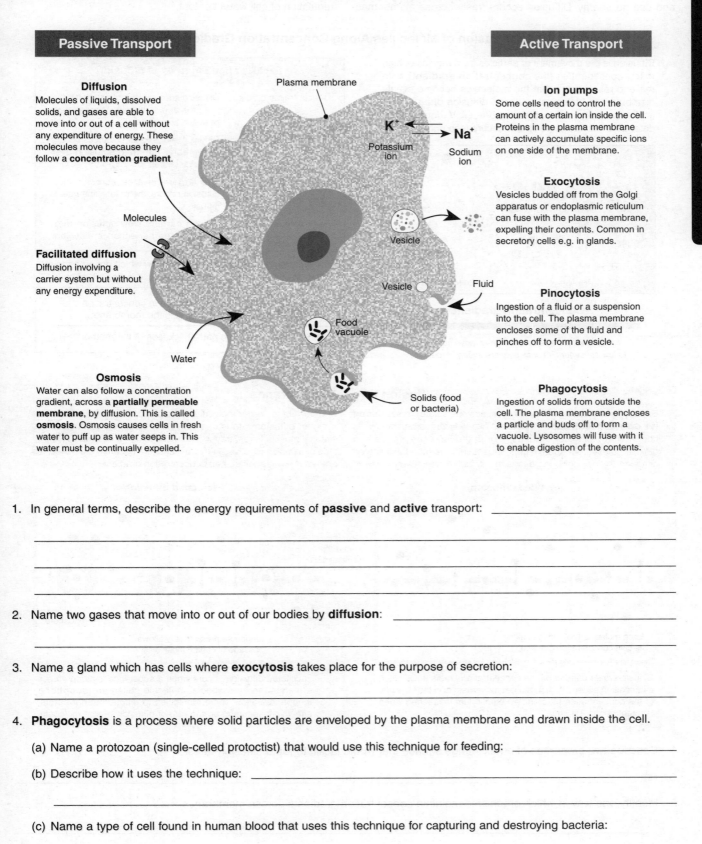

Passive Transport

Diffusion
Molecules of liquids, dissolved solids, and gases are able to move into or out of a cell without any expenditure of energy. These molecules move because they follow a **concentration gradient**.

Molecules

Facilitated diffusion
Diffusion involving a carrier system but without any energy expenditure.

Water

Osmosis
Water can also follow a concentration gradient, across a **partially permeable membrane**, by diffusion. This is called **osmosis**. Osmosis causes cells in fresh water to puff up as water seeps in. This water must be continually expelled.

Plasma membrane

K^+ Potassium ion

Na^+ Sodium ion

Vesicle

Vesicle   Fluid

Food vacuole

Solids (food or bacteria)

Active Transport

Ion pumps
Some cells need to control the amount of a certain ion inside the cell. Proteins in the plasma membrane can actively accumulate specific ions on one side of the membrane.

Exocytosis
Vesicles budded off from the Golgi apparatus or endoplasmic reticulum can fuse with the plasma membrane, expelling their contents. Common in secretory cells e.g. in glands.

Pinocytosis
Ingestion of a fluid or a suspension into the cell. The plasma membrane encloses some of the fluid and pinches off to form a vesicle.

Phagocytosis
Ingestion of solids from outside the cell. The plasma membrane encloses a particle and buds off to form a vacuole. Lysosomes will fuse with it to enable digestion of the contents.

1. In general terms, describe the energy requirements of **passive** and **active** transport: _____

_____

_____

_____

2. Name two gases that move into or out of our bodies by **diffusion**: _____

_____

3. Name a gland which has cells where **exocytosis** takes place for the purpose of secretion: _____

_____

4. **Phagocytosis** is a process where solid particles are enveloped by the plasma membrane and drawn inside the cell.

(a) Name a protozoan (single-celled protoctist) that would use this technique for feeding: _____

(b) Describe how it uses the technique: _____

_____

(c) Name a type of cell found in human blood that uses this technique for capturing and destroying bacteria:

_____

Related activities: Diffusion, Osmosis and Water Potential, Ion Pumps, Exocytosis and Endocytosis, Surface Area and Volume

RA 1

Diffusion

The molecules that make up substances are constantly moving about in a random way. This random motion causes molecules to disperse from areas of high to low concentration; a process called **diffusion**. The molecules move along a **concentration gradient**. Diffusion and osmosis (diffusion of water molecules across a partially permeable membrane) are **passive** processes, and use no energy. Diffusion occurs freely across membranes, as long as the membrane is permeable to that molecule (partially permeable membranes allow the passage of some molecules but not others). Each type of molecule diffuses along its own concentration gradient. Diffusion of molecules in one direction does not hinder the movement of other molecules. Diffusion is important in allowing exchanges with the environment and in the regulation of cell water content.

Diffusion of Molecules Along Concentration Gradients

Diffusion is the movement of particles from regions of high to low concentration (the **concentration gradient**), with the end result being that the molecules become evenly distributed. In biological systems, diffusion often occurs across partially permeable membranes. Various factors determine the rate at which this occurs (see right).

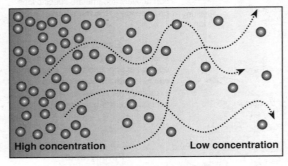

High concentration   **Low concentration**

Concentration gradient

If molecules are free to move, they move from high to low concentration until they are evenly dispersed.

Factors affecting rates of diffusion	
Concentration gradient:	Diffusion rates will be higher when there is a greater difference in concentration between two regions.
The distance involved:	Diffusion over shorter distances occurs at a greater rate than diffusion over larger distances.
The area involved:	The larger the area across which diffusion occurs, the greater the rate of diffusion.
Barriers to diffusion:	Thicker barriers slow diffusion rate. Pores in a barrier enhance diffusion.

These factors are expressed in **Fick's law**, which governs the rate of diffusion of substances within a system. It is described by:

$$\frac{\text{Surface area of membrane} \times \text{Difference in concentration across the membrane}}{\text{Length of the diffusion path (thickness of the membrane)}}$$

Diffusion through Membranes

Each type of diffusing molecule (gas, solvent, solute) moves **along its own concentration gradient**. Two-way diffusion (below) is common in biological systems, e.g. at the lung surface, carbon dioxide diffuses out and oxygen diffuses into the blood. Facilitated diffusion (below, right) increases the diffusion rate selectively and is important for larger molecules (e.g. glucose, amino acids) where a higher diffusion rate is desirable (e.g. transport of glucose into skeletal muscle fibres, transport of ADP into mitochondria). Neither type of diffusion requires energy expenditure because the molecules are not moving against their concentration gradient.

Unaided diffusion

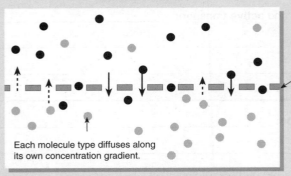

Each molecule type diffuses along its own concentration gradient.

Partially permeable membrane

Facilitated diffusion

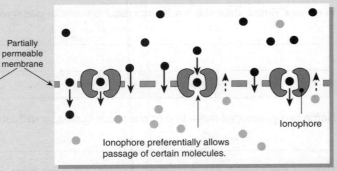

Ionophore

Ionophore preferentially allows passage of certain molecules.

Diffusion rates depend on the concentration gradient. Diffusion can occur in either direction but **net** movement is in the direction of the concentration gradient. An equilibrium is reached when concentrations are equal.

Facilitated diffusion occurs when a substance is aided across a membrane by a special molecule called an **ionophore**. Ionophores allow some molecules to diffuse but not others, effectively speeding up the rate of diffusion of that molecule.

1. Describe two properties of an exchange surface that would facilitate rapid diffusion rates:

   (a) _____ (b) _____

2. Identify one way in which organisms maintain concentration gradients across membranes: _____

   _____

3. State how facilitated diffusion is achieved: _____

Related activities: Active and Passive Transport, Osmosis & Water Potential, Surface Area and Volume   **Web links**: Osmosis and Diffusion

Osmosis and Water Potential

Osmosis is the term describing the diffusion of water along its concentration gradient across a partially permeable membrane. It is the principal mechanism by which water enters and leaves cells in living organisms. As it is a type of diffusion, the rate at which osmosis occurs is affected by the same factors that affect all diffusion rates (see earlier). The tendency for water to move in any particular direction can be calculated on the basis of the water potential of the cell sap relative to its surrounding environment. The use of water potential to express the water relations of cells has replaced the terms osmotic potential and osmotic pressure although these are still frequently used in areas of animal physiology and medicine. The concepts of osmosis, water potential, cell turgor, and plasmolysis are explained below and on the next page.

Osmosis and the Water Potential of Cells

Osmosis is simply the diffusion of water molecules from high concentration to lower concentration, across a partially permeable membrane. The direction of this movement can be predicted on the basis of the water potential of the solutions involved. The **water potential** of a solution (denoted with the symbol ψ) is the term given to the tendency for water molecules to enter or leave a solution by osmosis. Pure water has the highest water potential, set at zero. Dissolving any solute into pure water lowers the water potential (makes it more negative). *Water always diffuses from regions of less negative to more negative water potential*. Water potential is determined by two components: the **solute potential**, ψs (of the cell sap) and the **pressure potential**, ψp. This is expressed as a simple equation:

$$\psi cell = \psi s + \psi p$$

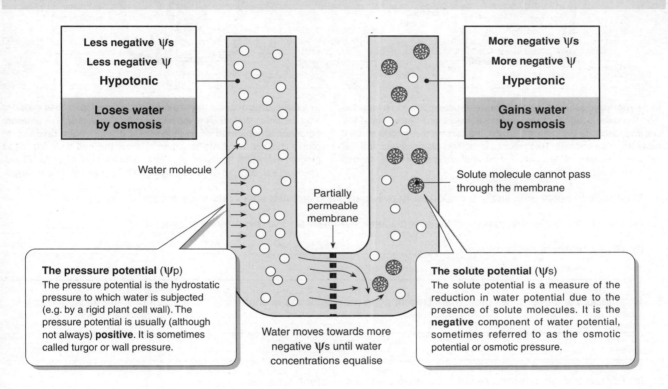

Less negative ψs
Less negative ψ
Hypotonic

Loses water by osmosis

Water molecule

The pressure potential (ψp)
The pressure potential is the hydrostatic pressure to which water is subjected (e.g. by a rigid plant cell wall). The pressure potential is usually (although not always) **positive**. It is sometimes called turgor or wall pressure.

Partially permeable membrane

Water moves towards more negative ψs until water concentrations equalise

More negative ψs
More negative ψ
Hypertonic

Gains water by osmosis

Solute molecule cannot pass through the membrane

The solute potential (ψs)
The solute potential is a measure of the reduction in water potential due to the presence of solute molecules. It is the **negative** component of water potential, sometimes referred to as the osmotic potential or osmotic pressure.

1. State the water potential of pure water at standard temperature and pressure: _____

2. The three diagrams below show the solute and pressure potential values for three hypothetical situations where two solutions are separated by a selectively permeable membrane. For each example (a) - (c) calculate ψ for the solutions on each side of the membrane, as indicated:

3. Draw arrows on each diagram to indicate the direction of net flow of water:

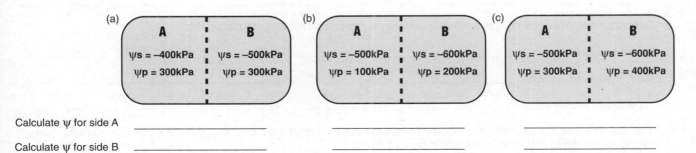

(a)

A	B
$\psi s = -400$kPa	$\psi s = -500$kPa
$\psi p = 300$kPa	$\psi p = 300$kPa

(b)

A	B
$\psi s = -500$kPa	$\psi s = -600$kPa
$\psi p = 100$kPa	$\psi p = 200$kPa

(c)

A	B
$\psi s = -500$kPa	$\psi s = -600$kPa
$\psi p = 300$kPa	$\psi p = 400$kPa

Calculate ψ for side A _____   _____   _____

Calculate ψ for side B _____   _____   _____

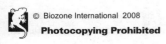

Related activities: Diffusion
Web links: Osmosis and Diffusion, Cellular Transport

DA 2

Water Relations in Plant Cells

The plasma membrane of cells is a partially permeable membrane and osmosis is the principal mechanism by which water enters and leaves the cell. When the external water potential is the same as that of the cell there is no net movement of water. Two systems (cell and environment) with the same water potential are termed **isotonic**. The diagram below illustrates two different situations: when the external water potential is less negative than the cell (**hypotonic**) and when it is more negative than the cell (**hypertonic**).

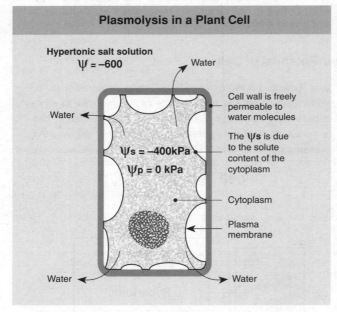

Plasmolysis in a Plant Cell

Hypertonic salt solution
$\Psi = -600$

Water

Water

Ψs = –400kPa

Ψp = 0 kPa

Water

Water

Cell wall is freely permeable to water molecules

The Ψs is due to the solute content of the cytoplasm

Cytoplasm

Plasma membrane

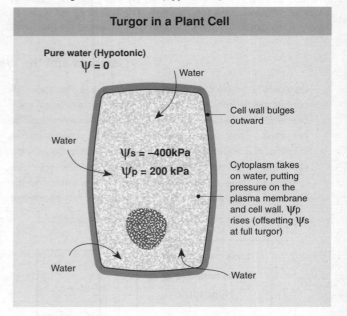

Turgor in a Plant Cell

Pure water (Hypotonic)
$\Psi = 0$

Water

Water

Ψs = –400kPa

Ψp = 200 kPa

Water

Water

Cell wall bulges outward

Cytoplasm takes on water, putting pressure on the plasma membrane and cell wall. Ψp rises (offsetting Ψs at full turgor)

In a **hypertonic** solution, the external water potential is more negative than the water potential of the cell (Ψcell = Ψs + ψp). Water leaves the cell and, because the cell wall is rigid, the plasma membrane shrinks away from the cell wall. This process is termed **plasmolysis** and the cell becomes **flaccid** (Ψp = 0). Full plasmolysis is irreversible; the cell cannot recover by taking up water.

In a **hypotonic** solution, the external water potential is less negative than the Ψcell. Water enters the cell causing it to swell tight. A pressure potential is generated when sufficient water has been taken up to cause the cell contents to press against the cell wall. Ψp rises progressively until it offsets Ψs. Water uptake stops when Ψcell = 0. The rigid cell wall prevents cell rupture. Cells in this state are **turgid**.

4. Fluid replacements are usually provided for heavily perspiring athletes after endurance events.

   (a) Identify the preferable tonicity of these replacement drinks (isotonic, hypertonic, or hypotonic): _____

   (b) Give a reason for your answer: _____
   _____

5. *Paramecium* is a freshwater protozoan. Describe the problem it has in controlling the amount of water inside the cell:
   _____
   _____

6. (a) Explain the role of pressure potential in generating cell turgor in plants: _____
   _____

   (b) Explain the purpose of cell turgor to plants: _____
   _____

7. Explain how animal cells differ from plant cells with respect to the effects of net water movements: _____
   _____

8. Describe what would happen to an animal cell (e.g. a red blood cell) if it was placed into:

   (a) Pure water: _____

   (b) A hypertonic solution: _____

   (c) A hypotonic solution: _____

9. The malarial parasite lives in human blood. Relative to the tonicity of the blood, the parasite's cell contents would be hypotonic / isotonic / hypertonic (circle the correct answer).

Ion Pumps

Diffusion alone cannot supply the cell's entire requirements for molecules (and ions). Some molecules (e.g. glucose) are required by the cell in higher concentrations than occur outside the cell. Others (e.g. sodium) must be removed from the cell in order to maintain fluid balance. These molecules must be moved across the plasma membrane by active transport mechanisms. **Active transport** requires the expenditure of energy because the molecules (or ions) must be moved **against** their concentration gradient. The work of active transport is performed by specific carrier proteins in the membrane. These transport proteins harness the energy of ATP to pump molecules from a low to a high concentration. When ATP transfers a phosphate group to the carrier protein, the protein changes its shape in such a way as to move the bound molecule across the membrane. Three types of membrane pump are illustrated below. The sodium-potassium pump (below, centre) is almost universal in animal cells and is common in plant cells also. The concentration gradient created by ion pumps such as this and the proton pump (left) is frequently coupled to the transport of molecules such as glucose (e.g. in the intestine) as shown below right.

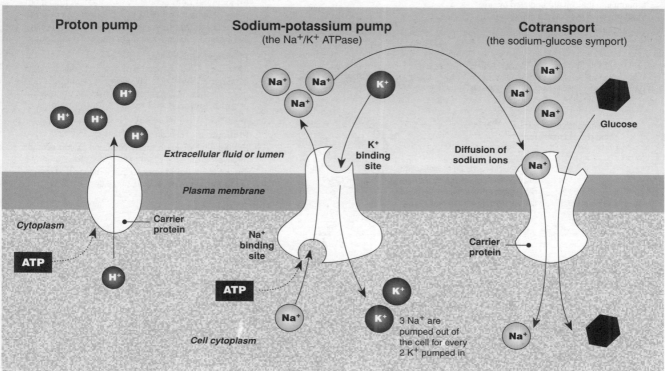

Proton pumps

ATP driven proton pumps use energy to remove hydrogen ions (H$^+$) from inside the cell to the outside. This creates a large difference in the proton concentration either side of the membrane, with the inside of the plasma membrane being negatively charged. This potential difference can be coupled to the transport of other molecules.

Sodium-potassium pump

The sodium-potassium pump is a specific protein in the membrane that uses energy in the form of ATP to exchange sodium ions (Na$^+$) for potassium ions (K$^+$) across the membrane. The unequal balance of Na$^+$ and K$^+$ across the membrane creates large concentration gradients that can be used to drive transport of other substances (e.g. cotransport of glucose).

Cotransport (coupled transport)

In the intestine, a gradient in sodium ions is used to drive the active transport of **glucose**. The specific transport protein couples the return of Na$^+$ down its concentration gradient to the transport of glucose into the intestinal epithelial cell. A low intracellular concentration of Na$^+$ (and therefore the concentration gradient) is maintained by a sodium-potassium pump.

1. Explain why the ATP is required for membrane pump systems to operate: _____

_____

2. (a) Explain what is meant by cotransport: _____

_____

(b) Explain how cotransport is used to move glucose into the intestinal epithelial cells: _____

_____

_____

(c) Explain what happens to the glucose that is transported into the intestinal epithelial cells: _____

_____

3. Describe two consequences of the extracellular accumulation of sodium ions: _____

_____

_____

Related activities: Active and Passive Transport, Absorption and Transport
Web links: Cellular Transport, Symport

A 2

Exocytosis and Endocytosis

Most cells carry out **cytosis**: a form of **active transport** involving the in- or outfolding of the plasma membrane. The ability of cells to do this is a function of the flexibility of the plasma membrane. Cytosis results in the bulk transport into or out of the cell and is achieved through the localised activity of microfilaments and microtubules in the cell cytoskeleton. Engulfment of material is termed **endocytosis.** Endocytosis typically occurs in protozoans and certain white blood cells of the mammalian defence system (e.g. neutrophils, macrophages). **Exocytosis** is the reverse of endocytosis and involves the release of material from vesicles or vacuoles that have fused with the plasma membrane. Exocytosis is typical of cells that export material (secretory cells).

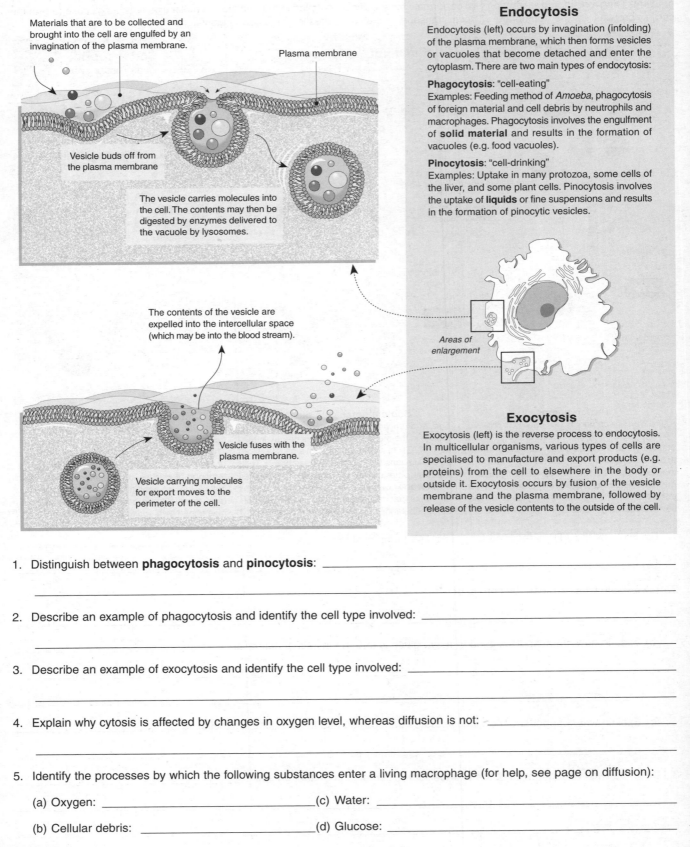

Materials that are to be collected and brought into the cell are engulfed by an invagination of the plasma membrane.

Plasma membrane

Vesicle buds off from the plasma membrane

The vesicle carries molecules into the cell. The contents may then be digested by enzymes delivered to the vacuole by lysosomes.

The contents of the vesicle are expelled into the intercellular space (which may be into the blood stream).

Vesicle fuses with the plasma membrane.

Vesicle carrying molecules for export moves to the perimeter of the cell.

Areas of enlargement

Endocytosis

Endocytosis (left) occurs by invagination (infolding) of the plasma membrane, which then forms vesicles or vacuoles that become detached and enter the cytoplasm. There are two main types of endocytosis:

Phagocytosis: "cell-eating"
Examples: Feeding method of *Amoeba*, phagocytosis of foreign material and cell debris by neutrophils and macrophages. Phagocytosis involves the engulfment of **solid material** and results in the formation of vacuoles (e.g. food vacuoles).

Pinocytosis: "cell-drinking"
Examples: Uptake in many protozoa, some cells of the liver, and some plant cells. Pinocytosis involves the uptake of **liquids** or fine suspensions and results in the formation of pinocytic vesicles.

Exocytosis

Exocytosis (left) is the reverse process to endocytosis. In multicellular organisms, various types of cells are specialised to manufacture and export products (e.g. proteins) from the cell to elsewhere in the body or outside it. Exocytosis occurs by fusion of the vesicle membrane and the plasma membrane, followed by release of the vesicle contents to the outside of the cell.

1. Distinguish between **phagocytosis** and **pinocytosis**: _____

   _____

2. Describe an example of phagocytosis and identify the cell type involved: _____

   _____

3. Describe an example of exocytosis and identify the cell type involved: _____

   _____

4. Explain why cytosis is affected by changes in oxygen level, whereas diffusion is not: _____

   _____

5. Identify the processes by which the following substances enter a living macrophage (for help, see page on diffusion):

   (a) Oxygen: _____ (c) Water: _____

   (b) Cellular debris: _____ (d) Glucose: _____

Related activities: Active and Passive Transport, Diffusion
Web links: Cellular Transport

Cholera

Cholera is an acute intestinal infection caused by the bacterium *Vibrio cholerae*. The bacterium produces an **enterotoxin** which binds to membrane receptors on the small intestine, opening the ion channels and increasing permeability of the mucosal epithelium to chloride ions. According to the principles of osmosis, water follows the salt across the membrane resulting in copious, painless, watery diarrhoea that can lead to severe dehydration, kidney failure, and death within hours if left untreated. Cholera can be prevented by hygienic disposal of human faeces, provision of an adequate supply of safe drinking water, safe food handling and preparation (e.g. preventing contamination of food and water), and effective general hygiene (e.g. hand washing with soap). Once contracted, the only treatment for cholera is the administration of **oral rehydration solutions (ORS)** to prevent dehydration or death. In severe cases the rehydration solution is administered intravenously, and the patient may be prescribed antibiotics to reduce the infection time. With prompt and appropriate ORS treatment, the fatality rate from cholera infection is less than 1%.

Development of Oral Rehydration Solutions

Many scientific disciplines have been involved in developing modern ORS. Key discoveries include:

1950s: Physiologists first noted that glucose and sodium were transported together across the intestinal epithelium.

1960s: The first ORS formulations were developed to treat severe diarrhoea. In addition to electrolytes, they also contained glucose which had been proven to increase water reabsorption.

The discovery that the cholera enterotoxin was responsible for fluid loss (diarrhoea) by interfering with membrane cAMP activity and G-proteins.

Current: The development of low osmolarity solutions which use alternative carbohydrate sources such as rice, instead of sugars to minimise diarrhoeal effect.

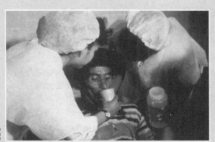
Administering ORS to a cholera patient

Vibrio cholerae

Oral Rehydration Solutions

Diarrhoea causes water and electrolytes to be lost from the body, resulting in dehydration and electrolyte imbalance. This in turn can alter osmotic gradients in the body, affecting hydration, blood pH, and nerve and muscle function. Drinking water alone to treat diarrhoea is ineffective for two reasons: during bouts of diarrhoea the large intenstine is losing rather than absorbing water, and secondly, electrolyte loss is not addressed. Instead, **oral rehydation solutions** (ORS) are prescribed and can be administered with no medical training. Modern ORS are a very simple, inexpensive product containing water and salts in specific ratios designed to replenish fluids and electrolytes. Carbohydrates, such as glucose or sucrose, are added to enhance electrolyte absorption in the intestinal tract. Although the presence of sugars can increase the rate of diarrhoea, they still have an overall benefit because they increase fluid replacement and improve patient hydration.

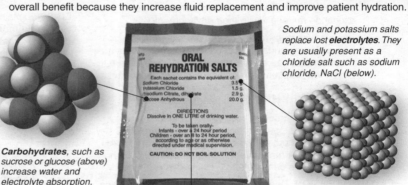

*Sodium and potassium salts replace lost **electrolytes**. They are usually present as a chloride salt such as sodium chloride, NaCl (below).*

ORAL REHYDRATION SALTS
Each sachet contains the equivalent of:
Sodium Chloride .... 3.5 g.
potassium Chloride .... 1.5 g.
Sodium Citrate, dihydrate . 2.9 g.
Glucose Anhydrous .... 20.0 g.

DIRECTIONS
Dissolve in ONE LITRE of drinking water.

To be taken orally-
Infants - over a 24 hour period
Children - over an 8 to 24 hour period,
according to age or as otherwise
directed under medical supervision.

CAUTION: DO NOT BOIL SOLUTION

Carbohydrates, such as sucrose or glucose (above) increase water and electrolyte absorption.

Sodium bicarbonate or sodium citrate (right) help maintain homeostatic blood pH and revert metabolic acidosis which occurs if blood pH falls below 7.35.

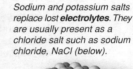

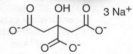

3 Na⁺

---

1. Identify the pathogen that causes cholera: _____

2. Describe why severe diarrhoea caused by cholera infection can be so dangerous if not treated quickly:

   _____

   _____

   _____

3. Briefly describe why ORS are more effective in treating the symptoms of cholera than water alone:

   _____

   _____

4. Explain why a patient taking an ORS with glucose might feel that their symptoms were worsening and stop treatment:

   _____

   _____

5. Discuss some of the ethical issues associated with trialing new ORS formulations on humans: _____

   _____

   _____

Gas Exchange at the Lungs

Unit 1: Biology and Disease
1.4 The lungs as an interface with the environment

Gas exchange in the lungs, pulmonary ventilation and breathing, gas transport, and lung disease

Learning Objectives

☐ 1. Compile your own glossary from the **KEY WORDS** displayed in **bold type** in the learning objectives below.

The Basics of Gas Exchange *(pages 105, 111)*

☐ 2. Distinguish between **cellular respiration** and **gas exchange** and explain why organisms need to exchange materials with their environment.

☐ 3. Explain how **respiratory gases** are exchanged across gas exchange surfaces. Describe the essential features of an efficient gas exchange surface. With reference to **Fick's law**, explain the significance of these features.

Gas Exchange in Humans *(pages 106-112)*

☐ 4. Describe the structure, location, adaptations, and function of the gas exchange surfaces and related structures in humans: **trachea, bronchi, bronchioles, lungs, alveoli** (and **alveolar epithelium**). Explain how these features contribute to efficient gas exchange.

☐ 5. EXTENSION: Describe the distribution of the following tissues and cells in the **trachea**, **bronchi**, and **bronchioles**: **cartilage, ciliated epithelium, goblet cells**, and **smooth muscle cells**. Describe the function of the **cartilage, cilia, goblet cells, smooth muscle**, and **elastic fibres** in the gas exchange system.

☐ 6. Recognise the relationship between gas exchange surfaces (alveoli) and the blood vessels in the lung tissue. Draw a simple diagram of an **alveolus** (air sac) to illustrate the movement of O_2 and CO_2, into and out of the blood in the surrounding capillary.

☐ 7. Describe the mechanism of ventilation (**breathing**) in humans. Include reference to the following:
  (a) The role of the rib cage, **diaphragm, intercostal muscles**, and **pleural membranes** in breathing.
  (b) The role of **surfactants** in lung function.
  (c) The distinction between **inspiration** (inhalation) as an active process and **expiration** (exhalation) as a passive process (during normal, quiet breathing).

☐ 8. Explain how the breathing (ventilation) rate and **pulmonary ventilation** (PV) rate are calculated and expressed. Provide some typical values for **breathing rate, tidal volume**, and **PV**. If required, describe the use of a **spirometer** to measure aspects of breathing.

The Basis of Lung Disease *(pages 113-117)*

☐ 9. Explain how both pathogens and environmental factors (e.g. tobacco smoking and pollution) contribute to lung diseases with specific, recognisable symptoms.

☐ 10. Describe the cause, course of infection, symptoms, and modes of transmission of pulmonary tuberculosis (TB). Explain the symptoms of the disease in terms of the effect of infection on lung function and gas exchange.

☐ 11. Describe the causes and symptoms of pulmonary **fibrosis, asthma**, and **emphysema**. Explain the effect of each disease on lung function and gas exchange.

☐ 12. Analyse and/or interpret data related to:
  • the effect of pollution and smoking on the incidence of lung disease
  • specific risk factors associated with the incidence of lung disease

---

 **Textbooks**

 See the 'Textbook Reference Grid' on page 7 for textbook page references relating to material in this topic.

Supplementary Texts
See pages 5-6 for additional details of these texts:
■ Adds, J. *et al.*, 2004. **Exchange & Transport, Energy & Ecosystems** (NelsonThornes), pp. 2-26.
■ Clegg, C.J., 1998. **Mammals: Structure and Function** (John Murray), pp. 24-31.
■ Fullick, A., 2000. **Human Health and Disease** (Heinemann), chpt. 3 especially pp. 69-73.

 **Periodicals**

See page 6 for details of publishers of periodicals:

STUDENT'S REFERENCE
■ **Lungs and the Control of Breathing** Bio. Sci. Rev. 14(4) April 2002, pp. 2-5. *The mechanisms, control, and measurement of breathing. This article includes good, clear diagrams and useful summaries of the important points.*

■ **Gas Exchange in the Lungs** Bio. Sci. Rev. 16(1) Sept. 2003, pp. 36-38. *The structure and function of the alveoli of the lungs, with an account of respiratory problems and diseases such as respiratory distress syndrome and emphysema.*

■ **Air Pollution and Asthma** Bio. Sci. Rev. 9(4) March 1997, pp. 32-36. *The link between air pollution and allergens and airway hyperactivity.*

■ **Smoking** Biol. Sci. Rev. 10(1) Sept. 1997, pp. 14-16. *The effects on human physiology of tobacco smoking, including the types and symptoms of smoking related diseases.*

■ **Environmental Lung Disease** New Scientist, 23 September 1995 (Inside Science). *An excellent supplement on lung disorders, with good diagrams illustrating lung functioning and gas transport.*

■ **Dust to Dust** New Scientist, 21 September 2002 (Inside Science). *The human respiratory system and the impact of polluting dust on health.*

 **Internet**

See pages 8-9 for details of how to access **Bio Links** from our web site: **www.biozone.co.uk**. From Bio Links, access sites under the topics:

ANIMAL BIOLOGY: • Anatomy and physiology • Human physiology lecture notes … *and others* > **Gas Exchange:** • Gas exchange • Lesson 11: The respiratory system • Respiratory system • Respiratory system: Chpt 4
HEALTH & DISEASE: > **Non-Infectious Diseases:** • Asthma • Chemicals and human health • American Cancer Society .. *and others*

Introduction to Gas Exchange

Living cells require energy for the activities of life. Energy is released in cells by the breakdown of sugars and other substances in the metabolic process called **cellular respiration**. As a consequence of this process, gases need to be exchanged between the respiring cells and the environment. In most organisms (with the exception of some bacterial groups) these gases are carbon dioxide (CO_2) and oxygen (O_2). The diagram below illustrates this process for an animal. Plant cells also respire, but their gas exchange budget is different because they also produce O_2 and consume CO_2 in photosynthesis.

The Need for Gas Exchange

Gas exchange is the process by which oxygen is acquired and carbon dioxide is removed. Cellular respiration creates a constant demand for oxygen (O_2) and a need to eliminate carbon dioxide gas (CO_2).

Gas exchange surfaces provide a means for gases to enter and leave the body. Some organisms use the body surface as the sole gas exchange surface, but many have specialised gas exchange structures (e.g. lungs, gills, or stomata). Amphibians use the body surface and simple lungs to provide for their gas exchange requirements.

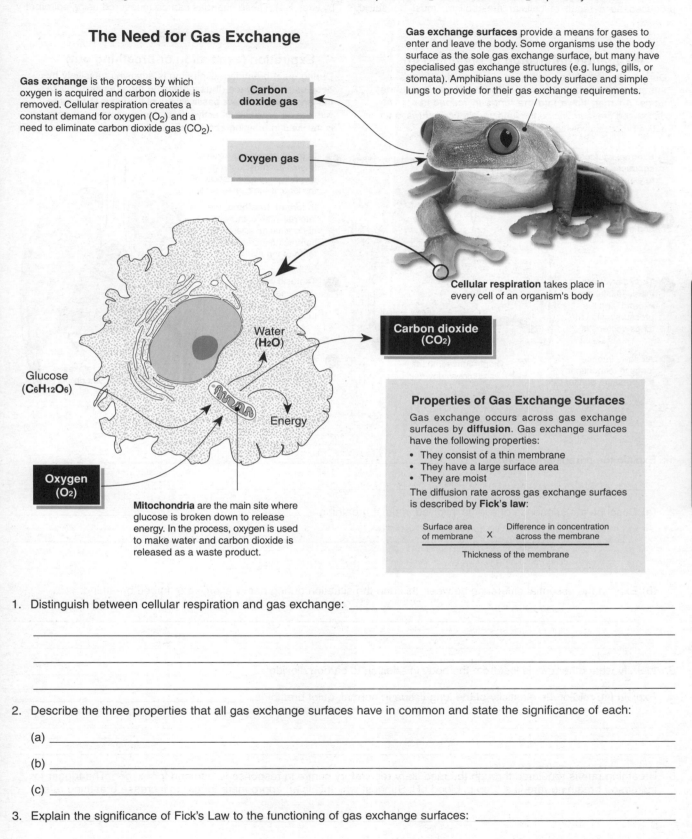

Carbon dioxide gas

Oxygen gas

Cellular respiration takes place in every cell of an organism's body

Water (H_2O)

Carbon dioxide (CO_2)

Glucose ($C_6H_{12}O_6$)

Energy

Oxygen (O_2)

Mitochondria are the main site where glucose is broken down to release energy. In the process, oxygen is used to make water and carbon dioxide is released as a waste product.

Properties of Gas Exchange Surfaces

Gas exchange occurs across gas exchange surfaces by **diffusion**. Gas exchange surfaces have the following properties:

- They consist of a thin membrane
- They have a large surface area
- They are moist

The diffusion rate across gas exchange surfaces is described by **Fick's law**:

$$\frac{\text{Surface area of membrane} \times \text{Difference in concentration across the membrane}}{\text{Thickness of the membrane}}$$

Gas Exchange at the Lungs

1. Distinguish between cellular respiration and gas exchange: _____

_____

_____

_____

2. Describe the three properties that all gas exchange surfaces have in common and state the significance of each:

(a) _____

(b) _____

(c) _____

3. Explain the significance of Fick's Law to the functioning of gas exchange surfaces: _____

_____

_____

Related activities: Diffusion, Surface Area and Volume

A 1

Breathing in Humans

In mammals, the mechanism of breathing (ventilation) provides a continual supply of fresh air to the lungs and helps to maintain a large diffusion gradient for respiratory gases across the gas exchange surface. Oxygen must be delivered regularly to supply the needs of respiring cells. Similarly, carbon dioxide, which is produced as a result of cellular metabolism, must be quickly eliminated from the body. Adequate lung ventilation is essential to these exchanges. The cardiovascular system participates by transporting respiratory gases to and from the cells of the body. The volume of gases exchanged during breathing varies according to the physiological demands placed on the body (e.g. by exercise). These changes can be measured using spirometry.

Inspiration (inhalation or breathing in)

During quiet breathing, inspiration is achieved by increasing the space (therefore decreasing the pressure) inside the lungs. Air then flows into the lungs in respeonse to the decreased pressure inside the lung. Inspiration is always an active process involving muscle contraction.

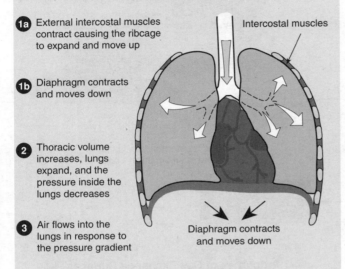

1a External intercostal muscles contract causing the ribcage to expand and move up

1b Diaphragm contracts and moves down

2 Thoracic volume increases, lungs expand, and the pressure inside the lungs decreases

3 Air flows into the lungs in response to the pressure gradient

Intercostal muscles

Diaphragm contracts and moves down

Expiration (exhalation or breathing out)

During quiet breathing, expiration is achieved passively by decreasing the space (thus increasing the pressure) inside the lungs. Air then flows passively out of the lungs to equalise with the air pressure. In active breathing, muscle contraction is involved in bringing about both inspiration and expiration.

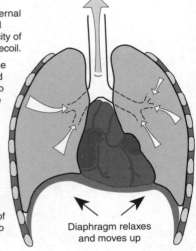

1 In **quiet breathing**, external intercostal muscles and diaphragm relax. Elasticity of the lung tissue causes recoil.

In **forced breathing**, the internal intercostals and abdominal muscles also contract to increase the force of the expiration

2 Thoracic volume decreases and the pressure inside the lungs increases

3 Air flows passively out of the lungs in response to the pressure gradient

Diaphragm relaxes and moves up

1. Explain the purpose of breathing: _____

_____

2. (a) Describe the sequence of events involved in quiet breathing: _____

_____

_____

(b) Explain the essential difference between this and the situation during heavy exercise or forced breathing:

_____

_____

3. Identify what other gas is lost from the body in addition to carbon dioxide: _____

4. Explain the role of the elasticity of the lung tissue in normal, quiet breathing: _____

_____

_____

5. Breathing rate is regulated through the medullary respiratory centre in response to demand for oxygen. The trigger for increased breathing rate is a drop in blood pH. Suggest why this is an appropriate trigger to increase breathing rate:

_____

_____

_____

Related activities: Measuring Lung Function, Gas Transport in Humans, Haemoglobins   **Web links**: Respiratory Basics Learning Activity

The Human Respiratory System

Lungs are internal sac-like organs found in most amphibians, and all reptiles, birds, and mammals. The paired lungs of mammals are connected to the outside air by way of a system of tubular passageways: the trachea, bronchi, and bronchioles. Ciliated, mucus secreting epithelium lines this system of tubules, trapping and removing dust and pathogens before they reach the gas exchange surfaces. Each lung is divided into a number of lobes, each receiving its own bronchus. Each bronchus divides many times, terminating in the respiratory bronchioles from which arise 2-11 alveolar ducts and numerous **alveoli** (air sacs). These provide a very large surface area (70 m²) for the exchange of respiratory gases by diffusion between the alveoli and the blood in the capillaries. The details of this exchange across the **respiratory membrane** are described opposite.

Morphology of the Respiratory System

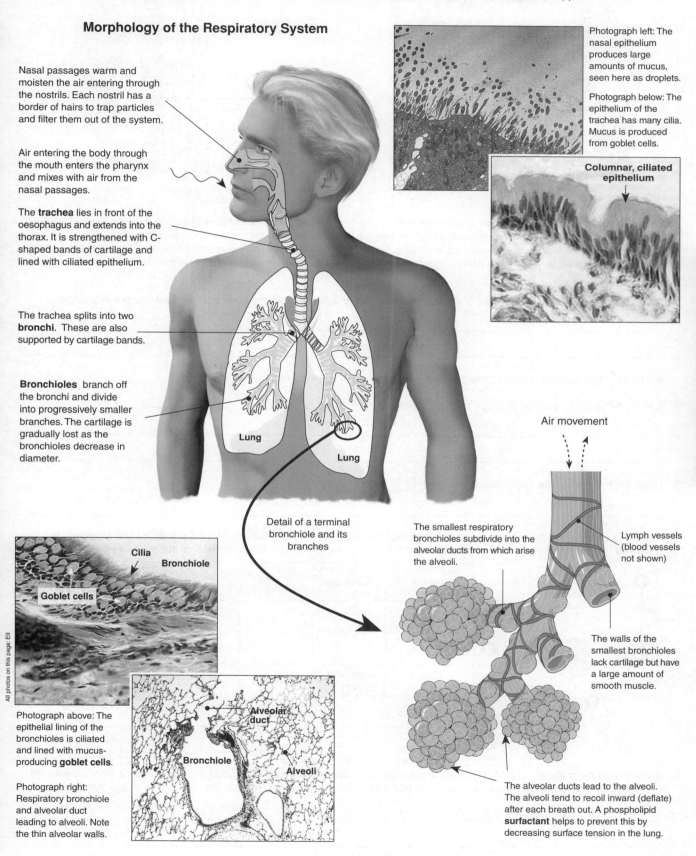

Nasal passages warm and moisten the air entering through the nostrils. Each nostril has a border of hairs to trap particles and filter them out of the system.

Air entering the body through the mouth enters the pharynx and mixes with air from the nasal passages.

The **trachea** lies in front of the oesophagus and extends into the thorax. It is strengthened with C-shaped bands of cartilage and lined with ciliated epithelium.

The trachea splits into two **bronchi**. These are also supported by cartilage bands.

Bronchioles branch off the bronchi and divide into progressively smaller branches. The cartilage is gradually lost as the bronchioles decrease in diameter.

Lung

Lung

Detail of a terminal bronchiole and its branches

Photograph left: The nasal epithelium produces large amounts of mucus, seen here as droplets.

Photograph below: The epithelium of the trachea has many cilia. Mucus is produced from goblet cells.

Columnar, ciliated epithelium

Cilia
Bronchiole
Goblet cells

All photos on this page: EII

Photograph above: The epithelial lining of the bronchioles is ciliated and lined with mucus-producing **goblet cells**.

Photograph right: Respiratory bronchiole and alveolar duct leading to alveoli. Note the thin alveolar walls.

Alveolar duct
Bronchiole
Alveoli

Air movement

The smallest respiratory bronchioles subdivide into the alveolar ducts from which arise the alveoli.

Lymph vessels (blood vessels not shown)

The walls of the smallest bronchioles lack cartilage but have a large amount of smooth muscle.

The alveolar ducts lead to the alveoli. The alveoli tend to recoil inward (deflate) after each breath out. A phospholipid **surfactant** helps to prevent this by decreasing surface tension in the lung.

Gas Exchange at the Lungs

Related activities: Gas Transport in Humans, Breathing in Humans, Review of Lung Function

RA 2

An Alveolus

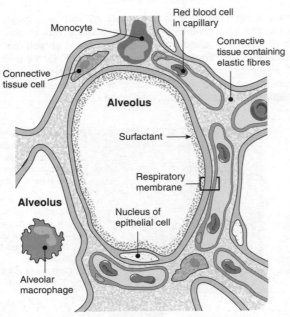

Monocyte

Red blood cell in capillary

Connective tissue containing elastic fibres

Connective tissue cell

Alveolus

Surfactant

Respiratory membrane

Alveolus

Nucleus of epithelial cell

Alveolar macrophage

The diagram above illustrates the physical arrangement of the alveoli to the capillaries through which the blood moves. Phagocytic monocytes and macrophages are also present to protect the lung tissue. Elastic connective tissue gives the alveoli their ability to expand and recoil.

The Respiratory Membrane

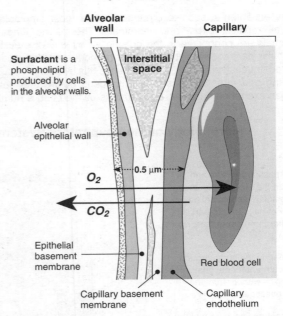

Alveolar wall

Capillary

Surfactant is a phospholipid produced by cells in the alveolar walls.

Interstitial space

Alveolar epithelial wall

O_2

0.5 μm

CO_2

Epithelial basement membrane

Red blood cell

Capillary basement membrane

Capillary endothelium

The **respiratory membrane** is the term for the layered junction between the alveolar epithelial cells, the endothelial cells of the capillary, and their associated basement membranes (thin, collagenous layers that underlie the epithelial tissues). Gases move freely across this membrane.

1. (a) Explain how the basic structure of the human respiratory system provides such a large area for gas exchange:

   _____

   _____

   (b) Identify the general region of the lung where exchange of gases takes place: _____

2. Describe the structure and purpose of the respiratory membrane: _____

   _____

   _____

3. Describe the role of the surfactant in the alveoli: _____

   _____

4. Using the information above and opposite, complete the table below summarising the **histology of the respiratory pathway**. Name each numbered region and use a tick or cross to indicate the presence or absence of particular tissues.

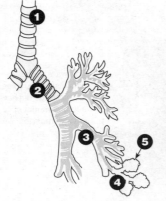

	Region	Cartilage	Ciliated epithelium	Goblet cells (mucus)	Smooth muscle	Connective tissue
1						✓
2						
3		gradually lost				
4	Alveolar duct		✗	✗		
5					very little	

5. Babies born prematurely are often deficient in surfactant. This causes respiratory distress syndrome; a condition where breathing is very difficult. From what you know about the role of surfactant, explain the symptoms of this syndrome:

   _____

   _____

Measuring Lung Function

Changes in lung volume can be measured using a technique called **spirometry**. Total adult lung volume varies between 4 and 6 litres (dm3) and is greater in males. The **vital capacity**, which describes the volume exhaled after a maximum inspiration, is somewhat less than this because of the residual volume of air that remains in the lungs even after expiration. The exchange between fresh air and the residual volume is a slow process and the composition of gases in the lungs remains relatively constant. Once measured, the tidal volume can be used to calculate the **pulmonary ventilation rate** or PV, which describes the amount of air exchanged with the environment per minute. Measures of respiratory capacity provide one way in which a reduction in lung function can be assessed (for example, as might occur as result of disease or an obstructive lung disorder such asthma).

Determining changes in lung volume using spirometry

The apparatus used to measure the amount of air exchanged during breathing and the rate of breathing is a **spirometer** (also called a respirometer). A simple spirometer consists of a weighted drum, containing oxygen or air, inverted over a chamber of water. A tube connects the air-filled chamber with the subject's mouth, and soda lime in the system absorbs the carbon dioxide breathed out. Breathing results in a trace called a spirogram, from which lung volumes can be measured directly.

During inspiration
Air is removed from the chamber, the drum sinks, and an upward deflection is recorded on the paper on the rotating drum.

During expiration
Air is added to the chamber, the drum rises, and a downward deflection is recorded.

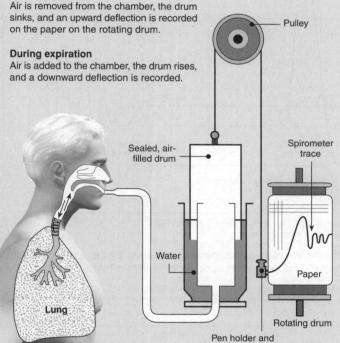

Pulley

Sealed, air-filled drum

Spirometer trace

Water

Paper

Lung

Rotating drum

Pen holder and counter balance

Lung Volumes and Capacities

The air in the lungs can be divided into volumes. Lung capacities are combinations of volumes.

DESCRIPTION OF VOLUME	Vol / dm3
Tidal volume (TV) Volume of air breathed in and out in a single breath	0.5
Inspiratory reserve volume (IRV) Volume breathed in by a maximum inspiration at the end of a normal inspiration	3.3
Expiratory reserve volume (ERV) Volume breathed out by a maximum effort at the end of a normal expiration	1.0
Residual volume (RV) Volume of air remaining in the lungs at the end of a maximum expiration	1.2

DESCRIPTION OF CAPACITY	
Inspiratory capacity (IC) = TV + IRV Volume breathed in by a maximum inspiration at the end of a normal expiration	3.8
Vital capacity (VC) = IRV + TV + ERV Volume that can be exhaled after a maximum inspiration.	4.8
Total lung capacity (TLC) = VC + RV The total volume of the lungs. Only a fraction of TLC is used in normal breathing	6.0

PRIMARY INDICATORS OF LUNG FUNCTION

Forced expiratory volume in 1 second (FEV_1)
The volume of air that is maximally exhaled in the first second of exhalation.

Forced vital capacity (FVC)
The total volume of air that can be forcibly exhaled after a maximum inspiration.

---

1. Describe how each of the following might be expected to influence values for lung volumes and capacities obtained using spirometry:

   (a) Height: _____

   (b) Gender: _____

   (c) Age: _____

2. A percentage decline in FEV_1 and FVC (to <80% of normal) are indicators of impaired lung function, e.g in asthma:

   (a) Explain why a forced volume is a more useful indicator of lung function than tidal volume: _____

   _____

   (b) Asthma is treated with drugs to relax the airways. Suggest how spirometry could be used during asthma treatment:

   _____

Related activities: The Human Respiratory System
Web links: Respiratory Basics Learning Activity

DA 2

Respiratory gas	Approximate percentages of O_2 and CO_2		
	Inhaled air	Air in lungs	Exhaled air
O_2	21.0	13.8	16.4
CO_2	0.04	5.5	3.6

Above: The percentages of respiratory gases in air (by volume) during normal breathing. The percentage volume of oxygen in the alveolar air (in the lung) is lower than that in the exhaled air because of the influence of the **dead air volume** (the air in the spaces of the nose, throat, larynx, trachea and bronchi). This air (about 30% of the air inhaled) is unavailable for gas exchange.

Left: During exercise, the breathing rate, tidal volume, and PV increase up to a maximum (as indicated below).

Spirogram for a male during quiet and forced breathing, and during exercise

Lung volume / dm³ (y-axis)

Inspiratory reserve volume (IRV) = 3.3 dm³

A, B, C, D, E, F, G

Resting   Exercise

PV   = breathing rate X tidal volume
dm³ min⁻¹ = breaths min⁻¹   X dm³

Time

3. Using the definitions given on the previous page, identify the volumes and capacities indicated by the letters **A-F** on the spirogram above. For each, indicate the volume (vol) in dm³. The inspiratory reserve volume has been identified for you:

(a) A: _____ Vol: _____ (d) D: _____ Vol: _____

(b) B: _____ Vol: _____ (e) E: _____ Vol: _____

(c) C: _____ Vol: _____ (f) F: _____ Vol: _____

4. Explain what is happening in the sequence indicated by the letter **G**: _____

_____

5. Calculate PV when breathing rate is 15 breaths per minute and tidal volume is 4.0 dm³: _____

6. (a) Describe what would happen to PV during strenuous exercise: _____

(b) Explain how this is achieved: _____

_____

7. The table above gives approximate percentages for respiratory gases during breathing. Study the data and then:

(a) Calculate the difference in CO_2 between inhaled and exhaled air: _____

(b) Explain where this 'extra' CO_2 comes from: _____

(c) Explain why the dead air volume raises the oxygen content of exhaled air above that in the lungs: _____

_____

Gas Transport in Humans

The transport of respiratory gases around the body is the role of the blood and its respiratory pigments. Oxygen is transported throughout the body chemically bound to the respiratory pigment **haemoglobin** inside the red blood cells. In the muscles, oxygen from haemoglobin is transferred to and retained by **myoglobin**, a molecule that is chemically similar to haemoglobin except that it consists of only one haem-globin unit. Myoglobin has a greater affinity for oxygen than haemoglobin and acts as an oxygen store within muscles, releasing the oxygen during periods of prolonged or extreme muscular activity. If the myoglobin store is exhausted, the muscles are forced into oxygen debt and must respire anaerobically. The waste product of this, lactic acid, accumulates in the muscle and is transported (as lactate) to the liver where it is metabolised under aerobic conditions.

Gas Exchange and Transport

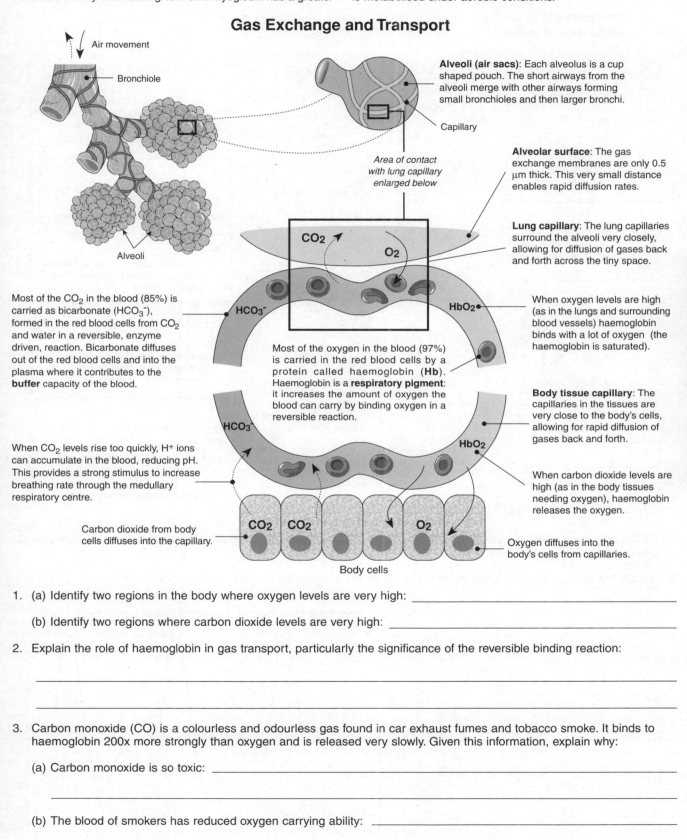

Air movement

Bronchiole

Alveoli

Alveoli (air sacs): Each alveolus is a cup shaped pouch. The short airways from the alveoli merge with other airways forming small bronchioles and then larger bronchi.

Capillary

Area of contact with lung capillary enlarged below

Alveolar surface: The gas exchange membranes are only 0.5 µm thick. This very small distance enables rapid diffusion rates.

Lung capillary: The lung capillaries surround the alveoli very closely, allowing for diffusion of gases back and forth across the tiny space.

CO_2 O_2

HCO_3^-

HbO_2

Most of the CO_2 in the blood (85%) is carried as bicarbonate (HCO_3^-), formed in the red blood cells from CO_2 and water in a reversible, enzyme driven, reaction. Bicarbonate diffuses out of the red blood cells and into the plasma where it contributes to the **buffer** capacity of the blood.

When oxygen levels are high (as in the lungs and surrounding blood vessels) haemoglobin binds with a lot of oxygen (the haemoglobin is saturated).

Most of the oxygen in the blood (97%) is carried in the red blood cells by a protein called haemoglobin (**Hb**). Haemoglobin is a **respiratory pigment**: it increases the amount of oxygen the blood can carry by binding oxygen in a reversible reaction.

HCO_3^-

HbO_2

Body tissue capillary: The capillaries in the tissues are very close to the body's cells, allowing for rapid diffusion of gases back and forth.

When CO_2 levels rise too quickly, H^+ ions can accumulate in the blood, reducing pH. This provides a strong stimulus to increase breathing rate through the medullary respiratory centre.

When carbon dioxide levels are high (as in the body tissues needing oxygen), haemoglobin releases the oxygen.

Carbon dioxide from body cells diffuses into the capillary.

CO_2 CO_2 O_2

Body cells

Oxygen diffuses into the body's cells from capillaries.

1. (a) Identify two regions in the body where oxygen levels are very high: _____

    (b) Identify two regions where carbon dioxide levels are very high: _____

2. Explain the role of haemoglobin in gas transport, particularly the significance of the reversible binding reaction:

    _____

    _____

3. Carbon monoxide (CO) is a colourless and odourless gas found in car exhaust fumes and tobacco smoke. It binds to haemoglobin 200x more strongly than oxygen and is released very slowly. Given this information, explain why:

    (a) Carbon monoxide is so toxic: _____

    _____

    (b) The blood of smokers has reduced oxygen carrying ability: _____

    _____

Related activities: The Human Respiratory System, Haemoglobins

A 2

Review of Lung Function

The respiratory system in humans and other air breathing vertebrates includes the lungs and the system of tubes through which the air reaches them. Breathing (ventilation) provides a continual supply of fresh air to the lungs and helps to maintain a large diffusion gradient for respiratory gases across the gas exchange surface. The basic rhythm of breathing is controlled by the respiratory centre in the medulla of the hindbrain. The volume of gases exchanged during breathing varies according to the physiological demands placed on the body. These changes can be measured using spirometry. Lung function and lung capacities can be affected by both obstructive and restrictive lung diseases and disorders.

Components of the respiratory system

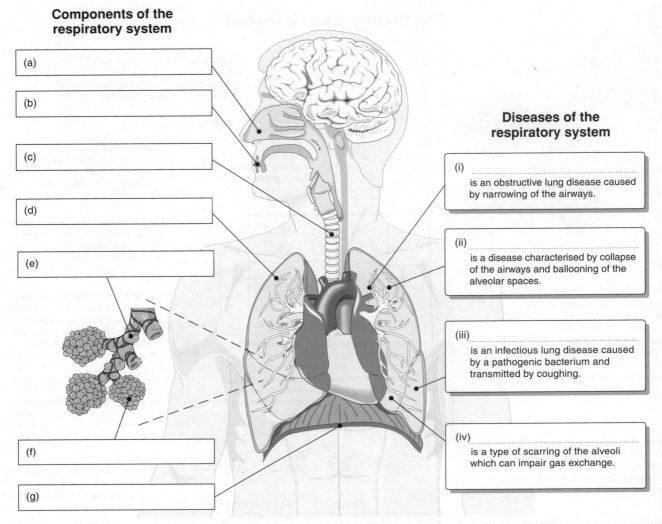

(a)

(b)

(c)

(d)

(e)

(f)

(g)

Diseases of the respiratory system

(i) _____ is an obstructive lung disease caused by narrowing of the airways.

(ii) _____ is a disease characterised by collapse of the airways and ballooning of the alveolar spaces.

(iii) _____ is an infectious lung disease caused by a pathogenic bacterium and transmitted by coughing.

(iv) _____ is a type of scarring of the alveoli which can impair gas exchange.

1. On the diagram above, label the components of the respiratory system (a-g) and the components that control the rate of breathing (i - vi).

2. Identify the volumes and capacities indicated by the letters **A - E** on the diagram of a spirogram below.

A = _____

B = _____

C = _____

D = _____

E = _____

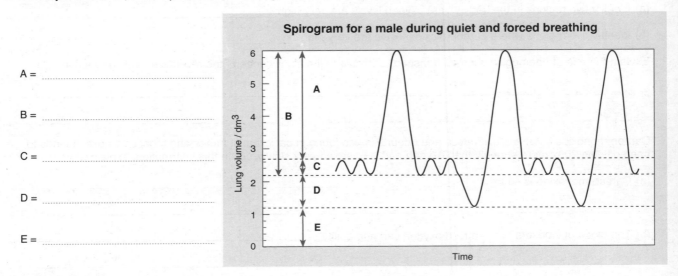

Spirogram for a male during quiet and forced breathing

Related activities: The Human Respiratory System, Breathing in Humans, Measuring Lung Function, Gas Transport in Humans

Respiratory Diseases

Respiratory diseases are diseases of the respiratory system, including diseases of the lung, bronchial tubes, trachea, and upper respiratory tract. Respiratory diseases include mild and self-limiting diseases such as the common cold, to life-threatening infections such as such as tuberculosis. One in seven people in the UK is affected by some form of chronic lung disease, the most common being asthma and chronic obstructive pulmonary disease (including emphysema and chronic bronchitis). Non-infectious respiratory diseases are categorised according to whether they prevent air reaching the alveoli (obstructive) or whether they affect the gas exchange tissue itself (restrictive).

Such diseases have different causes and different symptoms (below) but all are characterised by difficulty in breathing and the end result is similar in that gas exchange rates are too low to meet metabolic requirements. Non-infectious respiratory diseases are strongly correlated with certain behaviours and are made worse by exposure to air pollutants. Obstructive diseases, such as emphysema, are associated with an inflammatory response of the lung to noxious particles or gases, most commonly tobacco smoke. In contrast, scarring (**fibrosis**) of the lung tissue underlies restrictive lung diseases such as **asbestosis** and **silicosis** Such diseases are often called occupational lung diseases.

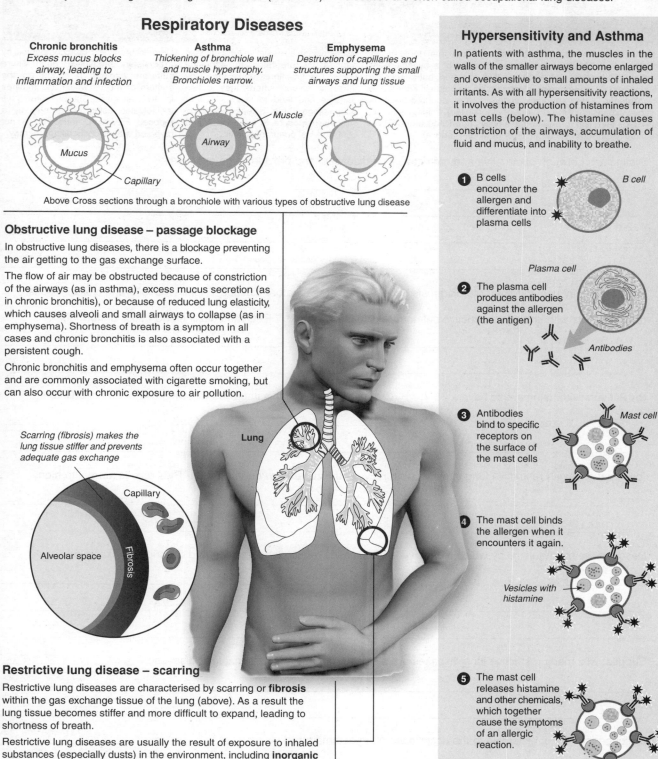

Respiratory Diseases

Chronic bronchitis
Excess mucus blocks airway, leading to inflammation and infection

Asthma
Thickening of bronchiole wall and muscle hypertrophy. Bronchioles narrow.

Emphysema
Destruction of capillaries and structures supporting the small airways and lung tissue

Mucus

Airway

Muscle

Capillary

Above Cross sections through a bronchiole with various types of obstructive lung disease

Obstructive lung disease – passage blockage

In obstructive lung diseases, there is a blockage preventing the air getting to the gas exchange surface.

The flow of air may be obstructed because of constriction of the airways (as in asthma), excess mucus secretion (as in chronic bronchitis), or because of reduced lung elasticity, which causes alveoli and small airways to collapse (as in emphysema). Shortness of breath is a symptom in all cases and chronic bronchitis is also associated with a persistent cough.

Chronic bronchitis and emphysema often occur together and are commonly associated with cigarette smoking, but can also occur with chronic exposure to air pollution.

Scarring (fibrosis) makes the lung tissue stiffer and prevents adequate gas exchange

Lung

Capillary

Alveolar space

Fibrosis

Restrictive lung disease – scarring

Restrictive lung diseases are characterised by scarring or **fibrosis** within the gas exchange tissue of the lung (above). As a result the lung tissue becomes stiffer and more difficult to expand, leading to shortness of breath.

Restrictive lung diseases are usually the result of exposure to inhaled substances (especially dusts) in the environment, including **inorganic dusts** such as silica, asbestos, or coal dust, and **organic dusts**, such as those from mouldy hay or bird droppings. Like most respiratory diseases, the symptoms are exacerbated by poor air quality.

Hypersensitivity and Asthma

In patients with asthma, the muscles in the walls of the smaller airways become enlarged and oversensitive to small amounts of inhaled irritants. As with all hypersensitivity reactions, it involves the production of histamines from mast cells (below). The histamine causes constriction of the airways, accumulation of fluid and mucus, and inability to breathe.

1 B cells encounter the allergen and differentiate into plasma cells

B cell

Plasma cell

2 The plasma cell produces antibodies against the allergen (the antigen)

Antibodies

3 Antibodies bind to specific receptors on the surface of the mast cells

Mast cell

4 The mast cell binds the allergen when it encounters it again.

Vesicles with histamine

5 The mast cell releases histamine and other chemicals, which together cause the symptoms of an allergic reaction.

Gas Exchange at the Lungs

Related activities: Measuring Lung Function, Antibodies, Diseases Caused by Smoking

RA 2

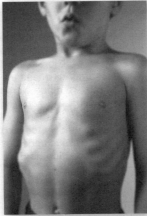  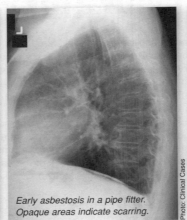 

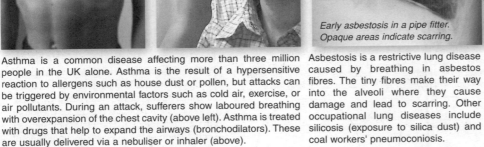

Early asbestosis in a pipe fitter.
Opaque areas indicate scarring.

Photo: Clinical Cases

Asthma is a common disease affecting more than three million people in the UK alone. Asthma is the result of a hypersensitive reaction to allergens such as house dust or pollen, but attacks can be triggered by environmental factors such as cold air, exercise, or air pollutants. During an attack, sufferers show laboured breathing with overexpansion of the chest cavity (above left). Asthma is treated with drugs that help to expand the airways (bronchodilators). These are usually delivered via a nebuliser or inhaler (above).

Asbestosis is a restrictive lung disease caused by breathing in asbestos fibres. The tiny fibres make their way into the alveoli where they cause damage and lead to scarring. Other occupational lung diseases include silicosis (exposure to silica dust) and coal workers' pneumoconiosis.

Chronic bronchitis is accompanied by a persistent, productive cough, where sufferers attempt to cough up the sputum or mucus which accumulates in the airways. Chronic bronchitis is indicated using **spirometry** by a reduced FEV_1/FVC ratio that is not reversed with bronchodilator therapy.

1. Distinguish between obstructive and restrictive lung diseases, and provide some examples:

   _____
   _____
   _____
   _____

2. Physicians may use spirometry to diagnosis certain types of respiratory disease. Explain the following typical results:

   (a) In patients with chronic obstructive pulmonary disease, the FEV_1 / FVC ratio declines (to <70% of normal):

   _____
   _____

   (b) Patients with asthma also have a FEV_1 / FVC ratio of <70%, but this improves following use of bronchodilators:

   _____
   _____

   (c) In patients with restrictive lung disease, both FEV_1 and FVC are low but the FEV_1 / FVC ratio is normal to high:

   _____
   _____

3. Describe the mechanisms by which restrictive lung diseases reduce lung function and describe an example:

   _____
   _____
   _____

4. Suggest why many restrictive lung diseases are also classified as occupational lung diseases: _____

   _____
   _____

5. Describe the role of histamine in the occurrence of an asthma attack: _____

   _____
   _____

Diseases Caused by Smoking

Tobacco smoking has only recently been accepted as a major health hazard, despite its practice in developed countries for more than 400 years, and much longer elsewhere. Cigarettes became popular at the end of World War I because they were cheap, convenient, and easier to smoke than pipes and cigars. They remain popular for the further reason that they are more addictive than other forms of tobacco. The milder smoke can be more readily inhaled, allowing **nicotine** (a powerful addictive poison) to be quickly absorbed into the bloodstream. **Lung cancer** is the most widely known and most harmful effect of smoking. Tobacco smoking is also directly associated with coronary artery disease, emphysema, chronic bronchitis, peripheral vascular disease, and stroke. Despite recent indications that mortality due to smoking may be declining in the UK, one third of all deaths from cancer, including around 80% of lung cancer deaths, are linked to this cause. The damaging components of cigarette smoke include tar, carbon monoxide, nitrogen dioxide, and nitric oxide. Many of these harmful chemicals occur in greater concentrations in sidestream smoke (**passive smoking**) than in mainstream smoke (inhaled) due to the presence of a filter in the cigarette.

Long term effects of tobacco smoking

Smoking damages the arteries of the brain and may result in a **stroke**.

All forms of tobacco-smoking increase the risk of **mouth cancer, lip cancer**, and **cancer of the throat** (pharynx).

Lung cancer is the best known harmful effect of smoking.

In a young man who smokes 20 cigarettes a day, the risk of **coronary artery disease** is increased by about three times over that of a nonsmoker.

Smoking leads to severe constriction of the arteries supplying blood to the extremities and leads to **peripheral vascular disease**.

Short term effects of tobacco smoking

- Reduction in capacity of the lungs.
- Increase in muscle tension and a decrease in steadiness of the hands.
- Raised blood pressure (10-30 points).
- Very sharp rise in carbon monoxide levels in the lungs contributing to breathlessness.
- Increase in pulse rate by up to 20 beats per minute.
- Surface blood vessel constriction drops skin temperature by up to 5°C.
- Dulling of appetite as well as the sense of smell and taste.

How smoking damages the lungs

Non-smoker

Normal alveoli arrangement

Thin layer of mucus

Cilia

Cells lining airways

Smoker

Coalesced alveoli

Extra mucus produced

Smoke particles

Cancerous cell

Smoke particles indirectly destroy the walls of the lung's alveoli.

Cavities lined by heavy black tar deposits.

SPECIMEN A-73-309 DATE

Gross pathology of lung tissue from a patient with emphysema. Tobacco tar deposits can be seen. Tar contains at least 17 known carcinogens.

Gas Exchange at the Lungs

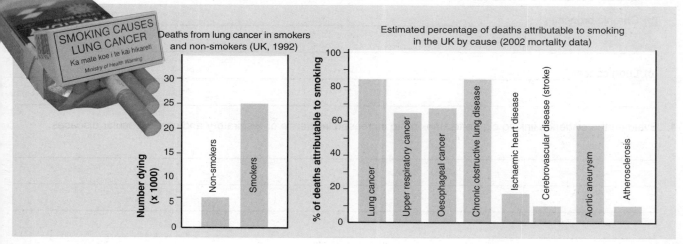

SMOKING CAUSES LUNG CANCER
Ka mate koe i te kai hikareti
Ministry of Health Warning

Deaths from lung cancer in smokers and non-smokers (UK, 1992)

Number dying (x 1000)

Non-smokers / Smokers

Estimated percentage of deaths attributable to smoking in the UK by cause (2002 mortality data)

% of deaths attributable to smoking

Lung cancer / Upper respiratory cancer / Oesophageal cancer / Chronic obstructive lung disease / Ischaemic heart disease / Cerebrovascular disease (stroke) / Aortic aneurysm / Atherosclerosis

Related activities: Respiratory Diseases, Cardiovascular Disease

RDA 2

Components of Cigarette Smoke

Particulate Phase

Nicotine: a highly addictive alkaloid

Tar: composed of many chemicals

Benzene: carcinogenic hydrocarbon

Gas Phase

Carbon monoxide: a poisonous gas

Ammonia: a pungent, colourless gas

Formaldehyde: a carcinogen

Hydrogen cyanide: a highly poisonous gas

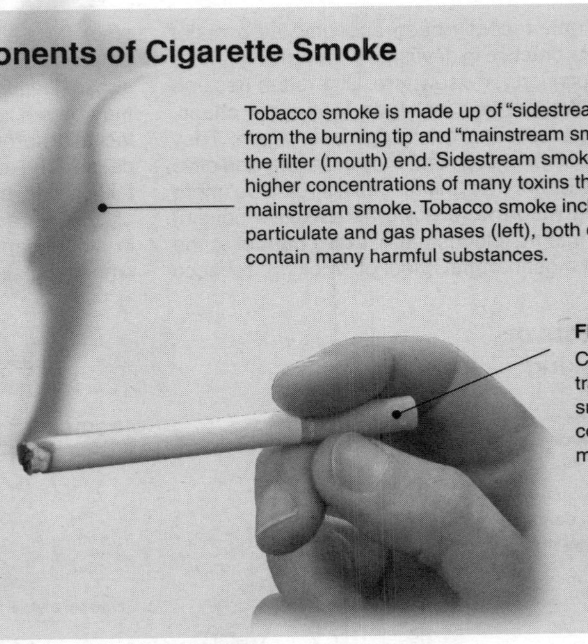

Tobacco smoke is made up of "sidestream smoke" from the burning tip and "mainstream smoke" from the filter (mouth) end. Sidestream smoke contains higher concentrations of many toxins than mainstream smoke. Tobacco smoke includes both particulate and gas phases (left), both of which contain many harmful substances.

Filter
Cellulose acetate filters trap some of the tar and smoke particles. They cool the smoke slightly, making it easier to inhale.

1. Discuss the physical changes to the lung that result from long-term smoking:

_____

_____

_____

_____

2. Determine the physiological effect of each of the following constituents of tobacco smoke when inhaled:

(a) Tar: _____

_____

(b) Nicotine: _____

_____

(c) Carbon monoxide: _____

_____

3. Describe the symptoms of the following diseases associated with long-term smoking:

(a) Emphysema: _____

_____

(b) Chronic bronchitis: _____

_____

(c) Lung cancer: _____

_____

4. Evaluate the evidence linking cigarette smoking to increased incidence of respiratory and cardiovascular diseases:

_____

_____

_____

_____

Tuberculosis

Tuberculosis (TB) is a contagious disease caused by the bacterium *Mycobacterium tuberculosis* (MTB). TB can affect many areas of the body, but the most common form, **pulmonary TB**, affects the lungs. Symptoms of pulmonary TB include a productive cough, and presence of the disease is indicated on a chest X-ray by opaque areas and large thick walled cavities in the lungs resulting from bacterial damage. Globally, TB is very widespread, and the emergence of drug resistance is contributing to the increasingly harmful impact of the disease. Effective treatment requires an aggressive and prolonged regime of antibiotics, and patient compliance with treatment is one problem to overcome. Given its current rate of spread, the WHO anticipate that approximately 1000 million people will be newly infected, over 150 million people will get sick, and 36 million will die from TB between 2002 and 2020.

Pulmonary Tuberculosis

Infection and Transmission

TB is a contagious disease, and is spread through the air when infectious people cough, sneeze, talk, or spit (below). Transmission of TB does not require a large inoculum; a person needs to inhale only a small number of *Mycobacterium tuberculosis* (MTB) to be infected.

Left untreated, each person with active TB will infect on average between 10 and 15 people every year. People infected with MTB will not necessarily become ill with the disease. The immune system can 'wall off' the MTB which can lie dormant for years, protected by a thick waxy coat. When the immune system is weakened, the chance of becoming ill (showing active symptoms) is much greater.

Symptoms

TB usually affects the lungs, but it can also affect other parts of the body, such as the brain, the kidneys, and the spine. The general symptoms of TB include weakness and nausea, weight loss, fever, and night sweats. The specific symptoms of pulmonary TB of include coughing, chest pain, and coughing up blood. The bacteria can spread from the bronchioles to other body systems, where the symptoms depend on the part of the body that is affected.

Effect on Lung Function

When MTB is inhaled, bacilli reach the lungs, where they are ingested by an alveolar macrophages (by phagocytosis). Usually the macrophages destroy the bacteria, but if they do not, they protect the microbes from the body's defences, and the bacilli survive and multiply within the macrophages. More macrophages are attracted to the area and a tubercle forms (hence the name of the disease). The disease may become dormant or the tubercle may rupture, releasing bacilli into the bronchioles (diagram, lower right).

Affected tissue is replaced by scarring (fibrosis) and cavities filled with cheese-like white necrotic material. During active disease, some of these cavities are joined to the air passages and this material can be coughed up. It contains living bacteria and can therefore pass on infection.

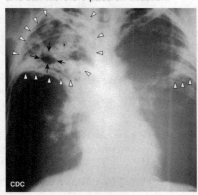

Above: Xray of lungs affected by pulmonary TB. The white triangles indicate areas where the airspaces of the lung are congested with fluid, and the dark arrows indicate a cavity, from which infective material is coughed up. Surface area for gas exchange is reduced and lung function is adversely affected.

Stages in TB Infection

The series below illustrates stages in MTB infection.

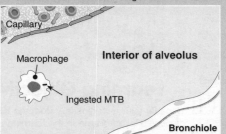

MTB enter the lung and are ingested by macrophages (phagocytic white blood cells).

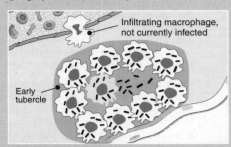

The multiplying bacteria cause the macrophages to swell and rupture. The newly released bacilli infect other macrophages. At this stage a tubercle may form and the disease may lie dormant.

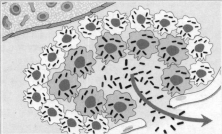

Eventually the tubercle ruptures, allowing bacilli to spill into the bronchiole. The bacilli can now be transmitted when the infected person coughs.

Gas Exchange at the Lungs

1. (a) Describe how TB infection affects the structure and function of the lung: _____

   _____

   _____

   _____

   (b) Relate this to the way in which TB is transmitted: _____

   _____

2. Explain how MTB may exist in a dormant state in a person for many years without causing disease symptoms:

   _____

   _____

Related activities: Prokaryotic Cells, The Human Respiratory System, Respiratory Diseases   **Web links**: Microbiology in Motion

RA 2

The Human Heart

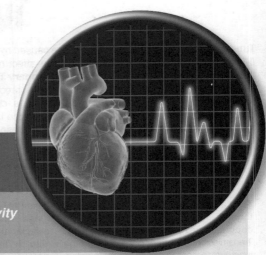

Unit 1: Biology and Disease

1.5 The human heart

Structure of the human heart, control of heart activity (including the effects of exercise), heart disease

Learning Objectives

☐ 1. Compile your own glossary from the **KEY WORDS** displayed in **bold type** in the learning objectives below.

Heart Structure & Function *(pages 119-126)*

☐ 2. Describe the internal and external gross structure of the human **heart** in relation to its function. On diagrams identify **atria**, **ventricles**, **atrioventricular valves**, and **semilunar valves**, as well the major vessels and the coronary circulation. Relate the differences in the thickness of the heart chambers to their functions.

☐ 3. Describe the **cardiac cycle**, relating stages in the cycle (**atrial systole**, **ventricular systole**, and **diastole**) to the maintenance of blood flow through the heart. Describe valve movements during the cycle. Analyse and interpret data relating to changes in blood pressure and myocardial volume during the cardiac cycle.

☐ 4. Describe how the heart beat is initiated and maintained, identifying the role of the **sinoatrial node** (SAN), the **atrioventricular node** (AVN), the **bundle of His**, and the **Purkinje fibres**. Relate the activity of the SAN to the **intrinsic heart rate**.

☐ 5. If required, describe the extrinsic regulation of **heart rate** through the **autonomic nervous system**.

☐ 6. Interpret and explain an electrocardiogram (ECG) with respect to both normal and abnormal heart activity.

☐ 7. Describe how **cardiac output** is calculated as a product of **stroke volume** and **heart rate**. Interpret data relating to cardiac output in different situations, for example at rest and during exercise.

Cardiovascular Disease *(pages 127-130)*

☐ 8. Recognise the term **cardiovascular disease** (CVD), as a broad term encompassing a variety of diseases, including **coronary heart disease**. Distinguish between different forms of cardiovascular disease, e.g. **atherosclerosis** and **hypertension**.

☐ 9. Describe the biological basis of **coronary heart disease**, including the development of atheromata (*sing*. **atheroma**) in the vessels associated with the heart. Recognise atherosclerosis (hardening of the arteries) as a chronic inflammatory disease of the arteries characterised by the presence of multiple atheromata. Explain the link between atheromata and:
  (a) Increased risk of aneurysm
  (b) Increased risk of thrombosis and stroke.

☐ 10. Explain the causes and symptoms of myocardial infarction. Describe risk factors associated with the development of coronary heart disease, including:
  (a) Diet (highly processed, high fat) and obesity
  (b) Blood cholesterol (particular the LDL;HDL ratio)
  (c) Cigarette (tobacco) smoking
  (d) Hypertension (high blood pressure)

☐ 11. Describe and explain data relating to the relationship between specific risk factors and the incidence of coronary heart disease.

☐ 12. EXTENSION: Explain how exercise reduces the risk of developing certain diseases, including coronary heart disease, stroke, diabetes, and obesity. Explain how regular, moderate exercise can counter the influence of other risk factors.

Textbooks

See the 'Textbook Reference Grid' on page 7 for textbook page references relating to material in this topic.

Supplementary Texts

See pages 5-6 for additional details of these texts:
■ Adds, J. *et al*., 2004. **Exchange & Transport, Energy & Ecosystems** (Nelson Thornes), chpt. 2.
■ Clegg, C.J., 1998. **Mammals: Structure and Function** (John Murray), pp. 24-47.
■ Fullick, A., 2000. **Human Health and Disease** (Heinemann), chpt. 3 especially pp. 74-85.

Presentation MEDIA to support this topic:

HEALTH & DISEASE: Non-Infectious Disease

Periodicals

See page 6 for details of publishers of periodicals:

STUDENT'S REFERENCE
■ **Keeping Pace - Cardiac Muscle and Heartbeat** Biol. Sci. Rev., 19(3), Feb. 2007, pp. 21-24. *Cardiac muscle cells generate electrical activity like nerve impulses, and these impulses produce smooth contraction of the heart muscle.*
■ **A Fair Exchange** Biol. Sci. Rev., 13(1), Sept. 2000, pp. 2-5. *Formation and reabsorption of tissue fluid (includes disorders of fluid balance).*
■ **Mending Broken Hearts** National Geographic, 211(2), Feb. 2007, pp. 40-65. *Heart disease is becoming more prevalent- assessing susceptibility is the key to treating the disease more effectively.*
■ **Heart Disease and Cholesterol** Biol. Sci. Rev., 13(2) Nov. 2000, pp. 2-5. *The links between dietary fat, cholesterol level, and heart disease.*
■ **Coronary Heart Disease** Biol. Sci. Rev., 18(1) Sept. 2005, pp. 21-24. *Cardiovascular disease: symptoms, risk factors and treatments.*

■ **Atherosclerosis: The New View** Sci. American, May 2002, pp. 28-37. *The pathological development and rupture of plaques in atherosclerosis.*

Internet

See pages 8-9 for details of how to access **Bio Links** from our web site: **www.biozone.co.uk**. From Bio Links, access sites under the topics:

GENERAL BIOLOGY ONLINE RESOURCES
• Biology I interactive animations *... and others*
> **Online Textbooks and Lecture Notes**: •
Human biology help • Learn.co.uk *... and others*

ANIMAL BIOLOGY: • Anatomy and physiology • Human physiology lecture notes... *and others*
> **Circulatory System**: • How the heart works •
The matter of the human heart *... and others*

HEALTH & DISEASE: > **Non-Infectious Diseases**: • Cardiology compass • Heart disease • NOVA Online: Cut to the heart

The Human Heart

The heart is the centre of the human cardiovascular system. It is a hollow, muscular organ, weighing on average 342 grams. Each day it beats over 100 000 times to pump 3780 litres of blood through 100 000 kilometres of blood vessels. It comprises a system of four muscular chambers (two **atria** and two **ventricles**) that alternately fill and empty of blood, acting as a double pump.

The left side pumps blood to the body tissues and the right side pumps blood to the lungs. The heart lies between the lungs, to the left of the body's midline, and it is surrounded by a double layered **pericardium** of tough fibrous connective tissue. The pericardium prevents overdistension of the heart and anchors the heart within the **mediastinum**.

Human Heart Structure
(sectioned, anterior view)

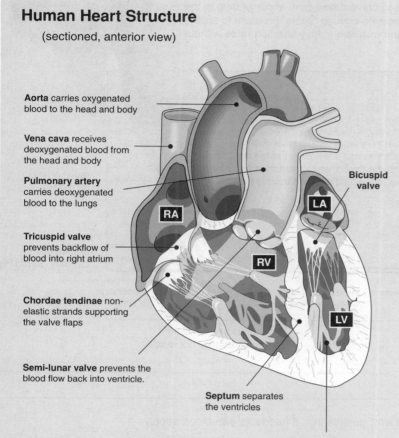

Aorta carries oxygenated blood to the head and body

Vena cava receives deoxygenated blood from the head and body

Pulmonary artery carries deoxygenated blood to the lungs

Tricuspid valve prevents backflow of blood into right atrium

Chordae tendinae non-elastic strands supporting the valve flaps

Semi-lunar valve prevents the blood flow back into ventricle.

Bicuspid valve

RA
RV
LA
LV

Septum separates the ventricles

The heart is not a symmetrical organ. Although the quantity of blood pumped by each side is the same, the walls of the left ventricle are thicker and more muscular than those of the right ventricle. The difference affects the shape of the ventricular cavities, so the right ventricle is twisted over the left.

Key to abbreviations

RA Right atrium; receives deoxygenated blood via anterior and posterior vena cavae

RV Right ventricle; pumps deoxygenated blood to the lungs via the pulmonary artery

LA Left atrium; receives blood returning to the heart from the lungs via the pulmonary veins

LV Left ventricle; pumps oxygenated blood to the head and body via the aorta

Top view of a heart in section, showing valves

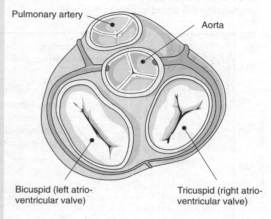

Pulmonary artery

Aorta

Bicuspid (left atrio-ventricular valve)

Tricuspid (right atrio-ventricular valve)

Posterior view of heart

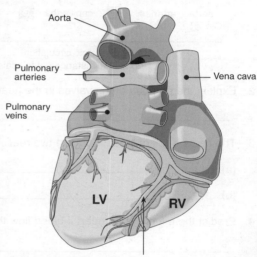

Aorta

Pulmonary arteries

Vena cava

Pulmonary veins

LV

RV

Coronary arteries: The high oxygen demands of the heart muscle are met by a dense capillary network. Coronary arteries arise from the aorta and spread over the surface of the heart supplying the cardiac muscle with oxygenated blood. Deoxygenated blood is collected by cardiac veins and returned to the right atrium via a large coronary sinus.

1. In the schematic diagram of the heart, below, label the four chambers and the main vessels entering and leaving them. The arrows indicate the direction of blood flow. Use large coloured circles to mark the position of each of the four valves.

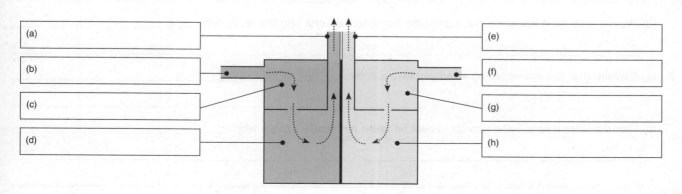

(a)
(b)
(c)
(d)
(e)
(f)
(g)
(h)

Related activities: Review of the Human Heart
Web links: Anatomy of the Heart

RA 2

Pressure Changes and the Asymmetry of the Heart

The heart is not a symmetrical organ. The left ventricle and its associated arteries are thicker and more muscular than the corresponding structures on the right side. This asymmetry is related to the necessary pressure differences between the pulmonary (lung) and systemic (body) circulations (not to the distance over which the blood is pumped per se). The graph below shows changes blood pressure in each of the major blood vessel types in the systemic and pulmonary circuits (the horizontal distance not to scale). The pulmonary circuit must operate at a much lower pressure than the systemic circuit to prevent fluid from accumulating in the alveoli of the lungs. The left side of the heart must develop enough "spare" pressure to enable increased blood flow to the muscles of the body and maintain kidney filtration rates without decreasing the blood supply to the brain.

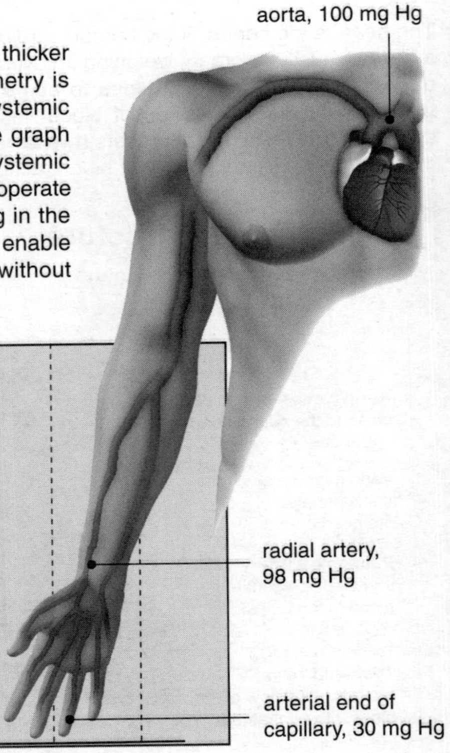

aorta, 100 mg Hg

Blood pressure during contraction (systole)

Blood pressure during contraction (diastole)

The greatest fall in pressure occurs when the blood moves into the capillaries, even though the distance through the capillaries represents only a tiny proportion of the total distance travelled.

Pressure /mm Hg

radial artery, 98 mg Hg

arterial end of capillary, 30 mg Hg

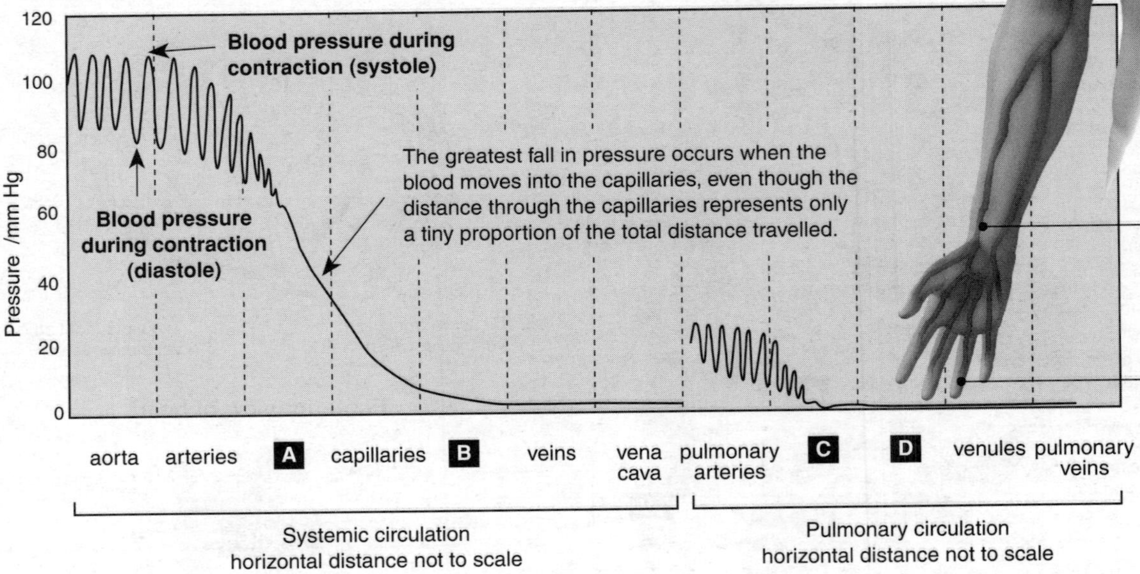

aorta   arteries   **A**   capillaries   **B**   veins   vena cava   pulmonary arteries   **C**   **D**   venules   pulmonary veins

Systemic circulation
horizontal distance not to scale

Pulmonary circulation
horizontal distance not to scale

2. Explain the purpose of the valves in the heart: _____

_____

3. The heart is full of blood. Suggest two reasons why, despite this, it needs its own blood supply:

(a) _____

(b) _____

4. Predict the effect on the heart if blood flow through a coronary artery is restricted or blocked: _____

_____

_____

5. Identify the vessels corresponding to the letters **A-D** on the graph above:

A: _____   B: _____   C: _____   D: _____

6. (a) Find out what is meant by the pulse pressure and explain how it is calculated: _____

_____

(b) Predict what happens to the pulse pressure between the aorta and the capillaries: _____

_____

7. (a) Explain what you are recording when you take a pulse: _____

_____

(b) Name a place where pulse rate could best be taken and briefly explain why: _____

_____

_____

Control of Heart Activity

When removed from the body the cardiac muscle continues to beat. Therefore, the origin of the heartbeat is **myogenic**: the contractions arise as an intrinsic property of the cardiac muscle itself. The heartbeat is regulated by a special conduction system consisting of the pacemaker (**sinoatrial node**) and specialised conduction fibres called **Purkinje fibres**. The pacemaker sets a basic rhythm for the heart, but this rate is influenced by the cardiovascular control centre in the medulla in response to sensory information from pressure receptors in the walls of the heart and blood vessels, and by higher brain functions. Changing the rate and force of heart contraction is the main mechanism for controlling cardiac output in order to meet changing demands.

Generation of the Heartbeat

The basic rhythmic heartbeat is **myogenic**. The nodal cells (SAN and atrioventricular node) spontaneously generate rhythmic action potentials without neural stimulation. The normal resting rate of self-excitation of the SAN is about 50 beats per minute.

The amount of blood ejected from the left ventricle per minute is called the **cardiac output**. It is determined by the **stroke volume** (the volume of blood ejected with each contraction) and the **heart rate** (number of heart beats per minute).

Cardiac output

= stroke volume x heart rate

Cardiac muscle responds to stretching by contracting more strongly. The greater the blood volume entering the ventricle, the greater the force of contraction. This relationship is known as **Starling's Law**.

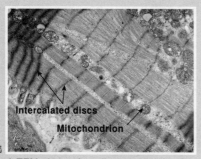

A TEM photo of cardiac muscle showing branched fibres (muscle cells). Each muscle fibre has one or two nuclei and many large mitochondria. **Intercalated discs** are specialised electrical junctions that separate the cells and allow the rapid spread of impulses through the heart muscle.

Sinoatrial node (SAN) is also called the **pacemaker**. It is a mass of specialised muscle cells near the opening of the superior vena cava. The pacemaker initiates the cardiac cycle, spontaneously generating action potentials that cause the atria to contract. The SAN sets the basic pace of the heart rate, although this rate is influenced by hormones and impulses from the autonomic nervous system.

Atrioventricular node (AVN) at the base of the atrium briefly delays the impulse to allow time for the atrial contraction to finish before the ventricles contract.

Bundle of His (atrioventricular bundle) containing Purkinje tissue. A tract of conducting fibres that distribute the action potentials over the ventricles causing ventricular contraction.

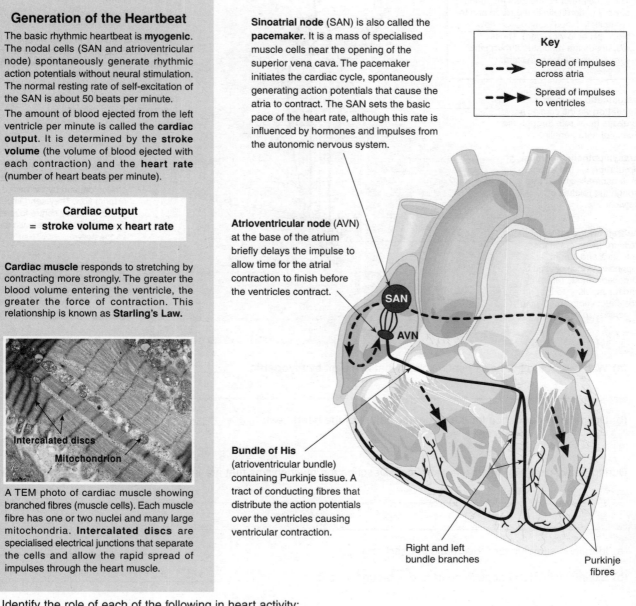

Key

- - → Spread of impulses across atria

- - ►► Spread of impulses to ventricles

SAN

AVN

Right and left bundle branches

Purkinje fibres

---

1. Identify the role of each of the following in heart activity:

   (a) The sinoatrial node: _____

   (b) The atrioventricular node: _____

   (c) The bundle of His: _____

2. Explain the significance of the delay in impulse conduction at the AVN: _____

   _____

3. (a) Calculate the cardiac output when stroke volume is 70 cm^3 and the heart rate is 70 beats per minute:

   _____

   (b) Trained endurance athletes have a very high cardiac output. Suggest how this is achieved: _____

   _____

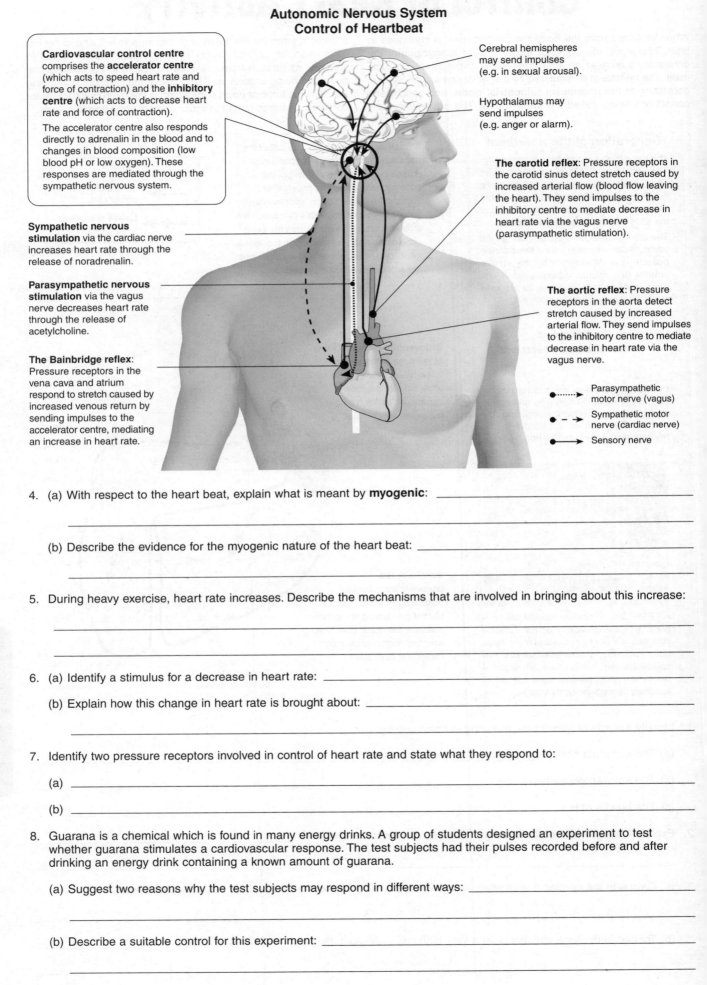

Autonomic Nervous System
Control of Heartbeat

Cardiovascular control centre comprises the **accelerator centre** (which acts to speed heart rate and force of contraction) and the **inhibitory centre** (which acts to decrease heart rate and force of contraction).

The accelerator centre also responds directly to adrenalin in the blood and to changes in blood composition (low blood pH or low oxygen). These responses are mediated through the sympathetic nervous system.

Sympathetic nervous stimulation via the cardiac nerve increases heart rate through the release of noradrenalin.

Parasympathetic nervous stimulation via the vagus nerve decreases heart rate through the release of acetylcholine.

The Bainbridge reflex: Pressure receptors in the vena cava and atrium respond to stretch caused by increased venous return by sending impulses to the accelerator centre, mediating an increase in heart rate.

Cerebral hemispheres may send impulses (e.g. in sexual arousal).

Hypothalamus may send impulses (e.g. anger or alarm).

The carotid reflex: Pressure receptors in the carotid sinus detect stretch caused by increased arterial flow (blood flow leaving the heart). They send impulses to the inhibitory centre to mediate decrease in heart rate via the vagus nerve (parasympathetic stimulation).

The aortic reflex: Pressure receptors in the aorta detect stretch caused by increased arterial flow. They send impulses to the inhibitory centre to mediate decrease in heart rate via the vagus nerve.

● ······▶ Parasympathetic motor nerve (vagus)

● – –▶ Sympathetic motor nerve (cardiac nerve)

● ——▶ Sensory nerve

4. (a) With respect to the heart beat, explain what is meant by **myogenic**: _____

_____

   (b) Describe the evidence for the myogenic nature of the heart beat: _____

_____

5. During heavy exercise, heart rate increases. Describe the mechanisms that are involved in bringing about this increase:

_____

_____

6. (a) Identify a stimulus for a decrease in heart rate: _____

   (b) Explain how this change in heart rate is brought about: _____

_____

7. Identify two pressure receptors involved in control of heart rate and state what they respond to:

   (a) _____

   (b) _____

8. Guarana is a chemical which is found in many energy drinks. A group of students designed an experiment to test whether guarana stimulates a cardiovascular response. The test subjects had their pulses recorded before and after drinking an energy drink containing a known amount of guarana.

   (a) Suggest two reasons why the test subjects may respond in different ways: _____

_____

   (b) Describe a suitable control for this experiment: _____

_____

The Cardiac Cycle

The heart pumps with alternate contractions (**systole**) and relaxations (**diastole**). The **cardiac cycle** refers to the sequence of events of a heartbeat and involves three major stages: atrial systole, ventricular systole and complete cardiac diastole. Pressure changes within the heart's chambers generated by the cycle of contraction and relaxation are responsible for blood movement and cause the heart valves to open and close, preventing the backflow of blood. The noise of the blood when the valves open and close produces the heartbeat sound (**lubb-dupp**). The heart beat occurs in response to electrical impulses, which can be recorded as a trace, called an **electrocardiogram** or **ECG**. The ECG pattern is the result of the different impulses produced at each phase of cardiac cycle, and each part is identified with a letter code. An ECG provides a useful method of monitoring changes in heart rate and activity and detection of heart disorders. The electrical trace is accompanied by volume and pressure changes (below).

The Cardiac Cycle

The **pulse** results from the rhythmic expansion of the arteries as the blood spurts from the left ventricle. Pulse rate therefore corresponds to heart rate.

Stage 1: Atrial systole and ventricular filling The ventricles relax and blood flows into them from the atria. Note that 70% of the blood from the atria flows passively into the ventricles. It is during the last third of ventricular filling that the atria contract.

Stage 2: Ventricular systole The atria relax, the ventricles contract, and blood is pumped from the ventricles into the aorta and the pulmonary artery. The start of ventricular contraction coincides with the first heart sound.

Stage 3: (not shown) There is a short period of atrial and ventricular relaxation (diastole). Semilunar valves (**SLV**) close to prevent backflow into the ventricles (see diagram, left). The cycle begins again. For a heart beating at 75 beats per minute, one cardiac cycle lasts about 0.8 seconds.

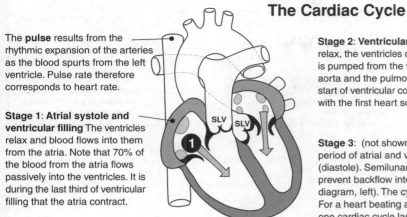

Heart during ventricular filling

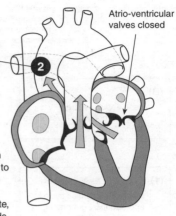

Atrio-ventricular valves closed

Heart during ventricular contraction

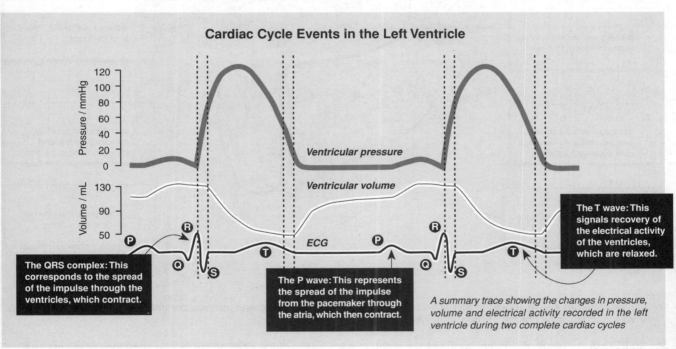

Cardiac Cycle Events in the Left Ventricle

Ventricular pressure

Ventricular volume

ECG

The QRS complex: This corresponds to the spread of the impulse through the ventricles, which contract.

The P wave: This represents the spread of the impulse from the pacemaker through the atria, which then contract.

The T wave: This signals recovery of the electrical activity of the ventricles, which are relaxed.

A summary trace showing the changes in pressure, volume and electrical activity recorded in the left ventricle during two complete cardiac cycles

The Human Heart

1. Identify each of the following phases of an ECG by its international code:

   (a) Excitation of the ventricles and ventricular systole: _____

   (b) Electrical recovery of the ventricles and ventricular diastole: _____

   (c) Excitation of the atria and atrial systole: _____

2. Suggest the physiological reason for the period of electrical recovery experienced each cycle (the T wave):

   _____

3. Using the letters indicated, mark the points on trace above corresponding to each of the following:

   (a) E: Ejection of blood from the ventricle

   (b) AVC: Closing of the atrioventricular valve

   (c) FV: Filling of the ventricle

   (d) AVO: Opening of the atrioventricular valve

Related activities: The Human Heart, Review of the Human Heart
Web links: Electrocardiogram, Cardiac Cycle Animation

RA 2

Review of the Human Heart

Large, complex organisms require a circulatory system to transport materials because diffusion is too inefficient and slow to supply all the cells of the body adequately. The circulatory system in humans transports nutrients, respiratory gases, wastes, and hormones, aids in regulating body temperature and maintaining fluid balance, and has a role in internal defence. All circulatory systems comprise a network of vessels, a circulatory fluid (blood), and a heart. This activity summarises key features of the structure and function of the human heart. The information for this activity can be found in the pages earlier in this topic.

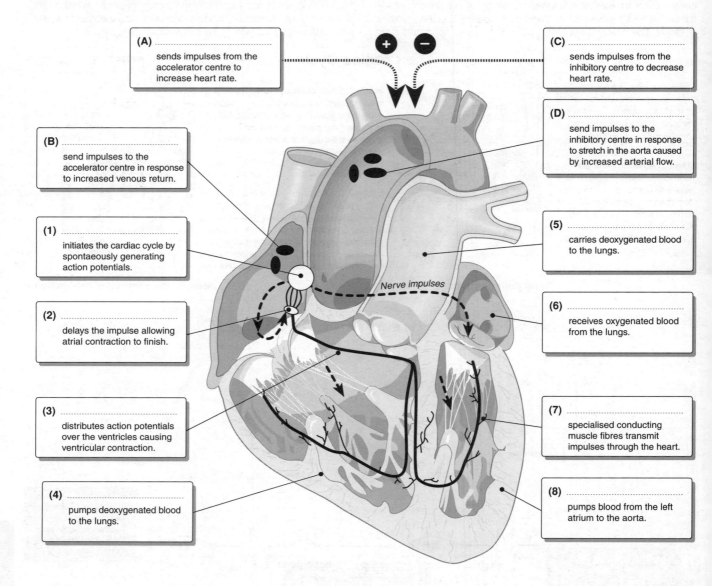

(A) ....
sends impulses from the accelerator centre to increase heart rate.

(C) ....
sends impulses from the inhibitory centre to decrease heart rate.

(D) ....
send impulses to the inhibitory centre in response to stretch in the aorta caused by increased arterial flow.

(B) ....
send impulses to the accelerator centre in response to increased venous return.

(1) ....
initiates the cardiac cycle by spontaeously generating action potentials.

(5) ....
carries deoxygenated blood to the lungs.

(2) ....
delays the impulse allowing atrial contraction to finish.

(6) ....
receives oxygenated blood from the lungs.

Nerve impulses

(3) ....
distributes action potentials over the ventricles causing ventricular contraction.

(7) ....
specialised conducting muscle fibres transmit impulses through the heart.

(4) ....
pumps deoxygenated blood to the lungs.

(8) ....
pumps blood from the left atrium to the aorta.

1. On the diagram above, label the identified components of heart structure and intrinsic control (**1-8**), and the components involved in extrinsic control of heart rate (**A-D**).

2. An **ECG** is the result of different impulses produced at each phase of the **cardiac cycle** (the sequence of events in a heartbeat). For each electrical event indicated in the ECG below, describe the corresponding event in the cardiac cycle:

A ---
The spread of the impulse from the pacemaker (sinoatrial node) through the atria.

B ---
The spread of the impulse through the ventricles.

C ---
Recovery of the electrical activity of the ventricles.

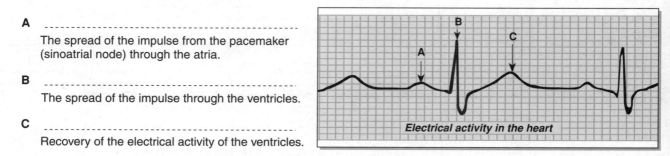

Electrical activity in the heart

3. Describe one treatment that may be indicated when heart rhythm is erratic or too slow: _____

_____

Exercise and Blood Flow

Exercise promotes health by improving the rate of blood flow back to the heart (called the venous return). This is achieved by strengthening all types of muscle and by increasing the efficiency of the heart. During exercise blood flow to different parts of the body changes in order to cope with the extra demands of the muscles, the heart, and the lungs.

1. The following table gives data for the **rate** of blood flow to various parts of the body at rest and during strenuous exercise. **Calculate** the **percentage** of the total blood flow that each organ or tissue receives under each regime of activity.

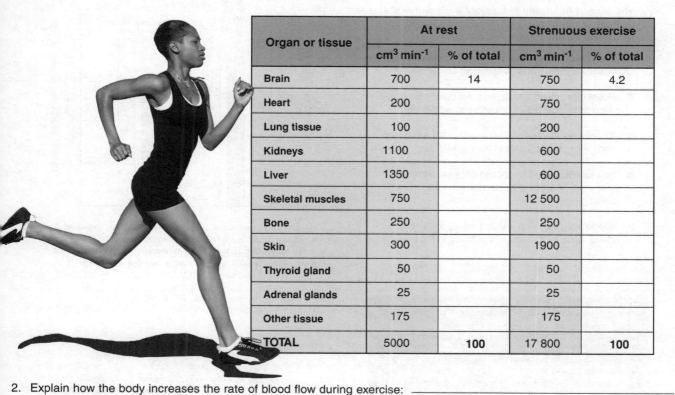

Organ or tissue	At rest		Strenuous exercise	
	cm³ min⁻¹	% of total	cm³ min⁻¹	% of total
Brain	700	14	750	4.2
Heart	200		750	
Lung tissue	100		200	
Kidneys	1100		600	
Liver	1350		600	
Skeletal muscles	750		12 500	
Bone	250		250	
Skin	300		1900	
Thyroid gland	50		50	
Adrenal glands	25		25	
Other tissue	175		175	
TOTAL	5000	**100**	17 800	**100**

2. Explain how the body increases the rate of blood flow during exercise: _____

_____

_____

3. (a) State approximately how many times the total rate of blood flow increases between rest and exercise: _____

(b) Explain why the increase is necessary: _____

_____

_____

4. (a) Identify which organs or tissues show no change in the rate of blood flow with exercise: _____

_____

(b) Explain why this is the case: _____

_____

_____

5. (a) Identify which organs or tissues show the most change in the rate of blood flow with exercise: _____

_____

(b) Explain why this is the case: _____

_____

_____

_____

The Human Heart

Related activities: Control of Heart Activity, The Health Benefits of Exercise

DA 2

Endurance refers to the ability of the muscles and the cardiovascular and respiratory systems to carry out exercise. Muscular endurance allows sprinters to run fast for a short time or body builders and weight lifters to lift an immense weight and hold it for a few seconds. Cardiovascular and respiratory endurance refer to the body as a whole: the ability to endure a high level of activity over a prolonged period. This type of endurance is seen in marathon runners, and long distance swimmers and cyclists. Different sports ("short burst sports" compared with endurance type sports) require different training methods and the physiologies (muscle bulk and cardiovascular fitness) of the athletes can be quite different.

The human heart and circulatory system make a number of adjustments in response to aerobic or endurance training. These include:

- **Heart size**: Increases. The left ventricle wall becomes thicker and its chamber bigger.

- **Heart rate**: Heart rate (at rest and during exercise) decreases markedly from non-trained people.

- **Recovery**: Recovery after exercise (of breathing and heart rate) is faster in trained athletes.

- **Stroke volume**: The volume of blood pumped with each heart beat increases with endurance training.

- **Blood volume**: Endurance training increases blood volume (the amount of blood in the body).

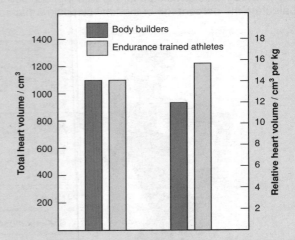

Difference in heart size of highly trained body builders and endurance athletes. Total heart volume is compared to heart volume as related to body weight. Average weights as follows: Body builders = 90.1 kg. Endurance athletes = 68.7 kg.

Weightlifters have good muscular endurance; they lift extremely heavy weights and hold them for a short time. Typical sports with high muscular endurance but lower cardiovascular endurance are sprinting, weight lifting, body building, boxing and wrestling.

Distance runners have very good cardiovascular and respiratory endurance; they sustain high intensity exercise for a long time. Typical sports needing cardiovascular endurance are distance running, cycling, and swimming (triathletes combine all three).

6. Suggest a reason why heart size increases with cardiovascular endurance activity: _____

_____

7. In the graph above right, explain why the relative heart volume of endurance athletes is greater than that of body builders, even though their total heart volumes are the same:

_____

8. Heart stroke volume increases with endurance training. Explain how this increases the efficiency of the heart as a pump:

_____

9. Resting heart rates are much lower in trained athletes compared with non-active people. Explain the health benefits of a lower resting heart rate:

_____

_____

Cardiovascular Disease

Cardiovascular disease (CVD) is a term describing all diseases involving the heart and blood vessels. It includes coronary heart disease (CHD), atherosclerosis, hypertension (high blood pressure), peripheral vascular disease, stroke, and congenital heart disorders. CVD is responsible for 20% of all deaths worldwide and is the principal cause of deaths in developed countries. In the UK, deaths due to CVD have been declining since the 1970s due to better prevention and treatment. Despite this, CVD is still the leading cause of mortality, and accounted for 37% of all deaths in 2004. The continued prevalence of CVD is of considerable public health concern, particularly as many of the **risk factors** involved, such as cigarette smoking, obesity, and high blood cholesterol, are controllable. Uncontrollable risk factors include advancing age, gender, and heredity.

Cardiovascular Diseases

Atherosclerosis: Atherosclerosis is a disease of the arteries caused by **atheroma** (fattty deposits) on the inner walls of the arteries. An atheroma is made up of cells (mostly macrophages) or cell debris, with associated fatty acids, cholesterol, fatty acids, calcium, and varying amounts of fibrous connective tissue. The lining of the arteries degenerates due to the accumulation of fat and plaques. Atheroma weakens the arterial walls and eventually restricts blood flow through the arteries, increasing the risk of **aneurysm** and **thrombosis** (blood clot formation). Complications arising as a result of atherosclerosis include **infarction**, stroke, and gangrene.

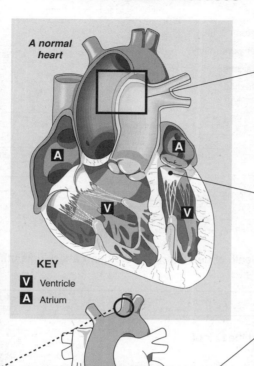

KEY

V Ventricle
A Atrium

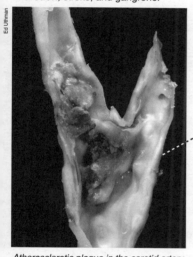

Atherosclerotic plaque in the carotid artery. Plaque material can detach from the artery wall and enters the circulation, increasing the risk of thrombosis.

Restricted supply of blood to heart muscle resulting in myocardial infarction

Aortic aneurysm: Ballooning of the wall of the aorta. Atheroma increases the risk of aneurysm in arteries because it weakens the artery wall. Aneurysms usually result from generalised heart disease and high blood pressure.

Valve defects: Unusual heart sounds (murmurs) can result when a valve (often the mitral valve) does not close properly, allowing blood to bubble back into the atria. Valve defects may be congenital (present at birth) but they can also occur as a result of rheumatic fever.

Myocardial infarction (*heart attack*): Occurs when an area of the heart is deprived of blood supply resulting in tissue damage or death. It is the major cause of death in developed countries. Symptoms of infarction include a sudden onset of chest pain, breathlessness, nausea, and cold clammy skin. Damage to the heart may be so severe that it leads to heart failure and even death (myocardial infarction is fatal within 20 days in 40 to 50% of all cases).

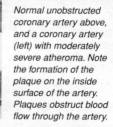

Normal unobstructed coronary artery above, and a coronary artery (left) with moderately severe atheroma. Note the formation of the plaque on the inside surface of the artery. Plaques obstruct blood flow through the artery.

Cholesterol and Risk of CVD

Cholesterol is a sterol lipid found in all animal tissues as part of cellular membranes. Cholesterol is transported within complex spherical particles called **lipoproteins**. One form of cholesterol-transporting molecule is called **high density lipoprotein** or **HDL**. HDL helps remove cholesterol from the bloodstream by transporting it to the liver. Another form of lipoprotein, called **LDL (low density lipoprotein)** deposits cholesterol onto the walls of blood vessels to form **plaques**.

Abnormally high concentrations of LDL and lower concentrations of functional HDL are strongly associated with CVD because these promote development of atheroma in arteries. This disease process leads to heart attack. It is the **LDL:HDL ratio**, rather than total cholesterol itself, that provides the best indicator of risk of cardiovascular disease, and the risk profile is different for men and women (tables right). The LDL:HDL ratio is mostly genetically determined but can be changed by body build, diet, and exercise regime.

Ratio of LDL to HDL		
Risk	**Men**	**Women**
Very low (half average)	1.0	1.5
Average risk	3.6	3.2
Moderate risk (2X average risk)	6.3	5.0
High (3X average risk)	8.0	6.1

Related activities: Diseases Caused by Smoking, The Human Heart, The Health Benefits of Exercise

RDA 3

The Human Heart

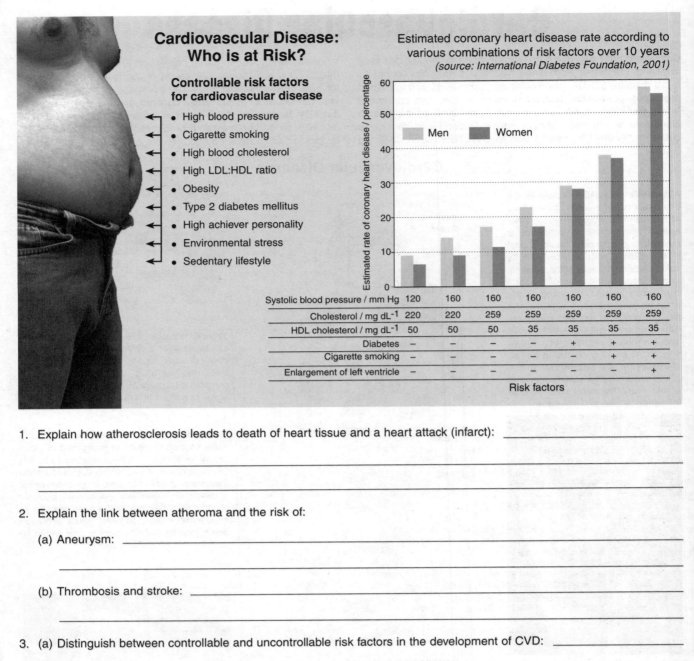

Cardiovascular Disease: Who is at Risk?

Controllable risk factors for cardiovascular disease

- High blood pressure
- Cigarette smoking
- High blood cholesterol
- High LDL:HDL ratio
- Obesity
- Type 2 diabetes mellitus
- High achiever personality
- Environmental stress
- Sedentary lifestyle

Estimated coronary heart disease rate according to various combinations of risk factors over 10 years
(source: International Diabetes Foundation, 2001)

Risk factors						
Systolic blood pressure / mm Hg	120	160	160	160	160	160	160
Cholesterol / mg dL^{-1}	220	220	259	259	259	259	259
HDL cholesterol / mg dL^{-1}	50	50	50	35	35	35	35
Diabetes	−	−	−	−	+	+	+
Cigarette smoking	−	−	−	−	−	+	+
Enlargement of left ventricle	−	−	−	−	−	−	+

1. Explain how atherosclerosis leads to death of heart tissue and a heart attack (infarct): _____

_____

_____

2. Explain the link between atheroma and the risk of:

   (a) Aneurysm: _____

   _____

   (b) Thrombosis and stroke: _____

   _____

3. (a) Distinguish between controllable and uncontrollable risk factors in the development of CVD: _____

   _____

   (b) Suggest why some of the controllable risk factors often occur together: _____

   _____

   _____

   (c) Evaluate the evidence supporting the observation that patients with several risk factors are at higher risk of CVD:

   _____

   _____

4. (a) Explain the link between high LDL:HDL ratio and the risk of cardiovascular disease: _____

   _____

   _____

   (b) Explain why this ratio is more important to medical practitioners than total blood cholesterol *per se*:

   _____

   _____

The Health Benefits of Exercise

Regular exercise helps protect against a range of health problems, improves mood, and assists in managing stress. Exercise promotes health by improving the rate of blood flow back to the heart (**venous return**). This is achieved by strengthening all types of muscle and by increasing the efficiency of the heart. During exercise blood flow to different parts of the body changes in order to cope with the extra demands of the muscles, the heart and the lungs. Over time, regular exercise leads to greater **endurance**, and improves the body's ability to respond to everyday demands of physical activity.

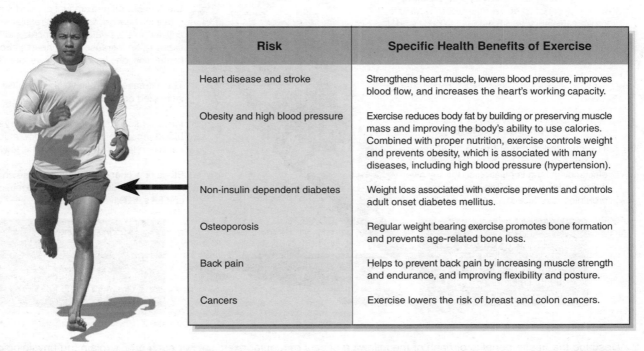

Risk	Specific Health Benefits of Exercise
Heart disease and stroke	Strengthens heart muscle, lowers blood pressure, improves blood flow, and increases the heart's working capacity.
Obesity and high blood pressure	Exercise reduces body fat by building or preserving muscle mass and improving the body's ability to use calories. Combined with proper nutrition, exercise controls weight and prevents obesity, which is associated with many diseases, including high blood pressure (hypertension).
Non-insulin dependent diabetes	Weight loss associated with exercise prevents and controls adult onset diabetes mellitus.
Osteoporosis	Regular weight bearing exercise promotes bone formation and prevents age-related bone loss.
Back pain	Helps to prevent back pain by increasing muscle strength and endurance, and improving flexibility and posture.
Cancers	Exercise lowers the risk of breast and colon cancers.

Regular, moderate exercise promotes psychological well-being, improves immune function, reduces muscular and mental tension, and increases concentration and energy levels.

Strength and resistance exercises, often with machines or weights, are an important component of physiotherapy for people recovering from trauma or illness.

Exercise is a social activity for many, providing a reason for regular social contact. Exercise also increases self-esteem and confidence, and reduces feelings of anxiety and depression.

A basic level of fitness is essential for maintaining muscular strength and flexibility into old age. Without it, people lose the ability to do everyday activities such as housework or lifting.

1. (a) Explain how the body increases the rate of blood flow during exercise: _____

_____

(b) Describe the physiological effects of this when exercise is performed on a regular basis: _____

_____

(c) Explain how these changes benefit health in the long term: _____

_____

_____

_____

The Human Heart

Related activities: Exercise and Blood Flow

ERA 2

Exercise and the Pulmonary and Cardiovascular Systems

The body has an immediate response to exercise but also, over time, responds to the stress of repeated exercise (which is called training) by adapting and improving its capacity for exercise and the efficiency with which it performs. Many of the health benefits of exercise stem from this improved efficiency, which means the body works with less effort during everyday activity.

Cardiovascular Performance

Heart rate: Heart rate increases during exercise but aerobic training leads to a lower steady state heart rate overall for any given level of work.

Stroke volume (the amount of blood pumped with each beat) increases with regular aerobic activity. This is related to an increased heart capacity, an increase in the heart's force of contraction, and an increase in venous return.

The increase in stroke volume results in an increased **cardiac output**.

In response to training, the **resting systolic blood pressure** (a measure of how much the heart is relaxing between beats) is lowered.

Blood flow changes during exercise so that more blood is diverted to working muscles and less is delivered to the gut.

Ventilation Rate

The rate and depth of breathing increases during exercise. Training improves the efficiency of lung ventilation so for any given exercise level, the effort associated with breathing is reduced.

Overall result:
Improved exchange of gases. For any given exercise level, breathing takes less effort.

Overall result:
The increased demands of exercise are met more efficiently. Everyday activity requires less effort.

2. Describe the health benefits of each of the following effects of regular exercise. For each one, explain the physiological mechanisms behind the health benefits:

(a) Increase in stroke volume and cardiac output: _____

_____

_____

(b) Increased ventilation efficiency: _____

_____

_____

(c) Increase in lean muscle mass and decreased body fat: _____

_____

_____

(d) Increased muscular strength and endurance: _____

_____

_____

(e) Maintenance of stable, healthy body weight: _____

_____

_____

3. Suggest why irregular or very low intensity exercise does not provide the health benefits of regular activity:

_____

_____

_____

Immunology

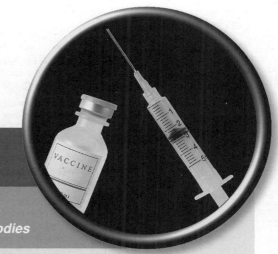

Unit 1: Biology and Disease
1.6 Mammalian defence systems

*The body's defences, the role of blood in defence,
Immune response, vaccination, monoclonal antibodies*

Learning Objectives

☐ 1. Compile your own glossary from the **KEY WORDS** displayed in **bold type** in the learning objectives below.

Recognising Self and Non-self *(pages 133-134)*

☐ 2. Explain the importance of **self-recognition** and explain its biological basis.

☐ 3. Explain the basis of the **Rh** and **ABO blood group systems** in humans. Explain what is meant by **agglutination** and how this reaction forms the basis of blood grouping. Explain the consequences of blood type incompatibility in **blood transfusions**.

The Blood and Defence *(pages 135-136, 139)*

☐ 4. Describe the nature and/or composition of **blood** including reference to the role of each of the following:

Non-cellular components: **plasma** (water, mineral ions, blood proteins, hormones, nutrients, urea, vitamins).

Cellular components: **erythrocytes**, **leucocytes** (**lymphocytes**, **monocytes**, **granulocytes**), **platelets**.

☐ 5. Describe the role of **blood clotting** in the resistance of the body to infection by sealing off damage and restricting invasion of the tissues by microorganisms.

Non-specific defences *(pages 137-138142)*

☐ 6. Explain what is meant by a **non-specific defence mechanism**. Distinguish between first and second lines of defence. Describe the nature and role of each of the following in protecting against pathogens:
- Skin (including sweat and sebum production)
- Mucus-secreting and ciliated membranes
- Body secretions (tears, urine, saliva, gastric juice)
- Natural anti-bacterial and anti-viral proteins such as **interferon** and **complement**
- The **inflammatory response**, **fever**, and cell death
- **Phagocytosis**

☐ 7. Recognise the term phagocyte as referring to any of a number of phagocytic leucocytes (e.g. macrophages).

Specific defences *(pages 137, 148)*

☐ 8. Describe the role of **specific resistance** in body's resistance to infection. Contrast specific and non-specific defences in terms of time for activation and action towards a pathogen.

☐ 9. Explain how the **immune response** involves recognition and response to foreign material. Explain the significance of the immune system having both **specificity** and **memory**. Providing examples, distinguish between **naturally acquired** and **artificially acquired immunity** and between active and passive immunity. Compare the duration of the immunity gained by active and passive means.

☐ 10. Recognise the role of the **lymphatic system** in the production and transport of leucocytes.

The Immune System *(pages 143-146, 153-154)*

☐ 11. Distinguish between: **cell-mediated immunity** and **humoral (antibody-mediated) immunity**.

☐ 12. Recall that other types of white blood cells are involved in non-specific defence mechanisms.

☐ 13. Explain the role of the **thymus** in the immune response. Describe the nature, origin, and role of **macrophages** (a type of phagocyte). Appreciate the role of macrophages in processing and presenting foreign antigens and in stimulating lymphocyte activity.

☐ 14. Explain the origin and maturation of **B lymphocytes** (cells) and **T lymphocytes** (cells). Describe and distinguish between the activities of the B and T lymphocytes in the immune response.

☐ 15. Explain how the immune system is able to respond to the large and unpredictable range of antigens in the environment. In your explanation, include reference to clonal selection. Appreciate that **self-tolerance** occurs during development as a result of the selective destruction of B cells that react to self-antigens.

Cell-mediated immunity

☐ 16. T cells are responsible for **cell-mediated immunity**. Describe how T cells recognise **specific** foreign antigens. Describe the functional roles of named T cells, including the **cytotoxic** (killer) **T cells** (T_C) and the **helper T cells** (T_H). Identify the organisms against which these T cells act.

Humoral immunity

☐ 17. Describe how B cells bring about **humoral (antibody-mediated) immunity**. Identify the organisms that are the main targets for the humoral response.

☐ 18. Describe and contrast the functional roles of **plasma cells** and **memory cells** and explain the basis for **immunological memory**. Discuss the role of immunological memory in long term immunity (ability to respond quickly to previously encountered antigens).

☐ 19. Identify common **antigens (immunoglobulins)** and explain their role in provoking an immune response. Describe the structure of an **antibody**, identifying the constant and variable regions, and the antigen binding site. Relate the structure of antibodies to their function.

☐ 20. Describe the methods by which antibodies inactivate antigens and facilitate their destruction.

☐ 21. Explain how **monoclonal antibodies** are produced and describe how they enable the targeting of specific substances and cells. Describe the importance of these properties when monoclonal antibodies are used in **diagnostic medicine** and in treating disease.

Vaccination and Public Health *(pages 148-156)*

☐ 22. Appreciate that **immunisation** involves the production of immunity by artificial means and that **vaccination** usually refers to immunisation by inoculation. Know that these terms are frequently used synonymously.

☐ 23. Recognise that vaccination provides **artificially acquired immunity**. Recall the difference between **passive** and **active immunity**.

☐ 24. Describe what is meant by a **primary** and a **secondary response** to infection. Explain the role of these responses and the immune system memory in the success of vaccines against specific pathogens.

☐ 25. Explain the role of **vaccination** programmes in preventing disease. Discuss the role of aggressive vaccination programmes in the eradication (or near-eradication) of some (named) infectious diseases.

☐ 26. Using the influenza virus as an example, explain what is meant by **antigenic variability** and describe its biological basis and its effects on immunity. Including reference to this, explain the biological and sociological reasons why vaccination has been successful in eradicating some diseases (such as smallpox) but not others (such as influenza).

☐ 27. Discuss how governments and health organisations respond to changing patterns of infection each year, e.g. the seasonal appearance of new strains of influenza or meningococcal disease.

☐ 28. Outline the vaccination schedule for the UK, identifying critical times for vaccination against specific diseases. With reference to the concept of **herd immunity**, comment on the role of effective vaccination programmes in public health and the incidence of infectious disease in the UK.

☐ 29. Describe the principles involved in producing vaccines and explain how vaccines are administered. Distinguish between types of vaccines, e.g. **subunit** vs **whole-agent vaccines** and **inactivated** (dead) vs **live** (attenuated) **vaccines**.

☐ 30. Evaluate the methodology, evidence, and data relating to the use of vaccines and monoclonal antibodies. Consider the following:
- The risks associated with vaccination relative to the risks associated with contracting the disease itself.
- The risks and benefits associated with live (attenuated) and dead vaccines.
- The incidence of disease before and after the implementation of vaccination programmes
- The role of preventative programmes in public health
- Potential ethical issues associated with the use of monoclonal antibodies

See the 'Textbook Reference Grid' on page 7 for textbook page references relating to material in this topic.

Supplementary Texts
See pages 5-6 for additional details of these texts:
- Clegg, C.J., 1998. **Mammals: Structure and Function** (John Murray), pp. 40-41.
- Freeland, P., 1999. **Microbes, Medicine and Commerce** (Hodder & Stoughton), pp. 92-99.
- Fullick, A., 1998. **Human Health and Disease** (Heinemann), pp. 27-36.

See page 6 for details of publishers of periodicals:

STUDENT'S REFERENCE
- **Skin, Scabs and Scars** Biol. Sci. Rev., 17(3) Feb. 2005, pp. 2-6. *The many roles of skin, including its importance in wound healing and the processes involved in its repair when damaged.*
- **Looking Out for Danger: How White Blood Cells Protect Us** Biol. Sci. Rev., 19 (4) April 2007, pp. 34-37. *The various types of lymphocytes (white blood cells) and they work together to protect the body against infection.*
- **Antibodies** Biol. Sci. Rev., 11(3) Jan. 1999, pp. 34-35. *The structure and function of antibodies: their roles and how they can be used in medicine.*
- **Monoclonals as Medicines** Biol. Sci. Rev., 18(4) April 2006, pp. 38-40. *The use of monoclonal antibodies in therapeutic and diagnostic medicine.*
- **Inflammation** Biol. Sci. Rev., 17(1) Sept. 2004, pp. 18-20. *The role of this nonspecific defence response to tissue injury and infection. The processes involved in inflammation are discussed.*

- **Lymphocytes - The Heart of the Immune System** Biol. Sci. Rev., 12(1) Sept. 1999, pp. 32-35. *An excellent account of the role of the various lymphocytes in the immune response.*
- **Fanning the Flames** New Scientist, 22 May 2004, pp. 40-43. *Inflammation is one of the first lines of internal defence, but it has been implicated in a host of disparate diseases.*
- **Fight For Your Life** Biol. Sci. Rev., 18(1) Sept. 2005, pp. 2-6. *Internal defence: pathogen recognition, the immune response, and the nature of adaptive and maladaptive immune reactions.*
- **Immunotherapy** Biol. Sci. Rev., 15(1), Sept. 2002, pp. 39-41. *Medical research is uncovering ways in which our immune system can be used in developing vaccines for cancer.*
- **A Jab in Time** Biol. Sci. Rev., 9(4) March 1997, pp. 17-20. *Infection and transmission of disease and the use of vaccination to combat diseases.*
- **Let Them Eat Dirt** New Scientist, 18 July 1998, pp. 26-31. *It seems that normal immune function requires some early exposure to microorganisms.*

TEACHER'S REFERENCE
- **Life, Death, and the Immune System** Scientific American, Sept. 1993. *An entire special issue on human infection, immune system, and disease.*
- **Immunity's Early-warning System** Scientific American, Jan. 2005, pp. 24-31. *The immune response is mediated by a family of molecules made by defensive cells. When they detect an invader, they trigger the production of signalling proteins that initiate an immune response.*
- **Edible Vaccines** Scientific American, Sept. 2000, pp. 48-53. *Vaccines in food may be the way of future immunisation programmes.*
- **Peacekeepers of the Immune System** Scientific American, Oct. 2006, pp. 34-41. *Regulatory T cells suppress immune activity and combat autoimmunity.*
- **Disarming Flu Viruses** Scientific American, January 1999, pp. 56-65. *The influenza virus, its life cycle, and vaccine development for its control.*
- **The Long Arm of the Immune System** Sci. American, Nov. 2002, pp. 34-41. *The role of dendritic cells, a class of leucocytes with a role in activating the immune system (good extension).*

- **Preparing for Battle** Scientific American, Feb. 2001, pp. 68-69. *Preparation and mode of action of the influenza vaccine. Includes discussion of the problems associated with the changing virus.*
- **No Need to Panic about Vaccines** New Scientist, 8 Mar 2008, pp. 8-9. *Debate about whether vaccination is linked to autism.*
- **Filthy Healthy** New Scientist, 12 Jan 2008, pp. 34-37. *Exposure to dirt and infections may aid our long term immunity, and help fight cancer.*

See pages 8-9 for details of how to access **Bio Links** from our web site: **www.biozone.co.uk**. From Bio Links, access sites under the topics:

GENERAL BIOLOGY ONLINE RESOURCES > **General Online Biology Resources**: • AP interactive animation • Biointeractive • Ken's BioWeb Resources > **Online Textbooks and Lecture Notes**: • S-Cool! A level biology revision guide • Biology Online.org • Human Biology Help • Welcome to the Biology Web... *and others*

ANIMAL BIOLOGY: • Anatomy and physiology • Human physiology lecture notes ... *and others*

HEALTH & DISEASE > **Defence and the Immune System**: • Blood group antigens • Immune defence against microbial pathogens • Inducible defences against pathogens • Microbiology and immunology • Constitutive defences against pathogens • The immune system: An overview • Understanding the immune system ... *and others*

Presentation MEDIA to support this topic:

Health & Disease CD-ROM:
• **Defence & Immunity**

Targets for Defence

In order for the body to present an effective defence against pathogens, it must first be able to recognise its own tissues (self) and ignore the body's normal microflora (e.g. the bacteria of the skin and gastrointestinal tract). In addition, the body needs to be able to deal with abnormal cells which, if not eliminated, may become cancerous. Failure of self/non-self recognition can lead to autoimmune disorders, in which the immune system mistakenly attacks its own tissues. The body's ability to recognise its own molecules has implications for procedures such as tissue grafts, organ transplants, and blood transfusions. Incompatible tissues (identified as foreign) are attacked by the body's immune system (**rejected**). Even a healthy pregnancy involves suppression of specific features of the self recognition system, allowing the mother to tolerate a nine month gestation with the foetus.

The Body's Natural Microbiota

After birth, normal and characteristic microbial populations begin to establish themselves on and in the body. A typical human body contains 1×10^{13} body cells, yet harbours 1×10^{14} bacterial cells. These microorganisms establish more or less permanent residence but, under normal conditions, do not cause disease. In fact, this normal microflora can benefit the host by preventing the overgrowth of harmful pathogens. They are not found throughout the entire body, but are located in certain regions.

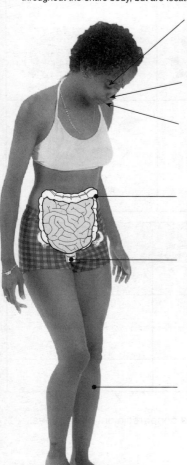

Eyes: The conjuctiva, a continuation of the skin or mucous membrane, contains a similar microbiota to the skin.

Nose and throat: Harbours a variety of microorganisms, e.g. *Staphylococcus spp.*

Mouth: Supports a large and diverse microbiota. It is an ideal microbial environment; high in moisture, warmth, and nutrient availability.

Large intestine: Contains the body's largest resident population of microbes because of its available moisture and nutrients.

Urinary and genital systems: The lower urethra in both sexes has a resident population; the vagina has a particular acid-tolerant population of microbes because of the low pH nature of its secretions.

Skin: Skin secretions prevent most of the microbes on the skin from becoming residents.

Distinguishing Self from Non-Self

The human immune system achieves self-recognition through the **major histocompatibility complex** (MHC). This is a cluster of tightly linked genes on chromosome 6 in humans. These genes code for protein molecules (MHC antigens) that are attached to the surface of body cells. They are used by the immune system to recognise its own or foreign material. **Class I MHC** antigens are located on the surface of virtually all human cells, but **Class II MHC** antigens are restricted to macrophages and the antibody-producing B-lymphocytes.

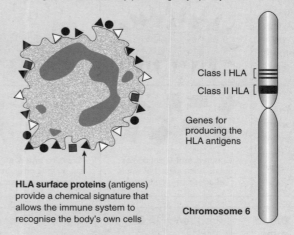

Class I HLA

Class II HLA

Genes for producing the HLA antigens

Chromosome 6

HLA surface proteins (antigens) provide a chemical signature that allows the immune system to recognise the body's own cells

Tissue Transplants

The MHC is responsible for the rejection of tissue grafts and organ transplants. Foreign MHC molecules are antigenic, causing the immune system to respond in the following way:

- T cells directly lyse the foreign cells

- Macrophages are activated by T cells and engulf foreign cells

- Antibodies are released that attack the foreign cell

- The complement system injures blood vessels supplying the graft or transplanted organ

To minimise this rejection, attempts are made to match the MHC of the organ donor to that of the recipient as closely as possible.

1. Explain why it is healthy to have a natural population of microbes on and inside the body: _____

_____

2. (a) Explain the nature and purpose of the **major histocompatibility complex** (MHC): _____

_____

_____

_____

(b) Explain the importance of such a self-recognition system: _____

_____

3. Name two situations when the body's recognition of 'self' is undesirable: _____

Immunology

Related activities: The Body's Defences, The Immune System

RA 2

Blood Group Antigens

Blood groups classify blood according to the different marker proteins on the surface of red blood cells (RBCs). These marker proteins act as **antigens** and affect the ability of RBCs to provoke an immune response. The **ABO blood group** is the most important blood typing system in medical practice, because of the presence of anti-A and anti-B antibodies in nearly all people who lack the corresponding red cell antigens (these antibodies are carried in the plasma and are present at birth). If a patient is to receive blood from a blood donor, that blood must be compatible otherwise the red blood cells of the donated blood will clump together (agglutinate), break apart, and block capillaries. There is a small margin of safety in certain blood group combinations, because the volume of donated blood is usually relatively small and the donor's antibodies are quickly diluted in the plasma. In practice, blood is carefully matched, not only for ABO types, but for other types as well. Although human RBCs have more than 500 known antigens, fewer than 30 (in 9 blood groups) are regularly tested for when blood is donated for transfusion. The ABO and rhesus (Rh) are the best known. Although blood typing has important applications in medicine, it can also be used to rule out individuals in cases of crime (or paternity) and establish a list of potential suspects (or fathers).

	Blood type A	Blood type B	Blood type AB	Blood type O
Antigens present on the **red blood cells**	antigen **A**	antigen **B**	antigens **A** and **B**	Neither antigen **A** nor **B**
Anti-bodies present in the **plasma**	Contains **anti-B** antibodies; but no antibodies that would attack its own antigen **A**	Contains **anti-A** antibodies; but no antibodies that would attack its own antigen **B**	Contains neither **anti-A** nor **anti-B** antibodies	Contains both **anti-A** and **anti-B** antibodies

Blood type	Frequency in UK Rh⁺	Frequency in UK Rh⁻	Antigen	Antibody	Can donate blood to:	Can receive blood from:
A	36%	7%	A	anti-B	A, AB	A, O
B	8%	1%				
AB	2%	1%				
O	38%	7%				

1. Complete the table above to show the antibodies and antigens in each blood group, and donor/recipient blood types:

2. Describe how blood typing could be effectively used in each of the following situations:

   (a) As forensic evidence: _____

   _____

   (b) In paternity cases: _____

   _____

   (c) In trauma medicine: _____

   _____

3. Explain why the discovery of the ABO system was such a significant medical breakthrough: _____

   _____

   _____

   _____

Related activities: Blood
Web links: Blood Typing Game

Blood

Blood makes up about 8% of body weight. Blood is a complex liquid tissue comprising cellular components suspended in plasma. If a blood sample is taken, the cells can be separated from the plasma by centrifugation. The cells (formed elements) settle as a dense red pellet below the transparent, straw-coloured plasma. Blood performs many functions: it transports nutrients, respiratory gases, hormones, and wastes; it has a role in thermoregulation through the distribution of heat; it defends against infection; and its ability to clot protects against blood loss. The examination of blood is also useful in diagnosing disease. The cellular components of blood are normally present in particular specified ratios. A change in the morphology, type, or proportion of different blood cells can therefore be used to indicate a specific disorder or infection (right).

Non-Cellular Blood Components

The non-cellular blood components form the plasma. Plasma is a watery matrix of ions and proteins and makes up 50-60% of the total blood volume.

Water
The main constituent of blood and lymph.
Role: Transports dissolved substances. Provides body cells with water. Distributes heat and has a central role in thermoregulation. Regulation of water content helps to regulate blood pressure and volume.

Mineral ions
Sodium, bicarbonate, magnesium, potassium, calcium, chloride.
Role: Osmotic balance, pH buffering, and regulation of membrane permeability. They also have a variety of other functions, e.g. Ca^{2+} is involved in blood clotting.

Plasma proteins
7-9% of the plasma volume.
Serum albumin
Role: Osmotic balance and pH buffering, Ca^{2+} transport.
Fibrinogen and prothrombin
Role: Take part in blood clotting.
Immunoglobulins
Role: Antibodies involved in the immune response.
α-globulins
Role: Bind/transport hormones, lipids, fat soluble vitamins.
β-globulins
Role: Bind/transport iron, cholesterol, fat soluble vitamins.
Enzymes
Role: Take part in and regulate metabolic activities.

Substances transported by non-cellular components
Products of digestion
Examples: sugars, fatty acids, glycerol, and amino acids.
Excretory products
Example: urea
Hormones and vitamins
Examples: insulin, sex hormones, vitamins A and B_{12}.
Importance: These substances occur at varying levels in the blood. They are transported to and from the cells dissolved in the plasma or bound to plasma proteins.

Cellular Blood Components

The cellular components of the blood (also called the formed elements) float in the plasma and make up 40-50% of the total blood volume.

Erythrocytes (red blood cells or RBCs)
5-6 million per mm^3 blood; 38-48% of total blood volume.
Role: RBCs transport oxygen (O_2) and a small amount of carbon dioxide (CO_2). The oxygen is carried bound to haemoglobin (Hb) in the cells. Each Hb molecule can bind four molecules of oxygen.

7-8 μm

Platelets
Small, membrane bound cell fragments derived from bone marrow cells; about 1/4 the size of RBCs.
0.25 million per mm^3 blood.
Role: To start the blood clotting process.

2 μm

Leucocytes (white blood cells)
5-10 000 per mm^3 blood
2-3% of total blood volume.
Role: Involved in internal defence. There are several types of white blood cells (see below).

Lymphocytes
T and B cells.
24% of the white cell count.
Role: Antibody production and cell mediated immunity.

Neutrophils
Phagocytes.
70% of the white cell count.
Role: Engulf foreign material.

Eosinophils
Rare leucocytes; normally 1.5% of the white cell count.
Role: Mediate allergic responses such as hayfever and asthma.

Basophils
Rare leucocytes; normally 0.5% of the white cell count.
Role: Produce heparin (an anti-clotting protein), and histamine. Involved in inflammation.

Immunology

Related activities: Gas Transport in Humans, The Body's Defences

A 2

The Examination of Blood

Different types of microscopy give different information about blood. A SEM (right) shows the detailed external morphology of the blood cells. A fixed smear of a blood sample viewed with a light microscope (far right) can be used to identify the different blood cell types present, and their ratio to each other. Determining the types and proportions of different white blood cells in blood is called a **differential white blood cell count**. Elevated counts of particular cell types indicate allergy or infection.

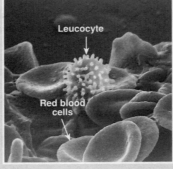

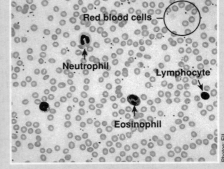

SEM of red blood cells and a leucocyte.   **Light microscope** view of a fixed blood smear.

1. For each of the following blood functions, identify the component(s) of the blood responsible and state how the function is carried out (the mode of action). The first one is done for you:

   (a) **Temperature regulation**. *Blood component involved:* <u>Water component of the plasma</u>

   Mode of action: <u>Water absorbs heat and dissipates it from sites of production (e.g. organs)</u>

   (b) **Protection against disease**. *Blood component:* _____

   Mode of action: _____

   (c) **Communication between cells, tissues, and organs**. *Blood component:* _____

   Mode of action: _____

   (d) **Oxygen transport**. *Blood component:* _____

   Mode of action: _____

   (e) **CO$_2$ transport**. *Blood components:* _____

   Mode of action: _____

   (f) **Buffer against pH changes**. *Blood components:* _____

   Mode of action: _____

   (g) **Nutrient supply**. *Blood component:* _____

   Mode of action: _____

   (h) **Tissue repair**. *Blood components:* _____

   Mode of action: _____

   (i) **Transport of hormones, lipids, and fat soluble vitamins**. *Blood component:* _____

   Mode of action: _____

2. Identify a feature that distinguishes red and white blood cells: _____

3. Explain two physiological advantages of red blood cell structure (lacking nucleus and mitochondria):

   (a) _____

   (b) _____

4. Suggest what each of the following results from a differential white blood cell count would suggest:

   (a) Elevated levels of eosinophils (above the normal range): _____

   (b) Elevated levels of neutrophils (above the normal range): _____

   (c) Elevated levels of basophils (above the normal range): _____

   (d) Elevated levels of lymphocytes (above the normal range): _____

The Body's Defences

If microorganisms never encountered resistance from our body defences, we would be constantly ill and would eventually die of various diseases. Fortunately, in most cases our defences prevent this from happening. Some of these defences are designed to keep microorganisms from entering the body. Other defences remove the microorganisms if they manage to get inside. Further defences attack the microorganisms if they remain inside the body. The ability to ward off disease through the various defence mechanisms is called **resistance**. The lack of resistance, or vulnerability to disease, is known as **susceptibility**. One form of defence is referred to as **non-specific resistance**, and includes defences that protect us from any invading pathogen. This includes a first line of defence such as the physical barriers to infection (skin and mucous membranes) and a second line of defence (phagocytes, inflammation, fever, and antimicrobial substances). **Specific resistance** is a third line of defence that forms the **immune response** and targets specific pathogens. Specialised cells of the immune system, called lymphocytes, produce specific proteins called antibodies which are produced against specific antigens.

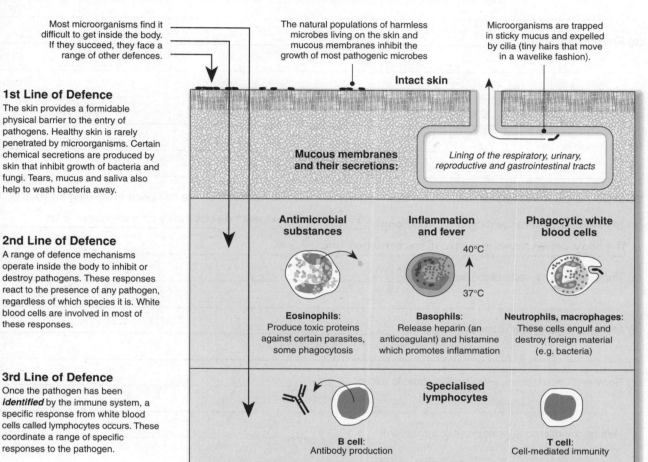

Most microorganisms find it difficult to get inside the body. If they succeed, they face a range of other defences.

The natural populations of harmless microbes living on the skin and mucous membranes inhibit the growth of most pathogenic microbes

Microorganisms are trapped in sticky mucus and expelled by cilia (tiny hairs that move in a wavelike fashion).

1st Line of Defence

The skin provides a formidable physical barrier to the entry of pathogens. Healthy skin is rarely penetrated by microorganisms. Certain chemical secretions are produced by skin that inhibit growth of bacteria and fungi. Tears, mucus and saliva also help to wash bacteria away.

2nd Line of Defence

A range of defence mechanisms operate inside the body to inhibit or destroy pathogens. These responses react to the presence of any pathogen, regardless of which species it is. White blood cells are involved in most of these responses.

3rd Line of Defence

Once the pathogen has been *identified* by the immune system, a specific response from white blood cells called lymphocytes occurs. These coordinate a range of specific responses to the pathogen.

Intact skin

Mucous membranes and their secretions:

Lining of the respiratory, urinary, reproductive and gastrointestinal tracts

Antimicrobial substances

Eosinophils:
Produce toxic proteins against certain parasites, some phagocytosis

Inflammation and fever

40°C
37°C

Basophils:
Release heparin (an anticoagulant) and histamine which promotes inflammation

Phagocytic white blood cells

Neutrophils, macrophages:
These cells engulf and destroy foreign material (e.g. bacteria)

Specialised lymphocytes

B cell:
Antibody production

T cell:
Cell-mediated immunity

1. Compare and contrast the type of response against pathogens carried out by each of the three levels of defence:

_____

_____

_____

_____

_____

_____

_____

_____

_____

_____

_____

Immunology

Related activities: The Action of Phagocytes, Inflammation, Fever, The Immune System   **Web links**: Immunoanimations

RA 2

138

2. Distinguish between specific and non-specific resistance: _____
_____
_____
_____
_____

3. Describe and explain features of the following white blood cells in relation to their role in the second line of defence:

   (a) Macrophages: _____
   _____

   (b) Eosinophils: _____
   _____

   (c) Basophils: _____
   _____

   (d) Neutrophils: _____
   _____

4. Describe the functional role of each of the following defence mechanisms (the first one has been completed for you):

   (a) Skin (including sweat and sebum production):   *Skin helps to prevent direct entry of pathogens into*
   the body. Sebum slows growth of bacteria and fungi.

   (b) Phagocytosis by white blood cells: _____
   _____

   (c) Mucus-secreting and ciliated membranes: _____
   _____

   (d) Body secretions: tears, urine, saliva, gastric juice: _____
   _____

   (e) Natural antimicrobial proteins (e.g. interferon): _____
   _____

   (f) Antibody production: _____
   _____

   (g) Fever: _____
   _____

   (h) Cell-mediated immunity: _____
   _____

   (i) The inflammatory response: _____
   _____

5. Infection with HIV results in the progressive destruction of T lymphocytes. Suggest why this leads to an increasing number of opportunistic infections in AIDS sufferers:
   _____
   _____
   _____

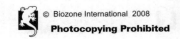

Blood Clotting and Defence

Apart from its transport role, **blood** has a role in the body's defence against infection and **haemostasis** (the prevention of bleeding and maintenance of blood volume). The tearing or puncturing of a blood vessel initiates **clotting**. Clotting is normally a rapid process that seals off the tear, preventing blood loss and the invasion of bacteria into the site. Clot formation is triggered by the release of clotting factors from the damaged cells at the site of the tear or puncture. A hardened clot forms a scab, which acts to prevent further blood loss and acts as a mechanical barrier to the entry of pathogens.

Blood Clotting

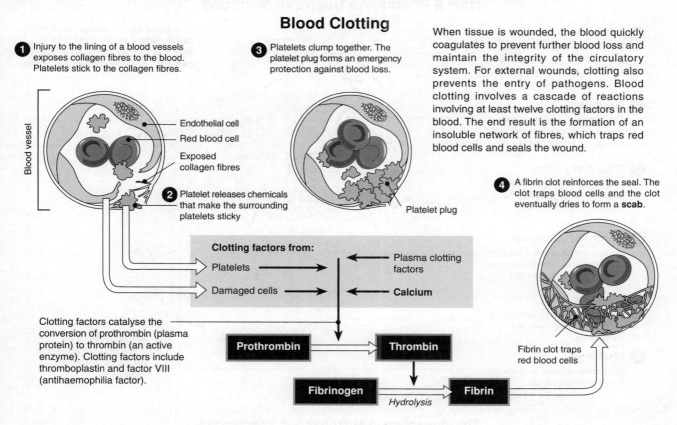

1 Injury to the lining of a blood vessels exposes collagen fibres to the blood. Platelets stick to the collagen fibres.

3 Platelets clump together. The platelet plug forms an emergency protection against blood loss.

When tissue is wounded, the blood quickly coagulates to prevent further blood loss and maintain the integrity of the circulatory system. For external wounds, clotting also prevents the entry of pathogens. Blood clotting involves a cascade of reactions involving at least twelve clotting factors in the blood. The end result is the formation of an insoluble network of fibres, which traps red blood cells and seals the wound.

Blood vessel

Endothelial cell
Red blood cell
Exposed collagen fibres

2 Platelet releases chemicals that make the surrounding platelets sticky

Platelet plug

4 A fibrin clot reinforces the seal. The clot traps blood cells and the clot eventually dries to form a **scab**.

Clotting factors from:

Platelets ⟶   ⟵ Plasma clotting factors

Damaged cells ⟶   ⟵ **Calcium**

Clotting factors catalyse the conversion of prothrombin (plasma protein) to thrombin (an active enzyme). Clotting factors include thromboplastin and factor VIII (antihaemophilia factor).

Prothrombin ⟹ Thrombin

Fibrinogen ⟶ Fibrin
Hydrolysis

Fibrin clot traps red blood cells

1. Explain two roles of the blood clotting system in internal defence and haemostasis:

   (a) _____

   (b) _____

2. Explain the role of each of the following in the sequence of events leading to a blood clot:

   (a) Injury: _____

   (b) Release of chemicals from platelets: _____
   _____

   (c) Clumping of platelets at the wound site: _____
   _____

   (d) Formation of a fibrin clot: _____
   _____

3. (a) Explain the role of clotting factors in the blood in formation of the clot: _____
   _____

   (b) Explain why these clotting factors are not normally present in the plasma: _____
   _____

4. (a) Name one inherited disease caused by the absence of a clotting factor: _____

   (b) Name the clotting factor involved: _____

Immunology

Related activities: Proteins, Enzymes, Blood
Web links: Haemostasis

RA 2

The Action of Phagocytes

Human cells that ingest microbes and digest them by the process of **phagocytosis** are called **phagocytes**. All are types of white blood cells. During many kinds of infections, especially bacterial infections, the total number of white blood cells increases by two to four times the normal number. The ratio of various white blood cell types changes during the course of an infection.

How a Phagocyte Destroys Microbes

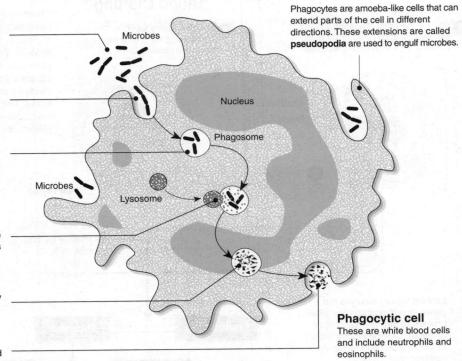

1 Detection
Phagocyte detects microbes by the chemicals they give off (chemotaxis) and sticks the microbes to its surface.

2 Ingestion
The microbe is engulfed by the phagocyte wrapping pseudopodia around it to form a vesicle.

3 Phagosome forms
A phagosome (phagocytic vesicle) is formed, which encloses the microbes in a membrane.

4 Fusion with lysosome
Phagosome fuses with a lysosome (which contains powerful enzymes that can digest the microbe).

5 Digestion
The microbes are broken down by enzymes into their chemical constituents.

6 Discharge
Indigestible material is discharged from the phagocyte cell.

Microbes

Nucleus

Phagosome

Microbes

Lysosome

Phagocytes are amoeba-like cells that can extend parts of the cell in different directions. These extensions are called **pseudopodia** are used to engulf microbes.

Phagocytic cell
These are white blood cells and include neutrophils and eosinophils.

The Interaction of Microbes and Phagocytes

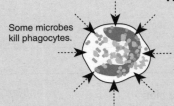

Some microbes kill phagocytes.

Microbes enter phagocytes and evade the immune response.

Dormant microbes may hide inside phagocytes.

Some microbes kill phagocytes
Some microbes produce toxins that can actually kill phagocytes, e.g. toxin-producing staphylococci and the dental plaque-forming bacteria *Actinobacillus*.

Microbes evade immune system
Some microbes can evade the immune system by entering phagocytes. The microbes prevent fusion of the lysosome with the phagosome and multiply inside the phagocyte, almost filling it. Examples include *Chlamydia*, *Mycobacterium tuberculosis*, *Shigella*, and malarial parasites.

Dormant microbes hide inside
Some microbes can remain dormant inside the phagocyte for months or years at a time. Examples include the microbes that cause brucellosis and tularemia.

1. Identify the white blood cells capable of phagocytosis: _____

   _____

2. Describe how a blood sample from a patient may be used to determine whether they have a microbial infection (without looking for the microbes themselves):

   _____

   _____

3. Explain how some microbes are able to overcome phagocytic cells and use them to their advantage: _____

   _____

   _____

Related activities: The Body's Defences, Blood

Inflammation

Damage to the body's tissues can be caused by physical agents (e.g. sharp objects, heat, radiant energy, or electricity), microbial infection, or chemical agents (e.g. gases, acids and bases). The damage triggers a defensive response called **inflammation**. It is usually characterised by four symptoms: pain, redness, heat and swelling. The inflammatory response is beneficial and has the following functions: (1) to destroy the cause of the infection and remove it and its products from the body; (2) if this fails, to limit the effects on the body by confining the infection to a small area; (3) replacing or repairing tissue damaged by the infection. The process of inflammation can be divided into three distinct stages. These are described below.

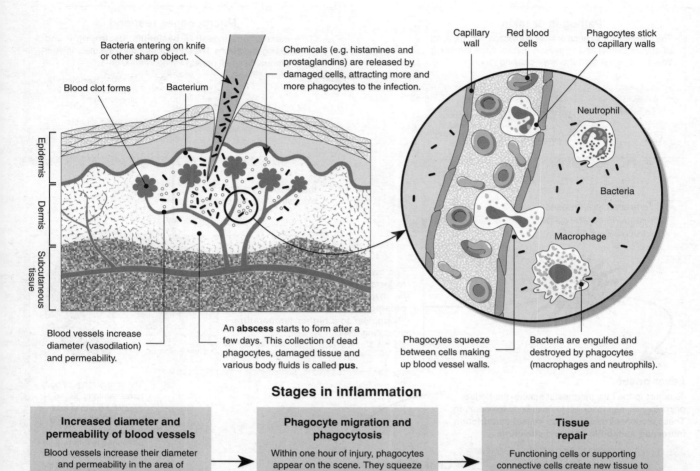

Bacteria entering on knife or other sharp object.

Chemicals (e.g. histamines and prostaglandins) are released by damaged cells, attracting more and more phagocytes to the infection.

Blood clot forms

Bacterium

Epidermis

Dermis

Subcutaneous tissue

Blood vessels increase diameter (vasodilation) and permeability.

An **abscess** starts to form after a few days. This collection of dead phagocytes, damaged tissue and various body fluids is called **pus**.

Capillary wall

Red blood cells

Phagocytes stick to capillary walls

Neutrophil

Bacteria

Macrophage

Phagocytes squeeze between cells making up blood vessel walls.

Bacteria are engulfed and destroyed by phagocytes (macrophages and neutrophils).

Stages in inflammation

Increased diameter and permeability of blood vessels	**Phagocyte migration and phagocytosis**	**Tissue repair**
Blood vessels increase their diameter and permeability in the area of damage. This increases blood flow to the area and allows defensive substances to leak into tissue spaces.	Within one hour of injury, phagocytes appear on the scene. They squeeze between cells of blood vessel walls to reach the damaged area where they destroy invading microbes.	Functioning cells or supporting connective cells create new tissue to replace dead or damaged cells. Some tissue regenerates easily (skin) while others do not at all (cardiac muscle).

1. Outline the three stages of inflammation and identify the beneficial role of each stage:

   (a) _____

   _____

   (b) _____

   _____

   (c) _____

   _____

2. Identify two features of phagocytes important in the response to microbial invasion: _____

   _____

3. State the role of histamines and prostaglandins in inflammation: _____

4. Explain why pus forms at the site of infection: _____

   _____

Immunology

Related activities: The Body's Defences, The Action of Phagocytes

A 1

Fever

Fever describes a condition where the internal body temperature increases to above-normal levels. It arises because of an increase in the body's thermoregulatory set-point so that the previous "normal body temperature" is considered hypothermic. Fever is not a disease, but it is a symptom of infection and, to a point, it is beneficial, because it assists a number of the defence processes. The release of the protein **interleukin-1** helps to reset the thermostat of the body to a higher level, and increases production of **T cells** (lymphocytes). High body temperature also intensifies the effect of **interferon** (an antiviral protein) and may inhibit the growth of some bacteria and viruses. High temperatures also speed up the body's **metabolism**, so promote more rapid tissue repair. Fever also increases heart rate so that white blood cells are delivered to sites of infection more rapidly.

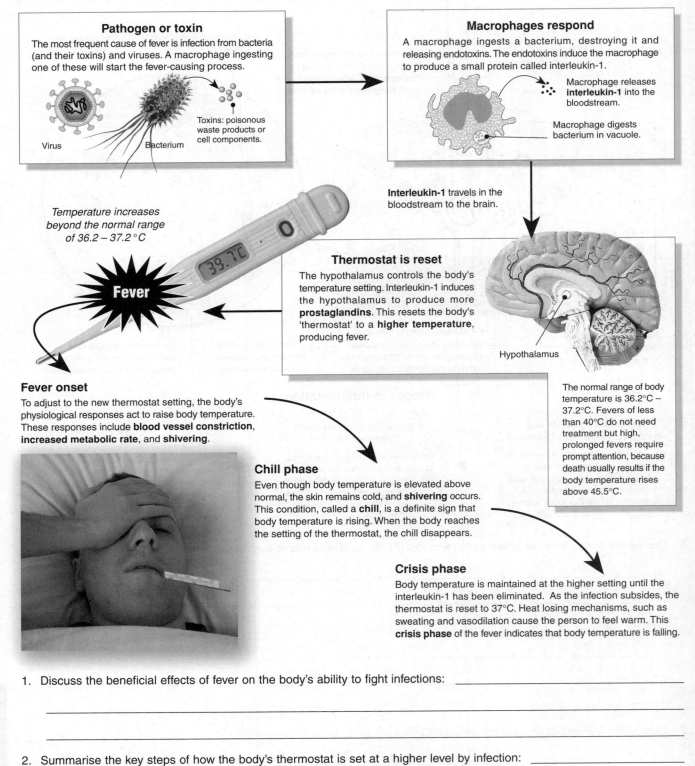

Pathogen or toxin

The most frequent cause of fever is infection from bacteria (and their toxins) and viruses. A macrophage ingesting one of these will start the fever-causing process.

Virus

Bacterium

Toxins: poisonous waste products or cell components.

Macrophages respond

A macrophage ingests a bacterium, destroying it and releasing endotoxins. The endotoxins induce the macrophage to produce a small protein called interleukin-1.

Macrophage releases **interleukin-1** into the bloodstream.

Macrophage digests bacterium in vacuole.

Interleukin-1 travels in the bloodstream to the brain.

Thermostat is reset

The hypothalamus controls the body's temperature setting. Interleukin-1 induces the hypothalamus to produce more **prostaglandins**. This resets the body's 'thermostat' to a **higher temperature**, producing fever.

Hypothalamus

Temperature increases beyond the normal range of 36.2 – 37.2 °C

Fever

39.7°C

Fever onset

To adjust to the new thermostat setting, the body's physiological responses act to raise body temperature. These responses include **blood vessel constriction**, **increased metabolic rate**, and **shivering**.

The normal range of body temperature is 36.2°C – 37.2°C. Fevers of less than 40°C do not need treatment but high, prolonged fevers require prompt attention, because death usually results if the body temperature rises above 45.5°C.

Chill phase

Even though body temperature is elevated above normal, the skin remains cold, and **shivering** occurs. This condition, called a **chill**, is a definite sign that body temperature is rising. When the body reaches the setting of the thermostat, the chill disappears.

Crisis phase

Body temperature is maintained at the higher setting until the interleukin-1 has been eliminated. As the infection subsides, the thermostat is reset to 37°C. Heat losing mechanisms, such as sweating and vasodilation cause the person to feel warm. This **crisis phase** of the fever indicates that body temperature is falling.

1. Discuss the beneficial effects of fever on the body's ability to fight infections: _____

_____

_____

2. Summarise the key steps of how the body's thermostat is set at a higher level by infection: _____

_____

_____

_____

The Immune System

The efficient internal defence provided by the immune system is based on its ability to respond specifically against a foreign substance and its ability to hold a memory of this response. There are two main components of the immune system: the humoral and the cell-mediated responses. They work separately and together to protect us from disease. The **humoral immune response** is associated with the serum (non-cellular part of the blood) and involves the action of **antibodies** secreted by B cell lymphocytes. Antibodies are found in extracellular fluids including lymph, plasma, and mucus secretions. The humoral response protects the body against circulating viruses, and bacteria and their toxins. The **cell-mediated immune response** is associated with the production of specialised lymphocytes called **T cells**. It is most effective against bacteria and viruses located within host cells, as well as against parasitic protozoa, fungi, and worms. This system is also an important defence against cancer, and is responsible for the rejection of transplanted tissue. Both B and T cells develop from stem cells located in the liver of foetuses and the bone marrow of adults. T cells complete their development in the thymus, whilst the B cells mature in the bone marrow.

Lymphocytes and their Functions

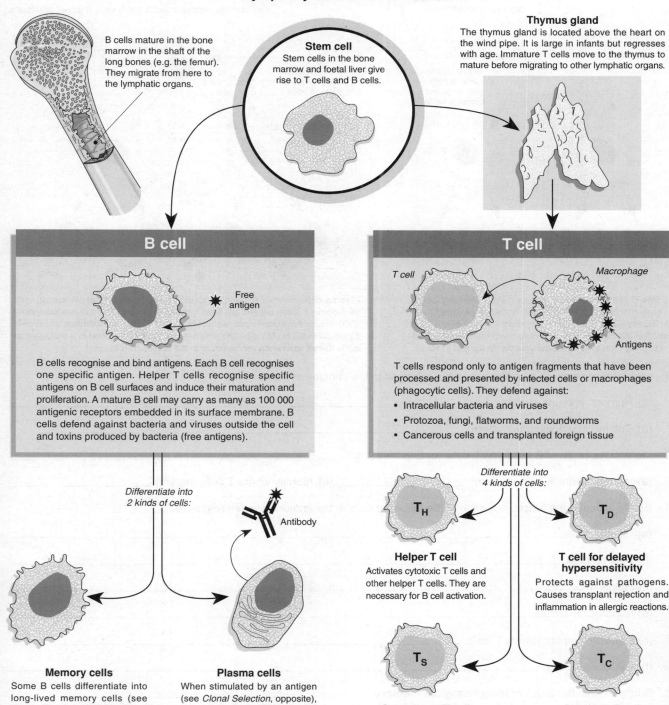

B cells mature in the bone marrow in the shaft of the long bones (e.g. the femur). They migrate from here to the lymphatic organs.

Stem cell
Stem cells in the bone marrow and foetal liver give rise to T cells and B cells.

Thymus gland
The thymus gland is located above the heart on the wind pipe. It is large in infants but regresses with age. Immature T cells move to the thymus to mature before migrating to other lymphatic organs.

B cell

Free antigen

B cells recognise and bind antigens. Each B cell recognises one specific antigen. Helper T cells recognise specific antigens on B cell surfaces and induce their maturation and proliferation. A mature B cell may carry as many as 100 000 antigenic receptors embedded in its surface membrane. B cells defend against bacteria and viruses outside the cell and toxins produced by bacteria (free antigens).

T cell

T cell   Macrophage

Antigens

T cells respond only to antigen fragments that have been processed and presented by infected cells or macrophages (phagocytic cells). They defend against:
- Intracellular bacteria and viruses
- Protozoa, fungi, flatworms, and roundworms
- Cancerous cells and transplanted foreign tissue

Differentiate into 2 kinds of cells:

Antibody

Differentiate into 4 kinds of cells:

T_H

T_D

Helper T cell
Activates cytotoxic T cells and other helper T cells. They are necessary for B cell activation.

T cell for delayed hypersensitivity
Protects against pathogens. Causes transplant rejection and inflammation in allergic reactions.

T_S

T_C

Memory cells
Some B cells differentiate into long-lived memory cells (see opposite). When these cells encounter the same antigen again (even years or decades later), they rapidly differentiate into antibody-producing plasma cells.

Plasma cells
When stimulated by an antigen (see *Clonal Selection*, opposite), some B cells differentiate into plasma cells, which secrete antibodies into the blood system. The antibodies then inactivate the circulating antigens.

Suppressor T cell
Regulates immune response by turning it off when no more antigen is present.

Cytotoxic T cell
Destroys target cells on contact. Recognises tumour (cancer) or virus infected cells by their surface (antigens and MHC markers).

Immunology

The immune system has the ability to respond to the large and unpredictable range of potential antigens encountered in the environment. The diagram below explains how this ability is based on **clonal selection** after antigen exposure. The example illustrated is for B cell lymphocytes. In the same way, a T cell stimulated by a specific antigen will multiply and develop into different types of T cells. Clonal selection and differentiation of lymphocytes provide the basis for **immunological memory**.

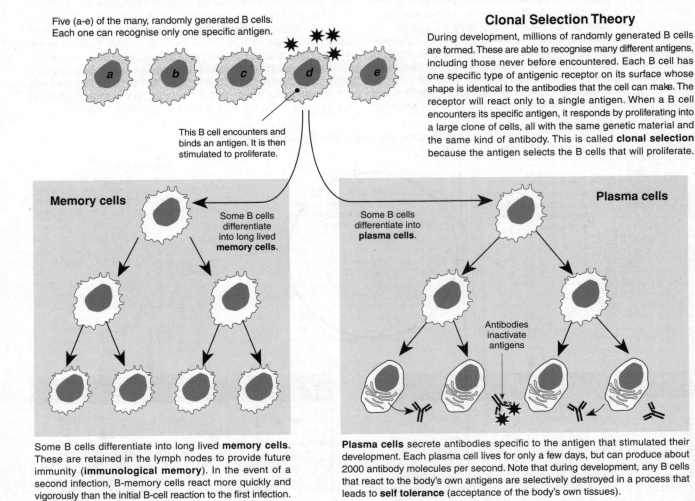

Five (a-e) of the many, randomly generated B cells. Each one can recognise only one specific antigen.

This B cell encounters and binds an antigen. It is then stimulated to proliferate.

Clonal Selection Theory

During development, millions of randomly generated B cells are formed. These are able to recognise many different antigens, including those never before encountered. Each B cell has one specific type of antigenic receptor on its surface whose shape is identical to the antibodies that the cell can make. The receptor will react only to a single antigen. When a B cell encounters its specific antigen, it responds by proliferating into a large clone of cells, all with the same genetic material and the same kind of antibody. This is called **clonal selection** because the antigen selects the B cells that will proliferate.

Memory cells

Some B cells differentiate into long lived **memory cells**.

Plasma cells

Some B cells differentiate into **plasma cells**.

Antibodies inactivate antigens

Some B cells differentiate into long lived **memory cells**. These are retained in the lymph nodes to provide future immunity (**immunological memory**). In the event of a second infection, B-memory cells react more quickly and vigorously than the initial B-cell reaction to the first infection.

Plasma cells secrete antibodies specific to the antigen that stimulated their development. Each plasma cell lives for only a few days, but can produce about 2000 antibody molecules per second. Note that during development, any B cells that react to the body's own antigens are selectively destroyed in a process that leads to **self tolerance** (acceptance of the body's own tissues).

1. State the general action of the two major divisions in the immune system:

   (a) Humoral immune system: _____

   (b) Cell-mediated immune system: _____

2. Identify the origin of B cells and T cells (before maturing): _____

3. (a) Identify where B cells mature: _____ (b) Identify where T cells mature: _____

4. Briefly describe the function of each of the following cells in the immune system response:

   (a) Memory cells: _____

   (b) Plasma cells: _____

   (c) Helper T cells: _____

   (d) Suppressor T cells: _____

   (e) Delayed hypersensitivity T cells: _____

   (f) Cytotoxic T cells: _____

5. Briefly explain the basis of **immunological memory**: _____

   _____

   _____

   _____

Antibodies

Antibodies and antigens play key roles in the response of the immune system. Antigens are foreign molecules that are able to bind to antibodies (or T cell receptors) and provoke a specific immune response. Antigens include potentially damaging microbes and their toxins (see below) as well as substances such as pollen grains, blood cell surface molecules, and the surface proteins on transplanted tissues. **Antibodies** (also called **immunoglobulins**) are proteins that are made in response to antigens. They are secreted into the plasma where they circulate and can recognise, bind to, and help to destroy antigens. There are five classes of **immunoglobulins**. Each plays a different role in the immune response (including destroying protozoan parasites, enhancing phagocytosis, protecting mucous surfaces, and neutralising toxins and viruses). The human body can produce an estimated 100 million antibodies, recognising many different antigens, including those it has never encountered. Each type of antibody is highly specific to only one particular antigen. The ability of the immune system to recognise and ignore the antigenic properties of its own tissues occurs early in development and is called **self-tolerance**. Exceptions occur when the immune system malfunctions and the body attacks its own tissues, causing an **autoimmune disorder**.

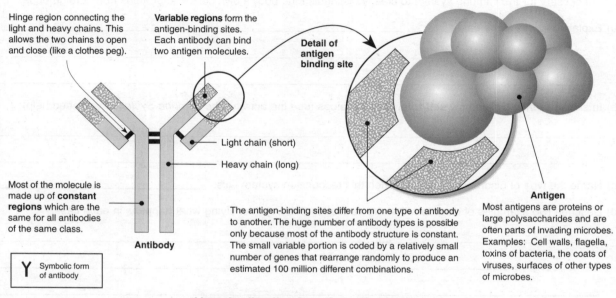

Hinge region connecting the light and heavy chains. This allows the two chains to open and close (like a clothes peg).

Variable regions form the antigen-binding sites. Each antibody can bind two antigen molecules.

Detail of antigen binding site

Light chain (short)

Heavy chain (long)

Most of the molecule is made up of **constant regions** which are the same for all antibodies of the same class.

Antibody

Y Symbolic form of antibody

The antigen-binding sites differ from one type of antibody to another. The huge number of antibody types is possible only because most of the antibody structure is constant. The small variable portion is coded by a relatively small number of genes that rearrange randomly to produce an estimated 100 million different combinations.

Antigen
Most antigens are proteins or large polysaccharides and are often parts of invading microbes. Examples: Cell walls, flagella, toxins of bacteria, the coats of viruses, surfaces of other types of microbes.

How Antibodies Inactivate Antigens

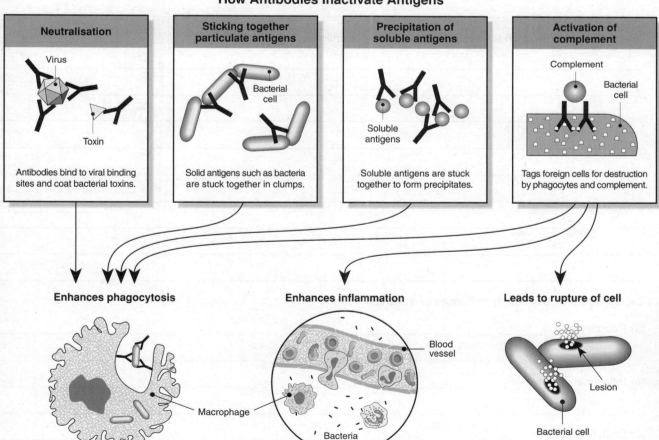

Neutralisation	Sticking together particulate antigens	Precipitation of soluble antigens	Activation of complement
Virus — Toxin	Bacterial cell	Soluble antigens	Complement — Bacterial cell
Antibodies bind to viral binding sites and coat bacterial toxins.	Solid antigens such as bacteria are stuck together in clumps.	Soluble antigens are stuck together to form precipitates.	Tags foreign cells for destruction by phagocytes and complement.

Enhances phagocytosis

Macrophage

Enhances inflammation

Blood vessel

Bacteria

Leads to rupture of cell

Lesion

Bacterial cell

Immunology

Related activities: Targets for Defence, The Immune System, Acquired Immunity, Vaccination

RA 2

1. Distinguish between an antibody and an antigen: _____

_____

_____

_____

_____

_____

_____

2. It is necessary for the immune system to clearly distinguish the body's own cells and proteins from foreign ones.

   (a) Explain why this is the case: _____

   _____

   _____

   (b) In simple terms, explain how **self tolerance** develops (see the activity *The Immune System* if you need help):

   _____

   _____

   (c) Name the type of disorder that results when this recognition system fails: _____

   (d) Describe two examples of disorders that are caused in this way, identifying what happens in each case:

   _____

   _____

   _____

   _____

3. Discuss the ways in which antibodies work to inactivate antigens: _____

   _____

   _____

   _____

   _____

   _____

   _____

   _____

   _____

4. Explain how antibody activity enhances or leads to:

   (a) Phagocytosis: _____

   _____

   (b) Inflammation: _____

   _____

   (c) Bacterial cell lysis: _____

   _____

Antigenic Variability in Pathogens

Influenza (flu) is a disease of the upper respiratory tract caused by the viral genus *Influenzavirus*. Globally, up to 500 000 people die from influenza every year, including 3000-4000 people in the UK. Three types of *Influenzavirus* affect humans. They are simply named *Influenzavirus* A, B, and C. The most common and most virulent of these strains is *Influenzavirus* A, which is discussed in more detail below. Influenza viruses are constantly undergoing genetic changes. **Antigenic drifts** are small changes in the virus which happen continually over time. Such changes mean that the influenza vaccine must be adjusted each year to include the most recently circulating influenza viruses. **Antigenic shift** occurs when two or more different viral strains (or different viruses) combine to form a new subtype. The changes are large and sudden and most people lack immunity to the new subtype. New influenza viruses arising from antigenic shift have caused influenza pandemics that have killed millions people over the last century. *Influenzavirus* A is considered the most dangerous to human health because it is capable of antigenic shift.

Structure of *Influenzavirus*

Viral strains are identified by the variation in their H and N surface antigens. Viruses are able to combine and readily rearrange their RNA segments, which alters the protein composition of their H and N glycoprotein spikes.

The *influenzavirus* is surrounded by an **envelope** containing protein and lipids.

The genetic material is actually closely surrounded by protein capsomeres (these have been omitted here and below right in order to illustrate the changes in the RNA more clearly).

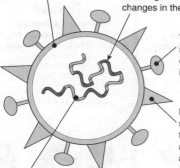

The **neuraminidase (N) spikes** help the virus to detach from the cell after infection.

Hemagglutinin (H) spikes allow the virus to recognise and attach to cells before attacking them.

The viral genome is contained on **eight RNA segments**, which enables the exchange of genes between different viral strains.

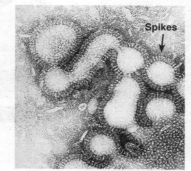

Spikes

Photo right: *Electon micrograph of Influenzavirus showing the glycoprotein spikes projecting from the viral envelope*

Antigenic Shift in *Influenzavirus*

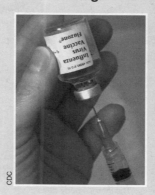
CDC

Influenza vaccination is the primary method for preventing influenza and is 75% effective. The ability of the virus to recombine its RNA enables it to change each year, so that different strains dominate in any one season. The 'flu' vaccination is updated annually to incorporate the antigenic properties of currently circulating strains. Three strains are chosen for each year's vaccination. Selection is based on estimates of which strains will be predominant in the following year.

CDC

H1N1, H1N2, and H3N2 (below) are the known *Influenza A* viral subtypes currently circulating among humans. Although the body will have acquired antibodies from previous flu strains, the new combination of N and H spikes is sufficiently different to enable new viral strains to avoid detection by the immune system. The World Health Organisation coordinates strain selection for each year's influenza vaccine.

H1N1   **H1N2**   **H3N2**

1. The *Influenzavirus* is able to mutate readily and alter the composition of H and N spikes on its surface.

   (a) Explain why this is the case: _____

   _____

   _____

   (b) Explain how this affects the ability of the immune system to recognise the virus and launch an attack:

   _____

   _____

   _____

2. Discuss why a virus capable of antigenic shift is more dangerous to humans than a virus undergoing antigenic drift:

   _____

   _____

   _____

Immunology

Related activities: The Immune System, Antibodies, Acquired Immunity, Vaccination, Disease and Public Health

A 2

Acquired Immunity

We have natural or **innate resistance** to certain illnesses; examples include most diseases of other animal species. **Acquired immunity** refers to the protection an animal develops against certain types of microbes or foreign substances. Immunity can be acquired either passively or actively and is developed during an individual's lifetime. **Active immunity** develops when a person is exposed to microorganisms or foreign substances and

the immune system responds. **Passive immunity** is acquired when antibodies are transferred from one person to another. Recipients do not make the antibodies themselves and the effect lasts only as long as the antibodies are present, usually several weeks or months. Immunity may also be **naturally acquired**, through natural exposure to microbes, or **artificially acquired** as a result of medical treatment.

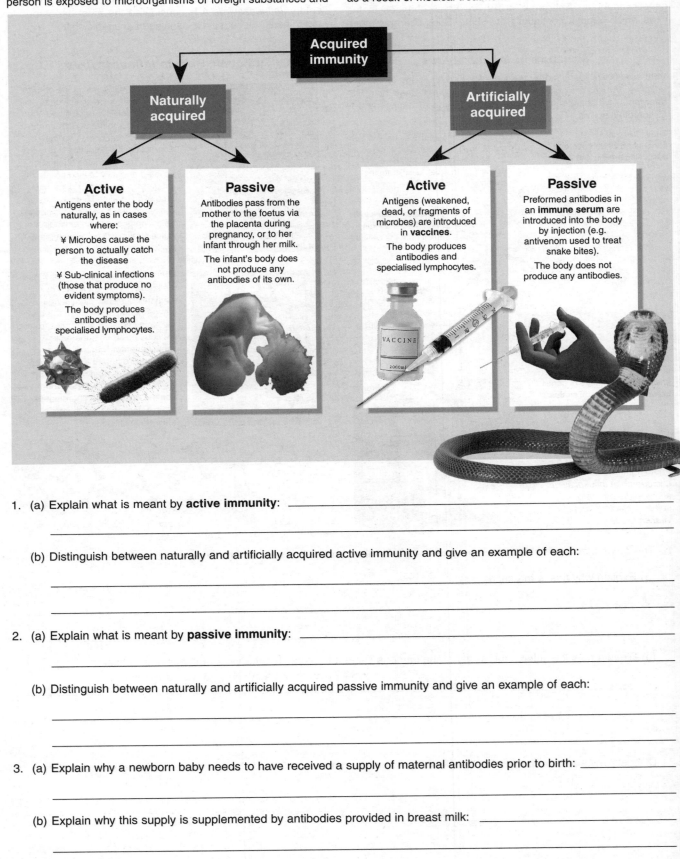

1. (a) Explain what is meant by **active immunity**: _____

   _____

   (b) Distinguish between naturally and artificially acquired active immunity and give an example of each:

   _____

   _____

2. (a) Explain what is meant by **passive immunity**: _____

   _____

   (b) Distinguish between naturally and artificially acquired passive immunity and give an example of each:

   _____

   _____

3. (a) Explain why a newborn baby needs to have received a supply of maternal antibodies prior to birth: _____

   _____

   (b) Explain why this supply is supplemented by antibodies provided in breast milk: _____

   _____

Related activities: Vaccination

Vaccination

A vaccine is a suspension of microorganisms (or pieces of them) that protects against disease by stimulating the production of antibodies and inducing **immunity**. **Vaccination** (often used synonymously with **immunisation**) is a procedure that provides **artificially acquired active immunity** in the recipient. A concerted vaccination campaign led to the eradication (in 1977) of **smallpox**, the only disease to have been eradicated in this way. Once eradicated, a pathogen is no longer present in the environment and vaccination is no longer necessary. Features of smallpox made it particularly suitable for complete eradication. It was a very recognisable and visible disease, with no long-term, human carriers and no non-human carriers. In addition, people who had not been vaccinated against the disease were identifiable by the absence of a vaccination scar on the upper arm. Disease control (as opposed to eradication) does not necessarily require that everyone be immune. **Herd immunity**, where most of the population is immune, limits outbreaks to sporadic cases because there are too few susceptible individuals to support an epidemic. Vaccination provides effective control over many common bacterial and viral diseases. Viral diseases in particular are best prevented with vaccination, as they cannot be effectively treated once contracted.

Primary and Secondary Responses to Antigens

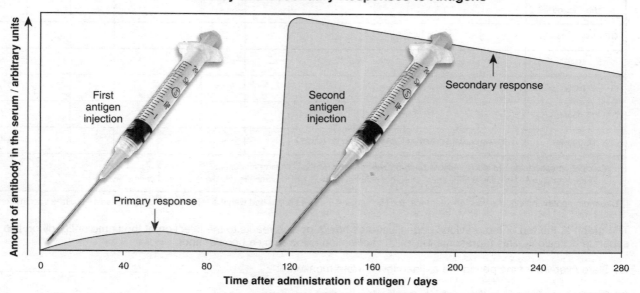

First antigen injection

Primary response

Second antigen injection

Secondary response

Amount of antibody in the serum / arbitrary units

Time after administration of antigen / days

0   40   80   120   160   200   240   280

Vaccines to protect against common diseases are administered at various stages during childhood according to an immunisation schedule.

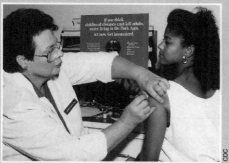

While most vaccinations are given in childhood, adults may be vaccinated against specific diseases (e.g. tuberculosis) if they are in a high risk group or if they are travelling to a region in the world where a disease is prevalent.

Selected Vaccines Used To Prevent Diseases In Humans		
Disease	**Type of vaccine**	**Recommendation**
Diphtheria	Purified diphtheria toxoid	From early childhood and every 10 years for adults
Meningococcal meningitis	Purified polysaccharide of *Neisseria menigitidis*	For people with substantial risk of infection
Whooping cough	Killed cells or fragments of *Bordetella pertussis*	Children prior to school age
Tetanus	Purified tetanus toxoid	14-16 year olds with booster every 10 years
Meningitis caused by *Haemophilus influenzae* b	Polysaccharide from virus conjugated with protein to enhance effectiveness	Early childhood
Influenza	Killed virus (vaccines using genetically engineered antigenic fragments are also being developed)	For chronically ill people, especially with respiratory diseases, or for healthy people over 65 years of age
Measles	Attenuated virus	Early childhood
Mumps	Attenuated virus	Early childhood
Rubella	Attenuated virus	Early childhood; for females of child-bearing age who are not pregnant
Polio	Attenuated or killed virus (enhanced potency type)	Early childhood
Hepatitis B	Antigenic fragments of virus	Early childhood

Immunology

Related activities: Acquired Immunity, Types of Vaccine

RDA 2

1. The table below provides a list of the vaccines used in the standard vaccination schedule for children and young adults in the United Kingdom. Additional vaccinations are available for those at high risk of contracting certain diseases.

   (a) List the diseases that each vaccine protects against.

   (b) Consult your family doctor, medical centre or other medical authority to determine the ages that each vaccine should be administered. Place a tick (✔) in each age column as appropriate (the last one has been done for you).

Vaccination Schedule Available to Children in the United Kingdom								
Vaccine	**Diseases protected from**	**Age in months**				**Age in years**		
		2	3	4	12-15	3-5	10-14	13-18
DTP (Triple antigen)								
Hib vaccine*								
OPV (Sabin vaccine)								
MMR								
BCG								
DT booster								
Td booster	Tetanus, diphtheria (low strength dose)							✔

Vaccination schedules are also available *for high risk groups* for the following diseases: anthrax, hepatitis A, hepatitis B, influenza, pneumococcal disease, typhoid, varicella (chickenpox), and yellow fever.

* Depending on an individual's vaccine tolerance, the Hib vaccine may be conjugated with the DTP vaccine or given as a separate vaccination

2. The graph at the top of the previous page illustrates how a person reacts to the injection of the same antibody on two separate occasions. This represents the initial vaccination followed by a booster shot.

   (a) State over what time period the antigen levels were monitored: _____

   (b) State what happens to the antibody levels after the first injection: _____

   _____

   (c) State what happens to the antibody levels after the booster shot: _____

   _____

   (d) Explain why the second injection has a markedly different effect: _____

   _____

3. The whole question of whether young children should be vaccinated has been a point of hot debate with some parents. The parents that do not want their children vaccinated have strongly held reasons for doing so. In a balanced way, explore the arguments for and against childhood vaccination:

   (a) State clearly the benefits from childhood vaccination: _____

   _____

   _____

   (b) Explain why some parents are concerned about vaccinating their children: _____

   _____

   _____

4. Consult your family doctor or medical centre and list three vaccinations that are recommended for travellers to overseas destinations with high risk of infectious disease:

   (a) Country/region: _____ Vaccine required: _____

   (b) Country/region: _____ Vaccine required: _____

   (c) Country/region: _____ Vaccine required: _____

Types of Vaccine

There are two basic types of vaccine: subunit vaccines and whole-agent vaccines. **Whole-agent vaccines** contain complete nonvirulent microbes, either **inactivated** (killed), or alive but **attenuated** (weakened). Attenuated viruses make very effective vaccines and often provide life-long immunity without the need for booster immunisations. Killed viruses are less effective and many vaccines of this sort have now been replaced by newer subunit vaccines. **Subunit vaccines** contain only the parts of the pathogen that induce the immune response. They are safer than attenuated vaccines because they cannot reproduce in the recipient, and they produce fewer adverse effects because they contain little or no extra material. Subunit vaccines can be made using a variety of methods, including cell fragmentation (acellular vaccines), inactivation of toxins (toxoids), genetic engineering (recombinant vaccines), and combination with antigenic proteins (conjugated vaccines). In all cases, the subunit vaccine loses its ability to cause disease but retains its antigenic properties so that it is still effective in inducing an immune response. Some of the most promising types of vaccine under development are the DNA vaccines, consisting of naked DNA which is injected into the body and produces an antigenic protein. The safety of DNA vaccines is uncertain but they show promise for use against rapidly mutating viruses such as influenza and HIV.

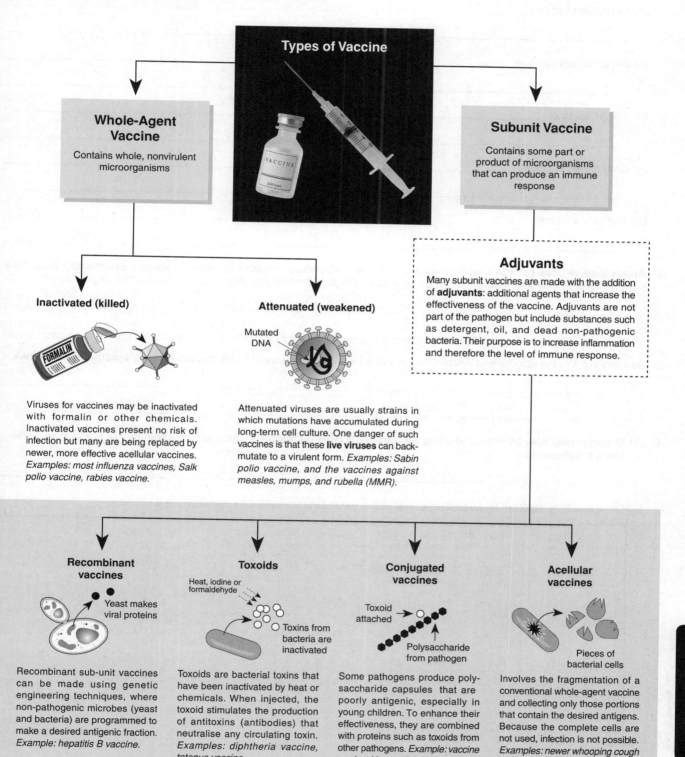

Types of Vaccine

Whole-Agent Vaccine
Contains whole, nonvirulent microorganisms

Subunit Vaccine
Contains some part or product of microorganisms that can produce an immune response

Inactivated (killed)

FORMALIN

Viruses for vaccines may be inactivated with formalin or other chemicals. Inactivated vaccines present no risk of infection but many are being replaced by newer, more effective acellular vaccines. *Examples: most influenza vaccines, Salk polio vaccine, rabies vaccine.*

Attenuated (weakened)

Mutated DNA

Attenuated viruses are usually strains in which mutations have accumulated during long-term cell culture. One danger of such vaccines is that these **live viruses** can back-mutate to a virulent form. *Examples: Sabin polio vaccine, and the vaccines against measles, mumps, and rubella (MMR).*

Adjuvants
Many subunit vaccines are made with the addition of **adjuvants**: additional agents that increase the effectiveness of the vaccine. Adjuvants are not part of the pathogen but include substances such as detergent, oil, and dead non-pathogenic bacteria. Their purpose is to increase inflammation and therefore the level of immune response.

Recombinant vaccines

Yeast makes viral proteins

Recombinant sub-unit vaccines can be made using genetic engineering techniques, where non-pathogenic microbes (yeast and bacteria) are programmed to make a desired antigenic fraction. *Example: hepatitis B vaccine.*

Toxoids

Heat, iodine or formaldehyde

Toxins from bacteria are inactivated

Toxoids are bacterial toxins that have been inactivated by heat or chemicals. When injected, the toxoid stimulates the production of antitoxins (antibodies) that neutralise any circulating toxin. *Examples: diphtheria vaccine, tetanus vaccine.*

Conjugated vaccines

Toxoid attached

Polysaccharide from pathogen

Some pathogens produce poly-saccharide capsules that are poorly antigenic, especially in young children. To enhance their effectiveness, they are combined with proteins such as toxoids from other pathogens. *Example: vaccine against Haemophilus influenzae b.*

Acellular vaccines

Pieces of bacterial cells

Involves the fragmentation of a conventional whole-agent vaccine and collecting only those portions that contain the desired antigens. Because the complete cells are not used, infection is not possible. *Examples: newer whooping cough and typhoid vaccines.*

Immunology

Related activities: Vaccination

RA 3

1. Describe briefly how each of the following types of vaccine are made and name an example of each:

(a) Whole-agent vaccine: _____

_____

(b) Subunit vaccine: _____

_____

(c) Inactivated vaccine: _____

_____

(d) Attenuated vaccine: _____

_____

(e) Recombinant vaccine: _____

_____

(f) Toxoid vaccine: _____

_____

(g) Conjugated vaccine: _____

_____

(h) Acellular vaccine: _____

_____

2. **Attenuated viruses** provide long term immunity to their recipients and generally do not require booster shots. Suggest a possible reason why attenuated viruses provide such effective long-term immunity when inactivated viruses do not:

_____

_____

3. Bearing in mind the structure of viruses, explain why heat cannot be used to kill viruses to make **inactivated vaccines**:

_____

_____

4. (a) Vaccines may now be produced using **recombinant DNA technology**. Describe an advantage of creating vaccines using these methods:

_____

(b) Draw a simple diagram to illustrate the use of the recombinant method to manufacture a vaccine:

Monoclonal Antibodies

A **monoclonal antibody** is an artificially produced antibody that binds to and inactivates only one specific protein (antigen). Monoclonal antibodies are produced in the laboratory by stimulating the production of B-lymphocytes in mice injected with the antigen. These B-lymphocytes produce an antibody against the antigen. When isolated and made to fuse with immortal tumour cells, they can be cultured indefinitely in a suitable growing medium (as shown below). Monoclonal antibodies are useful for three reasons: they are totally uniform (i.e. clones), they can be produced in very large quantities at low cost, and they are highly specific. The uses of antibodies produced by this method range from diagnostic tools, to treatments for infections and cancer, and prevention of tissue rejection in transplant patients. Many of the diagnostic tests, e.g. for some sexually transmitted or parasitic infections, previously required relatively difficult culturing or microscopic methods for diagnosis. In addition, newer diagnostic test using monoclonal antibodies are easier to interpret and often require fewer highly trained personnel.

Making Monoclonal Antibodies

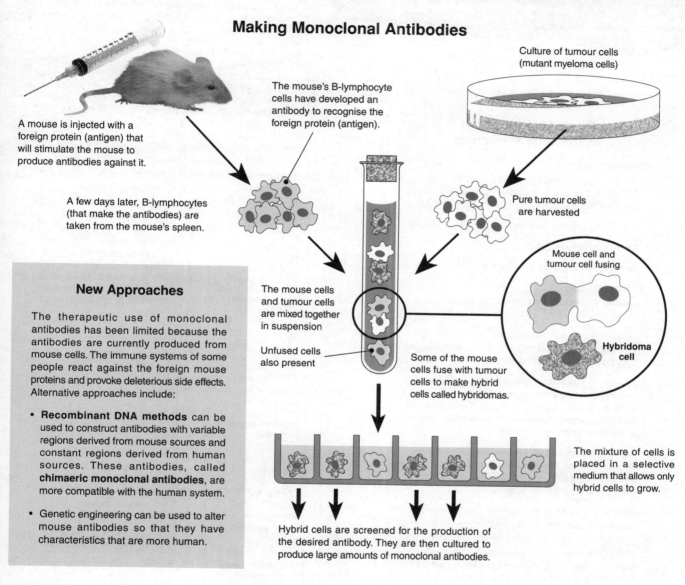

A mouse is injected with a foreign protein (antigen) that will stimulate the mouse to produce antibodies against it.

The mouse's B-lymphocyte cells have developed an antibody to recognise the foreign protein (antigen).

A few days later, B-lymphocytes (that make the antibodies) are taken from the mouse's spleen.

Culture of tumour cells (mutant myeloma cells)

Pure tumour cells are harvested

Mouse cell and tumour cell fusing

Hybridoma cell

The mouse cells and tumour cells are mixed together in suspension

Unfused cells also present

Some of the mouse cells fuse with tumour cells to make hybrid cells called hybridomas.

New Approaches

The therapeutic use of monoclonal antibodies has been limited because the antibodies are currently produced from mouse cells. The immune systems of some people react against the foreign mouse proteins and provoke deleterious side effects. Alternative approaches include:

* **Recombinant DNA methods** can be used to construct antibodies with variable regions derived from mouse sources and constant regions derived from human sources. These antibodies, called **chimaeric monoclonal antibodies**, are more compatible with the human system.

* Genetic engineering can be used to alter mouse antibodies so that they have characteristics that are more human.

The mixture of cells is placed in a selective medium that allows only hybrid cells to grow.

Hybrid cells are screened for the production of the desired antibody. They are then cultured to produce large amounts of monoclonal antibodies.

1. Identify the mouse cells used to produce the monoclonal antibodies: _____

2. Describe the characteristic of tumour cells that allows an ongoing culture of antibody-producing lymphocytes to be made:

_____

_____

3. Compare the method of producing monoclonal antibodies using mice with the alternative methods now available:

_____

_____

_____

_____

Immunology

Related activities: Antibodies   **RA 2**

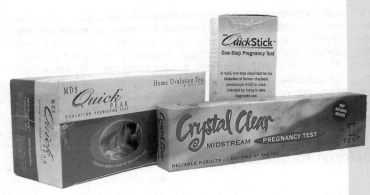

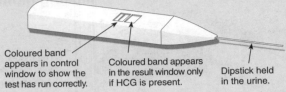

Detecting Pregnancy using Monoclonal Antibodies

When a woman becomes pregnant, a hormone called **human chorionic gonadotropin** (HCG) is released from the placenta. HCG accumulates in the bloodstream and is excreted in the urine. HCG is a glycoprotein, which means antibodies can be produced against it and used in simple test kits (below) to determine if a woman is pregnant. Monoclonal antibodies are also used in other home testing kits, such as those for detecting ovulation time (far left).

Coloured band appears in control window to show the test has run correctly.

Coloured band appears in the result window only if HCG is present.

Dipstick held in the urine.

Other Applications of Monoclonal Antibodies

Diagnostic uses

- Detecting the presence of pathogens such as *Chlamydia* and streptococcal bacteria, distinguishing between *Herpesvirus* I and II, and diagnosing AIDS.

- Measuring protein, toxin, or drug levels in serum.

- Blood and tissue typing.

- Detection of antibiotic residues in milk.

Therapeutic uses

- Neutralising endotoxins produced by bacteria in blood infections.

- Used to prevent organ rejection, e.g. in kidney transplants, by interfering with the T cells involved with the rejection of transplanted tissue.

- Used in the treatment of some auto-immune disorders such as rheumatoid arthritis and allergic asthma. The monoclonal antibodies bind to and inactivate factors involved in the cascade leading to the inflammatory response.

- Immunodetection and immunotherapy of cancer. Newer methods specifically target the cell membranes of tumour cells, shrinking solid tumours without harmful side effects.

- Inhibition of platelet clumping, which is used to prevent reclogging of coronary arteries in patients who have undergone angioplasty. The monoclonal antibodies bind to the receptors on the platelet surface that are normally linked by fibrinogen during the clotting process.

How home pregnancy detection kits work

The test area of the dipstick (below) contains two types of antibodies: free monoclonal antibodies and capture monoclonal antibodies, bound to the substrate in the test window.

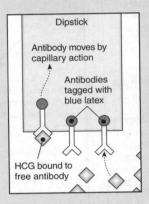

Dipstick

Antibody moves by capillary action

Antibodies tagged with blue latex

HCG bound to free antibody

The free antibodies are specific for HCG and are colour-labelled. HCG in the urine of a pregnant woman binds to the free antibodies on the surface of the dipstick. The antibodies then travel up the dipstick by capillary action.

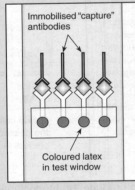

Immobilised "capture" antibodies

Coloured latex in test window

The capture antibodies are specific for the HCG-free antibody complex. The HCG-free antibody complexes travelling up the dipstick are bound by the immobilised **"capture" antibodies**, forming a sandwich. The colour labelled antibodies then create a visible colour change in the test window.

---

4. For each of the following applications, suggest why an antibody-based test or therapy is so valuable:

(a) Detection of toxins or bacteria in perishable foods: _____

_____

_____

(b) Detection of pregnancy without a doctor's prescription: _____

_____

(c) Targeted treatment of tumours in cancer patients: _____

_____

Disease and Public Health

Most of the information about the state of health of a nation's population comes from studying disease. **Epidemiology** is the study of the occurrence and the spread of disease. The **health statistics** collected by epidemiologists are used by health authorities to identify patterns of disease in their country. These patterns, including the **incidence** and **prevalence** of a disease are important in planning health services and investigating causes of disease. For example, an increase in disease prevalence on a local level (an **outbreak**) will require a different scale of public health response than would an **epidemic** (an increase in disease prevalence on a national scale) or a **pandemic** (a global epidemic). Health statistics enable the effectiveness of health policies and practices, such as vaccination programmes and quarantine procedures, to be monitored.

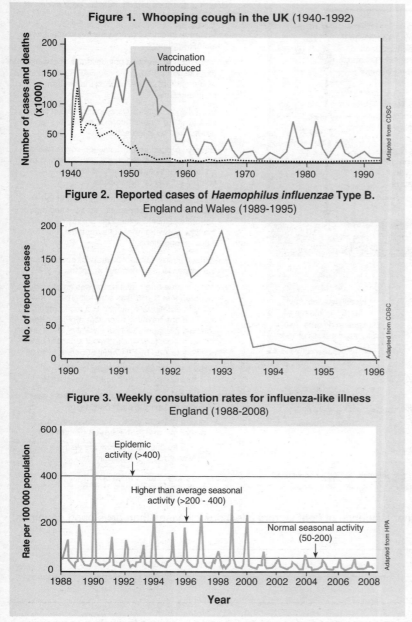

Figure 1. Whooping cough in the UK (1940-1992)

Number of cases and deaths (x1000)

Vaccination introduced

Adapted from CDSC

Figure 2. Reported cases of *Haemophilus influenzae* Type B.
England and Wales (1989-1995)

No. of reported cases

Adapted from CDSC

Figure 3. Weekly consultation rates for influenza-like illness
England (1988-2008)

Rate per 100 000 population

Epidemic activity (>400)

Higher than average seasonal activity (>200 - 400)

Normal seasonal activity (50-200)

Adapted from HPA

Year

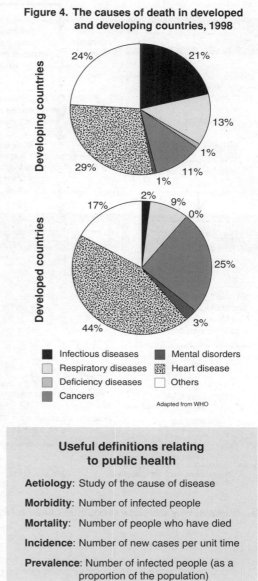

Figure 4. The causes of death in developed and developing countries, 1998

Developing countries

24%   21%

13%

1%

29%   1%   11%

Developed countries

2%

17%   9%

0%

25%

44%   3%

■ Infectious diseases   ■ Mental disorders
□ Respiratory diseases   ▦ Heart disease
▨ Deficiency diseases   □ Others
■ Cancers

Adapted from WHO

Useful definitions relating to public health

Aetiology: Study of the cause of disease

Morbidity: Number of infected people

Mortality: Number of people who have died

Incidence: Number of new cases per unit time

Prevalence: Number of infected people (as a proportion of the population)

1. (a) Suggest a probable reason for the pattern of reported cases of *Haemophilus influenzae* (Figure 2) prior to 1993:

_____

_____

(b) Suggest a possible cause for the decline in the incidence of *Haemophilius influenzae* after 1993:

_____

2. With reference to the influenza data (Figure 3), describe the event in 1990 and suggest what may have caused it:

_____

_____

_____

Immunology

Related activities: Vaccination, Antigenic Variability in Pathogens

RA 3

The Initial Spread of SARS in Toronto, Canada
(February – April, 2003)

Kwan Sui-Chu travels to Hong Kong in February, contracts **Severe Acute Respiratory Syndrome** (SARS) at the Metropole Hotel from a "super spreader", and returns home to Toronto where she infects her family. She later dies of SARS on March 5.

Kwan's Family

Tse Chi Kwai (son) → Wife of **Tse's** doctor

Tse shares a room with other patients, infecting two of them: "**Mr. D.**" and **Joseph Pollack**

"**Mr. D.**"

"**Mr. D.**" is transferred to York Central

Scarborough Grace Hospital

Joseph Pollack

Pollack's wife, **Rose**, is infected while in waiting room

Rose sits next to a prayer group **patriarch** and his **two sons**

In addition, at least 14 hospital staff develop symptoms

Mount Sinai Hospital

A patient had visited a Scarborough clinic; four on Mount Sinai staff develop symptoms

Filipino Prayer Group
(Bukas Loob Sa Diyos)

York Central Hospital

Health officials say "**Mr. D.**" could have exposed dozens. Two other patients die at York

One son travels to a Montreal conference

Patriarch's sons attend father's funeral and two other group functions. At least 30 members are infected.

One son travels to Pennsylvania

Source: *"How One Case Spawned Dozens More"*, TIME Magazine, May 5, 2003, page 36-37.

KEY: Infected   Known dead

The Containment of an Epidemic

The global SARS outbreak in 2003 developed quickly and dramatically. Its containment required heroic efforts and extraordinary measures. Health systems at every major outbreak site were strained to the limits of their capacity. The last reported case of SARS from this initial epidemic was detected and isolated, in Taiwan, on 15 June 2003.

Health authorities rapidly introduced a series of sweeping measures, including:

- Vigorous tracing of every possible contact with a SARS patient.

- Immediate quarantine of individuals suspected (but not confirmed) of having SARS (enforced with the threat of execution in the case of mainland China).

- Surveillance systems were upgraded and began to deliver the kind of information needed for prompt and targeted action.

- Hospital procedures for infection control were tightened, and procedures were developed to ensure the efficient delivery of protective equipment and other supplies.

- Mass education campaigns persuaded the population to check frequently for fever and report promptly at fever clinics. This greatly reduced the time between onset of symptoms and isolation of patients.

- A mechanism was established for coordinating the response of all relevant agencies.

- WHO issued rare travel advisories as evidence mounted that SARS was spreading by air travel along international routes. WHO recommended that persons traveling to certain regions/cities consider postponing all but essential travel until further notice. This was the most stringent travel advisory issued by WHO in its 55-year history.

- WHO set up three networks of leading laboratories around the world to investigate:
  - speeding up detection of the causative agent and developing a diagnostic test;
  - pooling clinical knowledge on symptoms, diagnosis, and management (treatment);
  - SARS epidemiology (how the disease is spread through a population).

Source: World Health Organisation (WHO)

3. Suggest why developing countries have a higher incidence of deaths from infectious diseases than developed countries:

_____

_____

_____

4. (a) Suggest why it is important to establish the **incidence** of a disease when it begins to spread through a community:

_____

_____

(b) Describe how knowledge of disease incidence was used in responding rapidly to contain the spread of SARS:

_____

_____

_____

_____

_____

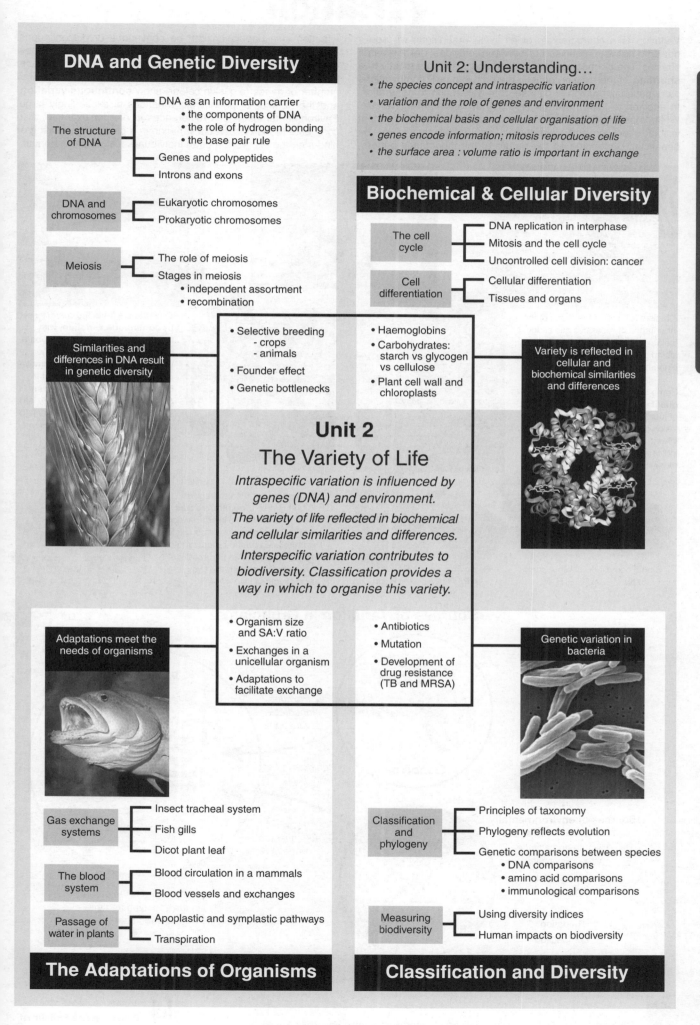

DNA and Genetic Diversity

The structure of DNA
- DNA as an information carrier
  - the components of DNA
  - the role of hydrogen bonding
  - the base pair rule
- Genes and polypeptides
- Introns and exons

DNA and chromosomes
- Eukaryotic chromosomes
- Prokaryotic chromosomes

Meiosis
- The role of meiosis
- Stages in meiosis
  - independent assortment
  - recombination

Unit 2: Understanding…
- *the species concept and intraspecific variation*
- *variation and the role of genes and environment*
- *the biochemical basis and cellular organisation of life*
- *genes encode information; mitosis reproduces cells*
- *the surface area : volume ratio is important in exchange*

Biochemical & Cellular Diversity

The cell cycle
- DNA replication in interphase
- Mitosis and the cell cycle
- Uncontrolled cell division: cancer

Cell differentiation
- Cellular differentiation
- Tissues and organs

Similarities and differences in DNA result in genetic diversity

- Selective breeding
  - crops
  - animals
- Founder effect
- Genetic bottlenecks

- Haemoglobins
- Carbohydrates: starch vs glycogen vs cellulose
- Plant cell wall and chloroplasts

Variety is reflected in cellular and biochemical similarities and differences

Unit 2
The Variety of Life

Intraspecific variation is influenced by genes (DNA) and environment.

The variety of life reflected in biochemical and cellular similarities and differences.

Interspecific variation contributes to biodiversity. Classification provides a way in which to organise this variety.

Adaptations meet the needs of organisms

- Organism size and SA:V ratio
- Exchanges in a unicellular organism
- Adaptations to facilitate exchange

- Antibiotics
- Mutation
- Development of drug resistance (TB and MRSA)

Genetic variation in bacteria

Gas exchange systems
- Insect tracheal system
- Fish gills
- Dicot plant leaf

The blood system
- Blood circulation in a mammals
- Blood vessels and exchanges

Passage of water in plants
- Apoplastic and symplastic pathways
- Transpiration

Classification and phylogeny
- Principles of taxonomy
- Phylogeny reflects evolution
- Genetic comparisons between species
  - DNA comparisons
  - amino acid comparisons
  - immunological comparisons

Measuring biodiversity
- Using diversity indices
- Human impacts on biodiversity

The Adaptations of Organisms

Classification and Diversity

Variation

Variation is a characteristic of all living organisms; we see it not only between species but between individuals of the same species. The genetic variability within species is due mostly to a **shuffling** of the existing genetic material into new combinations as genetic information is passed from generation to generation. In addition to this, **mutation** creates new alleles in individuals. While most mutations are harmful, some are 'silent' (without visible effect on the phenotype), and some may even be beneficial. Depending on the nature of the inheritance pattern, variation in a population can be continuous or discontinuous. Traits determined by a single gene (e.g. ABO blood groups) show **discontinuous variation**, with a very limited number of variants present in the population. In contrast, traits determined by a large number of genes (e.g. skin colour) show **continuous variation**, and the number of phenotypic variations is exceedingly large. Environmental influences (differences in diet for example) also contribute to the observable variation in a population, helping or hindering the expression of an individual's full genetic potential.

Albinism (above) is the result of the inheritance of recessive alleles for melanin production. Those with the albino phenotype lack melanin pigment in the eyes, skin, and hair.

Comb shape in poultry is a **qualitative trait** and birds have one of four phenotypes depending on which combination of four alleles they inherit. The dash (missing allele) indicates that the allele may be recessive or dominant.

Quantitative traits are characterised by **continuous variation**, with individuals falling somewhere on a normal distribution curve of the phenotypic range. Typical examples include skin colour and height in humans (left), grain yield in corn (above), growth in pigs (above, left), and milk production in cattle (far left). Quantitiative traits are determined by genes at many loci (polygenic) but most are also influenced by environmental factors.

Single comb
rrpp

Walnut comb
R_P_

Pea comb
rrP_

Rose comb
R_pp

Flower colour in snapdragons (right) is also a **qualitative trait** determined by two alleles. (red and white) The alleles show incomplete dominance and the heterozygote ($C^R C^W$) exhibits an intermediate phenotype between the two homozygotes.

$C^R C^R$

$C^W C^W$

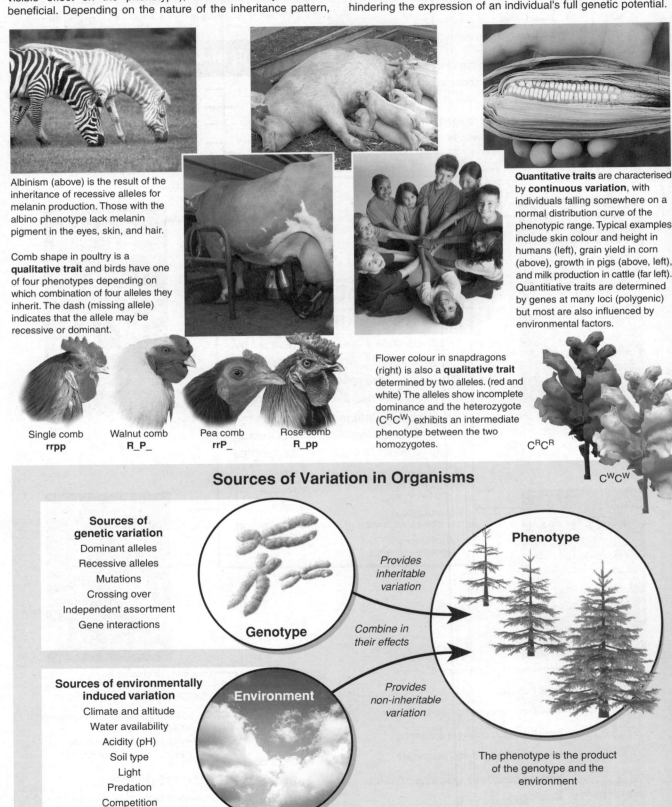

Sources of Variation in Organisms

Sources of genetic variation
Dominant alleles
Recessive alleles
Mutations
Crossing over
Independent assortment
Gene interactions

Genotype

Provides inheritable variation

Combine in their effects

Phenotype

Sources of environmentally induced variation
Climate and altitude
Water availability
Acidity (pH)
Soil type
Light
Predation
Competition

Environment

Provides non-inheritable variation

The phenotype is the product of the genotype and the environment

Related activities: Descriptive Statistics, Interpreting Sample Variability

The Effects of Environment on Phenotype

Severe stunting (krummholz)

Growth to genetic potential

Cline

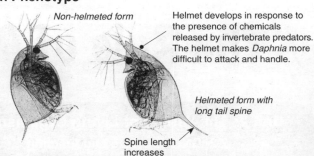

Non-helmeted form

Helmet develops in response to the presence of chemicals released by invertebrate predators. The helmet makes *Daphnia* more difficult to attack and handle.

Helmeted form with long tail spine

Spine length increases

Altitude and achievement of genetic potential in plants
Increasing altitude can stunt the phenotype of plants with the same genotype. In some conifers, e.g. **Engelmann spruce**, plants at low altitude grow to their full genetic potential, but become progressively more stunted as elevation increases, forming gnarled growth forms (krummholz) at the highest elevations. Continuous gradation in a phenotypic character within a species, associated with a change in an environmental variable, is called a **cline**.

Phenotypic response to predation in zooplankton
Some organisms respond to the presence of other, potentially harmful, organisms by changing their morphology or body shape. Invertebrates such as *Daphnia* will grow a large helmet when a predatory midge larva (*Chaoborus*) is present. Such responses are usually mediated through the action of chemicals produced by the predator (or competitor), and are common in plants as well as animals.

1. Describe the differences between **continuous** and **discontinuous** variation, giving examples to illustrate your answer:

_____

_____

_____

_____

_____

2. Identify each of the following phenotypic traits as continuous (quantitative) or discontinuous (qualitative):

(a) Wool production in sheep: _____

(d) Albinism in mammals: _____

(b) Kernel colour in maize: _____

(e) Body weight in mice: _____

(c) Blood groups in humans: _____

(f) Flower colour in snapdragons: _____

3. In the examples above, identify those in which an environmental influence on phenotype could be expected:

_____

4. From a sample of no less than 30 adults, collect data (by request or measurement) for one continuous variable (e.g. height, weight, shoe size, or hand span). On a separate sheet, record your results, produce a tally chart, and then plot a frequency histogram of the data, Staple the sheet into your workbook:

(a) Calculate the mean, median, and mode of your data (review the activity on descriptive statistics if you need help):

Mean: _____ **Mode**: _____ **Median**: _____

(b) Describe the pattern of distribution shown by the graph, giving a reason for your answer: _____

_____

_____

(c) Explain the basis of this distribution: _____

_____

(d) Explain the importance of random sampling and large sample size when gathering data relating to variation in a population. Include reference to the importance of chance in contributing to differences between samples:

_____

_____

_____

_____

The Role of DNA

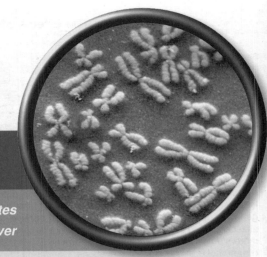

Unit 2: The Variety of Living Organisms
2.2 DNA structure and function

DNA structure, chromosome structure in prokaryotes and eukaryotes, genetic code, meiosis, crossing over

Learning Objectives

☐ 1. Compile your own glossary from the **KEY WORDS** displayed in **bold type** in the learning objectives below.

The Structure of DNA *(pages 165-171)*

☐ 2. Give examples of **nucleic acids** and describe their roles in biological systems.

☐ 3. Describe the components of a (mono)**nucleotide**: a 5C sugar (**ribose** or **deoxyribose**), a nitrogenous base (**purine** or **pyrimidine**), and a phosphate. Identify the purines and pyrimidines that form **nucleotides**.

☐ 4. Understand the role of **condensation** reactions in the formation of **polynucleotides** (nucleic acids).

☐ 5. Describe the Watson-Crick **double-helix** model of DNA structure. Include reference to the **base pairing rule**, the **antiparallel strands**, and the role of **hydrogen bonding** between **purines** and **pyrimidines**. Contrast the structure and function of **DNA** and **RNA**.

Genes and Polypeptides *(pages 171-173)*

☐ 6. Outline the basis by which information is transferred from DNA to polypeptide. Give a concise definition of a **gene**, and distinguish it from an **allele**.

☐ 7. Explain the features of the **genetic code**, including:
- The 4-letter alphabet and the 3-letter **triplet code** (**codon**) of base sequences.
- The **non-overlapping**, linear nature of the code which is read from start to finish point in one direction.
- Specific punctuation codons and their significance.
- The **universal nature** and **degeneracy** of the code.

☐ 8. Explain what is meant by the **one gene-one polypeptide hypothesis** and describe the extent to which it still applies. Explain how the hypothesis has been modified in the light of evidence indicating that much of eukaryotic DNA does not code for protein.

Chromosome Structure *(pages 162-164)*

☐ 9. Describe the structure of eukaryote **chromosomes**, explaining how DNA is packaged and organised in the nucleus (including the role of histone proteins).

☐ 10. Describe the structure of a prokaryotic chromosome, including reference to its location in the cell. Contrast prokaryotic and eukaryotic chromosomes, including reference to amount of protein-coding DNA (see #8).

Meiosis and Recombination *(pages 161, 174-177)*

☐ 11. Describe the role of meiosis in generating genetic variation. Define: **homologous chromosomes**, **genome**, **chromatid**, **centromere**. Describe how chromosome numbers can vary between somatic cells (**diploid** 2N) and gamete cells (**haploid** 1N).

☐ 12. Recognise that meiosis, like mitosis, involves DNA replication during interphase in the parent cell, but that this is followed by <u>two</u> cycles of nuclear division.

☐ 13. Summarise the principal events in meiosis, to include:
- (a) Pairing of **homologous chromosomes** (synapsis).
- (b) The **recombination** of segments of maternal and paternal homologues in **crossing over**.
- (c) The **independent assortment** of maternal and paternal chromosomes.
- (d) Production of **haploid cells**.

Textbooks

 See the 'Textbook Reference Grid' on page 7 for textbook page references relating to material in this topic.

Supplementary Texts

See pages 5-6 for additional details of these texts:

■ Adds, J., *et al.*, 2003. **Molecules and Cells**, (NelsonThornes), chpt. 2.

■ Jones, N., *et al.*, 2001. **The Essentials of Genetics**, (John Murray), pp. 123-188, 257.

Presentation MEDIA to support this topic:
GENES AND INHERITANCE
• The Genetic Code

Periodicals

See page 6 for details of publishers of periodicals:

■ **Gene Structure and Expression** Biol. Sci. Rev., 12 (5) May 2000, pp. 22-25. *An account of gene function, including a comparison of gene regulation in pro- and eukaryotes.*

■ **What is a Gene?** Biol. Sci. Rev., 15(2) Nov. 2002, pp. 9-11. *A good synopsis of genes and their role in heredity, mutations, and transcriptional control of gene expression.*

■ **Control Centre** New Scientist, 17 July 1999, (Inside Science). *The organisation of DNA in eukaryotic cells, how genes code for proteins, and the role of ribosomes and RNA in translation.*

■ **The Hidden Genetic Program** Scientific American, Oct. 2004, pp. 30-37. *Large portions of the DNA of complex organisms may encode RNA molecules with important regulatory functions.*

■ **DNA: 50 Years of the Double Helix** New Scientist, 15 March 2003, pp. 35-51. *A special issue on DNA: structure and function, repair, the new-found role of histones, and the functional significance of chromosome position in the nucleus.*

Internet

See pages 8-9 for details of how to access **Bio Links** from our web site: **www.biozone.co.uk**. From Bio Links, access sites under the topics:

GENETICS: • DNA glossary • Virtual library on genetics > **Molecular Genetics (DNA)**: • Beginners guide to molecular biology • DNA and molecular genetics • DNA from the beginning • DNA Interactive • Molecular genetics • Primer on molecular genetics • Protein synthesis

The Genome

Genome research has become an important field of genetics. A **genome** is the entire haploid complement of genetic material of a cell or organism. Each species has a unique genome, although there is a small amount of genetic variation between individuals within a species. For example, in humans the average genetic difference is one in every 500-1000 bases. Every cell in an individual has a complete copy of the genome. The base sequence shown below is the total DNA sequence for the genome of a virus. There are nine genes in the sequence, coding for nine different proteins. At least 2000 times this amount of DNA would be found in a single bacterial cell. Half a million times the quantity of DNA would be found in the genome of a single human cell. The first gene has been highlighted grey, while the start and stop codes are in black rectangles.

Genome for the φX174 bacterial virus

Start

The grey area represents the nucleotide sequence for a single gene

```
CCGTCAGGATTGACACCCTCCCAATTGTATGTTTTCATGCCTCCAAATCTTGGAGGCTTTTATGGGTTCGTTCTTATTACCCTTCTGAATGTCACGCTG
ACGAATACCTTCGGTTCGTAACCCCTAACTCTTTCTCATCTTTACGGTGTTCGGAGTTATCGTCCAAATTCTGGGAGCTATGGGAGTTTCAGTTTTATTA
GATGGATAACCGCATCAAGCTCTTGGAAGAGATTCTGTCTTTTCGTATGCAGGCCCTTGAGTTCGATAATGGTGATATGTATGTTGACGGCCATAAGGCT
ACAATAATTATAGTTCAACCCCCTCGTGTAACATCGTAACACGGTTAAGTAGGTAATTGAAGAGTCATTGTCTATGTTTGAGTAGTGCTTGGAGTCTTGG
CTATAGACCACCGCCCCGAAGGGGACGAAAAATGGTTTTTACAGAACGAGAAGACGGTTACGCAGTTTTGCCGCAAGCTGGCTGGTGAACGCCCTCTTAA
TTTCGGACATGCGCTATAGAATCAGGTCCGGACCTCGGTAGAACTTGTGAGTAGGAATTATGGAAGAAAAACCCCATTAATATGAGTAGCGCTTATAGG
GCTATTCAGCGTTTGATGAATGCAATGCGACAGGCTCATGCTGATGGTTGGTTTATCGTTTTTGACAGTCTCACGTTGGCTGACGACCGATTAGAGGCGT
GTGAGGCGCACAGTTAGTAATCGGAACGCTCGGAGCCGTGGTTCTTGGTATGCTGGTTATAGTGCTTTTATCAGTGCGTTTCGTAACCCTAATAGTATTT
GTATCAGTATTTTTGTGTGGCTGAGTATCGTAGAGCTAATGGCCGTCTTCATTTCCATGCGGTGCACTTTATGGGGACACTTCGTAGAGGTAGCGTTGAG
CGCACATGGGTTGAGGCTACCCGTATGAGTTGGTATTCCGGTGCATAAAAGGTTCGATAAATTGAGCCGCGGTAACGCATAGGCTGCTGGTTTTAATCG
AGGACGCTTTTTCACGTTGGTCGTTGGTTGTGGCCTGTTGATGCTAAAGGTGAGCGCTTAAAGGTACCAGTTATATGGCTGTTGGTTTCTATGTGGCTAA
GAAGGCTTCATGGGTGTCGAACCAAAAATCAGTCAACAAGGTAAGAAATGGAACAACTCGAAATGGTCGTTCCAGGTATAGAGTGAAAAGAATTGCATA
AAGGTGTTCAGAATCAGAATGAGCCGCAAGTTCGGGATGAAAATGGTCACAATGAGAAATCTCTCCACGGAGTGGTTAATCGAAGTTAGCAAGGTGGGTT
ACGCGGCGGTTTTGCAGCCGATGTCATTGAAAAGGGTCGGAGTTAGATGACAGAAAAAGGCAAGACGAAGTTAGACCAACTTGCCGCAGCGCAGCA
AGCTGTGACGAGAAATCTGGTCAAATTTATGCGCGCTTGGATAAAAATGATTGGCGTATCCAACCTGGACAGTTTTATCGGTTCCATGAGGCAGAAGTTA
AAGGGGGTCGTCAGGTGAAGGTAAATTAAGCATTTGTTCGTCATCATTAAGGACGAAATAGTTCTATTAAAAAGGTGAGTAGTCTTTATAGGCTTTCACA
AATGA GAAAATTCGACCTATCCTTGCGCAGCTCGAGAAGCTCTTAGTTTGCGACGTTTCGCCATCAACTAACGATTGTGTCAAAAAGTGACGCGTTGGAT
AATTTTAGGATTGTTGTGTTAGAGATGGTACTTGTTTTTACAGTGACTATAGATTTGGTCAGGAGTCGTTGCAGGGTTCGTATAATTCGGTGAAGAGGAG
AAGAGCGTGGATTACTATCTGAGTCCGATGCTGTTCAAGGAGTAATAGGTAAGAAATCATGAGTCAAGTTAGTGAACAATCCGTACGTTTCCAGACCGCT
GCAGTCATCGTTAGGTTTGAAACAATGAGGAGTCTTTTAGCTTTAGTAGAAGCCAATTTAGGTTTTGCCGTCTTCGGACTTACTCGAATTATCTCCGGTT
GCTCTCGTGCTCGTCGCTGCGTTGAGGCTTGCGTTTATGGTACGC
GCCTGCGAGGTGCGGTAATTATTACAAAAGGGATTTAAGTCCGTAGGC
GTTAAAGCCGGTGAATTGTTCGGGTTTACCTTGCGTGTAGGCGGA
TCGCGGAAATGGGAACGGAAATCATCGAGGGTTGCCGACGGCTGC
CGTGTTTGGTATGTAGGTGGTCAACAATTTTAATTGCAGGGGCTT
TAGAGCTTCGTCAGCGGTCGCTATTGGCCTCATCAACTTTAGCAT
GGACGCCGTTGGCGCTGTCCGTCTTTGTGGATTGCGTCGTGGCGT
GTTCTTTTCGCCGTAGGAGTTATATTGGTCATCACAATTGTCAGC
GCACGATTAAGCCTGATACCAATAAAATCCCTAAGCATTTGTTTCA
GAGTCCTCGTTCGCGTGGTCAGGTTTACAAAAGTGTAGGGTGGT
ACTGAGCTTTCTGGCCAAATGAGGAGTTCTACCAGATCTATTGAC
GTCTCTAATGTCGCGTACTGTTCATTTCGTGCGAACAGTCGCAGT
GGCATCTGGGTATGATGTTGATGGAACTGAGCAAACGTCGTTAGG
TTCAGTTTCGTGGAAATCGCAATTCCATGACTTAGAGAAATCAGC
ATACCGATATTGGTGGCGACCCTGTTTTGTATGGCAACTTGGCGC
TCTTCGGCCAAGGAGTTACTTAGCCTTCGGAAGTTCTTCCACTAT
GGTGATTTGCAAGAACGCGTACTTATTCGCAACCATGATTATGAC
GGCCGTTTTTAATTTTAAAAATGGCGAAGCGAATATTGGAGTGTGAGTTAGAAAATAGTGGTTCAGTAGTAACTTAGCGGTCACCAGCCGTGTAACGCTA
TGAGGGGTTGACCAAGCGAAGCGGGGTAGGTTTTGTGCTTAGGAGTTTAATCATGTTTCAGACTTTTATTTGTCGCCACAATTGAAAGTTTTTTTCTGAT
ATTGGGAGTTTGATAGTTTTATATTGGAACTGGTACATCGAAATCCACAGACATTTTGTCCACGGCTTCTTCGAGGTGATTGTCTTCAGTCTTGGTGGAA
ATGCTGGTAATGGTGGTTTTCTTCATTGCATTCAGATGGATACATCTGTCAAGGCCGCGAATCAGGTTGTTTCGATATTGTTTCTGATATTTGATGG
TACGGCTGGTAGGTTTCCTATTTGTAGTTATCCGTCAGCCCTCCCATCTGAGCCTTCGGTCTTCTGAGTTTCGGTTGGTTTGTCGGTTTTTTAAATCCCAGC
GATGGTGGTTATTATACGGTCAAGGACTGTGTGACTATTGACGTCCTTCCCGCCCCGCAATAACGTGTACGTTGGTTTCATGGTTTGGTCTAAGT
TCGTGGTTTGTATTTAGTGGAGTGAATTCACCGACCTCTGTTTATTAGAGAAATTATTGGACTAAGTCGCTTTGGTTAGGGGCCGTAAATCATCGCCATT
ATTGGTGGCGGTATTGCTTGTGCTTGGTGGTGGCGCCATGTCTAAATTGTTTGGAGCCGGTCAAAAAGCGGCCTCCGGTGGCATTCAAGGTGATGTGG
TTTGATCCCCGCCGGACTAGTCCCAATCCTTGTAATGTCGGAAGTTACCGTCTAAATTATGGTCGTAGTGGGTACGGATGTCATAAGAATAGCCATCGTT
TGTTTCTGGTGGTATGGGTAAAGGTCGTAAAGGAGTTCTTGAAGGTACGTTGGAGGGTGGGAGTTCTGCCGTTTGTGATAAGTTGGTTGATTTGGTTGGA
GTACTCGTGGTCGTGGGAGGGTTCGTAATTCGAGTCCCTTAGGTCGTCGTTCTATTAGTGCTCATAGGAAAGGAAATAGTCGGCGTCTGAACGGTGGTTC
GTTCGTCTGCTGGTATCGTTGACGGCGGATTTGAGAATCAAAAAAGACCTTAGACTGGATTGGTAAGGAGTTACGTCAGATATGGACCAGAAAGCATAAGACCGCACTTGAGCGGGTGAGTTACGGTCGTTAGAGAAAAAGTCAG
GAAGACAACTATTCGTTCGTAGAGTAAAAGACGTATATGGACCAGAAAGCATAAGACCGCACTTGAGCGGGTGAGTTACGGTCGTTAGAGAAAAAGTCAG
GAGTCTAGTGCTCGGCTTGCGTCTATTATGGAAAAGACCAATCTTTCCAAGCAACAGCAGGTTTCCGAGATTATGGGCGAAATGCTTACTCAAGCTCAAA
ATGGGGAGTAAGAGGCAAAGGACTACTTGATTCAGTTGGAGTCCTGATTGGACGGTCAGTAAAGAAAGTAAACCAGTAACCATTTTATGACTGGTCGGC
TGGCTGTTGTCATATTGGCGCTAGTGCAAAGGATATTTCTAATGTCGTCACTGATGCTGCTTCTGGTGTGGTTGATATTTTTCATCGTATTGATAAAGCT
AATAAAGGATGTGTTTAATCTCGGTTATGGTAGTGGAAATGGGAGAAAGGTCTTTAACAAGGTTCATAGCCGTTG
```

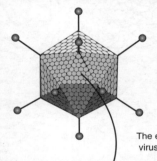

φX174 bacterial virus

This virus consists of a protein coat made up of a 20-sided polyhedron. Spikes made of protein at each of the 12 corners are used to attach itself to a bacterial cell.

The entire DNA sequence for the virus is made up of just 9 genes

1. Explain what is meant by the **genome** of an organism: _____

   _____

2. Determine the number of bases, kilobases, and megabases in this genome (100 bases in each row, except the last):

   1 kb = 1 kilobase = 1000 bases   **1 Mb** = 1 megabase = 1 000 000 bases

   (a) Bases: _____   (b) Kilobases: _____   (c) Megabases: _____

3. Determine how many bases are present in the gene shown above (in the grey area): _____

4. State whether the genome of the virus above is **small, average** or **large** in size compared to those viruses listed in the table on the earlier page *DNA Molecules*:

   _____

Related activities: DNA Molecules

Prokaryotic Chromosomes

DNA is a universal carrier of genetic information but the way in which it is packaged in the cells of prokaryotes and eukaryotes is fundamentally different. Unlike eukaryotic chromosomes, the prokaryotic chromosome is not enclosed in a nuclear membrane and is not associated with protein. It is a single circular (rather than linear) molecule of double stranded DNA and is located in a nuclear region called the **nucleoid**, which is in direct contact with the cytoplasm. The nucleoid can be variously shaped, and in actively growing cells it may occupy as much as 20% of the cell's volume. The chromosome is attached to the plasma membrane, and proteins in the plasma membrane are responsible for DNA replication and segregation of the new chromosome to a daughter

cell in cell division. As well as the bacterial chromosome, bacteria often contain small circular, double-stranded DNA molecules called **plasmids**. Plasmids are not connected to the main bacterial chromosome and they replicate independently of it. They usually contain 5-100 genes that are not crucial to cell survival under normal conditions and they may be gained or lost without harming the cell. However, in certain environments, they may confer a selective advantage as they may carry genes for properties such as antibiotic resistance, heavy metal tolerance, and synthesis of certain enzymes. The horizontal gene transfer of plasmid DNA by bacterial **conjugation** is a major factor in the spread drug resistance and in rapid bacterial evolution.

Organisation of the Prokaryotic Chromosome

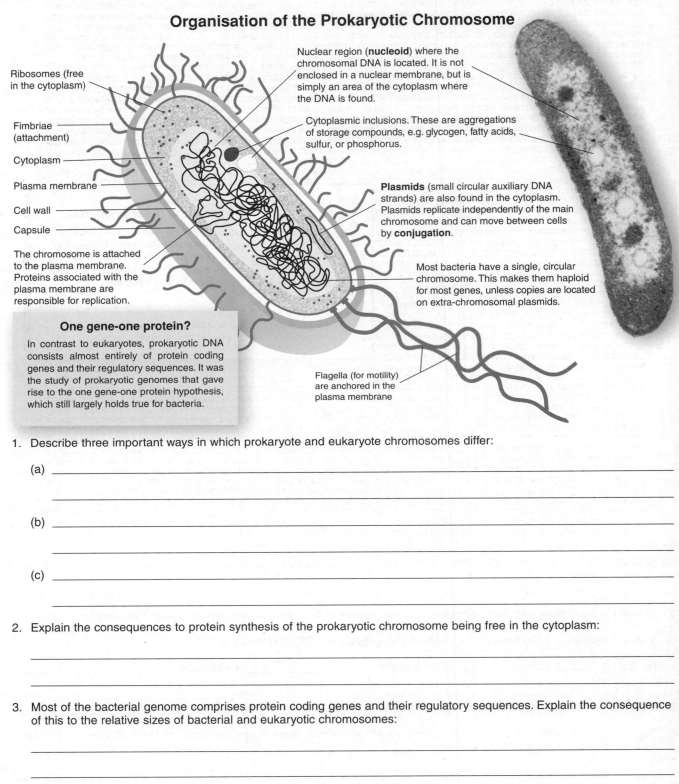

Ribosomes (free in the cytoplasm)

Fimbriae (attachment)

Cytoplasm

Plasma membrane

Cell wall

Capsule

The chromosome is attached to the plasma membrane. Proteins associated with the plasma membrane are responsible for replication.

Nuclear region (**nucleoid**) where the chromosomal DNA is located. It is not enclosed in a nuclear membrane, but is simply an area of the cytoplasm where the DNA is found.

Cytoplasmic inclusions. These are aggregations of storage compounds, e.g. glycogen, fatty acids, sulfur, or phosphorus.

Plasmids (small circular auxiliary DNA strands) are also found in the cytoplasm. Plasmids replicate independently of the main chromosome and can move between cells by **conjugation**.

Most bacteria have a single, circular chromosome. This makes them haploid for most genes, unless copies are located on extra-chromosomal plasmids.

Flagella (for motility) are anchored in the plasma membrane

One gene-one protein?

In contrast to eukaryotes, prokaryotic DNA consists almost entirely of protein coding genes and their regulatory sequences. It was the study of prokaryotic genomes that gave rise to the one gene-one protein hypothesis, which still largely holds true for bacteria.

1. Describe three important ways in which prokaryote and eukaryote chromosomes differ:

(a) _____

_____

(b) _____

_____

(c) _____

_____

2. Explain the consequences to protein synthesis of the prokaryotic chromosome being free in the cytoplasm:

_____

_____

3. Most of the bacterial genome comprises protein coding genes and their regulatory sequences. Explain the consequence of this to the relative sizes of bacterial and eukaryotic chromosomes:

_____

_____

Related activities: Prokaryotic Cells, Eukaryote Chromosome Structure, DNA Molecules   **Web links**: Structure and Function of Bacterial Cells

Eukaryote Chromosome Structure

The chromosomes of eukaryote cells (such as those from plants and animals) are complex in their structure compared to those of prokaryotes. The illustration below shows a chromosome during the early stage of meiosis. Here it exists as a chromosome consisting of two chromatids. A non-dividing cell would have chromosomes with the 'equivalent' of a single chromatid only. The chromosome consists of a protein coated strand which coils in three ways during the time when the cell prepares to divide.

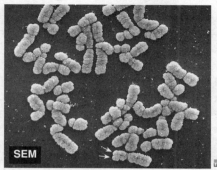

A cluster of human chromosomes seen during metaphase of cell division. Individual chromatids (arrowed) are difficult to discern on these double chromatid chromosomes.

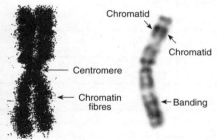

Chromatid

Chromatid

Centromere

Chromatin fibres

Banding

Chromosome TEM   Human chromosome 3

A human chromosome from a dividing white blood cell (above left). Note the compact organisation of the chromatin in the two chromatids. The LM photograph (above right) shows the banding visible on human chromosome 3.

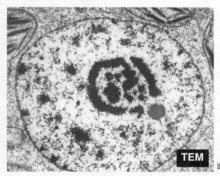

TEM

In non-dividing cells, chromosomes exist as single-armed structures. They are not visible as coiled structures, but are 'unwound' to make the genes accessible for transcription (above).

Looped domains

The evidence for the existence of looped domains comes from the study of giant lampbrush chromosomes in amphibian oocytes (above). Under electron microscopy, the lateral loops of the DNA-protein complex have a brushlike appearance.

The Packaging of Chromatin

Chromatin structure is based on successive levels of DNA packing. **Histone proteins** are responsible for packing the DNA into a compact form. Without them, the DNA could not fit into the nucleus. Five types of histone proteins form a complex with DNA, in a way that resembles "beads on a string". These beads, or **nucleosomes**, form the basic unit of DNA packing.

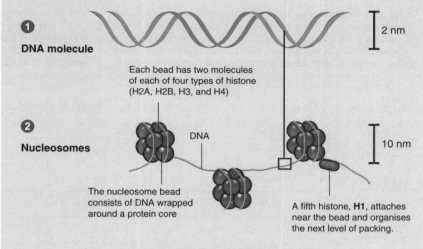

1 DNA molecule

2 nm

Each bead has two molecules of each of four types of histone (H2A, H2B, H3, and H4)

2 Nucleosomes

DNA

10 nm

The nucleosome bead consists of DNA wrapped around a protein core

A fifth histone, **H1**, attaches near the bead and organises the next level of packing.

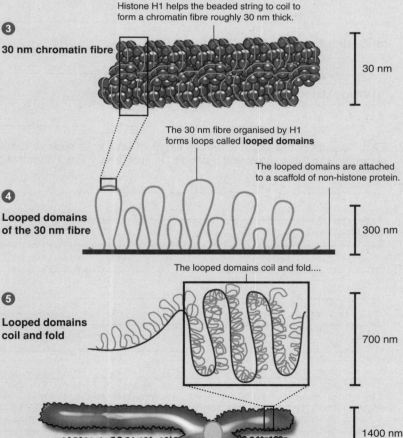

Histone H1 helps the beaded string to coil to form a chromatin fibre roughly 30 nm thick.

3 30 nm chromatin fibre

30 nm

The 30 nm fibre organised by H1 forms loops called **looped domains**

The looped domains are attached to a scaffold of non-histone protein.

4 Looped domains of the 30 nm fibre

300 nm

The looped domains coil and fold....

5 Looped domains coil and fold

700 nm

1400 nm

6 Metaphase chromosome

...making the chromatin even more compact and producing the characteristic metaphase chromosome.

Related activities: DNA Molecules
Web links: Chromosome Structure

EA 2

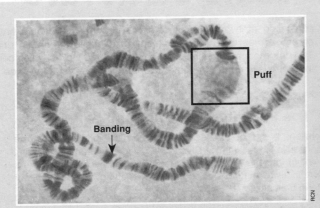

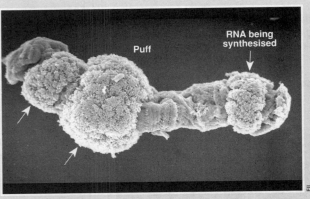

Banded chromosome: This light microscope photo is a view of the polytene chromosomes in a salivary gland cell of a sandfly. It shows a banding pattern that is thought to correspond to groups of genes. Regions of chromosome **puffing** are thought to occur where the genes are being transcribed into mRNA (see SEM on right).

A **polytene chromosome** viewed with a scanning electron microscope (SEM). The arrows indicate localised regions of the chromosome that are uncoiling to expose their genes (puffing) to allow transcription of those regions. Polytene chromosomes are a special type of chromosome consisting of a large bundle of chromatids bound tightly together.

1. Explain the significance of the following terms used to describe the structure of chromosomes:

   (a) DNA: _____

   _____

   (b) Chromatin: _____

   _____

   (c) Histone: _____

   _____

   (d) Centromere: _____

   _____

   _____

   (e) Chromatid: _____

   _____

2. Each human cell has about a 1 metre length of DNA in its nucleus. Discuss the mechanisms by which this DNA is packaged into the nucleus and organised in such a way that it does not get ripped apart during cell division:

   _____

   _____

   _____

   _____

   _____

   _____

   _____

   _____

   _____

   _____

   _____

   _____

   _____

   _____

Nucleic Acids

Nucleic acids are a special group of chemicals in cells concerned with the transmission of inherited information. They have the capacity to store the information that controls cellular activity. The central nucleic acid is called **deoxyribonucleic acid** (DNA). DNA is a major component of chromosomes and is found primarily in the nucleus, although a small amount is found in mitochondria and chloroplasts. Other **ribonucleic acids** (RNA) are involved in the 'reading' of the DNA information. All nucleic acids are made up of simple repeating units called **nucleotides**, linked together to form chains or strands, often of great length. The strands vary in the sequence of the bases found on each nucleotide. It is this sequence which provides the 'genetic code' for the cell. In addition to nucleic acids, certain nucleotides and their derivatives are also important as suppliers of energy (**ATP**) or as hydrogen ion and electron carriers in respiration and photosynthesis (NAD, NADP, and FAD).

Chemical Structure of a Nucleotide

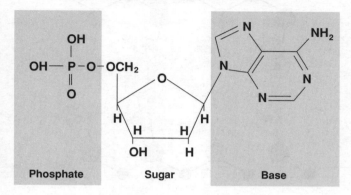

Phosphate   Sugar   Base

Symbolic Form of a Nucleotide

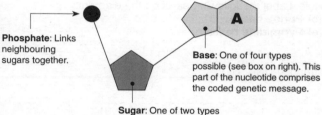

Phosphate: Links neighbouring sugars together.

Base: One of four types possible (see box on right). This part of the nucleotide comprises the coded genetic message.

Sugar: One of two types possible: ribose in RNA and deoxyribose in DNA.

Nucleotides are the building blocks of DNA. Their precise sequence in a DNA molecule provides the genetic instructions for the organism to which it governs. Accidental changes in nucleotide sequences are a cause of mutations, usually harming the organism, but occasionally providing benefits.

Bases

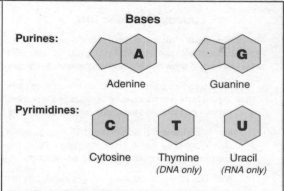

Purines:

Adenine   Guanine

Pyrimidines:

Cytosine   Thymine   Uracil
                  (DNA only)   *(RNA only)*

The two-ringed bases above are **purines** and make up the longer bases. The single-ringed bases are **pyrimidines**. Although only one of four kinds of base can be used in a nucleotide, **uracil** is found only in RNA, replacing **thymine**. DNA contains: A, T, G, and C, while RNA contains A, U, G, and C.

Sugars

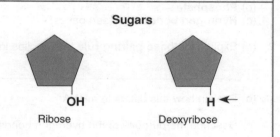

Ribose   Deoxyribose

Deoxyribose sugar is found only in DNA. It differs from **ribose** sugar, found in RNA, by the lack of a single oxygen atom (arrowed).

RNA Molecule

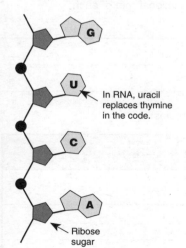

In RNA, uracil replaces thymine in the code.

Ribose sugar

DNA Molecule

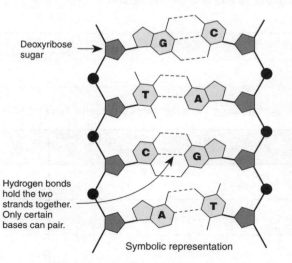

Deoxyribose sugar

Hydrogen bonds hold the two strands together. Only certain bases can pair.

Symbolic representation

DNA Molecule

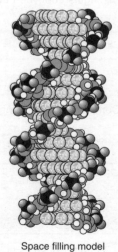

Space filling model

Ribonucleic acid (RNA) comprises a *single strand* of nucleotides linked together.

Deoxyribonucleic acid (DNA) comprises a *double strand* of nucleotides linked together. It is shown unwound in the symbolic representation (left). The DNA molecule takes on a twisted, double helix shape as shown in the space filling model on the right.

Related activities: DNA Molecules, Creating a DNA Molecule

A 2

Formation of a nucleotide

Condensation
(water removed)

A nucleotide is formed when phosphoric acid and a base are chemically bonded to a sugar molecule. In both cases, water is given off, and they are therefore condensation reactions. In the reverse reaction, a nucleotide is broken apart by the addition of water (**hydrolysis**).

Formation of a dinucleotide

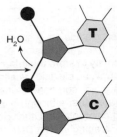

Two nucleotides are linked together by a condensation reaction between the phosphate of one nucleotide and the sugar of another.

Double-Stranded DNA

The **double-helix** structure of DNA is like a ladder twisted into a corkscrew shape around its longitudinal axis. It is 'unwound' here to show the relationships between the bases.

- The way the correct pairs of bases are attracted to each other to form hydrogen bonds is determined by the number of bonds they can form and the shape (length) of the base.

- The **template strand** the side of the DNA molecule that stores the information that is transcribed into mRNA. The template strand is also called the **antisense strand**.

- The other side (often called the **coding strand**) has the same nucleotide sequence as the mRNA except that T in DNA substitutes for U in mRNA. The coding strand is also called the **sense strand**.

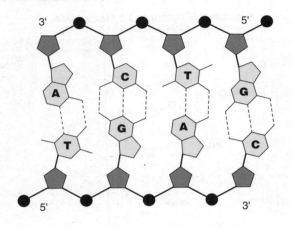

1. The diagram above depicts a double-stranded DNA molecule. Label the following parts on the diagram:
   (a) **Sugar** (deoxyribose)
   (b) **Phosphate**
   (c) **Hydrogen bonds** (between bases)
   (d) **Purine** bases
   (e) **Pyrimidine** bases

2. (a) Explain the **base-pairing rule** that applies in double-stranded DNA: _____

   _____

   (b) Explain how this differs in mRNA: _____

   (c) Describe the purpose of the hydrogen bonds in double-stranded DNA: _____

   _____

3. Describe the functional role of nucleotides: _____

   _____

4. Distinguish between the **template strand** and **coding strand** of DNA, identifying the functional role of each:

   _____

   _____

   _____

5. Complete the following table summarising the differences between DNA and RNA molecules:

	DNA	RNA
Sugar present		
Bases present		
Number of strands		
Relative length		

Creating a DNA Model

Although DNA molecules can be enormous in terms of their molecular size, they are made up of simple repeating units called **nucleotides**. A number of factors control the way in which these nucleotide building blocks are linked together. These factors cause the nucleotides to join together in a predictable way. This is referred to as the **base pairing rule** and can be used to construct a complementary DNA strand from a template strand, as illustrated in the exercise below:

DNA Base Pairing Rule			
Adenine	is always attracted to	**Thymine**	A ←→ T
Thymine	is always attracted to	**Adenine**	T ←→ A
Cytosine	is always attracted to	**Guanine**	C ←→ G
Guanine	is always attracted to	**Cytosine**	G ←→ C

1. Cut around the nucleotides on page 139 and separate each of the 24 nucleotides by cutting along the columns and rows (see arrows indicating two such cutting points). Although drawn as geometric shapes, these symbols represent chemical structures.

2. Place one of each of the four kinds of nucleotide on their correct spaces below:

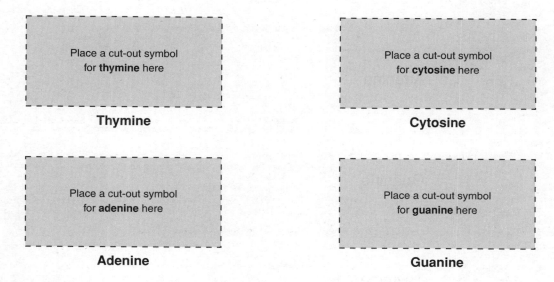

Place a cut-out symbol for **thymine** here	Place a cut-out symbol for **cytosine** here
Thymine	**Cytosine**
Place a cut-out symbol for **adenine** here	Place a cut-out symbol for **guanine** here
Adenine	**Guanine**

3. Identify and **label** each of the following features on the *adenine* nucleotide immediately above:
   phosphate, sugar, base, hydrogen bonds

4. Create one strand of the DNA molecule by placing the 9 correct 'cut out' nucleotides in the labelled spaces on the following page (DNA molecule). Make sure these are the right way up (with the **P** on the left) and are aligned with the left hand edge of each box. Begin with thymine and end with guanine.

5. Create the complementary strand of DNA by using the base pairing rule above. Note that the nucleotides have to be arranged upside down.

6. Under normal circumstances, it is not possible for adenine to pair up with guanine or cytosine, nor for any other mismatches to occur. Describe the two factors that prevent a mismatch from occurring:

   (a) Factor 1: _____

   _____

   (b) Factor 2: _____

   _____

7. Once you have checked that the arrangement is correct, you may glue, paste or tape these nucleotides in place.

> **NOTE:** There may be some value in keeping these pieces loose in order to practise the base pairing rule. For this purpose, *removable tape* would be best.

168

DNA Molecule

Put the named nucleotides on the left hand side to create the template strand

Put the matching **complementary** nucleotides opposite the template strand

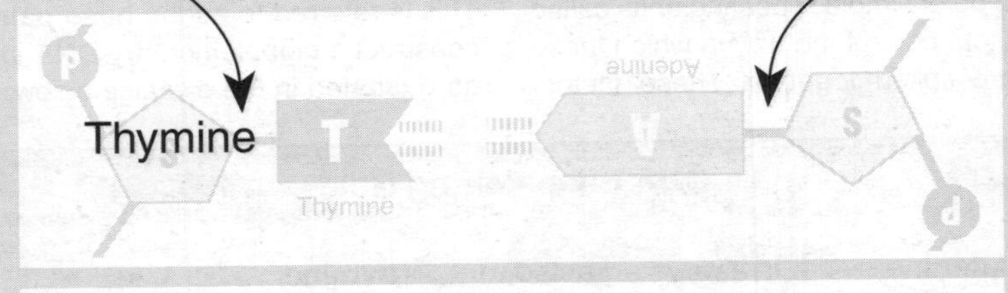

Thymine

Cytosine

Adenine

Adenine

Guanine

Thymine

Thymine

Cytosine

Guanine

Nucleotides

Tear out this page along the perforation and separate each of the 24 nucleotides
by cutting along the columns and rows (see arrows indicating the cutting points).

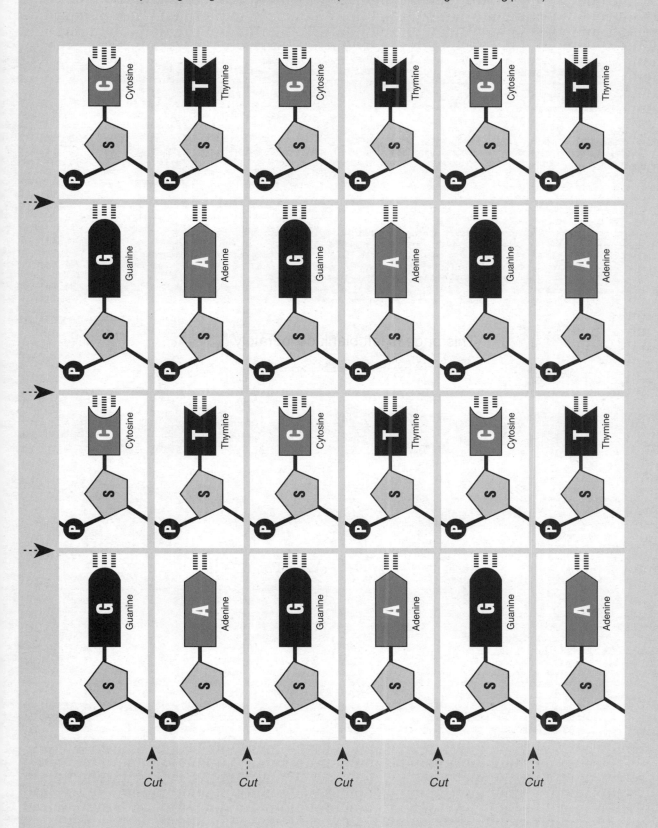

This page is left blank deliberately

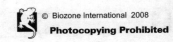

DNA Molecules

Even the smallest DNA molecules are extremely long. The DNA from the small *Polyoma* virus, for example, is 1.7 µm long; about three times longer than the longest proteins. The DNA comprising a bacterial chromosome is 1000 times longer than the cell into which it has to fit. The amount of DNA present in the nucleus of the cells of eukaryotic organisms varies widely from one species to another. In vertebrate sex cells, the quantity of DNA ranges from 40 000 **kb** to 80 000 000 **kb**, with humans about in the middle of the range. The traditional focus of DNA research has been on those DNA sequences that code for proteins, yet protein-coding DNA accounts for less than 2% of the DNA in human chromosomes. The rest of the DNA, once dismissed as non-coding 'evolutionary junk', is now recognised as giving rise to functional RNA molecules, many of which have already been identified as having important regulatory functions. While there is no clear correspondence between the complexity of an organism and the number of protein-coding genes in its genome, this is not the case for non-protein-coding DNA. The genomes of more complex organisms contain much more of this so-called "non-coding" DNA. These RNA-only 'hidden' genes tend to be short and difficult to identify, but the sequences are highly conserved and clearly have a role in inheritance, development, and health.

Total length of DNA in viruses, bacteria, and eukayotes

Taxon	Organism	Base pairs (in 1000s, or kb)	Length
Viruses	Polyoma or SV40	5.1	1.7 µm
	Lambda phage	48.6	17 µm
	T2 phage	166	56 µm
	Vaccinia	190	65 µm
Bacteria	Mycoplasma	760	260 µm
	E. coli (from human gut)	4600	1.56 mm
Eukaryotes	Yeast	13 500	4.6 mm
	Drosophila (fruit fly)	165 000	5.6 cm
	Human	2 900 000	99 cm

Kilobase (kb)

A kilobase is unit of length equal to 1000 base pairs of a double-stranded nucleic acid molecule (or 1000 bases of a single-stranded molecule). One kb of double stranded DNA has a length of 0.34 µm. (1 µm = 1/1000 mm)

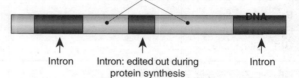

Exons: protein coding regions

Intron   Intron: edited out during protein synthesis   Intron

Most protein-coding genes in eukaryotic DNA are not continuous and may be interrupted by 'intrusions' of other pieces of DNA. Protein-coding regions (**exons**) are interrupted by non-protein-coding regions called **introns**. Introns range in frequency from 1 to over 30 in a single 'gene' and also in size (100 to more than 10 000 bases). Introns are edited out of the protein-coding sequence during protein synthesis, but probably, after processing, go on to serve a regulatory function.

Giant lampbrush chromosomes

Lampbrush chromosomes are large chromosomes found in amphibian eggs, with lateral loops of DNA that produce a brushlike appearance under the microscope. The two scanning electron micrographs (below and right) show minute strands of DNA giving a fuzzy appearance in the high power view.

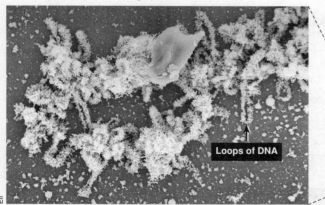

Loops of DNA

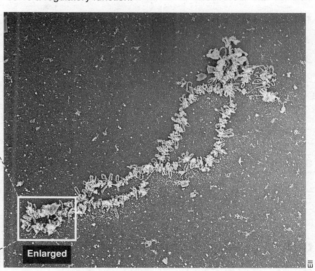

Enlarged

1. Consult the table above and make the following comparisons. Determine how much more DNA is present in:

   (a) The bacterium *E. coli* compared to the Lambda Phage virus: _____

   (b) Human cells compared to the bacteria *E. coli*: _____

2. State what proportion of DNA in a eukaryotic cell is used to code for proteins or structural RNA: _____

3. Describe two reasons why geneticists have reevaluated their traditional view that one gene codes for one polypeptide:

   (a) _____

   _____

   (b) _____

   _____

Related activities: The Simplest Case: Genes to Proteins, Prokaryotic Chromosomes

DA 2

The Genetic Code

The genetic information that codes for the assembly of amino acids is stored as three-letter codes, called **codons**. Each codon represents one of 20 amino acids used in the construction of polypeptide chains. The **mRNA-amino acid table** (bottom of page) can be used to identify the amino acid encoded by each of the mRNA codons. Note that the code is **degenerate** in that for each amino acid, there may be more than one codon. Most of this degeneracy involves the third nucleotide of a codon. The genetic code is **universal**; all living organisms on Earth, from viruses and bacteria, to plants and humans, share the same genetic code (with a few minor exceptions representing mutations that have occurred over the long history of evolution).

Amino acid		Codons that code for this amino acid	No.	Amino acid		Codons that code for this amino acid	No.
Ala	Alanine	GCU, GCC, GCA, GCG	4	**Leu**	Leucine		
Arg	Arginine			**Lys**	Lysine		
Asn	Asparagine			**Met**	Methionine		
Asp	Aspartic acid			**Phe**	Phenylalanine		
Cys	Cysteine			**Pro**	Proline		
Gln	Glutamine			**Ser**	Serine		
Glu	Glutamic acid			**Thr**	Threonine		
Gly	Glycine			**Try**	Tryptophan		
His	Histidine			**Tyr**	Tyrosine		
Iso	Isoleucine			**Val**	Valine		

1. Use the **mRNA-amino acid table** (below) to list in the table above all the **codons** that code for each of the amino acids and the number of different codons that can code for each amino acid (the first amino acid has been done for you).

2. (a) State how many amino acids could be coded for if a codon consisted of just two bases: _____

   (b) Explain why this number of bases is inadequate to code for the 20 amino acids required to make proteins:

   _____

   _____

3. Describe the consequence of the degeneracy of the genetic code to the likely effect of a change to one base in a triplet:

   _____

   _____

mRNA-Amino Acid Table

How to read the table: The table on the right is used to 'decode' the genetic code as a sequence of amino acids in a polypeptide chain, from a given mRNA sequence. To work out which amino acid is coded for by a codon (triplet of bases) look for the first letter of the codon in the row label on the left hand side. Then look for the column that intersects the same row from above that matches the second base. Finally, locate the third base in the codon by looking along the row from the right hand end that matches your codon.

Example: Determine **CAG**

C on the left row, A on the top column, G on the right row
CAG is Gln (**glutamine**)

Read second letter here · Read first letter here

Second Letter · Read third letter here

First Letter		U	C	A	G	Third Letter
U		UUU Phe UUC Phe UUA Leu UUG Leu	UCU Ser UCC Ser UCA Ser UCG Ser	UAU Tyr UAC Tyr UAA STOP UAG STOP	UGU Cys UGC Cys UGA STOP UGG Try	U C A G
C		CUU Leu CUC Leu CUA Leu CUG Leu	CCU Pro CCC Pro CCA Pro CCG Pro	CAU His CAC His CAA Gln CAG Gln	CGU Arg CGC Arg CGA Arg CGG Arg	U C A G
A		AUU Iso AUC Iso AUA Iso AUG Met	ACU Thr ACC Thr ACA Thr ACG Thr	AAU Asn AAC Asn AAA Lys AAG Lys	AGU Ser AGC Ser AGA Arg AGG Arg	U C A G
G		GUU Val GUC Val GUA Val GUG Val	GCU Ala GCC Ala GCA Ala GCG Ala	GAU Asp GAC Asp GAA Glu GAG Glu	GGU Gly GGC Gly GGA Gly GGG Gly	U C A G

Related activities: Amino Acids, The Simplest Case: Genes to Proteins

The Simplest Case: Genes to Proteins

The traditionally held view of genes was as sections of DNA coding only for protein. This view has been revised in recent years with the discovery that much of the nonprotein-coding DNA encodes functional RNAs; it is not all non-coding "junk" DNA as was previously assumed. In fact, our concept of what constitutes a gene is changing rapidly and now encompasses all those segments of DNA that are transcribed (to RNA). This activity considers only the simplest scenario: one in which the gene codes for a functional protein. **Nucleotides**, the basic unit of genetic information, are read in groups of three (**triplets**). Some triplets have a special controlling function in the making of a polypeptide chain. The equivalent of the triplet on the mRNA molecule is the **codon**. Three codons can signify termination of the amino acid chain (UAG, UAA and UGA in the mRNA code). The codon AUG is found at the beginning of every gene (on mRNA) and marks the starting point for reading the gene. The genes required to form a functional end-product (in this case, a functional protein) are collectively called a **transcription unit**.

This polypeptide chain forms one part of the functional protein.

This polypeptide chain forms the other part of the functional protein.

Functional protein

Polypeptide chain

A triplet codes for one amino acid

Polypeptide chain

← Amino acids

Translation

5' A U G C C G U G G A U A U U U C U U U U A U A U U A G 3'   5' A U G C A G C C A G G U A A A G U U C C G U G A 3' ← mRNA

Transcription

3' T A C G G C A C C T A T A A A G A A A A T A T A A T C 5'   3' T A C G T C G G T C C A T T T C A A G G C A C T 5' → DNA: **Template** strand

START Triplet Triplet Triplet Triplet Triplet Triplet **STOP**   **START** Triplet Triplet Triplet Triplet Triplet Triplet **STOP**

5' A T G C C G T G G A T A T T T C T T T T A T A T T A G 3'   A T G C A G C C A G G T A A A G T T C C G T G A 3' → DNA: **Coding** strand

├──────────── **Gene** ────────────┤   ├──────── **Gene** ────────┤

Transcription unit

Note: This start code is for the **coding strand** of the DNA. The template DNA strand from which the mRNA is made has the sequence: **TAC**.

*Three **nucleotides** make up a **triplet***

Nucleotide

● ⬠ G

In models of nucleic acids, nucleotides are denoted by their base letter. (In this case: **G** is for guanine)

1. Describe the structure in a protein that corresponds to each of the following levels of genetic information:

   (a) Triplet   codes for: _____

   (b) Gene   codes for: _____

   (c) Transcription unit   codes for: _____

2. Describe the basic building blocks for each of the following levels of genetic information:

   (a) **Nucleotide** is made up of: _____

   _____

   (b) **Triplet** is made up of: _____

   _____

   (c) **Gene** is made up of: _____

   _____

   (d) **Transcription unit** is made up of: _____

   _____

3. Describe the steps involved in forming a functional protein: _____

   _____

Related activities: DNA Molecules
Web links: Polyribosomes

A 2

Meiosis

Meiosis is a special type of cell division concerned with producing sex cells (gametes) for the purpose of sexual reproduction. It involves a single chromosomal duplication followed by two successive nuclear divisions, and results in a halving of the diploid chromosome number. Meiosis occurs in the sex organs of plants and animals. If genetic mistakes (**gene** and **chromosome mutations**) occur here, they will be passed on to the offspring (they will be inherited).

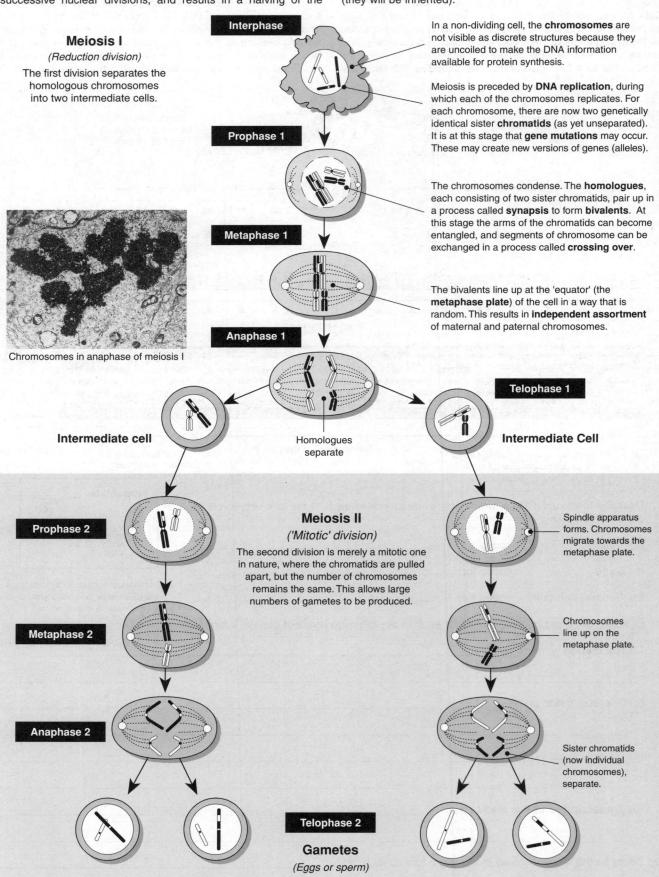

Meiosis I
(Reduction division)

The first division separates the homologous chromosomes into two intermediate cells.

Chromosomes in anaphase of meiosis I

Interphase

In a non-dividing cell, the **chromosomes** are not visible as discrete structures because they are uncoiled to make the DNA information available for protein synthesis.

Meiosis is preceded by **DNA replication**, during which each of the chromosomes replicates. For each chromosome, there are now two genetically identical sister **chromatids** (as yet unseparated). It is at this stage that **gene mutations** may occur. These may create new versions of genes (alleles).

Prophase 1

The chromosomes condense. The **homologues**, each consisting of two sister chromatids, pair up in a process called **synapsis** to form **bivalents**. At this stage the arms of the chromatids can become entangled, and segments of chromosome can be exchanged in a process called **crossing over**.

Metaphase 1

The bivalents line up at the 'equator' (the **metaphase plate**) of the cell in a way that is random. This results in **independent assortment** of maternal and paternal chromosomes.

Anaphase 1

Telophase 1

Intermediate cell

Homologues separate

Intermediate Cell

Meiosis II
('Mitotic' division)

The second division is merely a mitotic one in nature, where the chromatids are pulled apart, but the number of chromosomes remains the same. This allows large numbers of gametes to be produced.

Prophase 2

Spindle apparatus forms. Chromosomes migrate towards the metaphase plate.

Metaphase 2

Chromosomes line up on the metaphase plate.

Anaphase 2

Sister chromatids (now individual chromosomes), separate.

Telophase 2

Gametes
(Eggs or sperm)

Related activities: Variation
Web links: Meiosis Tutorial

The meiotic spindle normally distributes chromosomes to daughter cells without error. However, mistakes can occur in which the homologous chromosomes fail to separate properly at anaphase during meiosis I, or sister chromatids fail to separate during meiosis II. In these cases, one gamete receives two of the same type of chromosome and the other gamete receives no copy. This mishap, called **non-disjunction**, results in abnormal numbers of chromosomes passing to the gametes. If either of the aberrant gametes unites with a normal one at fertilisation, the offspring will have an abnormal chromosome number, known as an **aneuploidy**.

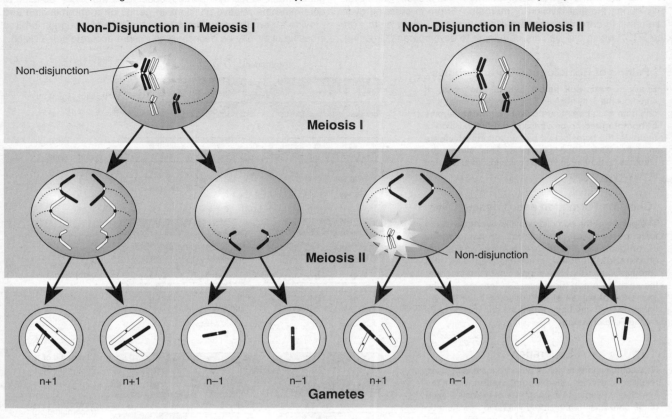

Non-Disjunction in Meiosis I

Non-Disjunction in Meiosis II

Non-disjunction

Meiosis I

Meiosis II

Non-disjunction

n+1 n+1 n–1 n–1 n+1 n–1 n n

Gametes

1. Describe the behaviour of the chromosomes in the first division of meiosis: _____

_____

_____

_____

_____

_____

2. Describe the behaviour of the chromosomes in the second division of meiosis: _____

_____

_____

3. Explain how mitosis conserves chromosome number while meiosis reduces the number from diploid to haploid:

_____

_____

4. Both these light micrographs (A and B) show chromosomes in metaphase of meiosis. State in what way they are different:

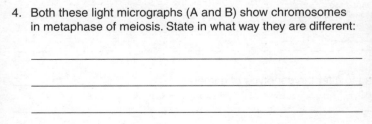
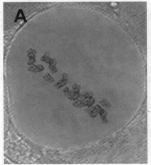
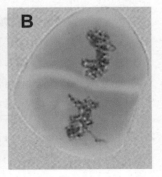

_____

_____

_____

_____

_____

Crossing Over

Crossing over refers to the mutual exchange of pieces of chromosome and involves the swapping of whole groups of genes between the **homologous** chromosomes. This process can occur only during the first division of **meiosis**. Errors in crossing over can result in **chromosome mutations** (see the activity on this on the TRC), which can be very damaging to development. Crossing over can upset expected frequencies of offspring in dihybrid crosses. The frequency of crossing over (COV) for different genes (as followed by inherited, observable traits) can be used to determine the relative positions of genes on a chromosome and provide a **genetic map**. There has been a recent suggestion that crossing over may be necessary to ensure accurate cell division.

Pairing of Homologous Chromosomes

Every somatic cell has a pair of each type of chromosome in its nucleus. These chromosome pairs, one from each parent, are called **homologous** pairs or **homologues**. In prophase of the first division of **meiosis**, the homologues pair up to form **bivalents** in a process called **synapsis**. This allows the chromatids of the homologous chromosomes to come in very close contact.

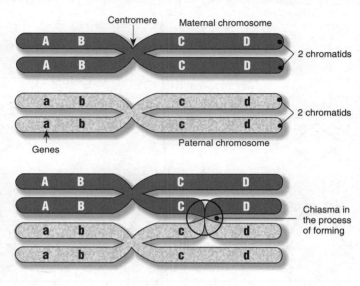

Chiasma Formation and Crossing Over

The pairing of the homologues allows **chiasmata** to form between the chromatids of homologous chromosomes. These are places where the chromatids become criss-crossed and the chromosomes exchange segments. In the diagram, the chiasma are in the process of forming and the exchange of pieces of chromosome have not yet taken place. Every point where the chromatids have crossed is a **chiasma**.

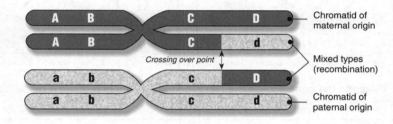

Separation

New combinations of genes arise from crossing over, resulting in what is called **recombination**. When the homologues separate at anaphase of meiosis I, each of the chromosomes pictured will have new genetic material (mixed types) that will be passed into the gametes soon to be formed. This process of recombination is an important source of variation for the gene pool of a population.

Gamete Formation

Once the final division of meiosis is complete, the two chromatids that made up each replicated chromosome become separated and are now referred to as chromosomes. Because chromatid segments were exchanged, **four** chromosomes that are quite different (genetically) are produced. If no crossing over had occurred, there would have been only two types (two copies of each). Each of these chromosomes will end up in a different gamete (sperm or egg).

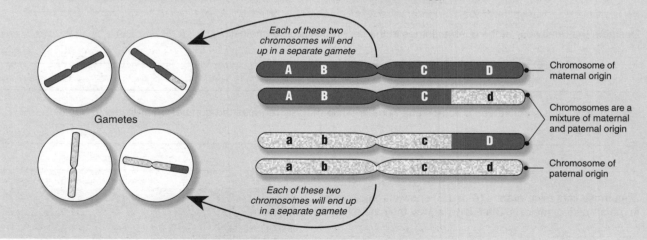

1. Briefly explain how the process of crossing over is going to alter the genotype of gametes: _____

   _____

2. Describe the importance of crossing over in the process of evolution: _____

   _____

Crossing Over Problems

The diagram below shows a pair of homologous chromosomes about to undergo chiasma formation during the first division of meiosis. There are known crossover points along the length of the chromatids (same on all four chromatids shown in the diagram). In the prepared spaces below, draw the gene sequences after crossing over has occurred on three unrelated and separate occasions (it would be useful to use different coloured pens to represent the genes from the two different chromosomes). See the diagrams on the previous page as a guide.

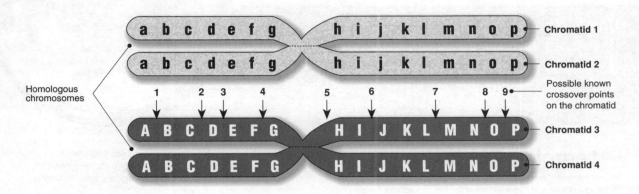

Chromatid 1

Chromatid 2

Homologous chromosomes

Possible known crossover points on the chromatid

Chromatid 3

Chromatid 4

1. Crossing over occurs at a **single** point between the chromosomes above.

   (a) Draw the gene sequences for the four chromatids (on the right), after crossing over has occurred at crossover point: **2**

   (b) List which genes have been exchanged with those on its homologue (neighbour chromosome):

   _____

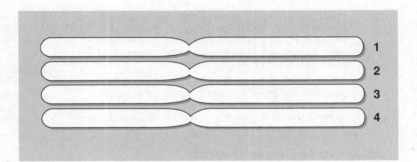

2. Crossing over occurs at **two** points between the chromosomes above.

   (a) Draw the gene sequences for the four chromatids (on the right), after crossing over has occurred between crossover points: **6** and **7**.

   (b) List which genes have been exchanged with those on its homologue (neighbour chromosome):

   _____

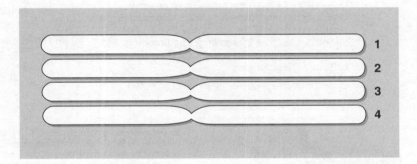

3. Crossing over occurs at **four** points between the chromosomes above.

   (a) Draw the gene sequences for the four chromatids (on the right), after crossing over has occurred between crossover points: **1** and **3**, and **5** and **7**.

   (b) List which genes have been exchanged with those on its homologue (neighbour chromosome):

   _____

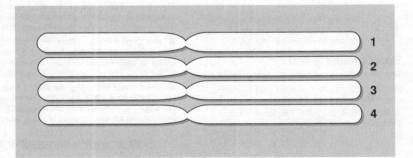

4. Explain the genetic significance of **crossing over**: _____

_____

_____

_____

Related activities: Crossing Over

RA 2

Variety and Complexity

Unit 2: The Variety of Living Organisms
2.3 DNA and genetic diversity

Genetic diversity, founder effect, population bottlenecks, genetic drift, artificial selection

Learning Objectives

☐ 1. Compile your own glossary from the **KEY WORDS** displayed in **bold type** in the learning objectives below.

The Nature of Variation *(pages 158-159)*

☐ 2. Describe examples of **intraspecific variation** and explain its basis (including reference to genes and environment). Appreciate that for many quantitative traits in a population, there is a normal distribution of phenotypic variation about a mean.

☐ 3. Recognise the need for **random sampling** and the importance of **chance** in contributing to differences between samples. Demonstrate an ability to collect and graphically display data pertaining to variation in the phenotype of a natural population.

Influences on Genetic Diversity

Selective breeding *(pages 179, 183-186)*

☐ 4. Describe and explain the influence of **selective breeding** on genetic diversity in domesticated animals. Include reference to the use of selective breeding techniques such as **inbreeding**, **line-breeding**, and **out-crossing**, which are used to produce breeds with particular characteristics.

☐ 5. Describe and explain the influence of selective breeding on genetic diversity in plants. Include reference to polyploidy, the use of genetic engineering, and techniques such as **inbreeding** to produce strains with particular qualities.

Events in Gene Pools *(pages 180-182)*

☐ 6. Recognise that special events in populations such as isolation can alter the amount of genetic diversity present in a gene pool. Appreciate that these changes may have evolutionary consequences.

☐ 7. Explain what is meant by **genetic drift** and describe the conditions under which it is important. Explain, using diagrams or a gene pool model, how genetic drift may lead to loss or **fixation of alleles** (where a gene is represented in the population by only one allele).

☐ 8. Using examples, explain the **founder effect**, including reference to its effects on genetic diversity and its evolutionary consequences.

☐ 9. Using an example, explain the **genetic (population) bottleneck effect**, including reference to its effects on genetic diversity and its evolutionary consequences.

☐ 10. Explain how the founder effect and genetic bottlenecks may accelerate the pace of evolutionary change. Explain the importance of **genetic drift** in populations that undergo these events.

See the 'Textbook Reference Grid' on pages 8-9 for textbook page references relating to material in this topic.

Supplementary Texts

See pages 5-7 for additional details of these texts:

■ Clegg, C.J., 1999. **Genetics and Evolution**, (John Murray), pp. 19-22, 34-39.

■ Jones, N., *et al.,* 2001. **The Essentials of Genetics**, pp. 190-232.

See page 7 for details of publishers of periodicals:

STUDENT'S REFERENCE

■ **What is Variation?** Biol. Sci. Rev., 13(1) Sept. 2000, pp. 30-31. *The nature of continuous and discontinuous variation in particular characters. The distribution pattern of traits that show continuous variation as a result of polygeny is discussed.*

■ **Polymorphism** Biol. Sci. Rev., 14(1), Sept. 2001, pp. 19-21. *An account of polymorphism in populations, with several case studies (including Biston moths) provided as illustrative examples.*

■ **Species and Species Formation** Biol. Sci. Rev., 20(3), Feb. 2008, pp. 36-39. *A summary feature covering the definition of species and how new species come into being through speciation.*

■ **The Engineering of Crop Plants** Biol. Sci. Rev., 20(4), April 2008, pp.30-33. *Engineering crops for better food value and to improve non-food crops as sources of raw material for industry.*

■ **The Cheetah: Losing the Race?** Biol. Sci. Rev., 14(2) Nov. 2001, pp. 7-10. *The evolutionary bottleneck experienced by cheetahs and its implications for the genetics of the species.*

TEACHER'S REFERENCE

■ **Skin Deep** Scientific American, Oct. 2002, pp. 50-57. *This article presents powerful evidence for skin color ("race") being the end result of opposing selection forces. Clearly written and of high interest, this is a perfect vehicle for student discussion and for examining natural selection.*

■ **Fair Enough** New Scientist, 12 Oct. 2002, pp. 34-37. *Skin color in humans: this article examines the argument for there being a selective benefit to being dark or pale in different environments.*

■ **Back to the Future of Cereals** Scientific American, August 2004, pp. 26-33. *Comparisons of the genomes of major cereal crops shows their close interrelationships and reveals the hand of humans in directing their evolution.*

See pages 10-11 for details of how to access **Bio Links** from our web site: **www.biozone.co.uk**. From Bio Links, access sites under the topics:

GENETICS > Population Genetics: • Introduction to evolutionary biology • Industrial melanism in *Biston betularia* • Micro-evolution and population genetics • Random genetic drift • Population genetics: lecture notes ... *and others*

RESOURCE MANAGEMENT & AGRICULTURE
> **Crop Production:** • Crop and grasslands service
> **Livestock Management and Improvement:** •
Breeds of livestock • Genetics Australia

Presentation MEDIA to support this topic:
EVOLUTION
• Population Genetics

Genetic Diversity

Genetic diversity refers to the variation in the nucleotides, genes, chromosomes, or genomes of organisms. Genetic diversity can express itself in a wide variety of observable characteristics (**phenotypes**). The domestic dog provides an excellent example of this. All breeds of dog are members of the same species, *Canis familiaris*. This species descended from a single wild species, the grey wolf *Canis lupus*, over 15 000 years ago. Five ancient dog breeds are recognised, from which all other breeds are thought to have descended by **selective breeding** (artificial selection). Selective breeding based on physical traits, and desirable behavioural characteristics (e.g. the ability to 'read' the body language of humans) have been selected for in dogs. As a result there are now over 400 different breeds ranging from the small chihuahua to the very tall great dane.

Grey wolf *Canis lupus pallipes*

The grey wolf is distributed throughout Europe, North America, and Asia. Amongst members of this species, there is a lot of variation in coat coloration. This accounts for the large variation in coat colours of dogs today.

The Ancestor of Domestic Dogs

Until recently, it was unclear whether the ancestor to the modern domestic dogs was the desert wolf of the Middle East, the woolly wolf of central Asia, or the grey wolf of Northern Hemisphere. Recent genetic studies (mitochondrial DNA comparisons) now provide strong evidence that the ancestor of domestic dogs throughout the world is the grey wolf. It seems likely that this evolutionary change took place in a single region, most probably China.

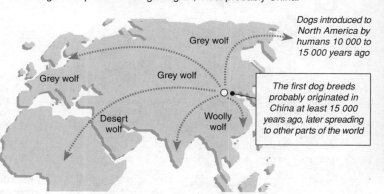

Dogs introduced to North America by humans 10 000 to 15 000 years ago

Grey wolf

Grey wolf

Grey wolf

Desert wolf

Woolly wolf

The first dog breeds probably originated in China at least 15 000 years ago, later spreading to other parts of the world

Mastiff-type
Canis familiaris inostranzevi
Originally from Tibet, the first records of this breed of dog go back to the Stoneage.

Greyhound
Canis familiaris leineri
Drawings of this breed on pottery dated from 8000 years ago in the Middle East make it one of the oldest.

Pointer-type
Canis familiaris intermedius
Probably derived from the greyhound breed for the purpose of hunting small game.

Sheepdog
Canis familiaris metris optimae
Originating in Europe, this breed has been used to guard flocks from predators for thousands of years.

Wolf-like
Canis familiaris palustris
Found in snow covered habitats in northern Europe, Asia (Siberia), and North America (Alaska).

1. Explain how selective breeding can result in changes in a gene pool over time: _____

_____

_____

_____

2. Describe the behavioural tendency of wolves that predisposed them to becoming a domesticated animal:

_____

3. List the physical and behavioural traits that would be desirable (selected for) in the following uses of a dog:

(a) Hunting large game (e.g. boar and deer): _____

(b) Game fowl dog: _____

(c) Stock control (sheep/cattle dog): _____

(d) Family pet (house dog): _____

(e) Guard dog: _____

Related activities: Selective Breeding in Crop Plants, Selective Breeding in Animals, The Species Concept   **Web links**: Dogs and More Dogs

RA 2

The Founder Effect

Occasionally, a small number of individuals from a large population may migrate away, or become isolated from, their original population. If this colonising or 'founder' population is made up of only a few individuals, it will probably have a non-representative sample of alleles from the parent population's gene pool. As a consequence of this **founder effect**, the colonising population may evolve differently from that of the parent population, particularly since the environmental conditions for the isolated population may be different. In some cases, it may be possible for certain alleles to be missing altogether from the individuals in the isolated population. Future generations of this population will not have this allele.

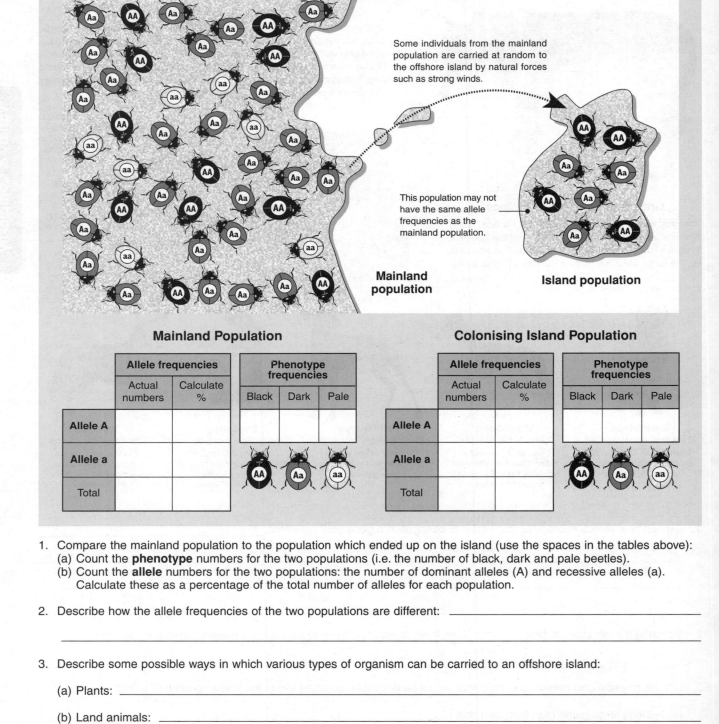

Some individuals from the mainland population are carried at random to the offshore island by natural forces such as strong winds.

This population may not have the same allele frequencies as the mainland population.

Mainland population

Island population

Mainland Population

	Allele frequencies		Phenotype frequencies		
	Actual numbers	Calculate %	Black	Dark	Pale
Allele A					
Allele a					
Total					

Colonising Island Population

	Allele frequencies		Phenotype frequencies		
	Actual numbers	Calculate %	Black	Dark	Pale
Allele A					
Allele a					
Total					

1. Compare the mainland population to the population which ended up on the island (use the spaces in the tables above):
   (a) Count the **phenotype** numbers for the two populations (i.e. the number of black, dark and pale beetles).
   (b) Count the **allele** numbers for the two populations: the number of dominant alleles (A) and recessive alleles (a). Calculate these as a percentage of the total number of alleles for each population.

2. Describe how the allele frequencies of the two populations are different: _____

   _____

3. Describe some possible ways in which various types of organism can be carried to an offshore island:

   (a) Plants: _____

   (b) Land animals: _____

   (c) Non-marine birds: _____

4. Since founder populations are often very small, describe another process that may further alter the allele frequencies:

   _____

   _____

Related activities: Genetic Drift
Web links: Genetic Drift Simulation, Oceanic Island Colonisers

Population Bottlenecks

Populations may sometimes be reduced to low numbers by predation, disease, or periods of climatic change. A population crash may not be selective; it may affect all phenotypes equally. Large scale catastrophic events, such as fire or volcanic eruption, are examples of such non-selective events. Humans may severely (and selectively) reduce the numbers of some species through hunting and/or habitat destruction. These populations may recover, having squeezed through a 'bottleneck' of low numbers. The diagram below illustrates how population numbers may be reduced as a result of a catastrophic event. Following such an event, the small number of individuals contributing to the gene pool may not have a representative sample of the genes in the pre-catastrophe population, i.e. the allele frequencies in the remnant population may be severely altered. Genetic drift may cause further changes to allele frequencies. The small population may return to previous levels but with a reduced genetic diversity.

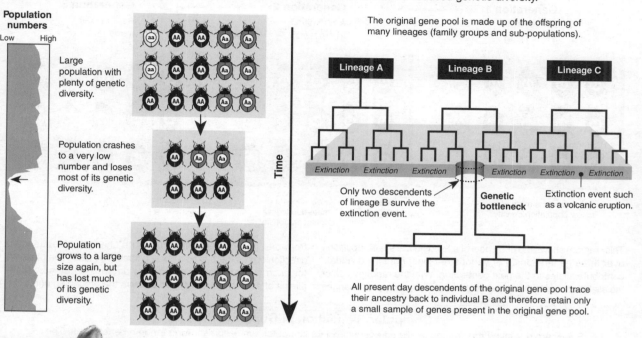

The original gene pool is made up of the offspring of many lineages (family groups and sub-populations).

Population numbers — Low / High

Large population with plenty of genetic diversity.

Population crashes to a very low number and loses most of its genetic diversity.

Population grows to a large size again, but has lost much of its genetic diversity.

Time

Lineage A   **Lineage B**   **Lineage C**

Extinction   *Extinction*   *Extinction*   *Extinction*   *Extinction*   *Extinction*

Only two descendents of lineage B survive the extinction event.

Genetic bottleneck

Extinction event such as a volcanic eruption.

All present day descendents of the original gene pool trace their ancestry back to individual B and therefore retain only a small sample of genes present in the original gene pool.

Variety & Complexity

Modern Examples of Population Bottlenecks

Photo: Dept. of Natural Resources, Illinois

Cheetahs: The world population of cheetahs currently stands at fewer than 20 000. Recent genetic analysis has found that the entire population exhibits very little genetic diversity. It appears that cheetahs may have narrowly escaped extinction at the end of the last ice age, about 10-20 000 years ago. If all modern cheetahs arose from a very limited genetic stock, this would explain their present lack of genetic diversity. The lack of genetic variation has resulted in a number of problems that threaten cheetah survival, including sperm abnormalities, decreased fecundity, high cub mortality, and sensitivity to disease.

Illinois prairie chicken: When Europeans first arrived in North America, there were millions of prairie chickens. As a result of hunting and habitat loss, the Illinois population of prairie chickens fell from about 100 million in 1900 to fewer than 50 in the 1990s. A comparison of the DNA from birds collected in the mid-twentieth century and DNA from the surviving population indicated that most of the genetic diversity has been lost.

1. Endangered species are often subjected to population bottlenecks. In relation to genetic diversity, explain how population bottlenecks affect the ability of a population of an endangered species to recover:

_____

_____

_____

2. Explain why the lack of genetic diversity in cheetahs has increased their sensitivity to disease: _____

_____

_____

3. Describe the effect of a population bottleneck on the potential of a species to adapt to changes (i.e. its ability to evolve):

_____

_____

Related activities: Genetic Drift

A 3

Genetic Drift

Not all individuals, for various reasons, will be able to contribute their genes to the next generation. **Genetic drift** (also known as the Sewell-Wright Effect) refers to the random changes in allele frequency that occur in all populations, but are much more pronounced in small populations. In a small population, the effect of a few individuals not contributing their alleles to the next generation can have a great effect on allele frequencies. Alleles may even become **lost** from the gene pool altogether (frequency becomes 0%) or **fixed** as the only allele for the gene present (frequency becomes 100%).

The genetic makeup (allele frequencies) of the population changes randomly over a period of time

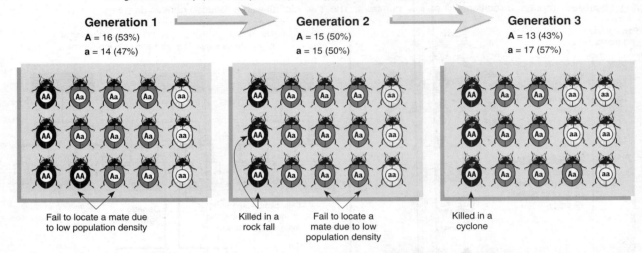

Generation 1
A = 16 (53%)
a = 14 (47%)

Generation 2
A = 15 (50%)
a = 15 (50%)

Generation 3
A = 13 (43%)
a = 17 (57%)

Fail to locate a mate due to low population density

Killed in a rock fall

Fail to locate a mate due to low population density

Killed in a cyclone

This diagram shows the gene pool of a hypothetical small population over three generations. For various reasons, not all individuals contribute alleles to the next generation. With the random loss of the alleles carried by these individuals, the allele frequency changes from one generation to the next. The change in frequency is directionless as there is no selecting force. The allele combinations for each successive generation are determined by how many alleles of each type are passed on from the preceding one.

Computer Simulation of Genetic Drift

Below are displayed the change in allele frequencies in a computer simulation showing random genetic drift. The breeding population progressively gets smaller from left to right. Each simulation was run for 140 generations.

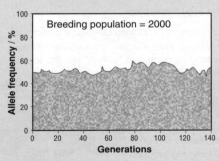

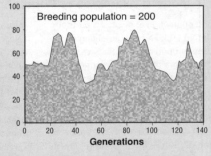

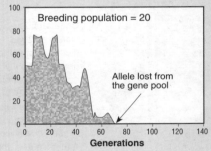

Allele lost from the gene pool

Large breeding population
Fluctuations are minimal in large breeding populations because the large numbers buffer the population against random loss of alleles. On average, losses for each allele type will be similar in frequency and little change occurs.

Small breeding population
Fluctuations are more severe in smaller breeding populations because random changes in a few alleles cause a greater percentage change in allele frequencies.

Very small breeding population
Fluctuations in very small breeding populations are so extreme that the allele can become fixed (frequency of 100%) or lost from the gene pool altogether (frequency of 0%).

1. Explain what is meant by **genetic drift**: _____

_____

2. Describe how genetic drift affects the amount of genetic variation within very small populations: _____

_____

_____

_____

3. Identify a small breeding population of animals or plants in Britain or Europe in which genetic drift could be occurring:

_____

Related activities: The Founder Effect
Web links: Genetic Drift Simulation

Selective Breeding in Crop Plants

For thousands of years, farmers have used the genetic variation in wild and cultivated plants to develop their crops. Genetic diversity gives species the ability to adapt to new challenges, such as new pests and diseases and new climatic conditions. The genetic diversity contained in different crop varieties provides farmers with options to develop, through selection, new and more productive crop plants. Wheat is a good example. It has been cultivated for more than 9000 years and has undergone many genetic changes during its domestication (below). Increasingly, researchers are focussed on enhancing the genetic diversity of this important crop to provide for future crop development. Several research centres and **seed** (gene) **banks** play a key role in this for wheat and other crop plants. They store the seeds of the species that collectively provide most of the food consumed by humans, and also keep a bank of seeds from less common or non-commercial varieties that may be threatened with loss.

The Evolution of Wheat

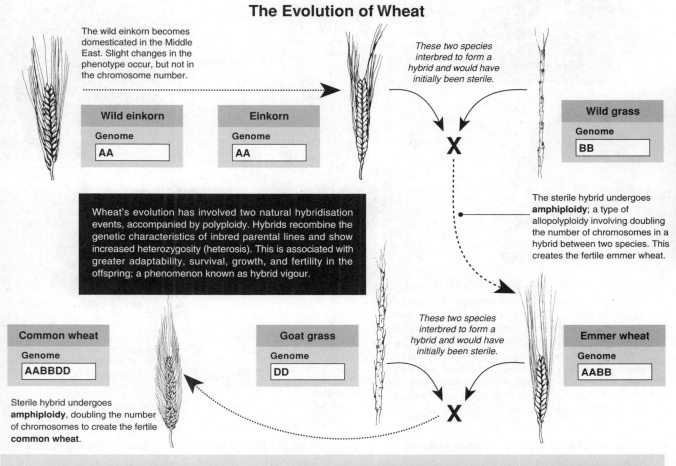

The wild einkorn becomes domesticated in the Middle East. Slight changes in the phenotype occur, but not in the chromosome number.

Wild einkorn
Genome
AA

Einkorn
Genome
AA

These two species interbred to form a hybrid and would have initially been sterile.

X

Wild grass
Genome
BB

The sterile hybrid undergoes **amphiploidy**; a type of allopolyploidy involving doubling the number of chromosomes in a hybrid between two species. This creates the fertile emmer wheat.

Wheat's evolution has involved two natural hybridisation events, accompanied by polyploidy. Hybrids recombine the genetic characteristics of inbred parental lines and show increased heterozygosity (heterosis). This is associated with greater adaptability, survival, growth, and fertility in the offspring; a phenomenon known as hybrid vigour.

Common wheat
Genome
AABBDD

Goat grass
Genome
DD

These two species interbred to form a hybrid and would have initially been sterile.

X

Emmer wheat
Genome
AABB

Sterile hybrid undergoes **amphiploidy**, doubling the number of chromosomes to create the fertile **common wheat**.

The number of apple varieties is now a fraction of the many hundreds grown a century ago. Apples are native to Kazakhstan and breeders are now looking back to this centre of diversity to develop apples resistant to the bacterial disease that causes fireblight.

Modern wheat (above) differs markedly from the ancestral grain it was. It has been selected for its non shattering heads, high yield, and high gluten (protein) content. Hybridisation to increase heterozygosity has been an important feature of its breeding.

In 18th-century Ireland, potatoes were the main source of food for about 30% of the population, and farmers relied almost entirely on one very fertile and productive variety. That variety proved susceptible to the potato blight fungus which resulted in a widespread famine.

Hybrid corn varieties have been bred to minimise harm inflicted by insect pests such as corn rootworm (above). Hybrids are important because they recombine the genetic characteristics of parental lines and show increased heterozygosity and hybrid vigour.

1. Describe why producing a hybrid from two inbred lines often has desirable effects in terms of crop characteristics:

_____

_____

_____

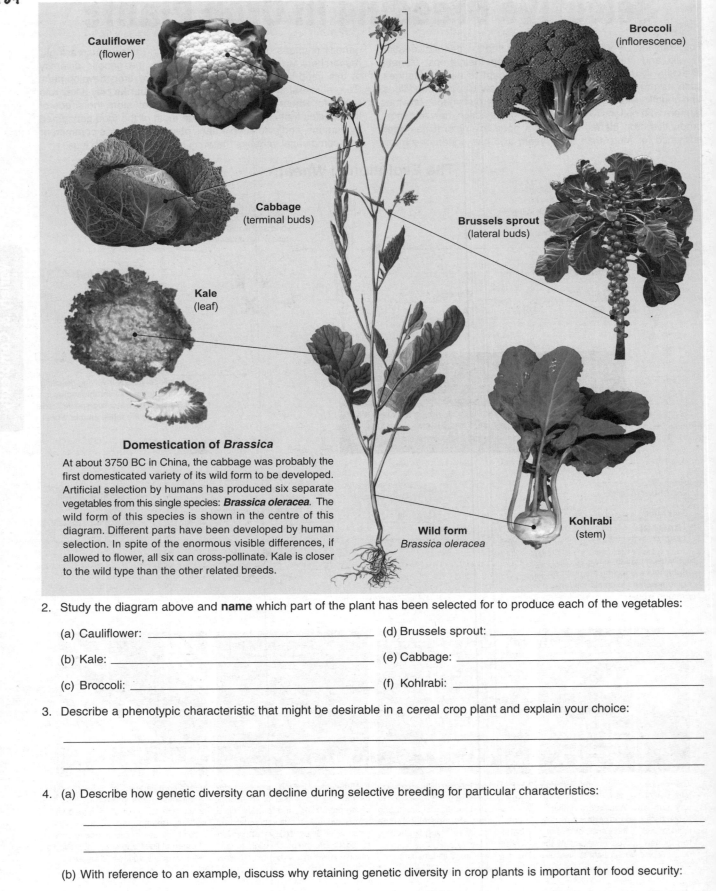

Cauliflower
(flower)

Broccoli
(inflorescence)

Cabbage
(terminal buds)

Brussels sprout
(lateral buds)

Kale
(leaf)

Domestication of *Brassica*

At about 3750 BC in China, the cabbage was probably the first domesticated variety of its wild form to be developed. Artificial selection by humans has produced six separate vegetables from this single species: ***Brassica oleracea***. The wild form of this species is shown in the centre of this diagram. Different parts have been developed by human selection. In spite of the enormous visible differences, if allowed to flower, all six can cross-pollinate. Kale is closer to the wild type than the other related breeds.

Wild form
Brassica oleracea

Kohlrabi
(stem)

2. Study the diagram above and **name** which part of the plant has been selected for to produce each of the vegetables:

(a) Cauliflower: _____

(d) Brussels sprout: _____

(b) Kale: _____

(e) Cabbage: _____

(c) Broccoli: _____

(f) Kohlrabi: _____

3. Describe a phenotypic characteristic that might be desirable in a cereal crop plant and explain your choice:

_____

_____

4. (a) Describe how genetic diversity can decline during selective breeding for particular characteristics:

_____

_____

(b) With reference to an example, discuss why retaining genetic diversity in crop plants is important for food security:

_____

_____

_____

_____

Selective Breeding in Animals

The domestication of livestock has a long history dating back at least 8000 years. Today's important stock breeds were all derived from wild ancestors that were domesticated by humans who then used **selective breeding** to produce livestock to meet specific requirements. Selective breeding of domesticated animals involves identifying desirable qualities (e.g. high wool production or meat yield), and breeding together individuals with those qualities so the trait is reliably passed on. Practices such as **inbreeding**, **line-breeding**, and **outcrossing** are used to select and 'fix' desirable traits in varieties. Today, modern breeding techniques often employ reproductive technologies, such as artificial insemination, so that the desirable characteristics of one male can be passed on to many females. These new technologies refine the selection process and increase the rate at which stock improvements are made. Rates are predicted to accelerate further as new technologies, such as genomic selection, become more widely available and less costly. Producing highly inbred lines of animals with specific traits can have disadvantages however. **Homozygosity** for a number of desirable traits can cause physiological or physical problems to the animal itself. For example, animals bred specifically for rapid weight gain often grow so fast that they have skeletal and muscular difficulties.

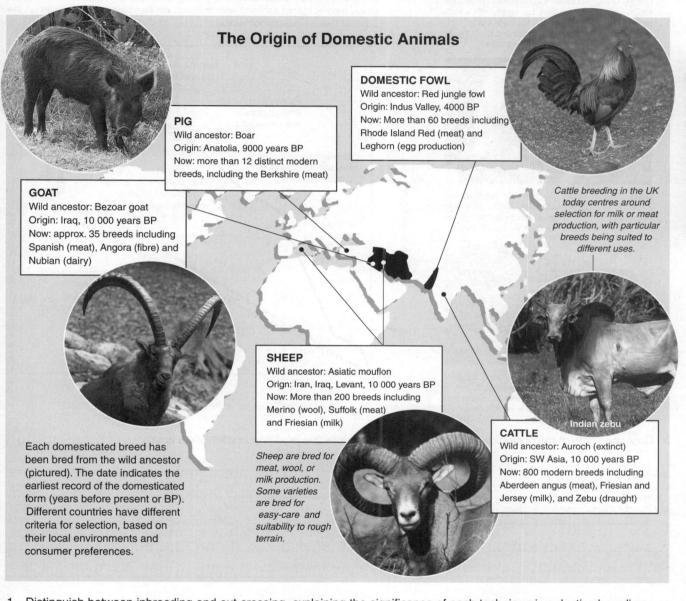

The Origin of Domestic Animals

DOMESTIC FOWL
Wild ancestor: Red jungle fowl
Origin: Indus Valley, 4000 BP
Now: More than 60 breeds including Rhode Island Red (meat) and Leghorn (egg production)

PIG
Wild ancestor: Boar
Origin: Anatolia, 9000 years BP
Now: more than 12 distinct modern breeds, including the Berkshire (meat)

GOAT
Wild ancestor: Bezoar goat
Origin: Iraq, 10 000 years BP
Now: approx. 35 breeds including Spanish (meat), Angora (fibre) and Nubian (dairy)

Cattle breeding in the UK today centres around selection for milk or meat production, with particular breeds being suited to different uses.

SHEEP
Wild ancestor: Asiatic mouflon
Origin: Iran, Iraq, Levant, 10 000 years BP
Now: More than 200 breeds including Merino (wool), Suffolk (meat) and Friesian (milk)

Indian zebu

CATTLE
Wild ancestor: Auroch (extinct)
Origin: SW Asia, 10 000 years BP
Now: 800 modern breeds including Aberdeen angus (meat), Friesian and Jersey (milk), and Zebu (draught)

Each domesticated breed has been bred from the wild ancestor (pictured). The date indicates the earliest record of the domesticated form (years before present or BP). Different countries have different criteria for selection, based on their local environments and consumer preferences.

Sheep are bred for meat, wool, or milk production. Some varieties are bred for easy-care and suitability to rough terrain.

1. Distinguish between inbreeding and out-crossing, explaining the significance of each technique in selective breeding:

_____

_____

_____

_____

2. Describe the contribution that new reproductive technologies are making to selective breeding:

_____

_____

Related activities: Genetic Diversity, Selective Breeding in Crop Plants

RA 2

Beef breeds: Simmental, Aberdeen-Angus, Hereford (above), Galloway, Charolais. Consumer demand has led to the shift towards continental breeds such as Charolais because they are large, with a high proportion of lean muscle. **Desirable traits**: high muscle to bone ratio, rapid growth and weight gain, hardy, easy calving, docile temperament.

Dairy breeds: Jersey, Friesian (above), Holstein, Aryshire. **Desirable traits**: high yield of milk with high butterfat, milking speed, docile temperament, and udder characteristics such as teat placement.

Special breeds: Some cattle are bred for their suitability for climate or terrain. Scottish highland cattle (above) are a hardy, long coated breed and produce well where other breeds cannot thrive.

Artificial Selection and Genetic Gain in Cattle

Cattle are selected on the basis of particular desirable traits (e.g. milk fat or muscle mass). Most of the genetic improvement in dairy cattle has relied on selection of high quality progeny from proven stock and extensive use of superior sires through artificial insemination (AI). In beef cattle, AI is useful for introducing new breeds.

Improved breeding techniques accelerate the **genetic gain**, i.e. the gain toward the desirable phenotype of a **breed**. The graph (below) illustrates the predicted gains based on artificial insemination and standard selection techniques (based on criteria such as production or temperament). These are compared with the predicted gains using breeding values and various reproductive technologies such as embryo multiplication and transfer (EMT) of standard and transgenic stock, marker (gene) assisted selection, and sib-selection (selecting bulls on the basis of their sisters performance).

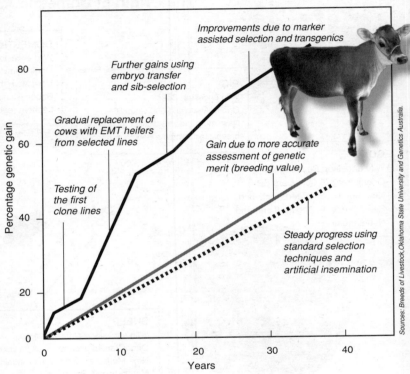

Sources: Breeds of Livestock, Oklahoma State University and Genetics Australia.

3. Describe some of the positive and negative outcomes of selective breeding in domestic animals: _____

    _____

    _____

    _____

    _____

    _____

4. Identify the two methods by which most of the genetic progress in dairy cattle has been achieved:

    (a) _____ (b) _____

5. Explain what is meant by the term **genetic gain** as it applies to livestock breeding: _____

    _____

    _____

6. Suggest why mixed breeds, such as Hereford-Friesian crosses, are popular for mixed beef/milk production:

    _____

    _____

Biochemical and Cellular Diversity

Unit 2: The Variety of Living Organisms
2.4-2.6 The biochemical and cellular basis of diversity

Haemoglobin, features of plant cells, DNA replication, mitosis and the cell cycle, cellular differentiation

Learning Objectives

☐ 1. Compile your own glossary from the **KEY WORDS** displayed in **bold type** in the learning objectives below.

Biochemical Diversity *(pages 55-60, 73, 188-190)*

☐ 2. Describe the structure of haemoglobin and its role as a **respiratory pigment**. Include reference to the loading and unloading of oxygen in relation to the oxygen dissociation curve and the effects of CO_2 concentration on the carrying capacity of haemoglobin. Relate types of haemoglobin to their oxygen transporting properties and the environment in which they operate.

☐ 3. Describe the basic structure of starch, glycogen, and **cellulose**, and relate the structure to the functional role in plants or animals in each case.

☐ 4. Describe the fundamental differences between plant and animal cells with reference to the structure of a palisade cell (as seen with light microscopy). Include reference to the appearance, ultrastructure, and function the **cell wall** and **chloroplasts**.

DNA Replication *(pages 191-192)*

☐ 5. Explain the **semi-conservative** replication of DNA during interphase, including:
  • the breaking of hydrogen bonds
  • attraction of new DNA nucleotides and base pairing
  • the role of **DNA helicase** and **DNA polymerase**.

☐ 6. Explain the significance of DNA replication in the **5' to 3' direction**. Relate this to the formation of the **leading strand** and the **lagging strand**.

Mitosis and the Cell Cycle *(pages 193-195)*

☐ 7. Describe the role of mitosis in growth and repair, and asexual reproduction (e.g. in yeast). Recognise the importance of **daughter nuclei** with chromosomes identical in number and type. Recognise cell division as a prelude to **cellular differentiation**.

☐ 8. Recognise and describe the following events in mitosis: **prophase**, **metaphase**, **anaphase**, and **telophase**. With respect to both plant and animal cells, understand the term **cytokinesis**, and distinguish between nuclear division and division of the cytoplasm.

☐ 9. Using diagrams, describe the stages of a mitotic **cell cycle** in eukaryotes. Include reference to: **mitosis**, **growth** (G_1 and G_2), and DNA replication (S).

☐ 10. Explain how **carcinogens** upset the normal controls regulating cell division. Relate your understanding of the cell cycle to cancer and its treatment.

Tissues and Organs *(pages 96-202)*

☐ 11. Recognise the hierarchy of organisation in multicellular organisms. With reference to specific examples, explain how cells are organised into **tissues**.

☐ 12. Using examples from both plants and animals, describe how the cells of a multicellular organism may **differentiate** to become adapted for different functions.

☐ 13. Discuss the importance of cooperation between cells, tissues, organs, and organ systems in the structure and function of multicellular organisms.

Textbooks

Periodicals

See the 'Textbook Reference Grid' on page 7 for textbook page references relating to material in this topic.

Supplementary Texts

See pages 5-6 for additional details of these texts:

■ Adds, J., *et al.,* 2003. **Molecules and Cells**, (NelsonThornes), chpt. 1-2, 4-5 as reqd.

■ Harwood, R., 2002. **Biochemistry**, (Cambridge University Press), chpt. 2 and 4.

Presentation MEDIA to support this topic:

CELL BIO & BIOCHEM The Molecules of Life Processes in the Nucleus

See page 6 for details of publishers of periodicals:

STUDENT'S REFERENCE

■ **Glucose & Glucose-Containing Carbohydrates** Biol. Sci. Rev., 19(1) Sept. 2006, pp. 12-15. *The structure of glucose and its polymers.*

■ **Red Blood Cells** Bio. Sci. Rev. 11(2) Nov. 1998, pp. 2-4. *The structure and function of erythrocytes and their role in oxygen transport.*

■ **Foetal Haemoglobin** Biol. Sci. Rev., 16(1) Sept. 2003, pp. 15-17. *The complex structure of haemoglobin molecules: the molecule in red blood cells that delivers oxygen to the tissues.*

■ **To Divide or Not to Divide** Biol. Sci. Rev., 11(4) March 1999, pp. 2-5. *The cell cycle: cell growth and stages of cell division and their control.*

■ **The Cell Cycle and Mitosis** Biol. Sci. Rev., 14(4) April 2002, pp. 37-41. *Cell growth and division, key stages in the cell cycle, and the complex control over different stages of mitosis.*

■ **Rebels without a Cause** New Scientist, 13 July 2002, (Inside Science). *The causes of cancer: the uncontrolled division of cells that results in tumour formation. Breast cancer is a case example.*

Internet WWW

See pages 8-9 for details of how to access **Bio Links** from our web site: **www.biozone.co.uk**. From Bio Links, access sites under the topics:

CELL BIOLOGY AND BIOCHEMISTRY: • Cell and molecular biology online • Cell structure and function web links > **Biochemistry and Metabolic Pathways:** • The Biology project: Biochemistry > **Cell Structure and Transport:** • Animal cells • CELLS alive! • Cell breakage and fractionation ... *and others* > **Cell Division:** • Cell division: Binary fission and mitosis • Cell cycle and mitosis tutorial

GENETICS: > **Molecular Genetics (DNA):** • Beginners guide to molecular biology • DNA and molecular genetics • Molecular genetics • Primer on molecular genetics

Chloroplasts and Cell Walls

The diagram illustrates features of a **palisade cell,** which is found in the leaves of dicotyledonous plants. It represents the general structure and organelles found in a typical plant cell. Plant cells are enclosed in a **cellulose cell wall**, which has a role in support and protection, as well as maintenance of cell volume. It does not interfere with the passage of materials into and out of the cell. Palisade cells contain **chloroplasts**, an organelle which enables plants to convert light energy into chemical energy by the process of photosynthesis. Palisade cells are the primary site for photosynthesis in most plants and are often clustered together at the top of a leaf to maximise light absorption. Both the cellulose cell wall and chloroplasts are features unique to plants.

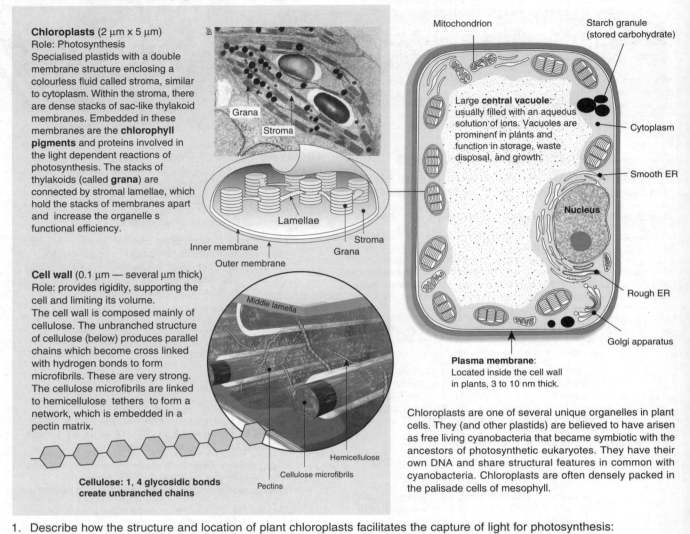

Chloroplasts (2 μm x 5 μm)
Role: Photosynthesis
Specialised plastids with a double membrane structure enclosing a colourless fluid called stroma, similar to cytoplasm. Within the stroma, there are dense stacks of sac-like thylakoid membranes. Embedded in these membranes are the **chlorophyll pigments** and proteins involved in the light dependent reactions of photosynthesis. The stacks of thylakoids (called **grana**) are connected by stromal lamellae, which hold the stacks of membranes apart and increase the organelle s functional efficiency.

Grana

Stroma

Lamellae

Inner membrane
Outer membrane
Stroma
Grana

Mitochondrion
Starch granule
(stored carbohydrate)

Large **central vacuole**:
usually filled with an aqueous solution of ions. Vacuoles are prominent in plants and function in storage, waste disposal, and growth.

Cytoplasm

Smooth ER

Nucleus

Rough ER

Golgi apparatus

Cell wall (0.1 μm — several μm thick)
Role: provides rigidity, supporting the cell and limiting its volume.
The cell wall is composed mainly of cellulose. The unbranched structure of cellulose (below) produces parallel chains which become cross linked with hydrogen bonds to form microfibrils. These are very strong. The cellulose microfibrils are linked to hemicellulose tethers to form a network, which is embedded in a pectin matrix.

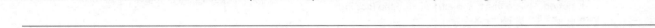

Middle lamella

Hemicellulose

Cellulose microfibrils

Pectins

Cellulose: 1, 4 glycosidic bonds create unbranched chains

Plasma membrane:
Located inside the cell wall in plants, 3 to 10 nm thick.

Chloroplasts are one of several unique organelles in plant cells. They (and other plastids) are believed to have arisen as free living cyanobacteria that became symbiotic with the ancestors of photosynthetic eukaryotes. They have their own DNA and share structural features in common with cyanobacteria. Chloroplasts are often densely packed in the palisade cells of mesophyll.

1. Describe how the structure and location of plant chloroplasts facilitates the capture of light for photosynthesis:

    _____

    _____

    _____

2. Describe two fundamental differences between plant and animal cells:

    (a) _____

    (b) _____

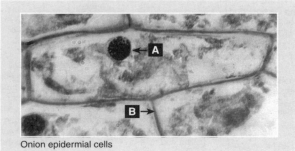

Onion epidermial cells

3. This photograph shows plant cells as seen by light microscopy. Identify the features labelled **A-B** and describe their function:

    A: _____

    _____

    B: _____

    _____

Related activities: Carbohydrates, Animal Cells, Cell Structures and Organelles, Plant Cell Specialisation   **Web links**: Review of Eukaryotic Cells

Haemoglobins

Regardless of the gas exchange system present, the amount of oxygen that can be carried dissolved in the blood is small. The efficiency of gas exchange in animals is enhanced by the presence of **respiratory pigments**. All respiratory pigments consist of proteins complexed with iron or copper. They combine reversibly with oxygen and greatly increase the capacity of blood to transport oxygen and deliver it to the tissues. For example, the amount of oxygen dissolved in the plasma in mammals is only about 2 cm^3 O$_2$ per litre. However the amount carried bound to haemoglobin is 100 times this. Haemoglobin is the most widely distributed respiratory pigment and is characteristic of all vertebrates and many invertebrate taxa. Other respiratory pigments include chlorocruorin, haemocyanin, and haemerythrin. Note that the precise structure and carrying capacity of any one particular pigment type varies between taxa (see the range of haemoglobins in the table below).

Respiratory Pigments

Respiratory pigments are coloured proteins capable of combining reversibly with oxygen, hence increasing the amount of oxygen that can be carried by the blood. Pigments typical of representative taxa are listed below. Note that the polychaetes are very variable in terms of the pigment possessed.

Taxon	Oxygen capacity / cm^3 O$_2$ per 100 cm^3 blood	Pigment
Oligochaetes	1 - 10	Haemoglobin
Polychaetes	1 - 10	Haemoglobin, chlorocruorin, or haemerythrin
Crustaceans	1 - 6	Haemocyanin
Molluscs	1 - 6	Haemocyanin
Fishes	2 - 4	Haemoglobin
Reptiles	7 - 12	Haemoglobin
Birds	20 - 25	Haemoglobin
Mammals	15 - 30	Haemoglobin

Mammalian Haemoglobin

Haemoglobin is a globular protein consisting of 574 amino acids arranged in four polypeptide sub-units: two identical **beta chains** and two identical **alpha chains**. The four sub-units are held together as a functional unit by bonds. Each sub-unit has an iron-containing haem group at its centre and binds one molecule of oxygen.

Chemical formula:
$$C_{3032}H_{4816}O_{872}N_{780}S_8Fe_4$$

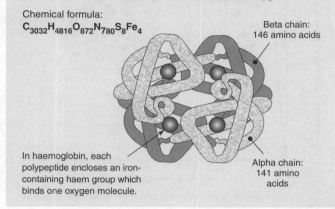

Beta chain: 146 amino acids

In haemoglobin, each polypeptide encloses an iron-containing haem group which binds one oxygen molecule.

Alpha chain: 141 amino acids

Aquatic polychaete fanworms e.g. *Sabella*, possess **chlorocruorin**.

Oligochaete annelids, such as earthworms, have **haemoglobin**.

Aquatic crustaceans e.g. crabs, possess **haemocyanin** pigment.

Vertebrates such as this fish have **haemoglobin** pigment.

Cephalopod molluscs such as *Nautilus* contain **haemocyanin**.

Birds, being vertebrates contain the pigment **haemoglobin**.

Many large active polychaetes, e.g. *Nereis*, contain **haemoglobin**.

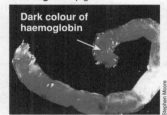

Dark colour of haemoglobin

Chironomus is one of only two insect genera to contain a pigment.

1. (a) Explain how respiratory pigments increase the carrying capacity of the blood: _____

_____

   (b) Identify which feature of a respiratory pigment determines its oxygen carrying capacity: _____

_____

2. With reference to haemoglobin, suggest how oxygen carrying capacity is related to metabolic activity: _____

_____

_____

3. Suggest why larger molecular weight respiratory pigments are carried dissolved in the plasma rather than within cells:

_____

Related activities: Proteins, Gas Transport in Humans

RA 2

Biochemical & Cellular Diversity

Haemoglobin and Oxygen Transport

In vertebrates, oxygen is carried in chemical combination with haemoglobin (Hb) in red blood cells. The most important factor determining how much oxygen is carried by Hb is the level of oxygen in the blood. As shown by an oxygen-haemoglobin dissociation curve, more oxygen combines with Hb at higher oxygen tensions (Fig. 1).

In the lung capillaries, (high O_2), a lot of oxygen is picked up and bound by Hb. In the tissues, (low O_2), oxygen is released. In skeletal muscle, myoglobin picks up oxygen from haemoglobin and therefore serves as an oxygen store when oxygen tensions begin to fall. The release of oxygen is enhanced by the **Bohr effect** (Fig. 2).

Fig. 1: Dissociation curves for haemoglobin and myoglobin at normal body temperature for foetal and adult human blood.

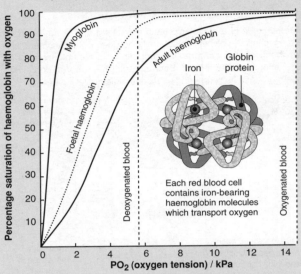

Fig. 2: Oxygen-haemoglobin dissociation curves for human blood at normal body temperature at different blood pH.

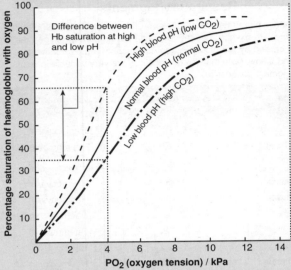

As oxygen level increases, more oxygen combines with haemoglobin. Hb saturation remains high, even at low oxygen tensions. Foetal Hb has a high affinity for oxygen and carries 20-30% more than maternal Hb. Myoglobin in skeletal muscle has a very high affinity for oxygen and will take up oxygen from haemoglobin in the blood.

As pH increases (lower CO_2), more oxygen combines with Hb. As the blood pH decreases (higher CO_2), Hb binds less oxygen and releases more to the tissues (**the Bohr effect**). The difference between Hb saturation at high and low pH represents the amount of oxygen released to the tissues.

4. Explain the significance of the **reversible binding** reaction of haemoglobin (Hb) to oxygen:

_____

_____

5. (a) Haemoglobin saturation is affected by the oxygen level in the blood. Describe the nature of this relationship:

_____

_____

(b) Comment on the significance of this relationship to oxygen delivery to the tissues: _____

_____

6. (a) Describe how foetal Hb is different to adult Hb: _____

(b) Explain the significance of this difference to oxygen delivery to the foetus: _____

_____

7. At low blood pH, less oxygen is bound by haemoglobin and more is released to the tissues:

(a) Name this effect: _____

(b) Comment on its significance to oxygen delivery to respiring tissue: _____

_____

8. Explain the significance of the very high affinity of myoglobin for oxygen: _____

_____

_____

DNA Replication

DNA replication is a necessary preliminary step for cell division (both mitosis and meiosis). This process ensures that each resulting cell receives a complete set of genes from the original cell. After DNA replication, each chromosome is made up of two chromatids, joined at the **centromere**. Each **chromatid** contains half original (parent) DNA and half new (daughter) DNA. The two chromatids will become separated during cell division to form two separate chromosomes. During DNA replication, nucleotides are added at a region called the **replication fork**. The position of the replication fork moves along the chromosome as replication progresses. This whole process occurs simultaneously for each chromosome of a cell and the entire process is tightly controlled by enzymes. The diagram below describes essential steps in the process, while that on the next page identifies the role of the enzymes at each stage.

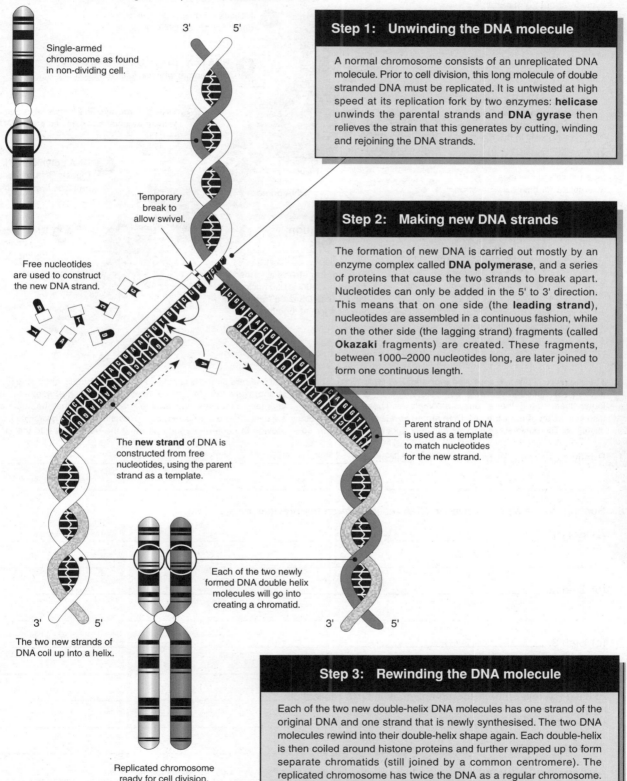

Single-armed chromosome as found in non-dividing cell.

Temporary break to allow swivel.

Free nucleotides are used to construct the new DNA strand.

The **new strand** of DNA is constructed from free nucleotides, using the parent strand as a template.

Parent strand of DNA is used as a template to match nucleotides for the new strand.

Each of the two newly formed DNA double helix molecules will go into creating a chromatid.

The two new strands of DNA coil up into a helix.

Replicated chromosome ready for cell division.

Step 1: Unwinding the DNA molecule

A normal chromosome consists of an unreplicated DNA molecule. Prior to cell division, this long molecule of double stranded DNA must be replicated. It is untwisted at high speed at its replication fork by two enzymes: **helicase** unwinds the parental strands and **DNA gyrase** then relieves the strain that this generates by cutting, winding and rejoining the DNA strands.

Step 2: Making new DNA strands

The formation of new DNA is carried out mostly by an enzyme complex called **DNA polymerase**, and a series of proteins that cause the two strands to break apart. Nucleotides can only be added in the 5' to 3' direction. This means that on one side (the **leading strand**), nucleotides are assembled in a continuous fashion, while on the other side (the lagging strand) fragments (called **Okazaki** fragments) are created. These fragments, between 1000–2000 nucleotides long, are later joined to form one continuous length.

Step 3: Rewinding the DNA molecule

Each of the two new double-helix DNA molecules has one strand of the original DNA and one strand that is newly synthesised. The two DNA molecules rewind into their double-helix shape again. Each double-helix is then coiled around histone proteins and further wrapped up to form separate chromatids (still joined by a common centromere). The replicated chromosome has twice the DNA as a regular chromosome. The two chromatids will become separated in the cell division process to form two separate chromosomes.

Biochemical & Cellular Diversity

Related activities: Mitosis and the Cell Cycle
Web links: DNA Replication

DA 3

Enzyme Control of DNA Replication

DNA replication occurs during interphase of the cell cycle at an astounding rate. As many as 4000 nucleotides per second are replicated. This explains how under ideal conditions, bacterial cells with as many as 4 million nucleotides, can complete a cell cycle in about 20 minutes.

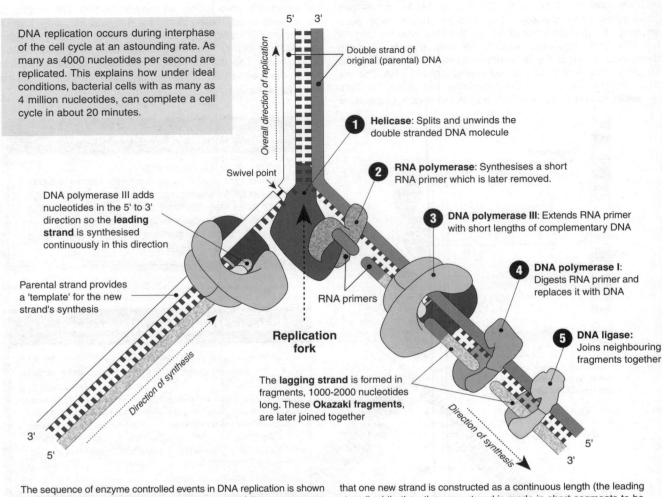

Double strand of original (parental) DNA

Overall direction of replication

Swivel point

Helicase: Splits and unwinds the double stranded DNA molecule

RNA polymerase: Synthesises a short RNA primer which is later removed.

DNA polymerase III: Extends RNA primer with short lengths of complementary DNA

DNA polymerase I: Digests RNA primer and replaces it with DNA

DNA ligase: Joins neighbouring fragments together

DNA polymerase III adds nucleotides in the 5' to 3' direction so the **leading strand** is synthesised continuously in this direction

Parental strand provides a 'template' for the new strand's synthesis

Direction of synthesis

RNA primers

Replication fork

The **lagging strand** is formed in fragments, 1000-2000 nucleotides long. These **Okazaki fragments**, are later joined together

Direction of synthesis

The sequence of enzyme controlled events in DNA replication is shown above (1-5). Although shown as separate, many of the enzymes are found clustered together as enzyme complexes. These enzymes are also able to 'proof-read' the new DNA strand as it is made and correct mistakes. The polymerase enzyme can only work in one direction, so that one new strand is constructed as a continuous length (the leading strand) while the other new strand is made in short segments to be later joined together (the lagging strand). **NOTE** that the nucleotides are present as deoxynucleoside triphosphates. When hydrolysed, these provide the energy for incorporating the nucleotide into the strand.

1. Briefly explain the purpose of DNA replication: _____

_____

2. Summarise the steps involved in DNA replication (on the previous page):

   (a) Step 1: _____

   _____

   (b) Step 2: _____

   _____

   (c) Step 3: _____

   _____

3. Explain the role of the following enzymes in DNA replication: _____

   (a) Helicase: _____

   (b) DNA polymerase I: _____

   (c) DNA polymerase III: _____

   (d) Ligase: _____

4. Determine the time it would take for a bacteria to replicate its DNA (see note in diagram above): _____

Mitosis and the Cell Cycle

Mitosis is part of the 'cell cycle' in which an existing cell (the parent cell) divides into two (the daughter cells). Mitosis does not result in a change of chromosome numbers (unlike meiosis) and the daughter cells are identical to the parent cell. Although mitosis is part of a continuous cell cycle, it is divided into stages (below). The example below illustrates the cell cycle in a plant cell. Note that in animal cells, cytokinesis involves the formation of a constriction that divides the cell in two. It is usually well underway by the end of telophase and does not involve the formation of a cell plate.

The Cell Cycle and Stages of Mitosis

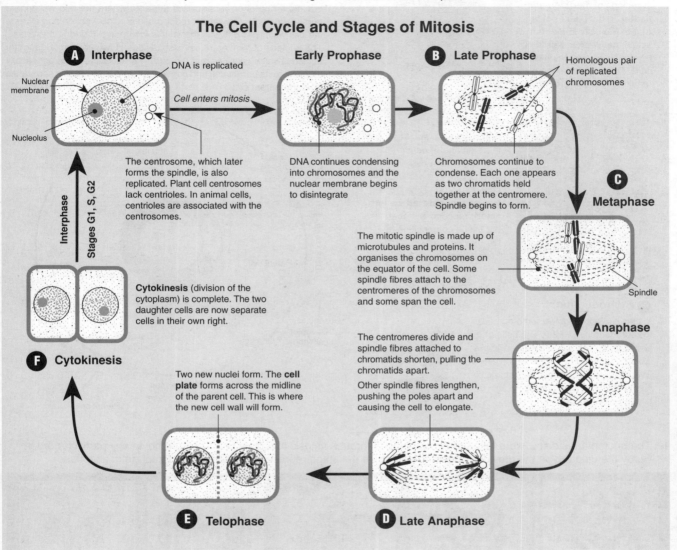

A Interphase — Nuclear membrane, Nucleolus, DNA is replicated. The centrosome, which later forms the spindle, is also replicated. Plant cell centrosomes lack centrioles. In animal cells, centrioles are associated with the centrosomes.

Early Prophase — DNA continues condensing into chromosomes and the nuclear membrane begins to disintegrate

B Late Prophase — Homologous pair of replicated chromosomes. Chromosomes continue to condense. Each one appears as two chromatids held together at the centromere. Spindle begins to form.

C Metaphase — The mitotic spindle is made up of microtubules and proteins. It organises the chromosomes on the equator of the cell. Some spindle fibres attach to the centromeres of the chromosomes and some span the cell. Spindle

Anaphase — The centromeres divide and spindle fibres attached to chromatids shorten, pulling the chromatids apart. Other spindle fibres lengthen, pushing the poles apart and causing the cell to elongate.

D Late Anaphase

E Telophase — Two new nuclei form. The cell plate forms across the midline of the parent cell. This is where the new cell wall will form.

F Cytokinesis — Cytokinesis (division of the cytoplasm) is complete. The two daughter cells are now separate cells in their own right.

Interphase Stages G1, S, G2

Cell enters mitosis

The Cell Cycle Overview

S Phase
Chromosome replication (DNA synthesis)

Second Gap Phase
The chromosomes begin condensing.

Mitosis
Nuclear division

Cytokinesis
Division of the cytoplasm and separation of the two cells. Cytokinesis is distinct from nuclear division.

First Gap Phase
Cell growth and development

The Cell Cycle — S, G2, M, C, G1

Homologous Chromosomes

In sexually reproducing organisms, the chromosomes of most cells are present as **homologous pairs**. One chromosome of a pair is supplied by the female parent and one by the male parent. Each homologue carries an identical assortment of genes, but the version of the gene (allele) from each parent may differ.

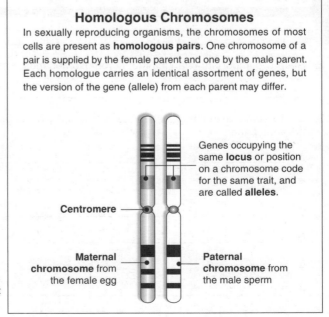

Genes occupying the same **locus** or position on a chromosome code for the same trait, and are called **alleles**.

Centromere

Maternal chromosome from the female egg

Paternal chromosome from the male sperm

Biochemical & Cellular Diversity

© Biozone International 2008
Photocopying Prohibited

Related activities: The Cell Cycle and Cancer, Root Cell Development

A 2

Mitotic cell division has several purposes (below left). In multicellular organisms, mitosis repairs damaged cells and tissues, and produces the growth in an organism that allows it to reach its adult size. In unicellular organisms, and some small multicellular organisms, cell division allows organisms to reproduce asexually (as in the budding yeast cell cycle below).

The Functions of Mitosis

❶ Growth

In plants, cell division occurs in regions of **meristematic tissue**. In the plant root tip (right), the cells in the root apical meristem are dividing by mitosis to produce new cells. This elongates the root, resulting in **plant growth**.

Root apical meristem

❷ Repair

Some animals, such as this skink (left), detach their limbs as a defence mechanism in a process called autotomy. The limbs can be **regenerated** via the mitotic process, although the tissue composition of the new limb differs slightly from that of the original.

Photo: AB Sheldon

❸ Reproduction

Mitotic division enables some animals to reproduce **asexually**. The cells of this Hydra (left) undergo mitosis, forming a 'bud' on the side of the parent organism. Eventually the bud, which is genetically identical to its parent, detaches to continue the life cycle.

Parent

Bud

The Budding Yeast Cell Cycle

Yeasts can reproduce asexually through **budding**. In *Saccharomyces cerevisiae* (baker's yeast), budding involves mitotic division in the parent cell, with the formation of a daughter cell (or bud). As budding begins, a ring of chitin stabilises the area where the bud will appear and enzymatic activity and turgor pressure act to weaken and extrude the cell wall. New cell wall material is incorporated during this phase. The nucleus of the parent cell also divides in two, to form a daughter nucleus, which migrates into the bud. The daughter cell is genetically identical to its parent cell and continues to grow, eventually separating from the parent cell.

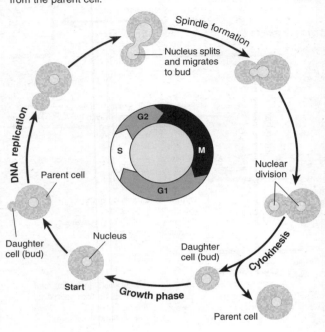

Spindle formation

Nucleus splits and migrates to bud

DNA replication

Parent cell

Daughter cell (bud)

Nucleus

Start

Growth phase

Daughter cell (bud)

Cytokinesis

Nuclear division

Parent cell

1. The photographs below were taken at various stages through mitosis in a plant cell. They are not in any particular order. Study the diagram on the previous page and determine the stage represented in each photograph (e.g. anaphase).

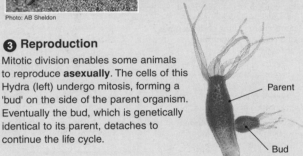

Photos: RCN

(a) _____ (b) _____ (c) _____ (d) _____ (e) _____

2. State two important changes that chromosomes must undergo before cell division can take place: _____

_____

3. Briefly summarise the stages of the cell cycle by describing what is happening at the points (**A-F**) in the diagram on the previous page:

A. _____

B. _____

C. _____

D. _____

E. _____

F. _____

The Cell Cycle and Cancer

Cancer is a term describing a large group of diseases characterised by the progressive and uncontrolled growth of abnormal cells. There is no single cause for all the forms of cancer; environmental, genetic, and biological factors are usually implicated. Certain risk factors increase a person's chance of getting cancer. Some risk factors, such as exposure to tobacco smoke, are controllable, while others, such as gender, are not. Because cancers arise as a result of damage to DNA, those factors that cause cellular damage, e.g. exposure to the chemicals in cigarette smoke, increase the risk of cancers developing.

Stages in the Formation of Cancer

The growth of a cancer begins when the genes controlling cell growth and multiplication (**oncogenes**) are transformed by agents known as **carcinogens**. Most well studied is the p53 gene which normally acts to prevent cell division in damaged cells. Scientists have found that the p53 gene is altered in 40% of all cancers. Once a cell is transformed into a tumour-forming type (**malignant**), the change in its oncogenes is passed on to all offspring cells:

Cancer cells ignore density-dependent inhibition and continue to multiply even after contacting one another, piling up until the nutrient supply becomes limiting.

1. Benign tumour cells
Defects (mutations) in one or two controlling genes cause the formation of a benign tumour. This is a localised population of proliferating cells where formation of new cells is matched by cell death.

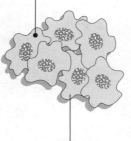

2. Malignant tumour cells
More mutations may cause the cells to become malignant. These cells stop producing a chemical that prevents blood vessels from forming. New capillaries grow into the tumour, providing it with nutrients.

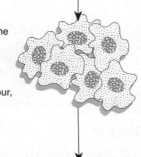

3. Metastasis
The new capillaries also provide a route for the malignant cells to break away from the tumour and travel to other parts of the body where they start new cancers.

Malignant cells break away from tumour mass and spread through the body through the **blood** or **lymphatic systems**.

Risk Factors for Cancer

The greatest **uncontrollable risk factor** for cancer is **ageing**; most cancers occur in people over the age of 65. Others include **genetic predisposition** (family history) and gender. **Controllable risk factors** include **lifestyle factors**, such as **tobacco use**. Not unexpectedly, different kinds of cancer are associated with different risk factors. For example, sunlight exposure increases the risk of skin cancers. Some major risk factors include the following:

Tobacco use is related to a wide range of cancers; smoking alone causes one third of all cancer deaths.

Excessive alcohol intake, especially when associated with tobacco use, is associated with oral cancers.

A highly processed, high fat diet is associated with higher risk of various cancers, including colon cancer.

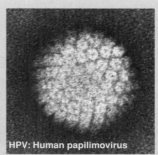

HPV: Human papilimovirus

Certain Infections are associated with the development of cancers. HPV is strongly linked to cervical cancer.

Ionising radiation and hazardous substances, such as asbestos and formaldehyde, cause cell damage that can lead to cancer.

Unprotected exposure to ultraviolet light causes early ageing of the skin and damage that can lead to the development of skin cancers.

Biochemical & Cellular Diversity

1. Explain the mechanism by which the risk factors described above increase the chance of developing cancer:

2. Explain why it can be difficult to determine the causative role of a single risk factor in the development of a cancer:

Differentiation of Human Cells

As the tissues and organs of an embryo take form, their cells become modified and specialised to perform particular functions. This process is known as **cellular differentiation**. Cellular differentiation begins as soon as cells have been formed by cell division. It is achieved via the action of regulatory genes (and, in some cases, hormones) that turn specific genes on or off. Cell differentiation is a serial process; the developmental options of a cell become more and more restricted as its development proceeds. Once the fate of a cell has been determined, it cannot alter its path and change into another cell type.

As the tissues and organs of an embryo take form, their cells become modified and specialised for particular functions. This process, called **cellular differentiation**, begins as soon as cells have been formed by cell division. It is achieved via the action of regulatory genes (and, in some cases, hormones) that turn specific genes on or off. Cell differentiation is a serial process; the developmental options of a cell become more and more restricted as its development proceeds. Once the fate of a cell has been determined, it cannot alter its path and change into another cell type.

The zygote (fertilised egg) has all the information stored in the chromosomes to make a complete new individual

Zygote

Cell word list

Sperm cell, sensory neurone, smooth muscle cell, pancreatic secretory cell, pigment cell, skin (epithelial) cells, egg cell (oocyte), white blood cell (leucocyte), striated muscle cell

At certain stages in the sequence of cell divisions, some genes are switched on, while others are switched off, depending on the destined role of the cell.

230 Different Cell Types

About 50 cell divisions

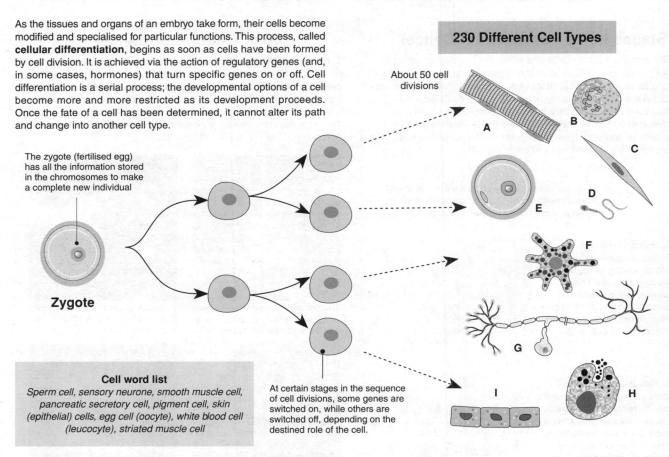

1. **Identify** the cells illustrated (A to I) in the diagram above by choosing names from the word list and state their **function**:

Cell Name	Function
(a) Striated muscle cell	Contractile element of skeletal muscle; creates movement
(b)	
(c)	
(d)	
(e)	
(f)	
(g)	
(h)	
(i)	

2. Describe two cells that continue dividing throughout an individual's life: _____

3. Explain how so many different types of cell can arise from one unspecialised cell (the zygote): _____

_____

_____

Human Cell Specialisation

Animal cells are often specialised to perform particular functions. The eight specialised cell types shown below are representative of some 230 different cell types in humans. Each has specialised features that suit it to performing a specific role.

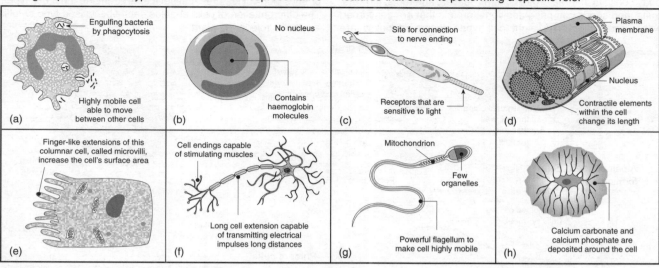

(a) Engulfing bacteria by phagocytosis. Highly mobile cell able to move between other cells.

(b) No nucleus. Contains haemoglobin molecules.

(c) Site for connection to nerve ending. Receptors that are sensitive to light.

(d) Plasma membrane. Nucleus. Contractile elements within the cell change its length.

(e) Finger-like extensions of this columnar cell, called microvilli, increase the cell's surface area.

(f) Cell endings capable of stimulating muscles. Long cell extension capable of transmitting electrical impulses long distances.

(g) Mitochondrion. Few organelles. Powerful flagellum to make cell highly mobile.

(h) Calcium carbonate and calcium phosphate are deposited around the cell.

1. Identify each of the cells (b) to (h) pictured above, and describe their **specialised features** and **role** in the body:

(a) Type of cell: _Phagocytic white blood cell (neutrophil)_

   Specialised features: _Engulfs bacteria and other foreign material by phagocytosis_

   Role of cell within body: _Destroys pathogens and other foreign material as well as cellular debris_

(b) Type of cell: _____

   Specialised features: _____

   Role of cell within body: _____

(c) Type of cell: _____

   Specialised features: _____

   Role of cell within body: _____

(d) Type of cell: _____

   Specialised features: _____

   Role of cell within body: _____

(e) Type of cell: _____

   Specialised features: _____

   Role of cell within body: _____

(f) Type of cell: _____

   Specialised features: _____

   Role of cell within body: _____

(g) Type of cell: _____

   Specialised features: _____

   Role of cell within body: _____

(h) Type of cell: _____

   Specialised features: _____

   Role of cell within body: _____

Biochemical & Cellular Diversity

Related activities: Animal Cells

RA 2

Plant Cell Specialisation

Plants show a wide variety of cell types. The vegetative plant body consists of three organs: stems, leaves, and roots. Flowers, fruits, and seeds comprise additional organs that are concerned with reproduction. The eight cell types illustrated below are representatives of these plant organ systems. Each has structural or physiological features that set it apart from the other cell types. The differentiation of cells enables each specialised type to fulfill a specific role in the plant.

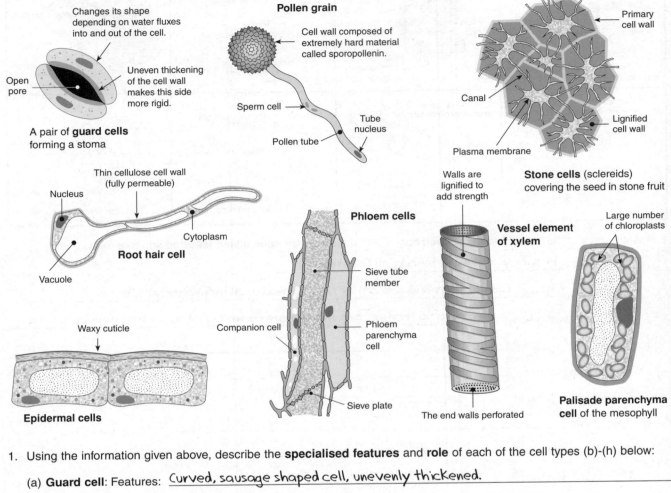

Pollen grain

Changes its shape depending on water fluxes into and out of the cell.

Open pore

Uneven thickening of the cell wall makes this side more rigid.

A pair of **guard cells** forming a stoma

Cell wall composed of extremely hard material called sporopollenin.

Sperm cell

Pollen tube

Tube nucleus

Primary cell wall

Canal

Plasma membrane

Lignified cell wall

Walls are lignified to add strength

Stone cells (sclereids) covering the seed in stone fruit

Nucleus

Thin cellulose cell wall (fully permeable)

Cytoplasm

Root hair cell

Vacuole

Phloem cells

Sieve tube member

Phloem parenchyma cell

Sieve plate

Companion cell

Vessel element of xylem

The end walls perforated

Large number of chloroplasts

Palisade parenchyma cell of the mesophyll

Waxy cuticle

Epidermal cells

1. Using the information given above, describe the **specialised features** and **role** of each of the cell types (b)-(h) below:

   (a) **Guard cell**: Features: _Curved, sausage shaped cell, unevenly thickened._

   Role in plant: _Turgor changes alter the cell shape to open or close the stoma._

   (b) **Pollen grain**: Features: _____

   Role in plant: _____

   (c) **Palisade parenchyma cell**: Features: _____

   Role in plant: _____

   (d) **Epidermal cell**: Features: _____

   Role in plant: _____

   (e) **Vessel element**: Features: _____

   Role in plant: _____

   (f) **Stone cell**: Features: _____

   Role in plant: _____

   (g) **Sieve tube member** (of phloem): Features: _____

   Role in plant: _____

   (h) **Root hair cell**: Features: _____

   Role in plant: _____

Related activities: Cell Walls and Chloroplasts

Root Cell Development

In plants, cell division for growth (mitosis) is restricted to growing tips called **meristematic** tissue. These are located at the tips of every stem and root. This is unlike mitosis in a growing animal where cell divisions can occur all over the body. The diagram below illustrates the position and appearance of developing and growing cells in a plant root. Similar zones of development occur in the growing stem tips, which may give rise to specialised structures such as leaves and flowers.

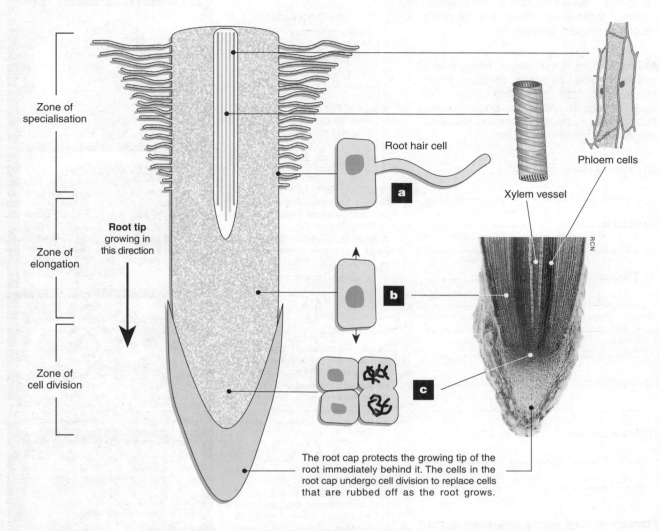

Zone of specialisation

Root hair cell

a

Xylem vessel

Phloem cells

Root tip
growing in this direction

Zone of elongation

b

Zone of cell division

c

The root cap protects the growing tip of the root immediately behind it. The cells in the root cap undergo cell division to replace cells that are rubbed off as the root grows.

1. Briefly describe what is happening to the plant cells at each of the points labelled (**a**) to (**c**) in the diagram above:

   (a) _____

   (b) _____

   (c) _____

2. The light micrograph (below) shows a section of the cells of an onion root tip, stained to show up the chromosomes.

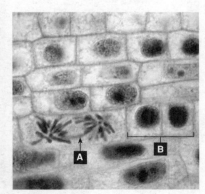

A

B

   (a) State the mitotic stage of the cell labelled A and explain your answer:

   _____

   (b) State the mitotic stage just completed in the cells labelled B and explain:

   _____

   (c) If, in this example, 250 cells were examined and 25 were found to be in the process of mitosis, state the proportion of the cell cycle occupied by mitosis:

   _____

   _____

3. Identify the cells that divide and specialise when a tree increases its girth (diameter): _____

Related activities: Mitosis and the Cell Cycle, Plant Cell Specialisation

RDA 2

Levels of Organisation

Organisation and the emergence of novel properties in complex systems are two of the defining features of living organisms. Organisms are organised according to a hierarchy of structural levels (below), each level building on the one below it. At each level, novel properties emerge that were not present at the simpler level. Hierarchical organisation allows specialised cells to group together into tissues and organs to perform a particular function. This improves efficiency of function in the organism.

In the spaces provided for each question below, assign each of the examples listed to one of the levels of organisation as indicated.

1. **Animals**: *adrenaline, blood, bone, brain, cardiac muscle, cartilage, collagen, DNA, heart, leucocyte, lysosome, mast cell, nervous system, neurone, phospholipid, reproductive system, ribosomes, Schwann cell, spleen, squamous epithelium.*

(a) Organ system: _____

_____

(b) Organs: _____

_____

(c) Tissues: _____

_____

(d) Cells: _____

_____

(e) Organelles: _____

_____

(f) Molecular level: _____

_____

_____

2. **Plants**: *cellulose, chloroplasts, collenchyma, companion cells, DNA, epidermal cell, fibres, flowers, leaf, mesophyll, parenchyma, pectin, phloem, phospholipid, ribosomes, roots, sclerenchyma, tracheid.*

(a) Organs: _____

_____

(b) Tissues: _____

_____

(c) Cells: _____

_____

(d) Organelles: _____

_____

(e) Molecular level: _____

_____

_____

The Organism

A complex, functioning whole that is the sum of all its component parts.

Organ System Level

In animals, organs form parts of even larger units known as organ systems. An organ system is an association of organs with a common function e.g. digestive system, cardiovascular system, and the urinogenital system.

Organ Level

Organs are structures of definite form and structure, comprising two or more tissues.

Animal examples include: heart, lungs, brain, stomach, kidney.

Plant examples include: leaves, roots, storage organs, ovary.

Tissue Level

Tissues are composed of groups of cells of similar structure that perform a particular, related function.

Animal examples include: epithelial tissue, bone, muscle.

Plant examples include: phloem, chlorenchyma, endodermis, xylem.

Cellular Level

Cells are the basic structural and functional units of an organism. Each cell type has a different structure and function; the result of cellular differentiation during development.

Animal examples include: epithelial cells, osteoblasts, muscle fibres.

Plant examples include: sclereids, xylem vessels, sieve tubes.

Organelle Level

Many diverse molecules may associate together to form complex, highly specialised structures within cells called cellular organelles e.g. mitochondria, Golgi apparatus, endoplasmic reticulum, chloroplasts.

Chemical and Molecular Level

Atoms and molecules form the most basic, level of organisation. This level includes all the chemicals essential for maintaining life e.g. water, ions, fats, carbohydrates, amino acids, proteins, and nucleic acids.

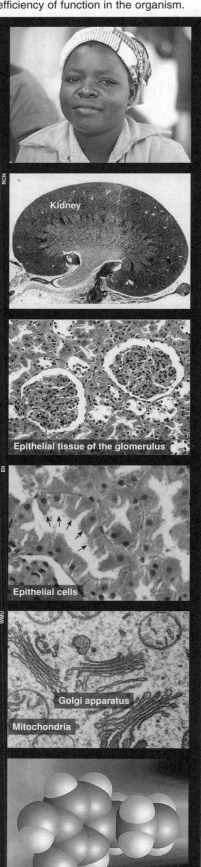

Kidney

Epithelial tissue of the glomerulus

Epithelial cells

Golgi apparatus

Mitochondria

Related activities: Animal Tissues, Plant Tissues

Animal Tissues

The study of tissues (plant or animal) is called **histology**. The cells of a tissue, and their associated intracellular substances, e.g. collagen, are grouped together to perform particular functions. Tissues improve the efficiency of operation because they enable tasks to be shared amongst various specialised cells. **Animal tissues** can be divided into four broad groups: **epithelial tissues**, **connective tissues**, **muscle**, and **nervous**

tissues. Organs usually consist of several types of tissue. The heart mostly consists of cardiac muscle tissue, but also has epithelial tissue, which lines the heart chambers to prevent leaking, connective tissue for strength and elasticity, and nervous tissue, in the form of neurones, which direct the contractions of the cardiac muscle. The features of some of he more familiar animal tissues are described below.

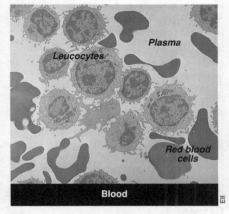

Blood

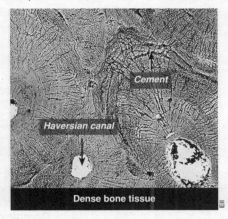

Dense bone tissue

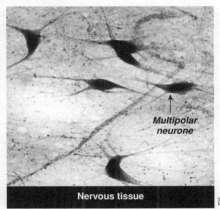

Nervous tissue

Connective tissue is the major supporting tissue of the animal body. It comprises cells, widely dispersed in a semi-fluid matrix. Connective tissues bind other structures together and provide support, and protection against damage, infection, or heat loss. Connective tissues include dentine (teeth), adipose (fat) tissue, bone (above) and cartilage, and the tissues around the body's organs and blood vessels. Blood (above, left) is a special type of liquid tissue, comprising cells floating in a liquid matrix.

Nervous tissue contains densely packed nerve cells (neurones) which are specialised for the transmission of nerve impulses. Associated with the neurones there may also be supporting cells and connective tissue containing blood vessels.

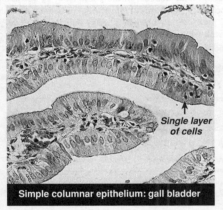

Simple columnar epithelium: gall bladder

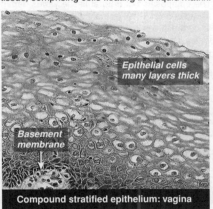

Compound stratified epithelium: vagina

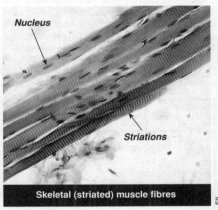

Skeletal (striated) muscle fibres

Epithelial tissue is organised into single (above, left) or layered (above) sheets. It lines internal and external surfaces (e.g. blood vessels, ducts, gut lining) and protects the underlying structures from wear, infection, and/or pressure. Epithelial cells rest on a basement membrane of fibres and collagen and are held together by a carbohydrate-based "glue". The cells may also be specialised for absorption, secretion, or excretion. Examples: stratified (compound) epithelium of vagina, ciliated epithelium of respiratory tract, cuboidal epithelium of kidney ducts, and the columnar epithelium of the intestine.

Muscle tissue consists of very highly specialised cells called fibres, held together by connective tissue. The three types of muscle in the body are cardiac muscle, skeletal muscle (above), and smooth muscle. Muscles bring about both voluntary and involuntary (unconscious) body movements.

Biochemical & Cellular Diversity

1. Explain how the development of tissues improves functional efficiency: _____

_____

_____

2. Describe the general functional role of each of the following broad tissue types:

(a) Epithelial tissue: _____ (c) Muscle tissue: _____

(b) Nervous tissue: _____ (d) Connective tissue: _____

3. Identify the particular features that contribute to the particular functional role of each of the following tissue types:

(a) Muscle tissue: _____

_____

(b) Nervous tissue: _____

_____

Related activities: Levels of Organisation

RA 2

Plant Tissues

Plant tissues are divided into two groups: simple and complex. **Simple tissues** contain only one cell type and form packing and support tissues. **Complex tissues** contain more than one cell type and form the conducting and support tissues of plants. Tissues are in turn grouped into tissue systems which make up the plant body. Vascular plants have three systems; the dermal, vascular, and ground tissue systems. The **dermal system** is the outer covering of the plant providing protection and reducing water loss. **Vascular tissue** provides the transport system by which water and nutrients are moved through the plant. The **ground tissue** system, which makes up the bulk of a plant, is made up mainly of simple tissues such as parenchyma, and carries out a wide variety of roles within the plant including photosynthesis, storage, and support.

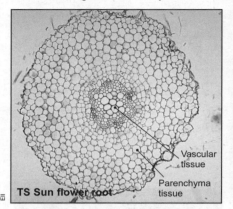

TS Sun flower root
Vascular tissue
Parenchyma tissue

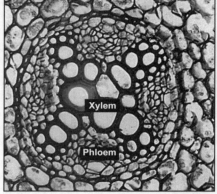

Xylem
Phloem

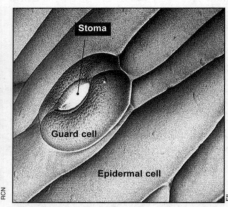

Stoma
Guard cell
Epidermal cell

Simple Tissues

Simple tissues consists of only one or two cell types. **Parenchyma tissue** is the most common and involved in storage, photosynthesis, and secretion. **Collenchyma tissue** comprises thick-walled collenchyma cells alternating with layers of intracellular substances (pectin and cellulose) to provide flexible support. The cells of **sclerenchyma** tissue (fibres and sclereids) have rigid cell walls which provide support.

Complex Tissues

Xylem and phloem tissue (above left), which together make up the plant **vascular tissue** system, are complex tissues. Each comprises several tissue types including tracheids, vessel members, parenchyma and fibres in xylem, and sieve tube members, companion cells, parenchyma and sclerenchyma in phloem. **Dermal tissue** is also complex tissue and covers the outside of the plant. The composition of dermal tissue varies depending upon its location on the plant. Root epidermal tissue consist of epidermal cells which extend to root hairs (**trichomes**) for increasing surface area. In contrast, the epidermal tissue of leaves (above right) are covered by a waxy cuticle to reduce water loss, and specialised guard cells regulate water intake via the stomata (pores in the leaf through which gases enter and leave the leaf tissue).

1. The table below lists the major types of simple and complex plant tissue. Complete the table by filling in the role each of the tissue types plays within the plant. The first example has been completed for you.

Simple Tissue	Cell Type(s)	Role within the Plant
Parenchyma	Parenchyma cells	Involved in respiration, photosynthesis, storage and secretion.
Collenchyma		
Sclerenchyma		
Root endodermis	Endodermal cells	
Pericycle		
Complex Tissue		
Leaf mesophyll	Spongy mesophyll cells, palisade mesophyll cells	
Xylem		
Phloem		
Epidermis		

Adaptation and Specialisation

Unit 2: The Variety of Living Organisms
2.7 Mass transport and gas exchange

Surface area and volume, gas exchange, blood vessels, plant transport systems and adaptations

Learning Objectives

☐ 1. Compile your own glossary from the **KEY WORDS** displayed in **bold type** in the learning objectives below.

Size and Surface Area *(page 205-206)*

☐ 2. Describe the relationship between an organism's size and its surface area (the **surface area: volume ratio** or **SA:V**). Explain the significance of this relationship to the exchange of gases with the environment.

☐ 3. Explain why diffusion is not an effective way to transport materials in larger, multicellular organisms. Describe systems in multicellular organisms that facilitate exchange of substances and heat transfer.

Gas Exchange Systems *(pages 107-108, 207-214)*

☐ 4. Explain that organisms need to exchange **respiratory gases** with their environment. Describe the structure and function of gas exchange systems in representative animals. In each case, relate the structure of the system to its suitability in the environment.
Body surface in a simple multicellular animal (e.g. flatworm) or in a single celled organism.
Tracheal tubes in insects, including the role of the **spiracles** and ventilation movements in gas exchange.
Gills in bony fish, including the significance of **countercurrent exchange**.
Lungs in mammals, including the role of breathing.

☐ 5. List the gases that plants exchange with their environment and identify the processes involved in using and producing these gases.

☐ 6. Describe the location, structure, function, and adaptations of the gas exchange surfaces and related structures in the leaves of **dicotyledonous plants**. Include reference the **mesophyll** and **stomata**.

☐ 7. Using **terrestrial insect**s and **xerophytic plants** as examples, describe some of the structural and functional compromises made between maximising the efficiency of gas exchange while minimising water loss.

Mammalian Transport *(pages 119, 217-221)*

☐ 8. With reference to transport systems in multicellular organisms, explain the role of **mass transport** in the efficient supply of material over large distances.

☐ 9. Describe the basic plan of the **mammalian circulation** system, identifying the name and location of the major **blood vessels** supplying the heart, liver and kidneys.

☐ 10. Describe and contrast the structure and role of the following vertebrate blood vessels: **arteries**, **arterioles**, **veins**. Relate the structure of each type of blood vessel to its specific function in the circulatory system.

☐ 11. Describe the structure and function of **capillaries**, including reference to how their structure facilitates their function in metabolic exchange.

☐ 12. Describe the formation of **tissue fluid** and explain how and where it is returned to the blood circulatory system.

Plant Transport Systems *(pages 222-225)*

☐ 13. Describe the structure of a dicot **primary root**, identifying the distribution and adaptations for function of the **root hairs**, **endodermis**, **xylem**, and **phloem**.

☐ 14. Describe the mechanism and pathways for water uptake in plant roots. Describe the role of **osmosis**, gradients in **water potential**, and the **symplastic**, **apoplastic**, and **vacuolar pathways** through the root.

☐ 15. Define the terms **transpiration** and **transpiration stream**. Recognise transpiration as a consequence of gas exchange and explain the role of **stomata** in these processes. Explain how transpiration benefits a plant.

☐ 16. Explain the roles of **cohesion-tension** (capillary action), **root pressure**, and **transpiration pull** in the movement of water through the xylem, identifying the relative importance of each.

☐ 17. Explain the effect of humidity, light, air movement, temperature, and water availability on transpiration rate. Describe how the factors affecting transpiration could be investigated experimentally.

Textbooks

See the 'Textbook Reference Grid' on page 7 for textbook page references relating to material in this topic.

Supplementary Texts

See pages 5-6 for additional details of these texts:
■ Adds, J. *et al.*, 2004. **Exchange & Transport, Energy & Ecosystems**, chpt.1-3
■ Clegg, C.J., 1998. **Mammals: Structure and Function** (John Murray).

Periodicals

See page 6 for details of publishers of periodicals:
■ **A Fair Exchange** Biol. Sci. Rev., 13(1), Sept. 2000, pp. 2-5. *Formation and reabsorption of tissue fluid (includes disorders of fluid balance).*
■ **How Trees Lift Water** Biol. Sci. Rev., 18(1), Sept. 2005, pp. 33-37. *An excellent account of the cohesion-tension mechanism by which plants move water through their tissues against gravity.*
■ **Cacti** Biol. Sci. Rev., 20(1), Sept. 2007, pp. 26-30. *The growth forms and structural and physiological adaptations of cacti.*

Internet

See pages 8-9 for details of how to access **Bio Links** from our web site: **www.biozone.co.uk**. From Bio Links, access sites under the topics:

ANIMAL BIOLOGY > Gas Exchange: • Gas exchange • Respiration in aquatic insects • Respiratory system • Respiratory system: Chpt 41 • Tracheal breathing > **Circulatory system** • Animal circulatory system • The circulatory system
PLANT BIOLOGY > Structure and Function: • Plant structure > **Nutrition and Gas Exchange**: • Gas exchange in plants > **Support and Transport**: • LAB: Measuring plant transpiration

Transport and Exchange Systems

Living cells require a constant supply of nutrients and oxygen, and continuous removal of wastes. Simple, small organisms can achieve this through **diffusion** across moist body surfaces without requiring specialised transport or exchange systems. Larger, more complex organisms require systems to facilitate exchanges as their surface area to volume ratio decreases. **Mass transport** (also known as mass flow or bulk flow)

describes the movement of materials at equal rates or as a single mass. Mass transport accounts for the long distance transport of fluids in living organisms. It includes the movement of blood in the circulatory systems of animals and the transport of water and solutes in the xylem and phloem of plants. In the diagram below, exchanges by diffusion are compared to mass transport to specific exchange sites.

Exchanges Across a Body Surface

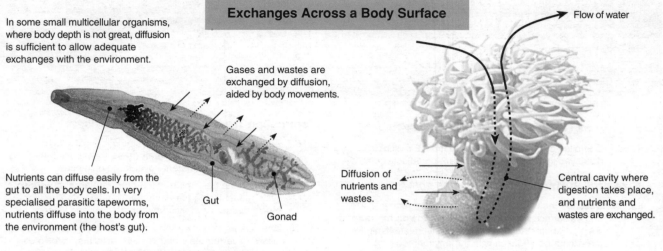

In some small multicellular organisms, where body depth is not great, diffusion is sufficient to allow adequate exchanges with the environment.

Gases and wastes are exchanged by diffusion, aided by body movements.

Nutrients can diffuse easily from the gut to all the body cells. In very specialised parasitic tapeworms, nutrients diffuse into the body from the environment (the host's gut).

Gut

Gonad

Platyhelminthes (liver fluke)

Flow of water

Diffusion of nutrients and wastes.

Central cavity where digestion takes place, and nutrients and wastes are exchanged.

Cnidarians (sea anemone)

Systems for Exchange and Transport

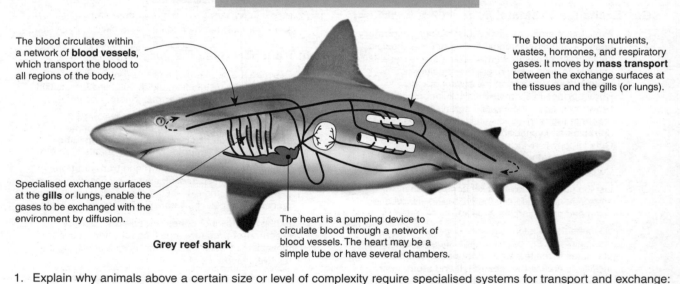

The blood circulates within a network of **blood vessels**, which transport the blood to all regions of the body.

The blood transports nutrients, wastes, hormones, and respiratory gases. It moves by **mass transport** between the exchange surfaces at the tissues and the gills (or lungs).

Specialised exchange surfaces at the **gills** or lungs, enable the gases to be exchanged with the environment by diffusion.

Grey reef shark

The heart is a pumping device to circulate blood through a network of blood vessels. The heart may be a simple tube or have several chambers.

1. Explain why animals above a certain size or level of complexity require specialised systems for transport and exchange:

_____

_____

_____

2. (a) Describe how materials move within the circulatory system of a vertebrate: _____

_____

(b) Contrast this with how materials are transported in a flatworm or single celled eukaryote: _____

_____

_____

(c) Identify two exchange sites in a vertebrate: _____

A 1

Related activities: Surface Area and Volume

Surface Area and Volume

When an object (e.g. a cell) is small it has a large surface area in comparison to its volume. In this case diffusion will be an effective way to transport materials (e.g. gases) into the cell. As an object becomes larger, its surface area compared to its volume is smaller. Diffusion is no longer an effective way to transport materials to the inside. For this reason, there is a physical limit for the size of a cell, with the effectiveness of diffusion being the controlling factor.

Diffusion in Organisms of Different Sizes

Respiratory gases and some other substances are exchanged with the surroundings by diffusion or active transport across the plasma membrane.

The **plasma membrane**, which surrounds every cell, functions as a selective barrier that regulates the cell's chemical composition. For each square micrometer of membrane, only so much of a particular substance can cross per second.

The surface area of an elephant is increased, for radiating body heat, by large flat ears.

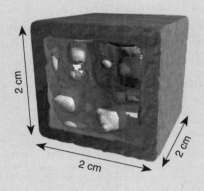

The nucleus can control a smaller cell more efficiently.

Oxygen

Food

Carbon dioxide

Wastes

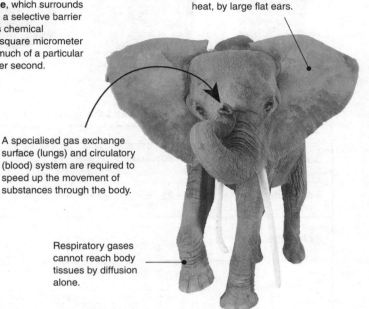

A specialised gas exchange surface (lungs) and circulatory (blood) system are required to speed up the movement of substances through the body.

Respiratory gases cannot reach body tissues by diffusion alone.

Amoeba: The small size of single-celled protoctists, such as *Amoeba*, provides a large surface area relative to the cell's volume. This is adequate for many materials to be moved into and out of the cell by diffusion or active transport.

Multicellular organisms: To overcome the problems of small cell size, plants and animals became multicellular. They provide a small surface area compared to their volume but have evolved various adaptive features to improve their effective surface area.

Smaller is Better for Diffusion

One large cube

2 cm

2 cm

2 cm

Eight small cubes

1 cm

1 cm

1 cm

Volume: = 8 cm³

Surface area: = 24 cm²

Volume: = 8 cm³ for 8 cubes

Surface area: = 6 cm² for 1 cube

= 48 cm² for 8 cubes

The eight small cells and the single large cell have the same total volume, but their surface areas are different. The small cells together have twice the total surface area of the large cell, because there are more exposed (inner) surfaces. Real organisms have complex shapes, but the same principles apply.

The surface-area volume relationship has important implications for processes involving transport into and out of cells across membranes. For activities such as gas exchange, the surface area available for diffusion is a major factor limiting the rate at which oxygen can be supplied to tissues.

Adaptation & Specialisation

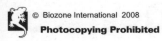

Related activities: Diffusion, Cell Sizes

DA 1

The diagram below shows four hypothetical cells of different sizes (cells do not actually grow to this size, their large size is for the sake of the exercise). They range from a small 2 cm cube to a larger 5 cm cube. This exercise investigates the effect of cell size on the efficiency of diffusion.

2 cm cube

3 cm cube

4 cm cube

5 cm cube

1. Calculate the volume, surface area and the ratio of surface area to volume for each of the four cubes above (the first has been done for you). When completing the table below, show your calculations.

Cube size	Surface area	Volume	Surface area to volume ratio
2 cm cube	2 x 2 x 6 = 24 cm² (2 cm x 2 cm x 6 sides)	2 x 2 x 2 = 8 cm³ (height x width x depth)	24 to 8 = 3:1
3 cm cube			
4 cm cube			
5 cm cube			

2. Create a graph, plotting the surface area against the volume of each cube, on the grid on the right. Draw a line connecting the points and label axes and units.

3. State which increases the fastest with increasing size, the **volume** or **surface area**.

_____

4. Explain what happens to the ratio of surface area to volume with increasing size:

_____

_____

_____

_____

5. Diffusion of substances into and out of a cell occurs across the cell surface. Describe how increasing the size of a cell will affect the ability of diffusion to transport materials into and out of a cell:

_____

_____

_____

_____

_____

Gas Exchange in Animals

The way in which gas exchange is achieved is influenced by the animal's general body form and by the environment in which the animal lives. Small, aquatic organisms such as sponges, flatworms and cnidarians, require no specialised respiratory structures. Gases are exchanged between the surrounding water (or moist environment) and the body's cells by diffusion directly across the organism's surface. Larger animals require specialised gas exchange systems. The complexity of these is related to the efficiency of gas exchange required, which is determined by the oxygen demands of the organism.

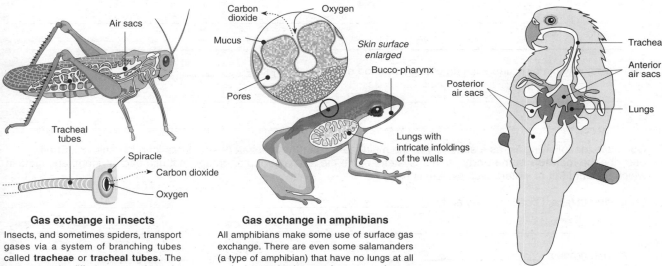

Gas exchange in insects

Insects, and sometimes spiders, transport gases via a system of branching tubes called **tracheae** or **tracheal tubes**. The gases move by diffusion across the moist lining directly to and from the tissues. The end of each tube contains a small amount of fluid which regulates the movement of gases by changing the surface area of air in contact with the cells.

Gas exchange in amphibians

All amphibians make some use of surface gas exchange. There are even some salamanders (a type of amphibian) that have no lungs at all and rely completely on surface gas exchange. This is only possible if the surface is kept moist by secretions from mucous glands. Frogs carry out gas exchange through the skin and in the lungs. At times of inactivity, the skin alone is a sufficient surface with either water or air.

Gas exchange in birds

A bird has air sacs in addition to lungs. The air sacs function in ventilating the lungs, where gas exchange takes place. Together, the anterior and posterior air sacs function as bellows that keep air flowing through the lungs continuously and in one direction.

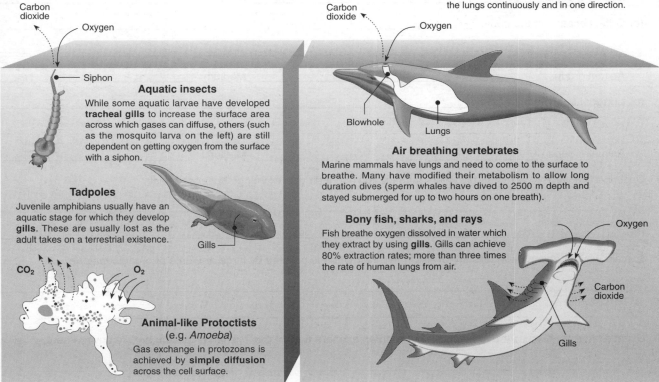

Aquatic insects

While some aquatic larvae have developed **tracheal gills** to increase the surface area across which gases can diffuse, others (such as the mosquito larva on the left) are still dependent on getting oxygen from the surface with a siphon.

Tadpoles

Juvenile amphibians usually have an aquatic stage for which they develop **gills**. These are usually lost as the adult takes on a terrestrial existence.

Animal-like Protoctists
(e.g. *Amoeba*)

Gas exchange in protozoans is achieved by **simple diffusion** across the cell surface.

Air breathing vertebrates

Marine mammals have lungs and need to come to the surface to breathe. Many have modified their metabolism to allow long duration dives (sperm whales have dived to 2500 m depth and stayed submerged for up to two hours on one breath).

Bony fish, sharks, and rays

Fish breathe oxygen dissolved in water which they extract by using **gills**. Gills can achieve 80% extraction rates; more than three times the rate of human lungs from air.

Jellyfish increase their surface area for gas exchange by having ruffles.

Nudibranch snails have elaborate exposed gills to assist gas exchange.

Some salamanders have no lungs and breathe solely through their skin.

Tube worms carry out gas exchange with feathery extensions in the water.

Related activities: Gas Exchange in Insects, Gas Exchange in Freshwater, Gas Exchange in Fish **Web links**: Vertebrate Lungs

RA 2

1. Suggest two reasons for the development of gas exchange structures and systems in animals:

   (a) _____

   (b) _____

2. (a) Explain why the air sacs of birds provide more efficient use of the air taken in with each breath:

   _____

   _____

   (b) Explain why birds require such an efficient method of gas exchange: _____

   _____

   _____

3. Complete the following list as a summary of the main features of the respiratory structures found in animals. Briefly describe the **location in the body** of each system, name the animal group or groups that use each system, and state in which medium (air or water) each system is used:

   (a) **Body surface**: Location in the body: _____

   _____

   Animal groups: _____   Medium: _____

   (b) **Tracheal tubes**: Location in the body: _____

   _____

   Animal groups: _____   Medium: _____

   (c) **Gills**: Location in the body: _____

   _____

   Animal groups: _____   Medium: _____

   (d) **Lungs**: Location in the body: _____

   _____

   Animal groups: _____   Medium: _____

4. Describe two ways in which air breathers manage to keep their gas exchange surfaces moist:

   (a) _____

   (b) _____

5. Explain why organisms with gills are at risk when their water is polluted by large amounts of organic material:

   _____

   _____

6. Using examples, discuss the relationship between an animal's type of gas exchange system and its environment:

   _____

   _____

   _____

   _____

   _____

   _____

Gas Exchange in Insects

Most insects are small terrestrial animals with a large surface area to volume ratio. They are at risk from desiccation by water loss through any exposed surface that is moist, thin, permeable, and vascular enough to serve as a respiratory membrane. To survive, they have adapted mechanisms to conserve water. Their bodies are covered by a hard exoskeleton with a waxy outer layer that minimises water loss. Insect excretory system are also developed to conserve water. Waste products and water pass through the excretory organs into the gut. Almost all the water is then reabsorbed from the rectum into the haemolymph. An almost dry excretory product (uric acid), is produced, minimising water losses to the environment. Tracheal systems are the most common gas exchange organs of terrestrial arthropods, including insects. Most body segments have paired apertures called spiracles in the lateral body wall through which air enters. Filtering devices in the spiracles prevent small particles from clogging the system, and valves control the degree to which the spiracles are open. In small insects, diffusion allows rapid gas exchange through the air-filled tubules. Larger, more active insects, such as locusts (below) have a tracheal system which includes air sacs that can be compressed and expanded to assist in moving air through the tubules.

Insect Tracheal Tubes

Insects, and some spiders, transport gases via a system of branching tubes called tracheae or tracheal tubes. The gases move by diffusion across the moist lining directly to and from the tissues. The end of each tube contains a small amount of fluid in which the respiratory gases are dissolved. The fluid is drawn into the muscle tissues during their contraction, and is released back into the tracheole when the muscle rests. Insects ventilate their tracheal system by making rhythmic body movements to help move the air in and out of the tracheae.

Spiracle openings on the abdomen

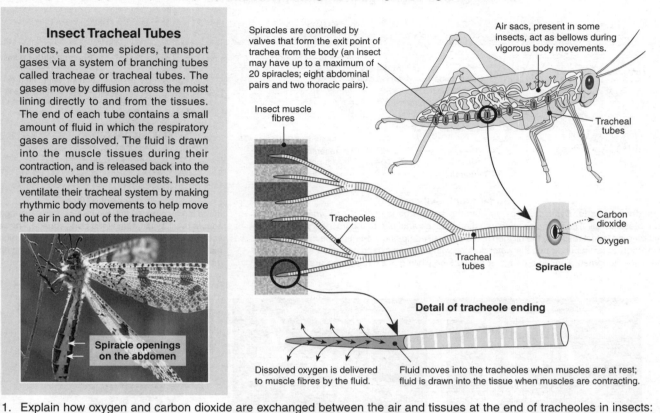

Spiracles are controlled by valves that form the exit point of trachea from the body (an insect may have up to a maximum of 20 spiracles; eight abdominal pairs and two thoracic pairs).

Air sacs, present in some insects, act as bellows during vigorous body movements.

Insect muscle fibres

Tracheoles

Tracheal tubes

Tracheal tubes

Carbon dioxide

Oxygen

Spiracle

Detail of tracheole ending

Dissolved oxygen is delivered to muscle fibres by the fluid.

Fluid moves into the tracheoles when muscles are at rest; fluid is drawn into the tissue when muscles are contracting.

1. Explain how oxygen and carbon dioxide are exchanged between the air and tissues at the end of tracheoles in insects:

_____

_____

_____

_____

2. Valves in the spiracles can regulate the amount of air entering the tracheal system. Suggest a reason for this adaptation:

_____

_____

3. Explain how ventilation is achieved in a terrestrial insect: _____

_____

_____

4. Even though most insects are small, they have evolved an efficient and highly developed gas exchange system that is independent of diffusion across the body surface. Suggest why this is the case:

_____

_____

_____

Adaptation & Specialisation

Related activities: Surface Area and Volume, Gas Exchange in Freshwater
Diffusion   **Web links**: Insect Respiratory System

RA 2

Gas Exchange in Freshwater

The availability of oxygen in water is very low relative to air: oxygen diffuses into water only very slowly and it is not very soluble (unlike CO_2). Moreover, as water temperature increases, the amount of oxygen that can be dissolved decreases. Despite these constraints, many invertebrate phyla, including the molluscs, annelids, and arthropods, have freshwater representatives. The majority of aquatic invertebrates are insects. As is the case in terrestrial insects, gases move to and from the tissues via the tracheae: the network of air-filled tubes that forms the insect respiratory system. What varies is the method by which oxygen enters this system. Like many aquatic invertebrates, aquatic insect larvae rely on **diffusion** across the body surface, with or without gills. Adult insects carry air with them when submerged. The air may be carried as a distinct bubble beneath the wings, or stay trapped by regions of unwettable (hydrofuge) hairs. A thin film of air trapped by hairs is called a **plastron**. It provides a source of oxygen and acts as a non-compressible diffusion gill, into which oxygen can diffuse from the water.

Gas Exchange in Aquatic Invertebrates

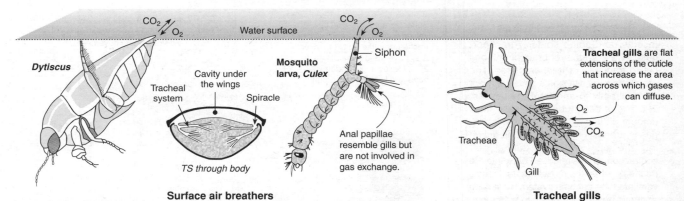

Surface air breathers

The **diving beetle**, *Dytiscus*, traps air from the surface beneath its wings where it forms a compressible gill. The spiracles open into the air space and lead to the tracheal tubes. As the submerged insect respires, the oxygen is gradually used up and the bubble decreases in size. A **mosquito larva** penetrates the water surface with a siphon extending from a spiracle at the tip of the abdomen. The larva hangs at the surface while gas exchange occurs by diffusion.

Tracheal gills

In the larvae of many aquatic insects, gas exchange occurs by diffusion across the body surface. This is enhanced by the presence of **tracheal gills** which may account for 20-70% of O_2 uptake depending on their surface area.

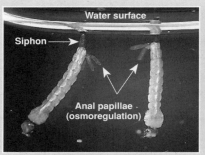

Gas exchange in mosquito larvae occurs with the air and is independent of O_2 content of the water.

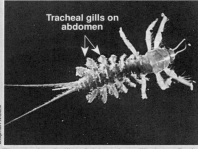

The tracheal gills of this spiny gilled mayfly (a very active species), are located on the abdomen.

Hydrophilid beetles use hydrofuge hairs to trap a film of air against the spiracles (a plastron).

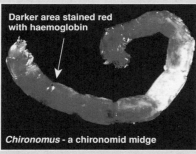

The blood of a few insect larvae, e.g. *Chironomus*, contains the O_2-carrying pigment **haemoglobin**, which allows them to survive when O_2 levels fall.

Anisops carries only a small air mass when diving but can exploit oxygen-poor waters because it has large haemoglobin-filled cells in its abdomen.

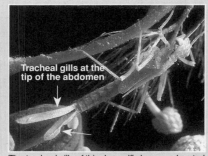

The tracheal gills of this damselfly larva are located at the tip of the abdomen (arrows). Like other insects with gills they are intolerant of low oxygen.

1. Giving an example for each, briefly describe two structural adaptations of freshwater invertebrates for gas exchange:

    (a) _____

    (b) _____

2. Describe one physiological adaptation of freshwater invertebrates for gas exchange: _____

    _____

Gas Exchange in Fish

Fish obtain the oxygen they need from the water by means of gills: membranous structures supported by cartilaginous or bony struts. Gill surfaces are very large and as water flows over the gill surface, respiratory gases are exchanged between the blood and the water. The percentage of dissolved oxygen in a volume of water is much less than in the same volume of air; air is 21% oxygen while in water dissolved oxygen is about 1% by volume. High rates of oxygen extraction from the water, as achieved by gills, are therefore a necessary requirement for active organisms in an aquatic environment. In fish, ventilation of the gill surfaces to facilitate gas exchange is achieved by actively pumping water across the gill or swimming continuously with the mouth open.

Bony fish have four pairs of gills, each supported by a bony arch. The operculum (gill cover) is important in ventilation of the gills.

Cartilaginous fish have five or six pairs of gills. Water is drawn in via the mouth and spiracle and exits via the gill slits (there is no operculum).

Circulation and Gas Exchange in Fish

Fish and other vertebrates have a **closed circulatory system** where the blood is entirely contained within vessels. Fish have a **single circuit system**; the blood goes directly to the body from the gills (the gas exchange surface) and only flows once through the heart in each circulation of the body. The blood loses pressure when passing through the gills and, on leaving them, flows at low pressure around the body before returning to the heart. The gas exchange and circulatory systems are closely linked because the blood has a role in the transport of respiratory gases around the body.

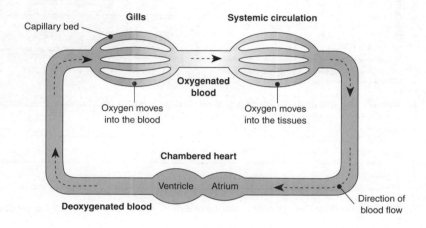

Fish Gills

The gills of fish have a great many folds, which are supported and kept apart from each other by the water. This gives them a high surface area for gas exchange. The outer surface of the gill is in contact with the water, and blood flows in vessels inside the gill. Gas exchange occurs by diffusion between the water and blood across the gill membrane and capillaries. The operculum (gill cover) permits exit of water and acts as a pump, drawing water past the gill filaments. Fish gills are very efficient and can achieve an 80% extraction rate of oxygen from water; over three times the rate of human lungs from air.

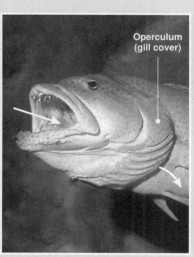

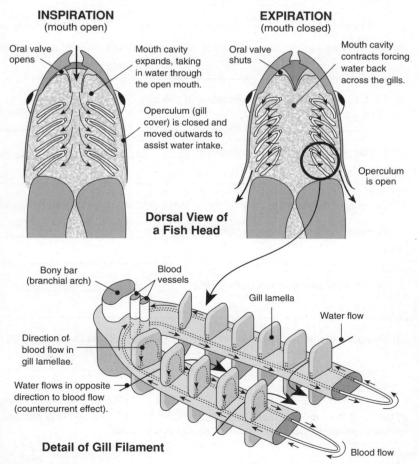

Source: C.J. Clegg & D.G. McKean (1994)

Adaptation & Specialisation

Related activities: Gas Exchange in Insects, Gas Exchange in Freshwater

RA 2

The structure of fish gills and their physical arrangement in relation to the blood flow ensure that gas exchange rates are maximised. A constant stream of oxygen-rich water flows over the gill filaments in the **opposite** direction to the direction of blood flow through the gills. This is termed **countercurrent flow** (below, left). Blood flowing through the gill capillaries therefore encounters water of increasing oxygen content. In this way, the concentration gradient (for oxygen uptake) across the gill is maintained across the entire distance of the gill lamella. A parallel current flow would not achieve the same oxygen extraction rates because the concentrations across the gill would quickly equalise (below, right).

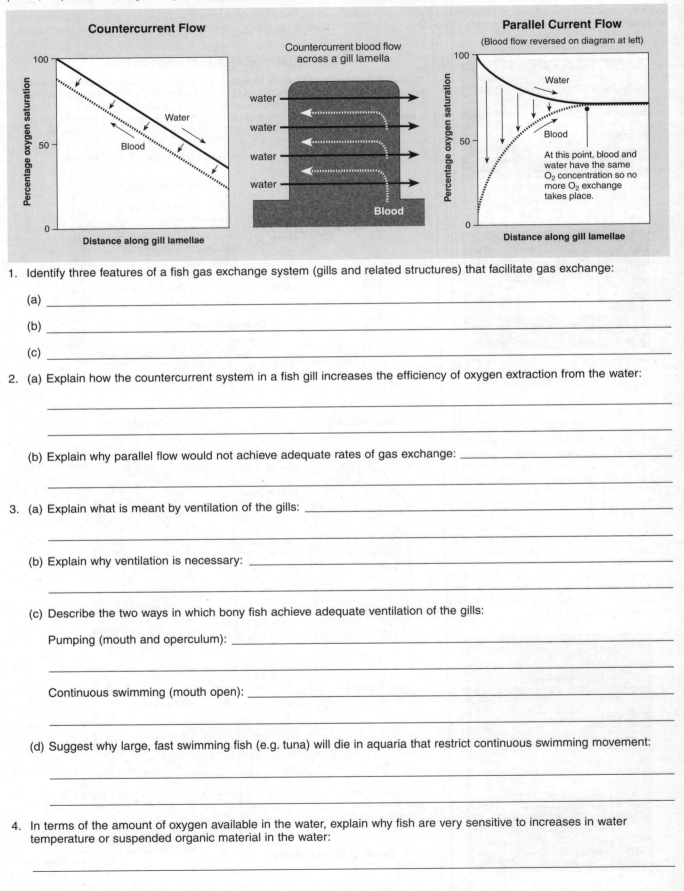

1. Identify three features of a fish gas exchange system (gills and related structures) that facilitate gas exchange:

   (a) _____

   (b) _____

   (c) _____

2. (a) Explain how the countercurrent system in a fish gill increases the efficiency of oxygen extraction from the water:

   _____

   _____

   (b) Explain why parallel flow would not achieve adequate rates of gas exchange: _____

   _____

3. (a) Explain what is meant by ventilation of the gills: _____

   _____

   (b) Explain why ventilation is necessary: _____

   _____

   (c) Describe the two ways in which bony fish achieve adequate ventilation of the gills:

   Pumping (mouth and operculum): _____

   _____

   Continuous swimming (mouth open): _____

   _____

   (d) Suggest why large, fast swimming fish (e.g. tuna) will die in aquaria that restrict continuous swimming movement:

   _____

   _____

4. In terms of the amount of oxygen available in the water, explain why fish are very sensitive to increases in water temperature or suspended organic material in the water:

   _____

   _____

Stomata and Gas Exchange

The **mesophyll** tissues of a dicot leaf are sandwiched between the epidermal layers. Palisade mesophyll is composed of regular cell layers, whereas in **spongy mesophyll** the cells are loosely arranged cells and there are many intracellular spaces. These allow for gas diffusion during photosynthesis and respiration. The leaf epidermis of angiosperms is covered with tiny pores, called **stomata**. Angiosperms have many air spaces between the cells of the stems, leaves, and roots. These air spaces are continuous and gases are able to move freely through them and into the plant's cells via the stomata. Each stoma is bounded by two guard cells, which together regulate the entry and exit of gases and water vapour. Although stomata permit gas exchange between the air and the photosynthetic cells inside the leaf, they are also the major routes for water loss through **transpiration**.

Dicot Leaf Structure

Respiring plant cells use oxygen (O_2) and produce carbon dioxide (CO_2). These gases move in and out of the plant and through the air spaces by diffusion. Angiosperms have many air spaces between the cells of the stems, leaves, and roots. These air spaces are continuous and gases are able to move freely through them and into the plant's cells via the **stomata** (*sing.* stoma).

When the plant is photosynthesising, the situation is more complex. Overall there is a net consumption of CO_2 and a net production of oxygen. CO_2 fixation maintains a gradient in CO_2 concentration between the inside of the leaf and the atmosphere. Oxygen is produced in excess of respiratory needs and diffuses out of the leaf. These **net** exchanges are indicated by the arrows on the diagram.

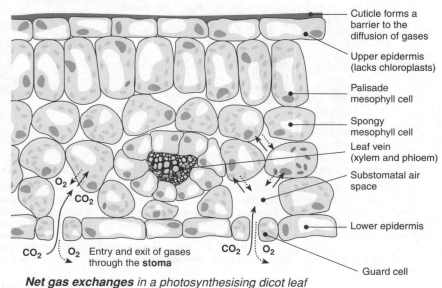

Net gas exchanges in a photosynthesising dicot leaf

- Cuticle forms a barrier to the diffusion of gases
- Upper epidermis (lacks chloroplasts)
- Palisade mesophyll cell
- Spongy mesophyll cell
- Leaf vein (xylem and phloem)
- Substomatal air space
- Lower epidermis
- Guard cell

Entry and exit of gases through the **stoma**

The surface of the leaf epidermis of a dicot illustrating the density and scattered arrangement of the pores or **stomata**. In dicots, stomata are usually present only on the lower leaf surface.

The leaves of dicots can be distinguished from those of monocots by their netted pattern of leaf veins. Monocots, in contrast, generally have leaves with parallel venation.

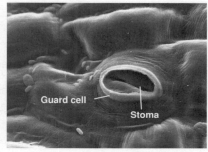

Guard cells on each side of a stoma (pl. stomata) regulate the entry and exit of gases and water vapour. Stomata permit gas exchange but are also the major routes for water loss.

The cycle of opening and closing of stomata

The opening and closing of stomata shows a daily cycle that is largely determined by the hours of light and dark.

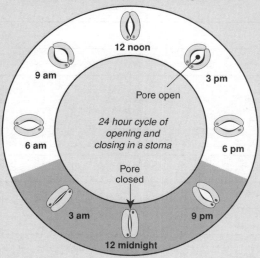

24 hour cycle of opening and closing in a stoma

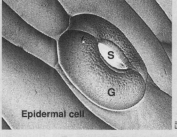

The image left shows a scanning electron micrograph (SEM) of a single stoma from the leaf epidermis of a dicot.

Note the guard cells (G), which are swollen tight and open the pore (S) to allow gas exchange between the leaf tissue and the environment.

Factors influencing stomatal opening

Stomata	Guard cells	Daylight	CO_2	Soil water
Open	Turgid	Light	Low	High
Closed	Flaccid	Dark	High	Low

Stomatal movements depend on environmental factors, especially light, carbon dioxide concentration in the leaf tissue, and water supply. Stomata tend to open during daylight in response to light, and close at night (left). Low CO_2 levels also promote stomatal opening. Conditions that induce water stress cause the stomata close, regardless of light or CO_2 level.

Adaptation & Specialisation

Related activities: Plant Cell Specialisation, Adaptations of Xerophytes
Web links: Gas Exchange and Stomata

The guard cells on each side of a stoma control the diameter of the pore by changing shape. When the guard cells take up water by osmosis they swell and become turgid, making the pore wider. When the guard cells lose water, they become flaccid, and the pore closes up. By this mechanism a plant can control the amount of gas entering, or water leaving, the plant. The changes in turgor pressure that open and close the pore result mainly from the reversible uptake and loss of potassium ions (and thus water) by the guard cells.

Stomatal Pore Open

K+ enters the guard cells from the epidermal cells (active transport coupled to a proton pump).

Water follows K+ by osmosis.

H_2O
K^+

H_2O

Guard cell swells and becomes turgid.

K^+

Thickened ventral wall

Pore opens

K^+
H_2O

K^+
H_2O

Nucleus of guard cell

ψguard cell < ψepidermal cell: water enters the guard cells

Stomata open when the guard cells actively take up K+ from the neighbouring epidermal cells. The ion uptake causes the water potential (ψ) to become more negative in the guard cells. As a consequence, water is taken up by the cells and they swell and become turgid. The walls of the guard cells are thickened more on the inside surface (the ventral wall) than the outside wall, so that when the cells swell they buckle outward, opening the pore.

Stomatal Pore Closed

K+ leaves the guard cell and enters the epidermal cells.

Water follows K+ by osmosis.

H_2O

H_2O
K^+

The guard cells become flaccid.

H_2O

Pore closes

K^+

H_2O

K^+

ψepidermal cell < ψguard cell: water leaves the guard cells

Stomata close when K+ leaves the guard cells. The loss causes the water potential (ψ) to become less negative in the guard cells, and more negative in the epidermal cells. As a consequence, water is lost by osmosis and the cells sag together and close the pore. The K+ movements in and out of the guard cells are thought to be triggered by blue-light receptors in the plasma membrane, which activate the active transport mechanisms involved.

1. Describe two adaptive features of leaves:

    (a) _____

    (b) _____

2. With respect to a mesophytic, terrestrial flowering plant:

    (a) Describe the **net** gas exchanges between the air and the cells of the mesophyll in the dark (no photosynthesis):

    _____

    (b) Explain how this situation changes when a plant is photosynthesising: _____

    _____

    _____

3. Describe two ways in which the continuous air spaces through the plant facilitate gas exchange:

    (a) _____

    (b) _____

4. Outline the role of stomata in gas exchange in an angiosperm: _____

    _____

5. Summarise the mechanism by which the guard cells bring about:

    (a) Stomatal opening: _____

    _____

    _____

    (b) Stomatal closure: _____

    _____

    _____

Adaptations of Xerophytes

Plants adapted to dry conditions are called **xerophytes** and they show structural (xeromorphic) and physiological adaptations for water conservation. These typically include small, hard leaves, and epidermis with a thick cuticle, sunken stomata, succulence, and permanent or temporary absence of leaves. Xerophytes may live in humid environments, provided that their roots are in dry microenvironments (e.g. the roots of epiphytic plants that grow on tree trunks or branches). The nature of the growing environment is important in many other situations too. **Halophytes** (salt tolerant plants) and alpine species may also show xeromorphic features in response to the scarcity of obtainable water and high transpirational losses in these environments.

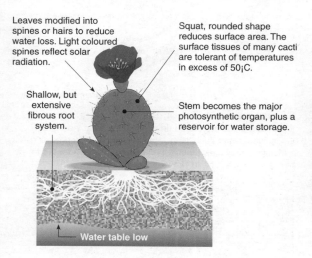

Leaves modified into spines or hairs to reduce water loss. Light coloured spines reflect solar radiation.

Squat, rounded shape reduces surface area. The surface tissues of many cacti are tolerant of temperatures in excess of 50¡C.

Shallow, but extensive fibrous root system.

Stem becomes the major photosynthetic organ, plus a reservoir for water storage.

Water table low

Seaweeds, which are protoctists, not plants, tolerate drying between tides even though they have no xeromorphic features.

A waxy coating of **suberin** on mangrove roots excludes 97% of salt from the water.

Dry Desert Plant

Desert plants, such as cacti, must cope with low or sporadic rainfall and high transpiration rates. A number of structural adaptations (diagram left) reduce water losses, and enable them to access and store available water. Adaptations such as waxy leaves also reduce water loss and, in many desert plants, germination is triggered only by a certain quantity of rainfall.

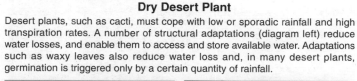

Acacia trees have **deep root systems**, allowing them to draw water from lower water table systems.

The outer surface of many succulents are coated in fine hairs, which traps air close to the surface reducing transpiration rate.

Ocean Margin Plant

Land plants that colonise the shoreline must have adaptations to obtain water from their saline environment while maintaining their osmotic balance. In addition, the shoreline is often a windy environment, so they frequently show xeromorphic adaptations that enable them to reduce transpirational water losses.

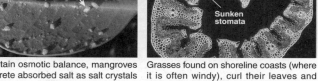
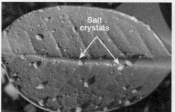
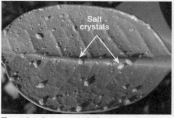

To maintain osmotic balance, mangroves can secrete absorbed salt as salt crystals (above), or accumulate salt in old leaves which are subsequently shed.

Grasses found on shoreline coasts (where it is often windy), curl their leaves and have sunken stomata to reduce water loss by transpiration.

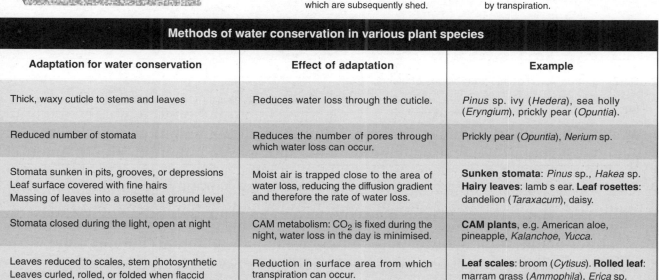

Methods of water conservation in various plant species

Adaptation for water conservation	Effect of adaptation	Example
Thick, waxy cuticle to stems and leaves	Reduces water loss through the cuticle.	*Pinus* sp. ivy (*Hedera*), sea holly (*Eryngium*), prickly pear (*Opuntia*).
Reduced number of stomata	Reduces the number of pores through which water loss can occur.	Prickly pear (*Opuntia*), *Nerium* sp.
Stomata sunken in pits, grooves, or depressions. Leaf surface covered with fine hairs. Massing of leaves into a rosette at ground level	Moist air is trapped close to the area of water loss, reducing the diffusion gradient and therefore the rate of water loss.	**Sunken stomata**: *Pinus* sp., *Hakea* sp. **Hairy leaves**: lamb s ear. **Leaf rosettes**: dandelion (*Taraxacum*), daisy.
Stomata closed during the light, open at night	CAM metabolism: CO_2 is fixed during the night, water loss in the day is minimised.	**CAM plants**, e.g. American aloe, pineapple, *Kalanchoe*, *Yucca*.
Leaves reduced to scales, stem photosynthetic. Leaves curled, rolled, or folded when flaccid	Reduction in surface area from which transpiration can occur.	**Leaf scales**: broom (*Cytisus*). **Rolled leaf**: marram grass (*Ammophila*), *Erica* sp.
Fleshy or succulent stems. Fleshy or succulent leaves	When readily available, water is stored in the tissues for times of low availability.	**Fleshy stems**: *Opuntia*, candle plant (*Kleinia*). **Fleshy leaves**: *Bryophyllum*.
Deep root system below the water table	Roots tap into the lower water table.	Acacias, oleander.
Shallow root system absorbing surface moisture	Roots absorb overnight condensation.	Most cacti

Adaptation & Specialisation

Related activities: Transpiration
Web links: Desert Plant Survival

A 1

Adaptations in halophytes and drought tolerant plants

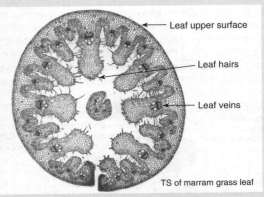

Leaf upper surface

Leaf hairs

Leaf veins

TS of marram grass leaf

Ice plant (*Carpobrotus*): The leaves of many desert and beach dwelling plants are fleshy or succulent. The leaves are triangular in cross section and crammed with water storage cells. The water is stored after rain for use in dry periods. The shallow root system is able to take up water from the soil surface, taking advantage of any overnight condensation.

Marram grass (*Ammophila*): The long, wiry leaf blades of this beach grass are curled downwards with the stomata on the inside. This protects them against drying out by providing a moist microclimate around the stomata. Plants adapted to high altitude often have similar adaptations.

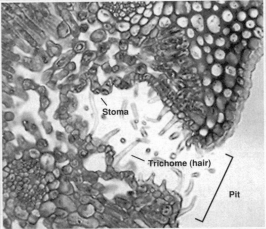

Stoma

Trichome (hair)

Pit

Ball cactus (*Echinocactus grusonii*): In many cacti, the leaves are modified into long, thin spines which project outward from the thick fleshy stem. This reduces the surface area over which water loss can occur. The stem stores water and takes over as the photosynthetic organ. As in succulents, a shallow root system enables rapid uptake of surface water.

Oleander is a xerophyte from the mediterranean region with many water conserving features. It has a thick multi-layered epidermis and the stomata are sunken in trichome-filled pits on the leaf underside. The pits restrict water loss to a greater extent than they reduce uptake of carbon dioxide.

1. Explain the purpose of **xeromorphic** adaptations: _____

_____

2. Describe three xeromorphic adaptations of plants:

   (a) _____

   (b) _____

   (c) _____

3. Describe a physiological mechanism by which plants can reduce water loss during the daylight hours:

_____

_____

4. Explain why creating a moist microenvironment around the areas of water loss reduces transpiration rate:

_____

_____

5. Explain why seashore plants (halophytes) exhibit many desert-dwelling adaptations: _____

_____

_____

_____

Mammalian Transport

Animal cells require a constant supply of nutrients and oxygen, and continuous removal of wastes. Simple, small organisms achieve this through simple diffusion across moist body surfaces. Larger, more complex organisms require a circulatory system to transport materials because diffusion is too inefficient and slow to supply all the cells of the body adequately. Circulatory systems transport materials, but also help to maintain fluid balance, regulate body temperature, and assist in defending the body against pathogens. The blood vessels form a vast network of tubes that carry blood away from the heart, transport it to the tissues, and then return it to the heart. The arteries, arterioles, capillaries, venules, and veins are organised into specific routes to circulate blood throughout the body. The figure below shows some of the **circulatory routes** through which the blood travels. The **pulmonary system** (or circulation) carries blood between the heart and lungs, and the **systemic system** (circulation) carries blood between the heart and the rest of the body. Two important subdivisions of the systemic circuit are the coronary (cardiac) circulation, which supplies the heart muscle, and the **hepatic portal circulation**, which runs from the gut to the liver.

The Mammalian Circulatory System

Deoxygenated blood (coloured grey below) travels to the right side of the heart via the vena cavae. The heart pumps the deoxygenated blood to the lungs where it releases carbon dioxide and receives oxygen. The oxygenated blood (coloured white below) travels via the pulmonary vein back to the heart from where it is pumped to all parts of the body. The **venous system** (figure, left) returns blood from the capillaries to the heart. The **arterial system** (figure right) carries blood from the heart to the capillaries. **Portal systems** carry blood between two capillary beds.

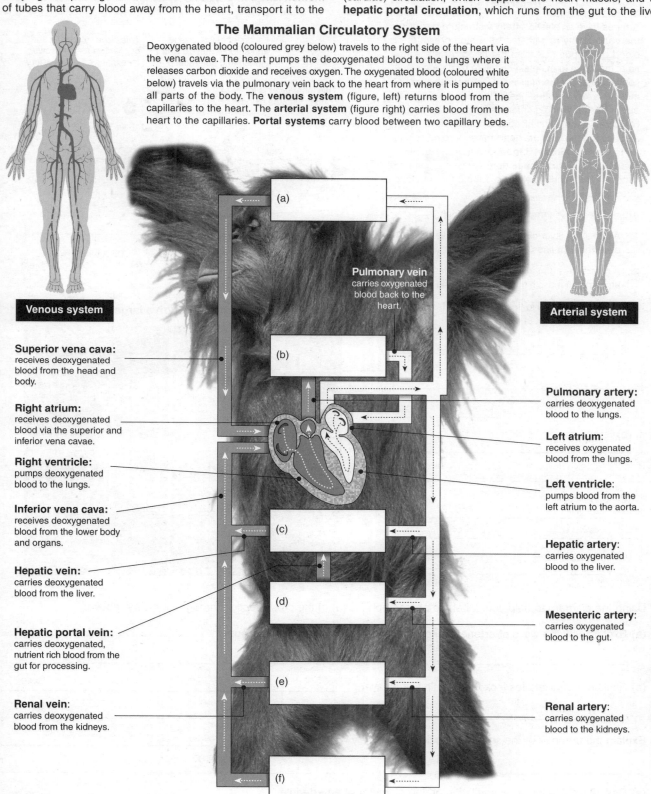

Venous system

Arterial system

Pulmonary vein
carries oxygenated blood back to the heart.

Superior vena cava:
receives deoxygenated blood from the head and body.

Right atrium:
receives deoxygenated blood via the superior and inferior vena cavae.

Right ventricle:
pumps deoxygenated blood to the lungs.

Inferior vena cava:
receives deoxygenated blood from the lower body and organs.

Hepatic vein:
carries deoxygenated blood from the liver.

Hepatic portal vein:
carries deoxygenated, nutrient rich blood from the gut for processing.

Renal vein:
carries deoxygenated blood from the kidneys.

Pulmonary artery:
carries deoxygenated blood to the lungs.

Left atrium:
receives oxygenated blood from the lungs.

Left ventricle:
pumps blood from the left atrium to the aorta.

Hepatic artery:
carries oxygenated blood to the liver.

Mesenteric artery:
carries oxygenated blood to the gut.

Renal artery:
carries oxygenated blood to the kidneys.

1. Complete the diagram above by labelling the boxes with the organs or structures they represent.

Related activities: The Human Heart

Adaptation & Specialisation

A 1

Arteries

In vertebrates, arteries are the blood vessels that carry blood away from the heart to the capillaries within the tissues. The large arteries that leave the heart divide into medium-sized (distributing) arteries. Within the tissues and organs, these distribution arteries branch to form very small vessels called **arterioles**, which deliver blood to capillaries. Arterioles lack the thick layers of arteries and consist only of an endothelial layer wrapped by a few smooth muscle fibres at intervals along their length. Resistance to blood flow is altered by contraction (**vasoconstriction**) or relaxation (**vasodilation**) of the blood vessel walls, especially in the arterioles. Vasoconstriction increases resistance and leads to an increase in blood pressure whereas vasodilation has the opposite effect. This mechanism is important in regulating the blood flow into tissues.

Arteries

Arteries have an elastic, stretchy structure that gives them the ability to withstand the high pressure of blood being pumped from the heart. At the same time, they help to maintain pressure by having some contractile ability themselves (a feature of the central muscle layer). Arteries nearer the heart have more elastic tissue, giving greater resistance to the higher blood pressures of the blood leaving the left ventricle. Arteries further from the heart have more muscle to help them maintain blood pressure. Between heartbeats, the arteries undergo elastic recoil and contract. This tends to smooth out the flow of blood through the vessel.

Arteries comprise three main regions (right):

1. A thin inner layer of epithelial cells called the **endothelium** lines the artery.

2. A central layer (the **tunica media**) of elastic tissue and smooth muscle that can stretch and contract.

3. An outer connective tissue layer (the **tunica externa**) has a lot of elastic tissue.

Artery Structure

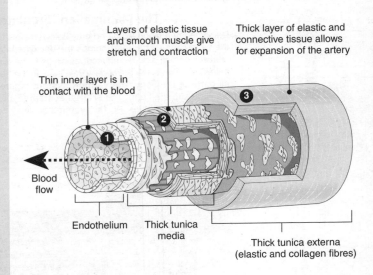

Layers of elastic tissue and smooth muscle give stretch and contraction

Thick layer of elastic and connective tissue allows for expansion of the artery

Thin inner layer is in contact with the blood

Blood flow

Endothelium

Thick tunica media

Thick tunica externa (elastic and collagen fibres)

Cross section through a large artery

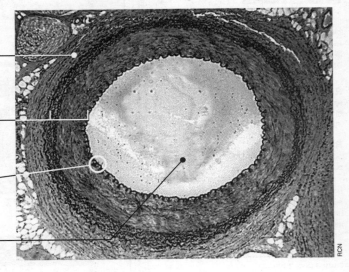

(a)

(b)

(c)

(d)

1. Using the diagram to help you, label the photograph (a)-(d) of the cross section through an artery (above).

2. (a) Explain why the walls of arteries need to be thick with a lot of elastic tissue: _____

    _____

    (b) Explain why arterioles lack this elastic tissue layer: _____

    _____

3. Explain the purpose of the smooth muscle in the artery walls: _____

    _____

4. (a) Describe the effect of vasodilation on the diameter of an arteriole: _____

    (b) Describe the effect of vasodilation on blood pressure: _____

Related activities: Veins, Capillaries and Tissue Fluid
Web links: Arteries

Capillaries and Tissue Fluid

In vertebrates, capillaries are very small vessels that connect arterial and venous circulation and allow efficient exchange of nutrients and wastes between the blood and tissues. Capillaries form networks or beds and are abundant where metabolic rates are high. Fluid that leaks out of the capillaries has an essential role in bathing the tissues. The movement of fluid into and out of capillaries depends on the balance between the blood (hydrostatic) pressure (HP) and the solute potential (ψs) at each end of a capillary bed. Not all the fluid is returned to the capillaries and this extra fluid must be returned to the general circulation. This is the role of the **lymphatic system**; a system of vessels that parallels the system of arteries and veins. The lymphatic system also has a role in internal defence, and in transporting lipids absorbed from the digestive tract. Note: A version of this activity (without reference to solute potential terminology), is available on the web and the Teacher Resource CD-ROM.

Exchanges in Capillaries

Blood passes from the arterioles into capillaries: small blood vessels with a diameter of just 4-10 μm. Red blood cells are 7-8 μm and only just squeeze through. The only tissue present is an **endothelium** of squamous epithelial cells. Capillaries form networks of vessels that penetrate all parts of the body. They are so numerous that no cell is more than 25 μm from any capillary. It is in the capillaries that the exchange of materials between the body cells and the blood takes place. Blood pressure causes fluid to leak from capillaries through small gaps where the endothelial cells join. This fluid bathes the tissues, supplying nutrients and oxygen, and removing wastes (right).The density of capillaries in a tissue is an indication of that tissue's metabolic activity. For example, cardiac muscle relies heavily on oxidative metabolism. It has a high demand for blood flow and is well supplied with capillaries. Smooth muscle is far less active than cardiac muscle, relies more on anaerobic metabolism, and does not require such an extensive blood supply.

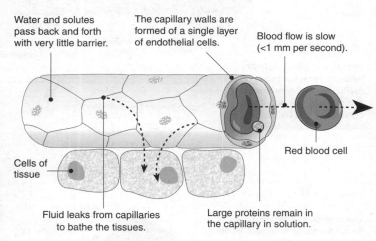

Water and solutes pass back and forth with very little barrier.

The capillary walls are formed of a single layer of endothelial cells.

Blood flow is slow (<1 mm per second).

Red blood cell

Cells of tissue

Fluid leaks from capillaries to bathe the tissues.

Large proteins remain in the capillary in solution.

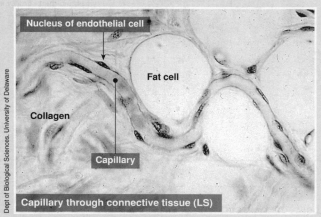

Nucleus of endothelial cell

Fat cell

Collagen

Capillary

Capillary through connective tissue (LS)

Dept of Biological Sciences, University of Delaware

Capillaries are found near almost every cell in the body. In many places, the capillaries form extensive branching networks. In most tissues, blood normally flows through only a small portion of a capillary network when the metabolic demands of the tissue are low. When the tissue becomes active, the entire capillary network fills with blood.

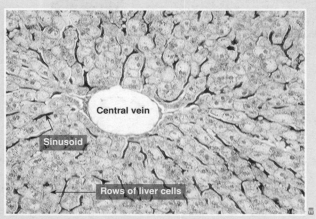

Central vein

Sinusoid

Rows of liver cells

Microscopic blood vessels in some dense organs, such as the liver (above), are called **sinusoids**. They are wider than capillaries and follow a more convoluted path through the tissue. Instead of the usual endothelial lining, they are lined with phagocytic cells. Like capillaries, sinusoids transport blood from arterioles to venules.

1. Describe the structure of a capillary, contrasting it with the structure of a vein and an artery:

_____

_____

_____

_____

2. Sinusoids provide a functional replacement for capillaries in some organs:

(a) Describe how sinusoids differ structurally from capillaries: _____

_____

(b) Describe in what way capillaries and sinusoids are similar: _____

_____

Related activities: Arteries, Veins

Web links: Microcirculation, Capillaries and Tissue Fluid

RA 2

Adaptation & Specialisation

The Formation of Tissue Fluid

Arteriole end of capillary bed

HP + Ψs (inside) > HP + Ψs (outside)

Hydrostatic pressure (HP) plus solute potential (Ψs) is high at arteriole end

Venule end of capillary bed

HP + Ψs (inside) < HP + Ψs (outside)

Hydrostatic pressure (HP) plus solute potential (Ψs) is low at venule end

As fluid leaks out through capillary walls, it bathes the cells of the tissues

RESULT: Net outward pressure: water and solutes leave the capillary

Capillary vessel

RESULT: Net inward pressure: water and solutes re-enter the capillary

Glucose, amino acids, water, ions, oxygen

Tissue fluid

Water, CO₂ and other wastes

Hydrostatic pressure (**HP**) tends to force fluids out of capillaries at the arteriolar end of a capillary bed. Most of the tissue fluid finds its way back into the capillaries.

Water will move to regions of more negative solute potential (ψ_S). ψ_S decreases towards the venous end of a capillary bed as a result of proteins remaining in the capillary as the tissue fluid forms.

Lymphatic vessel

The remaining tissue fluid drains into the **lymphatic vessels** where it is called **lymph**. Lymph is similar to tissue fluid but has more leucocytes.

Lymph is returned to the cardiovascular system near the heart.

The blood's hydrostatic pressure (blood pressure) is created by the pumping of the left ventricle. It can be measured using a **sphygmomanometer** (right); a cuff that is placed over the brachial artery and connected to a manometer. Blood pressure is the primary force in creating tissue fluid.

Lymph re-enters the general circulation when major lymphatic ducts empty into the subclavian veins.

Lymphatic duct

Lymphatic system

Cardiovascular system

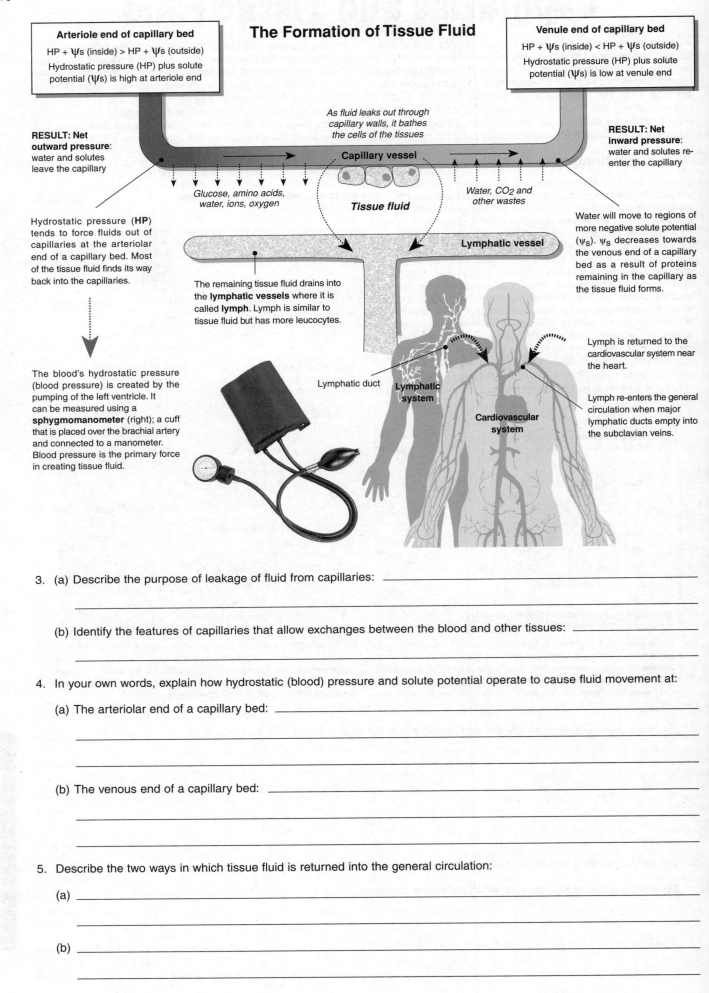

3. (a) Describe the purpose of leakage of fluid from capillaries: _____

_____

(b) Identify the features of capillaries that allow exchanges between the blood and other tissues: _____

_____

4. In your own words, explain how hydrostatic (blood) pressure and solute potential operate to cause fluid movement at:

(a) The arteriolar end of a capillary bed: _____

_____

_____

(b) The venous end of a capillary bed: _____

_____

_____

5. Describe the two ways in which tissue fluid is returned into the general circulation:

(a) _____

_____

(b) _____

_____

Veins

Veins are the blood vessels that return blood to the heart from the tissues. The smallest veins (**venules**) return blood from the capillary beds to the larger veins. Veins and their branches contain about 59% of the blood in the body. The structural differences between veins and arteries are mainly associated with differences in the relative thickness of the vessel layers and the diameter of the lumen. These, in turn, are related to the vessel's functional role.

Veins

When several capillaries unite, they form small veins called **venules**. The venules collect the blood from capillaries and drain it into **veins**. Veins are made up of essentially the same three layers as arteries but they have less elastic and muscle tissue and a larger **lumen**. The venules closest to the capillaries consist of an **endothelium** and a tunica externa of connective tissue. As the venules approach the veins, they also contain the tunica media characteristic of veins (right). Although veins are less elastic than arteries, they can still expand enough to adapt to changes in the pressure and volume of the blood passing through them. Blood flowing in the veins has lost a lot of pressure because it has passed through the narrow capillary vessels. The low pressure in veins means that many veins, especially those in the limbs, need to have valves to prevent backflow of the blood as it returns to the heart.

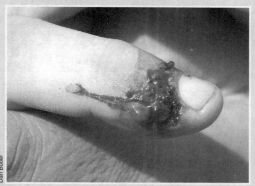

If a vein is cut, as is shown in this severe finger wound, the blood oozes out slowly in an even flow, and usually clots quickly as it leaves. In contrast, arterial blood spurts rapidly and requires pressure to staunch the flow.

Vein Structure

Inner thin layer of simple squamous epithelium lines the vein (**endothelium** or **tunica intima**).

Central thin layer of elastic and muscle tissue (**tunica media**). The smaller venules lack this inner layer.

Thin layer of elastic connective tissue (**tunica externa**)

One-way valves are located along the length of veins to prevent the blood from flowing backwards.

Blood flow

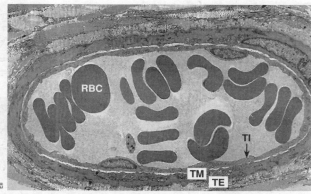

Above: TEM of a vein showing red blood cells (RBC) in the lumen, and the tunica intima (TI), tunica media (TM), and tunica externa (TE).

1. Contrast the structure of veins and arteries for each of the following properties:

   (a) Thickness of muscle and elastic tissue: _____

   _____

   (b) Size of the lumen (inside of the vessel): _____

   _____

2. With respect to their functional roles, give a reason for the differences you have described above: _____

   _____

   _____

3. Explain the role of the valves in assisting the veins to return blood back to the heart: _____

   _____

4. Blood oozes from a venous wound, rather than spurting as it does from an arterial wound. Account for this difference:

   _____

   _____

   _____

Adaptation & Specialisation

Related activities: Arteries, Capillaries and Tissue Fluid
Web links: Veins

RA 2

Root Structure

Roots are essential plant organs. They anchor the plant in the ground, absorb water and minerals from the soil, and transport these materials to other parts of the plant body. Roots may also act as storage organs, storing excess carbohydrate reserves until they are required by the plant. Roots are covered in an epidermis but, unlike the epidermis of leaves, the root epidermis has only a thin cuticle that presents no barrier to water entry. Young roots are also covered with **root hairs** (see below). Much of a root comprises a cortex of parenchyma cells. The air spaces between the cells are essential for aeration of the root tissue. Minerals and water must move from the soil into the xylem before they can be transported around the plant. Compared with stems, roots are relatively simple and uniform in structure. The structure of a dicot roots is described below.

The Structure of a Dicot Root

These photographs (left and below) show cross sections through a young dicot root (i.e. primary tissues). In the photograph to the left, note the large area of the root occupied by the cortex. The parenchyma (packing) cells of the cortex store starch and other substances. The air spaces between the cells are essential for aeration of the root tissue, which is non-photosynthetic. The vascular tissue, xylem (X) and phloem (P) forms a central cylinder through the root and is surrounded by the **pericycle**, a ring of cells from which lateral roots arise. The primary xylem of dicot roots forms a star shape in the centre of the vascular cylinder with usually 3 or 4 points. Unlike monocots, there is no central pith of parenchyma cells.

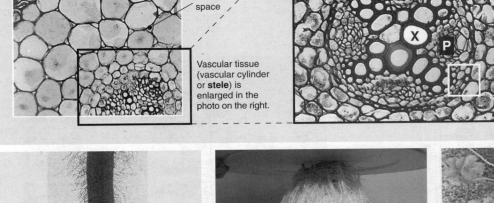

Root hairs

Cortex of parenchyma cells

Air space

Vascular tissue (vascular cylinder or **stele**) is enlarged in the photo on the right.

Cortex

Pericycle

Endodermis regulates water flow into the root

Root hairs are located behind the region of cell elongation in the root tip. They increase the surface area for absorption. The root tip is covered by a slimy root cap which protects the dividing cells of the tip and lubricates the root's movement through soil.

The roots and their associated root hairs provide a very large surface area for the uptake of water and ions, as shown in this photograph of the roots of a hydroponically grown plant.

Strawberry plants send out runners. These are above-ground, trailing stems that form roots at their nodes. The plant uses this mechanism to spread vegetatively over a wide area.

Runner

1. Describe three functions of roots: _____

_____

_____

2. Describe two distinguishing features of internal anatomy of a primary dicot root:

   (a) _____

   (b) _____

3. Explain the purpose of the root hairs: _____

_____

4. Explain how the endodermis regulates water flow into the root tissue: _____

_____

RA 2 **Related activities**: Uptake at the Root

Transpiration

Plants lose water all the time, despite the adaptations they have to help prevent it (e.g. waxy leaf cuticle). Approximately 99% of the water a plant absorbs from the soil is lost by evaporation from the leaves and stem. This loss, mostly through stomata, is called **transpiration** and the flow of water through the plant is called the **transpiration stream**. Plants rely on a gradient in water potential (ψ) from the roots to the air to move water through their cells. Water flows passively from soil to air along a gradient of decreasing water potential. The gradient in water potential is the driving force in the ascent of water up a plant. A number of processes contribute to water movement up the plant: transpiration pull, cohesion, and root pressure. Transpiration may seem to be a wasteful process, but it has benefits. Evaporative water loss cools the plant and the transpiration stream helps the plant to maintain an adequate mineral uptake, as many essential minerals occur in low concentrations in the soil.

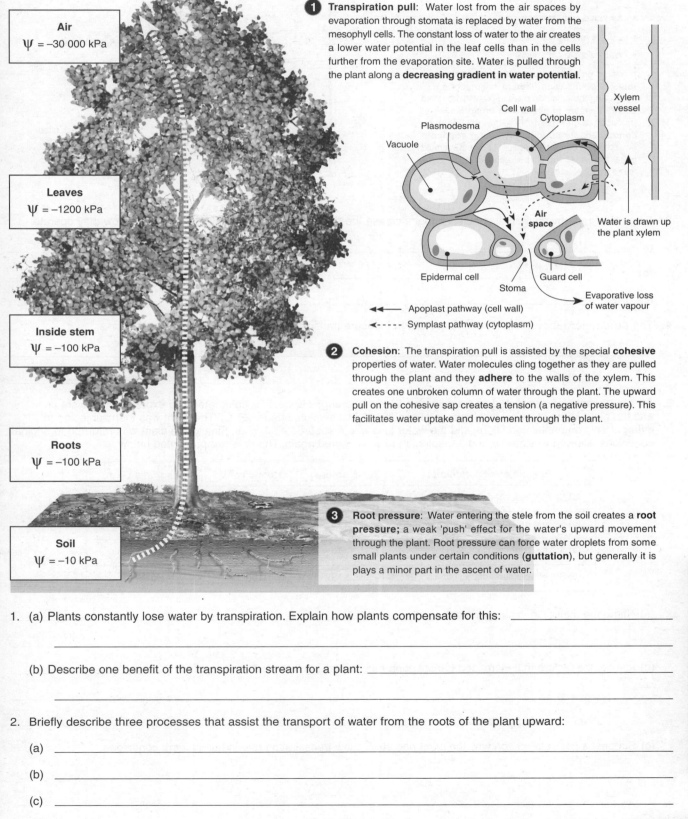

Air
$\psi = -30\ 000$ kPa

Leaves
$\psi = -1200$ kPa

Inside stem
$\psi = -100$ kPa

Roots
$\psi = -100$ kPa

Soil
$\psi = -10$ kPa

1 **Transpiration pull**: Water lost from the air spaces by evaporation through stomata is replaced by water from the mesophyll cells. The constant loss of water to the air creates a lower water potential in the leaf cells than in the cells further from the evaporation site. Water is pulled through the plant along a **decreasing gradient in water potential**.

Cell wall
Cytoplasm
Plasmodesma
Vacuole
Xylem vessel
Air space
Water is drawn up the plant xylem
Epidermal cell
Stoma
Guard cell
Evaporative loss of water vapour

◄◄ Apoplast pathway (cell wall)
◄----- Symplast pathway (cytoplasm)

2 **Cohesion**: The transpiration pull is assisted by the special **cohesive** properties of water. Water molecules cling together as they are pulled through the plant and they **adhere** to the walls of the xylem. This creates one unbroken column of water through the plant. The upward pull on the cohesive sap creates a tension (a negative pressure). This facilitates water uptake and movement through the plant.

3 **Root pressure**: Water entering the stele from the soil creates a **root pressure**; a weak 'push' effect for the water's upward movement through the plant. Root pressure can force water droplets from some small plants under certain conditions (**guttation**), but generally it is plays a minor part in the ascent of water.

1. (a) Plants constantly lose water by transpiration. Explain how plants compensate for this: _____

_____

(b) Describe one benefit of the transpiration stream for a plant: _____

_____

2. Briefly describe three processes that assist the transport of water from the roots of the plant upward:

(a) _____

(b) _____

(c) _____

Related activities: Osmosis and Water Potential
Web links: Transpiration, Transpiration Animation

Adaptation & Specialisation

DA 3

The Potometer

A potometer is a simple instrument for investigating transpiration rate (water loss per unit time). The equipment is simple and easy to obtain. A basic potometer, such as the one shown right, can easily be moved around so that transpiration rate can be measured under different environmental conditions

Some of the physical conditions investigated are:

- Humidity or vapour pressure (high or low)
- Temperature (high or low)
- Air movement (still or windy)
- Light level (high or low)
- Water supply

It is also possible to compare the transpiration rates of plants with different adaptations e.g. comparing transpiration rates in plants with rolled leaves vs rates in plants with broad leaves. If possible, experiments like these should be conducted simultaneously using replicate equipment. If conducted sequentially, care should be taken to keep the environmental conditions the same for all plants used.

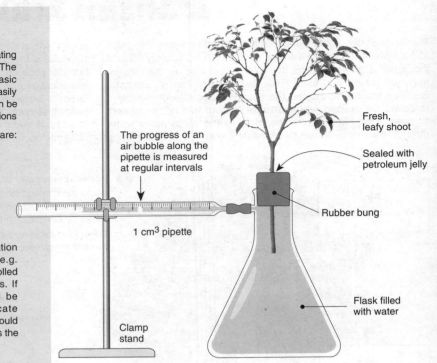

The progress of an air bubble along the pipette is measured at regular intervals

1 cm³ pipette

Clamp stand

Fresh, leafy shoot

Sealed with petroleum jelly

Rubber bung

Flask filled with water

3. Describe three environmental conditions that increase the rate of transpiration in plants, explaining how they operate:

(a) _____

(b) _____

(c) _____

4. The **potometer** (above) is an instrument used to measure transpiration rate. Briefly explain how it works:

_____

_____

5. An experiment was conducted on transpiration from a hydrangea shoot in a potometer. The experiment was set up and the plant left to stabilise (environmental conditions: still air, light shade, 20°C). The plant was then subjected to different environmental conditions and the water loss was measured each hour. Finally, the plant was returned to original conditions, allowed to stabilise and transpiration rate measured again. The data are presented below:

Experimental conditions	Temperature / °C	Humidity / %	Transpiration / gh⁻¹
(a) Still air, light shade, 20°C	18	70	1.20
(b) Moving air, light shade, 20°C	18	70	1.60
(c) Still air, bright sunlight, 23°C	18	70	3.75
(d) Still air and dark, moist chamber, 19.5°C	18	100	0.05

(a) Name the control in this experiment: _____

_____

(b) Identify the factors that increased transpiration rate, explaining how each has its effect: _____

_____

_____

(c) Suggest a possible reason why the plant had such a low transpiration rate in humid, dark conditions:

_____

_____

Uptake in the Root

Plants need to take up water and minerals constantly. They must compensate for the continuous loss of water from the leaves and provide the materials they need for the manufacture of food. The uptake of water and minerals is mostly restricted to the younger, most recently formed cells of the roots and the root hairs. Some water moves through the plant tissues via the plasmodesmata of the cells (the **symplastic route**), but most passes through the free spaces between cell walls (the **apoplast**). Water uptake is assisted by root pressure, which arises because the soil and root tissue has a higher water potential than other plant tissues. Two processes are involved in water and ion uptake: osmosis (in the case of water) and active transport. Note: An alternative version of this activity, without reference to water potential, is available in *Uptake in the Root* on the TRC (or see web links below).

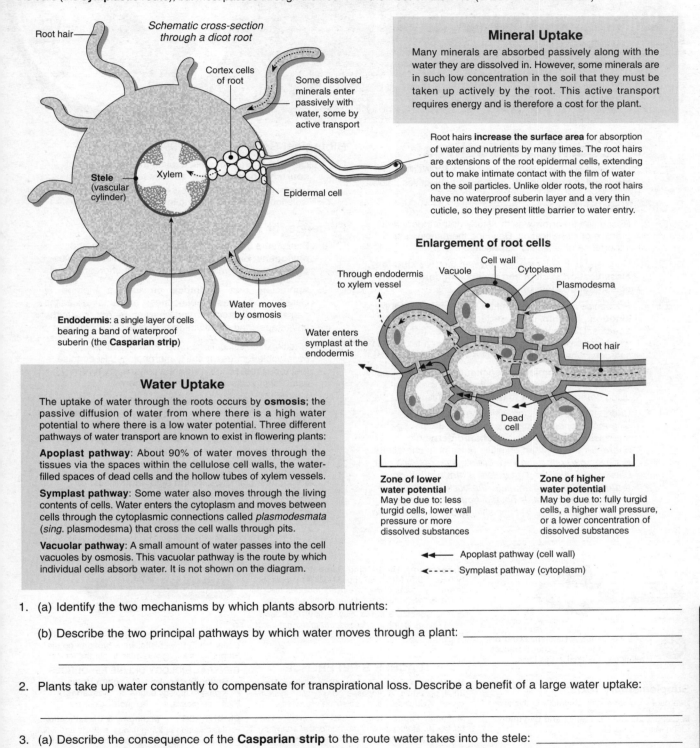

Schematic cross-section through a dicot root

Root hair

Cortex cells of root

Some dissolved minerals enter passively with water, some by active transport

Stele (vascular cylinder)

Xylem

Epidermal cell

Endodermis: a single layer of cells bearing a band of waterproof suberin (the **Casparian strip**)

Water moves by osmosis

Mineral Uptake

Many minerals are absorbed passively along with the water they are dissolved in. However, some minerals are in such low concentration in the soil that they must be taken up actively by the root. This active transport requires energy and is therefore a cost for the plant.

Root hairs **increase the surface area** for absorption of water and nutrients by many times. The root hairs are extensions of the root epidermal cells, extending out to make intimate contact with the film of water on the soil particles. Unlike older roots, the root hairs have no waterproof suberin layer and a very thin cuticle, so they present little barrier to water entry.

Enlargement of root cells

Through endodermis to xylem vessel

Vacuole

Cell wall

Cytoplasm

Plasmodesma

Root hair

Water enters symplast at the endodermis

Dead cell

Water Uptake

The uptake of water through the roots occurs by **osmosis**; the passive diffusion of water from where there is a high water potential to where there is a low water potential. Three different pathways of water transport are known to exist in flowering plants:

Apoplast pathway: About 90% of water moves through the tissues via the spaces within the cellulose cell walls, the water-filled spaces of dead cells and the hollow tubes of xylem vessels.

Symplast pathway: Some water also moves through the living contents of cells. Water enters the cytoplasm and moves between cells through the cytoplasmic connections called *plasmodesmata* (*sing*. plasmodesma) that cross the cell walls through pits.

Vacuolar pathway: A small amount of water passes into the cell vacuoles by osmosis. This vacuolar pathway is the route by which individual cells absorb water. It is not shown on the diagram.

Zone of lower water potential
May be due to: less turgid cells, lower wall pressure or more dissolved substances

Zone of higher water potential
May be due to: fully turgid cells, a higher wall pressure, or a lower concentration of dissolved substances

◄◄ —— Apoplast pathway (cell wall)

◄- - - - Symplast pathway (cytoplasm)

---

1. (a) Identify the two mechanisms by which plants absorb nutrients: _____

   (b) Describe the two principal pathways by which water moves through a plant: _____

   _____

2. Plants take up water constantly to compensate for transpirational loss. Describe a benefit of a large water uptake:

   _____

3. (a) Describe the consequence of the **Casparian strip** to the route water takes into the stele: _____

   _____

   (b) Suggest why this feature might be advantageous in terms of selective mineral uptake: _____

   _____

   _____

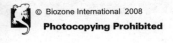
Adaptation & Specialisation

Related activities: Root Structure
Web links: Uptake at the Root

A 3

Classification and Evidence of Phylogeny

Unit 2: The Variety of Living Organisms

2.8-2.9 Classification

The principles of taxonomy, the species concept, tools for classification and evidence of phylogeny

Learning Objectives

☐ 1. Compile your own glossary from the **KEY WORDS** displayed in **bold type** in the learning objectives below.

Classification Systems *(pages 227, 231-232)*

☐ 2. Recognise **taxonomy** as the study of the theory and practice of classification. Describe the principles and importance of scientific classification.

☐ 3. Understand the differences between the **five kingdom classification system** and the **six kingdom classification system.**

☐ 4. Recognise at least seven major **taxonomic categories: kingdom**, **phylum**, **class**, **order**, **family**, **genus**, and **species**. Distinguish taxonomic categories from **taxa**, which are groups of organisms: "genus" is a taxonomic category, whereas the genus *Drosophila* is a taxon.

☐ 5. Explain how **binomial nomenclature** is used to classify organisms. Appreciate the problems associated with using **common names** to describe organisms.

☐ 6. Understand the basis for assigning organisms to different taxonomic categories. Appreciate that species are classified on the basis of **shared derived characters** rather than primitive (ancestral) characters. *For example, within the vertebrates, the presence of a backbone is a derived, therefore a **distinguishing feature**. Within the mammals, the backbone is an ancestral feature and is not distinguishing, whereas mammary glands (a distinguishing feature) are derived.*

Biological Species *(pages 228-229)*

☐ 7. Define the term **species**. Explain the importance of **courtship behaviours** in species recognition. Understand that behaviour is a means of prezygotic isolation which helps maintain species integrity.

Evidence for Phylogeny *(pages 227, 230-235)*

☐ 8. Explain the relationship between classification and **phylogeny**. Explain how newer classification schemes attempt to better reflect the **phylogeny** of organisms.

☐ 9. Appreciate that **cladistics** provides a method of classification based on relatedness, and emphasises the presence of **shared derived characters**. Appreciate the advantages and disadvantages of cladistic schemes.

☐ 10. Traditional classifications have been based on observable features (usually morphology). Recognise that today **molecular evidence** plays a key role in establishing classification and phylogeny.

☐ 11. Explain how **DNA hybridisaton** techniques can be used to compare the genetic relatedness of species. Describe how **molecular clock** data has been used by scientists recently to reclassify plants. Understand some of the limitations of such techniques.

☐ 12. Describe how **molecular evidence** such as comparisons of **DNA, amino acid sequences**, or **immunological proteins** can be used to compare the genetic relatedness of organisms.

See the 'Textbook Reference Grid' on pages 7 for textbook page references relating to material in this topic.

Supplementary Texts

See pages 5-7 for additional details of this text:

■ Clegg, C.J., 1999. **Genetics and Evolution**, (John Murray), pp. 62-63.

See page 6 for details of publishers of periodicals:

STUDENT'S REFERENCE

■ **A Passion for Order** National Geographic, 211(6) June 2007, pp. 73-87. *The history of Carl Linnaeus and the classification of plant species.*

■ **Taxonomy: The Naming Game Revisited** Biol. Sci. Rev., 9(5) May 1997, pp. 31-35. *New tools for taxonomy and how they are used (includes the exemplar of the reclassification of the kingdoms).*

■ **The Species Enigma** New Scientist, 13 June 1998 (Inside Science). *An account of the nature of species, ring species, and the status of hybrids.*

TEACHER'S REFERENCE

■ **What's in a Name?** Scientific American, Nov. 2004, pp. 20-21. *A proposed classification system called phyloclode, based solely on phylogeny.*

■ **Family Feuds** New Scientist, 24 January 1998, pp. 36-40. *Molecular and morphological analysis used for determining species inter-relatedness.*

■ **The Problematic Red Wolf** Sci. American, July 1995, pp. 26-31. *Is the red wolf a species or a long-established hybrid? Correctly naming and recognising species can affect conservation efforts.*

■ **Crumbling Foundations** SSR, Dec. 2005, pp. 65-74. *The current diminution of taxonomic expertise is nothing short of a disaster.*

■ **World Flowers Bloom after Recount** New Scientist, 29 June 2002, p. 11. *A systematic study of flowering plants indicates more species than expected, especially in regions of high biodiversity such as South American and Asia.*

See pages 8-9 for details of how to access **Bio Links** from our web site: **www.biozone.co.uk**. From Bio Links, access sites under the topics:

GENERAL BIOLOGY ONLINE RESOURCES
> **Online Textbooks and Lecture Notes:**
• Kimball's biology pages > **Glossaries:** • Evolution glossary • Taxonomy glossary

BIODIVERSITY > **Taxonomy & Classification:**
• Classification of living things • Birds and DNA • Taxonomy: Classifying life • The cockroach pylogeny • The phylogeny of life... *and others*

PLANT BIOLOGY > **Classification and Diversity:**
• Flowering plant diversity • Natural perspective: Plant Kingdom • Vascular plant families

Presentation MEDIA
to support this topic:

EVOLUTION
• Evolution

The New Tree of Life

With the advent of more efficient genetic (DNA) sequencing technology, the genomes of many bacteria began to be sequenced. In 1996, the results of a scientific collaboration examining DNA evidence confirmed the proposal that life comprises three major evolutionary lineages (domains) and not two as was the convention.

The recognised lineages were the **Eubacteria**, the **Eukarya** and the **Archaea** (formerly the Archaebacteria). The new classification reflects the fact that there are very large differences between the archaea and the eubacteria. All three domains probably had a distant common ancestor.

A Five (or Six) Kingdom World (right)

The diagram (right) represents the **five kingdom system** of classification commonly represented in many biology texts. It recognises two basic cell types: prokaryote and eukaryote. The domain Prokaryota includes all bacteria and cyanobacteria. Domain Eukaryota includes protoctists, fungi, plants, and animals. More recently, based on 16S ribosomal RNA sequence comparisons, Carl Woese divided the prokaryotes into two kingdoms, the Eubacteria and Archaebacteria. Such **six-kingdom systems** are also commonly recognised in texts.

A New View of the World (below)

In 1996, scientists deciphered the full DNA sequence of an unusual bacterium called *Methanococcus jannaschii*. An **extremophile**, this methane-producing archaebacterium lives at 85°C; a temperature lethal for most bacteria as well as eukaryotes. The DNA sequence confirmed that life consists of three major evolutionary lineages, not the two that have been routinely described. Only 44% of this archaebacterium's genes resemble those in bacteria or eukaryotes, or both.

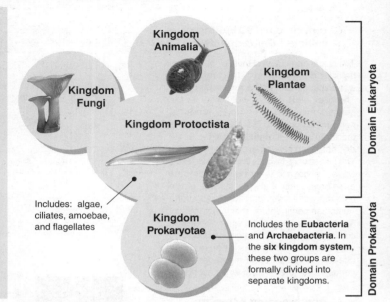

Kingdom Animalia
Kingdom Fungi
Kingdom Plantae
Kingdom Protoctista

Includes: algae, ciliates, amoebae, and flagellates

Kingdom Prokaryotae

Includes the **Eubacteria** and **Archaebacteria**. In the **six kingdom system**, these two groups are formally divided into separate kingdoms.

Domain Eukaryota

Domain Prokaryota

Domain Eubacteria

Lack a distinct nucleus and cell organelles. Generally prefer less extreme environments than Archaea. Includes well-known pathogens, many harmless and beneficial species, and the cyanobacteria (photosynthetic bacteria containing the pigments chlorophyll *a* and phycocyanin).

Domain Archaea

Closely resemble eubacteria in many ways but cell wall composition and aspects of metabolism are very different. Live in extreme environments similar to those on primeval Earth. They may utilise sulfur, methane, or halogens (chlorine, fluorine), and many tolerate extremes of temperature, salinity, or pH.

Domain Eukarya

Complex cell structure with organelles and nucleus. This group contains four of the kingdoms classified under the more traditional system. Note that Kingdom Protoctista is separated into distinct groups: e.g. amoebae, ciliates, flagellates.

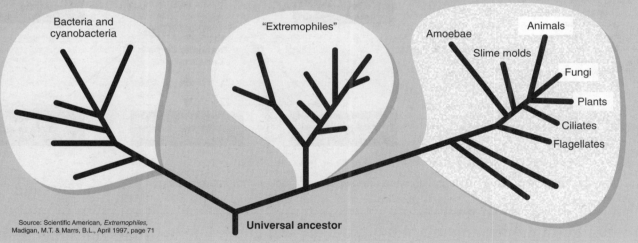

Bacteria and cyanobacteria

"Extremophiles"

Amoebae
Slime molds
Animals
Fungi
Plants
Ciliates
Flagellates

Source: Scientific American, *Extremophiles*, Madigan, M.T. & Marrs, B.L., April 1997, page 71

Universal ancestor

---

1. Explain why some scientists have recommended that the conventional classification of life be revised so that the Archaea, Eubacteria and Eukarya are three separate domains:

_____

_____

2. Describe one feature of the three domain system that is very different from the five kingdom classification:

_____

_____

3. Describe one way in which the three domain system and the six kingdom classification are alike: _____

_____

The Species Concept

The concept of a species is not as simple as it may first appear. Interbreeding between closely related species suggest that the boundaries of a species gene pool can be somewhat unclear. One of the best recognised definitions for a species is as "*a*

species is a group of actually or potentially interbreeding natural populations that is reproductively isolated from other such groups" (Ernst Mayr). Each species is provided with a unique classification name to assist with future identification.

Geographical distribution of selected *Canis* species

The global distribution of most of the species belonging to the genus *Canis* (dogs and wolves) is shown on the map to the right. The **grey wolf** (timber wolf) inhabits the cold, damp forests of North America, northern Europe and Siberia. The range of the three species of **jackal** overlap in the dry, hot, open savannah of Eastern Africa. The now-rare **red wolf** is found only in Texas, while the **coyote** is found inhabiting the open grasslands of the prairies. The **dingo** is found widely distributed throughout the Australian continent inhabiting a variety of habitats. As a result of the spread of human culture, distribution of the domesticated **dog** is global. The dog has been able to interbreed with all other members of the genus listed here, to form fertile hybrids.

Interbreeding between *Canis* species

Members of the genus to which all dogs and wolves belong present problems with the species concept. The domesticated dog is able to breed with numerous other members of the same genus to produce fertile hybrids. The coyote and red wolf in North America have ranges that overlap. They are also able to produce fertile hybrids, although these are rare. By contrast, the ranges of the three distinct species of jackal overlap in the Serengeti of Eastern Africa. These animals are highly territorial, but simply ignore members of the other jackal species and no interbreeding takes place.

For an excellent discussion of species definition among dogs see the article "The Problematic Red Wolf" in Scientific American, July 1995, pp. 26-31. This discusses whether or not the red wolf is a species or a long established hybrid of the grey wolf and coyote.

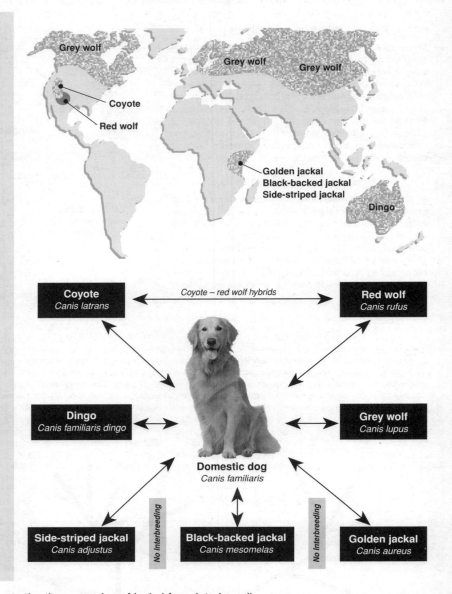

1. Describe the type of barrier that prevents the three species of jackal from interbreeding:

_____

_____

2. Describe the factor that has prevented the dingo from interbreeding with other *Canis* species (apart from the dog):

_____

3. Describe a possible contributing factor to the occurrence of interbreeding between the coyote and red wolf:

_____

_____

4. The grey wolf is a widely distributed species. Explain why the North American population is considered to be part of the same species as the northern European and Siberian populations:

_____

_____

Related activities: Variation, Classification System

Behaviour and Species Recognition

Many of the barriers observed in animals are associated with reproduction, reflecting the importance of this event in an individual's life cycle. Many types of behaviour are aimed at facilitating successful reproduction. These include **courtship behaviours**, which may involve attracting a mate to a particular breeding site. Courtship behaviours are aimed at reducing conflict between the sexes and are often stereotyped or ritualistic.

They rely on sign stimuli to elicit specific responses in potential mates. In addition, there are other reproductive behaviours which are associated with assessing the receptivity of a mate, defending mates against competitors, and rearing the young. Behavioural (ethological) differences between species are a type of **prezygotic** isolating mechanism to help preserve the uniqueness of a species gene pool.

Courtship and Species Recognition

Accurate species recognition when choosing a mate is vital for successful reproduction and species survival. Failure to choose a mate of the same species would result in reproductive failure or hybrid offspring which are infertile or unable to survive. Birds exhibit a wide range of species-specific courtship displays to identify potential mates of the same species who are physiologically ready to reproduce. They may use simple visual or auditory stimuli, or complex stimuli involving several modes of communication specific to the species.

Peacock courtship (left) involves a visually elaborate tail display to attract female attention. The male raises and fans his tail to display the bright colours and eye-spot patterns. Peahens tend to mate with peacocks displaying the best quality tail display which includes the quantity, size and distribution of eye-spots.

Bird song is an important behavioural isolation method for many species including eastern and western meadowlarks. Despite the fact that they look very similar and share the same habitat, they have remained as two separate species. Differences between the songs of the two species enables them to recognise individuals of their own species and mate only with them. This maintains the species isolation.

Eastern meadowlark

Some species use chemical cues as mating signals and to determine mate choice. The crested auklet (left) secretes aldehydes which smell like tangerines. Birds rub their bills in the scented nape of a partner during courtship. This "ruff-sniff" behaviour allows mate evaluation based on chemical potency. A potential partner might be seen as fitter and more attractive if it produces more aldehydes, because the chemical repels ectoparasites.

Courtship Behaviour is a Necessary Precursor to Sucessful Mating

Courtship behaviour occurs as a prelude to mating. One of its functions is to synchronise the behaviours of the male and female so that mating can occur, and to override attack or escape behaviour. Here, a male greater frigatebird calls, spreads its wings, and inflates its throat pouch to court a female.

In many bird and arthropod species, the male will provide an offering, such as food, to the female. These **rituals** reduce aggression in the male and promote appeasement behaviour by the female. For some **monogamous** species, e.g. the blue-footed boobies (left), the pairing begins a long term breeding partnership.

Courtship: Galapagos albatrosses

Although courtship rituals may be complex, they are very stereotyped and not easily misinterpreted. Males display, usually through exaggerated physical posturing, and the females then select their mates. Courtship displays are species specific and may include ritualised behaviour such as dancing, feeding, and nest-building.

1. (a) Suggest why courtship behavior may be necessary prior to mating: _____

   _____

   (b) Explain why courtship behavior is often ritualised and involves stereotyped displays: _____

   _____

   _____

2. In terms of species continuity, explain the significance of courtship behaviour in species recognition:

   _____

   _____

   _____

   _____

DNA and Taxonomy

Taxonomy is the study of classification. Ever since Darwin, the aim of classification has been to organise species, and to reflect their evolutionary history (**phylogeny**). Each successive group in the taxonomic hierarchy should represent finer and finer branching from a common ancestor. In order to reconstruct evolutionary history, phylogenetic trees must be based on features that are due to shared ancestry (homologies). Traditional taxonomy has relied mainly on **morphological characters** to do this. Modern technology has assisted taxonomy by providing **biochemical evidence** (from proteins and DNA) for the relatedness of species. The most familiar approach to classifying organisms is to use **classical evolutionary taxonomy**. It considers branching sequences and overall likeness. A more recent approach has been to use **cladistics**: a technique which emphasises phylogeny

or relatedness, usually based on biochemical evidence (and largely ignoring morphology or appearance). Each branch on the tree marks the point where a new species has arisen by evolution. Traditional and cladistic schemes do not necessarily conflict, but there have been reclassifications of some taxa (notably the primates, but also the reptiles, dinosaurs, and birds). Traditional taxonomists criticise cladistic schemes because they do not recognise the amount of visible change in morphology that occurs in species after their divergence from a common ancestor. Popular classifications will probably continue to reflect similarities and differences in appearance, rather than a strict evolutionary history. In this respect, they are a compromise between phylogeny and the need for a convenient filing system for species diversity.

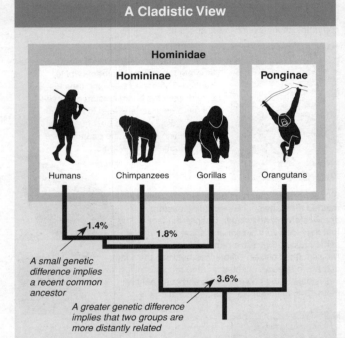

A Classical Taxonomic View

Hominidae — Humans

Pongidae — The 'great apes' — Chimpanzees, Gorillas, Orangutans

On the basis of overall anatomical similarity (e.g. bones and limb length, teeth, musculature), apes are grouped into a family (Pongidae) that is separate from humans and their immediate ancestors (Hominidae). The family Pongidae (the great apes) is not monophyletic (of one phylogeny), because it stems from an ancestor that also gave rise to a species in another family (i.e. humans). This traditional classification scheme is now at odds with schemes derived after considering genetic evidence.

A Cladistic View

Hominidae

Homininae — Humans, Chimpanzees, Gorillas

Ponginae — Orangutans

1.4% — A small genetic difference implies a recent common ancestor

1.8%

3.6% — A greater genetic difference implies that two groups are more distantly related

Based on the evidence of genetic differences (% values above), chimpanzees and gorillas are more closely related to humans than to orangutans, and chimpanzees are more closely related to humans than they are to gorillas. Under this scheme there is no true family of great apes. The family Hominidae includes two subfamilies: Ponginae and Homininae (humans, chimpanzees, and gorillas). This classification is monophyletic: the Hominidae includes all the species that arise from a common ancestor.

1. Briefly explain the benefits of classification schemes based on:

(a) Morphological characters: _____

_____

_____

(b) Relatedness in time (from biochemical evidence): _____

_____

_____

2. Describe the contribution of biochemical evidence to taxonomy: _____

_____

3. Based on the diagram above, state the family to which the chimpanzees belong under:

(a) A traditional scheme: _____   (b) A cladistic scheme: _____

Classification System

The classification of organisms is designed to reflect how they are related to each other. The fundamental unit of classification of living things is the **species**. Its members are so alike genetically that they can interbreed. This genetic similarity also means that they are almost identical in their physical and other characteristics. Species are classified further into larger, more comprehensive categories (higher taxa). It must be emphasised that all such higher classifications are human inventions to suit a particular purpose.

1. The table below shows part of the classification for humans using the seven major levels of classification. For this question, use the example of the classification of the European hedgehog, on the next page, as a guide.

   (a) Complete the list of the classification levels on the left hand side of the table below:

	Classification level	Human classification
1.	_____	_____
2.	_____	_____
3.	_____	_____
4.	_____	_____
5.	Family	Hominidae
6.	_____	_____
7.	_____	_____

   (b) The name of the Family that humans belong to has already been entered into the space provided. Complete the classification for humans (*Homo sapiens*) on the table above.

2. Describe the two-part scientific naming system (called the **binomial system**) that is used to name organisms:

   _____

   _____

3. Give two reasons why the classification of organisms is important:

   (a) _____

   _____

   (b) _____

   _____

4. Traditionally, the classification of organisms has been based largely on similarities in physical appearance. More recently, new methods involving biochemical comparisons have been used to provide new insights into how species are related. Describe an example of a biochemical method for comparing how species are related:

   _____

   _____

   _____

5. As an example of physical features being used to classify organisms, mammals have been divided into three major sub-classes: monotremes, marsupials, and placentals. Describe the main physical feature distinguishing each of these taxa:

   (a) Monotreme: _____

   _____

   (b) Marsupial: _____

   _____

   (c) Placental: _____

   _____

232

Classification of the European Hedgehog

Below is the classification for the **European hedgehog**. Only one of each group is subdivided in this chart showing the levels that can be used in classifying an organism. Not all possible subdivisions have been shown here. For example, it is possible to indicate such categories as **super-class** and **sub-family**. The only natural category is the **species**, often separated into geographical **races**, or **sub-species**, which generally differ in appearance.

Kingdom: **Animalia**
Animals: one of five kingdoms

Phylum: **Chordata**
Animals with a notochord (supporting rod of cells along the upper surface).
tunicates, salps, lancelets, and vertebrates

23 other phyla

Sub-phylum: **Vertebrata**
Animals with backbones.
fish, amphibians, reptiles, birds, mammals

Class: **Mammalia**
Animals that suckle their young on milk from mammary glands.
placentals, marsupials, monotremes

Sub-class: **Eutheria**
Mammals whose young develop for some time in the female's reproductive tract gaining nourishment from a placenta.
placentals

Order: **Insectivora**
Insect eating mammals.
An order of over 300 species of primitive, small mammals that feed mainly on insects and other small invertebrates.

17 other orders

Sub-order: **Erinaceomorpha**
The hedgehog-type insectivores. One of the three suborders of insectivores. The other suborders include the tenrec-like insectivores (*tenrecs and golden moles*) and the shrew-like insectivores (*shrews, moles, desmans, and solenodons*).

Family: **Erinaceidae**
The only family within this suborder. Comprises two subfamilies: the true or spiny hedgehogs and the moonrats (gymnures). Representatives in the family include the desert hedgehog, long-eared hedgehog, and the greater and lesser moonrats.

Genus: *Erinaceus*
One of eight genera in this family. The genus *Erinaceus* includes four Eurasian species and another three in Africa.

7 other genera

Species: *europaeus*
The European hedgehog. Among the largest of the spiny hedgehogs. Characterised by a dense covering of spines on the back, the presence of a big toe (hallux) and 36 teeth.

6 other species

The order *Insectivora* was first introduced to group together shrews, moles, and hedgehogs. It was later extended to include tenrecs, golden moles, desmans, tree shrews, and elephant shrews, and the taxonomy of the group became very confused. Recent reclassification of the elephant shrews and tree shrews into their own separate orders has made the Insectivora a more cohesive group taxonomically.

European hedgehog
Erinaceus europaeus

© Biozone International 2008
Photocopying Prohibited

DNA Hybridisation

DNA hybridisation refers to the molecular biology technique which measures the genetic similarity between the DNA samples of two species. The more closely the species are related, the fewer differences there will be in the exact sequence of bases. This is because there has been less time for the point mutations that will bring about these changes to occur. Modern species can be compared to see how long ago they shared a **common ancestor.** This technique gives a measure of 'relatedness',

and can be calibrated against known fossil dates to create a **molecular clock**. It is then possible to give approximate dates of common origin to species with no or poor fossil data. Angiosperms were the first large group to be reclassified based primarily on molecular characteristics of a photosynthetic gene. The study resulted in a new phylogenetic tree which was very different from the existing one based on morphology. Subsequent research using other genes later confirmed the new taxonomy.

DNA Hybridisation

1. Tissue samples (in this example blood) from each species are taken, from which the DNA is isolated.

2. The DNA from each species is made to unwind into single strands by applying heat (both human and chimpanzee DNA unwinds at 86°C).

3. Enzymes are used to snip the single strands of DNA into smaller pieces (about 500 base pairs long).

4. The segments from human and chimpanzee DNA are combined to see how closely they bind to each other (single strand segments tend to find their complementary segments and rewind into a double helix again).

5. The greater the similarity in DNA base sequence, the stronger the attraction between the two strands and therefore they are harder to separate again. By measuring how hard this hybrid DNA is to separate, a crude measure of DNA 'relatedness' can be achieved.

6. The degree of similarity of the hybrid DNA can be measured by finding the temperature that it unzips into single strands again (in this case it would be 83.6°C).

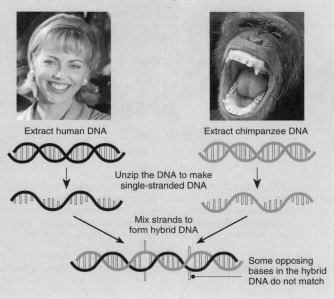

Extract human DNA   Extract chimpanzee DNA

Unzip the DNA to make single-stranded DNA

Mix strands to form hybrid DNA

Some opposing bases in the hybrid DNA do not match

Reclassifying Angiosperms

A large consortium of botanists (the **angiosperm phylogeny group**) radically rearranged angiosperm (flowering plant) classification in the 1990s by comparing DNA sequences of three genes. Although primarily based on molecular evidence, other techniques such as pollen morphology have been used to confirm the new classification.

The APG revised the system in 2003 and the **APG II** system is proving to be influential. Almost 25% of plant species have been reassigned to new taxonomic groups. One of the biggest changes was to the lily Order Liliales (lilies), below. Amongst the plants reclassified to other orders include the orchids which were found to be closely related to asparagus, and the sacred lotus, which was originally classed as a water lily, but was found to be more closely related to the plane tree under the revised system.

Reclassification of Order Liliales

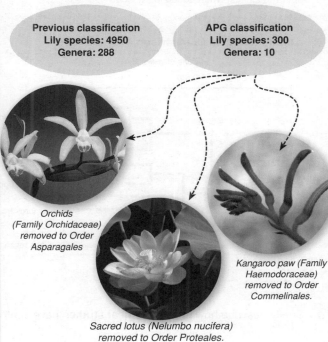

Previous classification
Lily species: 4950
Genera: 288

APG classification
Lily species: 300
Genera: 10

Orchids
(Family Orchidaceae)
removed to Order
Asparagales

Kangaroo paw (Family
Haemodoraceae)
removed to Order
Commelinales.

Sacred lotus (Nelumbo nucifera)
removed to Order Proteales.

---

1. Explain how **DNA hybridisation** can give a measure of genetic relatedness between species:

_____

_____

_____

2. Discuss why molecular evidence may be more accurate for correctly classifying plants than morphological evidence:

_____

_____

_____

Immunological Studies

Immunological studies provide a method of indirectly estimating the degree of similarity of proteins in different species. If differences exist in the proteins, then there must also be differences in the DNA that codes for them. The evolutionary relationships of a large number of different animal groups have been established on the basis of immunology. The results support the phylogenies developed from other areas: biogeography, comparative anatomy, and fossil evidence.

Method for Immunological Comparison

1. Blood serum (containing blood proteins but no cells) is collected from a human and is injected into a rabbit. This causes the formation of antibodies in the rabbit's blood. These identify human blood proteins, attach to them and render them harmless.

2. A sample of the rabbit's blood is taken and the rabbit's antibodies that recognise human blood proteins are extracted.

3. These anti-human antibodies are then added to blood samples from other species to see how well they recognise the proteins in the different blood. The more similar the blood sample is to original human blood, the greater the reaction (which takes the form of creating a precipitate, i.e. solids).

The five blood samples that were tested (on the right) show varying degrees of precipitate (solid) formation. Note that when the anti-human antibodies are added to human blood there is a high degree of affinity. There is poor recognition when added to rat blood.

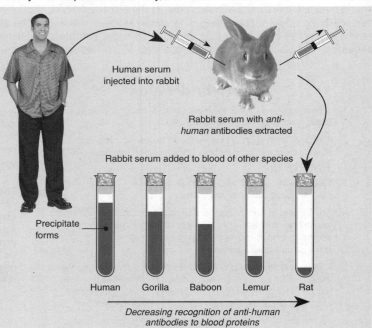

Human serum injected into rabbit

Rabbit serum with *anti-human* antibodies extracted

Rabbit serum added to blood of other species

Precipitate forms

Human Gorilla Baboon Lemur Rat

Decreasing recognition of anti-human antibodies to blood proteins

Immunological Comparison of Tree Frogs

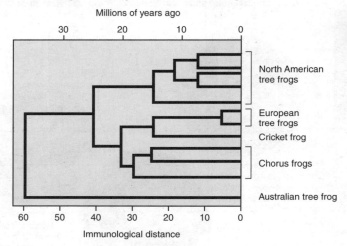

Millions of years ago

North American tree frogs

European tree frogs

Cricket frog

Chorus frogs

Australian tree frog

Immunological distance

The relationships among **tree frogs** have been established by immunological studies. The immunological distance is a measure of the number of amino acid substitutions between two groups. This, in turn, has been calibrated to provide a time scale showing when the various related groups diverged.

1. Briefly describe how **immunological studies** have contributed evidence that the process of evolution has taken place:

_____

_____

_____

_____

2. Study the graph above showing the immunological distance between tree frogs. State the immunological distance between the following frogs:

(a) Cricket frog and the Australian tree frog: _____ (b) The various chorus frogs: _____

3. Describe how closely the Australian tree frog is related to the other frogs shown:

_____

4. State when the North American tree frogs became separated from the European tree frogs: _____

Protein Comparisons

Protein sequencing provides an excellent tool for establishing **homologies** (similarities resulting from shared ancestry).

Phylogenetic trees based on protein homologies can then be compared to the those obtained using other methods.

Amino Acid Sequences

Each of our proteins has a specific number of amino acids arranged in a specific order. Any differences in the sequence reflect changes in the DNA sequence. The haemoglobin beta chain has been used as a standard molecule for comparing the precise sequence of amino acids in different species. Haemoglobin is the protein in our red blood cells that is responsible for carrying oxygen around our bodies. The haemoglobin in adults is made up of four polypeptide chains: 2 alpha chains and 2 beta chains. Each is coded for by a separate gene.

Example right: When the sequence of human haemoglobin, which is 146 amino acids long, was compared with that of 5 other primate species it was found that chimpanzees had an identical sequence while those that were already considered less closely related had a greater number of differences. This suggests a very close genetic relationship between humans, chimpanzees and gorillas, but less with the other primates.

Amino Acid Differences Between Humans and Other Primates

The 'position of changed amino acid' is the point in the protein, composed of 146 amino acids, at which the **different** amino acids occurs

Primate	No. of amino acids different from humans	Position of changed amino acids
Chimpanzee	Identical	–
Gorilla	1	104
Gibbon	3	80 87 125
Rhesus monkey	8	9 13 33 50 76 87 104 125
Squirrel monkey	9	5 6 9 21 22 56 76 87 125

Molecular Clocks

Protein homology refers to the similarity between different protein sequences. It allows scientists to draw phylogenetic trees to show the evolutionary relationships between species with a common ancestor. The divergence time of two species can be established by using a **molecular clock**, which measures the number of molecular differences between the proteins over time.

The technique can be used to determine the scientific classification of organisms and establish phylogenetic dates, especially when they can not be determined by other means, e.g. for the divergence of living taxa or if the fossil record is poor. The molecular clock for each species, and each protein, may run at different rates, so scientists calibrate the molecular clock data with other evidence (morphological, molecular) to confirm phylogenetic relationships. With protein homology, it is assumed that the more identical residues there are, the more recently the organsims evolved from a common ancestor. Phylogenetic trees can then be constructed to demonstrate this relationship.

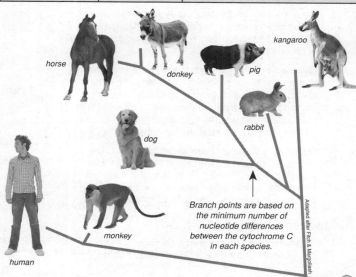

Branch points are based on the minimum number of nucleotide differences between the cytochrome C in each species.

Adapted after Fitch & Margoliash

The sequence homology of cytochrome C (right), a respiratory protein, has been used to construct a phylogenetic tree for several species of mammals. Overall, the phylogeny aligns well to other evolutionary data, although the tree indicates that primates branched off before the marsupials diverged from other placental mammals, which is incorrect based on a variety of other evidence. Cytochrome C is highly conserved, which means that its sequence changes very little despite speciation.

1. Explain why chimpanzees and gorillas are considered most closely related to humans, while monkeys are less so:

_____

2. (a) Explain why a respiratory protein like cytochrome C would be highly conserved: _____

_____

(b) Suggest why highly conserved proteins are good candidates for use in establishing protein homologies

_____

_____

3. Discuss some of the limitations of using protein homology, specifically molecular clocks to establish phylogeny:

_____

_____

Related activities: Immunological Studies

RDA 2

Evolution and Biodiversity

Unit 2: The Variety of Life
2.10-2.11 Evolution and biodiversity

Antibiotic resistance, evolution in bacteria, factors affecting biodiversity, measuring biodiversity

Learning Objectives

☐ 1. Compile your own glossary from the **KEY WORDS** displayed in **bold type** in the learning objectives below.

Antibiotics and Resistance (*pages 237-239*)

☐ 2. Describe how **antibiotics** act in a variety of ways to inhibit or kill bacteria. In particular, understand that some antibiotics function by acting upon the **cell walls** of certain bacteria.

☐ 3. Describe the changes to bacterial DNA (**mutations**) that enable them to develop **resistance** to certain drugs, including antibiotics. Explain the impact on human health in trying to treat people infected with methicillin resistant strains of *Staphylococcus aureus* (**MRSA**) and **drug resistant tuberculosis**.

☐ 4. Describe how bacteria are able to transfer drug resistance between generations by **vertical gene transfer** (vertical evolution). Distinguish this from **horizontal gene transmission**, whereby bacteria acquire genes for resistance through **conjugation**.

Biodiversity (*pages 240-241, 247*)

☐ 5. Define the term **biodiversity**. Recognise the different components of **biodiversity**: **species**, **habitat**, and **genetic diversity** and explain how biodiversity can be studied at each of these levels.

☐ 6. Explain the terms **species richness** and **species evenness**. Appreciate the role of appropriate sampling methods in fairly investigating these properties.

☐ 7. Explain the use of **diversity indices** in community ecology. Use a **diversity index**, such as the **Simpson's Index of Diversity**, to analyse and compare two local communities. Outline the significance of both high and low values of this diversity index. If required, describe the use of **biotic indices** (including **indicator species**) in monitoring change in the environment.

☐ 8. Discuss current estimates of global biodiversity. Identify regions of naturally-occurring high **biodiversity** (biodiversity hotspots) and describe the importance of these regions to global ecology.

Loss of Biodiversity (*pages 243-246*)

☐ 9. Recognise that areas of high biodiversity are under increasing pressure as human populations expand.

☐ 10. Using an example (e.g. rainforest destruction), discuss the ethical, ecological, economic, and aesthetic reasons for the conservation of biodiversity. Recognise the relationship between **diversity** and ecosystem **stability** and **resilience**. Appreciate the role of **keystone species** in ecosystem function and the possible consequences of removing these species.

☐ 11. Discuss the impact of **deforestation** and **agriculture** on species diversity. In terms of biodiversity, recognise the problems that can arise from both practices. Describe the practices that maintain or enhance biodiversity (e.g. the conservation of hedgerows in Britain) and discuss their benefits.

See the 'Textbook Reference Grid' on page 7 for textbook page references relating to material in this topic.

See page 6 for details of publishers of periodicals:

STUDENT'S REFERENCE

■ **MRSA: A Hospital Superbug** Biol. Sci. Rev., 19(4) April 2007, pp. 30-33. *An excellent account of how the evolution of MRSA has been driven by the misuse of antibiotics.*

■ **The Challenge of Antibiotic Resistance** Scientific American, March 1998, pp. 32-39. *An excellent article on the basis of antibiotic resistance in bacteria and its selective advantage.*

■ **March of the Superbugs** New Scientist (Inside Science),19 July 2003. *How antibiotic resistance arises and spreads through bacterial populations.*

■ **Biodiversity and Ecosystems** Biol. Sci. Rev., 11(4) March 1999, pp. 18-21. *The importance of biodiversity to ecosystem stability and sustainability.*

■ **Hot Spots** New Scientist, 4 April 1998, pp. 32-36. *An examination of the reasons for the very high biodiversity observed in the tropics.*

■ **Biodiversity: Taking Stock of Life** National Geographic, 195(2) Feb. 1999 (entire issue). *A special issue exploring the Earth's biodiversity and what we can do to preserve it.*

■ **Last of the Amazon** National Geographic, 211(1) Jan. 2007, pp. 40-71. *The current state of the Amazon forest, one of the world's most biologically diverse regions.*

TEACHER'S REFERENCE

■ **Conservation for the People** Scientific American, Oct. 2007, pp. 26-33. *Preserving biodiversity in ecological hotspots is not working as a conservation strategy. We need to protect ecosystems vital to ecosystem and human health.*

■ **Superbugs Bite Back** New Scientist, 29 Sep. 2007, pp. 37-39. *The difficulties of drug resistant bacteria such as MRSA in hospitals.*

See pages 8-9 for details of how to access **Bio Links** from our web site: **www.biozone.co.uk**. From Bio Links, access sites under the topics:

BIODIVERSITY > Biodiversity: • Convention on biological diversity • Ecology and biodiversity • World atlas of biodiversity … *and others*

CONSERVATION: > Habitat loss: • Causes of habitat loss and species endangerment • We need our forests • Rainforest destruction

HEALTH & DISEASE: > Prevention and Treatment: • Antimicrobial agents • Antibiotic resistance • How severe is antibiotic resistance • Resistance to antibiotics

Presentation MEDIA to support this topic:
ECOLOGY: Biodiversity & Conservation

Antibiotics

An **antibiotic** is a chemotherapeutic agent that inhibits or prevents microbial growth. Antibiotics are produced naturally by bacteria and fungi, but some synthetic (manufactured) **antimicrobial drugs** are also effective against microbial infections. Antimicrobial drugs interfere with the growth of microorganisms (see diagram below) by either killing microbes directly (**bactericidal**) or preventing them from growing (**bacteriostatic**). To be effective, they must often act inside the host, so their effect on the host's cells and tissues is important. The ideal antimicrobial drug has **selective toxicity**, killing the pathogen without damaging the host. Some antimicrobial drugs have a narrow **spectrum of**

activity, and affect only a limited number of microbial types. Others are **broad-spectrum drugs** and affect a large number of microbial species. When the identity of a pathogen is not known, a broad-spectrum drug may be prescribed in order to save valuable time. There is a disadvantage with this, because broad spectrum drugs target not just the pathogen, but much of the host's normal microflora also. The normal microbial community usually controls the growth of pathogens and other microbes by competing with them. By selectively removing them with drugs, certain microbes in the community that do not normally cause problems, may flourish and become **opportunistic pathogens**.

How Antimicrobial Drugs Work

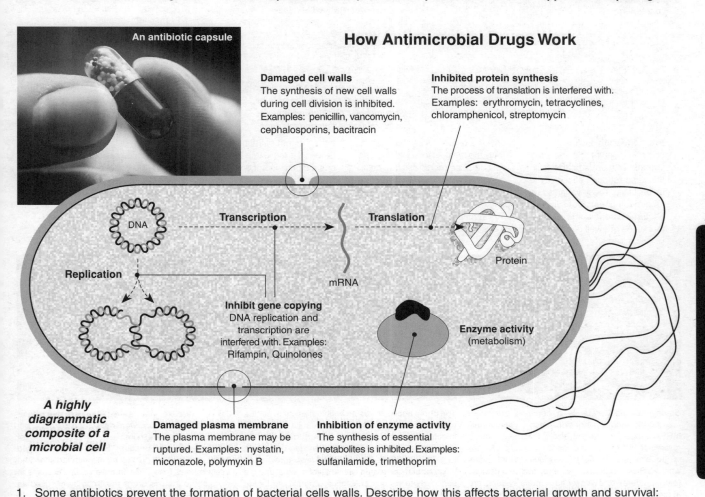

An antibiotic capsule

Damaged cell walls
The synthesis of new cell walls during cell division is inhibited. Examples: penicillin, vancomycin, cephalosporins, bacitracin

Inhibited protein synthesis
The process of translation is interfered with. Examples: erythromycin, tetracyclines, chloramphenicol, streptomycin

Transcription   Translation

DNA   mRNA   Protein

Replication

Inhibit gene copying
DNA replication and transcription are interfered with. Examples: Rifampin, Quinolones

Enzyme activity
(metabolism)

A highly diagrammatic composite of a microbial cell

Damaged plasma membrane
The plasma membrane may be ruptured. Examples: nystatin, miconazole, polymyxin B

Inhibition of enzyme activity
The synthesis of essential metabolites is inhibited. Examples: sulfanilamide, trimethoprim

Evolution and Biodiversity

1. Some antibiotics prevent the formation of bacterial cells walls. Describe how this affects bacterial growth and survival:

_____

_____

_____

2. Explain the advantages and disadvantages of using a **broad-spectrum drug** on an unidentified bacterial infection:

_____

_____

_____

3. Discuss the requirements of an "ideal" anti-microbial drug, and explain in what way antibiotics satisfy these requirements:

_____

_____

_____

Evolution of Drug Resistance

Resistance to drugs results from an adaptive response that allows microbes to tolerate levels of antibiotic that would normally inhibit their growth. This resistance may arise spontaneously as the result of mutation, or by transfer of genetic material between microbes. Over the years, more and more bacteria have developed resistance to once-effective antibiotics. Methicillin resistant strains of the common bacterium *Staphylococcus aureus* (MRSA) have acquired genes that confer antibiotic resistance to all penicillins, including **methicillin** and other narrow-spectrum pencillin-type drugs. Such strains, called "superbugs", were discovered in the UK in 1961 and are now widespread, and the infections they cause are exceedingly difficult to treat.

The Evolution of Drug Resistance in Bacteria

Susceptible bacterium

Less susceptible bacterium

Mutations occur at a rate of one in every 10^8 replications.

Bacterium with greater resistance survives

Drug resistance genes can be transferred to non resistant strains.

Any population, including bacterial populations, includes variants with unusual traits, in this case reduced sensitivity to an antibiotic. These variants arise as a result of mutations in the bacterial chromosome. Such mutations are well documented.

When a person takes an antibiotic, only the most susceptible bacteria will die. The more resistant cells remain and continue dividing. Note that the antibiotic does not create the resistance; it provides the environment in which selection for resistance can take place.

If the amount of antibiotic delivered is too low, or the course of antibiotics is not completed, a population of resistant bacteria develops. Within this population too, there will be variation in susceptibility. Some will survive higher antibiotic levels.

A highly resistant population has evolved. The resistant cells can exchange genetic material with other bacteria, passing on the genes for resistance. The antibiotic initially used against this bacterial strain will now be ineffective.

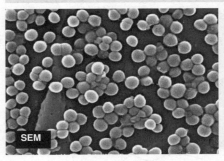

SEM

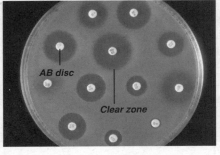

AB disc

Clear zone

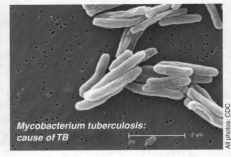

Mycobacterium tuberculosis: cause of TB

2 µm

All photos: CDC

Staphylococcus aureus is a common bacterium responsible various minor skin infections in humans. MRSA (above) is variant strain that has evolved resistance to penicillin and related antibiotics. MRSA is troublesome in hospital-associated infections where patients with open wounds, invasive devices (e.g. catheters), and weakened immune systems are at greater risk for infection than the general public.

The photo above shows an antibiogram plate culture of *Enterobacter sakazakii*, a rare cause of invasive infections in infants. An antibiogram measures the biological resistance of disease-causing organisms to antibiotic agents. The bacterial lawn (growth) on the agar plate is treated with antibiotic discs, and the sensitivity to various antibiotics is measured by the extent of the clearance zone in the bacterial lawn.

TB is a disease that has experienced spectacular ups and downs. Drugs were developed to treat it, but then people became complacent when they thought the disease was beaten. TB has since resurged because patients stop their medication too soon and infect others. Today, one in seven new TB cases is resistant to the two drugs most commonly used as treatments, and 5% of these patients die.

1. Explain what is meant by **antibiotic resistance**: _____

_____

2. (a) Explain how antibiotic resistance arises in a bacterial population: _____

_____

(b) Describe two ways in which antibiotic resistance can become widespread: _____

_____

_____

3. With reference to tuberculosis, discuss the implications to humans of widespread antibiotic resistance:

_____

_____

_____

Related activities: Antibiotics, The Basis of Resistance, Tuberculosis

The Basis of Resistance

Antibiotic resistance in bacteria occurs when their genetic material is altered in a way that makes them less susceptible to the action of an antibiotic. This may occur in several ways. Resistance can arise spontaneously when an organism's DNA is altered as a result of transcription error or it can be induced through exposure to mutagens. A bacterium can also transfer genetic material to bacteria other than its own offspring by **horizontal gene transmission** (HGT) (below left). The potential for genetic variation resulting from HGT is vast because material can pass between organisms that are not even of the same species, genus, or kingdom. In contrast, **vertical gene transmission** involves passing gene by descent, i.e. a bacterium receives genetic material directly from its ancestor. The mechanisms of resistance conferred are varied and include the production of enzymes that inactivate the drugs, or changes that prevent the antibiotic attaching to or penetrating the microbial surface.

Methods by which Bacteria Acquire Resistance

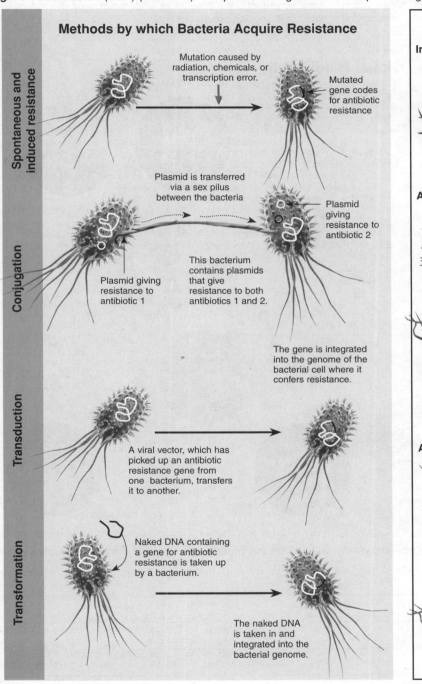

Spontaneous and induced resistance

Mutation caused by radiation, chemicals, or transcription error.

Mutated gene codes for antibiotic resistance

Conjugation

Plasmid is transferred via a sex pilus between the bacteria

Plasmid giving resistance to antibiotic 2

Plasmid giving resistance to antibiotic 1

This bacterium contains plasmids that give resistance to both antibiotics 1 and 2.

The gene is integrated into the genome of the bacterial cell where it confers resistance.

Transduction

A viral vector, which has picked up an antibiotic resistance gene from one bacterium, transfers it to another.

Transformation

Naked DNA containing a gene for antibiotic resistance is taken up by a bacterium.

The naked DNA is taken in and integrated into the bacterial genome.

Mechanisms of Resistance

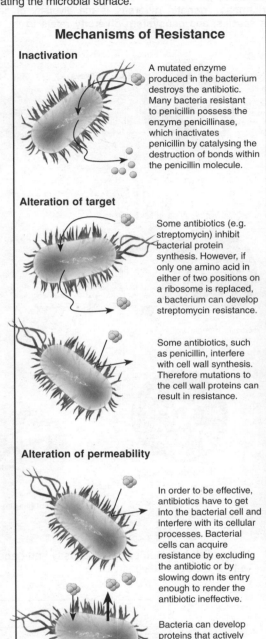

Inactivation

A mutated enzyme produced in the bacterium destroys the antibiotic. Many bacteria resistant to penicillin possess the enzyme penicillinase, which inactivates penicillin by catalysing the destruction of bonds within the penicillin molecule.

Alteration of target

Some antibiotics (e.g. streptomycin) inhibit bacterial protein synthesis. However, if only one amino acid in either of two positions on a ribosome is replaced, a bacterium can develop streptomycin resistance.

Some antibiotics, such as penicillin, interfere with cell wall synthesis. Therefore mutations to the cell wall proteins can result in resistance.

Alteration of permeability

In order to be effective, antibiotics have to get into the bacterial cell and interfere with its cellular processes. Bacterial cells can acquire resistance by excluding the antibiotic or by slowing down its entry enough to render the antibiotic ineffective.

Bacteria can develop proteins that actively pump antibiotics out of their cell faster than the antibiotics can enter.

Evolution and Biodiversity

1. Explain the major differences between **horizontal gene transmission** and **vertical gene transmission**:

_____

_____

2. Discuss the implications (to humans) of bacteria acquiring several different mechanisms of resistance:

_____

_____

Related activities: Antibiotics, Evolution of Drug Resistance, Prokaryotic Chromosomes

A 2

Global Biodiversity

The species is the basic unit by which we measure biological diversity or **biodiversity**. Biodiversity is not distributed evenly on Earth, being consistently richer in the tropics and concentrated more in some areas than in others. The simplest definition of biodiversity is as the sum of all biotic variation from the level of genes to ecosystems, but often the components of total biodiversity are distinguished. **Species diversity** describes the number of different species in an area (**species richness**), **genetic diversity** is the diversity of genes within a species, and **ecosystem diversity** refers to the diversity at

the higher ecosystem level of organisation. **Habitat diversity** is also sometimes described and is essentially a subset of ecosystem diversity expressed per given unit area. Total biological diversity is often threatened because of the loss of just one of these components. Conservation International recognises 25 **biodiversity hotspots**. These are biologically diverse and ecologically distinct regions under the greatest threat of destruction. They are identified on the basis of the number of species present, the amount of **endemism**, and the extent to which the species are threatened.

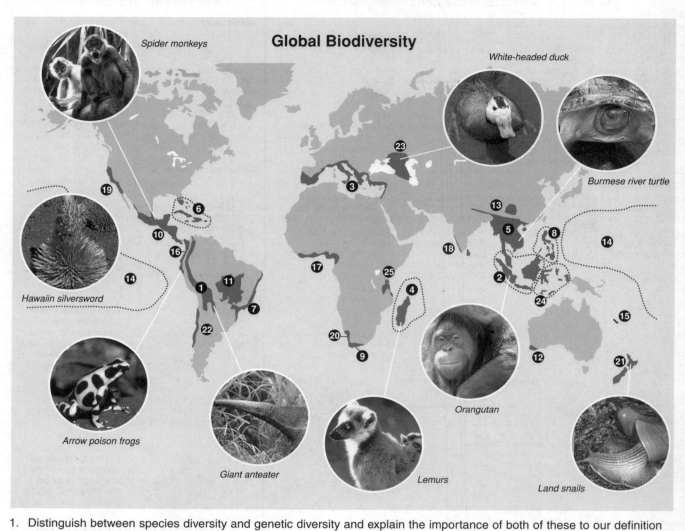

Global Biodiversity

Spider monkeys

White-headed duck

Burmese river turtle

Hawaiin silversword

Arrow poison frogs

Giant anteater

Lemurs

Orangutan

Land snails

1. Distinguish between species diversity and genetic diversity and explain the importance of both of these to our definition of total biological diversity:

   _____

   _____

   _____

   _____

2. Explain the importance of considering ecosystem (habitat) diversity when targeting regions for conservation purposes:

   _____

   _____

   _____

3. Use your research tools (e.g. textbook, internet, or encyclopaedia) to identify each of the 25 biodiversity hotspots illustrated in the diagram above. For each region, summarise the characteristics that have resulted in it being identified as a biodiversity hotspot. Present your summary as a short report and attach it to this page of your workbook.

Related activities: Loss of Biodiversity, Britain's Biodiversity

Britain's Biodiversity

The species is the basic unit by which we measure biodiversity. For some taxa, e.g. bacteria, the true extent of species diversity remains unidentified. Some data on species richness for the UK are shown below (note the bias towards large, conspicuous organisms). The biodiversity of the British Isles today is the result of a legacy of past climatic changes and a long history of human influence. Some of the most interesting, species-rich ecosystems, such as hedgerows, downland turf, and woodland, are maintained as a result of human activity. Many of the species characteristic of Britain's biodiversity are also found more widely in Europe. Other species (e.g. the Scottish crossbill), or species associations (e.g. bluebell woodlands) are uniquely British. With increasing pressure on natural areas from urbanisation, roading, and other human encroachment, maintaining species diversity is paramount and should concern us all today.

Peregrine falcon | Acorn barnacle | Bluebell woodland | Hedgehog
Hermit crab | Nuthatch | European otter | Red elf cup fungus
Red fox | Duke of Burgundy fritillary | Woodmouse | European badger
Oak (with gall) | Puffin | Common toad | Field vole

PHOTO CREDITS – see the front of the manual

Evolution and Biodiversity

Left: Fig. 1: British biodiversity, as numbers of terrestrial and freshwater species, compared with recent global estimates of described species in major taxonomic groups.

Major taxonomic group	Estimated no. of British species	Estimated no. of world species
Bacteria	*unknown*	> 4 000
Viruses	*unknown*	> 5 000
Protozoa	> 20 000	> 40 000
Algae	> 20 000	> 40 000
Fungi	> 15 000	> 70 000
Ferns and bryophytes	1 080	> 26 000
Lichens	1 500	> 17 000
Flowering plants	1 400	> 250 000
Invertebrate animals	> 28 500	> 1.28 million
Insects	22 500	> 1 million
Non-insect arthropods	> 3 000	> 190 000
All other invertebrates	> 3 000	> 90 000
Vertebrate animals	308	> 33 208
Fish (freshwater)	38	> 8 500
Amphibians	6	> 4 000
Reptiles	6	> 6 500
Birds (breeding residents)	210	9 881
Mammals	48	4 327

Source: Biodiversity: The UK Action Plan, 1994. HMSO

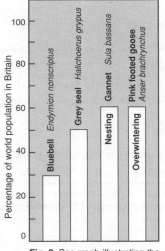

Fig. 2: Bar graph illustrating the percentage of world populations of various species permanently or temporarily resident in Britain.

Bluebell Endymion nonscriptus
Grey seal Halichoerus grypus
Gannet Sula bassana — Nesting
Pink footed goose Anser brachrynchus — Overwintering

Percentage of world population in Britain

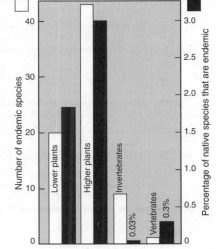

Fig 3: Bar graph illustrating the degree of endemism in Britain. Right axis indicates % endemism in relation to the number of described British native species.

Number of endemic species
Percentage of native species that are endemic

Lower plants | Higher plants | Invertebrates 0.03% | Vertebrates 0.3%

Related activities: Ecosystem Stability, Endangered Species, The Impact of Alien Species   **Web links**: Space for Species

RA 3

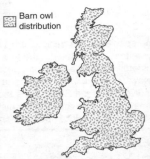
Barn owl distribution

Conservation of the barn owl (Tyto alba)

Status: The barn owl is one of the best known and widely distributed owl species in the world. It was once very common in Britain but has experienced severe declines in the last 50 years as a result of the combined impacts of habitat loss, changed farming practices, and increased sources of mortality.

Reasons for decline: Primarily, declines have been the result of changed farm management practices (e.g. increased land clearance and mechanisation) which have resulted in reduced prey abundance and fewer suitable breeding sites. Contributing factors include increases in road deaths as traffic speed and volume rises, and poorer breeding success and reduced chick survival as a result of pesticide bioaccumulation. In addition, more birds are drowned when attempting to bathe in the steep sided troughs which have increasingly replaced the more traditional shallow farm ponds.

Conservation management: A return to the population densities of 50 years ago is very unlikely, but current conservation measures have at least stabilised numbers. These involve habitat enhancement (e.g. provision of nest sites), reduction in pesticide use, and rearing of orphaned young followed by monitored release into suitable habitats.

Barn owls are predators of small mammals, birds, insects, and frogs. They are higher order consumers and, as such, have been badly affected by the bioaccumulation of pesticides in recent times. They require suitable nesting and bathing sites, and reliable sources of small prey.

Barn owls are widely distributed in Ireland and the UK, but numbers are not high.

Period of survey (England & Wales)	Breeding pairs (estimates)
1935	12 000
1968 – 1972	6000 – 9000
1983 – 1985	3800

1. Produce a pie graph below to show the proportions of British species in each taxonomic group (ignoring bacteria and viruses). Calculate the percentages from Fig. 1 (opposite) and tabulate the data (one has been completed for you). The chart has been marked in 5° divisions and each % point is equal to 3.6° on the pie chart. Provide a colour key in the space next to the tabulated figures. For the purposes of this exercise, use the values provided, ignoring the > sign:

Proportion of British species in different taxonomic groups

	Percentage of species in each taxon	Segment size	Key
Protozoa			
Algae			
Fungi			
Ferns and bryophytes			
Lichens			
Flowering plants			
Invertebrates	28 500 ÷ 87 788 X 100 = 32.5%	117°	⬛
Vertebrates			

2. Comment on the proportion of biodiversity within each taxonomic group: _____

3. (a) Contrast our knowledge of the biodiversity of bacteria and invertebrates with that of vertebrates: _____

(b) Suggest a reason for the difference: _____

4. Comment on the level of endemism in the UK and suggest a reason for it: _____

5. (a) Calculate the percentage decline in barn owls (England and Wales) over the 50 year period 1935 – 1985: _____

(b) Suggest why this species has been less difficult to stabilise against decline than other (more endangered) species: _____

Loss of Biodiversity

More than a third of the planet's known terrestrial plant and animal species are found within the biodiversity hotspot regions which cover only 1.4% of the Earth's land area. Unfortunately, biodiversity hotspots often occur near areas of dense human habitation and rapid human population growth. Most are located in the tropics and most are forests. Background (natural) extinction rates for all organisms (including bacteria and fungi) are estimated to be 10-100 species a year. The actual extinction rate is estimated to be 100-1000 times higher, mainly due to the effects of human activity. Over 41 000 species are now on the International Union for Conservation's (IUCN) red list, and 16 000 are threatened with extinction. Loss of biodiversity reduces the stability and resilience of natural ecosystems and decreases the ability of their communities to adapt to changing environmental conditions. Humans rely heavily on the biodiversity in nature and a loss of species richness has a deleterious effect on us all.

Insects make up 80% of all known animal species. There are an estimated 6-10 million insect species on Earth, but only 900,000 have been identified. Some 44 000 species may have become extinct over the last 600 years. The Duke of Burgundy butterfly (*Hamearis lucina*), right, is an endangered British species.

Just over 5% of the 8225 reptile species are at risk. These include the two tuatara species (right) from New Zealand, which are the only living members of the order Sphenodontia, and the critically endangered blue iguana. Only about 200 blue iguanas remain, all in the Grand Caymans.

	Total number of species*	Number of IUCN listed species
Plants	310 000 - 422,000	8474
Insects	6 -10 million	622
Fish	28 000	126
Amphibians	5743	1809
Reptiles	8225	423
Birds	10 000	1133
Mammals	5400	1027

* Estimated numbers

The giant panda (above), is one of many critically endangered terrestrial mammals, with fewer than 2000 surviving in the wild. Amongst the 120 species of marine mammals, approximately 25% (including the humpback whale and Hector's dolphin) are on the ICUN's red list.

Prior to the impact of human activity on the environment, one bird species became extinct every 100 years. Today, the rate is one every year, and may increase to 10 species every year by the end of the century. Some at risk birds, such as the Hawaiian crow (right), are now found only in captivity.

Current estimates suggest as many as 47% of plant species may be endangered. Some, such as the South African cycad *Encephalartos woodii* (above), is one of the rarest plants in the world. It is extinct in the wild and all remaining specimens are clones.

Threats to Biodiversity

Rainforests in some of the most species-rich regions of the world are being destroyed at an alarming rate as world demand for tropical hardwoods increases and land is cleared for the establishment of agriculture.

Illegal trade in species (for food, body parts, or for the exotic pet trade) is pushing some species to the brink of extinction. Despite international bans on trade, illegal trade in primates, parrots, reptiles, and big cats (among others) continues.

Pollution and the pressure of human populations on natural habitats threatens biodiversity in many regions. Environmental pollutants may accumulate through food chains or cause harm directly, as with this bird trapped in oil.

1. Discuss, in general terms, the effects of loss of biodiversity on an ecosystem: _____

_____

_____

_____

_____

Related activities: Global Biodiversity, Britain's Biodiversity, Tropical Deforestation

RA 2

Evolution and Biodiversity

Tropical Deforestation

Tropical rainforests prevail in places where the climate is very moist throughout the year (200 to 450 cm of rainfall per year). Almost half of the world's rainforests are in just three countries: **Indonesia** in Southeast Asia, **Brazil** in South America, and **Zaire** in Africa. Much of the world's biodiversity resides in rainforests. Destruction of the forests will contribute towards global warming through a large reduction in photosynthesis. In the Amazon, 75% of deforestation has occurred within 50 km of Brazil's roads. Many potential drugs could still be discovered in rainforest plants, and loss of species through deforestation may mean they will never be found. Rainforests can provide economically sustainable crops (rubber, coffee, nuts, fruits, and oils) for local people.

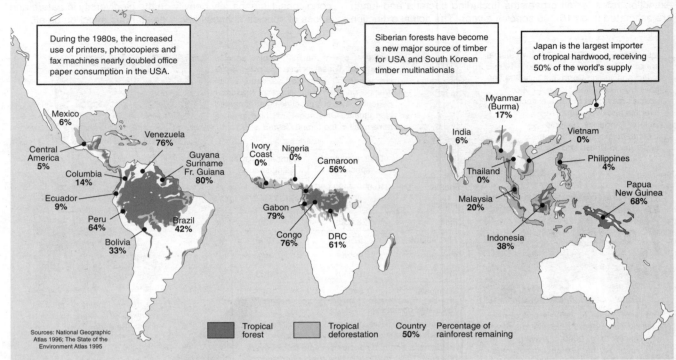

During the 1980s, the increased use of printers, photocopiers and fax machines nearly doubled office paper consumption in the USA.

Siberian forests have become a new major source of timber for USA and South Korean timber multinationals

Japan is the largest importer of tropical hardwood, receiving 50% of the world's supply

Mexico 6% · Central America 5% · Columbia 14% · Ecuador 9% · Peru 64% · Bolivia 33% · Venezuela 76% · Guyana Suriname Fr. Guiana 80% · Brazil 42% · Ivory Coast 0% · Nigeria 0% · Gabon 79% · Congo 76% · Camaroon 56% · DRC 61% · India 6% · Myanmar (Burma) 17% · Thailand 0% · Malaysia 20% · Indonesia 38% · Vietnam 0% · Philippines 4% · Papua New Guinea 68%

Sources: National Geographic Atlas 1996; The State of the Environment Atlas 1995

Tropical forest · Tropical deforestation · Country 50% · Percentage of rainforest remaining

The felling of rainforest trees is taking place at an alarming rate as world demand for tropical hardwoods increases and land is cleared for the establishment of agriculture. The resulting farms and plantations often have shortlived productivity.

Huge forest fires have devastated large amounts of tropical rainforest in Indonesia and Brazil in 1997/98. The fires in Indonesia were started by people attempting to clear the forest areas for farming in a year of particularly low rainfall.

The building of new road networks into regions with tropical rainforests causes considerable environmental damage. In areas with very high rainfall there is an increased risk of erosion and loss of topsoil.

1. Describe three reasons why tropical rainforests should be conserved:

   (a) _____

   (b) _____

   (c) _____

2. Identify the three main human activities that cause tropical deforestation and discuss their detrimental effects:

Agriculture and Diversity

The English countryside has been shaped by many hundreds of years of agriculture. The landscape has changed as farming practices evolved through critical stages. Farming has always had an impact on Britain's rich biodiversity (generally in a negative manner). Modern farming practices, such as increasing mechanisation and the move away from mixed farming operations, have greatly accelerated this decline. In recent years active steps to conserve the countryside, such as **hedgerow legislation**, policies to increase woodland cover, and schemes to promote environmentally sensitive farming practices are slowly meeting their objectives. Since 1990, expenditure on agri-environmental measures has increased, the area of land in organic farming has increased, and the overall volume of inorganic fertilisers and pesticides has decreased. The challenge facing farmers, and those concerned about the countryside, is to achieve a balance between the goals of production and conservation of diversity.

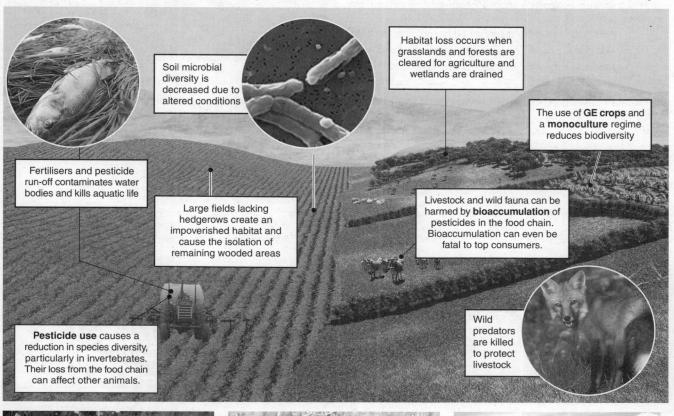

Soil microbial diversity is decreased due to altered conditions

Habitat loss occurs when grasslands and forests are cleared for agriculture and wetlands are drained

The use of **GE crops** and a **monoculture** regime reduces biodiversity

Fertilisers and pesticide run-off contaminates water bodies and kills aquatic life

Large fields lacking hedgerows create an impoverished habitat and cause the isolation of remaining wooded areas

Livestock and wild fauna can be harmed by **bioaccumulation** of pesticides in the food chain. Bioaccumulation can even be fatal to top consumers.

Pesticide use causes a reduction in species diversity, particularly in invertebrates. Their loss from the food chain can affect other animals.

Wild predators are killed to protect livestock

Evolution and Biodiversity

An increase in urban sprawl and the pressure on farmers to increase productivity are having a dramatic impact on the once common flowering plants of Britain's grasslands. Only through careful management and conservation of existing ecosystems will the diversity be maintained.

Conservation of grasslands is not only important for maintaining plant diversity Many birds, reptiles, invertebrates, and mammals rely on these ecosystems for food and shelter. A reduction in the diversity of grassland plant species translates to a reduction in the diversity of other species.

This woodland in Yorkshire, England, is home to numerous species of plants, animal and microbes. Clearing land for agriculture reduces both biodiversity and the ability of the community to adapt to changing environmental conditions. Natural ecosystem stability is decreased as a result.

1. One solution to the conflicting needs of conserving biodiversity and productivity is to intensively farm designated areas, leaving other areas for conservation. From the farmer's perspective, outline two advantages of this approach:

(a) _____

_____

(b) _____

_____

(c) Describe a disadvantage of this management approach: _____

_____

Related activities: Britain's Biodiversity, Loss of Biodiversity

RA 2

The Hedgerow Issue

A particularly significant factor of landscape change in recent years has been the amalgamation of fields and the removal of traditional hedgerows. Many traditional, mixed farms (right), which required hedgerows to contain livestock, have been converted to arable farms, and fields have become larger to accommodate modern machinery. In Britain, this conversion has resulted in the loss of thousands of kilometres of hedgerows each year.

Hedgerows are ecologically important because they increase the diversity of wildlife by:

- Providing food and habitats for birds and other animals.
- Acting as corridors, along which animals can move.
- Providing habitat for predators of pest species.

2. From an environmental perspective, outline two advantages of using hedgerows as a form of farm fencing:

(a) _____

(b) _____

3. From the perspective of the farmer, outline two disadvantages of using hedgerows:

(a) _____

(b) _____

Diversity of Wild Farmland Bird Populations in the UK, 1970 - 1999.

The hawfinch *(Coccothraustes coccothraustes)* is a common, but often hidden, member of the woodland communities in Britain.

Diversity Index (1970 = 100) plotted against *Year* (1970–1999).

Modified from: The Countryside Agency -State of the Countryside 2001 Report.

Populations of wild farmland bird species, because of their wide distribution and position near the top of the food chain, provide good indicators of the state of other wildlife species and of environmental health in general. Over the last 25 years, there has been a marked net decline in the diversity of farmland bird populations. However, since 1986, diversity has ceased to decline further and, in recent years, has actually showed an increase.

4. Suggest two possible reasons for this decline:

(a) _____

(b) _____

5. List three initiatives local and national government have implemented in an attempt to reverse this decline:

_____

_____

_____

_____

_____

Measuring Diversity

Measurements of biodiversity have essentially two components: **species richness**, which describes the number of species, and **species evenness**, which quantifies how equally the community composition is distributed. Both are important, especially when rarity is a reflection of how threatened a species is in an environment. Information about the biodiversity of ecosystems is obtained through **sampling** the ecosystem in a manner that provides a fair (unbiased) representation of the organisms present and their distribution. This is usually achieved through

random sampling, a technique in which every possible sample of a given size has the same chance of selection. Measures of biodiversity are commonly used as the basis for making conservation decisions and different measures of biodiversity may support different solutions. Often indicator species and species diversity indices are used as a way of quantifying biodiversity. Such indicators can be particularly useful when monitoring ecosystem change and looking for causative factors in species loss.

Quantifying the Diversity of Ecosystems

Reef community:
high density, clumped distribution

Measurements of biodiversity must be appropriate to the community being investigated. Communities in which the populations are at low density and have a random or clumped distribution will require a different sampling strategy to those where the populations are uniformly distributed and at higher density. There are many sampling options (below), each with advantages and drawbacks for particular communities. How would you estimate the biodiversity of this reef community?

 Random point sampling

 Point sampling: systematic grid

 Line and belt transects

 Random quadrats

 Marine ecologists use quadrat sampling to estimate biodiversity prior to works such as dredging.

 Line transects are appropriate to estimate biodiversity along an environmental gradient.

Keystone Species in Ecosystems

The stability of an ecosystem refers to its apparently unchanging nature over time, something that depends partly on its ability to resist and recover from disturbance. Ecosystem stability is closely linked to biodiversity, and more biodiverse systems tend to be more stable, partly because the many species interactions that sustain them act as a buffer against change. Some species are more influential than others in the stability of an ecosystem because of their pivotal role in some ecosystem function such as nutrient recycling or productivity. Such species are called **keystone species** because of their disproportionate effect on ecosystem function.

The **European beaver**, *Castor fiber*, was originally distributed throughout most of Europe and northern Asia but populations have been decimated as a result of both hunting and habitat loss. The beaver is a keystone species; where they occur, beavers are critical to ecosystem function and a number of species depend partly or entirely on beaver ponds for survival. Their tree-felling activity is akin to a natural coppicing process and promotes vigorous regrowth, while historically they helped the spread of alder (a water-loving species) in Britain.

Evolution and Biodiversity

1. (a) Distinguish between the two measures of biodiversity: species richness and species evenness:

(b) Explain why it is important to consider both these measures when considering species conservation:

Calculation and Use of Diversity Indices

One of the best ways to determine the health of an ecosystem is to measure the variety (rather than the absolute number) of organisms living in it. Certain species, called **indicator species**, are typical of ecosystems in a particular state (e.g. polluted or pristine). An objective evaluation of an ecosystem's biodiversity can provide valuable insight into its status, particularly if the species assemblages have changed as a result of disturbance.

Diversity can be quantified using a **diversity index (DI)**. Diversity indices attempt to quantify the degree of diversity and identify indicators for environmental stress or degradation. Most indices of diversity are easy to use and they are widely used in ecological work, particularly for monitoring ecosystem change or pollution. One example, which is a derivation of **Simpson's index**, is described below. Other indices produce values ranging between 0 and almost 1. These are more easily interpreted because of the more limited range of values, but no single index offers the "best" measure of diversity: they are chosen on their suitability to different situations.

Simpson's Index for finite populations

This diversity index (DI) is a commonly used inversion of Simpson's index, suitable for finite populations.

$$DI = \frac{N(N - 1)}{\Sigma n(n - 1)}$$

After Smith and Smith as per IOB.

Where:

DI = Diversity index
N = Total number of individuals (of all species) in the sample
n = Number of individuals of each species in the sample

This index ranges between 1 (low diversity) and infinity. The higher the value, the greater the variety of living organisms. It can be difficult to evaluate objectively without reference to some standard ecosystem measure because the values calculated can, in theory, go to infinity.

Example of species diversity in a stream

The example describes the results from a survey of stream invertebrates. The species have been identified, but this is not necessary in order to calculate diversity as long as the different species can be distinguished. Calculation of the DI using Simpson's index for finite populations is:

Species	No. of individuals
A (Common backswimmer)	12
B (Stonefly larva)	7
C (Silver water beetle)	2
D (Caddis fly larva)	6
E (Water spider)	5
Total number of individuals = 32	

$$DI = \frac{32 \times 31}{(12 \times 11) + (7 \times 6) + (2 \times 1) + (6 \times 5) + (5 \times 4)} = \frac{992}{226} = 4.39$$

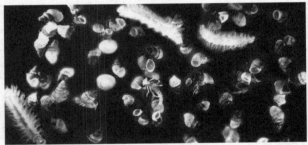

A stream community with a high macroinvertebrate diversity (above) in contrast to a low diversity stream community (below).

2. Describe two necessary considerations in attempting to make an unbiased measurement of biodiversity:

_____

_____

3. Explain why high biodiversity is generally associated with greater ecosystem stability: _____

_____

_____

4. Explain why the loss of a keystone species could be particularly disturbing for ecosystem diversity:

_____

_____

5. Describe a situation where a species diversity index may provide useful information: _____

_____

6. An area of forest floor was sampled and six invertebrate species were recorded, with counts of 7, 10, 11, 2, 4, and 3 individuals. Using Simpson's index for finite populations, calculate DI for this community:

(a) DI= _____   DI = _____

(b) Comment on the diversity of this community: _____

_____

Photo: Stephen Moore

Index

ABO blood group 134
Absorption, nutrients 70
Acquired immunity 148
Activation energy 61
Active transport 97, 101-102
Agriculture, effect on biodiversity 245
Alveoli 107-108
Amino acid 57-58
 - coding table 172
 - comparisons 235
 - condensation 58
 - hydrolysis 58
Anabolic reaction 62
Aneurysm 127
Angiosperm classification 233
Animal
 - cells 73-74
 - gas exchange in 207-212
 - tissues 200-201
Antibiotics 237
 - resistance 239
Antibodies 145
Antigenic
 - drift 147
 - shift 147
 - variability 147
Antigens, blood group 134
Apoplastic pathway 225
Appendicitis 69
Arteries 218
Arterioles 218
Assumptions 17
Asthma 113
Atherosclerosis 127
Arterial system 217
Atrioventricular node 121

Bacteria,
 - cell structure 79
 - effect of antibiotics 237
Bar graphs 26
Base pairing, of DNA 167
B-cell 143
Behaviour, animal 229
Benedicts test for sugar 54
Binomial classification 231-232
Biochemical tests 54
Biodiversity 240-246
 - and agriculture 245
 - Britain's 241-242
 - global 240
 - loss of 243
Biological drawings 41-42
Biology and disease 50
Biuret test for protein 54
Blood
 - clotting 139
 - composition of 135-136
 - flow, effect of exercise 125-126
 - group antigens 134
 - pressure 120
 - supply, to heart 119
 - types 134
 - vessels 204, 218-221
Body's defences 137
Bohr effect 190
Brassica 184
Breathing 106
Bronchi 107
Bronchioles 107
Bundle of His 121

Cancer
 - formation of 195
 - lung 115
 - risk factors 195
Capillaries 219
Carbohydrates 55-56
 - condensation 55
 - hydrolysis 55
Cardiac
 - cycle 123
 - output 121
Cardiovascular disease 127-128
Catabolic reaction 62
Cell cycle 193-194
 - and cancer 195
 - in yeast 194

Cell
 - animal 73-74
 - bacterial 79
 - differentiation, humans 196
 - eukaryotic 75
 - fractionation 85
 - intestinal 73
 - organelles 73, 77-78
 - prokaryotic 79-80
 - size 76
 - structures 86-88
 - types 196
Cell-mediated immune response 143
Cell specialisation
 - in humans 197
 - in plants 198
Cell walls, plants 188
Cellular processes 90
Cellulose 55
Chloroplasts 188
Cholera, membrane permeability 103
Cholesterol, and CVD 127
Chromatin 163
Chromatography 54
Chromosome
 - eukaryote 163-164
 - prokaryote 162
Cigarette smoke 115-116
Circulatory system, of fish 211
Citation, of references 47-48
Cladistics 230
Classification
 - hedgehogs 232
 - plants 233
 - systems 231-232
Clonal selection 144
Closed circulatory system 211
Clotting, of blood 139
Codon 172, 173
Cofactors 64
Collenchyma tissue 202
Compartmentation 95
Complex tissue 202
Compound microscope 81
Concentration gradient 98
Condensation reaction,
 - of amino acids 58
 - of carbohydrates 56
 - of lipids 91
 - of nucleotides 166
Connective tissue 201
Conservation, of the barn owl 242
Continuous variation 158
Control
 - experimental 14
 - of digestion 71
 - of heart activity 121-122
 - of heart beat 122
Controlled variables 14, 17
Countercurrent flow 212
Courtship behaviour 229
Crop plants 183-184
Crossing over 176-177
Cytochrome C 235
Cytokinesis 193

Data 22
 - analysis 37-40
 - distribution of 37-38
 - measuring spread in 38
 - presentation 25
 - transformation 23
Defence system 133
Deforestation 244
Denaturation, of protein 59
Denaturation of enzymes 63
Dependent variable 14, 17
Dermal tissue, of plants 202
Descriptive statistics 37-38
Diastole 123
Dicot, root structure 222
Differential centrifugation 85
Diffusion 97, 98, 204, 205
Digestion, control of 71
Digestive
 - enzymes 68
 - tract, human 65-66
Dinucleotide 166

Disaccharide 55
Discontinuous variation 158
Discussion writing 46
Disease
 - and public health 155-156
 - asthma 113
 - cardiovascular 127-128
 - causes of 51
 - of exchange systems 51
 - respiratory 113-117
 - smoking 113, 115-116
 - tuberculosis 117
 - types 51
Dissecting microscope 81
Distribution of data 37-38
Diversity
 - index 248
 - in dogs 179
 - measurement of 247-248
DNA
 - hybridisation 233
 - replication 191-192
 - junk 171
 - sizes 171
 - structure 165-166
DNA molecule, construction 167-170
Dog, evolution of 228
Domains 227
Drawings, biological 41-42
Drug resistance 238-239

Electrocardiogram (ECG) 123
Electron micrographs, 87-88
Electron microscopes 83-84
Emphysema 113
Emulsion test for lipids 54
Endocytosis 97, 102
Environmentally induced variation 158, 159
Enzyme(s) 61-64
 - activity 61
 - cofactors 64
 - denaturation 63
 - digestive 68
 - reaction rates 63
 - inhibitors 64
 - in DNA replication 191-192
Epidemiology 155
Epithelial tissue 201
Erythrocytes 135
Essential amino acid 57
Eukaryote chromosome 163-164
Eukaryotic cell, types of 75
Evidence for phylogeny 233-235
Evolution, of drug resistance 238-239
Exchange surface 105, 108
Exchange systems, and disease 51
Exercise, and blood flow 125-126
Exercise, and health 129-130
Exocytosis 97, 102
Experimental method 19
Expiration 106

Facilitated diffusion 97, 98
Fats 91
Fatty acids 91
Fever 142
Fibrosis 113
Fibrous protein 60
Fick's law 105
Fish gills 211
Fluid mosaic model 93
Food tests 54
Forced breathing 106
Founder effect 180
Fractionation, of cells 85

Gamete formation 176
Gas Exchange 105, 111
 - in amphibians 207
 - in animals 207-212
 - in aquatic insects 210
 - in birds 207
 - in fish 211-212
 - in freshwater 210
 - in insects 207, 209
 - in plants 213-214
Gas transport, human 111

Genetic code 172
Genetic Diversity 179, 240
Genetic drift 180, 181, 182
Genetic gain, in cattle 186
Genetic variation 158
Genome 161
Gills, 211
Globular protein 60
Glucose transport 101
Glycogen 55
Graph
 - interpretation of 33
 - presentation 26-34
 - types of 26-34
Guard cell 213-214

Haemoglobin 59, 111, 189-190
Halophyte 215-216
Health 51
Health statistics 155
Health, benefits of exercise 129-130
Heart
 - activity 121-122
 - beat, control of 122
 - structure of, human 119-120
Hedgehog classification 232
Hedgerow legislation 245-246
Hepatic portal system 70
Histograms 27
Homologous chromosome 174, 176, 193
Horizontal gene transfer 239
Hormones, role in digestion 71
Hot spot, biodiversity 240
Human
 - digestive tract 65-66
 - heart 124
 - respiratory system 107-108
Humoral response 143
Hydrolysis
 - of amino acids 58
 - of carbohydrates 56
Hypertonic solution 100
Hypothesis
 - forming 15
 - types 16
Hypotonic solution 100

Immune response, types of 143-144
Immune system 143-144
Immunisation 149-150
Immunity
 - acquired 148
 - passive 148
Immunoglobulins 145
Immunological comparisons 234
Immunology 234
Inbreeding 185
Independent assortment 174
Independent variable 14, 17
Induced fit model 61
Infectious disease 51
Inflammation 141
Influenza 147
Influenzavirus, genetic variability 147
Inhibitors of enzymes 64
Inspiration 106
Intestinal cell 73
Intestine
 - large 69
 - small 67
Intron 171
Investigations flow chart 35-36
Iodine test for starch 54
Ion pump 97, 101
Irreversible enzyme inhibitors 64
Isomer
 - amino acids 58
 - carbohydrate 56

Junk DNA 171

Keystone species 247
Kingdom systems 227
Kite graphs 29

Large intestine 69
Leucocytes 135

Line breeding 185
Line graphs 30-33
Line of best fit 34
Lipids 91-92
- functions of 92
Lock and key model 61
Loss of biodiversity 243
Lung 107
- cancer 115
- volume 109
Lung function, measuring 109-110
Lymphocytes 143

Macromolecule synthesis 96
Magnification 81
Major histocompatibility complex 133
Maltose hydrolysis 55
Mammalian circulatory system 217
Mating behaviour 229
Mass flow 204
Mass transport 204
Mean (average) of data 37
Median of data 37
Meiosis 174-175
- non-disjunction 175
Membrane
- role of 95
- structure 93
- transport 97-102
Membrane bound organelles 93
Meristematic tissue 199
Mesophyll 213
Methods writing 44
Microbiota, natural 133
Microscope
- comparison of types 84
- electron 83-84
- optical 81-82
Microscopy 81-84
- images 86-88
- stains 82
Microvilli 68, 73-74
Mineral uptake, in plants 225
Mitosis 193-194
Mode of data 37
Molecular clock 233, 235
Monoclonal antibodies 153-154
Monosaccharide 55
MRSA 238
Muscle tissue 201
Mutation 158
Myocardial infarction 127
Myoglobin 111

Nervous tissue 201
Non-disjunction at meiosis 175
Non-infectious disease 51
Notation, scientific 14
Nucleic acid 165
Nucleotide, condensation 166
Null hypothesis 15, 16
Nutrient absorption and transport 70

Obstructive lung disease 113-114
Oils 91
Optical microscope 81-82
Oral rehydration solution 103
Osmosis 97, 99-100
Outcrossing 185
Oxygen transport 190

Palisade cell 188
Parallel current flow 212
Parenchyma tissue 202
Passive
- smoking 115
- transport 97, 98-100
Pathogen 51-52
- genetic variability 147
Peristalsis 66
Phagocytes, action of 140
Phagocytosis 97, 102
Phenotype 158, 179
Phospholipids 91
Phylogeny 230
- evidence for 233-235
Pie graphs 28
Pinocytosis 97, 102
Plasmolysis, of plant cells 100
Planning an investigation 17
Plant
- adaptations of 215-216

- cell walls 188
- chloroplasts 188
- classification 233
- gas exchange 213-214
- root structure 222
- tissue 200, 202
- transpiration 223-224
Plasma membrane 93
Plasmid 162
Poisons 64
Polypeptide chain 57
Polysaccharide 55
Population bottlenecks 181
Portal system 217
Poster structure 43
Potometer 224
Prediction 15
Pregnancy testing 154
Pressure potential 99
Prezygotic mechanism 229
Prokaryotic
- cell 79-80
- chromosome 162
Protein 59-60
- comparison of 235
- denaturation 59
- fibrous 60
- globular 60
- homology 235
- structure 59
Proton pump 101
Public health and disease 155-156
Pulmonary
- circulatory system 217
- ventilation rate 109

QRS complex 123
Qualitative data 22
Quantitative data 22
Quiet breathing 106

Range, of data 37
Recording results 21
Red blood cells 135
Replication, in experiments 20
Report
- checklist 49
- writing 43
Resistance 137
Resolution 81
Respiratory
- disease 113-117
- membrane 107
- pigments 111, 189-190
Respiratory system, human 107-108
Restrictive lung disease 113-114
Results writing 45
Reversible enzyme inhibitors 64
Rf value 54
RNA structure 165
Root
- hairs 222
- structure of 222
- uptake at 225
Root cells, development of 199

SA:V ratio 205-206
Sample variability 39-40
Sampling 39, 247
SARS 156
Saturated fatty acids 91
Scanning electron microscope 83
Scatter plots 34
Scientific method 15
Scientific notation 14
Sclerenchyma tissue 202
Selective breeding
- in cattle 186
- in crop plants 183-184
- in dogs 179
- in domestic animals 185-186
Semi permeable membrane 99
Sewell-Wright effect 182
Simple tissue 202
Simpson's index 248
Sinoatrial node 121
Small intestine 67
Smoking related disease 113, 115-116
Sodium-potassium pump 101
Solute potential 99
Species
- concept 228

- diversity 240
- evenness 247
- richness 247
Species recognition, in courtship 229
Spirometry 109
Spontaneous resistance 239
Spiracle 209
Spirogram 110
Standard deviation 38, 39
Starch 55
Starling's law 121
Statistical analysis 36-40
Statistics, descriptive 37-38
Steroids 91
Stomach 67
Stomata 213-214
- control of opening 213-214
Surface area and volume 205-206
Symplastic pathway 225
Systemic circulatory system 217
Systole 123

Tables
- of results 21
- presentation of data 25
Taxonomy 230
T-cell 143
Terms, scientific 14
Tissue
- animal 200-201
- fluid 219-220
- organisation 200
- plant 200, 202
- transplant 133
- types 200-202
Toxicity, of antibiotics 237
Trachea 107
Tracheal
- gills 210
- system 209
Transcription unit 173
Translation 173
Transmission electron microscope 83
Transpiration 223-224
Transport
- across membranes 97-102
- of nutrients 70
- systems 204
Tree of life 227
Triplet code 173
Tube gut 66
Tuberculosis (TB) 117
Turgor, of plant cells 100

Unsaturated fatty acids 91

Vaccination 149-150
- UK schedule of 150
- against influenzavirus 147
Vaccine, types 151
Vacuolar pathway 225
Variables 14, 17
Variance 39
Variation 158-159
Variety of life 157
Vascular tissue, of plants 202
Veins 221
Venous system 217
Venules 221
Vertical gene transfer 239
Villi 67-68

Water potential 99-100
Water uptake, in plants 225
Wheat 183
White blood cells 135

Xerophytes 215-216

Yeast, cell cycle 194

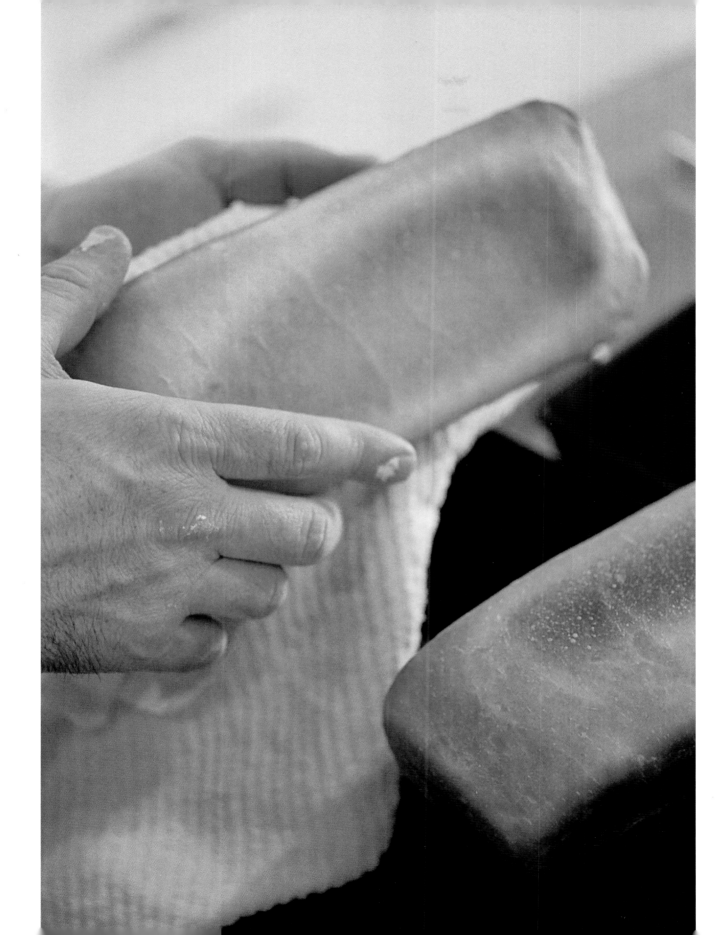

**shop-bought
loaf typically
contains**

wheatflour,
water,
yeast,
wheat protein,
salt,
vinegar,
dextrose,
soya flour,
vegetable fat,
emulsifier
E472e (mono-
and diacetyle
tartaric acid
esters of mono-
and diglycerides
of fatty acids),
flour treatment
agent E300
(absorbic acid),
preservative
calcium
propionate (to
inhibit mould
growth)

**home-made
loaf
contains**

flour,
yeast,
salt,
water

the dough

Each chapter that follows begins with a slightly different dough recipe and, from this 'parent' dough, you can bake a vast variety of styles of bread really easily. Just to keep things interesting, I have finished all but the Sweet Dough chapter with a slightly more challenging bread for you to try once you begin to feel comfortable with baking. Though the doughs vary the technique for making each one is identical.

Heating the oven

Your very first job is to preheat your oven to its highest temperature (250°C if possible – except for the Sweet Dough chapter, when the oven should start off a bit lower at 220°C) and put your baking stone or heavy baking tray (page 10) into the oven. Do this as early as you can, so that not only the oven, but the whole kitchen warms up – you'll find the dough is more responsive in a warm atmosphere.

For the Aga: with our recent move to Bath I have lost the gas oven in which all the bread for this book was baked and I have had to get used to an Aga. I was initially apprehensive but soon discovered some clear advantages: there is no need to preheat the oven and the kitchen is always at the perfect temperature for baking. To start with I put my baking stone directly onto the floor of the top oven, put an oven thermometer in to give me an accurate temperature reading and then adjust the control until I achieve a temperature of about 250°C. For most of the small loaves this has worked very well. When I tried larger loaves I found that they started to colour too quickly so I solved the problem by opening the door, so it is slightly ajar, to let some of the heat out, and then turning the loaf around a couple of times so it is evenly baked. I will continue to practice so I can include full Aga instructions in the next edition. I'm sure that the more I bake the more I will learn to trust it.

Weighing ingredients

Weigh all the ingredients carefully – I even weigh my water, as it is much more precise than trying to judge volume at eye level. You can see for yourself by measuring 350ml of water, then weighing it. Do it a few times and I bet that every time there will be a slight variation in the weight. In most cooking this would be neither here nor there, but in baking it is important to be accurate about your quantities.

Freezing bread

All of the breads in this book can be frozen, except for the Puff Ball. However, I would recommend you part-bake them first to retain freshness. Make sure the bread is thoroughly cool before freezing, wrap in greaseproof paper and seal in a plastic food bag. To use the bread, put into a cold oven, turned to 200°C – by the time the oven reaches the temperature (about 12–15 minutes) the loaves should be baked. If you are already using your oven or you have an Aga then just reduce the baking time to about 8–10 minutes. (Keep an eye on smaller breads that may take less time.) As an exception, breads made from sweet dough should always be fully baked before freezing. Defrost them fully at room temperature then reheat in a low oven (180°C) before serving.

make the dough

• Rub the yeast into the flour using your fingertips as if making a crumble until it disappears into the flour. Add the salt and then the water. Hold the bowl with one hand and mix the ingredients around with the other (or use the rounded end of your scraper) for 2–3 minutes until the dough starts to form.

• With the help of your plastic scraper, lift the dough onto your work surface. Even though the dough will feel quite soft and moist (and look like thick, sticky porridge) do not add any flour to the work surface.

add the water   mix the ingredients

lift out the dough   don't flour the surface

People are always amazed when I tell them that I work the dough by hand without flouring the work surface. Sometimes when I am giving breadmaking classes, to prove the point that you don't need any flour, I put some extra water into the dough, to make it really sticky. No one believes that it will really come together without flour, yet it does, simply by working it, stretching and folding, to trap the air inside. Think about it: if you continue adding flour at this stage – before you know it you can easily put another 100g into your dough, which will firm it up and change its make-up – then you are far more likely to end up with a 'brick'. If you work the dough without flour it allows you to keep the dough softer, so the finished bread is lighter, more airy and exciting.

work the dough

• Begin to work the dough. The idea is to stretch it and get as much air into it as possible. Forget the way you have probably been taught to knead the dough, by pummelling it with the heel of your hands and rotating it. The way to work it is to slide your fingers underneath it like a pair of forks[1], with your thumbs on top[2], swing it upwards and then slap it back down, away from you, onto your work surface (it will almost be too sticky to lift at this point)[3]. Stretch the front of the dough towards you, then lift it back over itself in an arc (to trap the air)[4], still stretching it forwards and sideways and tucking it in around the edges. Keep repeating this sequence[5]. At first this might seem to be too much to think about, but once you get the hang of it, you will find that you can work the dough easily in one quick, seamless movement[6/7]. The DVD will help with this.

1

2

3

4

5

6

• As you work the dough it will start to come together and feel alive and elastic in your hands[8]. Keep on working it until it comes cleanly away from the work surface[9], begins to look silky and feels smooth, firm-but-wobbly and responsive – you'll understand what I mean, when you feel it for yourself. I promise you the fascination with dough starts here! Once you get used to this technique, it should only take around 5 minutes, as opposed to 10–15 minutes of traditional kneading.

7

8

9

• Now you can flour your work surface lightly, place the dough on top and form it into a ball by folding each edge in turn into the centre[10] of the dough and pressing down well with your thumb, rotating the ball as you go[11]. Turn the whole ball over and stretch and tuck the edges under[12]. You will come across this technique in various stages throughout recipes – in each case follow this folding method. If the recipe calls for you to make a 'tight ball', then fold in a few more times into the centre.

10

11

12

If using a mixer with a dough hook

• Put the flour into your mixer bowl and rub in the yeast. Switch the mixer onto the slowest speed, add the salt and then the water and mix for 2 minutes, then turn up to the next slowest speed and mix for a further 6-7 minutes until the dough becomes smooth and elastic. Remove the dough from the bowl, transfer to a lightly floured surface and mould into a ball (page 25).

resting the dough

• Whichever method you use, once the dough has been mixed or worked lightly, flour the inside of your mixing bowl and put the ball of dough into it. Cover with a tea towel and rest in a draught-free place (page 14). Leave the dough for around 1 hour, until it is roughly double in volume – don't worry if this happens a bit quicker or takes a little longer, as the dough will react slightly differently according to the temperature of your kitchen. (A few of the recipes require you to rest the dough for a shorter or longer time anyway, so check before you start.) Once the dough has nearly doubled in volume, you are ready to carry on with whatever recipe you choose.

Note: In some of the recipes for flavoured bread you will need to incorporate extra ingredients – fruit, nuts, spices, etc. – at the end of working the dough by hand or mixing in a mixer, before resting, so check with the recipe you want to make before starting to make the dough. Having made your own wonderful, wholesome dough, make sure that when you flavour it you do it justice, by adding really good-quality ingredients.

keeping the dough going (making a ferment)

If you keep back a 200g piece of dough when you make your first batch of bread, you can leave it in the fridge, 'refreshing it' from time to time, to develop its flavour. Then you can add it to your next batch of dough to enhance it, keep back another 200g piece of that dough, and so on… that way you add more flavour and character to your dough and bread every time you bake. When you keep back your dough, put it in a bowl in the fridge, covered with clingfilm, leave it for 2 days, and add the same amount of water (200g) and double its weight of flour (400g). Mix well until you have a firm dough, then put it back in the fridge. If you aren't going to be baking for a while, refresh it every 7–10 days. To save your fridge from being over-run by growing dough, keep back 200g (throw away the rest) and again add the same amount of water and double the weight of flour and mix it in. Some people say you should leave the dough in ambient conditions, but if you keep it in the fridge you can control the temperature much better. You are in charge, not the dough. And as you become more confident and bake more regularly, you can increase the amount of dough you refresh so you can bake bigger batches of bread. Larger quantities of dough will mature more slowly so you can leave more time between feeding. I keep up to 2kg in my fridge, so if I go on holiday for two weeks I don't have to worry that it will have 'died' in the meantime – or take it with me in my suitcase. Don't laugh – I know people who have done it. I imagine them checking into their hotel, 'Yes there is me, my wife, my kids…and my ferment!'

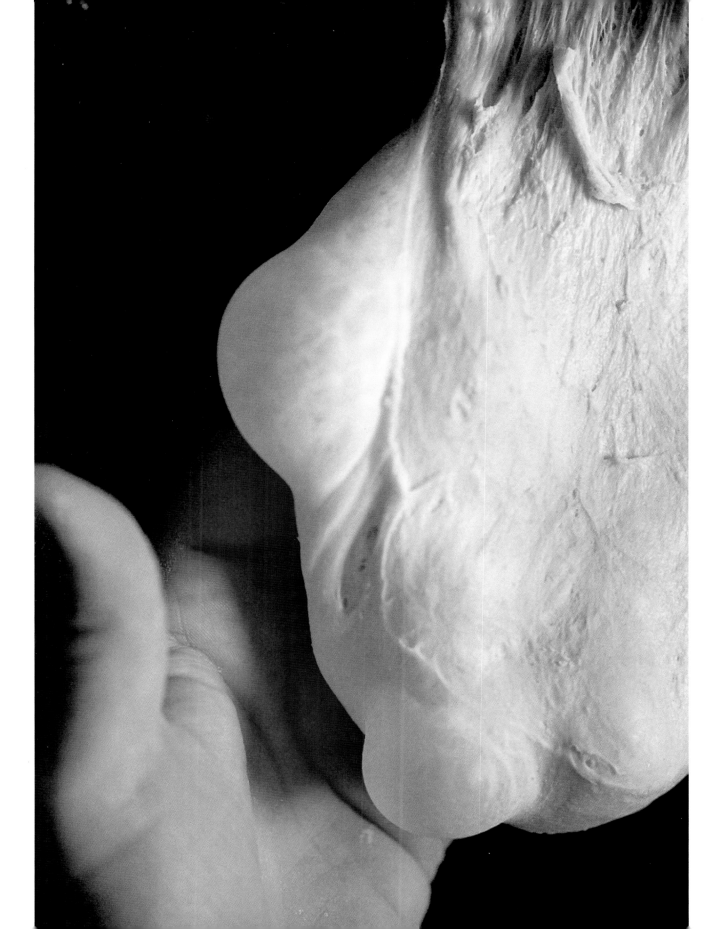

to roll into small balls

• After you have rested the dough, turn it out onto your surface. Divide into three. Flatten the dough with the heel of your hand into a rough oval shape. Fold one side of the flattened dough into the middle and use the heel of your hand to press it down and seal, then fold the other side into the middle and again press down firmly to seal. Finally fold in half lengthways so you end up with a long sausage shape and seal the long edge. By folding and pressing in this way – a technique that is repeated for many of the breads that are 'moulded' (shaped) – you give the dough extra strength and 'backbone'. Turn over so it is seam-side-down.

• Cut the log of dough into equal pieces as required for each recipe. To make these into small balls, you start off by using the same technique as for forming the worked dough into a ball before resting (page 25), i.e. fold each edge in turn into the centre of the dough and press down well with your thumb or fingers, rotating the ball as you go. If the recipe calls for a 'tight ball' fold into the centre a few more times. Turn the ball over and roll it in the palm of your hand, smoothing and easing the edges underneath.

to shape into long rolls

• Form each piece into balls (page 28). Flatten each ball into a circle with your fingers, then repeat the folding technique: fold one third into the centre and press down and seal with the side of your thumb, or heel of your hand, whichever feels more comfortable. Fold in the opposite third and seal again. Fold the roll in half lengthwise and seal the two sides together. Finally seal both ends. With the seam underneath, roll the dough evenly with your hands, easing the ends outwards, so that they become pointed.

to shape into loaves

• The technique is the same as for shaping rolls, except you will be using one big ball of dough or two, according to the recipe. First flatten the ball of dough a little with the heel of your hand. Fold one edge into the centre and press down with the heel of your hand. Fold the other edge over into the centre and press down again. Fold over in half and then press down again firmly to seal the edges. Turn over and place (seam-side-down) on a wooden peel or baking tray or in a greased loaf tin according to the recipe.

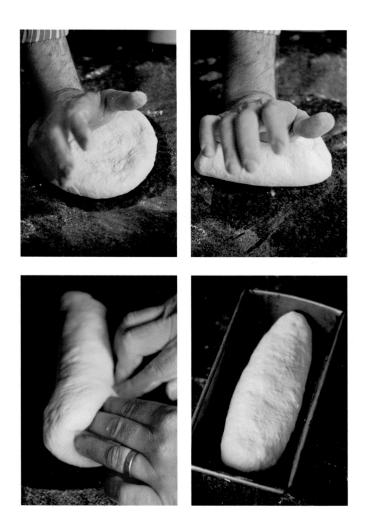

small breads are more fun...

When you make bread for the first time, I always suggest that you try some small breads first because if you make one big loaf and it collapses, you may never give it a go again. Small breads are more fun. So begin with the simplest dough of all, white dough, and I would suggest trying the fougasse – one of the easiest breads to make, and one of the biggest hits in my bread class.

1. White Dough

white: innocent, untainted

What is white dough? Flour, water, salt and yeast; that's all. This is the simplest, most fundamental dough you can make. But from just four basic elements, what possibilities, what endless variations, what fun... I never stop being amazed at how much you can do with four everyday ingredients. There is something so satisfying, addictive even, about experimenting with white dough. Even my son gets excited about making this bread with his dad.

10g Yeast (fresh if possible)
500g Strong bread flour
10g Salt
350g Water (or 350ml – you can use a measuring jug, but weighing is more accurate – page 20)

Remember to preheat the oven to 250°C. Rub the yeast into the flour using your fingertips as if making a crumble. Add the salt and water. Hold the bowl with one hand and mix the ingredients around with the other (or use the rounded end of your scraper) for 2–3 minutes until the dough starts to form. Make the dough according to the method on pages 22–23, but check your recipe to see if you need to add any other ingredients at this stage. Here is a reminder of the four stages of working the dough (pages 24–25).

1. Slide your fingers underneath with your thumbs on top.

2. Swing the dough upwards then slap it down away from you.

3. Stretch the front of the dough towards you.

4. Lift it back over itself in an arc to trap in the air.

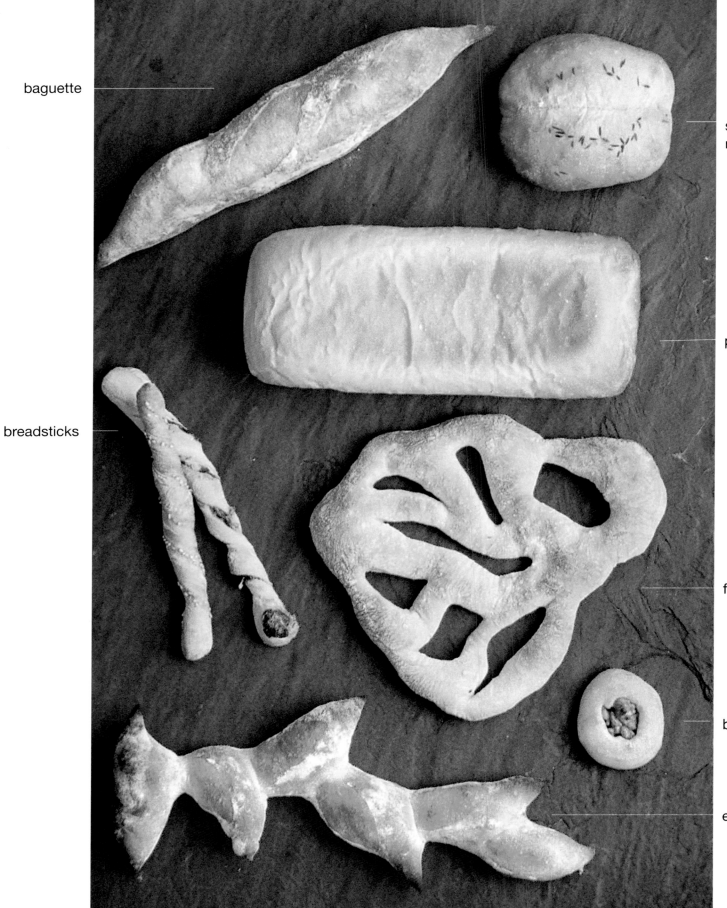

baguette

saffron roll

pain de

breadsticks

fougass

breadsh

epi

lemon
roll

layered roll

gruyère &
cumin loaf

spicy
roccan
roll

puff ball

façon
aucaire

fougasse

When I teach people to make bread this is always one of the first recipes I get them to try because fougasses are simple, and yet so smart and impressive looking, with a texture that is crunchy on the outside and soft inside. When they come out of the oven I see everyone wearing what I call, 'the fougasse grin' that says, 'Look what I've made!'

In all cookery, what goes around comes around as fashions constantly change. The contemporary-looking fougasses that you see are in fact just a reincarnation of an idea that has been around for a very long time. The original fougasse is a flatbread that belongs to the same family as focaccia – the word comes from the Latin word *focus* which means hearth – because the breads, which were like pancakes, were cooked under the cinders in the hearth.

I like to use maize flour for dusting this bread as it gives the crust a rich golden colour and creates the impression that the fougasse has been baked in a wood-fired oven. You can make fougasses with olive, rye or brown dough, too.

Quantity:	Makes 6 fougasses
Preparation:	20 minutes
Resting:	1 hour
Baking:	10–12 minutes

1 Batch White dough (page 33) rested for 1 hour

200g White or maize flour for dusting

To make

• Flour your work surface well. Use the rounded end of your plastic scraper to release the dough from the bowl, so that you can scoop it out easily in one piece and transfer it to the work surface without stretching it. Be careful not to deflate the dough when handling it but let it spread out to cove a square of your work surface. Generously flour the top of the dough.

• Using the flat edge of your scraper, cut the dough into two rectangles, and then cut each piece again into three roughly rectangular pieces. Again handle the dough as gently as you can so that it stays as light and full of air as possible. Keep the pieces well-floured.

• Take one of the pieces of dough and use the flat edge of your scraper to make a large diagonal cu across the centre, making sure that you don't go right to the edges of the dough, but cut all the way through the dough on to your work surface. Then make three smaller diagonal cuts fanning out on each side of the central one. Put your fingers into the slits and gently open them out to form holes. Be bold. In my classes, sometimes people try to make complicated patterns with lots of little cuts but of course when the dough bakes, they will close up. It is better to make fewer cuts and really open out the holes.

• Lift onto a lightly floured wooden peel or flat-edged baking tray and from here slide onto the hot baking stone or upturned tray in the preheated oven. Do this as quickly as possible, to avoid letting heat out of the oven. Using a water spray, mist the inside of the oven with water just before closing the door. Turn the heat down to 230°C and bake for 10–12 minutes until golden brown.

Variations: After the dough has been worked by hand or mixed, just before you leave it to rest, add some halved olives (buy good-quality ones with the stone in, and take the stone out yourself), roasted peppers, roasted onions, or just press some fresh rosemary or thyme leaves into each fougasse before baking.

Part-baking for the freezer: If you want to freeze your fougasse, 3/4-bake them for 6–7 minutes, then remove them from the oven, cool, wrap in freezer bags and freeze. To use, bake from frozen at 180–200°C for 12 minutes.

puff balls

These crispy thin balls of dough are a play on the classic idea of a salad with croûtons – but this way the bread is actually encasing the salad, which can be as simple as aromatic leaves and herbs, or if you want to be smart you could add some shaved truffle. The idea is to crack open the tops, like boiled eggs. The salad will spring out from the inside – I promise you, it always gets a good reaction!

   Remember that whatever you use as a filling shouldn't have any dressing, or the puff ball will become soggy. You can serve the dressing separately, for everyone to add once the puff balls are cracked open. This should give enough dough to make about 20 good-sized puff balls, but when you make them the first time, expect to break a few. Hopefully, you will end up with at least 10 perfect ones – you can use the broken ones as 'crisps' with some dipping sauces. With practice you can try shaping the dough into pillows or squares, rather than balls, or even make bite-sized ones for parties.

Quantity:	20 puff balls, or 10 puff balls and a bowlful of 'bread crisps'	**1 Batch** White dough (page 33) rested for 20 minutes	
Preparation:	20 minutes	Plain white flour for dusting	
Resting:	25 minutes	Salad of your choice	
Baking:	3–4 minutes		

To make

• Use the rounded end of your plastic scraper to scoop the dough from the bowl and use the flat edge to divide it into equal pieces (about 40g each).

• Round each piece of dough into a small ball (page 28), cover with a tea towel and leave to rest for a further 5 minutes.

• Make sure there are no tiny pieces of dried dough on your work surface or rolling pin, as any particles that get into the dough will stop it from puffing up. Dust your work surface with some flour – sieve it first, for the same reason.

• Roll out each piece of dough into a disc, turning it over a few times, and flouring well as you go. Continue rolling until the dough is really thin (1–2mm thick).

• You will need to bake the puff balls one or two at a time, depending on the size of your oven, so slide the first one or two onto a wooden peel or flat-edged baking tray, and use this to transfer the dough onto the baking stone or upturned tray in the preheated oven. Bake for about 3–4 minutes. The puff balls should inflate very quickly and are ready when they are completely puffed up, golden brown and sound hollow if you tap them (very!) gently with your finger.

• Carefully remove each one from the oven and cool on a wire rack. The puff balls are at their best about 3–4 hours after baking, but can be kept for a couple of days in an airtight tin. Don't store in a plastic bag or they will soften.

To serve

At the last minute, brush a small circle of the base with water to soften the crust, then carefully cut out this softened disc with a sharp knife. Just before serving push a good quantity of salad gently into each puff ball. Let everyone break the tops with a spoon or fork, and the salad will spring out.

Note: You can roll and bake in a continual process, rolling out one ball, putting it in the oven, then rolling out the next as the first one bakes, and so on.

bread shots

These are tiny pieces of dough, which make unusual little canapés to pass around with drinks. You simply roll out the pieces into little balls – try to do it as tightly as possible – then press your finger, or the end of a wooden spoon handle, into the centre to make a well, so that you can put in a filling such as cheese, pesto or even a walnut half or olive. When you leave the balls to prove, the dough will rise up around the filling.

Quantity:	About 30 bread shots
Preparation:	20 minutes
Resting:	1¼ hours
Proving:	45 minutes
Baking:	8–10 minutes

1 Batch White dough (page 33) rested for 1 hour
Flour for dusting
A little olive oil for greasing plus extra-virgin olive oil
  for finishing

A selection of 2 or more fillings:

- Pesto (page 72)
- Tomato paste (page 76) or mix some finely chopped herbs into some good-quality tomato purée
- Olive paste (page 122)
- Cheese: Choose a strong-flavoured mature hard cheese, cut into 1cm cubes
- Walnut halves
- Good-quality, whole, stoned olives

To make

- With the help of the rounded end of your plastic scraper, turn out the rested dough. With the flat edge, divide it first into 5 x 170g pieces, roll each piece into a log, halve each log, then cut each half into three, to make 30 pieces. Roll each piece into a tight, smooth ball (page 28). Place the balls onto a flat-edged baking tray, lightly greased with oil (make sure there is space between them or they will touch as they rise), and leave to rest for 15 minutes. Dip the handle of a wooden spoon or your index finger into the flour and then push it into the centre of the first ball. Put a little of your chosen filling into the well you have made. Repeat with the remaining balls. Leave the balls to prove for 45 minutes on a baking tray, covered with a tea towel.

- Put the tray into the preheated oven and mist the inside with a water spray. Turn down the heat to 220°C and bake for 8–10 minutes until they are light golden brown. Remove and allow to cool a little, so that they are just warm before serving. Brush with a little olive oil to give a nice sheen and an extra layer of flavour.

Part-baking in advance: Bake the shots for 4 minutes, leave to cool and store in a plastic bag in the fridge. When you are ready to serve, put them back in the oven (again at 220°C) for a few minutes until they colour.

layered rolls

These are really striking but very simple to make because you don't have to do any 'moulding' or shaping of the dough. You just roll it out, then cut it into discs with a cutter, and bake the discs one on top of the other. Such a simple idea, which you could do alternating two different types of dough: perhaps using some plain and some flavoured with Morrocan spice (page 53) or saffron (page 63).

Quantity: 10–12 rolls
Preparation: 20 minutes
Resting: 1 hour
Proving: 45 minutes
Baking: 10–12 minutes

1 Batch White dough (page 33) rested for 1 hour
Flour for dusting

To make

• Flour your work surface evenly and with the help of the rounded end of your scraper turn the dough out onto it. Flatten the dough a little with your hands and then roll it out to a thickness of about 5mm.

• Use the cutter to cut out rounds (or squares) and layer four pieces (brushed with a little water) on top of each other to make each roll.

• Place them on a flat-edged or upturned baking tray and leave to prove for 45 minutes.

• Transfer to your baking stone/upturned tray in the preheated oven. Mist the inside of the oven with a water spray just before closing the door. Turn down the heat to 230°C and bake for 10–12 minutes until dark golden brown. Cool on a wire rack.

lemon rolls

Lemon is a flavour that works particularly well with bread and, because you use the zest, the delicate, fragrant taste really shines through. I love these rolls in summer with a big bowl of salad, or even filled with smoked salmon. Of course you can make very simple rolls, without any lemon.

Quantity:	9–10 rolls
Preparation:	20 minutes
Resting:	65 minutes
Proving:	1 hour
Baking:	9–10 minutes

1 Batch White dough (page 33)
Zest of 2 large lemons
Flour for dusting

To prepare

Add the zest of the lemons to the dough just before you finish working by hand or mixing in a mixer, and ensure that it is evenly distributed through the dough. Form the dough into a ball (page 25) and place it into a lightly floured bowl to rest for 1 hour.

To make

• With the help of the rounded end of your scraper, turn the rested dough out onto a lightly floured work surface. Cut it into 9–10 pieces and form into balls (page 28). Cover with a tea towel and leave to rest for 5 minutes. Shape the balls into rolls (page 30). Line a tray with a clean tea towel and lightly flour it. Lay the rolls (seam-side-down) two abreast, parallel to the short edge of the tea towel and then make a pleat in the fabric to form a barrier between these rolls and the next two. Pleat again and repeat until all the rolls are laid out on the tray. Cover with another tea towel. Leave to prove for about 1 hour in a warm and draught-free place until the rolls have nearly doubled in volume.

• Place the rolls on a wooden peel or flat baking tray. Score the tops of the rolls with a razor blade or very sharp knife in a leaf pattern, i.e. one slash down the centre and three small ones fanning out on either side. Slide onto the baking stone/upturned tray in the preheated oven, mist the inside with a water spray and turn down the heat to 220°C. Bake for 9–10 minutes until golden brown.

Part-baking for the freezer: Bake the rolls for 5–6 minutes at 220°C, and then cool completely before freezing. To serve, bake from frozen at 210°C for 8–10 minutes until golden brown.

sesame & aniseed breadsticks

I made these because I love sesame seeds and I love aniseed – it's as simple as that. Perhaps it is to do with memories of drinking pastis in the sunshine, but I think these little sticks are great with an aperitif. Because the recipe only uses a half quantity of white dough I often make a full quantity and use the rest to make the variation that follows, with olives, herbs and pecorino. These breadsticks are a little chunkier than the Italian version (grissini), with slightly more of a bready texture. I like them quite soft and chewy – but the longer you bake them the crispier they will become.

Quantity:	10–12 breadsticks	**½ Batch** White dough (page 33) rested for 1 hour
Preparation:	20 minutes	**5** Star anise or 5g star anise powder
Resting:	1 hour	**50g** Sesame seeds
Proving:	20 minutes	Plain white flour for dusting
Baking:	8–10 minutes	

To prepare
Grind the star anise using a pestle and mortar and pass the powder through a fine sieve. Mix it with the sesame seeds on a tray.

To make
• With the help of the rounded end of your scraper turn the dough out onto the lightly floured work surface and flatten it with your hand into a rectangle about 15 x 30cm and about 1cm thick. Sprinkle some of the seed mixture on top and press it gently into the dough. Fold one third of the square into the centre, pressing down with your fingertips, sprinkle on some more of the seed mixture and fold the opposite third of the dough over on top, as if folding an A4 letter to put into an envelope. Press down again. Sprinkle some more of the seed mixture on top and press gently into the dough. With the flat edge of your scraper cut the dough widthways into 10–12 strips

about 1cm wide. Twist each strip, stretching it to the length of your baking tray and roll in the remaining sesame seed mixture. Place the strips on the tray leaving a gap between each one. Cover with a tea towel. Prove for 20 minutes. Put into the preheated oven, mist the inside with a water spray and bake them for 8–10 minutes until golden brown.

olive, herb & pecorino sticks

I love the flavours of these breadsticks – very southern Mediterranean. When we make them in the bread class people are enchanted by them. They look really smart on the table at lunch, or at a barbeque. I use purple Greek Kalamata olives, but you can substitute something similar: just don't buy cheap black shiny olives, which are really green olives subjected to oxygen to turn them black, and then coated with gum to keep them glossy. Buy them whole and take out the stones yourself – that way you will keep in all the flavour. Sometimes I make this with an herbes de Provence mix that has lavender in it, which I think is beautiful – but I know lavender is an acquired taste. If you like you can serve the breadsticks with a little pot of good extra-virgin olive oil to dip them into.

Quantity:	10–12 breadsticks	**½ Batch** White dough (page 33) rested for 1 hour
Preparation:	20 minutes	**100g** Purple olives, such as Kalamata, stone in
Resting:	1 hour	**50g** Pecorino cheese (or Parmesan if you prefer), grated
Proving:	30 minutes	**5g** Good herbes de Provence
Baking:	10–12 minutes	Maize flour for dusting

To prepare

Stone the olives and cut each one roughly into three. Mix the olives, cheese and herbs in a bowl.

To make

• With the help of the rounded end of your scraper, turn the dough out onto the work surface, lightly dusted with maize flour. Using your hand, flatten out into a rectangle about 2cm thick. Sprinkle the cheese and olive mixture on top and press it into the dough with your fingertips. Fold one third of the dough into the centre and press down with your fingertips. Then fold the opposite side over on top (as if you were folding an A4 letter to put into an envelope). Press with the palms of your hands to work the olives into the dough. With the flat edge of your scraper cut the dough widthways into 10–12 strips about 1cm wide. Flour your work surface with maize flour. Twist each strip and roll them a little on the work surface so they stretch to the length of your baking tray (non-stick, or covered with greaseproof paper so that the cheese in the dough doesn't stick to the tray) and place the strips on top, leaving a good gap between each one. Cover with a tea towel and leave to prove for 30 minutes. Put into the preheated oven. Mist the inside with a water spray, then bake them for 10–12 minutes until golden brown. Use a spatula or palette knife to lift them from the baking tray. Cool on a wire rack.

spicy moroccan rolls

One day I bought a packet of the traditional Moroccan spice mix, Ras-el-Hanout, and tried adding some of it to my bread dough. The flavours – which include the likes of cinnamon, nutmeg, turmeric, cardamom seeds, black pepper and cloves – came through really well. When I think of Morocco, I think of those wonderful squashy cushions that people sit on – so I decided to make these rolls in a similar shape. If you are making a tagine, or any dish using Moroccan spices, these would make a great accompaniment.

Quantity:	20 rolls	**1 Batch** White dough (page 33)	
Preparation:	20 minutes	**25g** Moroccan spice blend (Ras-el-Hanout)	
Resting:	45 minutes	**100g** Sesame seeds	
Proving:	30–45 minutes	Flour for dusting	
Baking:	10–12 minutes		

To prepare

Just before you have finished working the dough by hand, or at the end of mixing in the mixer, add the spices and work/mix a little more to make sure they are evenly distributed. Shape into a ball (page 25), cover with a tea towel and leave to rest for 45 minutes.

To make

• Turn the dough out onto a lightly floured work surface and flatten a little with the palm of your hand.

• Divide the dough into two and mould each piece into a log shape (using the folding technique on page 28). Divide each log into ten equal pieces – they will look a bit like overgrown marshmallows. Brush one cut side of each piece with water and then dip them into a bowl containing the sesame seeds.

• Cover with a tea towel and leave to prove for 30–45 minutes or until the rolls have nearly doubled in size.

• Mist the inside of your preheated oven with a water spray and slide the rolls onto your baking stone/upturned baking tray. Bake them for 10–12 minutes until light golden brown. Remove from the oven and cool on a wire rack.

baguettes

In France the word baguette has a very strict meaning: a baguette must weigh 320g and there must be seven cuts along the top, as opposed to five on le pain. The point of the cuts is to let the crust burst open so that it is good and crunchy. Every baker cuts the dough in his own way – it is his signature, which everyone else in the bakery recognises. But you don't need to worry about rules. Just try making some small baguettes first, and when you mould the bread do it as tightly as you can; then, just before you put the bread into the oven, spray it with water to create steam – these details will help you to create the fantastic thick crust that a good baguette should have. In France everyone likes their baguette baked differently. Personally I like the crust to be dark golden brown, not pale and insipid as you often see in this country (other people prefer them well cooked – *bien cuit*). Resting the dough for a minimum of 1 hour will give you the right light, airy texture inside, with plenty of holes running through the bread.

   Every time you make a baguette, keep back a piece (page 26) and add it to your next batch of dough; that way you will infuse more and more flavour into it each time you bake.

Quantity:	4 large or 8 mini baguettes	**1 Batch** White dough (page 33) rested for 1 hour
Preparation:	20 minutes	Plain white flour for dusting
Resting:	65 minutes	
Proving:	45-60 minutes	
Baking:	10–12 minutes	

To prepare
Line a baking tray with a lightly floured tea towel.

To make
• With the help of the rounded end of your scraper, turn the dough out onto a floured work surface. Using the sharp side of your scraper cut the dough into four pieces (weighing about 215g) if you are making full-sized baguettes or eight (weighing about 110g each) for the mini baguettes. Roll each piece into a ball (page 28) and rest for a further 5 minutes.

• Lightly dust your work surface with flour. To mould the baguettes, take the first ball, turn it rounded-side down and then flatten it with the heel of your hand into a rough oval shape. Fold one side of your flattened dough into the middle and again use the heel of your hand, or thumb, to press it down and seal. Bring the other side over to the middle and again press down to seal. By folding and pressing in this way, you give the dough some extra strength down the spine of the baguette. Finally fold in half lengthways and seal the edges so you end up with a long log shape. Roll each baguette a little to shape and extend it to the length of your tea towel-lined baking tray. Repeat with the other balls of dough.

• Lay the baguettes on the tea towel on your baking tray, making a pleat in the towel between each one (to stop them touching as they rise). Cover with another tea towel and leave to prove for 45-60 minutes, or until they have nearly doubled in volume.

• Transfer the baguettes to a very lightly floured wooden peel, flat-edged or upturned baking tray. Using a razor blade or sharp knife make 5 or 6 diagonal cuts across the top of the baguettes. Make the cuts swiftly and cleanly, taking care not to drag the dough.

• The crust on your baguettes will be crunchier if you bake them with a little steam, so mist the inside of the preheated oven using a water spray just before putting them in. Slide them onto your baking stone or tray in the oven. Spray again with water just before closing the door and bake for 10–12 minutes until the crust is a nice golden brown. (Once you have closed the door do not open it for the first 4-5 minutes so that you maintain the heat needed to form the crust.)

Variation: Epis

You see these all the time in French bakeries. Because there is more exposed surface area, they are even more crusty than the traditional baguette, and great to put in the middle of the table, letting people break off the 'ears'.

Follow the method for baguettes up to the point of laying the bread on a lightly floured flat baking tray. With a pair of scissors, held at a 45° angle to the dough, start at one end of the baguette and make snips (cutting three quarters of the way through the dough) at intervals all the way down the centre. This will create 'V' shaped points of dough which you can push to alternate sides of the bread, so that it looks like an ear of wheat. Bake, with steam (as above), for 10–12 minutes.

gruyère cheese & cumin bread

Cumin is a favourite spice of mine – I think its warmth marries brilliantly with Gruyère. I love to slice this bread and then use it instead of the more traditional Pain de Mie (page 64) to make croque monsieurs.

Quantity:	3 loaves
Preparation:	20 minutes
Resting:	1 1/2 hours
Proving:	1–1 1/2 hours
Baking:	15–20 minutes

1 Batch White dough (page 33) rested for 1 hour
2g Cumin seeds (just under 1/2 teaspoon)
2g Cumin powder (just under 1/2 teaspoon)
250g Gruyère cheese, coarsely grated
Flour for dusting
A little butter for greasing

To prepare
Grease 3 x 500g (20–22cm long) loaf tins with butter, and line them with non-stick silicon paper.

To make
• With the help of the rounded end of your scraper, turn the dough out onto a lightly floured work surface and flatten it with the base of your hands to about 1cm thick. Mix the cumin seeds and powder together and sprinkle on top of the dough. Sprinkle on the cheese and work this, and the cumin, into the dough by pressing firmly with your fingers. Fold a third of the dough into the centre, and then fold the other third over the top, to ensure that the cheese is evenly distributed through the dough. Then form the dough into a ball (page 25) and rest for a further 30 minutes.

• Divide the dough into three, mould each piece lightly into a loaf shape (page 31) and put one into each prepared tin. With a razor blade or sharp knife cut the top of each loaf diagonally four or five times. Cover with a tea towel and leave to prove for 1–1 1/2 hours until the loaves have nearly doubled in volume. The exact time taken will depend on the temperature of your proving place.

• Put the tins into the preheated oven, mist the inside with a water spray and turn down the heat to 210°C. Bake for 15–20 minutes until golden brown on top. Remove the loaves from the tins. Check that the base is also golden brown – if not, return to the oven without the tin for a few minutes. Cool on a wire rack.

pain façon beaucaire

The true Pain Beaucaire originates on the Côte d'Azur, and uses a special local wheat. This version uses white dough, but with the same folding technique, which looks really smart. I've found that once people get the hang of how easy it is to do, without having to mould the bread, they make it time and time again. Later on, when you feel confident to make pain de campagne (page 132) you can use the same folding technique with that dough.

Quantity: 8 small rolls
Preparation: 20 minutes
Resting: 1 hour
Proving: 30 minutes
Baking: 10–12 minutes

1 Batch White dough (page 33) rested for 1 hour
Maize or wholemeal flour for dusting
White flour for dusting

To make

• With the help of the rounded end of your scraper, turn out the dough and flatten it out with your hands into a rectangle. Brush with a little water and sprinkle on some maize or wholemeal flour. Fold over the dough lengthways, stopping 3cm before the edge. Brush this edge with water, fold it back over the dough and seal.

• Lay a tea towel on your work surface and sprinkle liberally with white flour. Place the dough, seam-side-down, on the tea towel and flour the exposed surface. Cover with another tea towel and leave to prove for 30 minutes somewhere warm and draught-free or until it has nearly doubled in size.

• With a sharp serrated knife, cut the dough widthways into 3cm slices. Place the pieces on a baking tray on their side, open out gently (so they look a bit like ring doughnuts but with a smaller and thinner hole), and bake in the preheated oven for 10–12 minutes or until golden brown.

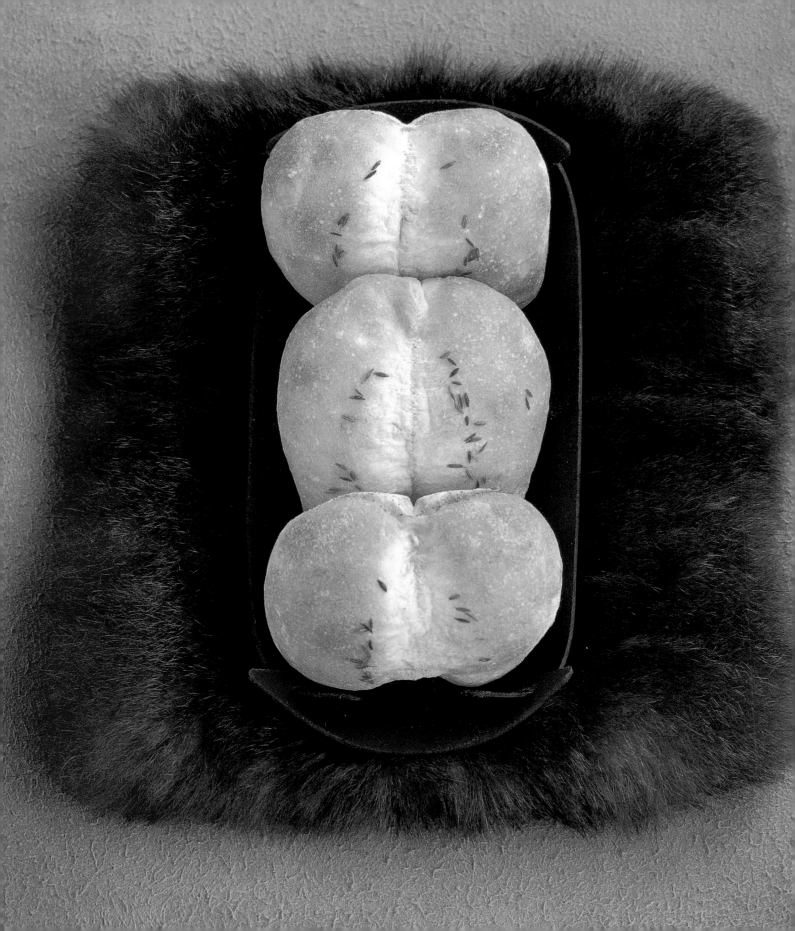

saffron rolls

Saffron (the dried stigma of a particular type of crocus) is another of those luxurious, glamorous ingredients that if you use with too heavy a hand can taste overpowering (and look too yellow) but, used in bread as a background flavour, it gives a lovely warm and delicate note. I love this bread with seafood chowder, or a fish stew like bouillabaisse – or you can use it to make crab or prawn mayonnaise sandwiches. Try to use saffron strands, rather than powder, as they give a smarter appearance to the bread, and a richer flavour.

Quantity:	9 or 10 rolls	**1 Batch** White dough (page 33)	
Preparation:	20 minutes	**Pinch** of Saffron strands (If you can't get strands	
Resting:	1 hour	powdered saffron will do)	
Proving:	45 minutes	**A few** Cumin seeds	
Baking:	12 minutes	White flour for dusting	

To prepare

When making the dough, dilute a few strands of saffron, or powder, in the water before mixing, then carry on as usual, resting for 1 hour.
Line a tray with a tea towel and dust with flour.

To make

• With the help of the rounded end of your scraper, turn out the dough, and with your hand, flatten it into a rectangle. Fold one third of the dough into the centre and press down with your fingertips; fold the opposite side over on top (as if you were folding an A4 letter to put into an envelope). With the flat edge of your scraper cut it into 9 or 10 pieces (weighing about 90–100g each) and mould each one into a ball (page 28). Flour the top of each ball and then place a floured rolling pin across the centre and press down firmly. The dough will rise up either side of the indent you have made, leaving you with a roll that resembles a coffee bean.

• Lay the rolls two abreast on the lined baking tray, making a pleat between each pair of rolls, cover with another tea towel and leave to prove for 45 minutes.

• Sprinkle a few cumin seeds on top of each roll, then slide onto your baking stone/upturned tray in the preheated oven. Mist the inside with a water spray and turn down the heat to 220°C. Bake them for 12 minutes. Cool on a wire rack.

pain de mie / everyday loaves

This is as close as you get to a sliced loaf in France; however, the dough is enriched with milk and butter. This is one of the few breads in France that is baked in a tin. 'Mie' means crumb, because this bread is all about the crumb rather than the crust ('croûte'). It is traditionally used for canapés and small toasts, where you don't want a crusty edge. So if you have a tin with a lid, bake it in that, or put a tray on top for most of the baking time, to prevent a proper crust from forming. This is also the typical bread to use for a croque monsieur (you could also use the Gruyère and Cumin bread, page 58, or Pain Viennois, page 154), the snack that all French kids grow up with: 2 slices spread with a little béchamel (page 150), sandwiched with a layer of ham, then topped with a thick layer of béchamel and some grated Gruyère cheese and put into a preheated oven at 200°C for about 12 minutes until the cheese melts and turns golden – brilliant!

I also use Pain de Mie to make summer pudding – one of my favourite British desserts; I love it so much that Jo and I even served it at our wedding.

Quantity:	2 loaves	**10g** Unsalted butter
Preparation:	20 minutes	**20g** Fresh yeast
Resting:	1 hour	**500g** Strong white flour
Proving:	1 hour	**50g** Full fat milk (50ml)
Baking:	25–30 minutes	**300g** Water (300ml)
		A little butter for greasing

To prepare
Grease 2 x 500g (20–22cm long) loaf tins with a little butter.

Preheat the oven to 250°C. Make the dough according to the method on pages 22-25, adding the butter with the yeast (rubbing them both in together) and the milk with the water, and rest for 1 hour.

To make

• With the help of the rounded edge of your scraper, turn out the dough onto a floured surface, and divide the dough into two equal pieces. Mould each piece very tightly into a loaf shape (page 31).

• Once the loaves are in their tins leave to prove in a warm draught-free place for 1 hour. Keep a close eye on the loaves while they are proving and when the dough is level with the top of the tin, cover with a lid or heavy tray weighed down so the dough can't rise any further.

• Put the tins into the preheated oven. Turn down the heat to 220°C and bake the loaves for 20–25 minutes, covered, and then a further 4–5 minutes uncovered, until light golden brown. Remove the loaves from the tins and cool.

summer pudding (serves 4-6)

Cut 6–8 slices of stale pain de mie – about 1¹/₂cm thick – and trim off the crusts. Keep back a couple of slices (for the lid) and use the rest to line the base and sides of a pudding basin – make sure the basin is completely covered (trim the bread to shape if necessary so that it fits closely together).

Remove the stalks and/or stones from 600g mixed soft fruits (include as many different fruits as you are able to get hold of, from strawberries, raspberries, blackberries, redcurrants, blackcurrants and sweet black cherries, but avoid adding too many blackcurrants as they can overpower the other fruits).

Put the fruit in a wide, heavy-bottomed pan, add 100g caster sugar, bring to the boil over a low heat and cook for a couple of minutes until the sugar has dissolved and the fruit has just started to soften and release its juice. Remove from the heat. Set aside 3 or 4 tablespoons of the juice, then spoon the fruit and the rest of the juice into the prepared bowl and cover with the remaining slices of bread. Place a plate, the same size as the rim of the bowl, on top of the pudding and weight it down (a tin or jar will do). Place the bowl, with the weight on top, in the fridge and leave to chill for at least 6 hours but preferably overnight.

To serve, remove the weight and the plate and slide a palette knife round the inside of the bowl to release the pudding. Cover the bowl with a serving plate and invert the bowl to turn the pudding out onto the plate. Add 2 tablespoons crème de cassis to the reserved juices then carefully pour them over the pudding so that all of the bread is soaked through and coloured.

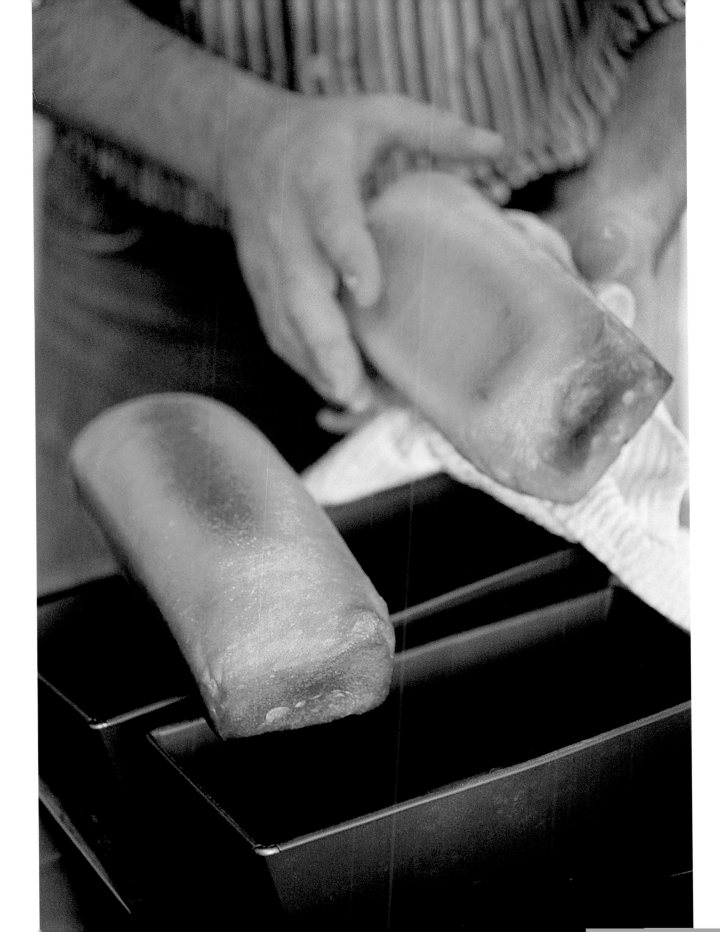

2. Olive Dough

olive oil: emollient; prized

This takes the basic White Dough on a stage further, adding olive oil which gives a lovely softness to the dough, making it very resilient, and resulting in bread with a fantastic texture and flavour, which also freezes well. There is also a recipe for ciabatta that uses avocado oil, to make a wonderfully tasty variation.

I like to use a light fruity olive oil, not a peppery intense one – and I also like to use a little semolina in the dough, to add character to the bread. The dough will feel slightly wetter than the white dough we made in the previous chapter, but once you have mastered the technique of working it, it will come together beautifully.

500g Strong bread flour
20g Coarse semolina
15g Yeast (fresh if possible)
10g Salt
50g Good-quality extra-virgin olive oil
320g Water (320ml – but weighing is more accurate)

Preheat the oven to 250ºC. Mix the bread flour and semolina together and rub in the yeast, using your fingertips as if making a crumble. Add the salt, olive oil and water, then continue, according to the method on pages 22–25, but check your recipe to see if you need to add any other ingredients at this stage.

flatbread

soup bowl

parmesan,
parma ham
& pine nut
slices

pizza

pancetta
& mixed
olive
bread

tomato,
garlic &
basil
bread

ciabatta

rock salt &
rosemary
focaccia

rock salt & rosemary focaccia

This is such an easy, popular bread to make and makes a generous slab that everyone can share. Just as every French baker has his own way of making a baguette, I'm sure every Italian baker lends his own individual style to focaccia. I'm not pretending that this is an authentic Italian recipe – just my way of making a fantastic Italian style of bread.

Quantity:	1 large slab	**1 Batch** Olive dough (page 69) rested for 1 hour
Preparation:	20 minutes	**4 tablespoons** Olive oil plus a little extra
Resting:	2¹/₄ hours	**A few sprigs** of Fresh rosemary
Proving:	45 minutes	Good-quality rock salt
Baking:	25–30 minutes	

To make

• With the help of the rounded end of your scraper, turn the dough out onto an oiled tray. Drizzle the oil over the dough, then, using your fingers, push and prod the dough so that it spreads from the centre towards the edges of the tray – but try not to stretch or pull it. Cover with a tea towel and leave to rest somewhere warm and draught-free for 45 minutes.

• Prod the dough again, dimpling it with your fingertips, and rest for a further 30 minutes.

• Take the leaves off the sprigs of rosemary and push them evenly into the dough. Sprinkle on the rock salt and immediately put into the preheated oven. Turn down the heat to 220°C and bake it for 25–30 minutes, until it is light golden brown. Remove from the oven and slide onto a wire rack to cool. Brush with a little more olive oil while it's still hot.

Variation: Pesto, Olive & Pepperdew
Pepperdew are little sweet yet piquant, and quite mild, peppers that come in a jar – you should be able to find them in most supermarkets. If you prefer something hotter, use red chillies. Follow the recipe above, but instead of topping with rock salt and rosemary, halve 20 cherry tomatoes, drain a jar of Pepperdew, and tear the peppers into pieces with your fingers. Remove the stones from a handful of Kalamata olives. Spread 4 tablespoons fresh pesto (page 76) onto the rested dough and work it evenly into the dough with your fingertips. Sprinkle the peppers on top, then the tomatoes and finally the olives. Push all of these ingredients gently into the dough. Leave to prove for 45 minutes and bake and finish with oil as above.

tomato, garlic & basil bread

Three beautiful flavours that work even better together and make a lovely moist bread that looks brilliantly colourful, is a lot more interesting than garlic bread and more tasty than tomato bread (much of which is made commercially with pre-mixed flavouring that reminds me of cheap tomato soup). When you dust the bread in maize flour it gives the finished loaf a rich colour.

Quantity:	3 loaves	**1 Batch** Olive dough (page 69) rested for 1 hour
Preparation:	20 minutes	**100g** Oven-dried tomatoes (page 76)
Resting:	1 hour	**20 cloves** Roasted garlic (page 76)
Proving:	30 minutes	**Large bunch** of fresh basil – leaves only
Baking:	20–25 minutes	A little extra-virgin olive oil to finish
		Flour for dusting (either white or maize flour)

To make

• Flour your work surface generously with white or maize flour. With the help of the rounded end of your scraper turn the rested dough out onto the work surface so that the sticky underside is uppermost. Sprinkle a little flour onto the dough and then, using your fingertips, spread it out gently into a rectangle about 35 x 25cm, prodding it gently, so you dimple it with your fingertips.

• Brush the excess flour from the top of the dough. Spread the tomatoes evenly over it and push them gently into it using your fingertips. Do the same with the garlic and then the basil leaves.

• Fold the right-hand third of the rectangle into the centre. Repeat with the left-hand third so that you end up with a smaller rectangle. Press the dough gently with your fingertips to work the additional ingredients better into the dough and tuck under the edges neatly all the way round.

• Cut the dough crossways into three equal pieces. Tuck the dough under one of the cut sides of the middle piece. Lightly oil a baking tray. Place the three pieces on it, cut-side up (so that you can see the tomato, garlic and basil). Cover with a tea towel and leave to prove somewhere warm and draught-free for 30 minutes.

• Put into the preheated oven, turn the heat down to 220°C and bake for 20–25 minutes until golden brown. Remove and transfer to a wire rack to cool. Brush with a little extra-virgin olive oil while still warm.

Part-baking for the freezer: If you want to freeze these loaves bake them for 15 minutes and then leave to cool for at least 1 hour. Wrap them well in freezer bags. To use, put them in a preheated oven at 180°C and bake for 12–15 minutes from frozen, or for 8–10 minutes if defrosted.

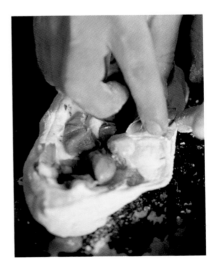

oven-dried tomatoes

Preheat the oven to 100°C. You need 1 punnet (250g) cherry tomatoes or 6–8 larger tomatoes. If you are using cherry tomatoes, halve them; if they are larger, quarter them and lay them on a baking tray, skin-side-down. Season with sea salt and freshly ground black pepper and sprinkle on a teaspoon of caster sugar and a couple of pinches of good-quality dried herbes de Provence (or a little fresh thyme and rosemary). Put in the preheated oven for 2 hours until dried but soft. After drying, the tomatoes should weigh about 100g and will be sufficient for the recipe for Tomato, Garlic & Basil Bread (pages 74–75).
Note: The tomatoes can be packed into a clean, sterile jar and covered with olive oil. You can store them like this for several weeks. You can also blitz them in a food processor to make a really tasty tomato sauce for the pizza on page 84, or a tomato paste for the bread shots on page 44.

roasted garlic

Preheat the oven to 180°C. Put an ovenproof pan on the hob and add 5 tablespoons olive oil, 25g butter and a teaspoon of caster sugar. When the butter has melted, add 20 peeled garlic cloves and toss them in the mixture, then transfer to the oven and cook for 20–25 minutes until the garlic has caramelised and is soft enough to offer no resistance to the point of a sharp knife. Remove the pan from the oven and let the garlic cool in its cooking juices. Once cool, lift the garlic from the juices and drain on a few sheets of kitchen paper.

fresh pesto

An Italian would probably throw up his hands in horror, but I like to add a little squeeze of lemon into my pesto. Put 100g pine nuts into a food processor with 3 garlic cloves and 100g grated Parmesan and blitz for a few seconds. Add 3–4 bunches of basil (enough to fill the bowl of the food processor loosely) and blitz again until it has all been chopped. Add the juice of half a lemon and 60g/4 tablespoons extra-virgin olive oil and blitz once more. Taste and season if necessary with sea salt and freshly ground black pepper. If the pesto is too thick add a little extra olive oil.
Note: The pesto can be kept in the fridge for a few days or in the freezer for several weeks.

soup bowl

I first thought of this after ordering an Indian takeaway. The food was tasty, but it looked so boring in its little plastic trays. I thought how much more fun it would be to serve it in bowls made from bread, which you could flavour with a little chilli or spice and then eat, as the sauces softened the bread. From the idea of a curry bowl it was only a short step to thinking about also using the bread containers as soup bowls – a nice play on soup with bread or croûtons.

Quantity:	8 bowls	**1 Batch** Olive dough (page 69) rested for
Preparation:	30 minutes	30 minutes
Resting:	40 minutes	A little olive oil for greasing
Baking:	20–25 minutes	White flour for dusting

To prepare

Lightly oil the outside of 8 earthenware bowls, about 12cm diameter (I use a set of soup or breakfast bowls).

To make

• With the help of the rounded end of your scraper, turn the dough out onto a lightly floured work surface and divide it into 100g pieces. Again lightly flour your work surface. Taking one piece at a time, roll out the dough into circles. Shake off any excess flour and shape over the upturned bowls. Press gently to ensure there are no air bubbles between the dough and the bowl. Rest for 10 minutes.

• Put (bowls upturned) into the preheated oven and turn down the heat to 200°C and bake for 20–25 minutes until golden brown. (You will probably need to bake in 2 batches.) Remove them from the oven and leave to cool for a few minutes. Using a fine-bladed knife, gently loosen the bread from the bowls and ease off. Cool on a wire rack.

For the freezer: The bowls freeze well for a few weeks. Stack them with a sheet of greaseproof paper between each one. Defrost for about 1 hour before warming them in the oven for 3 minutes at 180°C.

parmesan, parma ham & pine nut slices

These are a little like savoury pain aux raisins. You can even slice them in half if you like and fill them with rocket and slivers of Parmesan. I also like to make really small ones to serve with aperitifs – if you want to do this, cut the dough in half before you start, and when you roll it up, do so quite tightly to keep them small and neat (the larger ones can be a little looser).

Quantity:	12 slices
Preparation:	20 minutes
Resting:	1 hour
Proving:	45 minutes
Baking:	12–15 minutes

1 Batch Olive dough (page 69) rested for 1 hour

100g Parmesan cheese

100g Pine nuts

2 tablespoons Extra-virgin olive oil, plus a little extra for finishing

12 Slices of Parma ham

Maize flour for dusting

To prepare

Grate the Parmesan.

Scatter the pine nuts on a baking tray and toast under the grill or in a hot oven, turning from time to time until they are toasted. Leave to cool.

To make

• Sprinkle your work surface with maize flour. With the help of the rounded end of your plastic scraper, turn out the dough and with your fingers spread it out into a rough rectangle, dimpling it as you go, and brush with olive oil.

• Mix the nuts and grated cheese together and sprinkle half evenly over the dough. Lay the parma ham on top. Brush a little more oil over the ham then spread the remaining cheese and nuts on top.

• Roll the dough up like a roulade and seal the seam by pushing down on it with your fingers. Using a sharp serrated knife, cut the dough into 2cm slices and place them on their sides on a lightly greased baking tray.

• Cover with a tea towel and leave to prove for 45 minutes or until the slices have nearly doubled in volume.

• Put them in the preheated oven, turn down the heat to 240°C and bake for 12–15 minutes until golden brown. Remove and cool on a wire rack. Brush with a little more oil while still warm.

flatbread

This is very thin bread that you can use as a wrap or a pizza base. You can even bake it for a slightly longer time until it has completely dried then break it up and serve with dips as a low-fat alternative to crisps. You can also flavour the dough if you like – perhaps with some Thai spices or, alternatively, add a topping of fines herbes, rock salt, black pepper and (fresh or dried) chillies before baking.

Quantity:	4 flatbreads	**1 Batch** Olive dough (page 69) rested for
Preparation:	20 minutes	30 minutes
Resting:	55–60 minutes	Maize flour for dusting
Baking:	8–10 minutes	A little olive oil

To prepare

Lightly brush 4 non-stick 20 x 30cm trays with oil.

To make

• With the help of the rounded end of your scraper, turn out the dough and divide it into four equal pieces. Place a piece of dough onto a tray and, using your fingertips, push it out until it fills the tray. If the dough is very sticky, use a little maize flour to help you to do this. Don't worry if it doesn't quite fill the tray; there is no need to force it – it will expand during resting and you will be able to spread it out to fill the tray then. Repeat with the other three pieces of dough.

• Cover with a tea towel and rest for 15–20 minutes. Prod again with your fingertips to spread the dough out to fill the tray. Rest for a final 10 minutes before baking.

• To use as a wrap, put in the preheated oven, turn the heat down to 220°C and bake for 8–10 minutes until very lightly coloured (the colour of part-baked dough). Don't bake any longer, as the bread needs to be soft enough to roll. Serve filled with fresh vine tomatoes, salad, parma ham – the choices are endless.

To break up the bread into pieces to serve with a dip, bake for 15–18 minutes until crisp.

pizza

I don't use any semolina in this dough as I want it to be very smooth and elastic. The topping I have suggested is for a traditional margherita, but of course you can use any topping you like.

Quantity: 3 pizzas
Preparation: 15 minutes
Resting: 70 minutes
or overnight in the fridge
Baking: 10–12 minutes

Pizza base:
15g Fresh yeast
500g Strong white Italian flour
10g Salt
50g Olive oil (50ml)
320g Water (320ml)
Plain white flour for dusting

Topping for each pizza:
3/4 tablespoon Blitzed oven-dried tomatoes (page 76)
100g Buffalo mozzarella
Fresh basil leaves

To prepare

Preheat your oven to 250°C. Rub the yeast into the flour, using your fingertips as if making a crumble. Add the salt, olive oil and water, then continue according to the method on pages 22–25. Leave the dough to rest for 1 hour or, to achieve a better crust and taste, rest it overnight in the fridge. By doing this, you will enable the dough to rise very slowly and it will develop a little acidity that will improve its flavour and give a texture that is crispy on the outside and slightly chewy inside.

To make

• With the help of the rounded end of your scraper, turn out the dough, divide into three and shape into balls (page 25), and rest for a further 10 minutes. Lightly flour your work surface and place the balls of dough onto the flour. You need to make sure that the flour is evenly distributed so that your pizzas will not stick.

• Take one of the balls and place the heel of your hand in the centre of it and push it away from you so that it stretches the dough out. Turn the dough slightly and repeat. Keep stretching the dough until you have a roughly circular pizza shape of about 20–22cm in diameter. The edge should be slightly thicker than the dough in the middle. Repeat with the other two balls.

• Lift the pizza bases onto a floured baking tray and spread the tomato sauce evenly over them. Sprinkle with chunks of mozzarella and shredded basil leaves.

• Slide the pizzas onto the preheated baking tray or stone in the oven, turn the heat down to 240°C and bake for 10–12 minutes until the edges become golden brown and crispy.

pancetta & mixed olive bread

The combination of these really earthy flavours is beautiful and just melts into the bread – which makes fantastic sandwiches.

Quantity:	3 loaves	**1 Batch** Olive dough (page 69)
Preparation:	1 hour	**200g** Mixed (green and purple) olives, stone in
Resting:	1½ hours	**Bunch** of Sage, stalks removed
Proving:	1 hour	**1 tablespoon** Oil for frying
Baking:	30–35 minutes	**200g** Diced pancetta or lardons

To prepare

Stone the olives and roughly chop the sage. Heat the olive oil in a frying pan. When it's hot add the pancetta and stir. When the pancetta is starting to crisp, add the olives, stir and cook over a medium heat for about 2 minutes. Remove from the heat and add the sage. Stir well and spoon the mixture, including the cooking juices, into a bowl to cool.

During the last stage of working the dough by hand or mixing in a mixer, add the pancetta mixture, together with its cooking juices, and continue working/mixing the dough until the mixture is spread evenly through the dough. Lightly dust the inside of a clean bowl with flour and place the dough in it. Cover with a tea towel and rest for 1 hour in a draught-free place.

To make

• Turn the dough out onto a lightly floured work surface and form into a ball (page 25). Return to the bowl, cover and rest for a further 30 minutes.

• Flour the work surface again and turn the dough out onto it. Divide it into three equal pieces of about 440g each. Fold one side into the middle and again use the heel of your hand, or thumb, to press it down and seal. Bring the other side over to the middle and again press down to seal. Finally fold in half lengthways and seal the edges so you end up with a long log shape with rounded ends.

• Place the loaves on a baking tray and flour the tops with white or maize flour. With a razor blade or sharp knife, make six or seven diagonal cuts about 1cm deep across the top of each loaf. Cover the loaves with a tea towel and leave to prove for about 1 hour or until they have nearly doubled in volume.

• Open the preheated oven and mist with a water spray. Place the loaves in the oven, turn down the heat to 230°C, and bake for 30–35 minutes until they are a golden brown colour. Remove from the oven and cool on a wire rack.

ciabatta

The famous Italian 'slipper' bread needs a ferment or 'biga', as it is known in Italy, which helps to create a wonderful open structure and lightness. This is made simply with flour, water and yeast, which you need to make up and leave for 24 hours before using. I always prefer to work any dough by hand, rather than mix it in a mixer with a dough hook, but this is a bread that really benefits from working by hand, to get as much air into it as possible. It starts off very soft and sticky, but as you work it it will become more and more elastic and come away from your fingers.

   I make this with avocado oil, rather than olive oil. It is a bit more expensive, but worth trying as it makes beautiful bread and gives the dough a lovely, delicate avocado-green tinge.

Quantity:	4 loaves		
Preparation:	15 minutes		
Resting:	17–24 hours for the ferment		
	1¹/₂ hours for the dough		
Proving:	30–45 minutes		
Baking:	18–20 minutes		

For the ferment:

350g Flour

180g Water (180ml)

¹/₂ level teaspoon Fresh yeast

For the dough:

450g Strong white or Italian bread flour

10g Yeast

340g Water (340ml)

50g Olive or avocado oil (50ml)

15g Salt

A little olive or avocado oil for oiling

Flour for dusting

To prepare (24 hours in advance)

Mix the ingredients for the ferment together in a mixer or by hand for about 5 minutes until you have a rough dough. Place in a bowl, cover loosely with clingfilm and then a tea towel and leave it to rest in a draught-free place for 17–24 hours.

To make

• Remember to put your oven on at least 1 hour before you start making the dough to warm up the kitchen as well as the oven.

• Preferably make the dough by hand. Put the flour in a mixing bowl and rub in the yeast. Scoop the ferment into the bowl, then add the water, oil and salt, mixing well until all combined (use one hand to mix and hold the bowl with the other). Once the dough is no longer sticking to the bowl, transfer it to your work surface with the help of the rounded end of your scraper, and work it following the method on page 24. (If you prefer to use a mixer, combine the ingredients as above, mixing for a further 4–5 minutes on the second speed until the dough is light, supple and elastic.) Remove the dough from the bowl, transfer to a lightly oiled surface and mould into a ball (page 25).

• Lightly oil a bowl with either avocado or olive oil, place the dough in it and leave to rest for 1¹/₂ hours, covered with a tea towel, until it has risen and feels bubbly and light.

• Flour your work surface generously with white or maize flour and, with the help of the rounded end of your scraper, turn the dough out in one piece. Flour the top. Press the dough lightly and gently, dimpling it slightly with your fingers. Divide the dough into four roughly equal strips, and fold into three. Do this by folding one side of your flattened dough into the middle and use the heel of your hand to press it down and seal. Bring the other side over to the middle and again press down to seal. Finally fold in half lengthways and seal the edges so you end up with a long shape.

• Place the pieces of dough onto well-floured tea towels. Cover with another tea towel and leave to prove for 30–45 minutes.

• Flour a baking tray or wooden peel, pick up one ciabatta at a time, turn it over, stretch it lengthways a little at the same time, and lay on the peel or tray. (This stretch is what gives the bread its characteristic 'slipper' shape.) Spray the inside of your oven with a water spray and then quickly slide the ciabatta onto the baking stone or tray. Turn down the heat to 220°C and bake for 18–20 minutes until light golden brown.

Part-baking for the freezer: The bread can be part-baked for 15 minutes and then cooled, wrapped well in freezer bags, and frozen. To use them, bake from frozen for 12 minutes at 200°C.

Variation: Olive Ciabatta
Add 200g purple Kalamata or green, pitted and quartered olives during the last few minutes of working the dough.

The ferment

Leave the long shapes to prove

Stretch it lengthways

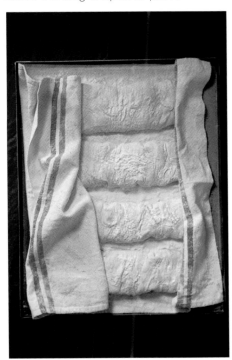

Many of the breads in this chapter have an autumnal, even Christmasy feel, because there is something earthy about brown bread which lends itself to fruit and spice and feels warming and cheering on a cold winter's day. Mostly I use a combination of white flour and wholemeal, which gives a lighter loaf than pure wholemeal and, though I have included one for 100% wholemeal, it is still lighter than most because it uses a ferment (page 14). Although the way of working the brown dough is the same as for the previous two chapters, don't worry if the dough seems slightly heavier.

300g Strong wholemeal flour
200g Strong white flour
10g Yeast (fresh if possible)
10g Salt
350g Water (350ml – but weighing is more accurate)

Preheat your oven to 250°C. Mix the two flours together and rub in the yeast, using your fingertips as if making a crumble. Add the salt and water, then continue according to the method on pages 22–25, but check your recipe to see if you need to add any other ingredients at this stage.

honey &
lavender
loaf

raisin,
hazeln
& shal
bread

poppy
seed s

apricot &
oat bread

sesame
plait

brown

seaweed
bread

pecan &
cranberry
bread

multiseed
bread

100%
wholemeal
bread

cardamom
& prune
bread

apricot & oat bread

I like this bread for breakfast – it's a little bit like muesli in bread form – but it's equally good toasted with cheese. The apricots (I use organic ones, with no artificial preservatives) give it a slight sweetness and the oats a little crunchiness.

Quantity:	4 small or 2 large loaves	**1 Batch**	Brown dough (page 93)
Preparation:	20 minutes	**200g**	Dried apricots (preferably organic),
Resting:	70 minutes		roughly chopped
Proving:	1 hour	**80g**	Oats (for coating)
Baking:	15 minutes baking for the small or		
	25 minutes for the large		

To prepare

Make the dough as explained on page 22 but add the apricots at the end of working it by hand or mixing in a mixer and continue working/mixing until the apricots are distributed evenly. Form the dough into a ball (page 25), place in a lightly floured bowl, cover with a tea towel and rest for 1 hour.

To make

• With the help of the rounded end of your scraper, turn the dough out onto a lightly floured work surface and divide it into two or four pieces depending on the size of loaf required. Shape into balls again, cover with a tea towel, and leave to rest for 10 minutes.

• Mould each ball into a loaf (page 31). Place the oats on a plate. Brush the tops and sides of each loaf with a little water then roll in the oats until they are coated generously. Place the loaves on a baking tray lined with a lightly floured tea towel, pleated in between the loaves so they don't touch as they rise.

• With a razor blade or sharp knife make a few diagonal cuts along the top of each loaf with a depth of at least 5mm, then leave to prove for 1 hour or until the loaves have nearly doubled in volume.

• Open the preheated oven and mist the inside with a water spray, then quickly slide the loaves onto the baking stone or tray and close the door. Turn down the heat to 220°C and bake for 15 minutes for the small loaves or about 25 minutes for the large ones. Once baked the loaves should sound hollow when tapped on the base with your finger. Cool on a wire rack.

honey & lavender loaf

Just a teaspoon of lavender gives the most extraordinary flavour, but I know not everyone likes it. If you don't, then forget this recipe! Personally I think this loaf is just beautiful toasted with soft goat's cheese. We love lavender so much we grow it in the garden, pick it at the end of the summer and then spend a somewhat tedious, if fragrant, evening taking off the heads and spreading them out to dry on baking trays. Once they are dry we put them into a plastic container which will keep us in lavender until it is in season again. If you have some lavender honey, you could use that as well – otherwise use another good-quality honey, preferably organic.

Quantity:	1 large loaf	**1 Batch** Brown dough (page 93)
Preparation:	20 minutes	**1 Heaped teaspoon** Lavender flowers (fresh/dried)
Resting:	1¹/₂ hours	**30g** Good-quality runny honey (or lavender honey)
Proving:	1–1¹/₂ hours	
Baking:	30–40 minutes	

To prepare

Make the dough following the method on page 22 but add the lavender at the same time as the flour, and the honey along with the salt. Shape the dough into a ball (page 25), place in a lightly floured bowl, cover with a tea towel and leave to rest for 45 minutes.

To make

• With the help of your plastic scraper, turn the dough out onto your work surface, then reshape it into a ball, put back into the bowl, cover, and rest for a further 45 minutes.

• Turn the dough out onto the work surface and press it down gently. Shape it into a square by drawing the four 'corners' into the centre. Flour the top of the loaf. Line a baking tray with a tea towel and place the loaf on it, folded-side down. Cover with another tea towel and leave to prove for 1–1¹/₂ hours until it has nearly doubled in volume.

• Place the loaf (folded-side-down) on a wooden peel or upturned baking tray and mark a double cross shape on the top of the loaf with a razor blade or sharp knife. Mist the inside of the preheated oven with a water spray and quickly slide the loaf onto the baking stone or tray and close the door. Turn down the heat to 220°C and bake for 10 minutes, then turn down again to 200°C and bake for a further 20–30 minutes. Once baked the loaf should sound hollow if tapped on the base with your finger. You will need to keep testing it, as with a large loaf such as this it's difficult to be absolutely accurate about timing.

cardamom & prune bread

I first tried using cardamom in a Danish-style pastry. I knew it was a spice that worked well with fruit, so I added some prunes, but I felt there was something missing. So, I cast my mind back to my days in Brittany, when we used to make Far Breton, a batter cake with prunes and good dark rum. When I tried adding the rum, the flavours really brought the bread alive, transforming it into something warm and earthy and Christmasy, almost like a traditional English afternoon tea bread or malt loaf, gorgeous toasted with butter.

Quantity:	2 loaves	
Preparation:	30 minutes	
Resting:	1³/₄ hours	
Proving:	1 hour	
Baking:	25–30 minutes	

1 Batch Brown dough (page 93)
100g Stoned prunes
4 tablespoons Rum
¹/₄ teaspoon Freshly ground cardamom

To prepare

Soak the prunes in the rum for at least 1 hour, or overnight if possible.

Make the dough following the method on page 22, but increase the quantity of yeast to 15g to counteract the heaviness of the fruit. Add the cardamom at the same time as the flour and the prunes shortly before the end of working by hand or mixing in a mixer. Continue working/mixing until everything is evenly distributed. Shape the dough into a ball (page 25), place in a bowl, cover with a tea towel and rest for 1 hour.

To make

• With the help of the rounded end of your scraper, turn out the dough onto a lightly floured work surface and reshape into a ball, put back in the bowl, cover with a tea towel and rest for a further 45 minutes.

• Again using the rounded end of your scraper, turn out the dough onto a lightly floured work surface and divide in half. Mould each half into a loaf (page 31). Place on a lightly floured tea towel on a shallow-edged or upturned baking tray. Flour the top of the loaves and then, with a razor blade or sharp knife, make four diagonal cuts (to a depth of 5mm) fanning out on either side of the loaf. Cover with a tea towel and leave to prove for 1 hour until they have nearly doubled in volume.

• Open the preheated oven and mist with a water spray. Slide the loaves onto the baking stone or tray and quickly close the door. Turn down the heat to 220°C and bake for 25–30 minutes. The loaves will sound hollow when tapped on the base when they are done. Remove from the oven and cool on a wire rack.

Top to bottom: cardamom & prune bread; apricot & oat bread; raisin, hazelnut & shallot bread; pecan & cranberry bread; seaweed bread

seaweed bread

If you ask people to identify the flavour of this bread, I doubt if they would be able to recognise it as seaweed – but everyone I have made this for has loved it. I used to do something similar in Brittany using local seaweed but here I find Japanese wakame works really well. Because of its affinity with the sea, it is fantastic with seafood, especially fresh oysters. This recipe uses equal measures of strong white and wholemeal flour.

Quantity:	1 loaf
Preparation:	30 minutes
Resting:	1³/₄ hours
Proving:	1 hour
Baking:	45 minutes

250g Strong white flour
250g Wholemeal flour
10g Yeast (fresh if possible)
10g Salt
340g Water (340ml)
10g Dehydrated wakame seaweed (this should give you about 50g rehydrated seaweed)

To prepare

Soak the seaweed in water, according to the instructions on the pack, until soft. Preheat the oven to 250°C. Mix the two flours and rub in the yeast, add the salt and then the water and make the dough following the method on pages 22–25. Add the seaweed at the end of working by hand or mixing in the mixer and continue working/mixing until it is evenly distributed through the dough. Shape the dough into a ball (page 25), place it in a lightly floured bowl, cover with a tea towel and rest for 1 hour.

To make

• With the help of the rounded end of your scraper, turn the dough out of the bowl and reshape into a ball, place it back in the bowl, cover with a tea towel and rest for a further 45 minutes.

• Turn the dough out onto a lightly floured work surface and mould it into a loaf shape (page 31). Leave to prove for 1 hour on a well-floured tea towel, seam-side-up.

• Turn the loaf over and place on a wooden peel or flat-edged baking tray. With a razor or sharp knife make three cuts on either side fanning out from the middle, along the top of the bread. Mist the inside of your preheated oven with a water spray and then slide the loaf onto the hot stone or upturned tray. Bake for about 45 minutes until well-coloured. The loaf should sound hollow when tapped on the base with your finger. Remove from the oven and cool on a wire rack.

sesame plaits

These are tiny plaited rolls which are good fun to make.

Quantity:	12 plaits
Preparation:	45 minutes
Resting:	65 minutes
Proving:	45 minutes
Baking:	12–15 minutes

1 Batch Brown dough (page 93) rested for 1 hour
50g Sesame seeds

To make

• Turn the rested dough out with the help of the rounded end of your scraper. With the flat edge, divide it into 12 equal pieces and roll them into balls (page 28). Cover with a tea towel and rest for 5 minutes.

• Lightly flour your work surface. Take one of the balls and flatten it to form a disc. Fold in two of the sides, to the centre, to form a rough rectangle, then turn it over so the folds are underneath. Using a sharp-bladed knife, make two parallel cuts straight through the dough starting just short of one end and going all the way down to the other, so that you end up with three strands joined together at one end by a strip of dough.

• Plait the strands by passing each one of the outer strands over the middle one in turn. Repeat until you reach the ends and seal by rolling each end of the plait until pointed. Repeat with the other eleven balls.

• Put the sesame seeds on a plate. Brush the tops of the rolls with a little water and dip (tops only) into the seeds. Place on a baking tray, cover with a tea towel, and leave to prove in a warm, draught-free place for 45 minutes or until they have nearly doubled in volume.

• Put into the preheated oven. Using a water spray, mist the inside of the oven just before you close the door. Turn down the heat to 220°C and bake for 12–15 minutes.

brown rolls

These are the wholemeal equivalent of the Lemon Rolls in chapter 1, but shaped more simply.

Quantity:	12 rolls
Preparation:	30 minutes
Resting:	65 minutes
Proving:	45 minutes
Baking:	10 minutes

1 Batch Brown dough (page 93) rested for 1 hour

To make

• Turn the dough out onto a lightly floured work surface with the help of the rounded end of your scraper. Divide it into twelve equal pieces and mould each one into a ball (page 28). Place them on a baking tray, cover with a tea towel and leave to rest on your work surface for 5 minutes.

• After resting, shape into balls again, roll a little into an oval shape, and place on a second baking tray, again leaving enough space for the rolls to rise without touching. Cover with a tea towel.

• Leave the rolls in a draught-free place to prove for 45 minutes until they have nearly doubled in volume.

• Using a razor blade or sharp knife, make one long cut lengthways, from one tip to the other. Open the preheated oven and mist with a water spray. Quickly put the rolls in the oven, turn down the heat to 230°C and bake for 10 minutes. Cool on a wire rack.

poppy seed stars

These look really pretty on a bread board alongside other shapes or styles of rolls and breadsticks.

Quantity: 12 stars
Preparation: 45 minutes
Resting: 65 minutes
Proving: 45 minutes
Baking: 10–12 minutes

1 Batch Brown dough (page 93) rested for 1 hour
50g Poppy seeds

To make

• With the help of the rounded end of your scraper, turn out the dough. With the flat edge divide it into 12 pieces (about 70g each) and roll them into balls (page 28), cover with a tea towel and rest for 5 minutes.

• Scatter the poppy seeds on a plate and fill a shallow bowl with water. Flatten one of the rolls with the palm of your hand, dip the top into the water, then immediately into the seeds and press them in with your hand. Place on your lightly floured work surface, seed-side-up, and flatten a little with your hand. Using the short end of a clean credit card make a diagonal cut across the centre of the dough – the cut shouldn't reach the edges of the roll but should go all the way through it to the work surface. Then make two other diagonal cuts that intersect the first one equally, so that the three cuts form a star shape. Carefully push the roll from underneath with your fingertips, and turn it inside out, so that the points of the star push upwards and outwards, resulting in the points being on the outside. Place the stars on a baking tray, seed-side-up, cover with a tea towel and leave to prove for about 45 minutes until the stars have nearly doubled in volume.

• Put them in the preheated oven, mist the inside with a water spray, and bake them for 10–12 minutes. Remove from the oven and cool on a wire rack.

multiseed brown bread

This is a very earthy, crunchy but simple bread, for which I use a multigrain flour.

Quantity:	2 loaves
Preparation:	15 minutes
Resting:	70 minutes
Proving:	1 hour
Baking:	15–20 minutes

200g Strong wholemeal flour
175g Strong white flour
125g Multigrain flour, plus some more for topping
10g Yeast
10g Salt
340g Water (340ml)
A little butter for greasing

To prepare

Grease 2 x 500g (20–22cm long) tins with a little butter. Preheat the oven to 250ºC.
Mix the three flours together and rub in the yeast, using your fingertips as if making a crumble. Add the salt and water, then continue according to the method on pages 22–25. Mould the dough into a ball (page 25), place in a lightly floured bowl, cover with a tea towel and leave to rest for 1 hour.

To make

• With the help of the rounded end of your scraper, turn the dough out onto your work surface and divide it into two equal pieces. Form each into a ball, cover with a tea towel and rest for a further 10 minutes.

• Mould each ball into a loaf (page 31) but, before putting the loaves into the tins, brush the tops with a little water and roll in some more multigrain flour. Cover with another tea towel and leave to prove for about 1 hour or until the loaves have nearly doubled in volume.

• Open the preheated oven and mist the inside with a water spray. Quickly place the tins on the baking stone or tray in the oven and close the door. Bake the loaves for 15–20 minutes. Remove and cool on a wire rack.

raisin, hazelnut & shallot bread

This is lovely toasted with some cheese and a spoonful of home-made chutney or ham and some good mustard. The idea is based on a confit of shallots I used to make to serve with duck, a long time ago – and the sweetness along with the nuts make a special combination.

Quantity:	2 loaves
Preparation:	45 minutes
Resting:	1½ hours
Proving:	1–1¼ hours
Baking:	30 minutes

1 Batch Brown dough (page 93)
1 teaspoon Good-quality runny honey (preferably organic)

A little Oil
A knob of Butter
80g Shallots, sliced
80g Hazelnuts, crushed
80g Raisins

To make

• Heat a frying pan on the hob until it is really hot. Add the oil and knob of butter. Put in the shallots and stir from time to time until they are soft and brown. Add the crushed hazelnuts, stir and cook over a medium heat for 1 minute, then add the raisins, stir again and cook for a further 30 seconds. Remove from the heat and transfer to a flat plate or tray to cool.

• Make the dough following the method on page 22, adding the honey along with the salt and water. Towards the end of working by hand or mixing in a mixer, add the shallots mixture and continue working/ mixing until it is evenly distributed. Form the dough into a ball (page 25), put it into a lightly floured bowl, cover with a tea towel and rest for 45 minutes. Turn the dough out onto your work surface and reshape it into a ball, put it back into the bowl, cover and rest for a further 45 minutes.

• Lightly flour your work surface. Divide the dough into two equal pieces and mould each one into a loaf (page 31). Lightly flour a tea towel with wholemeal flour and lay it on a tray. Lift the centre of the tea towel gently to form a ridge and place one loaf (smooth-side-down) on each side of the ridge. Cover with another tea towel and leave to prove for 1-1¼ hours or until the loaves have nearly doubled in volume.

• Turn the loaves over and place on a peel or flat-edged baking tray. With a razor blade or sharp knife, make one long cut the length of the top of each bread, to a depth of about 5mm. Mist the inside of your oven with a water spray and then slide the loaves onto the baking stone or tray. Bake them for about 30 minutes until well coloured. The loaves should sound hollow when tapped on the base with your finger. Remove from the oven and cool on a wire rack.

pecan & cranberry bread

I was thinking about Christmas and cranberries when I first made this, and because there happened to be some pecan nuts around I added those too. All the flavours just seemed to work really happily with the wholemeal flour, and I discovered that the bread goes brilliantly with Stilton.

Quantity:	1 large or 2 small loaves	**1 Batch** Brown dough (page 93)	
Preparation:	20 minutes	**100g** Shelled pecan nuts	
Resting:	65 minutes	**100g** Dried cranberries	
Proving:	1 hour	**Zest of 1** Large orange	
Baking:	20 minutes baking for small loaves or 40 minutes for a large loaf		

To prepare

Crush the pecan nuts – I do this with the end of a rolling pin or you could use a pestle and mortar.
Mix the pecans, cranberries and orange zest.
Make the brown dough following the method on page 22, but add the pecan and cranberry mix towards the end of working by hand or mixing in the mixer, and ensure that they are evenly distributed. Form the dough into a ball (page 25) and place in a lightly floured bowl covered with a tea towel to rest for 1 hour.

To make

• Turn the dough out onto a well-floured work surface and divide in half if you want to make two smaller loaves. Form into a ball or balls and leave to rest for a further 5 minutes.

• Mould again into a tight ball (or two) and place, smooth-side-down, in a floured wicker proving basket (if you have one) or a bowl lined with a well floured tea towel. Cover with another tea towel and leave to prove for about 1 hour until the dough has nearly doubled in volume.

• Turn the dough out of the bowl or basket and place on a peel or flat-edged baking tray. Cut a cross into the top of the loaf (loaves) with a razor blade or sharp knife. Open the preheated oven and mist the inside with a water spray. Quickly slide the loaf (or loaves) onto the baking stone or tray and close the door. Bake small loaves at 220°C for the first 5 minutes then turn the oven down to 200°C for the remaining 15 minutes. For a large loaf, bake for 5 minutes at 220°C, then a further 30-35 minutes at 200°C. Remove from the oven and cool on a wire rack.

100% wholemeal bread

This is heavier, but not as heavy as many breads made only with wholemeal flour, because it is made with a 'poolish', a style of ferment which was introduced into France by Polish bakers and which packs the bread with flavour and character, and helps lighten it.

Quantity: 2 loaves
Preparation: 15 minutes
Resting: 3–5 hours for the poolish
30 minutes for the bread
Proving: 1 hour
Baking: 30–35 minutes

For the poolish ferment:
5g Yeast (fresh if possible)
250g Tepid water (250ml)
250g Wholemeal flour

250g Wholemeal flour
5g Yeast (fresh if possible)
10g Salt
80g Water (80ml)
A little butter for
greasing

To prepare

Butter 2 x 500g (20–22cm long) loaf tins.

To make the poolish, whisk the yeast into the water until it has completely dissolved, then add the flour and whisk to obtain a batter. Cover with a tea towel and leave to rest for at least 3 hours, but no longer than 5, by which time it should have around doubled in volume – it is ready when it has formed into a dome and then slightly flattened out – at this point you need to use it quickly, because if you leave it any longer, it will start to collapse. Add the rest of the ingredients to the poolish, mix well using your scraper, and work by hand following the method on pages 24–25, until the dough is supple and no longer sticks to your hand or the work surface. Shape the dough into a ball and put into a lightly floured bowl, covered with a tea towel, to rest for 15 minutes. Preheat the oven to 250°C.

To make

• With the help of the rounded edge of your scraper, turn the dough out onto your work surface and divide it into two. Form each into a ball again, cover with a tea towel and rest for a further 15 minutes.

• Mould the two pieces of dough into tight loaves (page 31) and place in the greased tins. Cover with a tea towel and leave to prove for about 1 hour until they have nearly doubled in volume.

• Dust the tops of the loaves with a little wholemeal flour. Put them into the preheated oven. With a water spray mist the inside of the oven just before you close the door. Bake them for 30–35 minutes until they sound hollow when you tap the base with your finger. Remove from the oven and cool on a wire rack.

Most people associate rye bread with dark, heavy Scandinavian and Germanic-style breads such as pumpernickel. However, when you blend strong white flour with the rye flour, it lifts and lightens the texture, giving a really tasty, rustic bread that offers a wonderful base for ingredients like olives, fruit, nuts and spices. If you like your rye bread darker still, then just increase the ratio of rye flour to white, or if you prefer it lighter, you can increase the percentage of white flour.

400g Strong white flour
100g Dark rye flour
10g Yeast (fresh if possible)
10g Salt
350g Water (350ml – but weighing is more accurate)

Preheat the oven to 250°C. Mix the two flours together and rub in the yeast, using your fingertips as if making a crumble. Add the salt and water, then continue according to the method on pages 22–25, but check your recipe to see if you need to add any other ingredients at this stage.

dark rye
bread

somerset
cider bread

rye,
caraway
& raisin
bread

pain de
campagne

olive
bread

walnut
bread

aniseed
&
guinness
bread

moked
con &
onion
ead

walnut bread

I sometimes make this with a combination of walnuts and dates (while prunes have a natural affinity with wholemeal bread, dates are perfect with rye – raisins are good, too). If you are going to use fruit, reduce the quantity of walnuts to 150g, and add 125g chopped dates or raisins.

Quantity:	2 rings	
Preparation:	30 minutes	
Resting:	65 minutes	
Proving:	1 hour	
Baking:	20 minutes	

1 Batch Rye dough (page 117)
200g Shelled walnuts, crushed using a rolling pin or pestle and mortar (when broken unevenly they release their oil into the dough more easily)
Flour for dusting

To make

• Make the dough following the method on pages 22–25, adding the walnuts at the end of working by hand or mixing in the mixer and continue working/mixing until they are evenly distributed. Shape the dough into a ball, put it into a lightly floured bowl, cover with a tea towel and leave to rest for 1 hour. With the help of the rounded end of your scraper, turn out the dough onto a lightly floured work surface and divide into two. Shape each piece into a ball, cover with a tea towel and rest for a further 5 minutes, then remould the dough into a tight ball. Press the end of your rolling pin into the centre of each ball until you reach the work surface and make a hole. Flour your hands and then open up the hole to form a ring – the hole should be at least the size of a fist to prevent it from closing up as the dough rises. Lightly flour a tea towel and place the bread rings on top. Cover with another tea towel and leave to prove for about 1 hour until the rings have nearly doubled in volume. Transfer to a peel or flat-edged baking tray and, with a razor or sharp knife, make three cuts at equal points around the ring. Open the preheated oven and mist with a water spray. Quickly slide the rings onto the baking stone, turn down the heat to 220°C, and bake for 5 minutes, then turn down to 200°C and bake for a further 15 minutes. Remove and cool on a wire rack.

olive bread

This bread is inspired by the beautiful little pain de campagne-style loaves you find, filled with dark olive paste, in the markets of Provence – stunning.

Quantity:	3 loaves	
Preparation:	40 minutes	
Resting:	1 hour	
Proving:	1 hour	
Baking:	18–20 minutes	

1 Batch Rye dough (page 117) rested for 1 hour
100g Olive paste
Flour for dusting

To make

• With the help of the rounded end of your scraper, turn the dough out onto a lightly floured work surface and divide it into three pieces. Take the pieces one at a time, and flatten them with the palm of your hand into a rough rectangular shape. Spread about 2 tablespoons of the paste over the dough. Then fold and form into loaves (page 31).

• Place the loaves (seam-side-down) onto a lightly floured tea towel, flour the top of the loaves and pull the tea towel into low ridges in between the loaves so that they do not end up touching as they rise. Cover with a second tea towel and leave to prove for 1 hour or until the loaves have nearly doubled in volume.

• Transfer the loaves to a peel or flat-edged baking tray and make a single cut down the middle of each loaf with a razor blade or sharp knife. Open the preheated oven and mist the inside with a water spray, then quickly slide the loaves onto the preheated baking stone or tray and close the door. Bake them for 18–20 minutes. The loaves should sound hollow when tapped on the base with your finger. Cool on a wire rack.

olive paste

Drain and remove the stone from 180g Picholine (Provençal) olives (or similar). Put into a food processor with 2 teaspoons herbes de Provence and 20g extra-virgin olive oil and blitz until you have a coarse paste. You can store this in an airtight container in the fridge for a few days. Alternatively you can freeze the paste for several weeks, defrost it at room temperature and add a few drops of lemon juice to refresh it when you need it. This will make 200g.

rye, caraway & raisin bread

Rye and caraway are a classic combination, and the raisins just add a sweetness which works really well with cheese, especially blue cheese. Caraway is a favourite of mine – I love the aroma of the seeds when the bread is baking – but you can reduce the quantity if you are less partial to it.

Quantity:	2 loaves	**1 Batch** Rye dough (page 117)	
Preparation:	20 minutes	**250g** Raisins or sultanas	
Resting:	70 minutes	**1 teaspoon** Caraway seeds	
Proving:	1 hour	Flour for dusting	
Baking:	30 minutes		

To prepare

Mix the fruit and caraway seeds together.

Make the dough following the method on pages 22–25, adding the fruit and caraway shortly before the end of working by hand or mixing in the mixer. Continue working/mixing until they are evenly distributed. Shape the dough into a ball (page 25), place in a bowl, cover with a tea towel and rest for 1 hour.

To make

• With the help of the rounded end of the scraper, turn out the dough onto a lightly floured work surface and divide into two. Mould each into a ball, cover with a tea towel and leave on the work surface to rest for 10 minutes.

• Mould each ball into a tight loaf shape (page 31) of about 20cm length. Lightly flour a tea towel and place the loaves onto it, seam-side-up, making a pleat in the tea towel in between each one, so that they do not touch as they rise. Cover with another tea towel and leave to prove for 1 hour until they have nearly doubled in volume.

• Turn the loaves over and transfer to a peel or flat-edged baking tray and cut a leaf pattern (one cut down the centre, with four cuts fanning out on each side) in the top with a razor or sharp knife. Mist the inside of the preheated oven with a water spray. Slide the loaves onto the baking stone or tray and quickly close the door. Turn the heat down to 220°C and bake for 30 minutes. The loaves sound hollow when tapped on the base. Remove and cool on a wire rack.

smoked bacon & red onion bread

Smoked bacon and red onion are a great combination, which make a beautiful loaf to slice for sandwiches, or to serve with something like a chicken liver salad. Make sure you use good bacon, preferably dry-cured in the traditional fashion. The balsamic vinegar is only a dash to deglaze the pan, so it doesn't need to be the best quality – or you could use a tablespoon of red wine or red wine vinegar instead.

Quantity:	4 small loaves
Preparation:	30 minutes
Resting:	70 minutes
Proving:	1¼ hours
Baking:	20 minutes

1 Batch Rye dough (page 117)
1 tablespoon Olive oil
8 Thick slices Smoked, dry, cured bacon, snipped into strips
1 Large Red onion, finely sliced
1 tablespoon Balsamic vinegar
Flour for dusting

To make

• Preheat the oven to 250°C. Heat the oil in a frying pan and fry the bacon over a medium heat for a couple of minutes until it starts to brown and crisp, then add the onion and cook for another couple of minutes. Deglaze the pan by pouring in the vinegar and stirring well over the heat for a further minute or so, scraping all the bits of bacon from the bottom. Transfer the bacon, onion and juices into a dish to cool.

• Make the dough according to the method on pages 22–25, adding the bacon mixture towards the end of working by hand or mixing in a mixer and continue to work/mix until it is evenly distributed. Form the dough into a ball (page 25), put into a lightly floured bowl, cover with a tea towel and rest for 1 hour.

• With the help of the rounded end of your scraper, turn the dough out onto a lightly floured work surface and divide it into four roughly equal pieces. Mould each into a ball, cover with a tea towel and leave on the work surface to rest for a further 10 minutes. Reshape each of the pieces into a tight ball again. Lightly flour a tea towel (or two) and place the balls, smooth-side-up, on top. Cover with another tea towel (or towels) and leave to prove for about 1¼ hours until they have nearly doubled in volume.

• Transfer to a peel or flat-edged baking tray. Make a circular cut on the top of each loaf with a razor or sharp knife. Mist your preheated oven with a water spray, quickly slide the loaves onto the baking stone/tray and bake at 220°C for 5 minutes, turn down the heat to 190°C and bake for a further 15 minutes. The loaf should sound hollow if tapped on the base with your finger. Cool on a wire rack.

somerset cider bread

This was a bread I made to celebrate our move to Bath to set up my cookery school – using Burrow Hill Cider from Julian Temperley at the Somerset Cider Brandy Co. instead of the Breton cider I used to use for a similar bread in France. Adding cider, or ale, is a very traditional thing to do, and it lends the bread a real 'country,' rustic note, while the flavour is deepened by the addition of some fermented rye dough. This is a bread that is fabulous with some cured ham or a proper, traditional Cheddar. In this bread, I suggest you make a larger quantity of dough, as I feel the ferment works better with more bulk.

Quantity: 4 loaves
Preparation: 20 minutes
Resting: 4–6 hours for the ferment
1½ hours for the dough
Proving: 1¼–1½ hours
Baking: 45 minutes

For the ferment:
½ **Batch** Rye dough (page 117) left to ferment for 4–6 hours

10g Yeast (fresh if possible)
750g Strong white flour
250g Dark rye flour
20g Salt
450g Good-quality dry cider
150g Water (150ml)
Flour for dusting

To make

• Use your scraper to scoop the ferment from its container into your bowl, all in one piece, and add the rest of your ingredients (adding the cider with the water) and follow the method on pages 22–25. Shape the dough into a ball (page 25), put it into a lightly floured bowl, cover with a tea towel and rest for 45 minutes.

• With the help of the rounded end of your plastic scraper, turn the dough onto a lightly floured work surface and reshape into a ball, place it back into the bowl, cover with a tea towel and leave to rest for 45 minutes.

• Using the scraper, turn the dough out onto your lightly floured work surface and divide it into four equal pieces. Lightly flour a couple of tea towels. Mould the balls of dough into loaves (page 31) and place two on top of each tea towel, making a fold in the fabric between them to stop them touching when they rise. Cover with a tea towel and leave to prove for 1¼–1½ hours, or until they have nearly doubled in volume.

• Turn the loaves over, place on a peel or flat-edged baking tray and make one cut lengthways along the top of the loaves with a razor blade or sharp knife. Mist the inside of your preheated oven with a water spray and then slide the loaves onto the baking stone or tray. Bake for 10 minutes, then turn down the heat to 200°C, and bake for about 35 minutes until well coloured. The loaves should sound hollow when tapped on the base with your finger. Remove and cool on a wire rack.

aniseed & guinness bread

I love aniseed – particularly in pastis, and since I'm told that 'Black Velvet' can be made either with Champagne or pastis and Guinness (for which I have also developed a taste since coming to Britain), this seemed to me to be the perfect combination of flavours. I think it is brilliant served, Irish style, with seafood, especially oysters, and a drop more Guinness – cold, and in a glass, this time.

Quantity:	3 loaves
Preparation:	30 minutes
Resting:	3 hours 35 minutes
Proving:	1¹/₂ hours
Baking:	30 minutes

25g Yeast (fresh if possible)
700g Guinness, at room temperature (700ml)
250g Dark rye flour
750g Strong white flour
20g Salt
1 tablespoon Pastis
Flour for dusting

To make

• Whisk the yeast into the Guinness in a large mixing bowl until it has completely dissolved, then add the rye flour and 400g of the white flour and whisk to obtain a thick batter. Cover with a tea towel and rest for 2 hours.

• Preheat the oven to 250ºC. Add the rest of the ingredients to the batter, mix well and make the dough following the method on pages 22–25, until the dough is supple, elastic and no longer sticks to your hands. Shape into a ball and put into a lightly floured bowl, cover with a tea towel and leave to rest for 45 minutes.

• With the help of the rounded end of your scraper, turn the dough out onto a lightly floured work surface and reshape into a ball, place back in the bowl, cover with the tea towel and leave to rest for a further 45 minutes. With the help of the scraper, again turn the dough out and divide it into three equal pieces. Shape each into a ball again, and leave on the work surface, covered with a tea towel, to rest for a further 5 minutes. Lay a couple of tea towels on a baking tray and lightly flour them. Mould the balls into loaves (page 31) and place them on the tea towels, leaving a good space in between them. Cover with another tea towel and leave to prove for 1¹/₂ hours, or until they have nearly doubled in volume.

• Place the loaves on a peel or flat-edged baking tray, and make two diagonal cuts on the tops with a razor blade or sharp knife. Mist the inside of your preheated oven with a water spray and slide the loaves onto the baking stone/tray. Bake them for 5 minutes, reduce the heat to 220ºC and bake for a further 25 minutes until they are a rich dark colour. They should sound hollow when tapped on the base. Remove from the oven and cool completely on a wire rack.

pain de campagne

Think of pain de campagne as sourdough's little brother. Sourdough is enjoying a huge renaissance in popularity; however, making it in the traditional fashion is a serious breadmaking event: a long process in which a ferment is made without commercial yeast. The idea is that it attracts the natural, wild yeasts that are in the air all around us, allowing the dough to ferment very slowly, giving the bread its characteristicly robust flavour. In France the classic pain de campagne is used in a similar way to sourdough. You buy it to keep for a few days, as its flavour matures – and it lends itself beautifully to toasting and rubbing bruschetta-style with garlic and/or tomatoes, then adding a topping of your choice.

Quantity:	2 loaves	**For the ferment:**	**500g** Strong white bread
Preparation:	30 minutes	**1/2 batch** rye dough (page	flour
Resting:	4–6 hours for the ferment	117) left in a bowl (covered	**100g** Dark rye flour
	2 1/2 hours for the bread	with clingfilm) to ferment for	**5g** Yeast (fresh if possible)
Proving:	1 1/4 hours	4–6 hours, or overnight in the	**15g** Salt
Baking:	30–35 minutes	fridge and then brought	**400g** Water (400ml)
		back to room temperature	Flour for dusting

To make

• Use your scraper to scoop the ferment from its container into your bowl, all in one piece, and add the rest of your ingredients. Make the dough following the method on pages 22–25 and work it until you have a smooth dough which should be soft, supple and elastic, and shouldn't feel sticky. Form it into a ball (page 25) and place in a lightly floured bowl, covered with a tea towel, to rest for 1 hour.

• With the help of the rounded end of your scraper, turn the dough out onto a lightly floured work surface and shape it into a ball again, put back in the bowl, cover and leave to rest for a 1 hour.

• Repeat the above step, but rest for 30 minutes. Using the rounded end of the scraper again, turn the dough onto a well-floured work surface and divide it into two pieces of about 600g each. Shape each into a ball. Lightly flour two wicker proving baskets or line bowls with tea towels, well dusted with flour, and put a ball of dough into each one, seam-side-down. Cover with another tea towel and leave to prove for about 1 1/4 hours, or until they have nearly doubled in volume.

• Place the loaves on a peel or flat-edged baking tray, seam-side down, and cut a circle in the top of each loaf with a razor blade or sharp knife. Mist the inside of the preheated oven with a water spray. Quickly slide the loaves onto the baking stone or tray and bake for 5 minutes. Turn down the heat to 220°C and bake for a further 25–30 minutes until they are dark brown. The loaves should sound hollow if tapped on the base with your finger. Remove from the oven and cool on a wire rack.

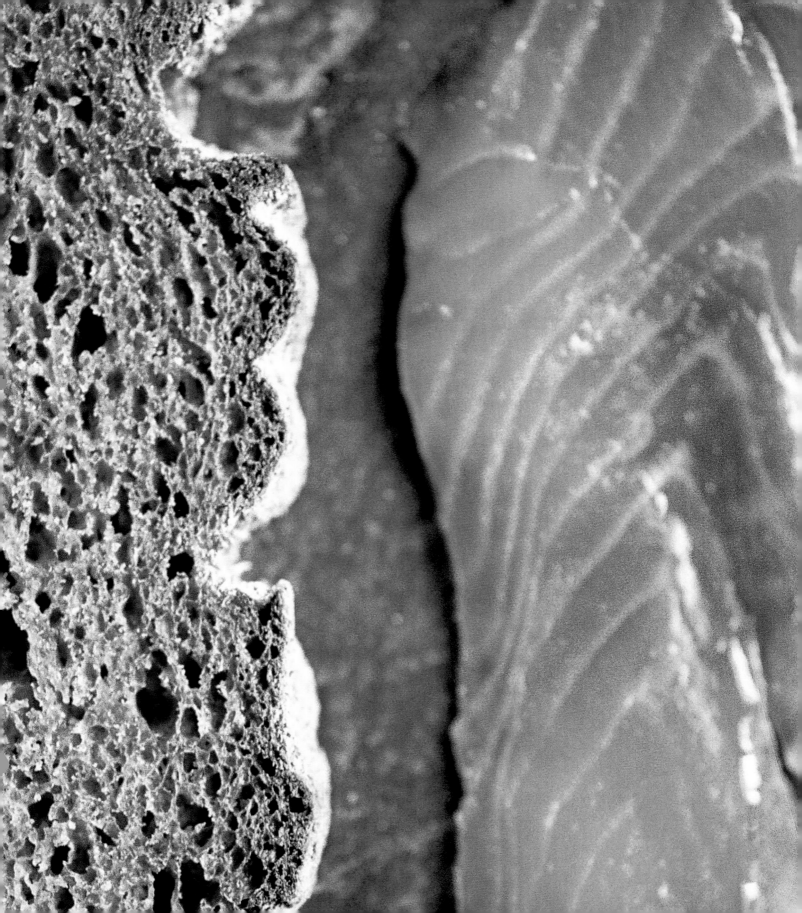

dark rye bread

This, again, is a slightly more complex loaf, boosted with extra flavour from the 'poolish' (page 114). While all bread should be allowed to cool before eating, dark rye bread, such as this one, can be especially indigestible if you eat it while still warm – so try to be patient and let it cool down properly for several hours, before cutting into it.

Quantity:	2 loaves	**For the poolish ferment:**	**200g** Dark rye flour
Preparation:	30 minutes	**6g** Yeast (fresh if possible)	**210g** Strong white flour
Resting:	3–5 hours for the poolish	**275g** Tepid water (275ml)	**15g** Salt
	95 minutes for the dough	**250g** Dark rye flour	**115g** Tepid water (115ml)
Proving:	1 hour		Flour for dusting
Baking:	45–50 minutes		

To prepare

To make the poolish, whisk the yeast into the water until completely dissolved, then add the flour and whisk to obtain a thick batter. Cover with a tea towel and leave to rest for at least 3 but no more than 5 hours. The poolish is ready to use when it forms a dome and then begins to flatten slightly. Once it reaches this point use it quickly, as if you leave it any longer, it will start to collapse. Add the poolish to the rest of the ingredients and work/mix following the method on pages 22–25. Shape the dough into a ball (page 25) and place in to a lightly floured bowl, covered with a tea towel, to rest for 45 minutes. Preheat the oven to 250°C.

To make

• With the help of the rounded end of your scraper, turn the dough out onto a lightly floured work surface and reshape it into a ball, place back in the bowl, cover with a tea towel and rest for a further 45 minutes.

• Again using your scraper, turn the dough out onto your lightly floured work surface and divide the dough into two equal pieces. Shape each into a ball and leave on the work surface, covered with a tea towel, to rest for a further 5 minutes. Line two proving baskets or bowls with well-floured tea towels. Mould the loaves into tight balls and place them, seam-side-down, on the tea towels. Cover with more tea towels and leave to prove for 1 hour or until they have nearly doubled in volume.

• Place the loaves on the peel or flat-edged baking tray, seam-side-down. Make four cuts in the top of each loaf, in each direction, to form a criss-cross pattern. Open the preheated oven and mist with a water spray, then quickly slide the loaves onto the baking stone or tray. Bake them for 5 minutes then turn down the heat to 200°C for a further 40–45 minutes. When the loaves are done they will look quite dark and sound hollow if tapped on the base with your finger. Remove and cool completely on a wire rack.

5. Sweet Dough

Sweet: melodious, gratifying

This dough is a cross between brioche and white bread and belongs to the family of 'milk doughs'. I love it because it isn't too sweet, yet it's sweet enough to carry the likes of chocolate and, although it is enriched with milk and butter, it isn't so rich that you couldn't use it, in its basic form, to make a brilliant tuna sandwich, croque monsieur or serve it lightly toasted with foie gras.

For the recipes in this chapter, preheat the oven to 220°C instead of 250°C.

250g Full-fat milk (250ml – weighing is more accurate)
15g Yeast (fresh if possible)
500g Strong bread flour
60g Unsalted butter at room temperature
40g Caster sugar
10g Salt
2 Large eggs

To make the dough

• Pour the milk into a pan and warm gently until it is about body temperature – it should feel neither warm nor cold when you dip your finger into it. (You can use a microwave to do this if you prefer – about 1¹/₂ minutes at full power.)

• To mix by hand, rub the yeast into the flour using your fingertips as if making a crumble. Rub in the butter, then add the sugar and salt, then the eggs and milk. Continue according to the method on pages 22–25, but check your recipe to see if you need to add any other ingredients at this stage.

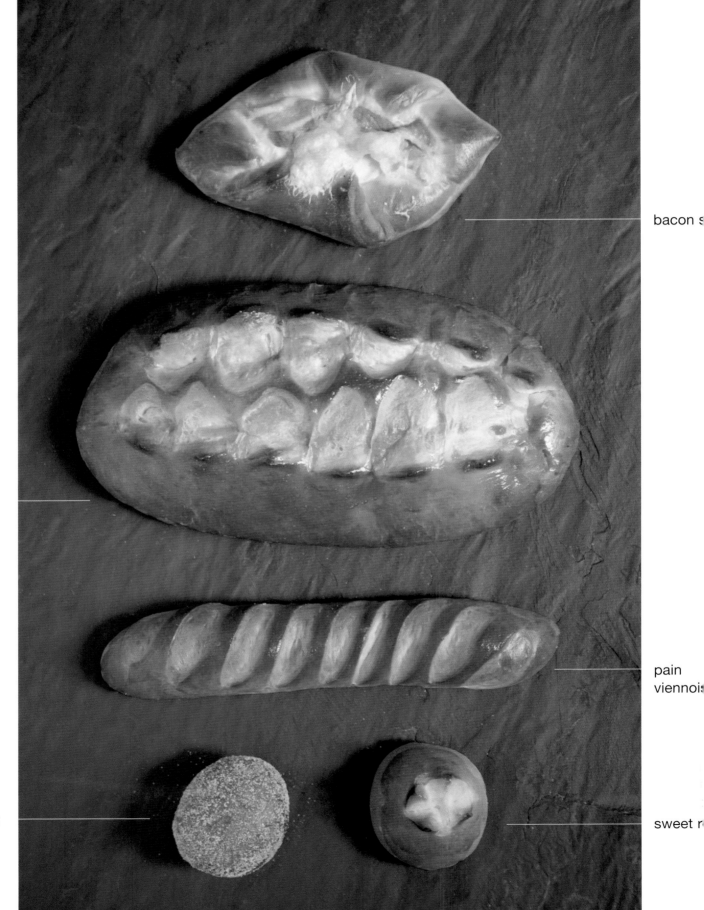

bacon s

orange &
mint loaf

pain
viennois

doughnut

sweet r

fruited tea
loaf

ck's
ocolate
n

scone

ricot &
mond
t

orange & mint loaf

I first made this when experimenting with a Marmalade Bread and Butter Pudding made with brioche and a dash of Grand Marnier. Instead of using brioche as a base, I wanted to try a more unusual bread that would really carry the flavour of the liqueur. From the starting point of orange, I tried infusing the dough with mint. The flavour was fantastic, and the bread kept well for several days, so I tried toasting it and serving it with a pot of fresh minted butter – and it was even better. I've also toasted it at breakfast time with scrambled eggs and crispy bacon. I love bread and butter pudding – such an English thing! However we do have something similar in France, which we used to do in the bakery to use up all the leftovers at the end of the day: croissants, pain au chocolat, you name it, everything would go into a big mixer with sultanas, crème anglaise and some alcohol, until it became a thick paste, which we would bake for about 2 hours, cut up into portions and then dust with sugar. It tasted fantastic.

Quantity:	2 large loaves
Preparation:	20 minutes
Infusing:	1 hour (for the milk)
Resting:	1 hour
Proving:	1½ hours
Baking:	22–32 minutes

1 Batch Sweet dough (page 137)
1 bunch of fresh mint
Zest of 2 Large oranges
1 tablespoon Cointreau
1 Egg beaten with a pinch of salt for an egg wash
Flour for dusting
A little butter for greasing

To prepare

Infuse the milk for the sweet dough with a bunch of mint by warming it through over a low heat, then take the pan off the heat and leave it for 1 hour before straining.

Mix the orange zest with the Cointreau. Lightly grease a baking tray with butter.

Make the sweet dough in the usual way (page 137) but using the mint-infused milk. At the end of working the dough by hand/mixing in a mixer add the orange zest and incorporate it well. Form it into a ball (page 25), lightly flour the bowl, and rest the dough for 1 hour.

To make

• With the help of the rounded end of your scraper, gently turn the dough out onto a very lightly floured work surface and divide it into two equal portions. Mould each piece into a loaf shape (page 31) and place on the lightly greased baking tray. Brush the top of each loaf with a little egg wash. Let the egg wash dry for a moment, then cover the loaves with a tea towel and leave to prove for 1½ hours, or until the dough has nearly doubled in volume and is springy when prodded with your finger. Brush again with a little egg wash. Using a pair of scissors held at 45° to the surface, make cuts along the length of each loaf. Put into the preheated oven, turn down the heat and bake at 210°C for the first 2 minutes, then turn down to 200°C for a further 20–30 minutes until the loaf is dark golden brown. Serve, toasted if you like, with mint butter.

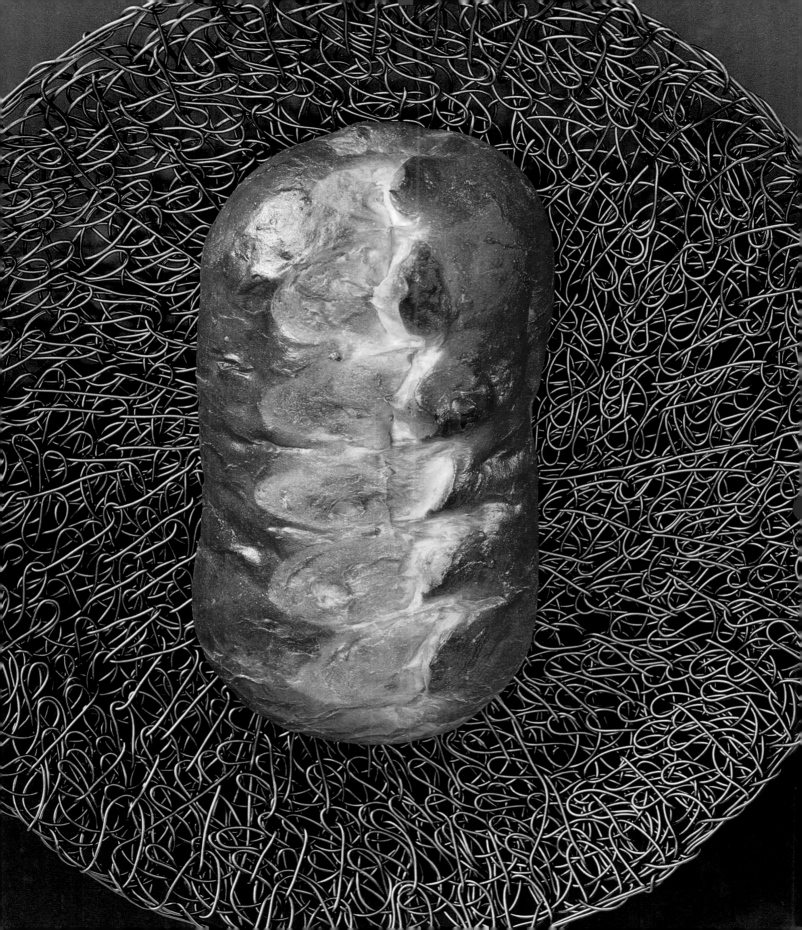

For the freezer: The loaf can happily be frozen, wrapped in freezer bags, and kept for 2–3 months.

mint butter

Put half a packet of butter and a bunch of mint (leaves only) into a food processor and blitz until combined. Chill in a bowl in the fridge until required.

marmalade bread & butter pudding (6–8 people)

You can use the Orange and Mint Loaf for this – or alternatively buy some brioche. Whatever you choose, you will need two loaves.

Preheat the oven to 210°C and soak 200g sultanas in 4 tablespoons of Grand Marnier, while you make the crème anglaise. Do this by bringing 1 litre of full-fat milk to the boil in a heavy–bottomed pan along with a vanilla pod (split lengthways and with the seeds scraped into the pan). In a bowl whisk 10 egg yolks and 150g caster sugar until they are a pale straw colour and take on a mousse-like appearance.

To make the crème anglaise: Pour the milk into the egg mixture, whisking well as you do so. Return the mixture to the pan over a medium heat. Using a wooden spoon stir continuously in a figure of 8 until it thickens enough to coat the back of a spoon. (To test, lift the spoon out of the crème and draw a line down the back of the spoon. If the line stays clean it is cooked.) Strain immediately into a clean bowl and continue stirring for 1 minute.

Slice the orange and mint loaf or brioche – the slices need to be about 1cm thick. Spread with marmalade then cut in half diagonally to form triangles. Strain the sultanas, but don't throw away the Grand Marnier. Overlap the triangles (points up) in an ovenproof dish, making sure there are no gaps between the slices. Scatter over the sultanas, pour the crème anglaise over the top, slowly, allowing time for the bread to absorb the liquid (there will probably be a good amount left, which you can keep back and serve with the pudding). Put in the preheated oven and cook for 20–30 minutes until golden brown on top.

To serve, warm the Grand Marnier in a small saucepan. Remove from the heat and light with a match. Pour over the pudding and then sprinkle with a little sifted icing sugar. Serve with crème fraîche, vanilla ice cream or any remaining crème anglaise.

jack's chocolate buns

My son Jack loves pain aux raisins – and chocolate – so he badgered me to make him something that was a cross between the two. You should have seen Jack's face, lit up and covered in chocolate, when he bit into the first one I made. They are pretty gooey, so he is on rations: only one, for a treat!

Quantity:	24 buns	**1 Batch** Sweet dough (page 137)
Preparation:	20 minutes	**25g** Good-quality cocoa powder
Resting:	45 minutes	**200g** Chocolate chips, milk or plain, or a mixture of both, as you prefer
Proving:	1^{1}/$_{2}$–1^{3}/$_{4}$ hours	**2** Eggs beaten with a pinch of salt for an egg wash
Baking:	12–15 minutes	**Crème Patissière** (page 158)
		15g cocoa powder

Quantity: 24 buns
Preparation: 20 minutes
Resting: 45 minutes
Proving: 1½–1¾ hours
Baking: 12–15 minutes

1 Batch Sweet dough (page 137)
25g Good-quality cocoa powder
200g Chocolate chips, milk or plain, or a mixture of both, as you prefer
2 Eggs beaten with a pinch of salt for an egg wash
Crème Patissière (page 158)
15g cocoa powder

To prepare

Make the sweet dough following the method on page 137, but add the cocoa powder at the same time as the milk and egg at the end of working by hand or mixing in the mixer. Cover with a clean tea towel and leave to rest for 45 minutes in a draught-free place.

Make the crème patissière following the recipe on page 158, but add 15g cocoa powder to the milk. Pour into a dish to cool.

To make

• Using the rounded end of your scraper, transfer the dough to a lightly floured work surface and, with a rolling pin, gently flatten it into a rough rectangle. Spread the chocolate crème patissière evenly over the dough and then sprinkle on the chocolate chips. Starting with one of the longer edges, roll the dough up until it resembles a Swiss roll. Using a sharp knife, cut the roll into 2cm slices and place them on their sides on a baking tray. Glaze with a little egg wash and leave to prove for 1¼–1¾ hours until the buns have roughly doubled in size.

• Glaze again and put into the preheated oven, turning the heat down to 180°C. Bake for 12–15 minutes. As the chocolate dough is quite dark it can be difficult to tell when the buns are properly baked, and you need to take care not to underbake them – the best way to tell when they are ready is to lift one gently with a spatula, and check that it is firm underneath.

For the freezer: If you don't want to bake the buns all in one go, you can freeze some. When they are cut, just before proving, put them on a small tray in the freezer, and when they are hard put them into a freezer bag. To use them, take them out, leave them to prove overnight and bake in the same way.

doughnuts

These doughnuts come with a warning – don't even think of making them when you are on your own, as you may well end up eating the lot in one go – though if you have immense willpower they will keep for a couple of days in the fridge as long as they haven't been dusted with sugar first. If I make a tray of them, they miraculously disappear, though mysteriously everyone says, 'Nothing to do with me!'

   Doughnuts ('beignets' in France) are of course a great classic, but I hate greasy ones, and I don't like ones with icing on them. I am locked into the memories of the beignets my grandmother used to make as a treat. I can still see the huge pan, with the risen dough bulging over the top (I would always be told off for prodding it) and I remember the wonderful smell and the anticipation as the first ones were fried, and then dusted in sugar or served with some jam or apple purée – which is still the only way I like to eat them.

Quantity:	30 doughnuts	
Preparation:	20 minutes	
Resting:	1 hour	
Proving:	45 minutes	
Frying:	15 minutes	

1 Batch Sweet dough (page 137) rested for 1 hour

500ml Good-quality groundnut oil for frying plus a little extra caster sugar for coating the doughnuts

To fill the doughnuts (optional) either apple compote (page 158), raspberry jam or crème patissière (page 158)

Flour for dusting

Oil for greasing

To make

• With the help of the rounded end of your scraper, turn out the dough onto a lightly floured work surface and form it into pieces (page 28) weighing about 30g each. Roll into tight balls (page 29). Lightly oil a baking tray and lightly dust it with flour. Arrange the doughnuts on top (seam-side-down), leaving sufficient space between them so that they will not touch as they rise. Cover the tray with a tea towel and leave to prove until the doughnuts have nearly doubled in size – about 45 minutes.

• Pour the oil into a 20cm saucepan (any bigger and the oil won't be deep enough) and place over a medium heat. When the oil is hot (allow about 15 minutes to reach the right heat – 180°C), use a fish slice to lift the first doughnut and flip it over carefully into the oil. The doughnut should start sizzling straight away. Add more doughnuts until you fill the pan (I fry a maximum of 5 at a time). Fry for about 30–45 seconds until the doughnuts start to colour and then turn over and fry the other side for the same amount of time. Use the fish slice to remove the doughnuts from the pan and drain on several sheets of kitchen towel. Leave to cool.

• For plain doughnuts, simply roll them in caster sugar before serving. For filled doughnuts, spoon the filling of your choice into a piping bag with a small nozzle and fill by inserting the nozzle into the doughnut at one side. How much filling you pipe in is up to you!

apricot & almond tart

You might wonder why I have included a tart in this book, but this is based on the sweet dough topped with mirabelles or gooseberries that my grandmother used to make. She would assemble the tart, then leave it for a while, so that the dough rose up around the fruit and then, when she baked it, the juice would ooze out and into the dough. We would sprinkle sugar over the top before eating it, and it was just gorgeous. This is a slightly more elaborate version, with crème d'amande. I promise you, if you make up a big batch of sweet dough one day and use some for this tart and the rest to make doughnuts, you will be very, very popular!

Quantity:	2 tarts
Preparation:	20 minutes
Resting:	95 minutes
Proving:	45 minutes
Baking:	20–25 minutes

1 Batch Sweet dough (page 137) rested for 1 hour
300g Crème d'amande (page 158)
12–15 Fresh ripe apricots, or plums if you prefer
1 Egg beaten with a pinch of salt for an egg wash
Flour for dusting
A little icing sugar or apricot jam, to serve

To make

• With the help of the rounded end of your scraper, turn out the dough onto a lightly floured work surface, divide it in half and shape each piece into a ball (page 25). Place in a floured bowl, cover with a tea towel and leave to rest for 20 minutes.

• Grease 2 baking trays or line with greaseproof paper. Roll out each piece of dough to a circle of about 25–30cm diameter, place on the trays and leave to rest for a further 15 minutes.

• Quarter the apricots or plums. Spread the crème d'amande over the tart bases starting from the middle and stopping about 2.5cm from the edge. Arrange the fruit quarters on top, skin-side down, packing them together as neatly as you can. Leave the tarts to prove for 45 minutes (when the edges will have risen to about double their original height).

• Brush egg wash evenly over the edges of the tart. Turn down the preheated oven to 200°C, and bake until the tips of the apricots or plums have browned (if the top colours too fast, turn down to 190°C) and the base is golden brown – about 20–25 minutes. Remove from the tray and cool on a wire rack. To serve, sprinkle a little icing sugar over the tart or glaze with clear apricot jam, heated in a pan until it melts.

Variation: Apple tart. Mix the almond cream with some apple compote (see page 158) and a drop of Calvados, and use peeled, sliced Cox's apples instead of apricots.

bacon slice

You know when you have that craving for bacon that nothing else will satisfy? Well, being French, when I was an apprentice in the bakery my cravings would be for a croque monsieur, made with lardons (our equivalent of bacon) and béchamel. We used to make an imitation by folding some bacon and béchamel into a piece of sweet dough and letting it prove, then baking it – wonderful!

Quantity: 6 slices
Preparation: 20 minutes
Resting: 1 hour
Proving: 45 minutes
Baking: 15 minutes

½ Batch Sweet dough (page 137) rested for 1 hour
200g Béchamel sauce (200ml)
1 Packet Good-quality, preferably dry-cured, organic bacon
1 Medium egg beaten with a pinch of salt for an egg wash
100g Grated Gruyère or Emmenthal

To make

• With the help of the rounded end of your scraper, turn out the dough onto a lightly floured surface and form it into a ball (page 25). Roll the dough out to a thickness of about 5mm then cut it into 6 x 12cm squares. Spoon a tablespoon of béchamel in the centre of a square and then fold two opposite corners to meet in the middle. Place a slice of bacon on top and then lift the whole slice onto a baking tray. Repeat with the other slices. Cover with greaseproof paper and then a tea towel and leave to prove for 45 minutes.

• Glaze the exposed dough with the egg wash. Sprinkle some of the cheese on top. Turn the preheated oven down to 200°C and bake them for about 15 minutes until they are a deep golden colour. Eat while they are still warm.

béchamel sauce

Melt 25g unsalted butter over a medium heat in a heavy-bottomed pan. When it has all melted and is bubbling gently, add 20g plain flour and whisk briskly off the heat until all of the butter has been absorbed and you have a putty-like paste that comes cleanly away from the pan. Add 150g (150ml) full-fat milk, a little at a time, whisking continuously to ensure that no lumps form. Once all the milk has been added and you have a smooth sauce, cook over a low to medium heat until it starts to bubble. Cook for 1 more minute. Season with sea salt and freshly ground black pepper and a little ground nutmeg to taste. Leave to cool. This makes 200g (200ml). For a richer sauce you can add 25g–40g grated cheese (Cheddar or Gruyère work well) to the sauce while it is over the heat – make sure it melts completely.

fruited tea loaf

Traditional 'tea bread' can sometimes be overly rich and heavy, but this one is nice and light – fantastic toasted, with fruit compote and fresh cream.

Quantity: 3 loaves
Preparation: 30 minutes
Resting: 65 minutes
Proving: 1¹/2 hours
Baking: 25–30 minutes

1 Batch Sweet dough (page 137)
150g Glacé cherries, quartered
50g Mixed peel or the grated zest of 2 large lemons and 2 large oranges
2 Large tablespoons Rum
125g Flaked almonds, plus some extra for topping
150g Sultanas
1 Medium egg beaten with a pinch of salt for an egg wash

To prepare

Grease 3 x 500g (20–22cm long) tins with butter.

Soak the cherries and peel or zest in the rum overnight.

Sprinkle the almonds on a baking tray and toast under the grill or in the hot oven, turning from time to time until they are golden brown. Leave to cool.

Mix all the fruit with the nuts and add the mixture to the dough towards the end of working by hand or mixing in the mixer, making sure it is evenly distributed. Shape the dough into a rough ball (page 25) and place in a lightly floured bowl. Leave to rest for 1 hour.

To make

• With the help of the rounded end of your scraper, turn the dough out onto a lightly floured work surface and divide it into three equal pieces. Mould each into a rough ball and leave to rest for a further 5 minutes.

• Mould each ball into a loaf (page 31) and place them in the tins. Brush the tops with the egg wash. Cover the tins with a tea towel and leave to prove for 1¹/2 hours or until the dough has nearly doubled in volume.

• Brush again with egg wash and, with a razor blade or sharp knife, make one cut along the top. Sprinkle over some extra almonds. Bake in the preheated oven for 25–30 minutes until the crust is dark golden brown. Remove from the tins and check that the sides and underneath are golden. If not, put them back in for a few minutes (out of the tins). Leave to cool on a wire rack.

pain viennois

This dough is the bread you see in parts of France as an alternative to brioche. It's a recipe I teach regularly in my bread classes, and everyone finds it very simple to make. As kids we used to eat small baguettes made with this dough for breakfast, or at tea-time – which we called 'le quatre-heure'. When we came home from school we would have them halved, with a bar of Poulain chocolate inside – these were the bars that every child ate, with the picture of a pony on the wrapper. You can also bake this in a tin and slice it for croque monsieur.

Quantity:	5 baguettes or 15 rolls	**1 Batch** Sweet dough (page 137) rested for 1 hour
Preparation:	20 minutes	**1** Medium egg beaten with a pinch of salt for an egg
Resting:	1 hour	wash
Proving:	1 hour	Flour for dusting
Baking:	8–12 minutes	

To make

With the help of the rounded end of your scraper, turn the dough out onto a lightly floured work surface and divide it into 5 pieces for baguettes or 15 pieces for rolls.

For the baguettes

• Flatten the pieces of dough with your hands into rough rectangles. Fold and roll according to the method on page 56. Place the baguettes on a tray with space between each, give them two coats of the egg wash, and then make a series of small deep cuts diagonally along the tops with a razor blade or sharp knife.

• Leave to prove for 1 hour then bake for 10–12 minutes in the preheated oven until the baguettes are dark golden brown.

For the rolls

• Form the pieces of dough into rolls (page 30).

• Place the rolls on a baking tray or trays, with space between each one.

• Glaze each roll with the egg wash, then with a knife or pair of scissors make a cross in the tops, about 5mm deep.

• Leave to prove for 1 hour, then bake in the preheated oven for 8–10 minutes until the rolls are dark golden brown.

scones

Everyone always asks me if I have a good recipe for scones. Well, I do – ever since I first tried them when I came to Britain, they have been my favourite British speciality. We are still talking about dough, and this one has cream in it, which is a bit of a play on the tradition of cream scones. I also like to make my scones square, rather than round.

Quantity:	12–15 scones
Preparation:	20 minutes
Resting:	15 minutes
Baking:	20 minutes

150g Salted butter
600g Plain flour
150g Caster sugar
40g Baking powder
280g Sultanas
190g Double cream
190g Milk (190ml)
2 Eggs, beaten with a pinch of salt for an egg wash

To prepare
Preheat the oven to 220°C.

To make
• Rub the butter into the flour in a mixing bowl. Add the sugar and baking powder. Add the sultanas and mix until they are evenly distributed.

• Add the cream and milk and mix with your scraper until all the ingredients are bound together. Lightly dust your work surface with flour and turn the dough out onto it. Press down, then fold it in half, then press down again, fold again the opposite way, and then repeat, until you have a rough square. Flour the top and bottom of the dough, cover with a tea towel and rest in a cool place for 15 minutes.

• Lightly flour the work surface and then roll the dough out to a thickness of 2½–3cm. Brush off any excess flour. With a sharp knife, cut out the scones into squares (about 6 x 6cm).

• Lay on a baking tray, making sure that the scones are not too close together. Roll out any scraps of dough and cut some more scones until you have used all of the dough.

• Glaze the scones with the egg wash. Wait for 2 minutes, then glaze again. Turn down the heat in the preheated oven to 200°C and bake the scones for around 20 minutes until they are well risen, and the top and underside is golden brown.

additional recipes

apple compote

Peel, core and quarter 2 large cooking apples. Melt a large knob of butter in a pan and add 1 teaspoon of sugar and a pinch of cinnamon. Add the apples and toss until well coated with butter. Cook for 1 minute or so, then reduce the heat, add a tablespoon of Calvados or brandy (if you like) and stir well. Cover the pan and leave over a low heat for 10–15 minutes, or until the apples are soft. Remove from the heat and cool for a few minutes, then, using a hand blender, blitz until smooth and leave to cool completely.

crème patissière

In a bowl whisk together 6 egg yolks, 70g caster sugar and 50g sifted flour. Put another 70g sugar into a saucepan with 500g (500ml) full-fat milk and a vanilla pod (split lengthways and seeds scraped in). Place over a low heat. Leave until the first bubble appears, then remove from the heat. Whisk $1/3$ of the milk into the egg mixture, then add the remaining $2/3$ of the milk and stir again. Pour back into the pan and put back on the heat. Bring to the boil and simmer for a couple of minutes, stirring constantly to ensure that the cream does not burn on the bottom of the pan. Pour into a dish to cool. Sprinkle a little icing sugar or flakes of butter on top to prevent a skin forming.

crème d'amande

Beat 125g butter (at room temperature) and 125g caster sugar by hand, or mix in a food processor with a paddle, until pale and fluffy. Add 125g ground almonds and mix again. Add 25g plain flour and continue to mix, finally adding 2 eggs, one at a time, along with 2 large tablespoons of rum (if you like), mixing well between each addition, until the mixture is light in consistency. Use immediately or store in an airtight container in the fridge for up to a week.

suppliers

BACON
Duchy Originals www.duchyoriginals.com
Available from most supermarkets

BAKING EQUIPMENT
The Bertinet Kitchen www.thebertinetkitchen.com

CIDER
Burrow Hill Cider www.ciderbrandy.co.uk
01460 240782

DELIS
L'Angolo (Carmelo Colosi)
College Road
Kensal Rise
London NW10

FLOUR
Shipton Mill
www.shiptonmill.com or by mail order from Flour Direct on 01666 505050 or
Leckford Strong White organic flour and Canadian Bread Flour both available from Waitrose

HERBS AND SPICES
Seasoned Pioneers www.seasonedpioneers.co.uk
Available from most supermarkets

OILS
Any good extra-virgin olive oil will do but I particularly like Belazu www.belazu.com
Available from most supermarkets
The avocado oil I use is made by Olivado Gourmet Foods www.olivado.com
and again is available from most supermarkets.

FRESH YEAST
All bakeries or supermarket in-store bakeries should be able to sell you some but you will need to ask. Many delis or health food stores may also stock it. Again, if they don't, ask, because they may be able to order it from their bakery supplier.

index

LEARNING RESOURCE CENTRE

Additives, 7
Almonds
  apricot & almond tart, 139, 148
  crème d'amande, 157, 158
Aniseed
  aniseed & guinness bread, 119, 130
  sesame & aniseed breadsticks, 48
Apples
  apple compote, 158
  apple tart, 148
Apricots
  apricot & almond tart, 139, 148
  apricot & oat bread, 94, 96
Avocado oil, 68, 88, 89

Bacon
  bacon slice, 138, 150
  pancetta & mixed olive bread, 71, 86, 87
  smoked bacon & red onion bread, 119, 127
Baguettes, 34
  epis, 34, 57
  keeping back dough, 54
  making, 56, 57
  meaning, 54
Baking, 14
Baking stone, 10
Béchamel sauce, 64, 150
Biga, 88
Bread & butter pudding, marmalade, 142
Bread shots, 34, 44
Breadsticks, 34
  olive, herb & pecorino, 50
  sesame & aniseed, 48
Brown dough
  apricot & oat bread, 96
  brown rolls, 105
  cardamom & prune bread, 101
  honey & lavender loaf, 98
  making, 93
  multiseed bread, 108
  pecan & cranberry bread, 112
  poppy seed stars, 107
  raisin, hazelnut & shallot bread, 110
  seaweed bread, 103
  sesame plaits, 104
  types of bread, 94, 95
  100% wholemeal bread, 114
Brown rolls, 94, 105
Brush, 11
Buns
  Jack's chocolate buns, 139, 145

Canadian strong white flour, 12
Caraway
  rye, caraway & raisin bread, 118, 124
Cardamom & prune bread, 95, 101

Cheese
  bread shots, 44
  gruyère cheese & cumin bread, 35, 58
  olive, herb & pecorino breadsticks, 50
  parmesan, parma ham & pine nut slices, 70, 80, 81
  pizza, 84, 85
Chocolate
  Jack's chocolate buns, 139, 145
  pain viennois, 64, 154
Chorleywood Bread Process, 8
Ciabatta, 71, 88–91
  olive, 91
Cider
  somerset cider bread, 118, 129
Colour chart, 16
Cranberries
  pecan & cranberry bread, 95, 112
Crème d'amande, 157, 158
Crème patissière, 158
Cumin
  gruyère cheese & cumin bread, 35, 58
  saffron rolls, 63

Dark rye bread 118, 135
Dough
  brown, 92–115
  keeping back, 26, 54
  kneading, 14, 24–26
  loaves, shaping into, 31
  making, technique for, 20–23
  olive, 68–91
  parent, 14
  resting, 14, 26
  rolls, shaping into, 30
  rye, 116–135
  small balls, rolling into, 28, 29
  sweet, 136–156
  white, 32–66
  working, 14, 23–26
Dough hook, using, 26
Doughnuts, 138, 146

Epis, 34, 57
Equipment, 10, 11
Everyday loaves, 64–67

Ferment, 14, 88
Flatbread, 70, 83
Flour, 12
Focaccia
  pesto, olive & pepperdew focaccia, 72
  rock salt & rosemary focaccia, 71, 72
Folding, 14
Fougasse, 34, 36–39
Fruit

fruited tea loaf, 139, 153
  summer pudding, 66
Fruited tea loaf, 139, 153

Garlic
  roasted, 76
  tomato, garlic & basil bread, 71, 74, 75
Gruyère cheese & cumin bread, 35, 58
Guinness
  aniseed & guinness bread, 119, 130

Ham
  parmesan, parma ham & pine nut slices, 70, 80, 81
Hazelnuts
  raisin, hazelnut & shallot bread, 94, 110
Herbs
  gruyère cheese & cumin bread, 35
  olive, herb & pecorino breadsticks, 50
  orange & mint loaf, 138, 140
  pesto bread shots, 44
  pesto, olive & pepperdew focaccia, 72
  rock salt & rosemary focaccia, 71, 72
  tomato, garlic & basil bread, 71, 74, 75
Home-made loaf, ingredients of, 19
Honey & lavender loaf, 94, 98

Ingredients, 12

Jack's chocolate buns, 139, 145

Kneading, 14, 24–26

Lavender
  honey & lavender loaf, 94, 98
Layered rolls, 35, 46
Leckford Estate, 12
Lemon rolls, 35, 47
Loaves
  shaping dough into, 31

Marmalade bread & butter pudding, 142
Mint
  mint butter, 142
  orange & mint loaf, 138, 140
Mixing bowl, 10
Multiseed bread, 95, 108

Nuts
  apricot & almond tart, 139, 148
  crème d'amande, 157, 158
  parmesan, parma ham & pine nut slices, 70, 80, 81
  pecan & cranberry bread, 95, 112
  raisin, hazelnut & shallot bread, 94, 110
  walnut bread shots, 44

Oats
  apricot & oat bread, 94, 96
Olive bread, 119, 122
Olive dough
  ciabatta, 88-91
  flatbread, 83
  making, 69
  pancetta & mixed olive bread, 86, 87
  parmesan, parma ham & pine nut slices,
    80, 81
  pizza, 84, 85
  rock salt & rosemary focaccia, 71, 72
  soup bowl, 78
  tomato, garlic & basil bread, 71, 74, 75
  types of bread, 70, 71
Olives
  bread shots, 44
  ciabatta, 91
  olive, herb & pecorino breadsticks, 50
  olive paste, 44, 120
  pancetta & mixed olive bread, 71, 86, 87
  pesto, olive & pepperdew focaccia, 72
Onions
  raisin, hazelnut & shallot bread, 94, 110
  smoked bacon & red onion bread, 119, 127
Oranges
  orange & mint loaf, 138, 140
  pecan & cranberry bread, 112
Oven, heating up, 20

Pain de campagne, 118, 132
Pain de mie, 34, 64–67
Pain façon beaucaire, 35, 60
Pain viennois, 64, 154
Pancetta & mixed olive bread, 71, 86, 87
Parmesan, parma ham & pine nut slices,
  70, 80, 81
Pecan & cranberry bread, 95, 112
Peppers
  pesto, olive & pepperdew focaccia, 72
Pesto
  bread shots, 44
  pesto, olive & pepperdew focaccia, 72
Pine nuts
  parmesan, parma ham & pine nut slices,
    70, 80, 81
Pizza, 84, 85
Plastic scraper, 11
Poolish, 135
  100% wholemeal bread, 114
  dark rye bread, 135
Poppy seed stars, 94, 107
Proving, 14
Prunes
  cardamom & prune bread, 95, 101
Puff balls, 35, 40–43
Pumpernickel, 117 Raisins

raisin, hazelnut & shallot bread, 94, 110
rye, caraway & raisin bread, 118, 124
Razor blade, 11
Resting dough, 14, 26
Rock salt & rosemary focaccia, 71, 72
Rolls
  brown, 94, 105
  layered, 35, 46
  lemon, 35, 47
  saffron, 34, 63
  shaping dough into, 30
  spicy moroccan, 35, 53
  sweet, 138
Rye, caraway & raisin bread, 118, 124
Rye dough
  aniseed & guinness bread, 130
  dark rye bread, 135
  making, 117
  olive bread, 122
  pain de campagne, 132
  rye, caraway & raisin bread, 124
  smoked bacon & red onion bread, 127
  somerset cider bread, 129
  types of bread, 118, 119
  walnut bread, 120

Saffron rolls, 34, 63
Salt, 12
Scones, 139, 156
Seaweed bread, 95, 103
Sesame seeds
  sesame & aniseed breadsticks, 48
  sesame plaits, 94, 104
Shallots
  raisin, hazelnut & shallot bread, 94, 110
Shipton Mill, 12, 158
Shop-bought loaf, ingredients of, 18
Sliced white bread, 8
Small breads, 31
Smoked bacon & red onion bread, 119, 127
Somerset cider bread, 118, 129
Soup bowl, 70, 78
Sourdough bread, 132
Spicy moroccan rolls, 35, 53
Summer pudding, 66
Sweet dough
  apricot & almond tart, 148
  bacon slice, 150
  doughnuts, 146
  fruited tea loaf, 153
  Jack's chocolate buns, 145
  making, 137
  orange & mint loaf, 140
  pain viennois, 154
  scones, 156
  types of bread, 138, 139
Sweet rolls, 138

Tarts
  apricot & almond tart, 139, 148
Tea towels, 10, 20
Timer, 11
Tomatoes
  bread shots, 44
  oven-dried, 76
  pizza, 84, 85
  tomato, garlic & basil bread, 71, 74, 75
  tomato paste, 76

Walnuts
  bread shots, 44
  walnut bread, 119, 120
Water, 12
Water spray, 11
Weighing ingredients, 20
Weighing scales, 10
Wheatsheaf, 57
White dough
  baguettes, 54–57
  bread shots, 44
  epis, 57
  everyday loaves, 64, 65
  fougasse, 36–39
  gruyère cheese & cumin bread, 58
  ingredients, 33
  layered rolls, 48
  lemon rolls, 49
  making, 33
  olive, herb & pecorino breadsticks, 50
  pain de mie, 64
  pain façon beaucaire, 60
  puff balls, 40–43
  saffron rolls, 63
  sesame & aniseed breadsticks, 48
  spicy moroccan rolls, 53
  types of bread, 34, 35
  wheatsheaf, 57
Wholemeal bread, 100% 95, 114
Wooden peel, 11
Work surface, 22, 25
Working dough, 14, 23–26

Yeast, 12
  rubbing in, 22